Routledge Revivals

England in the Nineteenth Century
Volume 1

Originally published in 1929, this volume discusses the early effects of the industrial revolution – the condition of the cotton spinners, the hardships for labouring children, the overcrowded prisons and other brutal punishments. At this time the principal branch of local government was the Poor Law and this book discusses how, in the monumental task of providing workhouses for the destitute, the England of the eighteenth century had completely failed. As well as social history, the book also covers military and political history.

England in the Nineteenth Century
1801-1805

A.F. Fremantle

First published in 1929 by George Allen & Unwin Ltd.

This edition first published in 2024 by Routledge
4 Park Square, Milton Park, Abingdon, Oxon, OX14 4RN

and by Routledge
605 Third Avenue, New York, NY 10158.

Routledge is an imprint of the Taylor & Francis Group, an informa business

© 1929 A.F. Fremantle.

The right of A.F. Fremantle to be identified as the author of this work has been asserted by him in accordance with sections 77 and 78 of the Copyright, Designs and Patents Act 1988.

All rights reserved. No part of this book may be reprinted or reproduced or utilised in any form or by any electronic, mechanical, or other means, now known or hereafter invented, including photocopying and recording, or in any information storage or retrieval system, without permission in writing from the publishers.

ISBN 13: 978-1-032-90139-8 (hbk)
ISBN 13: 978-1-003-54636-8 (ebk)
ISBN 13: 978-1-032-90159-6 (pbk)
Book DOI 10.4324/9781003546368

ENGLAND
IN THE NINETEENTH CENTURY
1801—1805

By

A. F. FREMANTLE

La puissance d'un peuple se compose de son histoire. NAPOLEON

LONDON
GEORGE ALLEN & UNWIN LTD
MUSEUM STREET

FIRST PUBLISHED IN 1929

All rights reserved
PRINTED IN GREAT BRITAIN BY
UNWIN BROTHERS LTD., WOKING

Considerate la vostra semenza:
Fatti non foste a viver come bruti,
Ma per seguir virtute e conoscenza.

DANTE

AUTHOR'S NOTE

IT will be observed that all account of several important parts of the Empire, notably Scotland, India, and Australia, has been omitted from this volume. Chapters on these subjects, together with a chapter on the state of Literature, Art, and Science, as well as the general narrative up to 1810, have all been prepared, and will be issued should the present volume receive a favourable verdict from the public.

CONTENTS

Chapter I

ENGLAND AT THE CLOSE OF THE EIGHTEENTH CENTURY

	PAGE
THE COUNTRY	17
THE AGRARIAN REVOLUTION	22
AGRICULTURAL WAGES	28
THE RISE IN PRICES	34
THE STOPPAGE OF CASH PAYMENTS	35
COUNTRY BANKS	36
CHANGES IN AGRICULTURAL METHODS	38
YORKSHIRE	40
MANCHESTER	41
LIVERPOOL	43
NEWCASTLE	44
BIRMINGHAM	45
WALES AND BRISTOL	47
EFFECTS OF MACHINERY ON THE CONDITION OF THE COTTON WEAVERS	48
CONDITION OF THE COTTON SPINNERS—RISE OF OWEN AND OTHERS	50
CONDITION OF LABOURING CHILDREN	51
OBSTACLES TO THE INTRODUCTION OF MACHINERY	53
WEALTH OF THE COUNTRY	55
TRADE	58
CANALS	61
ROADS	62
LONDON	64
MANNERS	68
THE RACE FOR WEALTH	74
TREATMENT OF WOMEN	75
NATIONAL PRIDE	83
THE CHURCH	84
THE EVANGELICALS	90
THE NONCONFORMISTS	91
PHILANTHROPY	94
INTELLECTUAL CONDITION OF THE PEOPLE	95
THE PRESS	97

	PAGE
HIGHER EDUCATION	98
RECREATIONS	102
NATIONAL VIGOUR	105

Chapter II

THE GOVERNMENT OF ENGLAND AT THE CLOSE OF THE EIGHTEENTH CENTURY

MERITS OF THE CONSTITUTION	108
THE HOUSE OF COMMONS	109
THE HOUSE OF LORDS	116
THE SOVEREIGN	117
THE CABINET	122
PITT'S EARLY CAREER	125
THE FRENCH WAR	129
PITT'S HOME POLICY	131
PITT'S COLLEAGUES	134
MINOR MINISTERS	138
THE OPPOSITION	140
FOX	140
THE PRINCE OF WALES	147
THE OPPOSITION, NOBILITY AND PRESS	148
THE OPPOSITION IN THE COUNTRY	151
THE JUDICATURE	154
THE CRIMINAL ADMINISTRATION	159
PRISONS AND PUNISHMENTS	161
INDEPENDENCE OF THE COURTS	164
ACTIVITIES OF THE CRIMINAL COURTS	166
POLICE	168
LOCAL GOVERNMENT	170
THE POOR LAW	171
THE MUNICIPAL CORPORATIONS	175
TRADE CONTROL	178
THE POST OFFICE	179
FINANCE—TAXATION	180
THE NATIONAL DEBT	182
EXCISE	185
CUSTOMS	186
MISCELLANEOUS TAXATION	186
INCOME TAX	187

CONTENTS

	PAGE
FINANCE—EXPENDITURE	188
THE MINT	191
IDEA OF THE THREE ESTATES	192
COMPOSITION OF THE HOUSE OF COMMONS	194
PARLIAMENTARY CONCEPTION OF INDUSTRIAL LEGISLATION	195
PARLIAMENTARY CONCEPTION OF COMMERCIAL LEGISLATION	198

Chapter III

IRELAND—THE FALL OF PITT'S ADMINISTRATION
(January—March, 1801)

IRELAND—NATIONAL CHARACTER AND ECONOMIC CONDITION	202
THE CAPITAL	209
THE SYSTEM OF GOVERNMENT	211
WEALTH OF IRELAND	215
THE VICEROYS AND PARLIAMENT	217
THE CATHOLIC QUESTION	221
THE REBELLION	224
THE UNION	231
THE TERMS OF THE UNION	235
THE SCARCITY OF CORN	241
FOREIGN AFFAIRS	243
MEETING OF PARLIAMENT	247
FALL OF PITT'S ADMINISTRATION	251
ADDINGTON'S SUCCESSION AS PREMIER	256
THE BUDGET	259
THE NEW ADMINISTRATION	260

Chapter IV

NORTH AMERICA—THE WEST INDIES—THE NAVY—THE ARMY—ADDINGTON'S ADMINISTRATION TILL THE CLOSE OF THE WAR
(March—October 1801)

DEBATES IN PARLIAMENT	264
THE SCARCITY	266
NORTH AMERICAN COLONIES	270
RELATIONS WITH THE UNITED STATES	277

	PAGE
THE BERMUDAS	277
THE WEST INDIES	278
THE NAVY	285
THE ARMY	296
THE PEACE OF LUNÉVILLE	308
THE EXPEDITION TO EGYPT	308
LANDING OF THE BRITISH	311
BATTLE OF CANOPUS	314
CONQUEST OF EGYPT	317
SAUMAREZ'S NAVAL ACTIONS	319
CHARACTER OF NELSON	322
EXPEDITION TO COPENHAGEN	326
BATTLE OF COPENHAGEN	329
DISSOLUTION OF THE ARMED NEUTRALITY	334
OPERATIONS IN THE ENGLISH CHANNEL	335

Chapter V

ADDINGTON'S ADMINISTRATION DURING THE PEACE

(October 1801—May 1803)

SIGNATURE OF PEACE PRELIMINARIES	338
THE ARMISTICE	342
PARLIAMENTARY DISCUSSION ON THE CIVIL LIST	344
TREATY OF AMIENS	345
BUDGET OF 1802	347
PARLIAMENTARY DEBATE ON BULL-BAITING	348
THE FIRST FACTORY ACT	349
POPULARITY OF PITT	350
TRIAL AND EXECUTION OF WALL	350
GENERAL ELECTION	352
GROWING ALARM AT FRENCH AGGRESSIONS	353
RUPTURE OF THE PEACE	356
PITT'S RELATIONS WITH ADDINGTON	363
BUDGET OF 1803	365
DISTURBANCES IN IRELAND	367
ADDINGTON'S ENDEAVOURS TO STRENGTHEN HIS POSITION	369

Chapter VI

ADDINGTON'S ADMINISTRATION AFTER THE OUTBREAK OF WAR

(May 1803—May 1804)

	PAGE
FEASIBILITY OF AN INVASION OF ENGLAND	370
BONAPARTE'S PLANS	372
THE NAVAL SITUATION	374
THE FRENCH FLOTILLA	378
DANCE'S ACTION WITH LINOIS	379
BONAPARTE'S ACTION ON THE OUTBREAK OF WAR	380
COLONIAL EXPEDITIONS	381
THE LAND DEFENCE OF THE UNITED KINGDOM	381
CRITICISM OF THE MEASURES OF GOVERNMENT	386
RESIGNATION OF ADDINGTON	390
PITT'S SECOND ADMINISTRATION	391

Chapter VII

PITT'S LAST ADMINISTRATION

(May 1804—January 1806)

THE NEW MINISTRY'S TASK IN THE NAVY AND ARMY	396
THE MENACE OF INVASION	400
OUTBREAK OF WAR WITH SPAIN	401
FORMATION OF THE THIRD COALITION	404
NAPOLEON'S NAVAL PLANS	405
NELSON'S PURSUIT OF VILLENEUVE TO THE WEST INDIES	407
MILITARY MEASURES OF THE GOVERNMENT	410
THE TENTH REPORT AND THE FALL OF MELVILLE	411
BUDGET OF 1805	413
DEBATES ON THE CATHOLIC PETITION	414
MEASURES TO COUNTERACT NAPOLEON'S NAVAL SCHEMES	415
BATTLE OF THE 22ND OF JUNE	417
VILLENEUVE'S RETIREMENT TO CADIZ	420
EXPEDITION TO THE CAPE OF GOOD HOPE	424
NELSON'S DEPARTURE FOR THE FLEET OFF CADIZ	424
BATTLE OF TRAFALGAR	428

	PAGE
DEATH OF NELSON	438
SEQUEL TO THE BATTLE OF TRAFALGAR	441
STRACHAN'S ACTION WITH DUMANOIR	443
NAPOLEON'S DEFEAT OF THE THIRD COALITION	444
PITT'S LAST DAYS	446
DEATH OF PITT	447
REFERENCES	455
BIBLIOGRAPHY	487
INDEX	503

ENGLAND IN THE NINETEENTH CENTURY
1801–1805

CHAPTER I

ENGLAND AT THE CLOSE OF THE EIGHTEENTH CENTURY

ENGLISH prints of the eighteenth century depict a countryside unenclosed, undrained, poorly timbered, and largely uncultivated, dotted with lonely cottages or small farmhouses. The members of the agricultural communities which lived there enjoyed their own independence. This conception was enshrined in an ancient statute of the reign of Queen Elizabeth, which had, however, fallen into disuse by 1775, when it was formally repealed. It provided that no more than one family should dwell in one cottage, and that each should have at least four acres of land. Near the church were a few gardens and closes, but elsewhere, all round the straggling village, lay the common field where each had his share. This was the plough-land, divided into wheat, spring corn, and fallow, or into some more elaborate rotation. In each of these divisions the shares were in long strips, bounded by narrow strips of unploughed land. As soon as the crop was cut the cattle could be turned on. In the low ground was usually the meadow, both for grazing and for hay. Beyond was waste land—wood, moor, and fen. Here were often more cottages, owned by squatters, who were no part of the village community, and had no share in plough-land or meadow. They had built their own huts and redeemed a part of the primeval wilderness. Here they cut their own fuel, and lived mainly upon the produce of wild or cultivated fruit trees, and cows, pigs, geese, and other livestock. Large farms were rare. Where there was more than one man could do, the farmer was helped by farm-servants who slept and boarded in his house, often the unmarried sons of the cottagers. When there was more work to be done the smaller holder himself could work for the larger. At harvest-time men would come from other parts of the country, and even from Ireland. In the winter, as there were no winter crops, no hedging and ditching, and not much to do besides threshing, there was time for cottage industries, which flourished in every county. But generally winter was the countryman's idle time, as it has been ever since the age of Hesiod and Virgil.

Never has the lot of the peasantry of England been happier. The landless field-labourer was almost unknown in the villages themselves outside the ranks of the few farm-servants who looked forward in due time to leaving their masters' houses, marrying, and having cottages and holdings of their own. If the squatter did not choose to appropriate a bit of ground near his hut, it was because the moor and woodland were free to him. Most of the cottagers in the villages kept cows, and perhaps a pig or two and other animals. The number which each one could graze on the common land was fixed, and there was no reason why he should part with his right. They had to work hard, as smallholders must do, and on the roughest fare, but there was no misery and no destitution. Meat, generally bacon, was a common article of diet. Farm-servants living with their masters received it regularly, along with small beer, except in the cider countries, where a gallon at a draught was not regarded as anything of a feat. A frequent allowance for poor-house inmates was meat three times a week, and broth on other days. The overseers would not have given old men and women better food to spin on than able-bodied labourers were earning outside. Many cottagers used their coppers for brewing ale, as well as for the laundry, and washed down their wholesome fare with their own home-brewed. In one of the attacks made during these times on the old unenclosed system as rendering the cottager upon whom the farmer relied for labour too independent, his prosperity is revealed in rather a surprising way. "If you offer them work", wrote a farmer, "they will tell you that they must go to look up their sheep, cut furzes, get their cow out of the pound, or, perhaps, say they must take their horse to be shod, that he may carry them to a horse-race or a cricket-match." This last sally at rural extravagance might almost pass as jest. But it is not without corroboration. Arthur Young, the great farmer and traveller, wrote in 1799 of the district known as the Isle of Axholme, in Lincolnshire: "A man will keep a pair of horses that has but three or four acres, by means of vast commons and working for hire." Nor were the outer signs of well-being neglected. In discussing the distinction between luxuries and necessities in his Wealth of Nations, Adam Smith wrote: "Through the greater part of Europe"—and most certainly he included England—"a creditable day-labourer would be ashamed to appear in public without a linen shirt." It was on account of the use of linen, he added, that soap was also necessary; and certainly that article figures prominently in the labourers' budgets of the times. The villagers went regularly to church— a thing which about the end of the century, when they could no longer afford decent clothes, they became ashamed to do.

There was a striking variety in the elements which made up the old village societies. Above the cottagers, who were themselves very small farmers, came the farmers proper, great and small, holding under leases which varied in different parts of the country, and under different landlords. Leases for the duration of the life of the survivor of three persons living at the commencement of the period of tenure were very common, particularly in the West of England. The notion appealed to the prevalent gambling spirit. A better system was that of twenty-one-year leases which became prevalent in Norfolk towards the end of the century on the initiative of the great Thomas Coke of Holkham.

A still superior class of tenure was that of the copyholder, or tenant entered in the manorial roll as being so according to the custom of the manor. All these classes of tenants usually paid only a money rent to the lord of the manor. But there were exceptions. Picturesque relics of feudalism survived into the nineteenth century. In Cheshire, noted for its cheeses, the lord of the manor has the right to choose a cheese at Christmas, and occasionally he enjoyed the right of a few days' team-work or two days' harvest-work as labourer from his tenant. In Cumberland the feudal services performed by the copyholders included ploughing, reaping, haymaking, and carrying letters. Above them came the yeomen—in the sense of petty proprietors—many of them differing from the tenant-farmer—if at all—in social standing and habits rather than in income. Some were worth six or seven hundred pounds a year; others enjoyed that fine old designation who were not much better off than cottagers, merely in virtue of their clear ownership of their lands. In the counties surrounding the capital, with the exception of Kent and Essex on the east, they were not numerous. There were many in Berkshire, in the west, in the mountainous districts of the north, and in the Isle of Man, where they owned nearly the whole. Above these a village might contain one or two small landholders who leased their land; and over them again was the lord of the manor, who might be anything from the lord of several other manors down to a small squire.

But variety by no means ended here. When communications were poor, industries unorganized, and wants simple, the indispensable clothes, tools, and utensils were made within the village, and some other services were performed there which, in a more advanced stage of society, were done outside. Young gave in 1804 a list of the employments of the heads of the 231 families which he found in 1789 in the parish of Redenhall with Harleston in Norfolk, a small market town with a population of 1,459 in 260 houses. There were 38 husbandmen, 26 spinners, 12 farmers, 12 publicans, and 8 carpenters. The list, of 57 classes in all, tails down through gentlemen and gentlewomen, 5; schoolmasters and schoolmistresses, 5; attorneys and surgeons, 3 each; and ends with rector, clerk, and molecatcher, 1 each, and sundries, 4.

It is difficult, moreover, to name a county which had not one or two thriving industries besides agriculture, carried on in the homes of the people. Some attempt was made at the first official census of Great Britain in 1801 to obtain separate returns of persons chiefly employed in agriculture, and those chiefly employed in trade, manufactures, or handicraft. No great reliance can be placed on the figures. But it is remarkable that, even in such a purely agricultural part as the cider county of Herefordshire, one person out of every three of those shown as having employment is returned as engaged in trade, manufactures, or handicraft. For England as a whole the agriculturists were found to be rather less than the others.

This variety extended to the employments of the agriculturists themselves, particularly in the north, where it would not have been possible to find all the miscellaneous trades and callings of Redenhall. The South of England had mainly passed beyond the stage where each family provides for almost all its own needs. the husbandman building his own house, cutting his tools, and shoeing his horse, the housewife spinning her own thread and knitting the garments for the family. Many southern homes, indeed, had their spinning-wheels at the end of the century, and in them the maidens still earned their name of spinster. But so little hard labour was done in the fields that the German chaplain, Wendeborn, called England the Paradise of women. He did not know the north. A more ungrateful soil, a harsher climate, and a more isolated life had still preserved in the north in their full vigour the first energies of mankind struggling out of barbarism. While in the south the fields at harvest were thronged with women gleaning behind the reapers, a Yorkshire girl would have been ashamed to be found so engaged. She would have been in front wielding the sickle, leaving that immemorable perquisite of the poor, gleaning, to old men, cripples, and children. This did not prevent the cooking and the household work from being better done north than south of the Trent. The labours of the north-country women were, indeed, unending. There is a book of Yorkshire poems by Thomas Brown, a young clergyman of the time, in which a jealous girl is made to say of a rival:

"She can't mak' cheese or spin like me."

But these were merely performances which exhibited the gracious promise of youth. As a matron she would have added a much larger number to the list.

In that valuable book, "The State of the Poor", published in 1797, Sir Frederick Eden, a baronet of Cumberland, gave a list of the requirements of a labourer living in that county. The cloth for his coat would be 10s., at 2s. 6d. a yard; his linen shirts would be 4s. 8d., at 1s. 5d. a yard; a pair of leather breeches, 3s. 6d. Most of the spinning and knitting would be done at home if he had a wife, and the making up would certainly be. Eden observes that there was much more variety in the cooking there than in the south. With rye-bread as their staple diet the housewives of the north had ingenuity forced upon them. The people of the south—though not of the west, the country of barley-bread, skim-milk, cheese, and potatoes—would touch only bread made with wheat, though mixtures with barley and rice were sometimes tolerated.

But all through the country the typical English village in its variety, its self-sufficiency, and its freedom from the extremes both of wealth and poverty, was passing away. The pasture counties of the west had never known the elaborate texture of a midland village community. The yeomen of Kent and Essex had early enclosed their land. It was mainly in the midlands and the counties near London that the old tenures and the old customs still prevailed up to the middle of the eighteenth century, and were then done away with by enclosure in village after village. Before that time enclosure had proceeded as a rule piecemeal within the village itself. But it now came to be a question of reconciling the interests of perhaps some hundreds of occupiers. Each possessed one or more small strips of land in each of the three or four fields which made up the arable land of the ancient village, not to speak of his share in the meadow and his right of grazing on the common waste. Some formal arrangement had become necessary, and this was usually carried out by legislation. But even in the county where there was the largest area of parliamentary enclosure, Northamptonshire, the area enclosed under Acts of Parliament during the eighteenth and nineteenth centuries scarcely exceeded one-half of the whole.

The change was one which seemed imperatively called for by economic law. Passing through the Vale of Aylesbury to Buckingham in 1770, Young was grieved to find land which he rightly foresaw might be made into as fine meadows as any in the world, hindered from being converted to its proper purpose by being still in open field and, consequently, largely tillage. Communications did not improve as rapidly as the capital grew. Cattle might be driven on the hoof from Scotland to Smithfield market to feed the mouths of London, but they would still require pasture on the way. The cows kept for dairy purposes in and about the city needed grass or hay, which were bulkier than grain. It seemed imperative to make every effort to devote the midland and south midland counties to the object for which they seemed to have been intended by nature, particularly when the lighter soils of the eastern counties which were equally near London were unsuited for pasture. Here the tendency was to specialize in precisely the opposite direction. But enclosure had advantages for the stock-breeder which it did not possess for the corn-grower. He could improve his breeds, which he was unable to do so long as his animals formed part of a general herd dependent upon the parish bull. The hedges, injurious to crops, were a relief to cattle from the heat of the day. Besides, when he had a meadow of his own, he could grow trees and make a pond. The existence of cattle cannot have been an enviable one in the old days—lying under the burning sun tethered in the grass balks which divided the strips of tilled land in the open field, until the hay was cut in the common meadow; and not very much better after it had been cut, and they had been set free to graze there. It was thus that the midland counties were led to follow the example of those of the extreme north, west, south-west, and south-east of England, almost all the cultivated part of which, as well as much of Wales, had been quietly enclosed before the eighteenth century.

Enclosure had few advantages in a plain of good natural arable land. But the rise in prices which set in soon after King George III's accession in 1760 revealed possibilities of fortunes to be made in agriculture. In the best districts men of enterprise chafed under the difficulties imposed by a common rule as to what crops should be grown. It was impossible to grow turnips when all the cattle in the village were turned on to everybody's land as soon as the corn was cut. But where the land was poor or uneven there were other reasons why the good farmer should desire to have his own land compact and undisturbed. He was able to drain it properly. He could improve sandy soil by mixing marl and clay. The best example of this was Norfolk, which, from being in the early part of the eighteenth century a country of miserable sheep-runs worth a yearly rent of two shillings an acre at best, had become long before its close the agricultural marvel of England, with its rich landlords and large farmers, and their turnips and clover.

Strong and reasonable as was the demand for parliamentary enclosure, it brought many evils in its train and met with fierce opposition. The legal expenses were con-

THE CLOSE OF THE EIGHTEENTH CENTURY 25

siderable. The cost of actual hedging was high, and, of course, larger in proportion, the smaller the area enclosed. But it was from the loss of their common rights that the people suffered most. They lost, with or without compensation, their rights of grazing over the common field and meadow, and in the case of an enclosure of the waste they lost rights not only of grazing but of cutting turf and wood for fuel. The common lost the half-famished cow and raw-ribbed pony—also the goose, that famous long-lived animal which supplied the cottager not only with eggs, but with a crop of a shilling's worth of feathers every year. The old village community lost its character. In many cases some of the classes which formed it disappeared. The squatters, living usually on the edges of moors and forests, had the reputation of being poachers and thieves—at best idlers, who could not be depended upon for honest work. Although in many cases their prescriptive rights in their habitations were recognized, in others they received short shrift and the land which they had taken in from the waste was treated as encroachment and taken from them. If they were allowed to keep it, they might still be unable to live now that they were prevented from using the land beyond. They became day-labourers, or drifted into the towns. They were followed by the cottagers of the village itself, who found that it paid to part with the land allotted to them and thus defray the legal expenses and save themselves the cost of fencing. If they remained as day-labourers they could but spend the balance in drink; if they elected to emigrate they had so much to face the world with. They could often have had no gardens round their cottages. The land which they had formerly possessed had formed part of the common field and meadow. They had to sell their cows and any other animals which they may have had. Such was the position in which the law and the Commissioners appointed by Parliament usually left them.

But there were numerous exceptions. Taking England

as a whole, it is probable that the number of occupiers of agricultural land who hired no labour still in 1800 greatly exceeded those who did. All through this period the landowners and farmers fluctuated between two ideals. One was that there should be a plentiful supply of daily labour always at command; the other demanded a longer view. It was that the men available should have some stake of their own in the village as well as being dependent upon labouring for others. Such men had some standing, could work better, and would not in their old age become a charge upon the parish. Young found in Lincolnshire in 1799 newly enclosed villages where each cottage was given its three acres on which a cow was kept. Cows in fact kept the poor-rates down. Lord Winchelsea's experiments in Rutland and Bucks in giving his cottagers good gardens and cow-pasture were completely successful, and found several imitators. They would have found more, but for the mixture of short-sighted selfishness and childlike faith in the working of economic laws which characterized the time.

It was this which in so many cases ruined the small farmer, who was the next to disappear. The movement, of which enclosure was only a part, was one to convert agriculture into an industry on a large scale, with a large turnover and big profits. The landlord's agent could not be bothered with a number of small tenants, and preferred to roll three or four into one. As the profits of corn and cattle rose, while the cost of wages lagged behind, there were farmers who could afford to take these large farms. The agent was also saved the trouble of seeing to the repairs of several small buildings instead of one large. The landlord was often misled as, although the cost of repairs was considerably reduced if there was only one farm, this did not make up for the loss of the higher rate of rent which the smaller farmer paid. But at a time when all rents were being enhanced this might easily escape notice.

Another frequent result of the change was the banishment

of the hired servant from the farmer's house, except in the north of England. The farmers were making fortunes, or at least becoming gentlemen—a word which in those days of industrial progress was rapidly ceasing to have any connection with birth. Once a tenant could set apart a couple of rooms in his house as parlours, and could dispense with the necessity of following his own plough, but merely managed and went to market, he could, like the Robert Martin of Jane Austen's Emma, claim the status of a gentleman farmer. He drank his bottle or two of port, and when a year of scarcity and high prices came, and he could make a 200 per cent. profit—so the Earl of Warwick complained in the House of Lords in 1800—he played guinea whist, and mixed brandy with his wine. No longer would he deign to sit down to table with cowherds and plough-boys. The labourer went into one of the deserted smaller farmhouses. He did not feed as well as he had done at his master's table, and meat no longer formed a regular part of his diet. Several rungs of the ladder were now taken away by which the industrious labourer formerly rose to the position of a substantial farmer or even a small proprietor, just as one who in the towns, starting from the bottom, becomes the owner of a large concern or factory. He had no standard of life before him, no hope of rising, no reason to wait. With the poor-law as the false friend of his youth and the one expected comfort of his age, he married as soon as he reached manhood, and surrounded himself with children, whom he could throw upon the parish for support.

A few more features complete the picture of the new village after the economic revolution had been completed. Hand-threshing had always given employment in the early winter months, and now hedging and ditching, the repair of roads, and the care of root crops were added. It was fortunate, for the old cottage industries were beginning to disappear, the spinning-wheel among the first. Everything was to be had at the market towns, brought there from the manufacturing centres. Even food could hardly be had in the village. The cottager had no longer a chicken-run. He could get no eggs. The price of butter and cheese had risen enormously against him. Milk he could scarcely get at all, and he was obliged to substitute the weakest of tea at twopence an ounce to drink with his meals, unless he was fortunate enough still to be able to brew his own ale or cider. The villager could rarely now carry his own grain to the miller, have it milled, and bake his own bread with his own flour. The miller dealt wholesale both with the grower and the baker, and the custom of baking at home went out, particularly as fuel had become so hard to get. In the north, however, there was still a considerable consumption of butter-milk and curds by the poor, and bread continued to be baked at home. The northern labourer had a little meat occasionally, whereas the southern had to be content with bread and cheese from one week's end to another.

Such were some of the changes which ruined the old rural life of a great part of England. By the end of the century the evil was only too obvious, but those who recognized it, caught up as they believed in the revolving wheels of an inexorable economic system, could not find the cure. A proposal to enact a scheme for the establishment of smallholdings, such as Winchelsea had introduced, would have shocked Parliament. Some impatience was occasionally expressed at the import of corn being in bad years promoted by bounties, which amounted to the encouragement of foreign agricultural improvements. It was pointed out that some of this money might have been spent in assisting agriculture at home by reducing the parliamentary cost of enclosure. This alone would have retained many of the poorer commoners in the possession of their lands. A general enactment might have been brought in, which would have reduced the cost to them of an enclosure still more, and have ensured them their proper shares. But although this was one of the objects of the General Enclosure Act of 1801, it was attained only to a very limited extent. The only remedy attempted for poverty was as blatant a breach of economic laws as any other could have been, and only intensified the evil which it was supposed to cure. In 1795 the wages difficulty came to a head in Berkshire. Here, as elsewhere, they had not kept pace with the growing cost of living, and had been supplemented from the poor-rate. To remedy so obvious an injustice, both to the labourer himself and to the poor ratepayer who did not employ labour, the magistrates of the county met at Speenhamland to fix the wages of day-labourers according to the ancient statutes. It was open to the Berkshire magistrates either to make use of the Elizabethan machinery or to suggest special legislation. But in an evil hour they were put off their course by the bugbear of the law of supply and demand. They supposed that, if the farmers had not raised wages upon the recent rise in prices, it must have been because they were naturally apprehensive of not being able to reduce them after a fall. It would not be fair to interfere with them. They were afraid to use their statutory powers, and took a step which stereotyped the growing practice which they had met in order to prevent. They merely recommended the farmers to pay their labourers in proportion to the price of provisions, while at the same time they provided for their not doing so if they did not wish. In that case the wages of the labourer were to be made up to him. A scale was drawn up. Every able-bodied man was to receive altogether in wages from his employer and in allowances from the poor-rate the value of six quartern loaves of wheaten bread of 4 lb. $5\frac{1}{2}$ oz. each for himself, and three each for his wife and every member of his family. The scale had just been fixed when England experienced one of the worst harvests of the century. The price of wheat ran up to 75s. a quarter. The average of the last five years had not been more than 50s. It was clear that a rise like this could not be permanent. This reinforced the view that the condition of affairs should be treated as distress, and the burden thrown upon the rates. The system was generally adopted elsewhere, and the principle was in the following year approved by Parliament.

Some eminent men, such as Lord Grenville and his brother Thomas, acutely perceived the absurdity of this arrangement. But they formed an insignificant minority. The mass of members of Parliament and even of economists appeared to take it for granted that the wages of able-bodied labour ought to be paid in part out of rates levied generally on the inhabitants of the parish. In 1799 a local magistrate furnished Arthur Young with an elaborate budget for a labourer with no children in prosperous Norfolk. He put the rent of a cottage low enough at sixpence a week, food for the man and his wife at only sixpence a day each, and the total at £30 9s. 2d. To meet this the labourer earned only 8s. a week for 48 weeks of the year; and this with his extra earnings at harvest, with what his wife got by gleaning and other labour, came only to £26 os. 6d. But Young offers no comment on the deficit. To a labourer so situated, what would usually be regarded as improvidence became an act of calculated self-interest. If the quartern loaf stood at a shilling, every infant brought into the world was worth three shillings to him under the Speenhamland scale. It was difficult, indeed, to save enough for food and clothing on the man's own allowance of a loaf for himself for six days out of seven in the week. But if he had a wife and half a dozen boys and girls his allowance was twenty-seven loaves, and that number of shillings was comparative affluence. The labourer was already prone to marry much earlier than the small farmer and the hired labourers who lived on the farm had been. The last had been in the habit of waiting until they could establish some standard of living. But the new labourers felt that to wait for this was to wait for ever. The result was a growth of population which went far to make up for the loss in rural districts through other causes.

In such circumstances a comparison between earnings and cost of living becomes an imperfect test of the condition of the people. Wages were unnaturally forced down by the system of a subsidy out of the rates. On the other hand, the labourers had the subsidy to fall back upon. In 1803, partly a year of peace, when the price of wheat averaged under 60s. a quarter, which was less than at any time for the past five years, one person in seven of the population of England and Wales was in receipt of parochial relief. Without such help it is difficult to understand how a labourer could exist, unless he had no family, or had some small holding of his own, or unless his family was able to supplement his earnings substantially by cottage industries. The ordinary weekly wage was eight shillings, or sometimes a little more in the north and midlands. In the fens of Lincolnshire it might be two or three shillings more. Farther north the old practice of boarding and generally also lodging with the farmer was retained on a yearly wage, which was £12 to £18 in 1794. In the south-west of England the wage was only 6s. a week. In the last twenty years of the century total earnings had risen by about one-half. But this was not enough with bread doubled in cost. Even cheese had begun to be a luxury and ale-drinking a vice.

A remedy for the labourer's destitution was furnished to some extent by the causes which produced it. Soldiers were required in ever-increasing numbers for the war with France; and the great manufacturing centres which were destroying the village industries demanded recruits as well. The labourer was, however, shackled to some extent by the law which made any newcomer, who had not acquired a settlement, as defined by certain conditions, liable to removal back to his birthplace if he were likely to become a burden upon the parish. Such was the law up to 1795; after that date he could only be removed if he actually became a pauper.

The injury done to the agricultural community did not go farther than this. There merely ceased to be a peasantry in England. The very word was no more in repute. Regardless of Goldsmith's famous lines, men imputed a sort of shame to those ties which, light as osier bands, yet firm as oak, bind a peasant to the land which he tills for himself. A heavy force had thrust itself into the old fluid society of the village. But while it had driven all that was on its left side down into destitution or poverty, it pressed that which was on its right into prosperity and even opulence. It is true that the smaller landed gentry were disappearing. But for this other causes were responsible. The standard of living rose for the poor country gentleman just at the time when taxation depressed him. "Lord North's American war", wrote Bishop Richard Watson, "rendered it difficult for a man of five hundred pounds a year to support the station of a gentleman, and Mr. Pitt's French war has rendered it impossible." But the rural revolution only tended—so far as he was concerned—to postpone the evil day. The yeomen were also among those who escaped. Some few were attracted into the growing industrial centres. Some sold their land in order to use their capital to farm larger areas as tenants. Many remained as they were, and their numbers were recruited from farmers who purchased their farms. Large farmers were much better off than they had been. Rents rose on enclosure, it is true, but it was because tenants were well able to pay them. A farm mainly of fair average pasture could, after enclosure, pay a pound an acre annually, fair arable and good pasture at least five shillings more. But in new leases of enclosed land granted in the last year or two of the century it was usual to enhance the rent by at least twenty per cent. It was, however, in reclaiming waste land, and improving stock and methods of cultivation, that fortunes could be made by landlords. All these three things were done by Thomas Coke of Holkham, whose history is a classic page in the romance of

THE CLOSE OF THE EIGHTEENTH CENTURY

agriculture. Between 1776 and 1818 he raised the rent of his estate on the bleak Norfolk coast from £2,200 to £20,000, and that without rack-renting or severity of any kind.

The actual progress of enclosure was very uneven. The outbreak of war in 1793 gave a powerful impulse to the movement, particularly in the counties best suited for corn-growing. At the end of the century, the open-field system prevailed in the south midlands only, where the growing-price of corn hindered the conversion of arable to pasture, and yet no great profit could be expected from enclosure while the land remained under the plough. Here in particular the movement met with considerable opposition, and was most irregular. It may easily be supposed that the violent contrasts presented by a country in which villages which had and villages which had not undergone a social revolution lay side by side, would not have escaped notice. In 1809 Arthur Young claimed that it was easy to distinguish the intelligent farmers who belonged to the enclosed villages in Oxfordshire from the others, who were a century behind in their ideas. Another contrast was drawn by Eden between two Buckinghamshire parishes not many miles apart—Winslow, enclosed in 1766, and Maids Morton, not as yet enclosed. The latter had the old system of small farms at annual rents varying from £17 to £90. The poor-rates from 1792 to 1795 averaged only 3s. 4d. Daily rates and piece-work are quoted for labourers, as that class did not depend upon a regular weekly wage. The earnings were 1s. 3d. to 1s. 6d. a day. In Winslow larger farms of £60 to £400 were the vogue. The poor-rates for the same years averaged 5s. 2d. Wages were no more than 7s. a week. It was not until he was a weekly labourer that the villager felt the rise in prices, and it was in Devonshire, which had become an enclosed county generations before the memory of living man, that the high prices of 1801 led to a serious outbreak.

The seasons of the last decade of the eighteenth century

had been poor, and the violent upward movement of prices in such years as 1795, 1796, 1799, and 1800 must be put down to this. But even the good seasons of 1796 and 1797 could not bring the average price of corn below 50s. a quarter in 1797 and 1798, and such a rate would have marked a bad and not a good year in the preceding decade. The rise in average prices was due to other causes than bad seasons. The first official census of England and Wales, held in 1801, gave a population of 8,872,980. In 1811 it was 10,150,615. A population which increased with such rapidity during the first decade of the nineteenth century must have been growing not much less rapidly during the years immediately preceding it. More food of every kind was required. At the same time the consumption of wheat was increasing in other ways. The midlands had begun to give up barley-bread. Cleanliness and vanity also took their toll. Starch absorbed about 40,000 quarters a year. When as a measure of enforced war economy a tax was put on hair-powder, one of the newspapers said that it would have been better to prohibit it altogether, instead of continuing to flour the heads of a quarter of a million men in the army and navy, and exempting them from the tax. Each of the country's defenders sprinkled his head with a pound of flour in the shape of hair-powder every week, which would have much better gone into a civilian stomach. All these circumstances occasioned a deficiency in the supply of wheat. The year 1792, the last year before the twenty years of scarcely interrupted war with France, was also the last in which ordinary wheat exports exceeded imports. England now began to depend upon foreign corn, and in the ten years from 1795 to 1804 her imports exceeded her exports by 6,152,000 quarters, at prices loaded with insurance at war risks. At a quarter a head yearly this was equivalent to the requirements of one person in every fourteen or fifteen. The acreage under wheat in the country was, in fact, insufficient. For over a hundred years the Government had successfully

THE CLOSE OF THE EIGHTEENTH CENTURY 35

pursued a policy of maintaining it by granting a bounty on export of 5s. a quarter whenever the price fell to 48s., or, later on, to 44s. It was now obliged to encourage import by heavy bounties, as well as becoming itself an importer.

Two other circumstances assisted in the general rise in prices. The first was somewhat late in its operation. It was connected with that peculiar institution, the Bank of England, which carried on the temporary financing of Government, and the arrangements for the National Debt, and the issue of notes current throughout the country. Sometimes it has been said to be under completely private and independent management, sometimes to be to all intents a State concern. But it is evident both that the Directors of the Bank, elected as they were by the proprietors of the Bank stock, were in themselves independent of the Government, and at the same time that the Government possessed considerable influence in the affairs of the Bank. When the latter was in difficulties it had recourse to the State. One of these occasions was in February of 1797, at a time when an invasion scare had led to a run on the country banks of the north. This in turn produced a run on the Bank of England, at a time when a considerable quantity of gold had left the country in payment of foreign subsidies. The Bank feared that it would not be able to fulfil its obligation to continue to pay cash for its notes. In order to save it from bankruptcy, the Chancellor of the Exchequer, William Pitt, with great promptitude issued an order prohibiting it from doing so. The return to cash payment was not made until 1821. It was obvious that during the interval it was open to the Bank substantially to increase its paper issue without any fear of bankruptcy. This was actually done. The practice of the Bank was to lend in notes at five per cent. as much as the public required, provided that good security was offered. This co-operated in the general rise of prices. The face value of Bank of England notes in circulation when the stoppage was ordered was rather more than

£8,500,000. It had been as much as £11,000,000. But now the Bank, having no longer any fear of the presentation of the notes, was able to go far beyond this figure, and beyond what was necessary in order to replace gold, which had passed out of circulation and was no longer minted. The average note circulation for 1800 was nearly £16,000,000.

The other factor in the rise of prices was the growth of country banks, another institution characteristic of English enterprise. In every country town there was probably some tradesman or other individual known as having more dealings than anyone else with the capital. Such a man would fall into the habit of purchasing his customers' bills on London, and sending them along with his own. Presently he would put up "The Bank" over his door. He would begin to take money on deposit, paying interest; and to issue loans in his turn. Finally, he would print notes and issue them. A full-blown country bank was now in existence. Other such concerns were started with the direct encouragement of London bankers. The bankers, being obliged to cash their own notes when presented, in gold, or Bank of England notes, or bills on London if required, were unable to issue as many notes as they liked. The notes of each country bank were current only in the restricted domain within which it was known and could be easily reached. It could not supply that area with more currency than was necessary for the transaction of ordinary business within it. Once it overstepped this margin, those in possession of more of its notes than were locally needed would desire to invest in the Funds, or to buy something from London or elsewhere. The bank would find this excess of notes returned to it over the counter, and Bank of England notes or bills upon London demanded in exchange; and it would be obliged to cut down its issue of notes until equilibrium was restored. The operations of country banks were thus harnessed to those of the Bank of England, in the same way as those of the latter had been through gold to the exchanges of the

THE CLOSE OF THE EIGHTEENTH CENTURY

world before the stoppage of cash payment. If the note issue of the Bank of England was henceforward unrestricted, that of the country banks was not. They did, however, increase the volume of currency within their domains to a very considerable extent. It was of course to their interest to do so as much as possible, and a competition grew up between each country bank and its neighbours, as well as the Bank of England. When the last increased its issues the former could increase theirs. In March 1801, during the scarcity, when the Earl of Suffolk proposed in the House of Lords to limit the circulation of the notes of country banks, he put it at £30,000 for each, or about £12,000,000 for the whole number—much the same amount as that of the Bank of England five-pound notes. It was, moreover, in the interest of the country banks to supply every individual locally known to them, who required a loan upon good security. Had there been no country bank, he would probably not have been able to get a loan at all. There were already on the computation of Henry Thornton, an eminent banker and member of Parliament, 353 banks in 1797, and the number had risen to 386 in 1800, and was rising rapidly. Every one of these banks had an interest in financing trade up to the full limit of its legitimate requirements. This was the second cause of the increase in the medium of exchange. It was an increase in that part of the currency which took the shape of paper only, and it did much more than merely take the place of the gold which had gone over to the Continent. There was more money in circulation; and had the harvest of 1800 been as good as that of 1796, prices must still have risen about ten per cent. owing to the relative fall in the value of money alone.

The establishment of country banks is responsible for one more of the causes of dearness. The throwing of farms together was much assisted by the increasing ease with which loans could be raised. Before there was a local bank, or some equivalent, a farmer whose stock was worth a thousand pounds, when compared with his neighbour who was worth fifty, was only by so much better off. But his advantages were immensely increased by the arrival upon the scene of a banker who knew what he was worth. He could easily borrow enough to enable him to rent and stock another farm of half the size of his own original one. At harvest-time he had another advantage. Being able to live on borrowed capital if necessary, until wheat had reached the top of its market, he was no longer obliged to sell at once. He could even buy up the stock of the small farmers, beating them down in price, and thus keep grain back. A complaint was made in a letter to The Times of January the 9th, 1801, that this was notoriously done. As the engrossment of farms proceeded, more and more of the corn of the country passed into the hands of the bigger men; and the consumer no longer enjoyed the advantage of the producer's extreme readiness to sell. Besides, the farmer could himself afford to produce less than three or four smaller men farming all together the same number of acres. Instead of growing as much wheat as before, and buying luxuries, he could grow less wheat and more oats, keep good horses, and ride to hounds. In any case, he would require more oats, for he would employ proportionately more and stronger horses on his land than the smaller farmer would do.

In spite of the fact that meat was not now eaten by the poorer labourer on the land as it formerly had been, the demand for cattle had risen. This was due to the growing standard of living among other classes, and the increasing requirements of the town, both in meat and dairy produce. This kept land under pasture, and acted as a counterpart to the growth of tillage through breaking up of waste land. The area under wheat was further reduced owing to changes in the method of agriculture. Turnips now began to form part of the rotation on all but the heaviest lands, and the turn of wheat came less often. Ploughs and carts had formerly been drawn by an animal which, when too old

THE CLOSE OF THE EIGHTEENTH CENTURY 39

to work, served its masters for food. But now the place of the ox was taken by the horse, a consumer of oats with a carcase of no value. It was the most significant novelty in agriculture in the last years of the eighteenth century, and it was connected with a number of other changes. Under the old method of husbandry the land was often so thick with weeds as to require a heavy plough, and this suited oxen. Time was not valued, and by lengthening the day if necessary they could finish their acre before night as well as horses could. There were no roads over the common field in the old unenclosed village, and the other roads were thick with mud, so that the expense of shoeing oxen used for carts was often saved. But enclosure brought early weeding and light ploughs; more and better roads were made; and time was more valued. The horses could work on a gentleman's farm one day, and draw the family coach the next; or, if a farmer fancied horse-dealing, he could break his horses in at home and send them to London to become carriage horses or something better. Oxen still persisted in the West of England, and in other places they were still occasionally reintroduced after being long unknown. The relative merits of the two animals were a subject of almost as keen discussion as those of enclosure and the old system. But where oxen had once disappeared, it was only large farmers or proprietors who could make it worth their while to bring them in again, and these would seldom care to do so.

Although its bucolic character had been lost, the husbandry of the country remained generally primitive. Threshing was almost universally carried out with the flail by hand—as was reaping. But it was a time of considerable enterprise. Threshing mills were started in several counties. In 1804 Young records the setting up in Norfolk of what was probably the first steam-engine to be used wholly for agricultural purposes—a ten horse-power machine to do threshing, grinding, and straw-cutting. In 1801 the Royal Society of

Arts gave a prize of a silver medal to a Northampton man for a cultivator of an advanced type. The same Society encouraged forestry, a science which lagged behind agriculture proper, by the grant in 1803 of a gold medal for the largest number of trees planted in a given time. It was won by the Earl of Fife, who planted millions of trees on his Scottish estate. Everywhere considerable interest was taken in the simpler sorts of agricultural machinery. Rotation of crops and the effects of the ordinary manures were carefully studied. Fancy prices were now given for fat cattle, and their breeders became famous. The traditional British meat had been beef, sheep being hitherto valued mainly for their wool—the established basis of English prosperity—and for their manure. Now this was changed. An invitation to dine often took the form of asking a man to eat his mutton with his host. But the fleece had not lost its importance. The Duke of Bedford's annual sheep-shearing was one of the great annual festivals of the country—far more notable than any race-meeting. The King himself hit the taste of his age by his interest in his own breed of Merino sheep, and in agriculture generally. From about the middle of the eighteenth century yeomen and farmers had begun to emancipate themselves from the common error of despising their own calling, and of educating their sons for the professions when they could afford to do so. They still educated them, but it was to become practical farmers afterwards. There has probably never been so highly civilized a nation in which agriculture as a pursuit was held in so much honour, or made the subject of so much intelligent discussion. Even the large manufacturers were interested in dairying and horse-breeding, and eagerly bought land and farmed it.

This was particularly the case in Yorkshire. The population of this great county was found in 1801 to be 858,892—not much less than one-tenth of the whole of England and Wales. Full of sturdy freeholders who voted for their county representative in Parliament, it was able to claim a political leadership of the whole country. A Yorkshire meeting was generally believed to give the political tone to the kingdom. Nor was its principal industry, the production of cloth, divorced from agriculture. Many of the clothiers, employing a few journeymen in their hand-looms, and doing some of the work themselves, were at the same time freeholders, possessing a few acres of land. Even where they did not, they enjoyed an independent position. William Wilberforce, speaking for his Yorkshire constituents in a debate upon the Union with Ireland in 1800, claimed a special superiority for the woollen industry. "It is", he said, "a domestic manufacture, not so much carried on in large factories where multitudes are collected together, and children learn prematurely the vices of a more advanced age; but any industrious individual possessing credit for a capital of £10 buys therewith a pack of wool, works it up with the assistance of his wife and family, and brings it to the public market for sale, just as the little farmers bring their little articles of produce; the wealth thus acquired and diffused is not obtained at the expense of domestic happiness, but in the enjoyment of it." Such men were scattered all over the West Riding of the county. Leeds itself stood only sixth in England with a population of 53,162, although that town was well to the fore in the adoption of steam-power for the purposes of manufacture, and although wool was the leading industry of the whole country.

On the opposite side of the Pennine Range was growing up the new industry which was rapidly supplanting it, and was destined to found a school of politics which would make the pre-eminence of Yorkshire forgotten. Its material had nothing to do with British soil. It brought wealth to a mushroom growth of cotton lords. Some of these, such as the first Sir Robert Peel, came from the yeoman class. But they maintained little connection with the land. They were before very long to be ranged in violent hostility to the landed interest, desiring above all cheap food and low wages for those who worked for them. The mills which they accumulated upon the banks of two streams running through a district which possessed the damp climate essential to the production of a fine thread brought the population of Manchester by 1801 up to 84,020, or nearly half as many again as that of Leeds. The town possessed a College and a small intellectual circle of inquirers, in which medical men were the leading spirits. Here shone John Dalton, discoverer of the atom; here, too, Robert Owen once disputed theology with Coleridge. But the tastes of the better-class residents appeared to a friendly observer, John Aikin, to exhibit, almost at the end of the eighteenth century, an interesting survival of primitive manners. The respectable males of the town met for conversation, news, and a sixpennyworth of punch every day after dinner in a dark dungeon of a public-house, kept by one who punctually cleared them out at closing time with the words, "Past eight o'clock, gentlemen!" enforced by a whip with a long lash which he held in his hand. It is not astonishing that masters who submitted to this should have employed the same means in their factories with children who dawdled on their way to work. It is only to be expected that those who eagerly left what Aikin calls their elegant drawing-rooms for such places should have thought almost anything good enough for those whom they employed. Although houses had been originally run up anyhow to meet the demand for hands, this did not prevent considerable overcrowding, particularly in damp cellars, resulting in tuberculosis, paralysis, and above all the deadly and virulent spotted fever. This last disease was worthily met by the institution of an infirmary by a local Board of Health in 1796, after which the health of the town improved. The new streets, which gradually took the place of the old lanes of wood-and-plaster houses, were creditable. The census figures of 1801 exhibit genuine overcrowding only in one quarter, where there were 276 families of 2,341 people in

271 of the small houses of that date. Moreover, there came a slight change for the better in the conditions of labour about 1800, when the waters of the Irwell and the Irk began to be replaced by steam as the motive-power of spinning machinery. Till this change was made, men, women, and children were expected to work an almost incredible number of hours in the twenty-four whenever there was a good rush of water, to make up for periods of enforced idleness when the mill-wheels did not run. By 1800 Manchester had 32 steam-engines.

The population of Lancashire as a whole was already 672,731, and was increasing much more rapidly than even that of the industrial or the West Riding of Yorkshire. It included not only the second but the third town in the kingdom in point of numbers, namely Liverpool, which had 77,653. Aided by the neighbouring system of canals, so much more important than roads, it had completely distanced Bristol, once second only to London, as the western port of Great Britain. 4,746 vessels entered its docks in 1800, paying over £23,000 in dues. It enjoyed an unenviable pre-eminence as the stronghold of that West Indian interest which carried on so pertinacious an opposition to the abolition of the African Slave Trade; and the West Indies formed at that time the principal source of Britain's mercantile and colonial wealth, and the quarter upon which her chief military energies were directed during the war with France, until the close of the century. Liverpool had also a growing trade with the United States of America, and was the principal port for Ireland. This was the cause of a considerable inflow of Irishmen, particularly during the distressed years of the close of the eighteenth century, which gave a permanent character to the lower strata of the town. The higher mercantile element was strongly reinforced by Scotsmen. Unlike the Irish, they did not form an alien colony. Sir John Gladstone, father of William Ewart Gladstone, had come from Leith. He founded two churches in Liverpool itself. The first was the Presbyterian Scottish church of the town; the second belonged to the Church of England. A cockpit in Cockspur Street illustrated a similar advance. It became first a Scottish dissenting chapel and finally Saint Andrew's Church.

Liverpool at this time occupied about a mile of the north bank of the Mersey, along which the docks lay, and stretched inland towards the hills for about two-thirds of that distance. Seen from outside, its windmills were its most prominent feature. Within doors pests of flies announced the existence in the town of numerous sugar warehouses. The civic sense of the people was strong. They had reason to be proud, not only of their docks, but of their waterworks, opened in 1801, and of the open streets which had, as in Manchester, taken the place of the narrow lanes which had formerly existed in the principal quarter of the town. There were other points of resemblance between the two towns. Although Liverpool had its Botanic Garden and its Athenæum, both founded by William Roscoe, then its greatest citizen, attempts at the encouragement of art, science, or literature were generally doomed to fail. Though the wealthiest people in the town did not meet habitually in taverns, the younger blades among them were little better than the Mohawks of the London of a much earlier generation. Riots in the streets, rowdiness in theatres, insults to women, and circulation of handbills in which young ladies were offered for sale, were among their curious diversions. So far as the poorer classes were concerned, the philanthropy of individuals and the public spirit of the Corporation, considerable as these were, could not keep pace with the evils incident to the rapid growth of an urban population. The inhabited houses, which had risen in number from 11,446 in the census of 1801 to 14,202 according to an enumeration made in 1807, were then found to include 2,920 cellars, often the residence of whole families, as in Manchester.

The engrossment of farms, which had depopulated the

Cheviots, had driven the people of the borderland between England and Scotland into the third great industry of the north. Newcastle, the centre of the northern coal trade, ranked next after Plymouth in the census, being eighth among the cities and towns of England, with a population of 28,366. The mines in this neighbourhood were the first in the country. Steam-power was used here, as elsewhere, for pumping and for bringing coal to the pit-head, whence it was conveyed to the wharves by iron railways run on self-acting inclined planes. The hewer's wage was 16s. a week, and a family with three or four boys working, the younger as trap-boys, the elder as "foals" drawing trams, could make 20s. to 30s. a week, and the fathers insisted on their boys going down the pit with them. The men were rough to their masters as they were to their children, and they would have been the last to submit to unfair treatment. So great was the demand for labour, that early in the new century the bounty for hewers rose from three to between twelve and eighteen guineas. They had a periodical dispute with the masters regarding their yearly bond of service, but at the moment there was no grievance. In some other parts of the country the mining population was even better off. In Monmouthshire, in the Forest of Dean, existed a class of forest-free miners. These could dig where they liked. In Derbyshire and Cornwall there was a system of contracting by which men were their own masters, often working only four or six hours a day.

The centre of the iron industry had grown up out of an ancient Warwickshire market town, in which smiths and cutlers had been tempted to set up their trade by the stock of coal and iron which lay to hand. Fourth in the kingdom, with its population of 73,670, Birmingham was already the first town in Europe in the enterprise of its inhabitants and the extraordinary variety of their productions. Building was among the most popular objects of speculation, and hence this town, with a smaller population, possessed more houses than either Manchester or Liverpool, and very nearly a house for every family. Their abodes were freely scattered on the slopes of the hill which gradually rises to the site of the classic Saint Martin's Church; they formed a rough half-moon with most of the barrack-like factories and homes of those who worked there below, and the better houses with their closes and gardens above. Two miles from the centre of the town was Soho, where Matthew Boulton, the greatest of England's industrial leaders, lived in feudal magnificence. It was a little town in itself with all its various industries. One was the construction of the steam-pumps for the tin-mines of Cornwall, another the minting of the copper coinage of the realm. Birmingham itself claimed to be the toy-shop of Europe by virtue of its pre-eminence in the production of a number of small articles of more or less fancy style, such as cheap jewellery, snuff-boxes, buckles, and buttons. It already bore an unenviable reputation for industrial charlatanism. Not only was it a great nursery of coiners of false—as well as genuine—money, but it turned out a great deal of shoddy stuff. Its cheap guns, which were sold to Africans, were more dangerous to the men who carried them than to their enemies. It specialized in false antiques. A contemporary squib pretended to advertise "Messrs. Humbug and Company" as having just received a large cargo of real antiques from Birmingham, manufactured there, consisting of Othos, Galbas, Neros, etc. But the alertness of its inhabitants was real enough. An idle person was not to be seen. They seemed to have not even time to wash their faces or to light and pave their streets. They worked hard and drank deep; they had their assembly-rooms or "Hotel", imitated London with their "Vauxhall" gardens, and boasted probably the best theatre outside the capital. The labourers were not badly off. They had their numerous clubs, which helped them to save money and at the same time to gratify a convivial and sometimes a gambling instinct. The contribution was usually sixpence a fortnight, and something was drunk for the good of the public-house in which they met. Besides the sick clubs, not uncommon elsewhere, Birmingham had its breeches clock and watch clubs. When there was enough money to purchase one of these articles, the members balloted for it, and this went on until all were served. For higher subscribers there were even clubs which drew for houses and capital. Most of the various products of the place could easily be manufactured by any clever and thrifty workman who had saved a hundred or even fifty pounds—as many did—and chose to set up for himself. A visitor to the town in 1791 has left his impressions: "Crusty knaves, that scud the street in aprons, seem ever ready to exclaim, 'Be busy and grow rich!'" Before that year it was thought safe to leave so loyal as well as industrious a town completely without police. It was never expected that Birmingham would become the scene of civil tumult. But loyalty itself fired the brand of anarchy. In that very year occurred the Church and King riots, directed against Doctor Priestley and other eminent Nonconformists of somewhat extreme reforming tendencies, one of the most ghastly outrages ever made by a mob upon the rights of free speech. No alteration was made in the government of the town, but the outbreak remained a warning that the notorious turbulence of the ship carpenters of Liverpool and the miners of Newcastle could find a counterpart in every large centre of population in the kingdom.

There was nothing on the west coast to disturb the rivalry between Liverpool and Bristol. The whole of Wales had only 541,546 inhabitants, and its largest town, Swansea, only 6,099. Though it had coal-mines in the south, where the Cornish ore went to be smelted, and a famous copper mine in Anglesey, it bore in general a rural and primitive stamp. The people had some strange superstitions. The belief for example in supernatural "knockers" who helped miners by imitating the sound of their work, and thus showing them where to search, was very prevalent. The people spoke their own language and had their own customs. The most picturesque of these was the maintenance of the old harper in families of importance, and occasionally at inns. The most useful was the practice of women working in the fields, one common enough certainly in most countries with the exception of England. The Welshwomen were very strong, and often went long distances to take up the heavier forms of domestic service. Their menfolk travelled to the English home counties for harvesting. Much of the communication with Wales, as well as with southern Ireland and the New World, was through Bristol. It imported wool from Spain, and was a market for the cloth trade of the south-west of England. It derived some advantage from being close to the Somersetshire coal-fields, and from its fine natural waterways in the Severn and the Wye. But all these sources of prosperity were failing. Partly owing to the greater energy of the northern people, partly to the advantages which they enjoyed in better water-power and, when that gave place to steam, to more abundant coal, the woollen manufactures of Gloucestershire, Wiltshire, Somerset, and Devon were gradually being superseded by those of Yorkshire. The canal system of the north and midlands balanced the rivers of Bristol. Its docks were poor, and when an improvement was made in 1803 it was already too late. It was now a long way behind Liverpool as a port, and although with a population of 63,645 it still stood fifth in the kingdom, it was steadily decreasing in importance relative to other large towns.

The industrial history of the country was still, however, very far from being the history of the large town or even of the towns in general. The first effect of the arrival of machinery had been to drive the manufacturer far from the centres of population. A tourist in Derbyshire, exploring the wild and romantic scenery of Matlock, suddenly found himself before a huge and barrack-like structure. It was the cotton mill of Richard Arkwright, the inventor of the water-frame. In the West of England, too, woollen manufacturers explored the river valleys for sites where water-power was available. In the eastern counties, with sluggish streams and no coal, the industry decayed. But before the end of the century both wool and worsted were being spun by Arkwright's frames, and Bradford, which had refused admission to a steam-engine as a "smoky nuisance" in 1793, accepted one in 1800. Yet even here the change from spinning by hand was very gradual. It was in cotton that the new inventions inaugurated the industrial revolution. Thirty years before the end of the century the weavers had still been unable to get all the yarn which they wanted, even when all the unattached women in the country were engaged as spinsters. They now found themselves fully employed. The cotton-weavers who lived in the Lancashire country-side on their tiny farms, much in the same prosperous way as the Yorkshire woollen weavers did, found it pay to engage half a dozen journeymen and apprentices, and convert their barns and empty rooms into loom-shops. Others lived and worked in cottages, each with its small garden, which rented at one or two guineas a year. The dwellings of each of these two classes of weavers were comfortable and well furnished. They had their handsome clocks, their pictures, their mahogany furniture, and their Staffordshire pottery. It was easy for them to afford such simple luxuries as they lived frugally. Oatmeal at about fourpence a pound was their principal food. Butchers' meat, costing sixpence a pound, was eaten at one meal a day with potatoes, three pounds of which could be got for a penny. Milk was largely drunk as well as ale.

Towards the end of the century a change set in. A new and entirely different class of weavers set up looms in the houses and cellars of Manchester and other towns. The power-loom had been invented, but it was not wanted in the cotton trade any more than in the woollen. The fly-shuttle was good enough. Even as it was, the weavers of the coarse cottons, many of whom had been attracted into the trade from other pursuits and had no special skill, were gradually ruined by the growing preference for the finer stuffs, and could seldom, even in better times, have earned much more than 15s. a week. The wages even of the highly paid cambric workers were brought down to 25s. in 1801. A number of causes co-operated to bring this about. The great burst of prosperity of about ten years earlier carried within it the germs of decay. The labour market was filled so quickly that it rose above its natural level. At the same time the war introduced a feverish race of price-cutting in the struggle to retain the Continental market. The great rise of food prices in 1800, the year of dearth as it was called, unfortunately operated to lower wages. Every weaver had to work full time in order to live at all, and there was a further glut of labour. By the end of the century the condition of no class of weavers in the cotton trade was prosperous.

The spinners were now the better off of the two classes. Women continued to be employed in spinning, as they had been while it was merely a home occupation. But the more complicated machines required men, and their wages on fine yarn at the beginning of the new century were about 35s. a week. It was easy to save on such earnings, and to become a master spinner in a small way, for spinning on mules and jennies—as distinct from the frame, which required power—still retained much of the character of a domestic industry. It was at this time that Manchester for a while outdistanced Birmingham as the nursery of the self-made man. Thrift had almost as much to do with this as enterprise. Among the numerous men who rose from the ranks whether of weavers or spinners was a saddler's son, Robert Owen. He would have been the first to say, in accordance with the ruling idea of his life, that he owed everything to his surroundings and nothing to himself. Getting on and growing rich was in the air even of Montgomery, where he was born in 1771. At nine years of age he wished to try his fortune in London. His parents made him wait only till he was ten. He was soon in good employment there, but he felt the lure of Manchester. Before he was a man, he had started his own small business in the cotton metropolis, with three spinners under him. The first factory in the town advertised for a manager on three hundred pounds a year, and Owen applied for the post. When told that he was young for such a salary—he was not yet twenty—he said that he could not take less, as he was able to prove that he was already making as much as this. He obtained the post. With his savings he was a few years later, when he wished to marry, in a position to join with others in a scheme to purchase the New Lanark Mills near Glasgow from his prospective father-in-law, David Dale, and so to render himself an eligible connection. He was only one of very many who rose, few of whom had his enterprise or abilities. It was not difficult to save in a community where this was the fashion, where hours were long and necessaries were cheap, where extravagance took repellent forms, and where there were few distractions. The hours of work followed the agricultural hours, which were generally from dawn to dusk in winter, and in summer twelve—and more at harvest-time—with short intervals for refreshment. But a full twelve hours could be worked in other industries, both in summer and winter. To save up for the Christmas festivities weavers thought little of working whole nights at the loom, singing carols such as "Christians, Awake" to keep themselves from sleep. In the good times when they worked sixty hours or less in a week, they worked a full twelve-hour day, and took a whole day off at a time.

William Cobbett, the son of a small farmer, related with pride in his delightful autobiography that he could not remember a time when he did not earn his own living. But the notion that there was nothing better than work was unfortunate in its effects upon the rising generation. It was taken for granted that, just as children helped their parents in agriculture and the domestic industries, they should continue to do so under the factory system. Sunday was their one idle day, and it was their most misspent day in the week. It was from observing this in the town of Gloucester that that friend of mankind, the journalist Robert Raikes, had been led to establish his Sunday schools. It was the general complaint that they picked up nothing but harm in the streets, and they would be much better employed attending church and learning to read. Only the enlightened Bishop Porteus dropped the suggestion that it was hard to deprive them of fresh air on their one free day in the week. The idea was brushed aside, partly because the votaries of Nature were still few, and those of religion and education many and enthusiastic, and partly because the fields themselves were a temptation to vice. On no day in the week was there so much crop-pilfering as on Sunday, and children took their full share. Rarely has a scheme originating in the brains of one or two individuals been more speedily and universally discovered to fill a genuine want than the institution of Sunday schools. The plan was eagerly taken up all over the country by numerous persons anxious to bestow on the children of the poor the rudiments of letters and religion. But it originated in the need of keeping them out of mischief. On weekdays this necessity was not felt. The children worked. In the manufacturing towns they could accompany their mothers to the warm factories; it seemed better for them than to be left for twelve or fifteen hours in the dismal cellars which were their homes. It seemed natural that they should be set at first to crawl about picking up the cotton-wool on the floor, and, as they grew older, put on to tasks suitable to their riper years, such as minding dangerous and unfenced machinery. In the letters of his imaginary Spanish traveller in England in the first years of the century, Southey made him write from Manchester: "I thought that if Dante had peopled one of his hells with children, here was a scene worthy to have supplied him with new images of torment." The hours he found were from five in the morning till six in the evening, with half an hour off for breakfast, and another half-hour for dinner. It must have been a comparatively humane factory, for fifteen hours a day were constantly worked. Not only did the children accompany their parents, but women were sent out to buy them, contractors would arrange for a wagon-load from the South of England, and poor-houses in London and elsewhere would send them by the score. Perhaps the lot of these children was better than that of the six-year-olds who spent twelve hours in pitch-darkness in the coal-mines opening and shutting trap-doors, or that of the climbing-boys or chimney-sweeps, sometimes the sons of master-sweeps, sometimes stolen boys, and sometimes boys who paid heavily for the crime of having gone the wrong way about the business of coming into the world at all.

It would be wrong to conclude that Lancashire men submitted to oppression either of themselves or of their families—at this period at least. Whatever the accumulated results of bad housing and long hours of work in heated rooms in a damp climate may have been later, the factory worker of 1801 still smacked of the country-side from which he came, and was one whom it was not safe to make into an enemy. Lancashire at this time bred the roughest men in England. They would fight together before the public in the most brutal manner, often till one or other was killed. The revival, early in the new century, of the cruel punishment of burning in the hand was not able to put down the custom. If the masters were hard they had good need to be. The history of the introduction of machinery, whether in that county or elsewhere, is a story of incessant intimidation —often successful. The masters had to go armed and to guard their factories as if they were fortresses. James Hargreaves, the inventor of the spinning-jenny, was driven out of Lancashire in fear for his life. One of Arkwright's mills was burnt down in spite of the presence of the police and troops, by a mob which marched through the country unopposed. A factory fitted with four hundred of Edmund Cartwright's new power-looms was destroyed in 1792, and the development of the weaving industry in this direction put off till the commencement of the nineteenth century.

Deplorable as all violence must be, it is most fortunate that the men had power to delay the introduction of machinery. Had power-looms been introduced before the war, as Cartwright intended, and the condition of the hand-loom weavers been gradually changing for the worse during the whole period of high prices, the result would have been a far greater shock to the social order than was the burning of a factory or two. This is true of other industries besides cotton. Wool lagged far behind, mainly because there were not the same fortunes to be made by the introduction of labour-saving appliances. Even the weaver's fly-shuttle, which generally increased the earnings of the men where it was introduced, was successfully resisted in parts of the West of England until far into the nineteenth century. The worsted weavers in particular were in no haste to adopt it, and appear to have taken a pride in their trade, even with its scanty earnings. About 1800, as related by a recognized authority, Edward Baines, one in a company of weavers betted that he was the only one present who had woven a five-shilling piece every week for the past twelve months. It is almost incredible, although it is the fact, that, aided no doubt by the earnings of their families in spinning and other subsidiary employments, the Yorkshire and Norwich men lived on scarcely more than this small sum weekly, and did not complain. But after 1800, with the arrival of the fly-shuttle, the wages even of worsted weavers rose to double and even treble as much. The other branches of the dispersed and complicated woollen industry were much better off. The spinners, who received least, got in the Leeds district 16s. 9d. in 1795, and 24s. 8d. in 1805. The operatives in one other

THE CLOSE OF THE EIGHTEENTH CENTURY 55

great industry, the frame-knitters of the Midlands, had been remarkable for the violence with which they enforced their demands. But the turn of the century was the time of fancy hose, and the knitters were now fairly prosperous. They were undisturbed by threatened innovation, and were able to maintain their earnings at a general average of fifteen shillings a week. There were two remaining localized industries of some importance, the steel industry of Sheffield and the Staffordshire potteries. The creators of the latter were the Wedgwood family, of whom the first Josiah, who died in 1795, had had the happy idea of hitting the classical taste of his age by producing from his workshop, which he called Etruria, appropriate designs which had been for many years the admiration of Europe. And this family was unique among the leading industrial families in the substantial encouragement which it gave to the English classics. It was through the munificence of the younger Josiah and Thomas Wedgwood that Coleridge was enabled by an allowance of £150 a year to devote himself to literature. They did not display their liberality only in the treatment of their workmen.

The object of all estimates of the wealth of the country as a whole must be a comparison either with that of foreign countries or with that of the same country at a different date. There can be no doubt that, compared with every other people existing in the world at that time, the British were extremely wealthy, whether judging by the impressions of travellers or by statistics. But for the second purpose, an estimate of the national resources in terms of what is conveniently called money is of very limited value. Regard must be had in the first place to its purchasing power. Food prices in average years were about 10d. or 11d. the quartern loaf of wheaten bread, 5d. or 6d. a pound for meat, 2d. a quart for milk, and about the same for ale and cider. Cotton fabrics were not cheap, and were as yet worn only by the few. A labourer's outfit of woollen and leathern garments, even in London, would not have been much above a couple of pounds. Bricks and mortar—or lath and plaster—could be obtained for very little. A good cottage could be built for £50, and many poor men put up their own. Quite large houses could be got for very little indeed. The lives of some celebrated men furnish interesting examples. One is that of "Hall-i'-th'-Wood" in Bolton, the glorious house with its beautiful oak staircase and mullioned windows, famous as the place where the spinning-mule was invented in 1779 by Samuel Crompton, who was, like his father, no more than a weaver and small farmer. No three people could have been much poorer in material wealth than Coleridge and William and Dorothy Wordsworth, whose banquets consisted of bread and cheese, washed down by a little brandy. Yet the last two, who were able to live for many years on a legacy of £900, rented a large mansion in Somersetshire for only £30 a year. There were already, indeed, signs of what afterwards became one of the most disgraceful scandals of the country, namely, the pulling down of cottages and deliberate laying waste of the country-side for fear of an increase in paupers and in the poor-rate. But the evil had not yet proceeded far. For the moment, the engrossing of farms had actually added to the accommodation in the village at all events, as the number of uninhabited houses shown in the 1801 census proves.

Where the three principal necessaries of life, food, clothing, and shelter, were cheap, and wants were few, it followed that the cost of labour and of all commodities produced wholly in the kingdom was low, and that moderate incomes still went a considerable way. But there is a second and a far more difficult point to consider in relation to any estimate of national wealth. Those who lived in the country produced most of their own food, their own furniture, and their own clothes. They were the vast majority. In computing the national wealth, these services could not be estimated, and yet the man who lived in the country might be better fed, and as well clothed and housed, as his cousin who had bought everything from persons whose names were in the trades directory. Moreover, there was not yet a vast organization of business and professional men who render services to one another which are paid for and assessed to income tax again and again, and so go to swell the total estimate of the national income. Nor was it replenished with the salaries of numbers of public servants, whether of Government or of local bodies, every penny of which is ultimately derived from production.

In 1798, before there had been any depreciation of the currency medium, William Pitt, as Chancellor of the Exchequer, made a careful estimate for income-tax purposes of the wealth of Great Britain, based upon the conclusions of Adam Smith, Arthur Young, and others. He estimated the cultivated land at 40,000,000 acres, yielding £25,000,000 a year to the landlord and £19,000,000 to the tenant. Tithes he put at £5,000,000; mines, canals, and timber at £3,000,000; the rent of houses at £6,000,000; the profits of the legal profession at £1,500,000; those of the medical and other professions at £500,000; and income derived by individuals from the public funds at £15,000,000. This gave a total of £75,000,000. He computed the total capital employed in foreign trade at £80,000,000, of which £30,000,000 were employed in the export of the leading manufactures of the country. He was without proper materials to enable him to carry out the task, always extremely difficult, of estimating the capital invested in the internal trade and leading manufactures. But he boldly took it at four times the sum employed in export of the principal manufactures, or £120,000,000. The profits upon this, as well as upon the foreign trade, were taken at £5 per cent., amounting, for both classes, to £30,000,000. To this remained to be added another rough estimate of the smaller or domestic trades, in which he included the brewing, distilling, and building trades, as well as those of the various classes of artisans. This he put for income-tax purposes at £10,000,000. Had he made no allowance for deductions he would probably have said £15,000,000. This would have brought the total yearly profits of trade and industry up to £45,000,000, still four millions less than those of the landlord, farmer, and tithe-receiver combined. Rents from the West Indies, £4,000,000, and from Ireland, £1,000,000, received and enjoyed by persons in Great Britain, brought the total of the national yearly income up to £125,000,000, exclusive of that of labourers and others who had less than £60 a year, or might completely escape income tax in other ways.

It is unlikely that Pitt's estimate was excessive, and there were no complaints in parliament on behalf of the landed interest, that the profits of the rival manufacturing and mercantile interests were rated too low. It may be taken, therefore, that, even if the wages and maintenance of labourers be left out of consideration, agriculture was still a source of somewhat greater wealth than all the remaining industries and trades taken together. But its primacy was being challenged. By 1800 the exports of Great Britain had risen, as officially valued, to over £24,300,000, the real, or declared, value being nearly £39,500,000. Those to America alone had doubled since the last year of peace, 1792, while the total was nearly half as much again as it had been in that year. The war had done something, but not much, to hinder the natural expansion of trade. Woollen goods stood first at nearly seven millions pounds, as officially valued, very soon to be outstripped by cotton, which in 1800 stood only second at five and a third millions. William Radcliffe, the proprietor of a weaving factory near Manchester, has left a vivid account of the growing market for this trade, lighting up at the same time the delightful relations then existing between employer and employed. On returning with his cash from market he would be accosted with the usual inquiry from one of the weavers: "Eh, mester, what a seet o' money yo han theer, I wonder weer yo'n git it?" He used to amuse them by naming the last place to which he had sent his bales, Frankfurt, Amsterdam, Moscow, even Paris; and on one occasion was able to say that he had got the money from "Bucharia," a rich trading country, lying north of Persia and "Hindostan."

Imports had also risen since 1792 by one-half, being officially valued at upwards of £30,500,000. The principal articles were sugar and coffee, mainly from the West Indies, each of which was valued at about £4,000,000. They were largely re-exported to the North Sea and the Baltic, and thus was England able to establish a control over the breakfast-tables of Europe, which had considerable influence upon warlike policy as it affected commerce. Tea from China, along with Indian piece-goods, the latter valued at over two and a half million sterling, were among the re-exports which she owed to the Eastern trade. The latter of these competed with the trade in British cotton piece-goods, and had been for some time regarded with considerable jealousy in Lancashire. But by now the advantages of machine-spun cotton had made themselves fully felt, and the Indian trade was declining. Corn was heavily imported in 1800, a year of great scarcity in England. A quantity valued at £2,675,000 was brought this year. The normal value of imported corn was hardly more than £1,000,000. The principal imports of raw materials of manufactures were 56,000,000 lb. of raw cotton, valued at £1,663,000, and 8,609,000 lb. of wool, valued at £500,000. A growing share of the cotton came from the United States, and a large but declining share of the wool from Spain.

The importance of the West Indian trade explains much of the war policy, both where it was wise and where it went wrong. Numbers of rich men in England derived a great part of their wealth from West Indian plantations. Their rents came to them in the form of sugar, coffee, and cotton; and nothing needed to be sent from home in exchange. The rest of what was needed to balance imports from the West Indies was supplied in various ways. Not much besides textiles was sent direct from England. A part reached those islands in the form of the most terrible of all trades—human merchandise from the east coast of Africa. The rest was made up by a round trade through the United States, which, in turn, received much more from Great Britain in the way of manufactures than it sent her in raw materials. This latter trade also helped to support British credit on the Continent, for whether or not England's merchandise was allowed to pass freely into the Baltic or upon the Italian coast, a bill drawn in St. Petersburg or Leghorn could always be discounted in New York. Inability to recognize this led to an undervaluing of the trade with the United States, which produced serious trouble in the latter part of the war. On the other hand, the value of the West Indian trade was fully appreciated. It was this which justified the policy of annexing the sugar islands in the possession of the enemy, particularly as the sugar of Martinique—as well as the coffee of Havana—was reputed much superior to that of the British colonies. It was this also which for years supported the African slave trade. Sugar was produced by slave labour. The supply could not, it was thought, be maintained except by the regular importation of fresh slaves. Upon this ground the slave trade was defended as the mainstay of British prosperity.

At the same time the trade with Northern Europe was far more important than either the American trade, the West Indian trade, the trade with the Iberian Peninsula or the Levant, or the trade under the control of the East India Company. While nearly one-fourth of the tonnage of British shipping which cleared from Great Britain—exclusive of that with Ireland—was for the West Indies, the proportion which went to the Baltic ports alone was not far short of a third. There was a great trade with these last in foreign vessels as well, and the United States carried nearly all its own trade. The total of neutral shipping which sailed from Great Britain was, however, not much more than half of the British share, so partial was the effect of the war upon commerce. In fact, six British ships, besides 206 foreign, actually cleared for France in 1800. One of these carried, besides a cargo of coffee, cotton, and sugar, a passenger by the name of Edwards, who unofficially entered into a friendly discussion with a French Minister upon the various difficulties in the way of exporting French corn to Great Britain at a time when his country was such a ready buyer. The ports which registered the largest number of ships after London and Liverpool were the northern ports of Newcastle, Hull, and Sunderland. The metropolis, with close on three thousand ships of a tonnage of over a million, was easily first. But she was not content with her primacy. In an endeavour to challenge again the supremacy which Liverpool had wrested from her in one trade, that with the West Indies, she had just built the West India Docks. The London Docks and the East India Docks followed a little later.

The internal trade of the country was only beginning to be of importance. The surplus production of the industrial centres consisted mainly of luxuries, in the sense of articles which were hardly consumed at all by the poorer classes—cotton piece-goods and refined sugar, for example. Had the country possessed a number of rivers navigable for long distances inland, a greater interest would have been taken in the development of the home market, more attention would have been paid to the growing impoverishment of the agricultural population, and the whole economic history of the country would have been different. As it was, reliance was placed on the coasting trade. Two-thirds of the average tonnage entering the Port of London consisted of coasting vessels; but more than half of this brought coal from the Tyne and the Wear. Comparatively little was employed in carrying the fabrics of Lancashire and Yorkshire to the metropolis. The place of rivers was to some extent taken by canals. It was in about the year 1790 that speculation in this form of enterprise was at its height. But it was justified, the usual rate of interest on a successful canal being ten per cent. The object usually was to connect some such inland town as Manchester or Birmingham with one of the ports, and this made it more dependent than before upon foreign trade. By the end of the century, 2,600 miles of canals were in existence. In 1801 the Paddington canal was opened with pomp and firing of cannon. Four years later permission was asked for coal to be brought by it to London. Newcastle had fine sea traditions, and there was considerable opposition from those who feared that, if coal ceased to be brought by sea, the breed of British seamen would be impoverished. But leave was granted, and the old name of sea-coal for the fuel burnt on London hearths now lost its meaning, although the quantity which actually arrived by canal was never considerable.

It was hopeless to expect to carry merchandise to any extent by land. In the extreme south-west, for example, there were next to no roads at all; only pack animals were used; even such towns as Bristol had sledges and not carts. Farther east, as the roads improved, carters were seen leading clumsy wagons drawn by teams of six or eight horses or oxen. In 1806 Parliament took note of the vigorous enforcement of the law that wagons with wheels six inches thick must not be drawn by more than four horses on turnpike roads. But this was the measure of the interest taken by Government in maintaining good roads. Not even did King George's travelling upon his own highway between Gloucester and Cheltenham make any difference, for Gloucestershire still kept up its reputation for the worst roads in England, perilous in summer and impassable in winter. But the Government had effected a great change in travelling during the last twenty years by the introduction of mail-coaches. There were now three public conveyances for passengers—the mailcoach travelling at seven miles an hour including stoppages, the ordinary stage-coach at six, and the slow coach at five. The first carried six inside passengers and four on the roof. Continental visitors such as Niebuhr, the future historian and statesman, found that the sacrifices which they were required to make to the speed and punctuality of the mails were more than they could bear. The mail-coaches went too fast to enable them to see the country; their luggage was knocked to pieces; only the briefest periods, and at long intervals, were allowed for refreshment; the time occupied in changing horses was of little or no use, as that often took only a minute; and these conveyances were particularly liable to be upset. The cost of coach-travelling was about sixpence a mile—in mail-coaches rather more. But the outlying parts of the country had no coaches. Travellers into Wales were obliged (unless they went by boat from Bristol) to take postchaise from Shrewsbury. Travelling in this way with a pair of horses cost no more than eighteen-pence a mile for three persons; but where the hills were steep four horses were necessary. But even postchaises were not always to be had in distant parts. In country neighbourhoods it was difficult to move about in winter, or in rough country at any time, without four horses. The simplest way of reaching the posting-road was on horseback, sending the luggage down by a farm-cart. In such circumstances country places were necessarily much isolated. But there was no lack of choice spirits who drove with reckless speed on those breakneck roads. What especially struck a foreign traveller was the numbers of all classes who were seen walking in the towns, while outside them all, except the very poorest, appeared to ride or drive. The roads in the neighbourhood of the metropolis in particular had a very gay appearance on a summer afternoon, crowded with vehicles of all kinds returning from pleasure parties, or bringing merchants back from their villas to start work early on the Monday morning.

The Londoner loved the country, or at any rate the road. Noblemen had their villas—sometimes large, ungainly mansions—scattered beyond the nursery gardens of Chelsea and Kensington. To those accustomed to the great houses of Continental capitals they seemed to be only encamped in the metropolis. In imitation City men kept their families, at least during summer, in what Coleridge satirized as "a cottage of gentility" in Clapham or Hampstead, instead of living with becoming splendour at or near the places where they worked. This custom happily hindered the growth of London. In 1801 it was found to contain a population of 864,845, comprised in 216,073 families in 121,229 inhabited houses. Most of it was included between a line drawn from the turnpike at Hyde Park Corner so as to meet the Thames where it turns to the east near Charing Cross, and to follow its left bank as far as the Tower of London, and another line parallel to it, drawn from about half a mile north of the north-east corner of the Park at Tyburn. The metropolis was actively extending its tentacles north of the Oxford Road, and in the last year of the expiring century new squares bearing the family names of Tavistock and Russell were rising in Bloomsbury on the site formerly occupied by the head of that house, the Duke of Bedford. Outside the area comprised between Hyde Park and the Tower of London there were three important districts, all included in the above enumeration. The populous City of Westminster provided a considerable area to the south as well as to the north of a line drawn from Hyde Park Corner along Piccadilly and continued to Charing Cross. The borough of Southwark, which extended only to about half a mile southwards of the river, was the second. The third was the straggling dock area which kept close to the northern bank for another couple of miles east of the Tower. The Thames itself was crossed by three bridges only, Westminster, Blackfriars, and London Bridge. The first two had been built in the middle of the century. London

Bridge was still the ancient thirteenth-century erection, but the dangerous houses which once stood on it had been removed.

The English custom, which stopped short at the Tweed as well as the English Channel, of only letting out whole houses and not single stories of flats to the heads of families, led to small houses and narrow streets. Little attention was paid to house property. The system of long building leases allowed a permanent interest to neither the landlord, nor the building speculator, nor the occupier. The number of houses in a dangerous state of dilapidation in London ran into thousands, and they were built of such poor bricks, with dirt as mortar, that complaints were made of their falling by their own weight before they were finished. The houses of ordinary persons were not supposed to come within the province of the architect. Nothing was done even to make them appear elegant, to use a favourite word of the day. There is an amusing example of this in one of the illustrations to Anecdotes of the Manners and Customs of London by James Malcolm, Fellow of the Society of Arts, who took a special interest in domestic architecture. It is entitled "In Goswell street", and "Ancient inconvenience contrasted with modern convenience". The bad old days are represented by a charming little row of Elizabethan houses with gables and bow-windows; modern improvement by an absolutely repulsive building erected in 1800. It was only upon the residences of the nobility, and such better-class houses as those in Fitzroy Square, that the architect employed his talent; and here the result of adapting severe classical ideas to modern needs was often rather dignified than pleasing. They owed their principal charm to a merit in which the eighteenth century excelled. Whatever its failings, it never lost a sense of proportion.

Foreigners admired the frequency with which Londoners changed their linen, although they added that it was forced upon them by the grimy atmosphere in which they lived, due to the use of sea-coal. This love of cleanliness, and the habit, even among the fastidious, of walking in the streets, led to the construction of pavements, in which the capital of England boasted a great superiority to Continental cities. As, even when the highest classes drove, they did not move about with any pomp, and were content even to hire hackney carriages, and to take the risk of having to wait behind a coal-wagon drawn by its team of six or eight horses, or a drove of oxen, no objection was raised to the streets, already narrow, being even more contracted. These were cleaned by the town scavengers, while the sweeping of the pavements was the province of the householders themselves. But both frequently failed in their duties, and the stench in mean streets and in the neighbourhood of public-houses, particularly on summer evenings, was appalling. Yet the Londoner had then a great love of air and open spaces. The custom of laying out squares with gardens in the centre was one example of this. Another was the general love of parks and of gardens where there was nothing to do but walk about and take light refreshment and listen to the band. The best of these, Vauxhall, was on the south side of the river. It was the fashionable night resort of London, with its concerts, its illuminations, its Lovers' Walk and its nightingales, real or feigned. Ten thousand persons sometimes visited Vauxhall in a night; but though the tariff of refreshments was reasonable—champagne being, even during the French war, ten shillings a bottle, old port half a crown, a quart of table-beer sixpence, and a chicken three shillings—the price of admittance, which included tea, coffee, and biscuits, had recently been raised to two shillings, and was beyond the means of any below the better class of tradesmen. The rest went to tea-gardens on a Sunday or holiday, or formed water-parties on the Thames—an amusement to which apprentices were much addicted. But unfortunately the disreputable behaviour of disorderly men and women caused the tea-gardens to be gradually first deserted by respectable tradesmen and artisans with their families, and then closed altogether.

It was not thirty years since Parliament itself had been overawed by the Spitalfields weavers, nor twenty since the followers of Lord George Gordon had converted the metropolis into a scene of riot and havoc; and London still contained many elements of violence. Water piracy on the Thames had only just been put down. In almost any part of London a brutal crowd of porters and loiterers could be collected in a moment. One of the magistrates, Patrick Colquhoun, wrote a Treatise on the Police of London, which was regarded by contemporaries as the standard work on the subject; and his figures, though they generally show some little exaggeration, are the best to be had. He estimated the loss by theft in the metropolis at £700,000 a year. Half the hackney coachmen, according to him, were in league with the thieves. Over £2,300,000 worth of fermented liquor was sold annually at $3\frac{1}{2}$d. a quart, almost all of it to the class of labourers, and the number of public-houses cannot have been much less than six thousand. This consumption was in addition to what was produced in the home. The painter Haydon, as late as 1808, was entertained by a porter of the Royal Academy with home-brewed ale; and there must have been many respectable labourers who supplied their own wants. But dram-drinking was a much greater evil. Colquhoun gives the amount spent on gin and other spirits as not much under a million pounds, and adds that the improvement in the condition of the poor, when the distilleries were temporarily closed owing to shortness of grain, was very noticeable. The same authority put the number of apprentices alone at 150,000, and suggests a reason for their growing tendency to lapse into a life of crime. It was characteristic of the Englishman to wish to get on in the social world. An alderman would be teased by his wife, if she were not already domiciled in a fashionable suburb, to make the move from Broad Street to Grosvenor

Square. In any case, it was only the poorest tradesman who now tolerated the greasy apprentice in his parlour; for the most part he was boarded out, and soon learned habits of vice. The numbers of women who lived wholly or partly by prostitution Colquhoun puts at the enormous figure of fifty thousand, including the wives of artisans and others who lived partly by these means. Allowing for the fact that London catered for an immense seafaring population, there can be no doubt that public morals were very low—as indeed was the case throughout the country, and particularly in the industrial districts. French visitors had reason to be shocked at English depravity.

The manufacturing parishes of London were the poorest. Three were unable to raise enough money within their own limits to maintain their own poor. These were St. Matthew, Bethnal Green; Mile End, New Town; and Christ Church, Spitalfields. In other parts unmerited destitution was not common. When an apprentice had served his time, and become a regular wage-earner or journeyman, he could, if he worked for ten hours between six in the morning and six in the evening, soon save enough to rise in the world as Owen had done. If he chose to celebrate "Saint Monday" in a more lively way, and to sleep out his drink on Tuesday, he could still make enough on the remaining four days to maintain his family. The journeyman, as well as the tradesman who employed him, could afford meat twice in the day. The difficulties of life only began with the class of more opulent tradesman or merchant, who was tempted to send his daughters to a boarding-school for their education. Dress, dancing, music, Vauxhall, the Park, the circulating library, a trip to Margate, or—much better—to Brighton, all the extravagance of the Half Fashion very soon ate up his income. Higher in the scale a higher level of absurdity was attained. There was a fashion of being late. To have breakfast at one o'clock, the tradesman's hour of dining, even later, dinner at six or seven, tea at nine or ten, and supper at midnight, were the height of fashion. The London "season" had been supposed to be during the winter, but it had grown more fashionable for those who needed the waters or gaieties of Bath to remain there at least until January, and as the new century wore on no woman who valued her reputation for elegance ventured to approach town till almost May; and the season crept on till long after the 4th of June, the King's birthday, its original limit. It was fortunate that in those days the finely proportioned rooms had very little furniture, their enormous gilt mirrors and cut-glass chandeliers being worth perhaps as much as every other article there. For it was the top of elegance to cram as many as possible of the thousand or so who then made up London Society on to the

"Forms with chalk
Painted on rich men's floors for one feast-night."

These receptions or "routs" were an endless subject of satire. It was said that a thermometer was the best test of whether one had really been a success or not.

The age was characterized by a barbarity of which—in some respects—savages themselves would have been ashamed. Public executions were a favourite spectacle. Wives were still occasionally brought to market and sold with halters round their necks. Unprotected women were assailed in the streets with coarse jokes. The crippled, the half-witted, the aged, were ridiculed. The last class lost all respect for themselves when they received none. French visitors to London commented on the old women whom they saw dressed like young, and the joke was passed in the English newspapers that an old woman was nowhere to be found in public places. A writer in the Lady's Monthly Museum for 1799 pretended to have met at Margate a lady who had remained in her fortieth year since 1780, and to have told her that he wished to know her object in coming there. " 'You do!' replied she, tossing her grey head in my face. 'Why, what do you think it should be but to dance?' " Yet the dancing, even at the best London houses, was without grace and spirit. The great Niebuhr, during his youthful visit to Great Britain, complained of the formalities of genteel conversation, which seemed to him only an introduction to insipidity; other travellers, with a pardonable exaggeration, described the conversation of men as consisting of little but a string of oaths. That of even fashionable women in mixed circles was coarse, although it had vastly improved in the last generation. Even in the liberal atmosphere of the East the entertaining William Hickey of Calcutta could not conceal his astonishment on seeing an elegant general indulging in so vulgar a herb as tobacco. He would no doubt have made an exception of snuff, for the great day of snuff-boxes was at hand. But smoking was not the custom in the higher ranks, and was generally regarded as rather vicious, and appropriate to public-houses, where pipes were supplied as well as tobacco. But quantities of beer and gin were drunk. To dine with a gentleman of that class which, in a later age, would have consisted almost completely of total-abstainers, was to hit the just mean of abundantly good living without excess. The French traveller Faujas Saint-Fond was so well entertained by a Quaker with champagne and Bordeaux that he wondered how he could become one; he knew no other people who had such happiness. But the average dinner-party in less strait-laced circles soon passed into an orgy. Food was coarsely cooked and coarsely eaten. It was the English who invented the table-knife with a rounded instead of a pointed end. They did not wish to prick their mouths. Saint-Fond was surprised when he reached Inverary Castle to find that he had at last reached a place where meat was eaten with a fork after the French fashion. Remarkable as the personal cleanliness of Londoners appeared to foreigners, it had not as yet reached a very high standard. Hot-baths were not used. Cold-baths, however, were not uncommon. They were subjects of correspondence and conversation. Lady Spencer joked with Windham about the difficulty of entering one; Arthur Young recorded how he stood in the pond up to his neck at four of a winter's morning; while the less intrepid Sir George Beaumont described to a friend his method—to bathe every limb in turn. All this was, however, done for health —not cleanliness.

But the times were tolerably free from that mean love of mean things which is usually termed vulgarity. It is true that there was a good deal of delight taken in ostentation. To a more fastidious generation the accounts in the Morning Post of the number of covers laid, the amount of plate shown, and all the tinsel and trappings of a magnificent entertainment of George III's reign, read like a nightmare. But a simpler age saw no necessity for throwing a decent veil over the undeniable fact that guests and gold and silver and equipages are collected at great houses for display. Homer would have shown much the same sort of innocent delight in the banquets of the Marquis of Abercorn, nicknamed Don Magnifico. The same nobleman wore the ribbon of the Order of the Garter when out shooting. He was not vulgar. He did not understand why, if it was legitimate to delight in receiving the highest purely personal honour which his King could bestow, there was any harm in wearing it. But he was behind the times. That Sovereign was himself a simple man, and it was ceasing to be the custom to parade distinctions of rank in public. A generation earlier a gentleman who lost his wig was in a sad predicament, But the fashion had gone out now, except for such personages as ecclesiastical and scholastic dignitaries and some professional men; and hair-powder had taken its place. When this was taxed, thousands of heads became black and brown. Charles Fox's was of the number, though in 1806, when he again became a Minister, he created a sensation by appearing powdered once more. When gentlemen took to not only wearing their own hair but displaying it in its own natural colour, aristocracy in dress was driven from its last fastness. The lowest labourer in London dressed on a holiday not unlike a man of the highest fashion; the round hat on the back of the head, muslin cravat over the stiff collar, dark blue or brown lapelled coat, breeches, white waistcoat, and stockings differed only in material or quality between man and man. Sharp as were the distinctions of rank, deep as was the gulf which separated, for instance, a duke from an earl (a thing which any prime minister or lord chancellor might hope to become) or an earl from one of Pitt's new barons, there was a tendency in a society which loved the republic of the turf and the hunting-field to set these distinctions aside. A tradesman's son might go to Eton and make friends with the nobility. A boarding-school such as that at Clapham, to which the poet Shelley's sisters went, might bring together the daughters of a baronet and of a tavern-keeper. Beau Brummell was said to have once complained to Sheridan of a predicament in which he found himself. He had business in the government offices. They were vulgarly situated at Somerset House, but he could not be seen on foot east of Charing Cross; his carriage would be recognized, and a hackney coach would be too common. But there were relatives of noblemen who had no objection to going into the City, such as the brother of the Marquis of Lansdowne, who became a cloth-merchant. This freedom from the exclusive spirit which prevailed among the nobility on the Continent had been noticed by the French traveller, Baron Baert, some years before the end of the eighteenth century, as one of the causes of British prosperity. The lighter element in society was represented by that extraordinary being the Bond Street lounger, a self-made caricature of a living man. Before the war Mary Wollstonecraft had complained that bodily strength was sunk into unmerited contempt. Even now the beau blanched his hands and browned his hair with walnut juice, was supposed to pay a Bond Street professor half a guinea to teach him to tie his neckcloth, and affected an effeminate drawl which left out all the hard consonants and broadened the vowels into a long "a". But as it was war-time he adopted a martial carriage, wore high Austrian boots and trunk breeches, carried a heavily knobbed cane, and was known to wear his arm in a sling after a defeat in Flanders. The contagion of military manners might even make him a duellist. Some very foolish examples of this custom occurred. Early in 1803, when the outbreak of war was again expected, two officers fought each other in consequence of a quarrel between their dogs in Hyde Park. One, a colonel, was killed; the other severely wounded. The parliamentary difference which led to the duel between Pitt and Tierney on a Sunday morning in 1798 at Putney was a hardly less petty cause of quarrel.

But all this warlike spirit was far from making up, in the eyes of the opponents of the war, for what they supposed the country to have lost. "Where", wrote a correspondent of the Morning Chronicle in 1801, "are the good old *pot-bellies*, the *double-chins*, and the gouty supporters? All swallowed up by the funding system." The breed of Englishmen, he complained, was lost; the upper classes mere skeletons and scarecrows. It might have been answered that he might still find the things the loss of which he deplored at Carlton House and on the front Opposition bench of the House of Commons. But generally speaking the observation was just. The old corpulence and fullness of face of the typical Englishman, John Bull, was steadily disappearing, along with hard drinking and heavy living. He was gradually effecting a curious exchange with his rival across the Channel. At the time of their Revolution, Frenchmen possessed a clear-cut decision of feature which they subsequently lost. The English generation which was distinguished by the faces hidden in layers of fat which Reynolds was obliged to paint, was now passing away. With the women it was different. If the testimony of not only the best, but even second and third-rate, artists is to be accepted, there was no need for improvement. Whether it is due to a tolerably sensible habit in dress, or to food being just at the due mean between coarseness and luxury, or to cool rooms and infrequent changes of climate, it is almost certain that never has there been a time when the daughters of England were more lovely.

Jean Fiévée, a journalist sent by Napoleon Bonaparte across the Channel during the peace to make a study of England, argued that its people were the least civilized in Europe. He gave three reasons: Their fondness for money, their inability to appreciate the society of women, and a preference for themselves as a nation which amounted to a mania. That some of the best interests of the country were being sacrificed to the mere accumulation of material wealth is true. Negro slavery, with its brutalizing effect upon whole ships' crews, as well as upon the individuals more directly concerned with the traffic, is only one example. The employment of children from the very earliest age in every possible trade, especially that of a pickpocket, is another. In general a materialism in thought and cynicism in morals combined with a misapprehension as to the economic requirements of the day to drive those considerations of national well-being, upon which the statesmen of Tudor times would have acted, into the background. The race for wealth must have been a bewildering sight to a foreigner. Southey's imaginary Spaniard had a paper advertising never-failing pills thrust into his hand at Temple Bar. Not far off were two rival blacking-makers on opposite sides of the street. One said that his was the best in the world; the other that his was so good that you might eat it. At another shop shoes and clothes were exhibited swimming in water to show that they were waterproof. It was an intelligent anticipation of the days of the real Mackintosh. Less innocent was the lottery office, advertising itself as the only lucky office—one of the many evil weeds which flourished

THE CLOSE OF THE EIGHTEENTH CENTURY 75

in the shade of the national system of gambling known as the State lotteries.

The second half of the eighteenth century saw a marked change in the position of women. Up to that time every branch of literature had been mainly composed from the man's point of view. But not long after George III ascended the throne the rough English novels of Fielding and Smollett were succeeded by something very different. Foreign observers towards the end of the century were struck by the existence of a large and intelligent female public, catered for by a band of female authors as well as male. Religious women such as the Countess of Huntingdon and Hannah More were not without considerable influence on society. The life of the middle and upper classes was, however, largely affected by two types of literature, which both expressed a revolt from the dullness of everyday life, but in different directions. Women were educated enough to be able to read, but not enough—so it was thought, at any rate—to render themselves fit companions for men. At dinner-parties it was common to invite men without their wives, and as late as the first years of the nineteenth century there would be at least twice as many men as women; and even those few women saw very little of the men once they had left the dinner-table and the general toasts had begun. Girls enjoyed considerable freedom in their movements, but could make little use of it. To walk far was thought unbecoming; women rode little except to get from place to place where it was impossible to drive; and there were no outdoor games which the two sexes could play together. There were some exceptions. Just as society had its political duchesses such as those of Devonshire and Gordon, and other great hostesses, who introduced a feminine influence into politics, sport had its fair votaries. On rare occasions women hunted, and even drove four-in-hands. The composer of an Address to the King and Queen at Weymouth in 1804 was tempted by the extravagances of the new women to compare the milder pursuits of "our grandmothers . . . who the Decalogue in cross-stitch wrought", and "my good aunt Deborah".—

> "What would she do to see the modern maid,
> With jockey sleeves and velvet cap array'd,
> Dashing thro' thick and thin to win the post,
> And swearing when she finds her wishes crost!"

But this was, after all, a reference to a single incident—the recent match at York ridden by a Mrs. Thornton, wife of another celebrated sporting character, for 500 guineas, and to the bad way in which her defeat was taken by the lady. She found no imitators, though she rode again for a higher stake—and won—in the following year.

It was much the same indoors. Ferdinand and Miranda are "discovered" in Shakespeare's Tempest playing at chess. It would have been a unique experience to have found a Bond Street lounger and a young woman of fashion of 1801 similarly employed; and in fact such games were almost unknown in private houses. Billiards had hardly been introduced. Card games, even the milder sort such as speculation—with which the Malmesburys kept William Pitt amused—were appropriated to the older generation. There was nothing to do, after they had put by the harp and closed the pianoforte, but to beautify the almost empty drawing-rooms where they were shut up, with variegated worsted bell-ropes, fireside screens and carpets, footstool covers and filigree work, unless they preferred to fill albums with "elegant" and usually worthless extracts. In this state of neglect they solaced themselves either with romances of the Gothic or German school, about castles and spectres and monks, or novels of the sentimental school. There was in both a tendency to deify mere passion, which sapped the moral fibre. But it was the school of sentiment which produced the more remarkable effects, both upon subsequent literature and upon contemporary life. It was at first mainly in the hands of men; and men fell largely under its influence as well as women. Works with such significant titles as Laurence Sterne's Sentimental Journey and Henry Mackenzie's Man of Feeling set the fashion, and were followed in the unworthy way in which fashions usually are followed. When all this inflammable material was caught by sparks thrown from the conflagration next door—the French Revolution—the results were dangerous. "Gratitude", so wrote a friend to James Mackintosh, afterwards the great law-reformer, "was said to be a vice, marriage an improper restraint, law an imposition." But it was reserved for a girl not far gone in her 'teens, in a skit never even thought worthy of publication till 1922, to give the best idea of the poisonous tendency of the novels of this class. Jane Austen's Love and Friendship burlesques in a few short letters most of the absurdities inseparable from the cult of the feelings alone, to the exclusion of all religious, moral, and even prudential restraints. Money, for instance, is to the imaginary writer of these letters nothing but worthless dross; and the man who has brutalized himself by acquiring such stuff deserves no consideration at all. The pure-souled heroine steals his bank-notes, and, being caught in the act, turns on him with a withering contempt. A man of similar mettle is so far advanced in independence that he erects disobedience into a duty. "Never shall it be said that I ever did anything after the age of fifteen to oblige my father." It is hardly necessary to add that the heroine and her friends considered it a duty to testify their sensibility on all occasions in every possible way—by tears, faintings, and the like. To see was to love, and to love was to unite oneself for ever with the object of one's choice.

It is not wonderful that a girl who was in the habit of escaping from the society of a cold father and a rough, hard-drinking brother, the only men, perhaps, whom she knew, to talk with a sister-soul about the beauty of sensibility and passion, should have been the ready victim of the first man who could patter the same cant, kept at any rate tolerably sober, and could string two or three sentences together without an oath. It was an age when everybody's income was pretty well known, and when the bounds within which it was prudent for a man to marry were very sharply defined, almost to the precise number of thousands of pounds which she ought to bring as her dowry, supposing her to be of well-to-do parents. Where marriage was in this way barred, it was deemed allowable to seduce a girl of slightly lower social status; a peer might so treat a baronet's daughter, or a squire the daughter of a clergyman. Seduction had succeeded hard drinking as the fashionable vice of the last quarter of the century. In the first place there were no circles, however refined, in which such subjects could not be mentioned with freedom, and there were few, indeed, in which it was thought disgraceful to make the attempt. Mothers—and their daughters, too, if they were prudent —had to be constantly on the watch, and an elaborate fortification of conventions came gradually to be erected around female virtue. Only after two generations had passed did the outworks extend to the exclusion of anything which might contaminate their conversation, or even their thoughts. The imagination of the creations of Jane Austen was unrestrained. Emma Woodhouse was a girl of twenty-one who had lived the most conventional existence possible in a small country neighbourhood—she had never even seen the sea. She was interested for a friend who was expecting an inheritance from a widowed and childless uncle against whom nothing was known. But this did not prevent her imagining that he might have had an illicit attachment, together with half a dozen natural children. It is a far cry from this to the time, half a century later, when George Meredith complained that his heroine, Clara Middleton, being "one of Society's hard-drilled soldiery, Prussians that must both march and think in step", could not so much as picture to herself the Egoist undergoing the personal chastisement of the nursery. Critics across the Channel, as

THE CLOSE OF THE EIGHTEENTH CENTURY 79

well as those in England who have emancipated themselves from such ideas, must reflect that, however absurd these later outworks around female chastity may appear, they were at least found necessary and erected by those who had the strongest interest in the defence of the main position.

Seduction was made easier in several ways besides the wrong turn taken by female education. The contemptuous attitude adopted by society towards religious observations had led to the custom of marriage being celebrated by special licence, and as privately as possible. It was thought vulgar to have the banns read, and absurdly pompous to have a train of carriages full of guests following the bride to church. A lover could often allege the opposition of a parent, in days when cutting off with a shilling was a reality, as a ground for postponing a ceremony which was regarded as unimportant. The distinction between wife and mistress was not sharply defined. Men and women often lived together for years whose friends scarcely knew whether they were married or not. Sometimes such couples never married at all, and yet this did not prevent the children from being well cared for and even reaching some of the highest posts in the service of the State. And, in days when parents were so apt to exert a very harsh authority, the only way of escape was extremely disagreeable. Rides to Gretna Green with heiresses and boarding-school misses were not infrequent, but they were avoided if possible. Posterity has seen the essence of romance in those frantic flights over rough roads through a winter's night with an irate father a stage behind, but those who lived then thought of them in the light of plain matter-of-fact as almost intolerable hardships. But even if marriage meant all this, it was better to go through with it. This was illustrated by the misfortunes of Mary Wollstonecraft, who published her Vindication of the Rights of Women in 1792. In the light of her principle of complete equality between man and woman, she set a low value upon an institution which often meant domestic slavery. She was easily induced to enter into an illicit union. She was deserted, and her life was ruined. It was given to few women to keep men faithful to them without the help of a legal union, as vanity made them believe that they could. Most of them suffered the usual fate of the fallen in all ages, and the streets were full of the daughters of country clergymen and others who had once borne the honourable name of gentlewoman. Female suicides were probably commoner in this period than in any other.

There was a better side to all this. Enlightenment sometimes took the form of severe pietism, as in Hannah More, or of severe rationalism, as in Mary Wollstonecraft. Still, it was an assertion of woman's place in the world by man's side, and it was supported by a real endeavour to deserve one. The help which the Duchess of Devonshire gave to the Whig party, and the services of the Duchess of Gordon in raising the regiment which bore her name, were examples of an influence which women had not enjoyed for many years. Deep drinking and high gambling had gone out of fashion; Brooks's Club ceased to monopolize the best hours of the most brilliant brains in London; and men and women began to meet in one another's houses, and more upon a level. A higher morality resulted as regards married people. The mere fact that debates in parliament, sermons, periodicals, and the light literature of the day were filled with complaints, was a proof that the public conscience was being aroused. Adultery was actually beginning to be less frequent, as was shown by the decrease in the number of law-suits brought by aggrieved husbands. Freedom of dress was another subject of incessant comment. In 1801 Lord Auckland introduced a bill to make adultery a criminal offence. It passed the House of Lords only. A facetious writer in the Morning Chronicle proposed the alternative of attacking the evil at the source, namely, female dress. He suggested that there should be "the Petticoat Lengthening Bill; the Jumps Stiffening Bill; the two-inch Waist Elongation Bill; the Bill to prohibit the use of flesh-coloured Stockings, etc." The nature and extent of the raiment which was supposed to require a reform of this kind is evident. It was an importation, of course, from Paris, and dated from a time when the French Revolution had thrown matrons into the background, and when the fashions were set by persons of a very different character. This is pointedly alluded to in one of Brown's dialect poems:

> "An' noo i' toon, as each yan passes,
> Yan can't tell ladies fra bad lasses."

The "Distresses of a Citizen" are vividly described in a letter to the True Briton newspaper from a supposed man on 'Change who had married the sixth cousin of a Welsh Baronet, and whose wife was therefore a "fashionable" and skipped with her grown-up daughters. He complained that, though he was by no means in Paradise, his females were almost as naked as Mother Eve before the fall. A similar satire on the liberal display of neck and limb in vogue was expressed in the epigram:

> "If Eve, in her innocence, could not be blam'd
> Because going naked she was not asham'd;
> Who e'er views the ladies, as ladies now dress—
> That again they grow innocent sure will confess;
> And that artfully too they retaliate the evil,
> By the Devil once tempted—they now tempt the Devil."

For a good many years there was fun in contrasting the man who, with his high Austrian boots and bellying Cossack pantaloons of broadcloth or leather, seemed to be trying how much weight he could carry, and the woman whose dress, such as it was, was of such flimsy material that it might go into a pocket-book. The Dandy's Songster, a collection of squibs relating to about 1810, described ladies

> "In their little jockey jackets,
> Their trinkets and their lockets,
> But the devil any pockets,
> For a basket now to carry's all the dandy, O!"

Another regrets:

> "The ladies, too, of ancient fame,
> With waist so taper, long, and small,
> Not like our modern tasty dames,
> For now they wear no waist at all."

All this looseness of dress and of morals, however deplorable it may have been to contemporaries, marked, nevertheless, a stage in the moral progress of society. Women were not so well guarded as they had been. A generation or two ago the adultery of a peeress had been uncommon, only because a nobleman would as soon have thought of carrying off the consort of another nobleman as a sovereign that of another sovereign. Both would have gratified their itch for novelty in other ways. Happy married life was the exception in the upper classes when George III ascended the throne. In one of his fits of madness in 1788, he imagined that all marriages were to be dissolved by Act of Parliament. According to George Rose he said (and the observation was regarded as a proof of shrewdness and not of delusion) that he did not think many of his friends would have desired to renew them. But he was speaking of a generation which was now passing away. Men were beginning to be captured by the attractions of their own class, and to see something more in the opposite sex than the mere freshness and beauty of extreme youth, which they could get anywhere. Hence the familiar "crim. con." case was a feature in the life of the earlier part of the reign which it had not been in the stricter past. Hence also the increasing frequency of such home lives as those of Fox and Grey, both of whom started as libertines and became ideally devoted husbands. The older way of life was left to men of the great Whig families such as the eleventh Duke of Norfolk and the fifth Duke of Bedford, who avoided the society of decent women, and when they wished for that of men sought it in places like Brooks's; and the club betting book indicates what sort of women formed the staple of conversation there. Another

THE CLOSE OF THE EIGHTEENTH CENTURY 83

Whig who held on ancient paths was the Duke of Clarence. By comparison with the lives of some of his relatives and friends, his own fruitful union with the actress Mrs. Jordan was almost respectable. Nevertheless, a birthday dinner which he gave in Bushy Park, when the Prince of Wales took her by the hand, led her into the dining-room, and seated her at the head of the table, was thought rather a scandal, although graced by the presence of Lord Chancellor Erskine, and the Earl and Countess of Athlone and daughter. Cobbett made great sport of it, demanding to know what the newspapers meant by recording that the Duke's children were present, considering that His Royal Highness was unmarried. Nor did he spare the presiding lady: "Mother Jordan who, the last time I saw her, cost me eighteen pence in her character of Nell Jobson!"

The third count in Fiévée's indictment has also considerable force. The Briton's assumption of superiority, usually made in its most repellent form, that of denying merit to others rather than claiming it for himself, was based neither upon knowledge of other nations nor a proper understanding of his own. He valued himself, for example, on the liberty he enjoyed, and while this prevented him from putting up with an adequate army or a respectable police, he tolerated the press-gang for the navy, and allowed himself to be imprisoned and starved for months, possibly years, for a trifling debt. It was easy, in fact, in criticizing so extraordinary a people, to pile contradiction upon contradiction until every advantage it appeared to enjoy became blotted out, and nothing definite remained—only the generalization which Shakespeare puts in the mouth of the Danish gravedigger in Hamlet: "They are all mad there." But oppositions of this kind are infructuous. It is more profitable to turn from what Englishmen thought of themselves, or foreigners thought of them, to a general view of the nation upon its spiritual, its intellectual, and its physical side.

The institutions and ceremonies which distinguished the religion of Rome had accompanied the Christianity which it sent to England in the early years of the Christian era. But long before the sixteenth century there had been a growing tendency to resist the authority claimed by the Pope. The opportunity of the Reformation was chosen by England to shake herself free, although in doing so she retained in great part the institutions and even the ceremonies and beliefs of Rome. The Church of England still traced the succession of her bishops back to the apostles chosen by Jesus Christ. Could she not do so, she could claim to be no more than a human institution, like any other society or corporation—an idea abhorrent to the mind of the High Churchman. This was repeatedly emphasized by Bishop Samuel Horsley, the leader of that particular school of thought, as well as the ablest prelate of any school at that time. It was, indeed, necessary for him to do so. The commoner view, even among the clergy, was that the Church was subordinate to the Civil Power, as indeed it must be when regarded merely upon its temporal side as a human institution consisting of subjects of the King, possessing property and performing duties towards other subjects. The idea of an even closer relation was assisted by the principal manner in which the clergy of the eleven thousand odd parishes of England and Wales were remunerated. The naïve directness of early Christianity had devoted one-tenth of the profits of every man's labour to the maintenance of the priesthood. In England tithes had become a legal obligation restricted to the produce of the fields. Some had passed into lay hands. In any case, it was a charge on the land, and one of a most vexatious character, as, unless other arrangements were made, it was calculated upon the gross produce of the farmer, and rose with his energy and enterprise. If he spent money on draining or manuring his land, or bought seed of a higher value, the parson knew nothing of this. When the crop was ready for harvest he came down for his tithe. The system was one of the many obstacles to the improvement of agriculture, and the opportunity of an enclosure was frequently taken to compensate him with other land. But where this had not been done the spectacle of the parson collecting his dues like a rate-collector, rather than obtaining his remuneration from voluntary contributions or some other less obvious source, led to his being regarded by those below him in station as the hired servant of the State or at least as a creature very similar to the lay rector or the landlord. On the other hand, as the appointment of bishops rested with the Sovereign, and that of the village clergy, or the presentation to benefices, with laymen, often the lords of the manor, the subordination of the clergy to the secular authority in things of the world was obvious, while their sacerdotal character was forgotten. And there was not much to keep it in evidence. A deep chill had been creeping over the Church for a hundred years. To become a parish priest was to acquire a "living", that is to say, to obtain at the gift of a relative or patron or even occasionally by purchase from whoever had the right of presentation, a stipend held on condition of arranging for the Sunday services and for the christening, marrying, and burying of the parishioners, and maintaining the necessary registers.

England owed much, even in those dark days, to its clergy. It was the country parsonages which produced many of her greatest sons—Nelson, for instance, and Coleridge; and it was to country parsons that she owed much of her best literature—Sydney Smith's wit and George Crabbe's poems, and a number of valuable researches into local subjects upon which the parish clergy were best qualified to write—above all, the condition of the poor. Some of the best were among those who combined clerical duties with other businesses such as husbandry and teaching. But many did not reside at all, and handed over the cure of souls for which they were responsible; and thus the word "curate", which originally meant parish priest, gradually came to mean a clergyman paid to do the duty of another. The new conception long survived in a familiar household word. Generations later there were many drawing-rooms on whose hearths the shining fire-irons existed more for show than use; but among them was a second poker of baser metal, which was made to do all the work, and save its brazen superior from being tarnished. This was known as the "curate". Other incumbents of livings received the emoluments and carried on the duties of two or three parishes from one centre. There was this much justification: The sons of the gentry who were intended for the Church, still the only profession open to them besides the army, the navy, and the law, naturally expected to live and to maintain their families in the way in which they had been accustomed to live. But this they could not do with a single benefice, even of three or four hundred pounds a year, and half the livings in the whole country were under a hundred. If they did not choose to farm or teach or write, they were obliged to endeavour to be pluralists, responsible for five or six parishes. There was another class of clergy, sometimes taken literally from the plough, often educated in one of the northern grammar schools and at Cambridge University by means of exhibitions and scholarships. These were ready to take cures at £40, £30, or as low as £10 a year. How a Cumberland clergyman was able to maintain a large family upon a stipend of £17, including £4, the estimated income of his garden, is described by Wordsworth in the Memoir of Robert Walker. This man also had the opportunity of becoming a pluralist in a small way, being offered a neighbouring curacy in addition to his own; but he refused. He spun wool, teaching the village school as he did so, in the chapel where he officiated as priest, and where he himself had been taught to read and write. He cultivated his garden, pastured cows and sheep on the mountain-side, and wrote out the petitions and deeds and even settled the affairs of his rustic neighbours. Latterly his income was raised

THE CLOSE OF THE EIGHTEENTH CENTURY 87

by the rent of land purchased for him for £800, and he became able to send his son to the university. He left £2,000 at his death. Robert Walker died before the end of the century; but the parish clergyman who was at once the poorest and most strenuous labourer in his parish, and the parish clergyman who did everything for his flock—who was schoolmaster, legal adviser, and doctor, and, if he was a man of some standing, magistrate also, as well as priest—had certainly not disappeared. A curacy was the natural destiny of an intelligent boy of humble origin from one of the northern counties. It was of this that George III was thinking when he said how greatly indebted he was to Lady Eldon for making her husband a lawyer and eventually his Lord Chancellor; he would otherwise have been only a country curate.

Besides these there existed two more groups of men who found no opening for their services as assistants at a time when the contracted sphere of a clergyman's regular duties did not leave room for any. These were the young priest who was waiting for a benefice and the old one who had failed. Each was only too glad to take a curacy on a low salary. The large numbers of all these classes enabled the beneficed clergyman to live in a manner which was not a scandal only because it was not thought to have any harm in it. He often did not even select one of his rectories or vicarages to live in. He was seen at watering-places abundantly. He dressed in black, but this did not really distinguish him from other men. He danced and went to the play as they did, and drank nearly as much. If he was a serious man, he might edit a newspaper like the duellist Henry Bate of the Morning Post, who had a living, and was not even content with one. How loosely these things were regarded may be illustrated from one who became an excellent example of a parish priest—George Austen, the father of the novelist. He was Rector of Steventon in Hampshire from 1761, but his biographers cannot find that he resided or did duty there until 1764, when he married and happened to need a home for his bride. The total number of parishes where the incumbents were not resident was put in the House of Commons in 1806 by Lord Porchester, who professed to give accurate figures, at 2,423. Others gave a higher figure. But there was great variety in different places. Arthur Young wrote in 1804 that half the clergy in Norfolk were non-resident, and was wont to complain bitterly of the "leather breeches parsons" of Suffolk. In Lincolnshire he found that services were held in some churches as seldom as once a month. In one the parish clerk was a woman who kept her goose in the pulpit, and would not let it be disturbed till the eggs were hatched. There is extant a strong letter from George Tomline, bishop of this diocese, written to Lord Buckingham in 1800, on putting down absenteeism. But he addressed it from the Deanery of St. Paul's, of which he was also an incumbent. The bishops, indeed, set an example of pluralism and non-residence. Richard Watson, Bishop of Llandaff, who lived permanently at Windermere, was an extreme case. But even the really excellent Horsley, who spent much of his own money in getting the minimum stipend of the curates of his Welsh diocese raised from £7 to £15, was as simple in these matters as Tomline. In a speech in the House of Lords in 1803 he mentioned the case of a Cardiganshire rector who declined to take up residence: "When I was preparing to come to town for the winter season, I sent for him", but the threat of a process was no use. "Upon my return to my diocese the ensuing summer I found my clerk"—the rector in question—"was not yet in residence."

The bishops were not at this time selected for administrative ability. Several had been the tutors of noblemen or ministers, others were of noble family themselves, a few, like Horsley and Watson, had distinguished themselves by their political writings. Beilby Porteus, Bishop of London, had come to the front as a preacher and theologian. The

THE CLOSE OF THE EIGHTEENTH CENTURY

deaneries and other minor dignities were regarded much in the light of endowments of learning, where they were not bestowed for less worthy reasons. Even the cathedral services were irreverently performed. Anthems were not well rendered. The psalms were sung in miserable paraphrases, and hymns were left mainly to the dissenters. The buildings were allowed to fall into disrepair. Inside, the churches were filled with private pews which the owners might keep under lock and key. The poor were often expected to stand throughout the services. This grievance becoming more pronounced with the growth of population, was one of the causes why the labouring man gave up going. Porteus complained that for 200,000 souls in the West of London there were only five parish churches, besides a few chapels built as a speculation in which popular preachers were paid to attract fashionable audiences. The church was the poor man's church no longer. It was thought a remarkable thing when, in 1798, what was said to be the first absolutely free church in England was built in Bath.

The emigrant Duke De Lévis, in a book on England at the commencement of the nineteenth century, observes that the commonest religion was a bare belief in God—simple theism, as he calls it. The eighteenth-century term for the fashionable religion was Deism, which ranged from the mere admission of the existence of the Supreme Being to a definite Unitarian religion, accepting all the teaching of Jesus Christ, but as man only. Outside the Church it had been a positive creed, prompting to earnest living; but it was now losing its strength. Among so-called churchmen the power of Deism was negative only, furnishing an excuse for religious apathy or even profligate life. But here, too, it was a waning force. Yet even up to the end of the century it could still be said that many of the clergy, including Bishop Watson himself, were strongly inclined in that direction. In 1771 a serious effort had actually been made to permit avowed

Deists openly to enter and remain in the Church. Many clergymen preached sermons which might almost have been composed by men who derived their religion and morals exclusively from Marcus Aurelius or Seneca. How little theology was supposed to be necessary, was amusingly shown in some remarks on his own father—a clergyman—by Leigh Hunt, who as a journalist is presumed to have understood what his readers must have thought. After writing of him that he read the Bible regularly to the end of his life, he hastily adds—as if to deprecate the obvious inference: "This was not hypocrisy." When such an attitude prevailed it is not strange that observances were neglected. Sunday was a day of engagements and amusements, and many of the shops were open. The churches had been originally intended to serve as common gathering places—an idea appropriate to an age when no real division was felt to exist between the temporal and spiritual concerns of the people. But the practice had become a scandal when the sacred building was profaned by the cries of partisans in local elections or by the muttered oath of the unfortunate whose name was drawn to serve in the militia ballot.

Upon this ocean of placid indifference William Wilberforce launched in 1797 his Practical View of the Prevailing Religious System of Professed Christians in the Higher and Middle Classes in this Country, contrasted with Real Christianity. Born at Hull of a mercantile family in 1759, the same year as his friend Pitt, a keen member of parliament, a clear reasoner, eloquent, witty, and a delightful companion and a man of the world, he had early in his career become disinclined to follow any but an actively Christian way of living. The sect in the Church of England of which he is to be regarded as the head, the Evangelical party, no doubt derived some indirect inspiration from the movement of Wesley of half a century earlier. But both he and Charles Simeon, the great Cambridge preacher, and Hannah More, took most of their fire from within, and from the questioning and awakening spirit of the times. Rational as the prevailing thought of the eighteenth century was, this had not prevented it from being vague. Either the Bible was a sacred book or it was not. Either it showed how to open direct relations between man and his Maker or it did not. To this question Deism, Socinianism, Unitarianism, or whatever name might be assumed by the half-belief of the moment, was felt not to supply a definite answer. The new age required something more, and such schools of theological thought found themselves thrust from position after position, till their votaries were compelled to find rest either in complete rejection or a full acceptance of Christianity. Small claim as can be made for the poet Coleridge to be taken as the type of the ordinary educated man, his changes of belief from orthodoxy to Unitarianism and back again to orthodoxy are typical of the movements of the contemporary mind. Wilberforce wrote his book for those for whom this work had been done or had never been necessary. He wrote for professed Christians, urging them to become what they called themselves, and not to rest satisfied with what was at best "a kind of sober settled plan of domestic dissipation, in which with all imaginable decency year after year wears away in unprofitable vacancy". His work appeared when, as he himself said, religion was in a declining state. But the soil was ready—much more than either he or his publisher believed. Many thousand copies of his book were sold in the first few months. It created a sensation, almost unique in the case of a religious work which was not even polemical. Its reception revealed spiritual forces, whose existence in the nation had not even been suspected.

The Evangelicals formed a great and growing body within the Church, and were closely allied to another which had been forced against its will outside it—that of the Methodists. At the death of their leader, John Wesley, in 1791, these numbered about half a million. Their work in

Wales was as yet hardly begun, but they were strongest in most other outlying parts—in the neglected quarters of the great towns, for example, among the miners of Northumberland, Durham, Staffordshire, and Cornwall, and in industrial districts, pressing up the valleys of Lancashire and Yorkshire to where the lonely weaver wrought and thought. There are parts of the Bible which seem to an Englishman to be inseparably associated with some passages in his own country's history. Instances of the confident valour of the chosen people—such a war-cry as "The sword of the Lord, and of Gideon"—bring to mind Oliver Cromwell surrounded by his Ironsides on the eve of some great victory. So the story of the wanderings from town to town of the primitive Christians, their persecutions, their rebuffs, their earnest disputes, the handicraft which the Apostle practised in order to live, the letters of encouragement which passed between one body of the faithful and another, seem to have been repeated in the life of Wesley and his followers. At the time of the great preacher's death the Methodism which he had founded was at its best; the first fires had not died down, and yet already families were growing up whose members had known no other form of religion but this one in all its freshness. Bamford gives a touching picture of the old piety of the Lancashire weavers among whom he was reared in his description of the head of such a household at meal-time: "Bending reverently forward and with his hands clasped he would say, 'Merciful God! bless this food to our temporal use, and sanctify ourselves to thy service, for Christ's sake.'" A similar thanksgiving followed when the meal was ended. The children of such families felt almost that the Divine Founder of their religion was visibly present in their homes.

This belief in the incessant participation of a special Providence in the common concerns of the world was admirable when confined to private life, but as inculcated from the pulpit or through the religious press it came to be

THE CLOSE OF THE EIGHTEENTH CENTURY 93

carried to absurd lengths. The whole body of Dissenters, as well as the evangelical party within the Church, was an object of equal loathing to High Church Tories and Latitudinarian Whigs. The great wit of these last, the Reverend Sydney Smith, did not lose the opportunity of ridiculing in the Edinburgh Review the stories of conversions, warnings, and punishments, with which the publications of what he styled a trumpery gospel faction were filled. The most absurd which he was able to find was that of a young man who on being stung by a bee uttered the most dreadful oaths and imprecations, whereupon the insect stung him again upon the offending member—the tongue. This was gravely published under the heading: "A sinner punished—a bee the instrument." But these vagaries did little harm. However justly the reviewer, secure in the emoluments of a church living, might gibe at the methodist preachers being "paid by the groan", and so on, it was none the less the case that their religion, with its hymns and its emotional appeal, was a more cheerful as well as a more earnest one than that of most established places of worship. It was Methodism, too, which breathed new life into the greatest of the three older dissenting sects, that of the Congregationalists, or Independents. Proud of several generations of doctrinal dissent from the Church of England, they would have nothing to do with the illiterate enthusiasm of the younger sects. But they had to admit that some of their best men owed much to Wesleyan influences. The Baptists also showed fresh energy about this time. The third of the regular Nonconformist bodies, that of the English Presbyterians, was suffering decay. The Society of Friends, or Quakers, stood apart. Inconsiderable in their numbers, and unable owing to their scruples to serve the State directly, they were in the front rank in such contests for the good of mankind as the struggle for the abolition of the Slave Trade, or the efforts made to humanize conditions in the factories. There was one other earnest religious body in

England—those who adhered to the faith of Rome. They did not at this time exceed 60,000.

Such was the state of the nation on its spiritual side—an upper class indifferent and half infidel, yet gradually awakening, a labouring class in which the process of revival—although by no means general throughout the kingdom—was in full swing, a middle class partaking of some of the enlightenment of the one class and the enthusiasm of the other, equipped to take the lead in religious matters. As might have been expected, it was just at this time that the sense of man's duty to his fellow-man began to take effective form. Thomas Clarkson, who worked more than any other man to remove the foulest stain from the national honour, recorded how gratified he was to find on his travels several towns in which a considerable number of people had given up sugar—the product of slave labour. Even if this was a puny way of assisting a great movement, it was often the only one in the power of those who adopted it; and at any rate it provided a complete answer to a certain class of argument. The view of a former Prime Minister, Lord Lansdowne, was even more honourable. Writing to a French correspondent as early as 1788, when the agitation for the abolition of the Slave Trade, conducted as it was by an inconsiderable band of men working over a country with primitive communications and a rudimentary provincial press, was hardly past its infancy, he observed: "Our people give no equivocal proof of it"—their capacity to comprehend and readiness to adopt liberal ideas—"by their conduct about the slave trade, when the majority of each town which profits by it are loud and enthusiastic for its abolition upon principles of morality, freedom, and commercial honour, and the manufacturers give away gratis the impressions of a pamphlet of which I send you six." Even in those early days, before the evils of the factory system had become apparent, the gibe often uttered later about sympathy for black slaves abroad and none for white slaves at home would have had point, especially as regards the parish apprentices and the chimney-sweepers. Yet here, too, something was being done. Many persons interested themselves in the labours of Hannah More and her sisters, who left cultivated society to live among and reclaim the savage miners of Cheddar in Somersetshire. From the Royal Family downwards many took up the Sunday-school movement. The proceedings of Sir Thomas Bernard's Society for Bettering the Condition of the Poor provided a common ground on which those engaged in such humble work as the relief of paupers, or the providing of cottagers with cows, might exchange their experiences. The first institution for training the blind to a trade was founded in Liverpool in 1791. It had to be confessed that a society which had produced terrible conditions of living, and fearful temptations to ruin of soul and body, had at least provided hospitals and infirmaries which were the admiration of Europe.

In her Silas Marner George Eliot gives a very striking picture of the ignorance of country people in the early years of the nineteenth century. She makes the old midland villager say of someone: "He came from a bit north'ard, so far as I could ever make out. But there's nobody rightly knows about those parts; only it wouldn't be far north'ard, not much different from this country, for he brought a fine breed of sheep with him, so there must be pastures there, and everything reasonable." Yet darkness such as this cannot have been very widely diffused. The travelled soldier and sailor brought news of distant counties and even of foreign countries. In the smallest towns, and even in large villages, there were charity schools in which some of the younger children were taught to read, usually by dames. The large towns had free grammar schools, particularly in the north, where a poor boy could go on from reading and writing to arithmetic, book-keeping, and navigation, if intended for commerce or the sea; or Latin and even Greek, if for the Church. In those agricultural districts where there was the highest standard of individual well-being and self-respect, such as parts of Cumberland, it was usual for labourers to be able to read. The same was the case with families who carried on domestic industries—even in the West of England. Reading was often taught at home, or recourse was had to one of the new Sunday schools. These in turn often stimulated interest in education sufficiently to produce the sacrifices necessary to enable it to be continued on weekdays. But writing was little taught. Generally speaking, a self-satisfied illiteracy prevailed; and this, to take one example, put great difficulties in the way of colonels of militia regiments. Intelligent men, often skilled artisans, were made non-commissioned officers. For such duties elementary education was required, but the men selected were usually illiterate, and sometimes refused to go to the schools which were specially provided for them.

With all this, as foreign observers recognized, the general intelligence of Englishmen was of a high standard. The speeches and writings of those whose business it was to make as direct an appeal as possible to the people are a proof. The shorthand version of the demagogue Thelwall's address to the famous Copenhagen Fields mob in 1795 is a straightforward appeal to the understandings of his listeners. It is vain to look in it for the foolish digressions, the cheap witticisms, the puerile anecdotes, with which a more modern orator would conciliate the impatience or pander to the ignorance of his audience. But the instance of Thelwall, who, experienced as he was in public speaking, could not make the people behave as he wished on this occasion, is not so good a one as that of Thomas Paine, who, although the prophet of a revolution which never took place, admittedly produced an enormous effect by his writings. His influence extended not only to the lowest grade of those able to read, but to large numbers who, though unable to read, were willing to listen to what was read to them. The last of his principal works, and the most influential, the Rights of Man, was far

THE CLOSE OF THE EIGHTEENTH CENTURY

from being a revolutionary squib, filled with appeals to greed and class jealousy. It was a sober treatise upon the form of government best able to secure the persons and property of the people whom it represents. To pass to a class slightly higher in the intellectual scale, that from which juries were taken, the addresses given by advocates at the famous State trials of the time, and in particular James Mackintosh's great defence of Peltier in 1803, presuppose an interest in their country's history most creditable to the craftsmen and shopkeepers of that day. There was probably much in the speeches, as there was in what Thelwall and even Paine said and wrote, which not all those who heard could completely understand, but at least they set themselves to do so and did not indignantly reject what was given them and demand trash.

The newspaper press in 1801 was extremely vigorous, and probably at no time in its history did it contain so many contributions from writers in the first rank. The files of Daniel Stuart's Morning Post for those years, for example, contain poems by Wordsworth and Coleridge, articles by the latter and jests by Charles Lamb. By 1803 the number of copies sold had reached 4,500, passing that of the Morning Chronicle, hitherto unquestionably the leading daily newspaper, edited as it was by one who was still among the forces of the age—the coarse, genial Aberdonian, James Perry. About the same time, the second John Walter introduced the public to another novelty. He believed that, were it possible to rely upon a paper for the accuracy of its news and its generally impartial outlook, that paper would take the first place in the public estimation. He proved this by what he was able to do for The Times. But while these men were transforming the newspaper into something considerably more powerful than it had been a few years before, a greater man, perhaps the most consummate of all journalists, was beginning to make his presence felt—William Cobbett. Son of a Hampshire farmer, after an adventurous career, mainly in America, as farm-boy, soldier, teacher, and journalist, he returned to England in 1800 at the age of thirty-seven, and started a patriotic paper, the Porcupine. He very soon concluded that a monthly organ was more suited to the expression of his views, and in 1802 he set up his Political Register. The society which maintained all these newspapers, costing as they did as much as sixpence each, was necessarily small. The sale was mainly in London. But the circulation was out of all proportion to the number of copies sold. Their advertisement columns showed that they were intended to reach the poorer orders of the community, and they did so. They were passed from hand to hand and read out in alehouses. Londoners loved politics, and the staple of them was the parliamentary debates.

Even among tradesmen in the metropolis the standard was high. A French traveller, Grosley, who visited London in 1765, mentioned what a large number of them could speak French, and Colquhoun made a similar observation thirty years later. No country in the world had so well informed a middle class. Higher in the scale, the quintessence of intelligence, was fully developed. It was a society which worshipped wit. The foreigners who found conversation so languid at mixed parties would have fared better had they visited the clubs. Even in private houses there were some dinners at which it was arranged for men like the poet Moore, Colonel Luttrell, Samuel Rogers, and Sydney Smith to shine. At such parties beauty was in little request in comparison with wit. It is true that the sallies of these professional diners-out were often artificial, and their impromptus carefully prepared. But a standard was set up, and the accomplishment was acquired by many others whose efforts, though less frequent, were more spontaneous, and therefore happier. More good sayings are recorded of King George III, in spite of his reputation for stupidity, than of most of the clever Englishmen of later generations. The leading public men of the day, Pitt, Fox, Windham, Wilberforce, and above all Sheridan, were noted for the good things they said. All of these used the rapier; their wit was sharp, like the best of every age and race, cutting into the vital parts, and scarcely felt until the point had been withdrawn. But there was another kind which descended like a steam-hammer, leaving its victim in crumbled pieces—more characteristic of an age which had just passed from beneath the intellectual sway of Doctor Johnson. Of this Doctor Parr's reply to James Mackintosh is an example. The conspirator O'Coigley had been executed. Mackintosh, who was regarded by his fellow-Whigs as a backslider—shortly about to be rewarded by the opposite side with a legal post—refused to mix his tears with Parr's, and called the Irishman a rascal. "Yes, Jamie," said the Doctor, "he was a bad man, but he might have been worse. He was an Irishman, but he might have been a Scotchman; he was a priest, but he might have been a lawyer; he was a republican, but he might have been an apostate."

When and how the governing classes received their high intellectual equipment, it is not easy to see. The problem is not difficult in cases where noblemen and even rich country gentlemen, appalled by the roughness of the public schools, or moved by a spirit of Patrician exclusiveness, had their sons educated by a clever young clerical tutor—such as Sydney Smith. But it is hard to say what boys actually learnt at school, and how they learnt it. That glorious idler, Charles Fox, boasted that no one really understood one important branch of classical attainment who had not been at Eton. Bishop Tomline, himself no Etonian, wrote: "It is certain that Eton school makes the best scholars in the world, and yet the boys never seem to do anything." It was the same at the Universities. At Cambridge in particular the undergraduates seemed to Baert to have little to do but to drink, and the self-indulgence and profligacy of the senior members of the University—who were in holy orders—was remarkable. Moreover, education finished very early, and a boy was often waiting till he came of age, so that he might take the seat which was waiting for him in parliament. The precocity of the youth of that age was, indeed, remarkable. Not to mention the fighting professions—Nelson commanding his ship at twenty and Arthur Wellesley his regiment at twenty-four—there was, in the diplomatic service, George Jackson. Full of weighty reflections, and—as his mother thought—of Westminster School conceit, he accompanied his brother to Paris during the armistice at the age of sixteen, and when only twenty acted at a most criticial moment as head of the Ministry at Berlin. While still at school, boys wrote such letters to one another as "Harry" Temple wrote in answer to his friend Francis Hare's exhortations to make progress in Greek and Latin, and to avoid the vices of a public school such as swearing and drunkenness, and not to think of marriage. The thirteen-year-old Harrovian, after a long digression upon the beauty of the classics, replied that he could find no pleasure in getting drunk. But he was unable to agree on the subject of matrimony, although he added: "I shall be by no means precipitate about my choice." Nor did young Temple become a prig. So far was this precocious flame from prematurely burning itself out, that as Lord Palmerston he displayed during a long career, ending with his death when still Premier at eighty years of age, a degree of vitality singular even for one born in that vigorous age.

It was certainly not in consequence of remarkable application, or any acquaintance on the part of their preceptors with the science of teaching, that the boys learnt so much and so quickly. The teaching in less aristocratic schools, such as Christ's Hospital, of which Lamb has told us so much, was no better. Here the highest honour was to be what was called a Grecian. It was the atmosphere created by traditions of this kind which set the inspired Coleridge reciting "Homer in his Greek" in the echoing cloisters of the old Grey Friars. All round the boys of that day, in their schools, their col-

THE CLOSE OF THE EIGHTEENTH CENTURY

leges, even their homes, there was an atmosphere of classical culture. The scepticism which had invaded religion had not yet touched the classics. Their fathers were incessantly reading and discussing those greatest productions of human thought. There came a time when the old Romans were read for the purpose of apt quotations in parliament. But at this period members were often so full of what they had just been reading that they positively could not keep it out of their speeches. Charges were even seriously made that boys were brought up to believe in the mythology of Greece and Rome. Certainly boys, and even girls, knew it better than Christianity. In 1831 Macaulay had a discussion with Lady Holland, then almost an old woman, on the word "talented". She was well read, and her brain had been sharpened by frequent contact with the keenest brains of the day in London. Macaulay was astonished to find that she did not seem to have heard of the Parable of the ten talents. Had the word under discussion been "mercurial" or "saturnine", she would have abounded in learned allusion. How classical was the outlook, even in the most unexpected quarters, is illustrated by the diary of a wild young cavalry officer, already distinguished, Robert Wilson. He makes no parade of scholarship. But wishing to jot down a brief note of what a certain chief whom he had met with in Egypt was like, he compares him to Sallust's Syphax, as to a well-known character. Officers of the army were also well acquainted with French. It was the language in which lectures were given at the High Wycombe College for officers; and it was useless, as Charles Napier—afterwards the General—found to enter there without a perfect conversational knowledge of it. Nor were other studies neglected. Parliamentary speakers were usually well versed in history, and would usually have read the Wealth of Nations, the greatest of all books on political economy. Mathematics, except to some extent at Cambridge, were neglected; and for medicine, and science generally, it was almost necessary to go to Edinburgh. There was a complaint that boys received no religious teaching at school, and learnt no science either there or at the English Universities. But some of them made up for it afterwards. Even statesmen and people of fashion studied Erasmus Darwin and crowded to the lectures of Humphry Davy on chemistry, of Porteus on the Gospel and Sydney Smith on moral philosophy. It was, indeed, a society which was not unwilling to learn, sitting at the feet of scientist or divine, when several famous men flourished, each of whom had a new idea or an old one in a new form, and set forth gallantly with it to reform the world, when men had great thoughts and were not afraid or ashamed to give them utterance, when a touch of the grand style was given even to a state paper or a leading article, when—although the trial of Warren Hastings was over—the golden age of English oratory had not yet passed.

Physically the English were a strong, healthy race. Most of them were occupied in agriculture. But the number of males who were regularly so employed in Great Britain in 1801, and who afterwards maintained, or sank to, the state of agricultural labourers, cannot have much exceeded a million and a half. Of these perhaps one-fifth, or 300,000, were from twenty to thirty years of age, and another sixth, or 250,000, from thirty to forty. In 1851 there were found to be, of male agricultural labourers, shepherds, indoor farm servants, and others connected with agriculture—not including paupers, dependents, and vagrants—as many as 40,002 of from seventy to eighty years of age, and 9,969 of eighty and upwards. Disregarding such slight immigration as there may have been into the rural tracts, which was out of all proportion small compared with the emigration from them, the conclusion may be drawn that—in spite of war losses—out of those male agricultural labourers who were between twenty and thirty in 1801, as many as twelve per cent. reached the age of seventy, while of those between thirty and forty, four per cent. lived to be eighty. This leaves out of

THE CLOSE OF THE EIGHTEENTH CENTURY 103

account all those who were ending their days as dependents or in workhouses or infirmaries. Such facts go to prove both the excellent stamina of the agricultural population, and that long hours of labour and coarse, or even insufficient, food had not sapped their strength.

Unfortunately there is little satisfactory to record on the subject of the amusements of the people. Wendeborn, who had travelled widely, noted as unique the absence in England of music in the fields. The principal sports were the cruel ones such as bull-baiting, at which they assisted only as spectators. Wrestling, single-stick, and boxing still lingered as village recreations in such counties as Cumberland, Lancashire, and Cornwall. They were gradually being superseded by cricket. But it was not until many years later that round-arm bowling was invented; and the national game was still in its earlier stages. Although Charles Fox had been known to play it as a mature statesman, and although the Duke of Dorset and others had drawn up its laws as early as 1774, it was not generally regarded as a game for young gentlemen after they had left school. Professional boxing and the inhuman sport of cockfighting took the first place among national recreations. Riding was the principal exercise of those who could afford it. A country gentleman kept his pointers; a spaniel was little esteemed, and, outside of Ireland, the setter was the poacher's dog. In a country where there was not much game besides partridges and hares, and only the latter were plentiful, it was not possible to get big bags, shooting over dogs with the slow-firing muzzle-loader, usually a single-barrel; and England had not yet acquired that primacy among the nations in the domain of sport which she has since enjoyed. Large shooting-parties were not yet in fashion. Coke of Holkham with his bags of five hundred in a day was a pioneer, and created almost a sensation. Hunting had, in many parts of the kingdom, emerged from the pleasant stage at which a few hard-riding gentlemen, joined by a farmer or two, met at daybreak to pursue fox or hare indifferently with a pack of heavy-built, slow-footed, trencher-fed dogs. But far into the new century the Roxby hounds in Yorkshire hunted fox and hare on alternate days, knowing by the huntsman's word of command which animal's scent they were to follow. The Quorn, the Cottesmore, and the Pytchley were old; so were the ducal packs; but a number of well-known hunts, such as the Bicester, the Warwickshire, and the Whaddon, were only coming into existence. Fox-hunting was a gradual development from hare-hunting, just as the foxhound was a stronger and fleeter variety of the harrier; and he was still so slow that runs of four or five hours were not uncommon. Racing was a third sport which hardly yet deserved to be called national. The great Epsom races had been started by the Earl of Derby twenty years before the end of the century. But it was not until the new one was in that they began to attract London crowds. Racing was, in fact, rather on its decline up to 1800. The famous sportsmen of the eighteenth century, like wicked "Old Quin"—the Duke of Queensberry—were growing old, and there were none as yet to take their places. Even Charles Fox had parted with his stable. Half a dozen starters at a classic race was quite a respectable field. Racing was an informal amusement, kept going by the enterprise of a few individual sportsmen. A common sporting event was a match between two horses on Newmarket Heath. But the public were interested in more manly trials of strength than those which, before steeplechases had been invented, depended almost entirely on the speed of a horse. It was common to offer to perform some feat of endurance for a wager. In 1806, for example, Edge of Macclesfield, aged sixty-two, walked 172 miles in 40 minutes under 50 hours for bets up to 20,000 guineas. Tradesmen or artisans would often wager to perform some sporting feat in connection with their employment. The villagers had their ploughing matches. They were an admirable means of testing agricultural theories, besides giving the ploughman a pride in himself and his horses.

The vigour of the nation had not yet found expression in those regularized games, and that enthusiastic addiction to field sports afterwards supposed to be the secret of England's greatness. The virtues which these things might have developed were fostered in other ways. The Briton enjoyed freedom; foreigners laughed at him; philosophers pointed to the chains which held him; but he still boasted of his freedom because he was conscious of it. This was pictured in the manners of society. There were some formalities which had to be maintained, some deferences which had to be observed, and all this gave an appearance of restraint. But it was an appearance only. There was as much of it at Court and on the quarter-deck of a flagship as elsewhere; and yet the King wandered about and chatted informally at his levees, and that greatest of disciplinarians who won the Battle of St. Vincent could be slapped on the back with impunity by one of the officers as they were going into action. It was the same all through the nation. To use a homely expression, there was elbow-room. There was a world outside the village where one might go and come back rich. There was nothing to prevent a poor boy, like Robert Owen and a hundred others, from rising to the place in the world to which his merits entitled him. It was certainly not because Wordsworth and Coleridge were poor that they were not fully appreciated. Tom Paine and Robert Blomfield the Farmer's Boy sold their works by the thousand. Never, perhaps, were those high in place so quick to recognize talent. Such were Lord Shelburne, afterwards Marquis of Lansdowne, the discoverer of Jeremy Bentham—who acknowledged that he owed to him the development of his attachment to the great cause of mankind—and the friend of many promising men of science and letters; William Windham, who saw at once on his return to England that young Cobbett would be a force to be reckoned with, and asked him to dinner to meet the Prime Minister; the Duke of Bedford, who gathered round him all who, he thought, could improve agriculture; Lord Mulgrave, who many times had Benjamin Haydon, an unsuccessful painter of an obscure provincial family, to dine alone with him at the Admiralty. The press was another power which brought abilities into notice and encouraged them; it had not yet become a deity which it was necessary to propitiate. Baert admired the almost romantic willingness of the English to venture their capital and so assist a rising man to make his efforts good. And the men of that country and day were capable of using those opportunities. It is Baert again who observes as a salient characteristic their thoroughness in performing what they had to do. Of their enterprise in industry, trade, and navigation it is not necessary to add more.

But of their aptitude for higher adventure it is but right to hear the founder of a great pacific school of thought. "What a common soldier may lose", wrote Adam Smith, "is obvious enough. Without regarding the danger, however, young volunteers never enlist so readily as at the beginning of a new war; and though they have scarce any chance of preferment, they figure to themselves, in their youthful fancies, a thousand occasions of acquiring honour and distinction which never occur. These romantic hopes make up the whole price of their blood." And he adds a little later that a tender mother among the inferior ranks of people is often afraid to send her son to school at a seaport town, lest he may be enticed to go to sea. It was in this spirit that John Shipp longed, while still a poorhouse child, to enter the army, enlisted as a boy, and twice won his commission. This it was that turned Cobbett's early fancies to the sea. He saw it from the top of Portsdown Hills. "But it was not", he wrote, "the sea alone that I saw: the grand fleet was riding at anchor at Spithead." And he called to mind "those memorable combats, that good and true Englishmen never fail to relate to their children about a hundred times a year." He was thinking of a small Hampshire farmstead, the place where, as he elsewhere says, he did not remember the time when he did not earn his own living. There must have been some good lessons learnt in the Englishman's home in those days. Even mutineers reverted to them when on the eve of their final punishment they exhorted their shipmates to do their duty to God, and to King and Country. Such were the men who in the first years of the nineteenth century foiled Napoleon Bonaparte, founded many a new Britain across the seas, and made their own land the workshop of the world.

CHAPTER II

THE GOVERNMENT OF ENGLAND AT THE CLOSE OF THE EIGHTEENTH CENTURY

THE numerous admirers of the British Constitution of the eighteenth century were apt to fall into a common error. They endeavoured to be clear and precise upon a subject which did not admit of precision. It is, obviously, just as much beside the mark to employ even tolerably concise expressions in describing the advantages of the British Constitution as to do so in describing that Constitution itself. There was good ground for the boast of Englishmen and the admiration of foreigners; but, carefully examined, it amounts to little more than this. The Sovereign's executive authority was secured, but he was obliged to choose his ministers from among the best persons; it was these also who made the laws and imposed taxation; but the whole people had the power to prevent the undertaking of an unpopular war, the enforcement of an unpopular law, or the collection of an unpopular tax. A final merit was the independence of the courts.

The constitution under which the political sense of the nation secured these advantages was anomalous and corrupt. The lowest but the most important of the three Estates of the Realm, the Commons, was represented in a very curious fashion. The House of Commons was intended as a legislative body standing for all descriptions of men in Great Britain. This was supposed to be secured by the variety of the interests represented. Even the word "constituency", which would have suggested, at least, the idea of uniformity, was not in use. The House of Commons consisted in 1800, of 558 members in all. To these Wales contributed 24, of whom half were returned by counties at the rate of one for each of the twelve, and half by boroughs or groups of boroughs. Of the 489 English members there were two for each of the two universities of Oxford and Cambridge

THE GOVERNMENT OF ENGLAND 109

Each of the forty English counties sent its two representatives. The rest of the English members were returned by cities and boroughs, usually two by each. There were several of these last which were not, and never had been, towns. This was particularly so in the West of England. Cornwall, for example, sent 44 members in all. The North and Midlands were by comparison neglected. But variety did not end here. The cities and towns in England and Wales fall into four groups, not very unequal in number. Of these the smallest and most curious is the burgage group. Here the right to vote attached to particular buildings or plots of land. Seventy members were returned from thirty-five places where the right of voting was vested in burgage or other tenures of a similar description, and the elections were a pure matter of form. The privileged houses and parcels of land were usually owned by some nobleman, who had merely to convey them temporarily by deed immediately before the election, and resume them immediately afterwards. A steward would go down and collect the tenants and servants round a table, and, after going through the necessary formalities, declare his lord's friend duly elected. A rather more numerous class was that of the corporations which governed, or were supposed to govern, the boroughs represented through them. A third was the scot and lot, and potwallopers, group. Here the franchise depended upon such things as the payment of a particular local tax, or the right and custom of separate cooking. In a few cases all the householders had the vote. But this did not render them independent, as all the houses might be owned by one man, who could turn them out if disobedient. The largest and most independent group, but that which for this very reason caused the most scandal, was that of the freemen. This right was sometimes a matter of heredity and custom, sometimes a gift of the corporation, the members of which, themselves possibly the nominees of some powerful individual, might bestow it on whomsoever they pleased. In some cases a residential or ratepaying qualification was required. But there were many instances of freemen, who had long ceased to live in the town, being brought at election time to vote in considerable numbers at the expense of a candidate. This was a comparatively minor evil. Nor were the large places especially disgraceful for bribery. The actual sale of votes was carried to perfection in the smaller boroughs, where the price might go to so much as fifty or sixty pounds a vote. The most open scandal of all in the great towns was the carnival of drunkenness and riot which took place at elections in those very places where the voters numbered thousands, and where, perhaps, one half of them were living on weekly wages. Here, and in several of the counties as well, the importance of getting the people on a candidate's side was fully appreciated. Hence the jokes, time-honoured even in those days, about the need for the candidate's being on the right side of the women, kissing the children, promising all that was asked, getting his name down upon all the stewardships of the public charities, "and down with your ten pounds—ten in capital letters!" as one of the exponents had it. Foreigners pointed to all this when they derided the boasted freedom of Englishmen as a freedom enjoyed only once in seven years, when a new parliament had to be called, and then disgracefully abused. It was more, indeed, than a freedom—it was a right; and a right that it was dangerous to question. At the general election of 1790 at Liverpool, the sitting members, feeling sure of their seats, did so. They turned the tap off. A friend of General Tarleton's realized the situation. He broached a cask of ale before the thirsty crowd, and won him the election. Yet there existed evils in comparison with which these outbursts once in several years were harmless. Manchester and Birmingham had other reasons to congratulate themselves, as for a long time they did, on having no vote. They were saved from what might have been a perpetual hindrance to the steady growth of their prosperity. The author of the Board of Agriculture's Survey of Somersetshire observed that party feeling at Taunton, a potwalloper borough with four hundred electors, never subsided between the elections, and did so much harm to trade that woollen manufacturers removed elsewhere.

In Scotland each of thirty counties returned one member —as in Wales—the Edinburgh Corporation one member, fourteen groups of boroughs a member each. The number of counties sending members had been reduced from thirty-three to thirty by an arrangement under which three out of a group of six outlying counties sent members in turn to alternate parliaments, while the other three remained unrepresented. There were in Scotland no gatherings of sturdy and independent freeholders at election time. Only those had the vote for their county who could show a charter for their lands from the Crown. Hence there were counties with scarcely more than ten electors. The boroughs were governed by self-elected corporations. These chose delegates, and groups of delegates chose representatives in Parliament. The forty-five county members were chosen by less than three thousand persons, and freedom of election was almost unknown. Scotland was, in the expressive language of the day, managed.

A petition was presented to the House of Commons in 1793 on behalf of the Society of the Friends of the People for a reform of Parliament. The facts upon which it was relied were not challenged. Besides the 35 places in which the elections were a mere form, there were in England 46 in which the voters were not more than 50 in number, 37 more where they were not more than 100, and 26 where they did not exceed 200. Most of these constituencies returned 2 representatives, so that they accounted in all for 249 members of Parliament. In Scotland there were actually 30 members for counties with less than 250 electors each, and 15 for districts of boroughs with less than 125. Thus 294 members, or a majority of the House, were elected by what was comparatively a mere handful of the population.

But the analysis did not end here. The Friends of the People went on to show that 84 individuals sent 157 men to Parliament by their own immediate authority, and estimated that 150 more were returned on the recommendation of another 70 patrons. An even greater majority of the House of Commons consisted, therefore, of the nominees of 154 persons.

It has to be added that the purchase and sale of seats was not reduced to a complete system. The price varied. Twenty years before the debate on this petition the Earl of Chesterfield had offered a borough jobber £2,500 for a secure seat. He was laughed at, the rich East and West Indians having just come into the market. The price was £3,000 at least. In 1793, as Sir Philip Francis told the House, it had touched £6,000. But this must have been its highest point In 1807 the reformer Romilly bought a seat for £2,000, which he thought more honourable than being a lord's nominee, and less trouble than facing a popular election; and the price a few years later was put at £5,000. In 1795, however, when Gatton in Surrey was auctioned for £110,000, nothing was thought of the rental in comparison with the right to nominate two Members. Thomas Holcroft, dramatist and democrat, published in that year the defence which he had meant to have made to a prosecution for High Treason which the Attorney-General had been so inconsiderate as to withdraw. He quoted some passages from the cynical speech of the successful auctioneer at that sale. The purchase of Gatton is recommended to "any Gentleman who has made a fortune in either of the Indies.... No tormenting claims of insolent electors to evade; no tinkers' wives to kiss; ... with this elegant contingency in his pocket, the honours of the state await his plucking, and with its emoluments his purse will overflow." Holcroft also quoted from The Times a somewhat confusing instance of the way in which these arrangements were described. "Councillor Baldwin, Secretary to the Duke of Portland, is to be elected for the borough of Malton, in the gift of Earl Fitzwilliam." One of the most famous of these noble proprietors was the Earl of Lonsdale, who called his nine seats his cat-o'-nine-tails, and sent forty labourers from his northern collieries to live house-free in Haslemere in Surrey, and to vote for him in that borough of inhabitant freeholders. About a dozen boroughs, usually seaports, were wholly or partly in the hands of the Admiralty, Ordnance, or Treasury. One of these, Harwich, regularly provided a seat for one of the Secretaries of the Treasury for the time being.

The nomination system had some very obvious advantages. It was an excellent means of introducing a promising youth into Parliament, and occasionally one who, like Pitt, could not afford to meet even a part of the cost of a contested election. On the other hand, a peer's son was frequently elected before he was of age to sit, as was Charles Fox. This use of borough patronage occasioned a curious incident, characteristic of the times, in the case of a much less important person. The electors were apt to be sensitive about their right to see the candidate, and in offering a seat it was common for the patron to mention whether it was necessary to go down. Reigate was one of these places, and on one occasion, when Lord Royston was elected, his absence had to be excused on the score of a commendable desire to finish his education. But absurd as such incidents were, these boroughs had their legitimate uses. Among them was the provision of safe seats for candidates of consequence who had failed elsewhere. Unpopular leaders were not driven for refuge to the House of Lords.

It is less easy to understand how the obvious disadvantages were overcome for the commons of England who were supposed to be represented. But some of the compensating factors are clear. Certain seats and classes of seats were considered much more honourable than others. A county member enjoyed great distinctions. As Knight of the shire he was, for example, privileged to wear spurs in the House itself. Wilberforce was very glad to exchange Hull for the

H

county of York, and would never have changed back again, although the expenses of his committee in 1807 reached the enormous amount of £58,000; a triumph of electoral economy however, by comparison with the £200,000 which his two rivals spent between them. Numerous clothiers and others who owned small properties expected their expenses in travelling to York in order to vote. It cannot have been very different elsewhere, so long as peasant proprietors remained, as the voting qualification was the possession of a freehold of a yearly value of forty shillings. The arrangement by which voting took place only at the capital of the county was at first sight anything but democratic. It usually either prevented the poorer freeholder from voting at all, or obliged him to owe his ability to do so to some rich man who paid his expenses, often on a very lavish scale. But as things were, it formed an essential part of the popular element in the county election. There would have been nothing impressive about a hundred or so of electors collecting quietly to vote, often under the eye of the great man of the neighbourhood, at each one of thirty or forty scattered polling centres. Nor would there have been much opportunity of a popular address to them. But, gathered as they were by thousands at their local capital to be addressed there by the candidates, it was quite a different matter. Now they really deserved the name of sturdy freeholders. Influence had shrunk to its proper proportions, and even the weak plucked up courage for a struggle. Such notably were the contests at York, almost Homeric in their vigour, in which Wilberforce was so invariably successful, especially his first victory in 1784, when the county electors threw off the interest of the great Whig families of Howard and Wentworth, and chose the man in whom they believed. So elected, the county members had a moral strength out of all proportion to their numbers. No ministry could have existed with every one of the 92 members for English and Welsh counties against it. Moreover, a member for an important borough carried much greater weight than a member for one of those places in which election was a farce. Had it been otherwise it would never have been necessary for Georgiana Duchess of Devonshire to kiss the cobblers and tailors about Covent Garden so as to secure her darling Charles Fox's return for Westminster. In days when men had such a contempt for uniformity they did not think much of the mere figures of a division list. Every member's vote was weighted in the estimation of his colleagues by the degree in which he represented a popular interest.

Other means by which public opinion made itself felt were the press and petitions. To these last Parliament was extremely sensitive. In 1801 Fox wrote that the growing strength in the House of Commons of the cause of the abolition of the Slave Trade had been principally due to petitions. Parliament was acutely conscious that it represented the people very imperfectly. Indeed, the doctrine of Edmund Burke, that he was a member not for Bristol but for the whole kingdom, was very generally accepted. It followed that attention was paid to regular and irregular expressions of public opinion which would have been neglected in a theoretically more perfect constitution. It was impossible to engage in an unpopular war in a country dependent upon private enterprise, where there was no general compulsory service, and where the standing army was kept very low. It was impossible to enforce unpopular laws through a numerous body of unpaid justices of the peace, who had to live in the country, and in any case thought much more about local interests than about what the Government wished to be done. It was impossible to collect an unpopular tax. The Excise Bill of 1733 had been withdrawn when it had nearly provoked a civil war, and the example of the discomfiture on that occasion of so shrewd a statesman as Robert Walpole made his successors cautious indeed. A nation which had no police worth the name possessed a very real check upon its Government.

The Estate of the Realm which came next above the

Commons consisted of the Lords. The Upper House of Parliament, or House of Lords, did not contain all the Lords or even all the Peers. Not only was this the case as to the younger sons of dukes and marquises, who were known by their christian names and surnames with the prefix "lord," just as the daughters of dukes, marquises, and earls as well, had the prefix "lady". Even the eldest son of a duke, a marquis, or an earl, who was allowed by courtesy to be known by one of his father's titles, did not sit in the House of Lords. Another class of lords who were not in the Upper House, but who were in their case excluded from the Lower also, consisted of those peers of Scotland who were neither peers of Great Britain nor had been chosen by their colleagues at the election held at the commencement of the life of a Parliament to represent the Scottish peerage at Westminster. The last Parliament of the century comprised 246 English lay and 26 spiritual peers. There were 23 dukes, of whom 4 were princes of the blood, 11 marquises, 88 earls, 14 viscounts, and 110 barons. The clergy were represented by 2 archbishops and 24 bishops. Scotland sent 16 lay peers, bringing the grand total to 288.

The general stock of influence and experience was greater, and that of ability not much less, in the Upper House than in the Lower. In several successive administrations nearly all the principal Ministers had been drawn from it. Throughout the eighteenth century it had received numerous recruits —above all under the younger Pitt. That Minister had definitely put an end to any notion which may have persisted that the nobility were a separate order in the State, in the sense in which this could have been said in some Continental countries. This was not done without hostile comment. But it would be entirely wrong to suppose that he travelled out of his way to find unworthy persons so as to ensure a majority over the Whig aristocracy. Many were already Scottish or Irish peers. Many were substantial country gentlemen. Of the rest almost all had distinguished themselves in public life, in the fighting or diplomatic services, or in law, and those were not times when it behoved a young Minister to be niggardly in his recommendations to honour. How little he had really degraded the peerage is evinced by the one case selected by the hostile wits of the day for attack. One of the new creations was a wealthy banker as well as an excellent landlord. His principal service to the public consisted in facilitating government loans. A charade was made on the new title:

> "My first is a passport to Fame,
> My second to Joy or Vexation,
> My third, though it is but a name,
> Has power to lead half the nation;
> My whole is a Title, but hush!
> My meaning is growing too clear:
> It put the whole court to the blush
> When His Majesty made him a Peer."

But no addition to the ranks of their lordships' House added much new life to it. Partly because the atmosphere of the place was unfavourable to rhetoric, partly because their true position in the State was felt to be as lord-lieutenants of counties or other local magnates rather than as debaters, partly because they had already much more influence in the Lower House than they had any right to have, their proceedings were not regarded as important. The House of Lords filled a comparatively unimportant part in the constitution. It was a reserve force at the disposal of the Crown, to be brought into use in an emergency.

At the turn of the century King George, the third sovereign of the House of Brunswick, was sixty-one years of age, and had been forty years on the throne. He was popular with a people who beheld in him a shining example of qualities supposed to be distinctively English. Religious, faultless in his family life, a patriot, an excellent man of business, full of common sense, fond of sport and of farming, he was at the same time stubborn generally, but particularly so upon questions affecting his religious convictions, mistrustful of ideas, and devoid of political imagination. Yet there was much about him which should rather have recalled the small German Court of Hanover from which his family had sprung, and the disposition which might have been developed in a prince who had never left it. Such were his meticulous accuracy in dating his notes to the exact minute, his passion for minute information on the affairs of his subjects, his parsimoniousness, his methods of statecraft, his lack of sympathy with freedom, and a coarseness and want of taste which prevailed in spite of an interest, genuine so far as it went, in science, art, and even literature. Some minor, usually personal, detail would come first in his mind. He was much more interested in the disputes of Royal Academicians than in their pictures. He knew enough of the classics to be able to enjoy a joke at the expense of Lord Kenyon, the Chief Justice, and his bad Latin. He was interested in Fanny Burney's novels, but when she presented him with a copy of Cecilia, he characteristically plunged into the subject of proof-reading. He was astonished, he told her, to hear that she read the proofs herself; he knew how difficult it was for a person to correct his own proofs, and could scarcely believe in her doing so. Many of his conversations are recorded, usually burlesqued with a plentiful sprinkling of "What? What?" and their habitual character is a series of questions on some trivial point—the answer scarcely heeded—followed by a trite reflection on his own part. In reality few men in his kingdom had more general information, but his passion for inquiry lent itself easily to ridicule. The most famous instance was Peter Pindar's jest, founded, no doubt, upon some actual incident, about his having asked a housewife how the apple got into the dumpling. It is not necessary to suppose that he was really so absurd as such stories, if literally taken, would suggest; any more than to believe that he really tried, as in Gillray's picture, to make his daughters drink their tea without sugar, while his German consort exhorted them: "O my dear Creatures, do but

Taste it! You can't think how nice it is without Sugar—and then consider how much work you'll save the poor Blackamoors by leaving off the use of it! and above all, remember how much expense it will save your poor Papa!"

He had a strong will, and, like most men so gifted, he recognized that quality in others, and had the tact of knowing when it was useless to persist, as well as when he could safely press his views. So much was the personal charm which he undoubtedly possessed taken for granted in his lifetime, that hardly any explicit notice of it has been passed down to posterity. But there is one remarkable tribute to it from the pen of Wilberforce, certainly no courtier, any more than those to whom he alludes. The first Earl Camden had once told him that when the King took him into his closet, and fairly gave himself to talking him over, he was almost irresistible. And Wilberforce added an observation of his own as to how courtly Fox himself became during the last months of his life, when he was again a Minister.

It is impossible to claim for George the intellectual accomplishment of understanding the British Constitution. But he realized perfectly well that, as the Parliament had the power of refusing supplies, it was impossible in the long run for a Sovereign to govern, except through Ministers who enjoyed its confidence. But how far the constitution permitted the King any voice in their selection, and how far they ought to be a definite body under a regular chief through whom he was bound to deal, were points upon which the popular party in the State was, owing to a curious combination of circumstances, the most favourable to royal pretensions. It is quite impossible to define the real law of the constitution upon either of these points. But it is certain that Fox and his followers thought it perfectly right, should George III be incapacitated by insanity from performing his duties, for his successor, if he chose, to dismiss his ministers and replace them by others, irrespective of any parliamentary decision. It is equally certain that the same party objected to the idea of collective cabinet responsibility, and even to the very words "cabinet" and "prime minister" as being unknown to the constitution. And yet, if ministers were to be independent of one another, they would be all the more dependent upon the King. For these reasons, one of the principles of the constitution in the eighteenth century —the principle, namely, that a policy of which the wisest men were in favour should be carried into effect—found imperfect expression. When he made the two great mistakes of his reign, George was also resisting the overwhelming sense of those, whether in office or out, who were best able to advise him. But in each of these cases, his persistence in the quarrel with the American Colonies, and his opposition to Irish Catholic Emancipation, he had the nation with him. He was not impressed by votes in the House of Commons. He knew that body to be corrupt. He had the best reason for knowing; he had so often corrupted it himself. Whether all this proves George's ignorance of the British Constitution, or proves that he knew it only too well, it is hardly worth while to conjecture.

The principle that some minister had to be held responsible for every one of the King's acts was, on the whole, generally accepted. But it did not in the least follow from this that he had, as an invariable rule, to act automatically upon advice, or even that he had to consult one of his ministers before he acted. Occasionally he conferred a title, granted a place in his household, or promoted a bishop, without advising with anyone. He usually abstained from making appointments in the army directly, but was satisfied by their being in great measure removed from the active control of any minister responsible to Parliament. They were in the hands of his second son, the Duke of York, as Commander-in-Chief. He had a considerable direct control over the diplomatic service, the expenses of which were defrayed out of the money voted for his personal service—the Civil List. Within the much wider range of subjects upon which it was impossible for him to act positively without the advice of his ministers he had large powers. He could in his turn advise them; and such advice coming from one with long experience, great knowledge of men, and considerable acquaintance with foreign affairs, it was not always wise to reject. If they were not unanimous, he could take advantage of their dissensions. He could delay, or even refuse to take, the action which they pressed upon him, and throw upon him the burden of forcing a constitutional crisis. He might even dismiss them and choose fresh ministers, provided that he was not deprived by so doing of a majority in Parliament. Even if he were, he might by their advice dissolve and appeal to the electors. George availed himself largely of all these powers.

It was William Pitt who, called to office in 1783 as Minister, as the Prime Minister was then more usually called, to release him from advisers under whose yoke he chafed, not only subjected the King generally to the ascendancy of his own powerful will and intellect, but made two definite inroads upon the royal prerogative. The Lord Chancellor held a very special position in the State. He had his own patronage, civil and ecclesiastical. While the First Lord of the Treasury merely led the House of Commons, the Lord Chancellor was at once the principal government member of the House of Lords and the president over its deliberations. Moreover, he was not only the head of the Judicature, but he was the keeper of the King's conscience. It was he who obtained the royal assent to Acts of Parliament. His confidential relations with the Sovereign enabled him to defy the head of the ministry himself. Till 1792 the Lord Chancellor had been one whose name had been connected with a last emphatic assertion of royal authority. Ten years earlier a great constitutional victory had been gained over the Crown. Against the Sovereign's wish, his favourite Minister, Lord North, had resigned in the face of a hostile House of Commons. Against the Sovereign's wish, the party which had expelled him had enforced their point that the new Premier should be their own leader, the Marquis of Rockingham, who was their own nominee and not the King's. But in one matter George prevailed. He successfully insisted on the retention of Lord Thurlow as Chancellor. It was this very man who now, secure in a position which appeared to be independent of changing administrations, openly leant to the side of opposition, and contested the cabinet policy in the House of Lords, but was to find that a Chancellor could do so with impunity no longer. Pitt gave the King his choice between him and Thurlow, and it was Thurlow who was dismissed. There were several subsequent occasions on which the Lord Chancellor showed a certain independence of the Minister, notably the cases of Eldon in 1804 and Erskine in 1807. But Pitt had established the definite principle that it was the head of the ministry, holding the office of First Lord of the Treasury, who led, and that none of his colleagues could publicly oppose him and keep their places. The King was no longer able to encourage one of his ministers, publicly at least, to thwart the others. The second point was one which could not have attracted attention at the time, and yet formed a constitutional precedent of some importance. When Pitt resigned in 1801 he left the King on the best terms, and was succeeded by a Minister with whom he agreed on all points except one, which had been—by common consent—removed from the sphere of practical politics. It was natural that George would have suggested on parting with him that the statesman whose regular services he was losing might still aid him with his counsels. It is almost impossible to conceive a situation in which such an arrangement could have been less objectionable—the two ministers the greatest of friends, the most perfect agreement of policy, the long experience and transcendent abilities of the outgoing Minister, the inexperience and mediocre attainments of the new, and above all the critical condition of public affairs. But Pitt had no hesitation on the subject. He practically informed the King that the proposal was entirely unconstitutional and would be most unfair to his successor. He was as good as his word, and avoided all conversation with him during the three years that he was out of office. It was difficult after this for a Sovereign to consult with persons prominent in political life outside the circle of his responsible advisers.

The system which Pitt did so much to introduce was, however, very far from being established as a distinct part of the constitution. The King was considered to act by the advice of the Privy Council, the members of which were chosen by him. The highest offices in the State carried with them admission into it, and admission into it in turn furnished an opportunity for other employment. Lord Granville Leveson Gower wrote in 1792 that he was willing to accept the post of Comptroller of the Household, because this would bring him into the Privy Council, and he would then be eligible to become a member of the Board of Trade. To be a Privy Councillor, who had the privilege of putting "Right Honourable" in front of his name, was regarded also as an honour not much, if at all, inferior to the red riband of the Order of the Bath. Charles Abbot, who was afterwards Speaker, has left a vivid account of the day when he was sworn a member: "We took the oaths of allegiance, kneeling, and then the privy councillors' oath was administered to us standing; after which we kissed the King's hand and shook hands with each privy councillor present." He describes the Sovereign as seated at the head, and the Prime Minister at the foot, of the table. When the proceedings were over the former walked round and talked and joked with those present. The Cabinet, a body never mentioned in official documents, consisted merely of those Privy Councillors who were His Majesty's advisers for the time being and held the principal offices of State, and had also been invited by the Prime Minister to become members. But the King might, if he wished, consult any member of his Privy Council.

Indeed, up to the end of the eighteenth century their reciprocal right of claiming an audience and tendering their counsels was occasionally exercised, as was also that equally possessed by peers. Fox obtained in 1797 an interview in which he urged his views upon the King in opposition to those of Ministers.

The business transacted at meetings of the Privy Council at which the King presided was formal only. The real business of the country was settled by the Cabinet, in whose deliberations he did not take a part. Upon occasions of extreme emergency, such as the Sunday when the decision was reached to stop cash payments at the Bank and when the King came up specially from Windsor to London for the purpose, the three stages, namely, a Cabinet meeting, an audience of the Sovereign in which the Minister explained its policy and obtained his approval, and the meeting of the Privy Council at which a formal order was passed putting it into effect, were scarcely distinguishable. On other occasions George III was usually aware of the views of his individual advisers, and was considered to have a right to his share in the shaping of a policy. The popular party gave him his full title to this. It was fully conceded to him by Fox. This was clearly implied by him, for example, in March, 1801, when he censured Pitt under the impression that he had kept his Irish policy a secret from the King until the time had come for putting it into effect. As late as 1812, Francis Jeffrey, writing in the Edinburgh Review, ascribed to the Sovereign a considerable direct authority with the Cabinet. That George took care to keep himself early and well informed follows naturally from his inquiring disposition and business-like habits. He gave frequent audiences to his ministers. When he was at Windsor Castle there was no loss of time. An Irish visitor to London was informed that the red boxes containing the official papers were forwarded from London at midnight; they were seen by the King between 4 and 7 a.m. For many years His Majesty had no assistance, but in later life he was helped by Lieutenant-Colonel Herbert Taylor. The boxes were back in their London offices by 10 a.m.; and it was after they had been dispatched that the King attended chapel and took his morning ride.

The head of the Cabinet invariably held the post of First Lord of the Treasury, and also at this time, when he was a commoner, that of Chancellor of the Exchequer. In the former capacity he had a large amount of ecclesiastical and other patronage; in the latter he not only managed finance, but had considerable control over the workings of the other departments. As Premier he presided over the Cabinet's deliberations, and was the regular channel of communication between it and the King. There were three Secretaries of State, in charge of the Home, the Foreign, and the War Departments respectively. The first of these dealt also with Ireland, Scotland, and the Colonies, but in 1801 a change was made, the last being handed over to the Secretary for War. There were two other ministers in the Cabinet, as it had been up to 1798, connected with the Army: the Master-General of the Ordnance, and the Secretary at War (not usually in the Cabinet), who had to do mainly with military finance. The Navy was represented by the First Lord of the Admiralty. The President of the Council, the Lord Privy Seal, and, occasionally, the Chancellor of the Duchy of Lancaster, had seats in the Cabinet, but the duties of their offices were little more than formal. The last was not a member in 1800, and the Master-General, being absent in Ireland as Viceroy, was no longer able to attend. The Lord Chancellor and Camden brought the number of the active members of the Cabinet, as it stood in 1800, up to ten.

The Prime Minister, William Pitt, was born in 1759, the second son of England's greatest war minister. It was the year when the first William Pitt reached the summit of his glory—when his country's fleets and armies triumphed in Quebec and Quiberon Bay, Lagos, Minden, and Guadeloupe.

The same father, the first Earl of Chatham, whose greatness and patriotism inspired his earliest years, directed the details of his education, as he was too delicate for school; and accustomed him to a practice of extempory translation of the classics, to which Pitt afterwards ascribed his own readiness of speech. At fourteen he went to Pembroke Hall, Cambridge, and studied mathematics, history, and politics as well as classics. Here he continued after he had taken his degree as Master of Arts at the early age of seventeen. He still remained at Cambridge studying civil law; and all these subjects, with the addition of a little French and such general reading as Adam Smith's Wealth of Nations, make up the sum-total of his education on the intellectual side. Its strength lay in the single-minded use which he made of it to the one end of becoming a statesman.

When he first went to Cambridge he was attacked by a serious illness. The doctor recommended riding exercise and copious draughts of port wine. The former he continued throughout life whenever his duties permitted him to do so, and he rarely allowed them to prevent him. The port wine he never neglected. A constitution poor, and re-established by such means, was bound to be precarious. He continued to be the same inelegant overgrown stripling, yet with a serious and a commanding expression and demeanour, and much of his great father's dignity of carriage. It would be a mistake to suppose that Pitt was a prig. He took part in field sports. He was convivial and popular at Cambridge. Though he never seemed to seek friends, he was courteous and communicative. With his intimates he showed an affectionate disposition. But he was correct in his relations with the opposite sex. The last quality was, indeed, that one upon which his political opponents were compelled to fasten for purposes of ridicule in default of a better; and men like Fox and Sheridan, who could never have been accused of being seduced by the engrossments of statesmanship to neglect the claims of gallantry, could never get over their amusement at the notion of anyone aspiring to govern an Empire who was a child where the opposite sex was concerned.

Pitt's father, the great Lord Chatham, died in 1778, leaving his family in somewhat distressed circumstances. It is true that his widow received a pension of £3,000 a year. But it was paid most irregularly, and economy was never one of the virtues of the Pitt family. William found himself beset by money difficulties. He had lost no time in being entered at Lincoln's Inn, was called to the bar at the age of twenty-one, and at once began to practise, with an eye on Parliament. He failed to obtain election for Cambridge University at the general election of 1780, but was presented with a seat soon after. He only obtained the honourable distinction of being Member of Parliament for his University in 1784. His first speech was made before he was twenty-two. He fell naturally into the first rank. Burke said: "It is not a chip of the old block; it is the old block itself." A few months later, Fox, on someone remarking, "Mr. Pitt, I think, promises to become one of the first men in Parliament," said emphatically, "He is so already."

It shows the even balance of his mind that he did not devote himself entirely to parliamentary labours, but went on working at the bar, and with considerable success. Yet he knew his value as a statesman. When he was still twenty-two he stated in his place in the House that he could not accept any situation in a new administration short of cabinet rank; and yet this disclaimer only kept him out of office a few months. He was Chancellor of the Exchequer to Lord Shelburne at twenty-three. That nobleman's ministry was overturned by the notorious coalition of North and Fox in a few months. Pitt was far too honourable to coalesce with North, whose conduct of the war with America he, as well as Fox, had bitterly opposed. It was owing to this that he gradually found himself in opposition to Fox and most of the Whigs, who followed him. Disraeli's saying,

"England does not love Coalitions", is truer of this one than of any. The King felt it to be so and, sooner than accept North and Fox, offered Pitt the Premiership in February, 1783. With extraordinary judgment the young Chancellor, who had not resigned with his chief, as it was not desired that he should do so, took time to consider, looked round the circle of his political friends, and came to the conclusion that it was not time for him to attempt to form a ministry until North and Fox had tried and failed. They fell after a few months; and on the 19th of December Pitt, at twenty-four, was First Lord of the Treasury and Chancellor of the Exchequer, posts which he filled for the next seventeen years:

> "A sight to make surrounding nations stare,
> A kingdom trusted to a schoolboy's care."

In contrast to his father's title of the greatest of England's war ministers Pitt may justly be termed the greatest of her peace ministers—and this although by his exertion when living and example when dead he brought her successfully through the mortal struggle with the greatest enemy which she had ever had. For his real genius lay with peace. His first task during the nine years which followed his accession to office was to restore and revive the country, which had emerged from the war with the United States of America, France, and Spain weaker than at almost any time in her history. He considered himself a disciple of Adam Smith. He reduced customs duties and made collection efficient. He carried out a commercial treaty with France. He made economies in expenditure. Abroad he had successfully contested Spain's claim to exclude England from the Pacific coast of North America, thus laying the foundation of the colony of British Columbia, he had saved Holland from falling under the yoke of France, and he had initiated the policy of defending British interests in the Levant from Russian aggression. In pursuing this last object, however, he had not been successful, and the country had lost prestige.

The consequence was that in 1792, when it became a primary object to prevent war breaking out on the Continent between revolutionary France and the powers threatened by the new order of things, he was either unwilling or unable to interfere effectually. Still less was he able to restore peace after war had actually broken out.

The series of political changes, usually accompanied with violence, known to history as the French Revolution, had continued since 1788. In August 1791 it had become clear that Louis XVI of France was no longer a free agent. The Emperor of Austria and the King of Prussia met at Pilnitz and issued a declaration inviting the other sovereigns of Europe to help re-establish him as a king with the usual powers attaching to sovereigns. This did not commit them or render war inevitable. Pitt thought little of it. It was followed next month by the forced acceptance by Louis of a position as the head of a constitutional monarchy with defined powers. In the beginning of 1792 Pitt reduced the army, expressing the belief that, now that Russia had made peace with Turkey, the general peace was secure for some considerable time—a class of prediction which has occurred with singular frequency in the mouths of British statesmen on the eve of devastating wars. But the relations between France and the two Central Powers grew gradually more bitter, and in April France declared war upon Austria. Paris became more and more turbulent, and on the 10th of August the mob rose and made Louis a prisoner. For the next few years it was generally this mob or the command of the military force at the capital which determined who should rule France. That country had now started downwards on a path on which there was no calling a halt. Already, in July, Prussia had declared war. But all this seemed to put war between England and France farther off than ever. No one could have expected that, surrounded by enemies, disorganized France could have held out for long. There was nobody in England, and there can have been few in

France, who could have foreseen that that country, in a sort of calculated madness, would have preferred to have all Europe against her at the same time. England was a partial exception. Those who ruled France during the half-year which followed the 10th of August were probably quite willing to let her have peace, at the price of submitting to insult and watching tamely, while France pursued her aggressions everywhere except upon actual British territory. On the 16th of November the French Convention issued two decrees encroaching upon Dutch independence. In particular it decreed freedom of navigation on the estuary of the River Scheldt, which was under control of that republic. In so doing it appealed to the Law of Nature. But there was no such law, and even if there had been, there were no recognized interpreters. This right had been secured to the Dutch by treaty after treaty with Great Britain, who had also pledged herself to support them against any violation of it by a treaty concluded so late as 1788. Charles Fox, leading the Opposition, had opposed even a commercial treaty with France as an inveterate enemy of hers under the old order. Now that that was changed he made excuse for her. But the ground upon which Pitt stood was that British interests and British treaty rights were violated, irrespective of the form of the Government which violated them. The French decree was very quickly followed by deeds. French gunboats forced the passage of the Scheldt held by the Dutch, and seized the city of Antwerp in Austrian Flanders. They had already driven out that Power and were now knocking loudly on the frontier posts of the Dutch Republic. Three days before the date of this decree the British Government had dispatched an assurance to that Government regarding assistance in the event of a French invasion; but it was not known to the French until it was too late—they had already committed themselves.

There was a further cause of war. On the 19th of November the Convention had issued another decree inviting general revolution and defying sovereigns indiscriminately throughout Europe. By itself such a decree was of no more importance than the Declaration of Pilnitz; it only became important when France showed by acts that she meant what she said. This she had already done, and was about to do on the largest scale. In such an atmosphere it was impossible amicably to settle a question relating to French aggression in the Low Countries, a question upon which Great Britain had fought time after time. Negotiations continued both with France and with Austria, but they were unavailing. The French ambassador was dismissed, but not before his Government had ordered his recall. On the 1st of February, 1793, France declared war both upon the kingdom of Great Britain and the Dutch republic.

Forced into war as he was, Pitt found himself assisted from a quarter which a year or two before could hardly have been expected to furnish him with help. Of the Whigs of the day who had formed the Opposition throughout this first half of his Ministry, Edmund Burke, the greatest of all British political thinkers, had long displayed eagerness to support a government that would declare war upon the French revolutionaries. He had his friend, the chivalrous and eloquent William Windham, with him. Others who did not any more than Pitt and his colleagues share this enthusiasm for a royalist crusade, were brought over during the year 1792 by a sense of the country's danger. Their leader was the Duke of Portland, formerly Prime Minister of the Coalition Ministry of 1783. The Opposition was left with little more than fifty members under Fox, but its abilities were out of all proportion to its numbers. Pitt's principal difficulties were, however, out of doors.

Few parts of his life are more to his credit than the success with which he carried out that most difficult of a statesman's duties, the prevention of civil disorder. A Minister who is attacked can always resign. But should he enjoy general support, and believe in the maintenance of himself in office, he is bound, in the interest of constitutional government itself, to take measures to prevent his being thrust out by mere violence, or the fear of it. Yet it is impossible for him to act so as to escape the most bitter criticism. If the disaffection is held to be widespread and dangerous, and he takes his steps accordingly, Burke is quoted at him, he is told that it is impossible to frame an indictment against a nation, and blamed for acting with indiscriminating severity. Suppose him on the other hand to make a careful selection. If he prosecutes a rascal who has just caught the sort of language which inflames the passions of the mob, he is ridiculed for giving a person of no account just the advertisement which his foolishness wants. If he has the courage to pick off the leaders—noblemen, landholders, men of letters, gentlemen of the long robe—he is angrily asked whether great respectability, services to the State, talents and learning are no security against prosecution. The rights of free speech and a free press are claimed—as if it were wrong to write a letter to an individual inciting him to murder, but right to print one addressed to the community—wrong to suggest a crime to a single person who is master of his actions, but right to excite immense numbers into a condition in which they know neither what their leaders nor what they themselves are doing, and in that state commit a hundred ghastly crimes which they bitterly regret when they come to themselves. If he forbears to prosecute at all, whether from policy or because the evidence is deemed insufficient, and disorder follows, he may be charged with desiring to provoke it, as has constantly been said of the Irish Government in the case of the rebellion of 1798.

These are general difficulties; but Pitt had a special one to face. There was no real police, and there were more than the usual objections to the use of the military arm in the suppression of riots. It was, until the passing of the Seditious Meetings Act, which was itself made the subject of severe criticism, necessary to allow huge crowds

THE GOVERNMENT OF ENGLAND   133

to collect and to be openly incited to disturbance. An example of the successful efforts of those who sympathized with revolution was the very occurrence of the year 1795 which led to the passing of this law. Under the auspices of the London Corresponding Society an immense meeting was held in Copenhagen Fields, which was claimed by its supporters to have amounted to the enormous number of 150,000 persons. It passed an "Address to the Nation" practically calling for civil war. Two days later a violent attack was made on the King himself when on the way to open Parliament, and repeated on his return. It was now impossible to say that the Government had discovered an imaginary conspiracy. The only resource left for the Opposition was to accuse Pitt of having engineered the tumult so as to have a pretext for his own tyrannical measures. It is strange that the Society was allowed to continue its labours long after this, and was not suppressed until after it had openly instigated rebellion in Ireland in 1798. Severe measures now had to be taken. But the number of individuals affected during those perilous years when Ireland was in rebellion, the fleet in mutiny, and numerous secret rebels actually watching for a French invasion, was never large. At the end of the century it was twenty-nine. The debates on what was described as the Suspension of the Habeas Corpus Act turned mainly, not upon the number of persons imprisoned without trial, but upon such matters as the exact size of the room in which a gentleman, Colonel Despard, was confined, and how much weight he had lost in prison. That officer became a greater danger when he had come out than before he went in. In 1802 he headed a definite conspiracy against the State. This circumstance certainly lent support to the belief that the suppression of sedition is worse than futile—a belief resting on the assumption that those desirous of overturning a government of whatever kind are usually gifted with such loftiness of spirit that no apprehension of danger or loss can turn them from their path. Yet the notion that the best way of rendering a man a popular idol was to punish him overlooked the fact that the men most worthy the notice of those in authority are precisely those who have obtained popularity already, and that those ingratiating qualities by which they have captivated mobs are unlikely to shine so brightly in a dungeon as in the streets. A man may, indeed, become a martyr if publicly punished. But those public punishments which still existed were then seldom employed upon seditious persons, except, of course, in the very rare cases when the death penalty had to be inflicted. So far as the minor ones are concerned, it would be unreasonable to suppose that ministers and legislators who have ordained the pillory and the stocks, for instance, as public examples were completely ignorant of human nature as it existed in their time. It is gratuitous to express a disbelief in the efficacy of punishment. Only a few exceptional characters among mankind continue a course—particularly a wrong one—in the face of all the deterrents which it is possible for a government to invent; and Pitt would have perfectly succeeded in suppressing sedition by the end of the century, had it not closed with the greatest scarcity of food known for many years. The view that such tendencies were bound to die out, however unwise the methods might be which Government employed in their repression, is not deserving of serious consideration. The events of history are only inevitable in the sense that the forces which have operated to bring them about are more powerful than those which have operated to prevent them. In this sense the French Revolution was inevitable. It was also inevitable that the forces which made for a contemporary revolution in England should fail. But this was only because those which upheld order were too powerful, and one of the mightiest of these was the brain and the tempered resolution of Pitt.

His principal colleagues were the Foreign Secretary, William Grenville, his first cousin, whom he had raised to the peerage, and the Secretary for War, Henry Dundas. Indeed, these three formed a sort of inner cabinet which met occasionally shortly before the Cabinet proper. Grenville, born in the same year as his cousin, was one of a family prominent in public service throughout the latter half of the eighteenth century—a family, too, which had risen into wealth largely through an accumulation of public offices and sinecures. Lord Grenville's father had been the Premier; his elder brother, the Marquis of Buckingham, had been Lord-Lieutenant of Ireland; his younger brother, Thomas, held a minor post in the Ministry. Apart from his ingrained appetite for public money in the form of places and sinecures he possessed a high rectitude of character and a remarkable indifference to most of the inducements which bring men into public life. Though he commanded in a considerable degree the esteem and even attachment of officials both British and foreign with whom he came into contact in the course of his duties, he was far from being a popular personage. After he had himself been for a year the head of an administration—in 1807—he expressed his anxiety to retire, and recorded, with a frankness perhaps unique among statesmen, his own incapacity for the management of men. He preferred books. Contemporaries, repelled by the Grenville pride, the reserve, the obstinacy, and the portentous manner and ponderous build of the Foreign Secretary, might have been reconciled could they have seen how he closed one of his letters on official matters to a minister abroad: "We sent you *Castle Rackrent* last week. Are you not delighted with it?"—or could they have stood with the Earl of Minto and watched him patting and petting a favourite old horse for ten minutes together. He could even jest. But of these sides of him little was known. He belonged essentially to the class of statesmen rather than that of politicians; of those who frame policies rather than those who move men; of those who foresee the future rather than those who live in the present. The causes wherein he succeeded no less than those wherein he failed—the emancipation of the slaves no less than that of the Catholics—showed that he held fast by the better part of Whiggism, the part in which he was at one with his cousin and chief.

The other, Henry Dundas, enjoyed a rather larger share of Pitt's confidence. It was assuredly not because the two men had the same ideas of what was meant by the public service that this was so. Dundas's notions went very little further than the management of men by jobbery. To this he devoted almost all his powers. He had some liberal ideas, upon the Irish Catholic claims for example. He was a clear-headed administrator and an excellent man of business. But, apart from his having, as was proved in 1806, connived while Treasurer of the Navy at actual dishonesty, he had, throughout his career, pursued a crooked path. This he attempted to conceal by affecting a bluff Scottish manner. His good-natured "Wha wants me?" was a standing joke in the House of Commons. His correspondence was full of places and promotions. It was mainly his own native country that he served in this way. Lady Holland told a story of his having sent for a gentleman who had rendered signal service to the King, and asked what he could do for him. "I wish that you would make me a Scotchman", was the reply. Dundas was not content with being Secretary of State. As President of the Board of Control he enjoyed the patronage of the East India Company. Many a Scot, who certainly fully justified his selection, owed the first step in his career to him. In the army the most important posts came in 1801 to be held by Scotsmen—his own namesake David Dundas, Abercromby, the Stuarts and Moore, for example—and these also did justice to his choice. His third office, that of Treasurer of the Navy, had no patronage attached. But afterwards, when he was First Lord of the Admiralty, Lord St. Vincent surmised that he would try to make a Scottish Navy, a thing which it was impossible to do. Pitt relied upon Dundas partly owing to the latter's superior knowledge of men; but their intimacy was also due to convivial reasons. Many were the bottles which the two emptied together, and many the Whig jokes cracked at their expense. One occasion was celebrated by a collection of 101 Bacchanalian Epigrams, some of which were very fair specimens of the wit of the day. They were in the form of dialogues between the two cronies, as they entered the House of Commons together. One was:

"P.—'I can't discern the Speaker, Hal; can you?'
"D.—'Not see the Speaker! damn me, I see *two*.'"

Another ran:

"P.—'Europe's true *balance* must not be o'erthrown.'
"D.—'Damn Europe's balance—try to *keep your own*.'"

The Secretary for Home Affairs was the third Duke of Portland, who was born in 1738. He had been once Prime Minister, presiding over the ill-famed North and Fox Coalition, and was to become so once again. His gifts were certainly not superficial. He scarcely ever made a speech— in fact he did not often utter a syllable. But he was no unworthy upholder of the traditions of the House of Bentinck. He was a man of iron determination. In 1806 he underwent the terrible operation of being cut for the stone. The old man was seven minutes under the knife without uttering a sound. He was liberal in his views on Irish matters, and through troublous times preserved—under Pitt—internal peace in England without undue severity. He carried, however, no weight in council. One of those who had come over with him in 1792, Earl Spencer, born in 1758, was First Lord of the Admiralty, and there has hardly ever been a better one. Pitt's elder brother, the Earl of Chatham, a man of the grossest indolence and self-indulgence, whose calculated taciturnity gained him an unmerited reputation for wisdom, was Lord President of the Council. The tenth Earl of Westmorland was Lord Privy Seal, an office which he held with a short interval in 1806 and 1807 for thirty years. The Secretary at War was William Windham. Born in 1750 of an old Norfolk family, although illegitimate, he has been always regarded as the type of a finished scholar and English gentleman. In little else did he conform to conventional standards. In a far from business-like cabinet he was the most erratic. He was always brilliant, and the one thing which could be safely prophesied about him was that what he would do would be something which no one would expect, and that the reasons which he would find would be such as would occur to no one else. Sir James Mackintosh very justly said of him: "Singular as it may sound, he often opposed novelties from a love of paradox." He was a Whig conservative, in which he followed his master, Burke. His other master had been Doctor Johnson, whose last pious advice to him he had deeply treasured, and it was one of the causes of an uprightness of character which he maintained to the last. A contemporary of Pitt, Earl Camden, who had been Viceroy of Ireland, was admitted to the Cabinet without office. The actual Viceroy, Marquis Cornwallis, still held his seat in the Cabinet as Master-General of the Ordnance, though he was unable to attend. The number was brought up to eleven by the Lord Chancellor, Lord Loughborough—soon to pass out of public life.

There were some men of note in minor posts. The most brilliant junior in parliament was George Canning. He was born in 1770, the son of a small country gentleman from the North of Ireland. His father died when he was a child, and his mother, who was a beautiful woman, went on the stage. His Irish origin, and this indirect connection with the theatre, as well as his brilliant wit, made him seem a younger counterpart of his friend Sheridan, already long established as one of the Opposition leaders. When he came out into the world, Canning was taken up by the great Whig houses. But although he had made many friends of good family at Eton College, where he had been educated, and afterwards in the golden period of his youth, an aristocracy repelled him—and this although he still remained a favourite of great Whig ladies such as Lady Bessborough, sister of Georgiana Duchess of Devonshire, and Lady Holland. Patriotism disgusted him with the views of Fox upon the war, and a strain of the romantic led him to attach himself to Pitt rather than any other, while still not much more than a boy. The Minister, who had now held the highest post in the State for ten years, was a perfect boy himself whenever he could unbend among his intimates, and repaid the young man's devotion with familiarity. He deigned to contribute to Canning's Anti-Jacobin, and added a stanza, and that not the least humorous, to the exquisite lament of the former student of "Gottingen." He gave him the post of Under-Secretary for Foreign Affairs under Grenville. Although Canning had actually resigned, and was holding other offices of less importance in 1800, his masterly gifts of style were still in request during that year for drafting dispatches.

Another was Viscount Castlereagh, son of the Earl of Londonderry. He was born in 1769. He was now Chief Secretary for Ireland. A third, the son of the Earl of Liverpool, an old Tory statesman raised to the peerage under Pitt, was Lord Hawkesbury, born in the same year as Canning. He was on the Board of Control for Indian affairs. A fourth was known as "Old George Rose". This minister's opinions on the subject of finance and on the condition of the poor were respected across the floor of the House, but his character was not. It was remembered that he had been a poor naval officer originally, and that his present prosperity was due to the number of minor offices in the State which he had contrived to absorb, and the nature of whose duties was obscure. At present he was Verderer of the New Forest, Clerk of the Parliaments, and Master of the Pleas in the Court of Exchequer. Another financial expert was in the House of Lords. This was Lord Auckland, created a peer for diplomatic services, and at this time Joint Postmaster-

General. The law advisers of the Crown were the Attorney-General, Sir John Mitford, and the Solicitor-General, Sir William Grant.

Opposed to Ministers in the House of Commons was a party which contrasted strangely with the ranks of large-acred noblemen who formed the Opposition in the House of Lords. There was Richard Sheridan, the son of an actor manager, born in 1751, the most brilliant man of his time as dramatist, orator, and wit. In any question he took the generous side; during the dark days of the Mutiny of the Nore he hastened to Pitt's support; later, when Addington, who was trying to restore peace in Europe, was being laughed at, he supported him too. Against such evils as oppression in India and in Ireland, the Slave Trade and cruelty to animals, he was a tower of strength. But he was a bad party man, not only in the sense that he would not put his party before his country, but that he would not sacrifice —even in minor things—his personal views, or their expression in public, for the sake of his political associates. Another was a confirmed boaster of his lineage, the Honourable Thomas Erskine. He bore no resemblance in fortune to a Russell or a Howard. The son of a very poor Scottish peer, he was born in one of the highest rooms in one of the stupendous warrens of the Edinburgh Old Town, and had been packed off as a boy to sea—just as if he had been the third son of an English country parson. Others were George Tierney, the son of a Spanish merchant, and Samuel Whitbread, the brewer. A very different man was the brilliant darling of the Whig drawing-rooms—Charles Grey. But the real link between the Commons and the patrician Whigs of the Upper House was furnished by the leader of the party.

Charles James Fox, born in 1749, the son of the first Lord Holland, resembled Pitt in belonging to a family ennobled by the then reigning monarch for brilliant political services. His father, while a commoner and still somewhat of an adventurer, had created a great sensation by a secret marriage with Lady Caroline Lennox, daughter of the Duke of Richmond, who had refused to allow the match. In this way Charles was descended from Charles II of England and Henri IV of France. His admirers traced resemblances between him and the great French King; and they were certainly striking. Both had wit, personal charm, great powers of leadership, intense vitality, and a prettily expressed sentimental philanthropy. Both were political opportunists and religious latitudinarians of the drabbest dye. Fox's genius was first ripened at Eton, where he spent the ages of nine to fifteen. Here he learnt to understand the classics as—in his own belief at least—he could have learnt them nowhere else. But his father, as great a cynic as ever lived, did not believe in letting his son go to the devil his own way, and thought it his parental duty to show him the road. He taught him, while still a boy, as much evil as a boy could learn in continental gaming hells, before he let him return to Eton for his last year to debauch the other boys. Charles was then, at fifteen, sent to Hertford College, Oxford. But University life, with its evening card-parties and its moderate drinking bouts, was thought too cramping for a youth of seventeen, and after less than two years it was time that his real education should be taken up again. Before the hour came for the finished man of the world to start life in as cynical a society as England has ever known, he spent two more years on the Continent, indulging a passion for literature and languages and art which the dissipations into which he was thrown had no power to dull.

For the most noteworthy thing about Fox was his extraordinary vitality. He enjoyed that perennial alertness of mind of which only the consummate idler seems to be capable. One day losing thousands, racing on Newmarket Heath or gambling at Brooks's Club, the next he was sitting down with equal zest to read a favourite classic, or magnificent in the House of Commons upholding views, which he did not care if he had to maintain alone, against the best speakers of the day. In middle age the profligate reappears as the most domestic of men, not with the weariness of the sated rake but with an almost boyish passion for the mistress whom he has now married, the classics, and the nightingales of Saint Anne's Hill. Urged by his friends to play his part in the nation's affairs again, he passes unwillingly to town, bears off against the greatest orators there the honours of a full-dress debate, and returns without a regret to the pleasures left behind. His life was consistent in one thing. Towards the end of it, when England stood alone under a feeble ministry against the arrayed might of Napoleon, he writes: "I do not see sufficient prospect of real good to make me give that sort of attention to public affairs which is inconsistent with my private comfort." Some of the portraits of his burly, good-humoured, gaily dressed if somewhat slovenly figure suggest a man of much intellectual power and forcible character, possibly a hearty squire or a man of sport and pleasure, a prosperous business man or even bookmaker; certainly not one who was troubled overmuch by matters of state. He had entered political life as if it was a game—no doubt the most fascinating of all games, and all the more so because he claimed the right in this one to make up the rules as he went along. It was a game, too, that he could drop when he chose, like any other game. He had the old loose eighteenth-century outlook, something of which is reflected in what Rogers told of his attachment to the old pronunciation of "London". He called it "Lonnon" to the last.

He was not without patriotism. But in him it took the form of admiration rather than of love. Few finer things have been said of England's sea-power than what Fox said of the sea after the naval failures of 1781: "It used to be the country of an English commander." But devotion to England he had none. To the last days of his life the parts of Virgil which he most admired were the sentimental and domestic passages, and not those describing the glories of the Roman

Empire, which might have been expected to appeal more closely to a statesman—in striking contrast to the William Pitt of thirteen who composed a tragedy which was entirely political. "Patriot" was a word which had acquired a bad name in the circles in which he moved in the impressionable time of his life. The cultivated Englishman of the eighteenth century loved to regard himself as a Citizen of the World. It was impossible for the intense patriotism of the ancient Greeks, or even the contemporary French, to appeal to Fox.

Political liberty was his guiding star. This was a natural result of his early training—brought up as he had been in the enjoyment of every sort of personal licence, so soon as his generous mind had assimilated the teaching of the greatest genius in the House of Commons, Edmund Burke. He thought that that cause had brought about more good than all others put together. Careless whether he remained in political life or not, he was free to adopt the views best recommended to his taste. He adhered to them with a strange pertinacity. While most of the leaders of his party, and not the least generous among them, passed over to the support of Pitt on the war, he remained the head of a forlorn band of friends of freedom who could not bear to be at war with a nation which had destroyed the Bastille, and the other monuments of the ancient order of things in France. But he had no other principles. He had attacked North as though that Minister were being impeached, which indeed he said he deserved to be. Yet very shortly after this he was sitting with him in the same Cabinet. He wrote of Pitt as a "mean, low-minded dog," and yet he was ready to do the same with Pitt. He did not attempt to render himself an authority on public finance, and his objection to rotten boroughs was not so much that they were rotten—he was himself a member for one—as that they were efficacious in upholding the strength of the Crown. He cared little for the voice of the people, "this rascally people" as he once called it. He made no endeavour to understand social and economic questions. William Wordsworth sent him in 1801 a copy of Lyrical Ballads, as an acceptable offering to a statesman of great sensibility of heart. He described in the admirable letter which accompanied his gift the manner in which the industrialization of the country and the administration of the poor law had loosened the bonds of domestic feeling. But he could not mention any remedy which Fox had proposed for those evils; nor did the statesman go into these matters at all, either when he replied to the poet's letter or on other occasions. And yet this, and not the repression of a few mob-orators, authors, or even dukes, was the greatest evil of the age, and took its share of the time of ministers, as well as of the other Opposition leaders.

Charles Fox had stupendous powers of mind, immense knowledge of men as well as of books, and a captivating geniality, which seems to have followed naturally from his large frame and his habits of indulgence. As a child his mother called him "dreadfully passionate". But as his mind grew he came to be rather violent than passionate. He could never have ended by taking his own life, like his supporter, Whitbread, or his opponent Castlereagh. In a period when duels were frequent, even among public men, he too fought one. He twice fired his pistol in the air, and, though wounded himself, so carried matters that his adversary afterwards became one of his most devoted friends. It was impossible not to love him. Even his opponents could not feel bitter against him. His violence took the form of showing in public that he did not care. The indiscretion of a course was almost a recommendation to him. He would bring forward a measure at the very moment which was most damaging to himself, to his own party, and to the measure's own eventual success. He would grasp at the most flimsy reasons for taking office along with his most inveterate adversaries. He would leave office on the flimsiest grounds. His mind grew with, or rather outgrew the strength of, his feelings, but it never overshadowed them. His readiness in fence made him the greatest of all parliamentary debaters. Yet he never forgot that men had hearts, and it is the peculiar note of his oratory that he was able to appeal to their hearts and their reasons in the same breath.

Fox has been praised as the ideal party chief, and in particular as the man who during dark days kept together a band of followers devoted to what seemed the forlorn causes of liberty and reform. Yet in point of fact in nothing did he show less talent than in his leadership while in opposition to Pitt. When his rival took office in 1783, Fox allowed himself to be outmanœuvred with incredible ease, in spite of his greater experience, his abler following, and his immense majority. His bungling of things in 1788, when the madness of the King made it appear as if his party might return to office, was appalling, and did lasting damage to his prestige. When the Revolution came, he vacillated; and then deprived vacillation of its one excuse by coming down on the wrong side. In April 1792 Grey, Erskine, Sheridan, Whitbread, and others founded "The Friends of the People", a club whose innocent object it was to obtain parliamentary reform. But Fox refused to join. Yet he did not condemn. He would not speak the word which, as Grey complained fifty years later, would have kept him out of "all the mess". He allowed what commenced as the convivial freak of heated bloods to rush him into breaking up his party for a cause for which he had at no time shown much enthusiasm. The name of the club, and the names of its promoters, which did not include those of the right wing of the Opposition, gave a very good excuse to those who saw in the movement much more than a mere effort after constitutional reform. Nor could they help connecting it with similar movements going on across the Channel and also on this side of the Channel, which made for anarchy rather than reform. Fox must have seen this, and seen, moreover, that the moderates of his party would have nothing to do with it, even if he could not see that they were bound to go over to Pitt, as they did. But as he failed to take control from the start, all these results were inevitable; and it was also inevitable that, being what he was, he should throw his shield over Grey and the hotheads. Started under these auspices, the new party—for, purified of such elements of caution and sense of responsibility as the former Opposition possessed, this is what it had become—fell from lower to lower deep of discredit. At last, in 1798, when Arthur O'Connor (who was related to an Irish peer) was tried for high treason, Fox, Sheridan, and the Duke of Norfolk actually stultified themselves by volunteering evidence of his virtue and patriotism, and helped to procure his acquittal. Not long afterwards he confessed the leading part which he had taken in the organization of the Irish rebellion which almost immediately followed.

But even as the leader of this forlorn band Fox did not fancy himself. His constant retirements to Saint Anne's Hill necessitated temporary transfers of the parliamentary leadership into other hands. "It must be from movements out of doors and not in Parliament that opposition can ever gain any strength", he wrote to his nephew as an excuse for refusing to go to town. But he started no such movements. The portrait of him as the man who kept the sacred fire alive is, indeed, a strange one. He did much by his factiousness to convert moderate men into opponents of reform in his lifetime, and the cause could not have succeeded when it did had not many Tories crossed over and become its champions after his death, as they would have done had he never existed. It was his country's misfortune rather than his own that he spent most of his time as a politician, and had few opportunities of displaying statesmanship. Yet it is upon his merits as a statesman, and not as a politician, that he rests his title to honour. It was not in partisan leadership, but in dealing with large questions of policy for which he had to own responsibility, that he showed his best self.

A more important member of the Whig party than anybody after Fox himself—in a social sense, at least—was one who on occasions styled himself its head—George, Prince of Wales. Born in 1762, he had received a sound though a contracted education both in the classical and modern languages. He was a consummate musician. His memory was remarkable. Sir Nathaniel Wraxall in his memoirs observed upon the astonishment of foreign officers at the extraordinary knowledge which he displayed in conversation of minute details relating to the Prussian Army. He had another, not very princely, gift. He was an excellent mimic. He was a fair speaker and a good talker. His judgment upon persons and affairs was by no means contemptible. In the most unfavourable circumstances he bore himself with some dignity and a certain royal tact. He must have had great charm of manner. For brilliant political leaders such as Fox, Burke, Sheridan, and Erskine, and great soldiers such as Moira and Lake, could not have become and remained his intimates merely in virtue of court glamour or personal ambition, while more than one woman, including one good woman, loved him with a constant affection; and there was much in him for which compensation had to be found. He had lost the slim figure and much of the good looks which had distinguished him in youth, and in his character as a man he was altogether loathsome. Totally devoid of truth, or of a sense of justice, entirely without self-control, completely abandoned to the unbridled gratification of his desires for women, food, and drink, and almost destitute of public spirit, his history is one dreary catalogue of heartless affairs of the heart, debts, and disputes with his parents and with his wives. His legal wife, Princess Caroline of Brunswick, had been married to him in 1795, and had borne him a daughter in the following year. Not long before the end of the century he had left her, and had persuaded Maria Fitzherbert, the wife of ten years earlier, who was his in the eyes of the Church though not of English law, to return to him. He was now leading a somewhat retired life, and had lost most of his popularity in a society which in his time he had done almost as much to corrupt as his exemplary father and mother to purify. Lady Holland records that, invited in 1798 to dine at her house, he arrived at six, and finding himself almost the first, seemed uneasy and afraid that the rest of those who had been asked had refused to meet him. The story shows at least how far from rigid the bands of etiquette were, and that no one felt obliged to pay court to him. His popularity, equally with his unpopularity, was his own. With Fox at this time he was no longer intimate. His chief adviser, when not called away by military duties, was the Earl of Moira, seconded by Sheridan and Erskine. Of the King's seven other sons, the second, Frederick, Duke of York, Commander-in-Chief of the Army since 1794, had become closely allied with the Government. But the third, William, Duke of Clarence, was a persistent speaker on the Opposition side in the House of Lords, and assisted to maintain the dignity—such as it was—of an Opposition Court.

Fox's natural friends were not the half-republicans of the Lower House, but the men of the great Whig families— the Russells, the Howards, the Cavendishes, the Grenvilles, and the Wentworths. Of these the last two were no longer his political friends, for the House of Buckingham had always adhered to Pitt, and Earl Fitzwilliam had held office under him. But they were not permanently estranged from Fox, as the Bentincks and Lennoxes were, in spite of his earlier political connection with the heads of those two families, the Dukes of Portland and Richmond, as well as his near relationship to the latter. It is, however, no matter of wonder that so many leading families should have followed or preceded Portland in adhering to a statesman bent to save England from a French revolution; the strange thing is that there were so many who stayed with Fox. This was partly owing to his personality. But it was mainly due to their pride, a pride different certainly from that of an Eastern pasha or a Spanish grandee, but as lofty in its kind as any that has been entertained by the sons of mankind. Men like Bedford and Norfolk openly despised religion and morality. What they did was right because they did it. Consistency was nothing to them. If Norfolk possessed more close parliamentary boroughs than even Lonsdale, was he not on the popular side? If Bedford sent in a false return of the number of his man-servants, was he not patriotically resisting iniquitous taxation? England existed for the great Whigs, who had the right to be the King's advisers; if they were not, so much the worse for him. When danger threatened from across the Channel, they were perfectly fearless. They did not dream that it would touch them, and, in any event, they would not give up their cherished opposition, or basely rally behind the sheltering arm of Pitt.

Their political creed was mainly negative—light taxation, no foreign entanglements—in a word, freedom. For this they were ready to make sacrifices. Fox's nephew, Lord Holland, thought nothing of the losses which he might incur on his West Indian estate by the abolition of the Slave Trade. But as the Whigs felt strongly on scarcely any subject except their right to rule the country, their convictions usually cost them very little. They disliked dissenters intensely, as being earnest people who denounced vice; but they won their support by being at all times ready to relieve them from restrictions, a zeal which cost nothing to men who cared so little for the Establishment. Yet they did not dislike the Church of England, so long as it was indifferent and worldly; when an attempt was made to reform it, they were loud in their remonstrance. If they were ready at all times to allow the existence of abuses in the tithe system, it was because they had hungry eyes on church property. The great Whig divine of the day was Doctor Parr. His view of the Church in which he ministered is startling. He wrote of a young man: "He has lately been ordained, and as he has no principle nor good feeling, he will make a truly loyal and orthodox Churchman." Had this come from the pen of an earnest church reformer, it might have passed as a piece of bitter satire on an abuse which the writer felt deeply. But Parr was no reformer, only a country clergyman with a grievance that he could not get the bishop's licence to hold two livings. The merit of having no narrow principle could certainly be claimed by some well-known persons in holy orders on the popular side. The Reverend Horne Tooke, the revolutionist, was something more than a Whig; but there were also the obscene Doctor Wolcote, who with characteristically execrable taste chose for himself the literary name of Peter Pindar, and the fighting parson Henry Bate. These were productions of an age which was passing away with much else that was typical of Whiggism. But the far more reputable Sydney Smith was at times an odd kind of clergyman. He frequently made it necessary to remember that he had become one against his will. Until well into the new century he maintained the Whig habit of satirizing Premiers for being regular in their lives, and poked fun at Perceval for living at Hampstead, and walking to church every Sunday followed by his eleven sons with their hair combed and their faces washed. The ethical breadth of a parish priest who is amused by this sort of thing is astonishing.

While the clergy had such unbridled pens, there need be no wonder that laymen used the press on the Whig side with an appalling disregard of decency. Until the exposures of Canning's Anti-Jacobin tempered James Perry's violence, the Morning Chronicle spared no one. In its anxiety, for example, to make Pitt's financial scheme a failure, it attacked a private lady by name in the vilest manner for the mere crime of having subscribed to a war fund. Later on it at least confined its disgusting allusions to public men. Yet there was about this time a revolutionary organ for which Lamb wrote, and which even Perry regarded as low and indecent, the Albion. The Morning Post was another newspaper which published the most infamous attacks upon Ministers, some from the pen of Coleridge. Apart from their scurrility, the opposition writers performed the difficult task of justifying their party and its violently hostile attitude towards the war, with considerable success. Only for a short time, in 1797 and 1798, when Canning drove them all before him in headlong flight, and again shortly before the Peace of Amiens, when Cobbett had just appeared upon the scenes, was their supremacy seriously challenged. George Rose's attempts to work up ministerial organs were failures. Ministers had one friend in The Times, but this such a very candid one, to use the word in the sense which Canning's line introduced into the language, that they were more pleased when it left them alone. But the pictured page told another story. Those were the palmy days of the caricaturists, when crowds daily thronged the shop-window in St. James's Street where Gillray's prints were exhibited, while the artist himself was feverishly drawing fresh cartoons in an upper story to satisfy their insatiable appetites. The Government succeeded in winning both him and Rowlandson. It was fortunate that it was able to do so; for the caricaturists could hit very hard indeed. They surely gave the image of the time. Hardly a single telling point in a debate, not one unpleasant habit or ungainly feature of a public man, not even the Royal Family itself, escaped them. Although upon the side of authority, they preserved a certain balance appropriate to art. The parsimony and awkwardness of the King was contrasted with the dissolute ease of his sons, the prim stiffness of Pitt with the unbuttoned grossness of Fox and Sheridan.

Of the distribution of parties throughout the country little that is definite can be said. The Whigs had always been strong in many of the English counties, and those who continued to follow Fox had lost little of their strength. Coke of Holkham, his intrepid friend, who had claimed a knight of the shire's right to appear before George III booted and spurred when presenting him with the distasteful address of the Commons in favour of the independence of the United States of America, was not always returned for Norfolk as county member. But he was usually successful. Parr levied his subscriptions in favour of Fox's depleted exchequer from country clergymen in the midlands. Earl Stanhope, whose revolutionary sympathies gained him the name of Citizen Stanhope, was able to use his feudal influence with great effect for the cause among the stalwart freeholders of Kent. When the time came for the agricultural interest to demand a higher duty on foreign corn, in 1804, the measure was not introduced by Pitt, who was then again Minister, but by a staunch Whig, Charles Western—Squire Western as he was called after the character in Fielding's Tom Jones. There was also a growing tendency to compromise the county membership between the parties, each returning one of the two members. This was another proof that the followers of Fox had lost little ground with the landed interest, apart from those who had seceded with Portland; and some of these were about to return during the first years of the new century. His second in the House of Commons, Grey, never needed to hide his ardent zeal for parliamentary reform from his constituents, the freeholders of Northumberland.

Fox's party was strong in the older manufacturing towns. The newer were for Government. Birmingham had no member, but had sufficient influence to return one of the two county members. It sent a supporter of Pitt. Lancashire was Tory. Manchester was devoted to the Church and King interest. It also had no member. But that same interest returned in 1802 one of its principal cotton-spinners, John Horrocks, as member for Preston, where all the inhabitant householders had votes; and there were over two thousand on the register. But both Birmingham and Manchester possessed growing reform parties which looked to Fox as their friend.

The Opposition enjoyed another increasing source of strength. There existed a number of complicated enactments passed with the object of excluding those who did not conform to the Church of England from political rights. It is easier to enter upon a long account of their contents than to describe how they were actually felt at any time by those against whom they were directed. In one matter the law certainly admitted of no evasion. No person who adhered to the religion of Rome could sit in either House of Parliament. The eleventh Duke of Norfolk became the only Protestant in the line of the heads of his house in order to become able to do so. But in most other matters the laws were evaded either by general connivance or with the direct assistance of the legislature. A member of the Catholic Jerningham family, for instance, voted in 1802 in the Middlesex election, and was pursued with jeers and abuse for doing so by Sir Francis Burdett's admirers. But they were too late. They should have applied to the sheriff beforehand to require the voter to take the oath that the Pope had no spiritual jurisdiction in the realm, and had this been put to him and he had then refused he could not have voted. Another member of this family held a commission in the English army, "by acquiescence", as it was called, and he was far from being the only one. But the Catholics had to be careful to prevent such cases from becoming in any way conspicuous. Protestant Nonconformists could both vote and sit in Parliament. But they could not hold offices without taking the sacrament according to the rites of the Church of England. This was regularly disregarded, and an act was passed every year indemnifying those who had done so. Nevertheless, there was a real grievance. The Catholics were prevented from taking any prominent part in the service of their country. The Dissenters were annually allowed a municipal, and to some extent a political, existence on sufferance. Pitt had been favourable to the cause of toleration, but not so much so as Fox, who had in 1792 endeavoured unsuccessfully to repeal the Test Act. Besides this the older Nonconformists had always been, and the Methodists were becoming more and more, the opponents of the Established Church. This led, in the circumstances of the time, to the entertainment of republican ideas; and threw even moderate men into opposition to Government. But for the few years which immediately followed the French Revolution the menace to religion and peace was felt to be so strong that the generality of Nonconformists eagerly dissociated themselves from extreme views. In 1794 the Baptists removed one of their ministers for merely throwing doubts upon the loyalty of some of them in a sermon. On the whole, the dissenting body was a moderating force in the country, in opposition alike to the Ministry and to the disruptive doctrines which had been brought over from France.

Such were the elements which formed the main strength of the Opposition. It was the only definite party in the State, and even it possessed elements which shaded off imperceptibly into a sediment rejected by every constitutional party. Earl Stanhope, for example, though he had once been Pitt's political friend besides being his brother-in-law, and though he had no desire to overthrow the Government by violence, yet associated freely with those who had. He was regarded as so extreme by Fox's own party that he was in the habit of forming a minority of one in the House of Lords. Nevertheless, the Opposition was sufficiently defined to form a strong contrast to the Government. On that side there was nothing but a mass kept together partly by loyalty to the throne, partly by confidence in the Minister, by the fear of anarchy, and by love of office, old Tories, followers of Pitt, followers of Portland, courtiers and placemen. It was the national party, if that phrase has any meaning.

In governing the country Ministers had to keep in mind that there was something which was generally regarded as above them and above the King and, in a certain sense, above Parliament itself. This was the Common Law. Its possession was the peculiar privilege of England as compared with the nations of the Continent. Even Scotland did not share it. Rights which had to be secured in foreign countries by positive enactments were the Englishman's birthright. A celebrated admirer of the English constitution, the Swiss Jean Louis de Lolme, was much struck by the distinction. "I used to take it for granted," he wrote in his book on the subject, "that every article of liberty the Subject enjoys in this Country was grounded upon some positive law by which this liberty was insured to him. In regard to the freedom of the press I had no doubt but it was so, and that there existed some particular law, or rather series of laws or legislative paragraphs, by which this freedom was defined and carefully secured; and as the liberty of writing happened at that time to be carried very far, and to excite a great deal of attention (the noise about the Middlesex election had not yet subsided), I particularly wished to see those laws I supposed, not doubting but there must be something remarkable in the wording of them." It was only after a long and vain search that he arrived at the conclusion which would have been obvious to every Englishman, that the liberty of the press was grounded upon the absence of prohibition. In contrast to the system which prevailed in other countries, he observed, it was the subject and not the Government which possessed inherent rights, and it was the duty of Ministers when they took any action to produce the law which enabled them to do so. These rights were rooted deeply in the general heart of man. They were a diviner thing than Sovereign or Parliament. It seemed only natural to Englishmen that the Common Law which embodied them should be veiled by mysteries of its own, like those of the divine right of Kings and the procedure of the Legislature. This explains much of the curious contradiction between a certain contempt for lawyers characteristic of a direct people, and its respect for anomalies of law and acquiescence in procedure made up of legal fictions, which were not so much antiquated as at no time suited to any rational scheme of things—preposterous in their original essence.

Some attempt was made in the eighteenth century to remedy a glaring defect in the system of civil jurisprudence. Little now remained of the jurisdiction of the old local courts and the gap required to be filled. The administration of the civil law rested mainly with the three ancient royal courts. These were the Courts of King's Bench and of Common Pleas, over which presided the two Chief Justices, and that of the Exchequer, whose head was styled Chief Baron and the judges Barons. Even trifling cases had to be decided by these courts sitting at the capital, or by their members on tour as judges of assize, in either case with a jury. A suit for a debt of twenty pounds would cost three times the amount. Besides, even if a case were tried at assize, a Birmingham man, for example, would have been obliged to drag every paltry dispute about a sick apprentice button-maker, or a defaulting benefit club, to an elaborate decision before a Court resplendent in wigs and ermine at Warwick, the assize town for the county, if it had not been for the institution of the Court of Requests. One of the commissioners of that court, William Hutton, has left a lively account of its working. Its jurisdiction extended only to cases of below forty shillings in value. It was assisted by two attorneys as clerks. It avoided taking formal evidence, and simply listened, as well as it was able, to what the parties and their friends had to say. In this it possessed one great advantage over superior courts, for there the parties themselves were disabled from giving evidence as presumably untrustworthy in their own cause. The fees only amounted to a few pence, and the procedure was astonishingly rapid. The defect of the court appears to have been that it was difficult to get the commissioners, who were unpaid, to attend regularly. It was a time when a knowledge of law was fairly widely diffused, as must always be the case where a large proportion of the population, including the tithe-owning clergy, who formed so considerable an element of the educated classes, had some connection with the land. But in the large towns in which these courts were established interest in law was less than elsewhere, and municipal public spirit was almost non-existent. Where such a spirit did exist it was possible to establish municipal civil courts. In Portsmouth there was a Court of Record consisting of the Mayor, Recorder, and Aldermen, which tried civil suits with the aid of a jury.

The regular law-courts had another grave defect, which could hardly have been expected, considering that they administered not a rigid code but a system of traditional law. This in its turn was both supplemented by statutes and explained from time to time by recorded judicial decisions. There was a complete scale of appeals ending in the House of Lords sitting as a judicial body. Such a system might well have been expected to be flexible. Yet with all this the courts were entirely unable to cover the whole field with which the civil law has to deal. There were simple grievances for which neither common law nor any statute provided the remedy; legal relationships, growing yearly more intricate, whose existence it did not recognize. Such matters, as well as the guardianship of wards, were the province of the Lord Chancellor as Keeper of the King's Conscience, sitting as a Court of Equity. He had only one judge to assist him in these growing duties, the Master of the Rolls, whose decisions were subject to an appeal to himself. The congestion of cases in chancery was a great and growing scandal. Merely to describe its procedure faithfully was to take rank as a satirist.

For one class of wrong the main remedy was actually left to the legislature. In case of adultery of a wife the husband could only obtain a separation in the Ecclesiastical Court. He had then to bring an action for criminal conversation against the paramour, usually demanding and often obtaining damages of some thousands of pounds. The last stage was to obtain a divorce by Act of Parliament. A man who was not wealthy could, of course, do none of these things, and if his wife left him and he wished to marry again, he was forced to commit bigamy. In another matter connected with marriage the common law bore very hardly upon all those who were not rich enough to afford marriage settlements. It treated husband and wife as one person in law. In other words, her property passed into his possession, her personal property absolutely, her landed estate under his control. But the Court of Chancery by its equitable jurisdiction had elaborated the system of marriage settlements, which secured for her the control of her separate estate through the means of a trustee.

A curious effect upon the social life of the country was produced by the state of the law regarding debt. Fiction and satire were full of the prodigal son who wasted his property as soon as he succeeded to possession, and it sometimes appears strange that, if he had many prototypes in real life, there were still so many old families remaining in possession of their ancestral acres. The explanation is to be found, apart from the safeguards provided by the right to entail, in the partiality of the law for landed property. For a debt of a few pounds a man could be haled to prison, and, if he happened to be in a strange place, cut off entirely from his friends for months and forced to keep himself from starving by begging through the prison gratings, so important was it deemed to safeguard the creditor's interests. Yet it was not possible to sell a rood of land in execution of a personal debt. The provision seemed to reformers at the time to be merely a grotesque survival of feudalism, although experience in many parts of the world has shown the value of the principle that, in the interests of the agricultural population generally, the estates of the landowners should be safeguarded from falling into the hands of money-lenders.

But the creditor availed himself to the full of his remedy against his debtor's person. Colquhoun estimated that forty thousand people were arrested for trifling debts yearly throughout the kingdom. It was the common lot of authors and artists to spend part of their days in a debtors' prison, and even the great did not always escape. They well deserved it when they thought it no shame to owe poor tradesmen their bills for many years, and then to speak of them, if they enforced payment, as "rascals", as Sir John Sinclair, a large landowner and prominent public man, did, when a saddler had him arrested. The real wife of the Prince of Wales, Mrs. Fitzherbert, while living with him and leading gay society, was in danger of a similar fate.

There was a far more convenient system of criminal than of civil jurisdiction. The supreme court, with certain appellate powers over justices of the peace, was the Court of King's Bench sitting on the Crown side. Judges of any of the three civil courts toured the country, and held criminal assizes in the capital towns of counties to try the graver classes of offences with the aid of a jury. But the five extreme northern counties were only visited once a year, and hence a man might spend nearly twelve months in jail after commitment by the magistrates, to find either that the grand jury at the sessions did not find a true bill against him so that he did not need to be tried at all, or that after the trial before the judge and the petty jury he was acquitted. Another evil was that the same maxim of the common law, that a man cannot be a witness in his own case, prevailed here as before the civil courts. But here it operated one-sidedly. It was merely the accused who was not allowed to tender himself as a witness. Another bad provision was that counsel was not allowed to defend prisoners charged with felony. This was to some extent balanced by a fourth; there was no public prosecutor. This tended to make both judge and jury exert themselves to master the real facts, for however great the advantages may be of hearing the case put alternately from two opposite points of view by two able lawyers, this must lead to a certain weakening of the sense of responsibility on the part of those with whom the decision rests. They acquire a tendency to regard themselves as umpires in a game. Colquhoun, who from the point of view of an energetic, although a humane, police magistrate had every reason to deplore the large proportion of acquittals, gave a bitter enumeration of a felon's chances of escape. "His first hope is that he shall intimidate the Prosecutor and Witnesses by the threatening of the gang with whom he is connected—his next that he may compound the matter; or bribe or frighten material witnesses, so as to keep back evidence; or induce them to speak doubtfully at the trial, though positive evidence was given before the Magistrate; or, if all should fail, recourse is had to perjury, by bringing the Receiver, or some other associate, to swear an *alibi*." The figures quoted by him bore this out to a considerable extent. In 1795 no less than 91 persons sent up before the old Bailey in London, and 253 before the provincial assizes, were discharged for want of prosecution. It is remarkable that, although prosecutors were bound over at the time the case was committed to appear, they so often failed to do so. They were intimidated, or they objected to the expense and trouble, or they were deterred by the severity of the punishment which might be, although, except for murder, highway robbery, and forgery, it rarely was, inflicted. Another fruitful cause of acquittal was a flaw in the indictment or other legal defect. The humane Romilly noted this, and added that so often were men acquitted on such grounds that merely to have been tried was generally sufficient alone to destroy a man's character, and to make it impossible for him to get employment. In the early years of the nineteenth century the number convicted was not nearly two-thirds of the number committed for trial, whereas forty years later, with six times the number of commitments, it had risen to almost three-fourths. Nor did the prisoner's chances of escape end here. The sanguinary code which, in striking contrast to the system prevalent on the Continent, imposed the penalty of death upon upwards of one hundred and fifty offences, some of which, such as those of stealing one shilling's worth of property from the person, or five shillings' worth from a shop, were exceedingly petty, had a further effect besides making prosecutors unwilling to prosecute and juries to return verdicts of guilty. The King's prerogative of mercy was freely used. In 1805 there were more executions than in any year up to the end of the decade. But of the 350 sentenced to death out of 2,783 convicted by judges in that year, only 68 were executed.

It was now nearly a generation since the time when the great John Howard had been obliged to travel on horseback between jail and jail as he visited them on his tours of mercy, because even the inspection of the prisoners made his clothes so offensive that an immediate prolonged disinfection in the open air was necessary. Something had been done to improve the prisons, especially in the metropolis. Yet even here the condition and management of the new Cold Bath Fields Prison was disgraceful, and both deserved and obtained the special attention of the House of Commons. Yet enough was not done, and the authorities were themselves to blame if it was popularly regarded out of doors as the English Bastille, and if terrible stories were abroad about the existence of underground cells where the tyrants of the people exercised their wickedness. In general, the nature and cause of the horrible jail fever, which made it necessary to avoid an accused when he was brought into court as if he were the pest itself, was not in the least understood. It was put down to overcrowding; and this there certainly was. There were places where the condition of the inmates could hardly have been worse. So late as 1807 the turnkey of Bristol jail told James Neild, a good man who carried on Howard's work, that when he unlocked the felons' sleeping-room in the morning the putrid steam issuing from it was enough to knock him down. In the Bridewell of the same town a cat had to be kept in each room to prevent the sewer-rats from gnawing the feet of the unfortunate people imprisoned there for debt. They could only wash three times a week. Most of these persons could have afforded themselves no comforts and must with difficulty have been even kept alive. But there were others, both debtors and criminals, who possessed means. In their case scandal took a different form. The Governor of Newgate, for example, was principally maintained out of the prisoners' fees. It became the practice, early in the new century, for those who were condemned for political crimes to suffer little but detention. When Leigh Hunt was in jail, his wife chose the place for her own confinement, lying in amid surroundings which he described as if they were among the prettiest in London. Cobbett had equally kind treatment. He was able to see all his friends, and he carried on his Political Register while still in jail. Setting altogether apart the expediency and justice of the prosecution of and the sentences awarded to Hunt and Cobbett, such treatment amounted to making a sentence of imprisonment into a farce. There was, indeed, an unending variety of prison administration, not astonishing in a country where the old dislike of uniformity and management by the State, or even by a local body, was carried to such a point that even jails were occasionally the private property of some county magnate.

The shortage of prisons was made good by hulks. These were shocking places. Their condition attracted much attention in 1802. A Member of Parliament, Sir Henry Mildmay, and James Neild were deputed by the Government to inspect them. One of their reports was very unfavourable. Some person with an even more intimate knowledge, probably a humane officer or warder, gave a vivid description of the effect of the life upon the newly joined convict. In a few days he is crawling with vermin, abject and miserable. Then there comes a change; he grows hardened and ruthless. "The Country Convict whose ideas before the Hulk confinement never went further than robbing a Hen-roost, or stealing out of an open field . . . becomes a profest and ingenious thief." The absence of real discipline assisted to bring about this result, as the smith convicts provided him on release with the requirements of a burglar's business. At the same time the hulk system was by no means economical. Transportation to New South Wales was condemned by Colquhoun on the same grounds. But it is difficult to realize what such critics can have regarded as a reasonable rate. Colquhoun himself calculated that £1,663,974 was spent in transporting about 15,000 convicts to that and to other colonies in twenty-five years. If a felon could be got rid of, to emerge some time afterwards at the opposite end of the world as, possibly, a useful colonist, for about a hundred pounds, the State might be considered to make a very fair bargain. Transportation was certainly popular with the convicts themselves, once they found themselves in prison.

The minor, usually brutal, punishments, regular and irregular, were certainly effective. An intelligent German of the name of Campe, who visited England in 1802, was delighted to see a bookseller responsible for a foul publication being well pelted for an hour in the pillory, previous to serving six months' imprisonment. It was a custom which he would have liked to have seen introduced into his own country. It is easy to imagine the zest with which the crowd must have taken its share in the punishment of an attorney condemned to stand in the pillory before Newgate, as Robert Patterson was in 1806, for defrauding a man of £130 under pretence of getting him a place in the Ordnance Office. Public whippings were common, and even women were not exempt. The entrances to country towns were plastered with large bills to the effect that any vagrants seen passing through would be arrested and would suffer this punishment, and pounds and stocks were in regular use for them. But most of the traditional popular modes of punishment were getting at least rare enough to cause a little sensation when they were carried out, for instance the ducking of a scold at Kingston in 1801. Yet it was still the custom in towns to drag a pickpocket caught in the act to the nearest pump, half-drown him, and then let him go.

The head of the judicature, the Lord Chancellor, in the person of Lord Loughborough, tried unsuccessfully in 1801 to reassert the right which Thurlow had enjoyed of retaining office upon a change of ministry. It was now settled custom of the constitution that he should resign along with the rest of the Cabinet. With this exception, and to a certain extent those of the Master of the Rolls and the Chief Justice of the King's Bench, the judges in general were independent of party as well as to all intents irremovable. Their judgments and the verdicts of the juries were almost invariably regarded as impartial. So little disposed were they to comply with executive requirements that, in order to deal with the special circumstances of the time, Pitt had been obliged to introduce the limited measure conveniently described under the comprehensive title of the Habeas Corpus Suspension Act. This did not give a general power to the police or to judges or magistrates to imprison without legal trial. Nor did it in terms give such power even to the Secretary of State. It merely made it impossible for any person imprisoned under a warrant signed by that authority to insist upon being either brought up for trial or set free. In ordinary circumstances the system of trial by jury was thought to be as great a security for liberty as everything else put together. Not but that this, too, had its defects. The ordinary class of London tradesmen could not be expected to follow complicated civil cases. To meet the difficulty the courts had a class of special jurymen drawn from a separate list, who were known from the amount of their fees as the Guinea Corps. It was a common complaint as regards the Court of Exchequer that the special juries consisted of almost the same individuals in every cause for years. Another defect was the power which a single determined juryman had of wearing the other eleven out. A third was that juries were occasionally subjected to influence. Of this a curious example can be produced from the very quarter where it might have been supposed that the jury system would have received most respect. Lady Holland wrote in her diary that her husband and Fox intended in 1798 to go over to Ireland to Lord Edward Fitzgerald's trial as a rebel. The object was "to make a show of friends and family; for a strong appearance in a man's favour has its effect upon a jury, especially where there are titles and celebrity!" Fitzgerald died in prison, but the same party had a similar opportunity in the case of O'Connor's trial in England, and made use of it with some success.

The independence of the courts which formed the subordinate criminal judicature throughout the country was equally secure. It was made up of upwards of 2,600 Justices of the Peace. The title marks the fact that it was their duty rather to maintain order than to sit in judgment. The country justices, mainly squires and parsons of the richer class, were now irremovable except for misconduct, as was also the Lord-Lieutenant of the County, upon whose recommendation they were appointed by the Lord Chancellor. In Petty Sessions two or more decided the simpler classes of offences; and four times a year they were united in Quarter Sessions to try more serious crimes with the aid of a jury. Responsible as they were, not merely for administering justice, but for police and for self-government generally, it was the justices of the peace who really governed the country-side, and under shifting ministries afforded that element of stability elsewhere produced by a bureaucratic hierarchy. The towns depended mainly upon the same system. The new urban areas which were springing up sometimes complained of a lack of magistrates. The inhabitants of rising industrial centres like Halifax, and young watering-places like Brighton, had to go outside for justice.

But there were not many towns without their own justices of the peace. The older large towns, and even some of the smaller towns, had their own courts and their own Borough Quarter Sessions. As regards powers there were some curious anomalies. A thief charged in the ancient and populous city of Bath had to be committed to the Taunton assizes, while the local court at Winchelsea, with only a few hundred inhabitants, could decide capital felonies. In general most of the corporations had a criminal jurisdiction, consisting usually of the Mayor and some of the aldermen and common councilmen. The City of London enjoyed a court of this character. But elsewhere in the metropolis the ordinary system of unpaid magistrates had broken down; and following the example of the court existing at Bow Street, several new stipendiary police magistrates were introduced from 1792 onwards. Patrick Colquhoun was one of these, a happy instance of one of Dundas's Scotsmen.

The sphere of action of the criminal courts generally was a narrow one. The volumes of the State Trials for the last ten years of the eighteenth century contain very few English cases, even for the years before the date of the Habeas Corpus Suspension Act. They include only a single instance of a prosecution on account of a speech made at a public meeting. But both the higher courts and the country magistrates were greatly occupied with a class of case which at first sight appears puerile, the prosecution of a half-drunken man for using some such expression as "Damn the King and Billy Pitt" upon licensed premises. But it was necessary to meet the methods of Jacobins wherever they were being employed with any hope of effect. Where the ordinary place of public resort was a public-house, where these were the common resort of soldiers, a class proverbially ignorant and easily moved to be discontented and dangerous when made so, where the mass of the people was illiterate, it was the best thing which a promoter of sedition could do, after fortifying himself with the excuse of a heavy draught of ale, to take the soundings of his audience with an expression like this. Where the seed fell on good ground the Magistrates would hear nothing of the matter; but if some of his hearers were loyal there would probably be an uproar at once, and yet they would have nothing but these bare words to report. When cases of this apparently trifling kind were referred to the Attorney-General for his advice, he was inclined to reply that a prosecution was undesirable for a few words uttered in drunkenness. But the agitator did not always escape. In one case in 1802 the magistrates had before them a man who had told a private soldier that he should have shot the King. He had frequently said similar things in public, and was committed to Quarter Sessions in spite of the excuse that he was drunk. There were, moreover, some cases which the authorities appear to have treated with unnecessary severity. The Morning Chronicle for January the 12th, 1801, records a sentence of six months at Stafford Quarter Sessions upon a man who said, "Damn the King and his peace officers", while intoxicated; and this prosecution was at the Treasury expense. But these were exceptions. This is clear from a perusal of the manuscripts left by Francis Place, the tailor, for several years a leader in the agitation against Government as well as its manuscript historian. The worst example which he could produce of the so-called Reign of Terror in England from 1797 to 1800 was that of a Lincolnshire blacksmith sentenced to a year's solitary confinement for damning the King and calling the Government a despotism. It was a most cruel sentence, but it seems to have stood alone; and there cannot have been many parallels even to the Stafford case.

Outside the domain of offences affecting the State, the work of the courts was limited, both by the absence of a regular police in the case of regular crimes and general negligence regarding many other matters. Little attention, for instance, was paid to nuisances, and such cases tended to be dealt with—if at all—by the old manorial courts, and in other more or less informal means. In some places such local authorities as were the Paving and Cleansing Commissioners in Portsmouth had a right to impose fines for obstruction of the road or petty offences against sanitary rules. False weights and measures used in small country places were a subject of very serious complaint. It was only in 1797, when special authority was given to the High Constables and others to examine them, that the grievance began to be met. A number of minor offences were taken up by the Society for the Suppression of Vice, for example three cases of cruelty to animals in 1803. But outside the capital very little can have been done as regards all minor matters, except vagrancy. Poaching was not as yet treated with severity. The complaint against the game laws was, not the cruel punishment awarded to a poor man for stealing a pheasant, but the prevention of a farmer whose land was overrun with hares from protecting his own crops. He would not be qualified to take out a licence, not having a freehold of £100 annual value.

With regard to more serious offences, the general view of foreign critics was that England had some shadow of police for the purpose of apprehending delinquents after crimes had been actually committed; but none for that of preventing them. A preventive force was bound either to wear uniform or not. In the latter case its members would have borne the character of detectives, and would have been loathed as spies. In the former they would have been hated as elements, however humble, of a permanent military force. "By the way, Seton," said King Gustavus III of Sweden to an English traveller, "how can the King of England possibly allow highway robberies? Were I there, I'd order three regiments of horse to patrol the road; but oh! that would be reckoned an infringement upon liberty." The King was perfectly right. George III's subjects had gone so far as to admit the rudiments of a detective force in the metropolis in the shape of a dozen police officers attached to the court at Bow Street, the celebrated Bow Street runners. They even tolerated a small horse-patrol, which guarded the main roads near London, and which was eventually raised in 1805 to above fifty men. But this was the limit of their endurance. In other respects, the theory that the maintenance of the peace was a personal duty incumbent upon the subject was pressed as far as it would go. Both in London and the provinces every able-bodied male in the parish was liable to serve for a year as parochial constable. He was usually appointed by the Justices. He was allowed to pay a Deputy to do his duty for him. The watchmen also were paid, as also that venerable parish functionary, the beadle. Whenever the system was found to be intolerably inefficient, the best course was for the inhabitants to form committees for the purpose of watching what their guardians were about. There were examples in London in 1808, and again in 1810, of arrangements being made by neighbouring parishioners to carry out inspections in Fleet Street between 7 p.m. and midnight.

There is a passage in Colquhoun's Treatise on the Functions and Duties of the Constable, published in 1803, which throws into high relief the utter helplessness of the ordinary authorities in a time of civil disturbance. "The instant a constable hears of any *unlawful assembly, mob*, or *concourse of people* being assembled for any purpose likely to produce danger or mischief within or near his district or constablewick, it is his bounden duty to give notice thereof to the nearest Justice, and to repair instantly to the spot with his long or short stave, and there to put himself under the direction of such Magistrate or Magistrates as may be in attendance." It must have been a strangely hopeless business. Everything depended upon the magistrates. If they proved unable to restore order by their personal authority, it was necessary to give misrule its head. If the people of a particular place had a fancy to fix the price of food, or to collect the weavers' shuttles by force to ensure the success of a strike, it was hopeless to interfere. It was, however, often possible to prevent the repetition of a riot by calling in the yeomanry. In 1797 the miners of Derbyshire evinced their objection to the militia levy by seizing and destroying the lists. An offer of the gentlemen of the town to be sworn in as special constables was refused, and nothing was done at the time. But the Roxburgh Fencibles were sent for by the next meeting, and on this occasion the mob was dispersed and half a dozen arrests were made. It was, indeed, impossible for magistrates, dotted as they were about the country, to act with severity in cases of this kind. Portland, the Home Secretary, was too prudent and too liberal a man to attempt to insist upon their doing so. It was easy to run into the opposite extreme. Ten years later a ludicrous instance occurred of a more lively sense of its responsibilities on the part of Government. In 1808 the Home Secretary, who was now Hawkesbury, wrote to the Horse Guards to point out the absurdity of quartering a party of cavalry at Dunstable to prevent a boxing match.

Thus was the government of the country generally left in the hands of the justices of the peace. The people entertained a horror of any approach towards a centralized system. In 1801 the justices of Richmond in Yorkshire actually refused to convict under a recent Act of Parliament on the ground that it was arbitrary and not fit to be put into execution. Doctor Johnson summed up the national prejudice against the excise in the definition which he inserted in his dictionary: "A hateful tax levied upon commodities, and adjudged not by the common judges of property but by wretches hired by those to whom excise is paid." But it was not so much the tax to which the people objected as the means of its collection. The customs was objectionable; but the customs officer might be avoided or evaded. The exciseman was a perpetual incubus. He was, however, almost the only reminder of the existence of a central authority. And the field of his operations was greatly contracted. Local taxation was subject to the justices sitting in quarter sessions. These administered the county rate, a sum which for the whole of England did not amount to as much as three hundred thousand pounds a year. Of this nearly £50,000 were for bridges, and almost all the rest for prisons and prisoners.

The small sum which the magistrates had to spend in the shape of the county rate was no measure of their executive duties. The bridges were maintained out of this source merely because they could not be kept up in the same manner as the roads. These last were by law kept in repair by the inhabitants of the parishes through which they passed. A statute duty of six days in the year was incumbent on them. The owner of a cart had to lend it, while the ordinary ablebodied man tendered personal service. Such a system was rapidly growing obsolete, and was unsatisfactory even when a money payment was substituted. It was not the least of the cares of quarter sessions to receive complaints that a particular parish had failed to keep up its part of the road, and to call upon it to make good the omission. For the main arteries of communication there was naturally a much better system. Turnpike trusts were set up by Act of Parliament, and the roads maintained out of the money collected at the pikes.

As neither the State nor local authorities spent a penny upon public instruction, the justices were spared the thorny mazes of educational controversy. The principal branch of local government was the poor law, a subject of perennial interest alike to Parliament and, judging from the number of books and pamphlets which were constantly appearing, to the general public. The object of the Elizabethan poor law had been to throw upon each parish the duties of supporting those of its poor who were unable to work, and of setting to work those who were able and providing them with maintenance. In this almost superhuman task the England of the eighteenth century had signally failed. There were some satisfactory poor-houses. That at Manchester as described both by Eden and by Bamford, whose father was for a short time its governor, was a shining example. One of the most striking things in that ghastly account of cruelty, the Life of Robert Blincoe, is the shock which the boy received after his decent religious upbringing in a London poor-house at the behaviour of his associates in the factory. But as a general rule the poor-houses were miserable places, as is shown by the frequency of legislative attempts to improve them. At this time they were not often called workhouses, and certainly did not deserve the name. Before the end of the century the difficulty of finding work for the able-bodied poor was generally regarded as insuperable, and the system of granting a subsidy in aid of wages was eagerly embraced. The rest of the administration of the poor law was vitiated by a false economy. The poor-house was often inadequate even as a last home for the aged and decrepit, who could not have wanted much. Pauper children were farmed out. With regard to this there is a heart-rending story which would hardly be credited if it were merely contained in the works of a professed reformer, or told in some speech of a philanthropic member of parliament. Long before Elizabeth Fry had commenced the work which made her famous, she met in London a beggar-woman who had a half-starved, half-naked child with her. Struck with compassion, she insisted on following her home. She found that she was a woman with whom pauper children were put out to nurse, and that she systematically starved them in order to make more money by begging with them, and, when they died, by concealing their deaths.

It was, indeed, the poor law which formed the thorny side of the justices' official activities. The actual administration did not rest with them, but with parish officials. The chief of these were the churchwardens, usually two in number. They were generally chosen yearly for each parish by the whole body of parishioners meeting in open vestry, or by some of them as a select vestry. In some cases one churchwarden was chosen by them, the other by the parish priest. These formed one class of overseers of the poor. Others were appointed by the justices, or by the parishioners at a vestry meeting. The overseers fixed the poor rate and administered the fund. But attempts were constantly being made to improve the administration of the poor law by bringing it more directly under magisterial control. The most famous of these measures, a law of 1782, commonly known as Gilbert's Act, provided that, if the ratepayers agreed, the justices might appoint a visitor and a governor for the poor-house, and a guardian for each parish. The scheme, where it was accepted, produced some improvement in the case of poor-houses, but caused a change for the worse in the position of the able-bodied unemployed. It excluded them from the poor-house and made no satisfactory arrangement for providing them with work outside it. It led directly to systems which fell into well-deserved disrepute. One was the arrangement for supplementing wages by allowances out of the rates, which is named after the small town of Speenhamland, where the Berkshire justices in 1795 set so notorious an example to the rest of the kingdom. Another was that adopted in a few parishes by which such labourers were sent on the rounds from one ratepayer's house to another for employment, the parish being responsible for a part of their maintenance or sometimes the whole, where there was not work for them. Another act, passed in 1796, permitted relief to be granted to poor persons in their own homes with the approval of the vestry or the sanction of a justice of the peace, and completed the charter of outdoor relief and consequent demoralization.

A year earlier the prevailing liberal tendency in poor-law matters had shown itself in a much less questionable manner. The law regarding settlement was altered. The rule had been that a newcomer likely to become a pauper, and so a burden upon the parish where he intended to live, could be removed. It was now provided that the justices could only send him back to the place of his last legal settlement after he had become actually chargeable. Even now there was much injustice and considerable waste. The treatment of a vagrant tended to resemble one of those games in which some article is rapidly passed from hand to hand, the person who is unsuccessful in getting rid of the objectionable deposit in time having to pay forfeit. The zeal occasionally shown by callous parish authorities to get rid of a sick or dying pauper, so that they might escape the expense of his funeral, was the subject of bitter satire. That it was a genuine scandal is shown by a provision being made against such removals in the act of 1795. But the strenuous competition between parishes to pass their paupers on found vent in other directions. Among the legal subtleties invented was that of arranging a marriage between two aged paupers resident in different parishes. As a settlement could be obtained by marriage, this device enabled one set of parish authorities to pass their pauper on. But in one case where this was tried the ingenuity of the opposing lawyer refused to be baffled. The law of conspiracy was brought into play, precisely as it would have been in the converse case of a conspiracy to elope with a wealthy heiress. An old pauper woman was an eligible subject to get rid of, and thus the overseer, churchwarden, and constable of her parish were indicted for conspiring to make up a match between her and a poor old man of another parish with intent to transfer the burden of her support.

It resulted that for every pound raised for relief of the poor almost another shilling was spent upon litigation and removals. The amount spent upon actual relief in 1803, when a full return was made, was £4,077,891. Of this, one quarter was spent upon above 83,000 inmates of poorhouses, and the remaining three-quarters on nearly twelve times that number who were relieved out of doors. The rapid growth of the poor rate, which had doubled in twenty years, was a source of recurrent perplexity to legislators and economists. The distractions of the war and the confusion engendered by the industrial revolution gave no opportunity of attacking the problem as a whole. It was thought, and with reason, that the best chance of keeping the rates down was to maintain local control as far as possible. But the parish authorities, even with the assistance of the justices, seldom solved the difficulty of administering an economical, and at the same time efficient, workhouse. Interest ceased to be taken in this branch of the subject. In spite of the immense growth in the population and in pauperism, it is doubtful whether there had been any increase in poor-house or workhouse accommodation in the last quarter of a century. Outdoor relief claimed all their attention. The requirements of economy were met by a jealous safeguarding of their right to maintain no paupers but their own (itself, as has been seen, the source of a fresh extravagance in the way of litigation and removals). On the other hand, they satisfied their benevolent impulses, and in a good many cases—it must be added—their wish to provide cheap labour for ratepayers, by a lavish expenditure upon relief of able-bodied persons in their own homes. Patriotism, moreover, claimed its share in the increase. The unfortunate individual who was drawn for the militia was regarded as a representative of his parish in the defensive force of the kingdom, and it was felt to be due to him to maintain his family from the parish rates. To this extent the increase in the poor rate was a war charge locally borne.

Outside the capital the prevailing stamp of local administration was the same whether in town or country. London, indeed, possessed a complicated constitution of its own, a compromise between the medieval system of guilds and the modern one of wards, as the basis of representation. A freeman of one of these guilds or companies could become a freeman of the City. The twenty-six aldermen represented the wards. They were elected for life by the freemen ratepayers. The Lord Mayor was chosen from those aldermen who had already served as Sheriff by the Court of Common Hall, a meeting of ten thousand or so of the liverymen of the companies, who constituted a higher grade than the freemen. But the administration of the City was mainly in the hands of the Court of Common Council, which consisted, besides the Lord Mayor and Aldermen, of some two hundred commoners chosen annually by the freemen ratepayers. The members of this body supplied the Commission of Sewers, which had the charge of many things besides drains, and the various committees.

The two hundred and sixty or so remaining municipal corporations of England and Wales were not bodies possessing an independent corporate life, elected by the inhabitants, and responsible for justice, policing, sanitation, paving, and lighting. Cases where there was any form of election were the exception. The most liberal institutions existed in those towns of which the freedom could be obtained by being bound to a trade for a number of years, as well as by inheritance and in other ways, and where the freemen chose the common councilmen and sometimes even the mayor and aldermen. But the freedom of the town could not always be so easily acquired, and there were hardly more than twenty in which the freemen chose the corporation. In nearly two-thirds of the whole number the common councilmen simply elected themselves for life. They chose one of their number to be mayor, and the aldermen usually consisted of those who had filled that office. There were a number of officials under them, but in few cases was substantial work done by either the Corporation itself or any of its servants, except as justices of the peace or as members of the grand jury. In this last capacity it might be their duty to present at Quarter Sessions the case of a shopkeeper who had not repaired the spout on his roof or the pavement in front of his shop. Generally speaking the Mayor and Corporation were supposed to have outlived their usefulness. They were regarded in the strange light of ornaments, and seldom in any other. The income which they received from various sources, such as dock dues, market dues, and landed property, was generally misapplied. When there was real work to be done, it was handed over to a lighting or paving commission or trust, of which their own more energetic members might form a part. The dirty and unhealthy city of Bristol, in which wheeled traffic was not allowed for fear of the road collapsing into the underground sewers, is a good example of a corrupt co-opting corporation. Compared with this, the condition of those towns which had no municipal institutions at all was enviable. Birmingham petitioned for a corporation in 1716. Since that date it had grown wiser, and was now satisfied to be governed by two constables and two bailiffs. Manchester was ruled by a borough reeve, who was a social figure-head, and two constables chosen annually at the ancient manorial institution of the court-leet, practically by the lord of the manor. In 1796, when the unwholesome conditions of life among factory workers attracted attention, it had appointed its unofficial Board of Health, which established an infirmary. In 1792 it obtained an Act of Parliament for lighting, watching, cleansing, and even replanning the town, and levying a police rate of 1s. 3d. in the £. The Commissioners who were to administer the Act consisted of the borough reeve and constables, the wardens and fellows of the Collegiate Church, and the owners and occupiers of buildings of £30 in value. Indeed, there were few places where the sense of a corporate life was so strong as in Manchester, which had no corporation. In 1785, for example, it gave Fox a grand reception on the occasion of an unpopular shop-tax which it desired his services to get removed. All the trades marched in procession, and twelve thousand persons signed the petition. In 1803 The Times published an article warmly praising the system introduced into this and some others of the great manufacturing towns (none of them, presumably, municipalities), whereby the

Gentlemen of the fourth class, who were not liable to be called up under the General Defence Act, had formed municipal corps for the preservation of the peace. Yet even its youth did not save Manchester from corruption. There were as many complaints of financial irregularities as if it had enjoyed a charter dating from Plantagenet times. Nor were the powers so recently bestowed upon the inhabitants by the Act of 1792 appreciated. Had they been properly utilized, Manchester would have been a very different place.

In a country so governed there was almost boundless scope for legislation of a reforming tendency. But the parliament men of that day took little interest in change outside the sphere of parliamentary reform and religious toleration. Government interference in order to correct local abuses would, moreover, have been resented. It would not have been thought right, for example, to regulate trade. At a time when there was considerable zeal for the abolition of useless posts, the case of the Board of Trade and Plantations had not been thought a hopeful one in Whig circles. Brooks's Club betting-book had an entry which displays it in strange company. "Mr. Crewe bets Sr. W. Aston five Guineas that the Board of Trade & five Guineas that the Board of Green Cloth are abolished in 1782." And so they both were by Burke's Act of that year. But the former was reintroduced by Pitt under its old name of the Committee of the Privy Council for the affairs of Trade and Plantations. It soon ceased to have anything to do with the colonies, the purpose for which it had been originally intended. There are no references to its meetings at this time, or to its activities, which were mainly confined to the collection of statistics. Even in this, it was overshadowed by the Treasury. The office of President of the Board carried little weight. Early in the nineteenth century, however, its possibilities began to be recognized. When he constructed his last administration in 1804 Pitt thought that it was an office which, when combined with that of Joint Postmaster-General, might carry a seat in the Cabinet. In the succeeding ministry so eminent a financier as Lord Auckland was glad to take the post. In accepting it, he told Grenville that he hoped to make it more useful and efficient than it had been in the past.

There was one department, however, outside the Treasury, which was brought into beneficial touch with every part of the country. This was the Post Office. That institution was, however, regarded much more as a useful source of revenue than as a function of government promoting trade and serving the general convenience. The details of its organization were thought beneath the notice of statesmen. But its possibilities as a means of raising money were a subject of the keenest interest to the Chancellor of the Exchequer himself, in an era which, however posterity may regard it, appeared to contemporaries as one of breakneck advance in the matter of communications. In the face of the most confident prognostications of failure, Pitt had sanctioned the introduction of mail-coaches in 1784 on the proposal of John Palmer, a Bath theatrical proprietor, who was appointed Controller-General at the Post Office to carry out his plan. Before this time letters had been carried all over the kingdom on horseback, usually by lads, and robberies were extremely frequent. But the mail-coaches were protected by an armed guard, and for years not a single one was attacked. Incidentally the advantage to the general traveller of this regular means of communication at seven miles an hour was very considerable. It was reserved for an even more humble person to reform the town post known as the penny and afterwards as the twopenny post. A letter-carrier named Edward Johnson reorganized the system in London so that it was actually possible for five letters to pass to and fro between Lombard Street and the Haymarket between eight in the morning and seven in the evening. The general control of the Post Office was in the hands of the celebrated Francis Freeling, Secretary from June 1798 almost until the accession of Queen Victoria. It was he who was made the butt of allusions in the letters of the time as the agent through whom the Government exercised its curiosity as to the contents of the correspondence of important personages. He co-operated vigorously with the Exchequer in plans for raising the rates on correspondence. The minimum outside London and a few other towns which had their internal penny post, was 3d. for a single letter not exceeding fifteen miles. An enclosure made it a double letter, two enclosures a treble, and an ounce paid four times the charge for a single letter. The scale rose to 8d. a single letter for a distance exceeding 150 miles. But in the first year of the new century the scale was extended beyond that limit, and a letter from London to Edinburgh paid 1s. instead of 8d. The supreme control of the Post Office was in the hands of that instrument of government so dear to Englishmen—a Board which did not sit. The Joint Postmasters-General were usually a couple of noblemen.

The titular heads of the Post Office did very little. This was the more striking in 1800, because the two Postmasters-General, Lord Auckland and Lord Gower, happened to be men who left some mark upon public affairs generally, although next to none on the Post Office. The Chancellor of the Exchequer did not complain so long as the net income from the department was three-quarters of a million—some twenty times as much as he had been glad to obtain three years before from additions to the taxes upon auction sales or bricks.

It was, indeed, principally as a tax-gatherer that the Government made its existence felt in every corner of the country. What this meant is illustrated by a communication made to Cobbett's Political Register in 1806, which, although it refers directly to a period when taxation had slightly risen compared with what it had been five years earlier, yet indicates clearly how hardly it was even then bearing upon that class of the community whose status was most adversely affected. The case is taken of a man with an income of £1,000 a year, farming his own estate of 200 acres valued at £200 a year with a house rated at £50. He would have to pay both a landlord's and tenant's income tax (or, as it was sometimes called, property tax) on the £200. This amounted to £35. On the estimated income from his house his tax was £3 15s. That on his remaining £750 at ten per cent. was £75. Thus income tax alone was £113 15s. The ancient land tax (which was distinct from the income tax) might be £10. There were two more burdens on his house, amounting to £32; the house tax proper at 2s. 6d. in the pound, and the window tax on, say, forty windows of £25 15s. Besides this he would have to pay £19 9s. for his six horses for riding, driving, and the farm, £10 for a carriage, and £9 for two outdoor and one indoor servant. The remaining items were two guineas for armorial bearings, three for a game licence, one for hair-powder, and a pound for a watch-dog and spaniel, amounting to £7 6s. The total thus paid in direct taxation was £201 10s. Moreover, this correspondent supposes poor, church, and highway rates at 8s. in the pound on his landed and house property of £250. This would account for another £100 a year. Added to this there was tithe at 5s. an acre, commonly regarded as a tax, which made another £50. Thus considerably more than a third of the man's total income went in direct payment to the State, to local bodies, or to the Church. It is startling to find that direct taxation was so heavy in the days of elaborate tariffs.

But the demands of the State were enormous for the national income of that time. The yearly expenditure upon the war amounted to about £35,000,000. Of this, the navy and the army accounted for between ten and fifteen millions each. The former generally claimed most, but the year 1797 was an exception. In that year the army took nearly fifteen and a half millions. Between one and two millions went to Ordnance and the remainder usually in subsidies to the allies and in miscellaneous services. No single budget can be taken as typical of the rest in all these respects. The ordinary expenses of the State, on the other hand, were regarded as subject to so little variation that they were not included in the annual budgets. They were defrayed out of the Consolidated Fund, an invention of Pitt. This, the permanent revenue, consisted of the customs, excise, stamps, land tax, and other taxes with the exception of the specially imposed war-taxes. They amounted in 1800 to nearly £25,000,000. This paid the King's Civil List—about £900,000, miscellaneous regular services, about £1,500,000, pensions and a few minor items, and a surplus of over £2,000,000 to the war budget. By far the greater part went to pay the charges of the National Debt.

When Pitt came into office he was faced with a debt of £238,000,000. He elaborated his plan of a Sinking Fund. The term was really a misnomer. So far from consisting in the gradual reduction of the mountain of the National Debt, it meant the construction of another mountain by its side, which would some day—it was hoped—be large enough to absorb it. The system was simplicity itself. Supposing a syndicate of Jews to lay by one million a year and to purchase stock with it, and every year thereafter to devote not only a fresh million, but all the interest received on what they had already invested, to the purchase of fresh stock, they would ultimately be able to absorb the whole. For such a syndicate let the State be substituted. All that was necessary was for the Government to become its own usurer. Over against the State, Pitt created a Board of Commissioners, whose duty it was to buy up the National Debt at the rate of a million pounds a year invested at compound interest. Not a penny of the Debt was written off, and the interest was not reduced. The same effect, nay, a much better, would have been obtained if a million only had been spent annually on the purchase of stock, and the entries in the books cancelled. For the cost of these elaborate operations would have been saved. Yet no one, even of Pitt's bitterest opponents, seems to have detected any fallacy in his lifetime. And from a point of view which considers not abstract finance, but things as they actually are, it was the Minister who was right and the economist who was wrong. Everyone took for granted that the Consolidated Fund should go on doing what it was there to do—pay the interest on the unreduced National Debt. On the other hand, men's imaginations were struck by the idea of this enormous fund, growing with inevitable and ever-increasing velocity. For Pitt succeeded in getting the Sinking Fund regarded as sacrosanct till years after his death. It was a gigantic tangible proof of the solvency of the nation. However much he might have to borrow in any one year for purposes of war, the million was always set aside. In 1792, the year in which he counted on a long peace, he permanently added £200,000. When war came he provided that one per cent. of all future loans was to be put aside to serve as a sinking fund which would pay them off in forty-five years. All this would have been the height of absurdity if the world had consisted of hard-headed financiers like some of his later critics. But if it had, there would have been no wars. It was not even the case that the sinews of war were supplied by strictly logical men of business. Government stock was purchased by ordinary people. Besides, the City itself was guided by ideas on the subject of credit into which intangible elements of sentiment entered. It regarded the Government as it would have regarded a man who, although obliged to incur fresh debt, was at least taking praiseworthy steps to pay it off, as well as his old debt, according to a definite system. It did not stop to ask whether it was wise to borrow at a high rate of interest in order to do so, instead of waiting until there was a natural surplus. It knew from experience in the past that if Government is not stern with itself it borrows more than it should in time of war, and reduces taxation more than it should in time of peace; and the Debt is left to shift for itself. Pitt's system did what was required in maintaining the credit of the country. £68,000,000 had been redeemed by the end of the century. The total funded debt, redeemed and unredeemed, now stood at £488,000,000, as £250,000,000 of new debt had been funded since 1792. But this amount did not represent a debt which the Government was bound to discharge at any particular date, but merely a liability to pay interest, now amounting to some £13,800,000. If the public was able to purchase a £100 stock with £60, the Commissioners were able to do the same; and as there was no compulsory date of repayment by the State it was no loser.

The method by which loans were actually raised was usually complicated, and, owing to the impracticability of inviting tenders generally from the public, it was in the hands of a few large banking houses, and one or two enterprising stockjobbers. Pitt made a far better bargain than his predecessors. But even in his time the successful tenderers always expected to get in at considerably below the proper market rate. In 1802 Lord Carrington, wishing to do Arthur Young a favour, got his name down for £5,000. The rise was four and a half per cent. In a day or two after the loan had been issued Young was astonished to receive a draft for over £220. A considerable portion of each loan was, moreover, reserved for the office of the Chief Cashier of the Bank of England, and when Abraham Newland retired from that post he was worth £200,000 as well as £1,000 a year from land. The Chancellor of the Exchequer was very much in the hands of the financiers, and it was because they insisted upon three per cents. that he was unable to float a loan at par. In 1793 Pitt had attempted to do so. But there was only one set of subscribers for the loan, and they would only take three per cents., then at 72. He was never afterwards so unsuccessful as this in getting what he wanted. The great banking firms came to be animated by a desire not to take an undue advantage of their country's difficulties, besides which a competition grew up between them and the Jewish stockjobbers, who at that time first came into the market. He was occasionally able to raise a part of his requirements at four or five per cent., thus selling his stock more nearly at par. In 1800, after eight years of war, he was unable to do this. But he succeeded in obtaining a loan of $18\frac{1}{2}$ millions, exchanging £157 three per cent. stock for each £100 which he received. The yield came to just under $4\frac{3}{4}$ per cent. The century closed with £100 three per cent. consols quoted at 61.

To meet all these growing charges the Chancellor found himself driven to every possible expedient, and all principles of taxation were thrown to the winds. The raw materials of trade were taxed. The course of trade itself was made subject to a duty. It had been a principle to exempt, so far as possible, the labouring class, because it was considered both that taxation bore too hardly upon it at the time when it was imposed and, on the other hand, that the eventual result was invariably a rise in wages and hence a general increase in all commodities. But that class was allowed to escape no longer. Finally, Pitt was driven to that hated thing, the income tax.

The principal head of revenue was the excise—upwards of £11,000,000. Beer was the chief item. The tax upon it was not a heavy one. There was no desire to abridge the people of what was an ordinary article of diet, or to drive them to gin or any still more unwholesome intoxicant. It was an old tax upon what had always been considered in the light of a general necessity, unlike tea and sugar, which were regarded as luxuries. It had consequently not been raised since the outbreak of war. Pitt had not, however, been able to keep his fingers off what was known to housewives as the salt box, and a tax of 10s. a bushel was imposed on salt. With regard to articles which he treated as luxuries he had no scruples. This was the light in which he regarded newspapers, and certainly he did his best to make them so. Paper was taxed, advertisements paid 3s. each, and every copy of a newspaper paid $3\frac{1}{2}$d. Not only was a house taxed twice over after it was built, but it was taxed heavily in building. Bricks paid 5s. a thousand.

Customs brought seven millions. Of this nearly two millions were furnished by the sugar duty at £1 the hundredweight, and one and a quarter by tea, which paid 40 per cent., except the coarser sorts of under 2s. 6d. a pound, which paid 20 per cent. Such taxes were imposed with regret as falling in some degree upon the lower classes of the people, but they were treated as inevitable. On the other hand, French wine (which there was no idea of excluding on account of the war) paid a duty of 10s. 6d. the imperial gallon, and other wine about one-third less. But there was a tariff on imports generally for the sake of revenue. Cotton, for example, paid 1d. a pound. On the other hand, some of the few protective duties in the tariff, those on East Indian calicoes and muslins, ranging from 25 to 30 per cent., were in the interest of Lancashire. Those on corn formed part of a national fiscal policy.

Besides excise and customs there was a miscellaneous body of taxes, most of which contributed to the Consolidated Fund. The most ancient of these was the land-tax, fixed at around two millions in 1798, since which almost a quarter had been redeemed. Objectionable attempts were made to take a toll from internal trade. Stage-coaches paid a mileage, and Pitt nearly succeeded in taxing canals and parcels sent by coach as well. A more justifiable tax upon communications was the convoy tax. Every merchant vessel was required to sail under protection, and in return duties on goods as well as tonnage were paid to about a million and a half. Stamps brought in nearly three millions. Succession duties were very low and lineal descendants paid nothing. A more interesting class of taxes, although bringing in comparatively little, was the group known as the assessed taxes. They formed a tax upon a person's general scale of living, his hairpowder, his dog, his clocks and watches, as well as his plate, his men-servants, his carriage, and his horses. Even farm-horses were included. Above all were the inhabited house and window taxes. This last, the celebrated tax upon the light of the sun, had a lasting prejudicial effect upon domestic architecture. But it did not affect the poor: houses with under seven windows were exempt.

The great majority of all these taxes was consistent with that principle of liberty which was potent even in matters of finance. The taxation was voluntary. An individual might always escape by declining to make use of the commodity taxed. Some taxes to which this could not be applied, such as those upon land and houses, were old, and obviously could not be done away with in a time of war. But a way was paved through the assessed taxes, which affected the establishment which a man was able to maintain, to the introduction of a revolution in finance. Resort was not had to it until one last appeal had been made to the voluntary principle. Persons not already taxed up to one-tenth of their income were in 1798 invited to make voluntary contributions to the Exchequer. The result compares unfavourably with those occasions of national sacrifice when rich men have melted down their plate and ladies made piles of their jewellery in the common cause. Nor was the appeal made in a manner to produce such effects. When this is borne in mind the event appears to have been not unsatisfactory. The gifts came to £2,300,000. The Duke of Bedford, in particular, showed that, if he was a sharp critic of direct taxation and had even been fined for evading it, this was not because he objected to his money going to Government, for he gave £100,000. But this was only a temporary expedient. In that same year Pitt introduced a direct tax upon all yearly incomes of £60 or over. On incomes of £200 or more it was at ten per cent. Below this there was a graduated scale, and an abatement was allowed in respect of children. The yield in 1800 was four and three quarter millions. In two points the tax outraged public opinion. It was unavoidable, and it entailed an inquisition into a man's affairs. It is true that under the existing order people were already beset by informers. Although it is not the fact that Pitt or Dundas or Portland was surrounded by political spies, the existing system of taxation bred an expert class of revenue informers. On one occasion Lady Bessborough was fined £60 because her servant, who had been given the money for the hair-powder tax, had omitted to pay it. She found that the informer knew everything which went on in her house. This state of things was very unpopular, but a general inquisition under authority was disliked still more. The income tax was only imposed as a war measure.

It is no matter for wonder that the system of expenditure was parsimonious. To have ventured government money on roads, on communications of any kind (outside the strictly commercial activities of the Post Office), on education, on sanitation, on medical services affecting the general public, on any institution for the encouragement of science, art, or literature, would have appeared financial lunacy. It would have been regarded as cramping independent effort. There were one or two exceptions more apparent than real. There was a British Museum. Edward Jenner received £10,000 for his discovery of vaccination, Henry Greathead £1,200 for the invention of the lifeboat. In 1793 a Board of Agriculture was established, of which Sir John Sinclair was the first President and Arthur Young the first Secretary. It received £3,000 a year. It was not a department of government, but did useful work in conducting agricultural surveys of England by counties, setting on foot various inquiries and publishing results. On the other hand, expenditure was sanctioned from time to time on a variety of charitable objects. For example, the four most impoverished East End parishes of London, being unable to maintain their own paupers, received £6,603 in 1800 for poor relief. The money was paid through Henry Thornton, the banker and philanthropic member of parliament. Expenditure upon political services, on the other hand, was lavish. Pitt's administration was pure relatively to what had gone before, and he was believed to have worthily carried on the work which Burke did in the cause of economic reform under Lord Rockingham. Yet the standard was still far from high. The name of Burke itself was prominent on the list of pensioners and sinecurists. There was no person more suited both by devotion and character to receive the mantle of Pitt than George Canning. Yet, when thirty years of age, he received from the incorruptible Minister a curious sinecure of nearly £450 a year, the Receiver-Generalship of the Alien Office. But perhaps nothing better illustrates the point of view with which the obligations of statesmen were regarded than some of the grounds upon which Pitt was praised at his death. He had £5,000 as First Lord of the Treasury, £2,450 as Chancellor of the Exchequer, and £3,080 as Lord Warden of the Cinque Ports. Yet he was praised for not having taken the Clerkship of the Pells (an office of which only the salary was important, afterwards given by his successor Addington to his own son, a boy). He was praised for having profited so little by the public money as to have died in debt. He was praised in an article in the Annual Register for not having forgotten his old tutor George Pretyman, afterwards Tomline. He had made him a bishop and a dean. The suggestion is unfair to Tomline, who justified his preferment by his solid work for the Church, for it is evident that the writer supposed that Pitt's merit in promoting him consisted in its being an act of favour and not a tribute to merit. In this state of public opinion it was not to be expected that any appreciable reduction could be made in the number of those posts like the Registrarship of the Admiralty, worth £10,000 a year, or the two Chief Justiceships in Eyre, worth £2,250 each, or even Lord Grenville's post of Auditorship of the Exchequer, worth £4,000, which had once had important duties attached to them, but now had few or none. In 1809 the Committee of Public Expenditure found that the principal sinecures amounted to above £350,000. Of these £100,000 worth was in Scotland and Ireland, and £57,000 colonial. A Chief Justiceship of a colony, which was never visited by the sinecurist, was a very lucrative office. Such posts were also the less likely to fall victims to the periodical knife of the financial purist, as they were paid for in several cases out of colonial revenues. A number of posts could have had only a pecuniary and etymological interest. The list of public servants was full of queer names and phrases—filazer and exigenter, Vice-Warden of the Stannaries, Clerk of the Pells, and Clerk of the Pipe.

It was not an uncommon thing for enterprising persons to engage to obtain, for a consideration, government appointments with easy duties attached to them. An amusing advertisement appeared in the Morning Chronicle on the very last day of the century:—

"PLACES UNDER GOVERNMENT, ETC.

"GENTLEMEN of Honour and Respectability may be informed of several genteel Civil Appointments under Government of 70*l.* 80*l.* 100*l.* 200*l.* 300*l.* 500*l.* 800*l.* and 1000*l.* per Annum, etc., both at Home and Abroad. Commissions in the Army for sale and exchange. A Troop, a Company, Lieutenancies, etc., etc. Enquire of Melville and Co., 7 Cecil Street, Strand, from eleven till two o'clock." From a continuation of the advertisement it appears that a man who wished to resign could expect three to six years' purchase of his salary from his successor. The name "Melville" almost suggests a squib on Dundas, whose home bore this name. But the advertisement of a few days later in The Times of January the 21st, 1801, was obviously a serious one. It offered a premium up to £3,000 to anyone who would procure the advertiser a place under Government. At the same time it is not to be supposed that the number of easy places drawing public money was large. Pitt saw to this. His reductions, particularly in the customs service, were very considerable. The total number of persons employed in the public departments of the United Kingdom in 1797 (the year before a number of further reductions were made) had been no more than 16,267, receiving £1,374,561 a year. The ancient justification of sinecures had been that after a gentleman had served His Majesty well for a number of years he had some claim to a post of which the duties were hardly more than nominal or could be performed by a deputy, much as an honest old office messenger who is past work could be accommodated with the duty of sitting at the bottom of the stairs with a small boy to help him. This system could only be removed if one of pensions took its place. Pitt was a pioneer in this also. His Chancellor Loughborough, on his retirement in 1801, was the first judge to receive the pension of £4,000 a year instituted under the statute of 1799.

One department of the State was far from efficient. The pages of Lord Liverpool's standard work, A Treatise on the Coins of the Realm, published in 1805, showed, cautiously and gently as the old man expressed himself, how ill he thought of the Royal Mint. The system was an extravagant one. The Mint was unable to do the work for which it existed. When copper twopences and pence were first coined under royal authority recourse had to be had to Boulton's Birmingham works, for lack of the requisite machinery to turn out a large quantity. But the Government was reluctant to attack the problem of silver coinage even with his help. For a long time few or no coins had been issued. Substitutes had become necessary. Occasionally they took the form of small local notes, which were known as silver notes. In 1804, for example, a Wolverhampton magistrate wrote that £20,000 worth of cards of under twenty shillings face value were in circulation in his neighbourhood. The shortage of silver to pay seamen and dockyard men led in 1804 to the issue by the Bank of Spanish dollars with fresh impressions stamped upon them.

It would have been impossible to cope with the difficulty by gradually issuing new coin. For the coins had become, as

Liverpool wrote, "mere counters" without any mark by which they could be identified as coin. The sixpences had lost weight most, and at a mint assay held in 1798 it was found that 200 sixpences were required to make up a pound Troy instead of the proper number of 124. It was obvious that as long as a recognized part of the currency was of this character, it was open to anybody to clip or otherwise remove a good portion of the new silver and still have something left which would pass as coin. As regards gold the Mint had no trouble. Since the stoppage of cash payments in 1797 gold had come to be very little used, and there was still, according to Liverpool's estimate, £30,000,000 worth of gold coin in the King's European dominions, even after allowing for the amount of bullion which had left the kingdom owing to war charges.

Liverpool addressed his treatise in the form of a letter to the King, coinage being the royal prerogative, and expressly omitted to discuss points which required the authority of Parliament. The distinction was characteristic of such a high old Tory, and yet would not altogether have found disfavour with Fox and those who thought like him. Although the theory that King, Lords, and Commons were separate elements in the State, balancing one another and neutralizing one another's powers for evil, and uniting in all that was good, was not very much better than nonsense, as Bentham showed in his amusing attack upon Blackstone, yet that theory exercised a real influence on the proceedings of all three. In one or two ways it was more potent than it had been in the age when Parliament had made war upon the King. The practice of petitioning the House of Commons was on the increase. It was a comparatively rare thing to send a deputation to Ministers. The House of Commons was generally treated as a separate authority in the State, much in the same way as Liverpool regarded it, and could be requested to take action. Its province was legislation. There was no regular question time during which Ministers could be catechized concerning their executive acts. Nor was it the custom to indicate disapproval of them, either by moving a reduction in the vote for a particular department or otherwise. Of debates in which the conduct of Ministers generally was arraigned on large questions of policy, there was no lack. A second class was financial. Here the House showed its independence. It frequently refused to vote taxes for which Pitt asked, in spite of having given him its general confidence. On the other hand, the House regarded itself as responsible as a whole for voting the necessary supplies. The leaders of the Opposition themselves avoided making the budget an opportunity to attack the ministry of the day. Two budgets early in the nineteenth century—those of 1801 and 1804—were passed without any objections at all. The third and most important of the House's activities was in the legislative sphere. This is not because bills—as laws were called before they had been what was known as read three times in both Houses and received the royal assent—were discussed in great detail. The committee stage, that between the second and third readings, when the bill was taken section by section, was not of much importance even in the House of Commons. Only in 1800 was it decided to make permanent the post of Chairman of Committees, who presided over this stage instead of the Speaker. This last dignity, which was regarded in a very different light, had now been held for several years by Henry Addington. The position of the House of Commons as an authority in the State, independent of the Ministry in which it reposed its confidence, was evinced by the great importance attached to the office of Speaker, apart from his position as President of an assembly for whose orderly deliberations he was responsible. He was the spokesman of the House, and at the close of the session attended the House of Lords, and there, in presenting the money bills, addressed the King on the work of the Commons during its progress. The existence of a special body of His Majesty's confidential servants forming the Cabinet was not hinted at in these speeches.

Another example of the manner in which each House was regarded as a separate Estate was evinced by the prominent part taken by members who were not ministers in the introduction of bills, as well as in modifying them when introduced. One of the most important measures passed in the last decade of the old century was Fox's bill, giving the jury the power to decide in trials for libel whether the matter complained of was libellous or not. A prominent member of the Opposition, Western, brought in the first definite protective measure for corn. Those who gave its shape to the first labour legislation were the first Sir Robert Peel and Wilberforce. In the immense sphere of local legislation, canal bills, turnpike bills, and above all enclosure bills, parliamentary committees entered into the minutest details of matters which would in a later generation have been left mainly to the settlement of government departments acting on general lines. An attempt by the Board of Agriculture to save Parliament this labour by incorporating certain principles into a General Enclosure Bill in 1796 was unsuccessful. Always suspicious of efforts after uniformity, the Englishman of that day restricted the activities of departments and boards. There did not exist an armoury of departmental policies and precedents brought out by the painstaking permanent official to control the vagaries of the party minister. There was, in fact, no bureaucracy. Where party ended, it was not the department but Parliament which began. The general parliamentary attitude towards matters outside the sphere of acute political controversy was partly determined by the composition of the House of Commons. The county members formed its most important element. They were practical; they did not take long views; they inclined to treat the affairs of the kingdom simply as county affairs on a larger scale. Others, such as the lawyers, with their gift for speaking on all subjects and their limitation of having, usually, no personal

THE GOVERNMENT OF ENGLAND

acquaintance with any, scarcely counted. The attitude of the county members was governed, partly by certain traditional conceptions, and partly by the advice of those few members who understood such things.

There were very few industrial employers in Parliament. Of the two most eminent, one, Samuel Whitbread, the brewer, was by far the most zealous social reformer in the House of Commons, and the other, Sir Robert Peel, took the lead in measures for the relief of children in cotton-mills, of which he was himself an owner. The unjust treatment by Parliament of industrial labour was due not to self-interest but partly to confusion of economic thought and partly to a misapprehension of the political situation. A traditional conception of freedom of trade in the interests of the consumer underlay the old English legal system. The producer or shipper was to bring his commodities into the open market and sell them to the consumer or retailer. This was the object of the ancient prohibitions of forestalling, engrossing, and regrating denounced by Adam Smith. Upon his principles the actions of the man who should buy up a large quantity of corn and keep it out of the market was itself subject to economic law, and any attempt to interfere with it would do evil rather than good. When Portland took action to prevent the common law from being put into force in 1800, Holland, although he hated the Ministry, and the renegade Whig leader in particular, went out of his way to assure him of his support. The same traditional view of freedom of trade underlay the way in which the law of conspiracy was applied. The idea was that a skilled labourer should individually bring his labour to market, and sell it for what it would fetch. It was thought unfair to the consumer, who was in this case the employer, that it should be "engrossed" and artificially kept out of the market till it would sell for a higher price. There was nothing whatever wrong in a strike, according to the broader view of free trade laid down by Adam Smith. When the question came up in the House of

Lords, Holland consistently argued, following the same authority, that the trade in hired labour should also be allowed to find its own level. But this time he was at issue with the ministers. They followed Adam Smith on the question of keeping back corn from the market. But on that of keeping back labour they clung to the older English principle that it was to be suppressed as a conspiracy in restraint of trade.

A particular body of employers, the master millwrights of London, had in 1799, become dissatisfied with what the common law permitted to be done. They petitioned Parliament for leave to bring in a Bill for the better preventing of unlawful Combinations of Workmen employed in the Millwright Business, and for regulating the Wages of such Workmen. It is significant that while they objected to their men being allowed the right of collective bargaining for the price of their labour, they did not object to the old Elizabethan method of its being fixed by the magistrates. But Parliament brushed this point aside. In its anxiety to counteract the activity of revolutionary propaganda in industrial centres it conceived itself to have done all that was either necessary or safe by way of not merely countenancing but actually encouraging legitimate combinations among labourers by passing a Friendly Societies Act in 1793. It now decided to pass a general law against combinations to obtain higher wages or shorter hours, and the Workmen's Combination Acts of 1799 and 1800 were the result. The old idea of protecting trade from restraints upon its freedom appears in the prohibition of combinations among masters. This was, however, a dead letter from the first. The political element is revealed in harsh provisions, such as one by which a man could be imprisoned for refusing to incriminate himself. It was believed that the organizations now coming into existence would prove a dangerous weapon in the hands of a political incendiary. It has never been easy either for the Legislature or for the members of a trade union themselves to define satisfactorily the legitimate sphere of its activities. Of what went on in the minds of operatives in the midlands and the north of England, Pitt himself and most of the rest of Parliament were supremely ignorant. But they knew that in 1773 the Spitalfields weavers after ten years of rioting, in the course of which they had on one occasion exhibited their strength under the walls of Parliament, succeeded in bending it to their desires. London in 1780 and Birmingham in 1792 had shown what a mob of labourers could do, once it interested itself in politics. From this point of view the Combination laws range themselves with other enactments limiting the rights of political agitation passed about the same time. But they did nothing to suppress Jacobinism, except in so far as they were an exhibition of the general determination of Government. Attempts to keep down wages might be directed against individuals with some success. It was with this view that additions were now made to the usual orders to sheriffs as to holding general sessions to the effect that justices of the peace and also free citizens should prefer the names of artificers and servants taking any excessive wages contrary to the form of the Statute. But the law was not effective in repressing combination, which it was, indeed, impossible to do. There were still societies with printed rules and tickets. Some of them had enormous power. The law rapidly became a dead letter. For five years after the passing of the first Act the obligation of prosecuting had been so bandied about between private persons and the Government, each party evading its responsibilities, that there were still unions throughout the trades of the country. It was absurd to attempt to make a selection, and Spencer Perceval as Attorney-General practically declined to do so, and got his view accepted. What the Acts had power to do was to force the movement underground to some extent, thus giving to these labourers' brotherhoods and clubs some of that very character of seditious confederacies which it had been feared that they might assume, and also, by making joint agreements between masters and their men illegal, giving to all such negotiations an atmosphere of insecurity.

The traditional fiscal policy in relation to trade was governed by three principles. The first was to guard the woollen manufacture. The Lord Chancellor presided in the Upper House of Parliament sitting upon the Woolsack; and that staple, still her greatest export, had been the mainstay of England's prosperity. It had been supposed that English fleeces enjoyed a special superiority owing to the temperate climate, and that only after mixing it with English wool could manufactures combining fineness and strength be obtained from the foreign material. Hence sprang a number of restrictions, among which the prohibitions of the export of sheep and of raw wool ranked first. Hence, also, those who resisted the introduction of machinery in the case of some processes of the woollen manufacture were able to obtain a consideration from the Legislature denied to the cotton-workers. So ancient was this industry that they were able to appeal to legislation as old as Tudor times prohibiting the use of the gigmills then invented for raising the nap on cloth. The interest of the agriculturist who produced the raw material, and that of the consumer who bought the finished product, were alike sacrificed to that of the manufacturer; and even the capitalist manufacturer was hampered by the existence of the old laws, which were not repealed till 1809.

The second principle was to ensure the wheat supply of the country in the interest of the consumer. It was thought that this could best be done by maintaining the area under that crop, and this was effected by the legislation of 1670 and 1689, which remained unaltered for nearly a century. In 1774 the scale at which the existing import duty of 16s. a quarter was imposed was set at 48s. a quarter and under, and it was complained that wheat-growing in consequence had ceased to pay, and that arable land was converted to pasture. In

1791, 50s. was taken as the price up to which agriculture required protection. The import duty was fixed at 24s. 3d. When the price was between 50s. and 54s. the duty was 2s. 6d. At and above 54s. there was a nominal duty of 6d. When the price fell below 44s. there was an export bounty of 5s., but at and above 46s. exportation was entirely prohibited. The maintenance of an adequate wheat-growing area at home was rendered imperative by the fact that the main supplies of foreign wheat came from northern Europe. No reliance could be placed on a good season there when there was a bad one at home.

But the war provided a new argument for protection. During the hostilities with the Baltic Powers in 1801 the people, already suffering from two bad seasons, saw this supply cut off. At the same time a clamour arose from the Board of Agriculture and the writers whom that body had called into existence for the cultivation of the waste lands. These were estimated at 7,000,000 acres, mostly culturable, in England alone. How ludicrous, it was urged, to seek riches in colonies and to hunt for markets for manufactures when there was this almost boundless source of wealth undeveloped at our doors, nay, on the heaths surrounding the metropolis itself, and now only given up to a few miserable sheep and infested with gipsies and highwaymen! But it was only a continuance of the high prices induced by the bad seasons of the last few years that preceded the Peace of Amiens, the interruption of supplies during the war, and the rise in prices due to the change in currency and the general growth of manufactures and wealth, that could enable these waste lands to be brought under the plough. On the land already under cultivation, moreover, rents had been raised and had to be paid. So accustomed had the agricultural interest grown to the high prices that when a good season brought wheat below 50s. a quarter in the spring of 1804 there was an outcry that the farmers were in distress, although such a price would have been thought a high one only ten years before. The duty of 24s. 3d. was now imposed when the price of wheat was at or below 63s. a quarter; the intermediate duty of 2s. 6d. when it was between 63s. and 66s.; and the nominal one of 6d. when it was at and above the last figure. On the other hand, the 5s. bounty on export was only now allowed when the home price was under 48s. and exportation was prohibited when it reached 54s. The opposition between the interest of agriculture and that of the rest of the community began to emerge in the discussion on this measure. But it was not yet pronounced. The law of 1804 was regarded as one more in the series of adjustments of the time-honoured scale of 1689 to suit altered conditions. It was not treated as important at the time. Nor was it even made a government measure. It was introduced by a member of the Opposition, who with Coke represented the Whig landed interest, Charles Western.

An even more important principle in certain respects was that which had found expression in the Navigation Act of 1660. This had provided that trade to England from Asia, Africa, or America should only be carried on in ships built in what was afterwards known as the British Empire, and that at least three-fourths of the mariners should be English. Adam Smith had pointed out that the monopoly so created did not in reality increase the wealth of a nation, though he added that, as defence was of much more importance than opulence, it was a wise measure as tending to reduce the naval strength of Holland, the only country which could then endanger the security of England. But the position during the war with revolutionary France had changed. As a measure of national defence the Navigation Act had lost its value. No danger remained of a country building up a maritime population which might threaten the safety of England. On the other hand, the great economist's arguments as regards the harmfulness of the measure to the national wealth had been strengthened. British ships could no longer cope with the West Indian trade. Successive

Governments found themselves forced to throw it open to vessels belonging to the United States, and necessary legislation was carried through, in the face of considerable hostile criticism, to enable this to be done. Examples of more exclusively protective measures existed in the prohibition of the export of yarn and machinery, in which Lancashire took considerable interest. Even the emigration from the country of skilled workmen was forbidden.

The sketch here given shows what degree of truth there was in the eighteenth-century theory, which Bentham turned to such effective ridicule, namely, that the country was governed by King, Lords, and Commons, each pair acting as checks upon the third. It was not yet fully realized that, so far from want of harmony being essential, such a triplicate Government was only possible where His Majesty's confidential servants were in complete possession of the confidence of Parliament, or at least the Lower House. An attempt to carry on the administration in another country in which this condition was absent, or, if present, only accidentally so, proved a failure. Had the real nature of cabinet responsibility to Parliament been understood, it is improbable that the experiment would have been made. How it failed, and the nature of the system which was substituted for it, is now to be described.

CHAPTER III

IRELAND—THE FALL OF PITT'S ADMINISTRATION

(January–March 1801)

PHILOSOPHERS, poets, and priests have united in holding up to admiration the man who is content with the barest necessities of life. Nowhere was it possible to realize this idea so well as in the prevailing type of Irishman, the Catholic peasant. He lived upon a single root, the easiest of all foods to grow, and to prepare for the table. He wore the same clothes in summer and winter. He did not trouble himself with shoes. He built the walls of his house of sods or of mud. He put together a roof out of the branches of a tree overlaid with a few swathes of rushes or heath. He occasionally saved himself labour by making use of the discovery that if he took the mud for his walls from the floor of his house the floor would go down as quickly as the walls would go up. Sometimes he was able to spare himself the trouble of building more than three walls by taking the side of a ditch for the fourth. He furnished his nest with a few wisps of straw. Nor were the results disappointing. The system bred the most intelligent peasantry in Europe, certainly one far more quickwitted, more anxious to learn, and better educated than the corresponding class on the opposite side of the Irish Channel. His social festivities were distinguished by a cultivated gaiety equally difficult to parallel in the peasantry of another country. For his religion he would make almost any sacrifice. He was pure in his life and devoted to a home where the loveliest of all women were to be found. Nor was he without virtues not generally found in a bucolic order of society—courtesy, generosity, and personal charm. Vices he had—cruelty, vindictiveness, and fanaticism. Yet it was possible to excuse these as sur-

THE FALL OF PITT'S ADMINISTRATION 203

vivals from a barbarous age, which no upbringing could be expected immediately to remove.

Yet his merits were almost completely overlooked. He was accused, various meanings being attached to the term according to the fancy of the critic, of being "miserable". It is true that Arthur Young, writing abour twenty years before the end of the century, contrasted his good fortune in the possession of a cow and a potato field with the lot of his English counterpart who had neither, but had the demoralizing poor law which the Irishman was better without. But the cottier system, in spite of bearing some resemblance to that which Lord Winchelsea and others were praised for attempting to introduce into England, was generally denounced. Economists who had read Adam Smith upon the division of labour could see no merit in the self-subsistent Irish home. "Except in the cotton branches and the curing of provisions", wrote Edward Wakefield in his Account of Ireland so late as 1812, "this pernicious system is everywhere observed; it pervades all ranks, from the nobleman, who makes his own candles, cultivates his own patch of flax, and has it spun by his servants, to the cotter, whose wife and daughters spin and manufacture their frieze and woollen stuffs, which serve them as clothing." Men of this school wished that the peasant had more, and more various wants; then he would work harder. Instead of comparing him with Diogenes, moralists merely called him lazy, and in so doing rendered him lazier. He became involved in a vicious circle. Those for whom he worked and to whom he paid rent abused his simplicity. If he had few wants, money would be no good to him, and he had best be kept at work. He was rack-rented for his miserable bit of land, while the daily wage which went to pay it was fined down by his landlord and employer, who came next above him in the scale, and who in his turn was in many cases not the proprietor of the soil but a farmer. A typical tenant rented about fifty acres. An immense gulf lay between him and both the landlord to whom he owed rent and the Protestant incumbent to whom he owed tithe, both of whom he very likely never saw. That gulf was filled by a host of evil creatures, who cheated the landlord and rector while they fleeced the peasant. First came the middleman, who knew how to wring a high rent from a crowd of small tenants whom the careless proprietor was incompetent to deal with. Towards the end of the century, as land went up in value, the landlord grew impatient of the profit which was made at his expense. The middleman began to die out. He was replaced as oppressor by the agent, though the same man was often both. The rent was only one of the things which the tenant had to pay. The agent took from him duty work, duty fowls, duty turkey, duty geese, glove-money, and sealing-money. Such feudal survivals were combined with a system as far as possible from anything possessing the true feudal spirit—that infamous system by which, when a tenant's lease was up, his land was put to auction by sealed tenders, and the unfortunate man was obliged to offer an exorbitant rent if he did not wish to see the land, which he had very probably reclaimed himself from moor or bog, pass into other hands. It was partly for this reason that the farmhouse could hardly be distinguished from the cottier's cabin. It was supposed to be in no one's interest to build. So he left his plough and harrow in the corner of the last field which he had tilled, and did not even keep a yard for his pigs. Towards the end of the century, however, there was some improvement in the system of leases. Instead of shorter terms such as twenty-one years farms were let for thirty-one years or three lives, whichever was longest. This latter arrangement appealed to the gambling instinct as in the West of England, and also satisfied the Irish electoral qualification of a freeholder. When the Catholics obtained the vote in parliamentary elections on the forty-shilling franchise in 1793 the landlords multiplied their tenants of this class and the number of voters who would follow them to the poll.

Between the farmer and the rector, again, there was in many cases the proctor or the tithe-farmer. The evils which attended the tithe system in England existed in Ireland also. But there were many others. The poverty of the farmer made it hard to contest a proctor's oppressive valuation. A poor man could not afford to keep his corn on the ground, or to be cited to the Bishop's court. The inequalities were a glaring example of Irish contempt for law. Graziers were rich, and the Irish Parliament had, merely by resolution and not by statute, declared pasture exempt. Except in the south, tithe could not be demanded for potatoes. In the south again, peasants drew home the tithe-farmers' corn, hay, and turf free. Last of all, the due was paid to an alien and a hated Church. Yet even here there was not much difficulty when the rector collected his tithes himself.

For if personal relations could once be established things were almost sure to run well. Richard Edgeworth's experience in the Irish midlands was a proof of this, and justified his daughter Maria's description in The Absentee of a tenantry still ready to love a landlord, who has lived away from them in London for many years, the moment of his return. The diary of Lady Bessborough discloses a truth which is even stranger. Her husband and she were typical absentees. Yet when they did at last visit their estate, in which their faces were unknown, they filled the people with delight, and found themselves invested with an authority to settle disputes in which the priests themselves could hardly have surpassed them. Had this impulsive affectionateness of disposition been valued as it should have been, Ireland might have been saved for England. It was not the greatest of the evils of absenteeism that perhaps two millions of the national rent-roll was spent by landlords who lived out of the country. The ill-effects of the example set by these great proprietors went much farther. The country-side and the country people were regarded with unmerited contempt. The large Irish proprietors aped the Englishman who owned land in Ireland,

and were aped in their turn by the smaller landlords who could not afford to live out of Ireland. If an Irishman could not live in London or in Bath, he could at least live in Dublin. This aspiring spirit spread through the whole social order, down to the buckeens or small proprietors and middlemen, who ought to have been improving their estates as well as drinking claret and keeping their packs of hounds, down to the squireens or large farmers of five hundred a year, who lived the same useless life; right down to the smaller farmers and even the cottier, who, if he could not live like a gentleman, could at least do his best to be as idle as it was possible for a gentleman to be. The same spirit had reached the Dublin tradesman who had his showy villa at the foot of the Wicklow hills. It was tacitly accepted that to speak Irish, the mother tongue of the great part of the country, was the mark of a savage. So was Catholicism. To the Protestant the Irish Catholic was not an object of hatred; he was merely an unfortunate being whom the lights of the Reformation had not yet reached. The Church shamelessly enjoyed the revenues of enormous landed properties, and made no attempt to proselytize. But to the nineteenth century the idea survived that conversion was bound to come. Catholics were certainly a class apart, but not completely so. An increasing number, for example, sent their sons to be educated at the Protestant institution of Trinity College, Dublin. Several men of note were not more than a generation or two removed from Catholics. Such were Lord Clare, Doctor Duigenan, Bishop O'Beirne of Meath, Dean Kirwan, and Lord Cloncurry. O'Beirne had a brother who was an Irish priest, and Kirwan had been one himself.

No crimes are more excusable than those which spring from fanaticism, which is nothing but a wrong-headed devotion to the highest ideas which a man can have. But there was nothing of this in the oppressions to which the Catholic was subjected in the eighteenth century. He was merely held to belong to an inferior order. It was thought quite natural that he should pay a higher rent than a Protestant for the same land. The penal legislation against Catholics had begun as a measure of national precaution, and was continued until the last quarter of the eighteenth century as an expression of contempt and, in the case of the prohibition to purchase land, in order to keep the price of land down and the rate of rent up. Even after it had been repealed, and after the legislature had declared them admissible to the grand jury, the bench of magistrates and municipal corporations, they were still generally excluded. The Protestant, whether he was of English or Irish descent or—as was more common—of the half-blood, felt himself to belong to the ruling race. It was natural for one of these landlords to be quick with his cane or horsewhip when he came across anything like sauciness. "Knocking down", observed Arthur Young in describing this trait, "is spoken of in the country in a manner that makes an Englishman stare. Nay," he added, "I have heard anecdotes of the lives of people being made free with without any apprehension of the justice of a jury. . . . But law gains ground." It did; yet thirty years later Wakefield saw a poor man's cheek laid open at Carlow races by a gentleman with his whip for standing in his way. A number of magistrates were present. But no one, either of the oppressed class or of those whose business it was to do justice, seemed to think anything of the matter.

Yet, if a people so treated showed no resentment, it was because they had long memories and could afford to wait. If the character of a nation may be looked for in the old women who forget nothing and are sensitive only to lasting impressions, there is much significance in the words which an old beggar-woman was overheard muttering to herself as she tottered along the road: "Revenge is sweet and I'll have it." Maria Edgeworth records this in the Life of her father as typical of the national character; and it is significant that this sinister trait is allowed to peep out in a work so much devoted—like the same author's works of fiction—to showing the amiable qualities of the Irish peasant. An even deeper colouring appears in the Memoirs of Miles Byrne, a Wexford rebel of 1798. Two years earlier he had, in an impulsive moment, allowed himself to be enrolled in the yeomanry. When his father heard what the boy had done he became outrageous. He would rather, he said, see his son dead than ever see him put on a red coat. "How often had he shown me", wrote Miles, "the lands that belonged to our ancestors now in the hands of the descendants of the sanguinary followers of Cromwell." These terrible passions could go to sleep for generations—overlaid by many kindlier feelings—but they did not die.

The Catholics must have formed nearly three-fourths of the total population of Ireland. The first census, held in 1813, was imperfect. At the second, held in 1821, the numbers were 6,801,827. Earlier estimates are generally low, but it is difficult to credit that the population could have increased by more than one-third during the first twenty years of the nineteenth century. The total number of Irish-born resident in Ireland may, therefore, be taken at 5,000,000. Of the Protestants, roughly 450,000 were members of the Church of England, and double that number dissenters—mainly Ulster Presbyterians. Till almost the end of the century these last had been alienated from the Government. They had been overbid in the rental of their farms by the Catholics, who could live on less; and were often forced to emigrate. They formed and maintained a connection with the great republic which was growing across the Atlantic. Mainly Scottish by race, they were Covenanters by tradition. But before the end of the century economic change had paved the way to a change in the political attitude of Ulster. The growth of flax, the spinning of linen yarn, and the weaving of linen were recognized as forming the national industry of the country. But Ulster was its peculiar home. The nearness of Belfast to Scotland afforded opportunities of intercourse with their cousins which encouraged the descendants of the Scottish settlers in industrious habits. Hence arose a second industry which for a while almost threatened linen. In 1784 the first water-mill for cotton-spinning was established at Belfast, and by the end of the century many thousands in the district were obtaining their livelihood out of cotton. The town itself had made a phenomenal advance in the last fifty years, although it still cannot have had much more than 20,000 inhabitants in 1800. As the new century opened it was observed that, following the Liverpool practice, a Presbyterian who became rich went over to the Church of England. He had lost his republicanism years before.

Dublin was a striking contrast; and, indeed, it was a true representative of the country of which it was the capital. It had at the end of the century a population of about 170,000. The city was a grotesque mixture of filth and finery—an epitome of the whole country. The French traveller Baert shrewdly observed that the difference between the Scots and the Irish was that, while both were poor, the former admitted it, but the latter did not, and ruined themselves by ostentation. He thought that they displayed more luxury in their horses and their retainers than was shown in any country in Europe. It is true that many of these last were of the type of Thady in Maria Edgeworth's Castle Rackrent, who wiped down the window-seat with his wig. Judges who went on circuit insisted upon the formality of being met by the sheriff at the bounds of the county. They entered the assize town attended by an immense train of dirty carriages with dirty harness, and miserably mounted javelin men with ancient large cocked-hats edged with tarnished lace. On one occasion a Chief Justice, having for once been properly attended on circuit, publicly thanked the sheriff at enormous length for the respectable manner in which he had met the King's commission. If fine names could give satisfaction, there was no want of that in Ireland.

Every innkeeper had his "lady"—never his wife, each county had its Governor, each corporate town its sovereign, the counties were divided into baronies, the city guilds of Dublin were called corporations. These had a magnificent procession every three years at the perambulation of the bounds; each corporation had a gilt carriage drawn by six or eight horses; among those who attended on horseback were a hundred and fifty tailors. Yet this was the city found by a traveller in 1791 to be swarming with beggars. "We saw", he wrote, "numbers of dirty wretches, whose sole employment seemed to consist in divesting each other of filth and vermin." Sometimes the contrast was to be seen in the same individual at the same time, as in the case of the broad-laced frills upon the shirts of the bare-legged children. The procession to College Green at the opening of Parliament was a grand affair, but the streets had to be specially cleaned beforehand. It was a far cry from the splendour of homes like those in Merrion Square, where these senators resided, to the filth and stench in which labourers and beggars lived only a few hundred yards off, between the Castle and the College. Here, as elsewhere throughout the pestilential city, small rooms were let for one or two shillings a week to between ten and twenty people who lived together, and slept on wads of filthy straw. After a very thorough inquiry, a contemporary clergyman, John Whitelaw, found that for all Dublin the average number of persons to a house was between eleven and twelve—an enormous number for the small houses of that time. It is hard to imagine how they could have lived. No industry prospered in Dublin, owing partly to the profligate example of the upper classes, which was followed by those who should have been engaged in the promotion of industry, and partly to the worthless and contentious character of the drunken labouring population, which ruined trade after trade. How little account was taken of life was evinced by the scandal of the Foundling Hospital, an institution for which Parliament was responsible,

THE FALL OF PITT'S ADMINISTRATION

as it was managed under an Act of Parliament and mainly supported by a government grant. Out of over two thousand infants annually admitted for several years up to the year of the rebellion very nearly one-half died.

In such a country of playboys it was impossible for the people to take either themselves or their government seriously. Although the system of local administration was closely modelled upon that of England, the magistracy, to which the people looked as the outward sign of power, was very different in its composition. So few were the resident country gentlemen that the ownership of landed property could not be imposed as a qualification for the office of justice of the peace. At the same time the whole Roman Catholic population was generally excluded. In 1793 the legal disability had been removed, but very little use was made of the fact. Wakefield wrote in 1812 that he had only met with one instance of a Catholic magistrate. In their recommendations the governors of counties fell back upon the class of squireens; but the country was ill-provided with schools for this class, and many of them could hardly write and—what was of much more importance—had no sense of public duty. So far as police was concerned, the baronial constable, who did the country duty, was a byword. It was almost everywhere necessary in matters of importance to employ soldiers. The constant disturbances of Oakboys and Whiteboys and others which disgraced Ireland during a great part of the century, and which had in every case an economic origin, were taken as a matter of course. Their agrarian character was just enough appreciated to give the authorities what they held to be a sufficient excuse not to deal with them as ordinary crime. But it did not lead them to the logical conclusion—to look for a constructive remedy. Men became habituated to disorder.

The close corporations of the towns were the same festive irresponsible bodies as in England. In two respects, however, the Irish system in the counties had an advantage.

Debts of under £10 were recoverable at Quarter Sessions, at which magistrates were provided with paid assistant barristers to assist them. Secondly, the excellence of the Irish roads, which was in such striking contrast to the general barbarism of the country, was due to the system by which, if the need of a new road could be proved to the satisfaction of the grand jury, it could order a rate to be imposed. This rate amounted to only a few pence an acre, and although the power was often grossly abused, yet the burden was much less, and produced much better results, than the corresponding burden, the poor rate, in England. Only the turnpike roads were bad.

A fatality appeared to attend every operation of Government. About the middle of the century it found itself with a surplus budget, a circumstance usually connected with prosperity in other countries. In Ireland it merely proved fatal to enterprise. The habit commenced of giving grants in aid for works, and the perennial jest of the canal or pier which nobody wanted, except the contractor and his friends who fattened by the job, took its rise from that time. Individual enterprise could not dream of competing with a Government ready to lavish money in unconditional grants without security upon projects which had not the remotest prospect of paying a dividend. At the same time, it is to the credit of the Government that, corrupt as it was, it recognized some sort of obligation to spend money upon objects then usually regarded across the Irish Channel as outside the purview of state expenditure, such as hospitals and educational institutions. The considerable grants to the national foundation of Trinity College Dublin, and, later on, to the Roman Catholic College of Maynooth, were certainly not wasted. £30,000 yearly was spent on an attempt to bring up the children of Catholics as Protestants in what were known as the charter schools. The system made more enemies than proselytes, and—although the schools were a failure—it is some testimony to the tolerance of the

THE FALL OF PITT'S ADMINISTRATION 213

time that the number in them was even allowed to reach so high a figure as 1,600. Not much better success attended a law dating from the reign of Henry VIII which should have ensured the provision of elementary education in every parish. Every clergyman of the Church of England was obliged on induction into a living to swear that he would teach, or cause to be taught, an English school within his Vicarage or Rectory. The oath was taken, and the duty generally disregarded. The real education of the country was in the hedge-schools, carried on in the open air or from one parent's house to another's by young Catholics who had received some learning, but were not quite good enough for priests. Here the young peasant acquired the English language and his letters together. He read Laugh and be Fat, Irish Rogues and Rapparees, and other such joyous and licentious publications.

As in England, the activities of the central Government were brought home to the people principally in connection with excise and currency. It does not appear that the exciseman was quite so hated in Ireland. On his approach the tell-tale materials could always be stowed away in a turf-heap or the nearest bog; nobody would peach and it was a jest to elude him. Until the end of the eighteenth century this was very easily done. Afterwards the Government showed more energy and used to seize about three thousand illicit stills annually. Excise officers were known as hearth-tax collectors, from the objectionable tax which fell upon almost every poor man's fireside until 1793, when houses with only one hearth were generally exempted. The tax fell at the rate of about two shillings a hearth. But upon the whole the peasant was very lightly taxed even when he did not elude payment. He was not really a heavy drinker, even of whisky, except upon occasions of festivity. It was not until 1797 that taxation in Ireland followed the example of Great Britain in departing from the principle of sparing the necessities of the poor. It was now, however, obliged to do so. The duties on leather and salt in particular were severely felt. But by this time the Government had scarcely any option. In time of peace it had easily paid its way, but it had no extra resources to draw upon in time of war; and it was now ludicrously impecunious. In 1796, when it wished to move troops in haste to meet the French landing in Bantry Bay, it was obliged to borrow £45,000 from a rich nobleman, Lord Cloncurry. Ireland, which until 1793 had balanced her finances with a net income and expenditure of about a million and a third and a debt of a million and a half, found after that year that her debt and her deficit alike were rising by leaps and bounds. This was not due to acquiescence in any unreasonable demands. She only paid for the services of 10,000 men outside her own limits, and her grants to the Navy were confined to one of £200,000 in 1795. In the last year alike of the century and the separate Parliament she had, indeed, raised her revenue to three millions, but her expenditure was more than double this, or, if the extraordinary expenses due to the disturbed state of Ireland be deducted, it still exceeded the revenue by more than a million. Although the sum would not have been considered large in a country of even moderate wealth, it was so for Ireland, making up one-half of her whole receipts from customs and excise, which formed the mainstay of her revenue. The only other important head was the characteristic one of lotteries, which brought in about half a million. By the end of the century her debt amounted to £28,500,000. It was impossible to raise all her requirements at home, and one-half had been funded in England.

The Irish currency system had been grossly neglected, and this caused considerable discontent, which was only prevented from becoming serious by the backward condition of the country. In many transactions the people were content to make payments by tally. The Bank of Ireland was opened in 1783. It issued notes, and also the silver tokens which took the place in Ireland of mint coins. The deficiency in currency

THE FALL OF PITT'S ADMINISTRATION 215

was only in part made up by the issues of private bankers. Failures of these were more frequent even than in England, and in 1800 there were only eleven remaining which issued notes. The gap was filled by a crowd of tradesmen and others, who circulated in their own neighbourhood what were known as silver notes. These ranged from 6s. to 3½d. On one occasion an English traveller in Killarney found, when he was about to return, that he was encumbered with a number of these scraps of paper, which would not, of course, have been taken at twenty miles' distance. He presented them at the office of issue, which turned out to be the shop of the local saddler. The man refused to receive them unless the amount was taken out in saddlery. In the end the beggars got the whole. The system, however, gave occasion to much more serious impositions. Rascally estate agents refused to receive rent in anything but guineas, on which they made a profit by selling again and again to the tenants.

In spite of the war, in spite even of internal disturbances, Ireland was, throughout the last twenty years of the century, in a condition of constantly increasing prosperity. It is true that the complaint that wages had not risen in proportion to the cost of living had even greater justification here than in England. The ordinary wage of an agricultural labourer, as given in the contemporary Statistical Survey of the County of Kilkenny, only rose from 8d. to 9d. between 1790 and 1800. It is thanks mainly to the comparatively high rates prevailing in Ulster that the average of the information contained in these surveys gives a higher weekly wage—5s. 1d.—for the following decade. The earnings of the Meath cottier, the typical Irish peasant, were £20 yearly in 1802—no considerable advance on the condition of things found by Young five-and-twenty years before. But the general wealth of the country was much increased. Exports had risen considerably, reaching in real values nearly six and a half million pounds. The rise in beef, pork, and bacon had been fairly steady. But greater signs of prosperity were to be discerned in the fall of the foreign trade. The Act of Parliament known after the name of the Chancellor of the Irish Exchequer as Foster's Corn Law, had given a great impulse in 1784 to the export of wheat and oats. But the value of these, which was nearly £500,000 in 1792, fell rapidly in the next few years, even when the seasons were good. There can be no doubt of tillage having enormously increased, and, allowing for the presence of additional troops, there must have been a greater consumption among the ordinary civil population. Her exports of woollen goods, again, fell almost to nothing. The peasant was better clothed. The greatest of Irish exports, linen, amounted to nearly 36,000,000 yards in 1800, valued at almost £2,400,000. Ireland's principal imports were woollens, iron, coal, and cottons from England, and sugar, tea, and tobacco from abroad. Her total average imports, at the official values, for the last three years of the century was £4,657,784; her exports, £4,350,640.

In spite of efforts to develop her resources, Ireland remained an agricultural country. The Irish never took to the sea. The inconsiderable coal-fields of Tyrone and Kilkenny remained almost her only minerals; nor was much use made of water-power, for the great rivers, themselves sluggish, were situated where the people were least enterprising. The large grazing areas of the south-west and west formed—next to linen—her principal wealth. She exported 260,000 hundredweight of butter and 150,000 barrels of beef. The centres of the trade were Cork, Waterford, and Limerick. Almost all of this was in the hands of Catholics, who had been stimulated into considerable commercial activity by the law which, until 1781, prevented them from investing in landed property. But this legislation had also the evil effect produced by all legislation which tends to create a money-lending class. The richer Catholic ought to have been some sort of link between the Catholic peasant

THE FALL OF PITT'S ADMINISTRATION 217

and the Protestant. But, deprived of the prospect of some day owning his little piece of land, he became a rent or tithe jobber, or a mere usurer; and he retained this character after the penal legislation had been repealed. The worst oppressors of the Catholics were Catholics. There was again an unsound element in such prosperity as the small farmers and cottiers themselves enjoyed. They had not always lived upon a single root. The crop of the earliest known potato only availed them for nine months of the year; and until two generations before 1800 the cottier had to grow a little corn to serve him for the remaining months. The introduction of the apple-potato, which kept for the whole year, had now made this unnecessary. This tempted the people to that dependence upon a single staff of existence which left them at any time exposed to such a calamity as finally burst with such terrible effect in 1846.

In 1782, England, under the stress of war, had yielded to the demand of the Irish patriot, Henry Grattan, backed by Protestant volunteers with arms in their hands, for the legislative independence of the Irish Parliament. It was the inauguration of a long period in which it has genuinely been believed in Ireland that what was refused to justice could only be extorted by violence. Yet Rockingham and Fox sanctioned the measure in the belief that it was right; and two opportunities immediately occurred under the next two administrations which showed that England was not to be compelled to yield to force what she denied to reason. Before the volunteers had been brought into action again, in 1783, after peace had been restored, Shelburne's Viceroy, Earl Temple, afterwards Marquis of Buckingham, induced the Government in London, as a matter of public faith, to fill up what was wanting in the measure of the year before; and a renunciation Bill was carried. A few months later there was another British administration, the Coalition of North and Fox, and another Viceroy. The volunteers were again in action. Their Convention sat in Dublin as a rival legislature, passed a reform bill through all its stages, and presented it to the Irish Parliament. On this occasion Fox insisted strongly and successfully upon the principle that it is an error not merely to make political concessions to men who approach Government with arms in their hands, but even to pay any attention to their petitions. The Irish Parliament refused to receive the Bill. The Convention was dissolved, and the country enjoyed some years of rest, until political agitation again started up into life under the influence of the French Revolution.

During the whole of this period Ireland continued to be governed by a Viceroy who was a nobleman of equal, or almost equal, political standing with a cabinet minister in England, and who was in close communication not only with the Home Secretary—first Dundas and afterwards Portland—but with Pitt himself. His Chief Secretary was usually an Englishman, to whom he gave one of the seats at his disposal in the Irish Parliament. Until towards the end of the century he governed with the aid of the Irish Privy Council. But there was so little agreement—even in principle—among its members, that business was delayed, and a cabinet system took its place. It consisted usually of the Lord Chancellor, the Chief Secretary, and the Attorney-General, frequently also of the Speaker of the House of Commons and the Primate. But Lord Camden when Viceroy found it a nuisance, and his successor, Lord Cornwallis, abolished it. In England the names of those who filled the high permanent posts in the offices of state are not generally remembered. But in Ireland such men were important, and the Viceroy found it necessary to depend upon them, particularly so long as his Chancellor and his Chief Secretary were Englishmen. This was invariably the case until a new departure was made in the very last appointments to those offices made in the century, those of the Earl of Clare and Viscount Castlereagh. Even then the Secretaries, Under-Secretaries, and others, who made up what was afterwards

THE FALL OF PITT'S ADMINISTRATION 219

known as "Dublin Castle" held the strings of administration. They required to be regularly consulted in any case, and a regular cabinet system had become an encumbrance.

As the Lord-Lieutenant or Viceroy was in Dublin Castle to carry out the policy of the English Cabinet, and not to enact the part of a constitutional sovereign, it was necessary for him to maintain a majority in the Irish Parliament. In the House of Lords this was easy. It had been the custom of successive Lord-Lieutenants to fill that House with their supporters, until at the close of the century it comprised 250 members, of whom 22 were spiritual peers. Very few were descended from Irish Kings, or from distinguished progenitors of any kind. There was only one duke—the Duke of Leinster. The number of barons alone created since the accession of George III was as many as 52 out of 65. The management of the House of Commons usually presented little difficulty. In one sense, indeed, it was not so corrupt as the English House. It is true that of its 300 members only 66 were representative of the 32 counties and Trinity College, Dublin, the remainder standing for 117 corporate boroughs, of which there were not a dozen free from the control of some patron or other. But a very large number were of the nature of colonies established by Stuart sovereigns, and expressly intended to be under the political control of some local landed proprietor. If they continued to be so, they merely maintained their original character. There had been no corruption. Uninhabited boroughs were only the natural consequence, for a colony could not always be a success. In this state of things the whole system of borough representation was weighted by proprietorship of this peculiar character. It furnished the enterprising Irish politician with a South Sea of adventure. Maria Edgeworth, in her novel Ormond, has given an example of a lampoon on one of these, as he was in the period immediately before the existence of Grattan's Parliament of 1782–1800.

> "At first he joined the patriot throng,
> But soon perceiving he was wrong,
> He ratted to the courtier tribe,
> Bought by a title and a bribe;
> But how that new-found friend to bind
> With any oath—of any kind,
> Disturbed the *premier's* wary mind.
> '*Upon his faith—upon his word.*'
> Oh! that, my friend, is too absurd.
> '*Upon his honour.*' Quite a jest.
> '*Upon his conscience.*' No such test.
> '*By all he has on earth.*' 'Tis gone.
> '*By all his hopes of heaven.*' They're none.
> 'How then secure him in our pay,
> He can't be trusted for a day?'
> How?—When you want the fellow's throat,
> Pay by the job—you have his vote."

In the atmosphere of somewhat frothy patriotism which existed in Grattan's Parliament these methods were tempered. The House had some title to respect, and the Government received a fair measure of support. But right up to the end it was hardly possible to take seriously an assembly which was so much a mad medley of rhetoricians and comedians, which would sit almost twice round the clock listening to an exuberance of eloquence on a single motion, which would suspend its deliberations for nearly half an hour to take its full enjoyment of one of Sir Boyle Roche's bulls, which sat in breathless and hopeful suspense while Grattan, the first man of the House, and Isaac Corrie, the Chancellor of the Exchequer, deliberately provoked one another to a duel. The employment of influence was not a regular incident of administration so far as even the House of Commons was concerned. In its saner moods Grattan's Parliament followed its patriot leader in offering little or no obstruction to the financial measures proposed by Government, and later on to the military requirements of the war, and even to laws needed to repress insurrection. But where it proved recalcitrant it was necessary to have recourse to the time-honoured inducements which had always had their

THE FALL OF PITT'S ADMINISTRATION

effect. Out of the 300 members of the House about 110 had places or pensions under the Crown, and about 30 more could be generally relied upon. In 1793 placemen and pensioners in the House of Commons divided between them about one-eighth of the whole public revenue of £1,600,000 a year. In an emergency a few more peerages could be granted in the lavish manner in which they had been distributed before as well as after 1782. But it was felt that this was not a satisfactory state of things. Besides, there had been difficulties even with this subservient parliament. In 1785 Pitt had attempted to carry through a measure of free trade between Great Britain and Ireland, but had failed because he had been unable to induce the parliaments of the two countries to agree. In 1789 the temporary madness of the King had thrown upon the parliaments of Great Britain and Ireland the duty of deciding who should be the Regent, and what should be his powers. The Dublin Parliament, having been declared legislatively independent of that in London, naturally refused to follow it, and an acute difference between the two parliaments was created, which was only terminated by George III's opportune recovery. Pitt became gradually convinced of the necessity of a parliamentary union.

A political question now came to the front which was soon found to have an important bearing on this larger problem. For many years past the policy of successive administrations in both countries had been gradually to relieve the Catholics of some of the disabilities to which they had been made subject at a period when it had been thought dangerous to give them political, and even some of the most ordinary civil, rights. In 1792 the time had arrived for considering the question of the parliamentary vote. Pitt looked upon it from three points of view. In the first place he believed in toleration and had, in 1791, removed a number of restrictions on Catholics in England. In the second place, the principles of the French Revolution, which were hostile to established order in other matters, had been bitterly so to Catholicism—the strongest conservative force in Europe. Pitt believed in enlisting that force upon his side, and it appeared even more politic to do so in Ireland, where the stronghold of sedition was not among the Catholics, but among the Presbyterians of the North. Thirdly, it would facilitate a parliamentary union. Ireland would no longer be held by a Protestant garrison. Protestant and Catholic alike having political power would both be inclined to turn to England as arbiter of their differences, and to accept union of the two parliaments as the best solution. In 1793 the Catholics were given the franchise, as well as permitted to become magistrates and to hold commissions in the Army. In the following year the Government turned its attention to the question of admitting them to parliament itself.

But it was soon found that ideas suffer a sea change when transported from one country to another. Hostile as the revolutionary spirit known as Jacobinism was to Catholicism in France, it had become an ally in Ireland. The violent faction fights which had been carried on between Presbyterians and Catholics in Ulster, and had spread to a part of the adjoining province of Leinster, had grown more intense. Both parties were disaffected towards Government. In Leinster, where Presbyterians were few and such landlords as were resident were mostly Protestant, the Catholic outrages took the form of sporadic insurrection. Such was the condition of affairs in January 1795, when a new Viceroy, Earl Fitzwilliam, landed to inaugurate a larger and more liberal policy. He pressed the measure for admitting Catholics to Parliament upon the Government in London. It could easily have been passed so far as Ireland was concerned. It appeared preposterous to have admitted the Catholic lower orders, ignorant and possibly disloyal, to the franchise, while continuing to exclude the higher orders, enlightened and almost universally loyal, from a seat in Parliament. But to carry the measure now would lay Government open to a damaging criticism. The admission of Catholics to the vote in 1793 had been granted in virtue of their loyalty. Their admission to the House in 1795 was proposed in virtue of their disloyalty. The good results expected from the earlier measure had not materialized. Meanwhile Pitt's mind, under pressure of the danger from French ideas, had been hardening against reform. And it was probable that the admission of Catholics to the Irish Parliament would have led to greater insistence in the demand which Grattan and his friends were already making. It would have become necessary either to take up a fresh position so as to resist an attack in Ireland on the subject of parliamentary reform, or to explain to the Opposition at Westminster why it could be safely granted on one side of the Irish Channel and not on the other. Fitzwilliam was, moreover, precipitate in allowing his eagerness to satisfy the Catholics to become known; and this was embarrassing to Government. At this point the King imposed his peremptory veto on any further consideration of the subject, and the Viceroy was recalled.

Earl Camden, who took his place, carried out one measure for the Catholics. He founded in 1795 a College for the education of priests at Maynooth, a town a few miles from Dublin. It took the place of those seminaries in France, where they had been educated hitherto, but which had now been closed. The new College was placed under a body of trustees, on which the Government was represented by the Chancellor and three judges, and a parliamentary grant was voted for the foundation. But Camden's main preoccupation was with endeavouring to preserve the public peace. It was not till 1798 that rebellion broke out in a definite form with rebel armies marching under regular leaders and towns under rebel administration. But for at least three years previously many parts of the country had been in a state of half-smothered insurrection. In February 1795 Fitzwilliam had written that the people were already alienated, and that if oaths and engagements entered into for the purpose of destroying the Government, and of assisting any foreign invaders, may be said to be a state of rebellion, the whole body of the lowest orders of the people had long been in rebellion.

The people of Ireland were too ignorant, and at the same time too intelligent, to be diverted from a consideration of their real grievances by agitations for a change in the political machinery. Almost every one of the evils by which they had been oppressed had been growing worse in the past few years. It is true that in 1793 cottages with only one hearth had been relieved of the hearth tax. But the tithe evil was as bad as ever. Rack-renting and oppression by middlemen were on the whole increasing. Meanwhile the cost of food was rising. Nothing better illustrates the straits to which those unfortunates were brought than the moderation of their demands, even in the extremity of disaffection. In the summer of 1795 Camden reported the existence of seditious notices threatening those who let potato grounds for more than four guineas an Irish acre—about five-thirds of an English one. At the same time a demand was made for labour to be paid at tenpence a day for one-half of the year, and a shilling for the other. The cottier was glad to obtain by means of intimidation the privilege of having to work not much more than three months of the year to pay the rent on his potato plot, let alone the grass for his cow. Men who were outside the ordinary political circles realized that the trouble was economic. The Earl of Bristol, Bishop of Londonderry, an acute observer if a disreputable ecclesiastic, wrote on the eve of the rebellion that the first cure for the troubles of the country was the substitution of land for tithe. Lieutenant-General Sir Ralph Abercromby, who was Commander-in-Chief at the same time, and had known the country twenty years before, wrote: "The disturbances which have arisen in the South are exactly similar to those

THE FALL OF PITT'S ADMINISTRATION

which have always prevailed in that part of the country, and they hold out the old grievances of tithes and oppressive rents. The country gentlemen and magistrates", he added, "do not do their duty." Brigadier-General John Knox, who owned property in the North, wrote in a similar strain. Within the regular political circles the character of the growing unrest was less clearly understood. Nor did either the Government or the reformers realize that Irishmen had long memories for injuries received and for those brief periods of supremacy which they had themselves enjoyed. Nor did they understand that, except for an intellectual handful, Irish nationalism was meaningless unless it included hatred for the English.

The British Parliament possessed some excuse for that ignorance which had been the bane of English efforts to govern Ireland. It was led astray by those very Irishmen who professed to stand for the Irish nation. So far from being too patriotic they were—in one sense—not patriotic enough. They modelled themselves on other nations. They did not suspect so much as the existence of Irish ideas. They framed false analogies between themselves and other countries. The leaders of 1782 had been misled by that of the colonies which had obtained their independence as the United States of America, and whose example Ireland had followed in demanding her legislative independence. What was peculiar to Ireland did not strike them. The Presbyterians of the North had gradually become permeated with the revolutionary spirit. It had been this sect which had sent men for many years to America; the Catholics did not emigrate. Religious differences were easy to adjust across the Atlantic, and it was supposed to follow that they must be so at home. There followed another connection with another country which was still more fatal. The Whigs of 1782 were followed by the Jacobins, who founded in 1791 the Society of United Irishmen at Belfast. In no place in Ireland had zeal for Catholic emancipation been more remarkable. In a transport of republican enthusiasm the new lights toasted the principles of the seceded colonies and of revolutionary France. Compliments exchanged between volunteers and Catholic bodies were the pledge of the fraternity which was to unite Presbyterians and Catholics for evermore. No Irishman was then able to warn Englishmen—or to warn his own countrymen—that in four years' time the strife between the two nations would have outgrown the stage of faction fights, and led to a state of almost regular warfare; or to predict the foundation of an Orange Society in which Presbyterians were gradually to range themselves against the Catholics on the side of order; or to foretell that in seven years' time the United Irishmen themselves would have goaded on the Catholics to rebel, by working upon ancient animosities and making them believe that the Protestants intended to massacre them.

The history of those years was full of surprises for those very Irishmen who were most closely in touch with the elements of disaffection. None of them could have supposed that at the end of 1796, in spite of the presence for several days of a French force in Bantry Bay, the South and West of Ireland would have remained staunch, and indeed given remarkable proofs of loyalty; or that rebellion would have broken out seriously not in the north where there had been most unrest, and where the United Irishmen were strongest, not in the west where Catholic refugees from the north had fanned the flames of discontent, not in the Catholic strongholds of the south-west, not even in the midlands where the contagion of revolutionary ideas from Dublin was most to be feared, but in the south-east—a part of the country where prosperity was much advanced, and where English was everywhere spoken. No one could have supposed that that insurrection would have been led by priests educated in the conservative seminaries of the Continent, and would have assumed most of the characteristics of a religious war. In his letter to the citizens of Dublin, written almost on the eve of the outbreak, Grattan said that it was the misfortune

THE FALL OF PITT'S ADMINISTRATION 227

of the ministry that they did not perceive that the influence of Pope, Priest, and Pretender was at an end. The easy tolerant way in which the different creeds had been existing together, characteristic of the eighteenth century, had, on the contrary, been gradually giving way to keener and more perilous attachments. Within the Catholic Church itself the Bishops had certainly lost authority. But this was a pure evil from the point of view of order. The inferior clergy was breaking away from conservative tradition. The laymen were thought to be highly influenced by Tom Paine's works, and so they were; but that influence stopped before it taught the people to throw off the authority of the priests. Multitudes did not even speak English, much less read, and the new notions permeated to them through many a devious channel. When taught to reject authority and to appeal to ideas, the authority which they rejected was that of their Government; and the first—the only—ideas to which they had recourse were those which formed part of the religion in which they had been brought up, and the vague traditions of the brief ascendancy of 1641 and 1689, the curse of Cromwell, and the spirit of vengeance. The Presbyterian, on his side, thought of the Bible, Derry, and the Boyne. The dream that the only effect of such a cataclysm as the French Revolution would be to quicken the pace of Whig rationalism was the wildest of fallacies. There was little need, indeed, to teach the Irish a contempt for order. They had plenty of examples in the wild, lawless lives of the gentry who composed the grand juries at assize and the benches of magistrates. A great many of the troubles of the country sprang from the disturbances in the Ulster county of Armagh, and the oppression of the Catholics there. At the end of 1795 Lord Gosford, the Governor, had convened a meeting of the magistrates, told them that their supineness was the talk of every corner of the kingdom, and got them to pass unanimously what amounted to a vote of censure on themselves. The evils of absenteeism and the failure of magistrates to do their duty were, however, a common subject of complaint over most of Ireland. When it became dangerous for country gentlemen to live in their homes, there was much excuse; but the evil originally sprang from inexcusable neglect of their duties. Yet in the circumstances of the time even the best magistrates could have done little without a regular police. Fitzwilliam had seen this and had outlined the plan of a disciplined constabulary. But it had gone no farther in his time. Even his idea had not included one essential point. To be useful such a force should have local knowledge without local connections. When actually adopted—in 1796—his plan took the form, in Camden's hands, of accepting the offers of the more well-to-do classes to enrol themselves as yeomanry, cavalry, and infantry. Most of them, particularly in Ulster, were violent Protestants, and tended to be swayed by local and sectarian prejudices. Outrage was repressed by outrage. There was some excuse for this in the fact that for many years unrest in Ireland took the form of the sporadic outrages of bands of desperate men who required to be hunted down. Large tracts of country were completely peaceful, peopled by a cheerful peasantry often warmly attached even to landlords of another faith. This encouraged that fatal adherence to the voluntary principle, that dislike of uniformity, characteristic of the Englishman—much more of the Irishman—of the eighteenth century. Exemplary visitations were made the inadequate substitutes of resolute moderated severity.

The rebel theory of the origin of the rebellion was an example of that veiling of a half-truth behind literal absurdity known as an Irish bull. It was said to have been caused by the cruelty of the methods employed in its suppression. "The insurrection", in the words of one of its leaders, Doctor MacNeven, "was occasioned by the house-burnings, the whippings to extort confessions, the torture of various kinds, the free quarters, and the murders committed upon the people by the magistrates and the army."

THE FALL OF PITT'S ADMINISTRATION 229

People were not murdered by the magistrates; but the other charges were justified; and he might have added that men had been illegally compelled to serve in the fleet. But it was not until after the King's troops had been repeatedly attacked by rebels that the Insurrection Act had been passed, compelling the registration of arms, and authorizing their surrender in proclaimed districts. This was early in 1796. A year of ineffectual administration by the civil authorities followed. Then came another year of military raids for arms, which were found to have been secreted by the people in enormous numbers and with baffling ingenuity, while assassinations and regular attacks upon the troops continued. The country was already in insurrection, and any severity which was not indiscriminate and which stopped short of inhumanity was justified in disarming it. Unfortunately the persistent refusals to give up weapons or to divulge anything combined with the system of assassination and outrage, which had been adopted in order to terrorize the loyal and the civil and military authorities, to exasperate the troops and some of the magistrates. They committed barbarities, which have left a lasting stain upon the British name, besides making the organized rebellion of 1798 unavoidable. When that hour came Ulster was almost everywhere quiet, and this was—it is true—partly due to that province, the one in which disaffection had originated, having been distinguished as an object of severity. But it was also due in part to the growing bitterness between Orangemen and Catholics, and in part to the growing disgust of the Presbyterians with the attitude of the French. The outbreak in the neighbourhood of Dublin took place as planned by the rebel Directory on the 23rd of May. It was easily put down. Regular rebellion was almost confined to the south-eastern county of Wexford. It began on the 26th of May, when the standard of revolt and religious war was raised by a Catholic priest, Father John Murphy. Fed on the terrible local tradition of Cromwellian severity, it continued till the recapture of Wexford on June the 21st.

So far as that war was anything more than a bitter struggle of infatuated priests and peasants for the satisfaction of the passions of fanaticism and revenge, it illustrated the essentially worthless character of the Irish Protestant gentry. Sir Jonah Barrington, a loyal member of parliament, afterwards related how, a few weeks before the outbreak, he had met several of the Protestant landowners of Wexford county at dinner. Struck by the looseness of their conversation on political subjects, he made out a list of those of the party likely to fall victims in the rebellion which seemed to be impending. He was right in every single case. He made a bargain with one of them, Captain Keugh, that the one who found himself on the victorious side would save the other from the hanging which awaited him in case of failure. "We shook hands", he added, "on the bargain, which created much merriment, and gave the whole after-talk a cheerful character." Everything turned out according to Barrington's predictions, except that when he tried to save Keugh he was too late. Within three months his friend was hanged by General Lake exactly where he had foretold— on the bridge of Wexford. Some disgust at Government for maintaining a system of influence and refusing parliamentary reform, and some feeling of reciprocal loyalty towards Catholic tenants who asked for their leadership even when engaged in a religious war, must have combined with much levity and turbulence and love of fighting for its own sake to induce these gentlemen to act as they did. A few years later Ireland had been pacified. But these passions were not even then eradicated, nor yet directed against the country's enemies. In 1808 eleven or twelve justices of Wexford county assisted at a duel which was fought between two candidates for Parliament. It was a mere election dispute. There had been no personal quarrel, and the combatants were in reality friends. They fired at one

THE FALL OF PITT'S ADMINISTRATION

another at less than ten paces, and one of them, a surviving member of one of those very families which had already suffered for bearing arms against the King, was shot through the heart. His opponent confidently surrendered himself for trial, and was acquitted by a Wexford jury.

The authority of the magistrates had been superseded by the yeomanry and militia, and these in turn by the regular forces of the Crown; and now Camden himself gave place to a soldier, Marquis Cornwallis, as the one hope of pacifying Ireland. He arrived the day before Wexford was recaptured, but he was in time to deal successfully with an ill-timed and inconsiderable French invasion, and a number of minor outbreaks. Within a fortnight of his arrival he was able to issue a proclamation of amnesty. The danger had been terrible, but the evil done had not been very serious. The loss of life was probably between 15,000 and 20,000 persons, of whom two-thirds had fallen in the field, 1,600 being King's troops; 400 loyal persons had been massacred or assassinated and 2,000 rebels hanged or exiled. Nor was the loss of property serious. For some months longer unrest continued in different parts of the country, houghing of cattle was rife in Connaught in the following spring, there was a tithe war in the south-west, and the hills of Wicklow immediately south of Dublin were given up to outlaws for some years more. It was what some thought a strange moment to add fuel to the flames by introducing a measure bound to rouse the most violent opposition and to alienate the Government's most loyal supporters.

Yet Pitt's Cabinet and the new Viceroy alike felt that the Union of the two Parliaments of Great Britain and Ireland could be no longer delayed. It was time to close the ranks in the face of a foe with whom peace seemed farther off than ever. The spirit of the time made for centralization and rejected particularism. In the face of this the existence of a separate legislature in Dublin kept alive the idea of complete separation, while the insurrection and the repeated attempts of the French to invade and conquer Ireland had brought that peril closer. No disastrous difference of opinion had emerged between the two parliaments during the last twenty years. Yet examples had not been wanting to show that differences must always exist, and at any moment the slender tie between the two countries, only maintained by means of the executive, might be severed. And what harmony there was, what smoothness in the working of administration, could only be maintained by that influence which some called by a grosser name. To keep up a majority in parliament required a perpetual tax on the public funds and on the fountain of honour. It was necessary, in Castlereagh's expressive language, "to buy out and secure to the Crown for ever the fee-simple of Irish corruption, which has so long enfeebled the powers of Government and endangered the connection". The poverty of the country was another consideration. Once Ireland was united with England, manufacturers and merchants would feel secure, and capital would cross the Irish Channel. It was in this connection that the example of Scotland in 1704 appealed to those in power. It is one of the benefits of a study of history that it enables men to correct the hasty analogies discovered by politicians; but the advantage was in this case confined to very few. Alone among the eminent British supporters of the Union with Ireland, Lansdowne expressly passed over the Union with Scotland as having no bearing on the present case. But it was impossible for others not to be influenced by the analogy of another country, which had a hundred years ago been turbulent and poor, and determined not merely to keep her own separate parliament, but to break away altogether, which had been managed into acquiescence, and where there could not now perhaps be found one thinking person who regretted that Great Britain had become one country. Finally there was the religious question. Camden had held the balance on the whole very fairly. Three months before he left Ireland he had refused to adopt a suggestion of Portland to give definite encouragement to the Orange Society. Yet it was impossible to escape the fact that Ireland was mainly ruled, as Lord Chancellor Clare was fond of reiterating, through a Protestant garrison. Moreover, the gradual removal of disability after disability from the Catholics had gone on until they stood knocking at the doors of Parliament itself for admission. To refuse was to perpetuate a grievance, to admit them was to introduce sectarian animosities within the Legislature itself. Within the wider area of an Imperial Parliament their aspirations might be satisfied without danger.

It was this last consideration which had most weight with the new Viceroy. Cornwallis was one of the justest as well as firmest of men. He had no weaknesses and no prejudices. He refused to be in the hands of the Dublin officials who claimed a right to govern the country on the plea of being the only people who knew it. On the other hand, he had no objection to natives of Ireland. He had, in fact, made an innovation in taking an Irishman, Lord Castlereagh, as his Chief Secretary; and he gave him his fullest confidence. His first business had been to restore order. But the French invaders had only just surrendered, and mischief at home was still afoot when he was looking beyond these immediate difficulties to a final pacification. "With regard to future plans", he wrote to Portland on the 16th of September, 1798, "I can only say that some mode must be adopted to soften the hatred of the Catholics to our Government. Whether this can be done by advantages held out to them from a union with Great Britain, by some provision for their clergy, or by some modification of tithe, which is the grievance of which they complain, I will not presume to determine. The first of these propositions is undoubtedly the most desirable, if the dangers with which we are surrounded will admit of our making the attempt, but the dispositions of the people at large, and especially of the North, must be previously felt." There can be no doubt that no single measure could have been more satisfactory to the Catholics than the removal of the grievances concerning tithes, while no better means of bringing government influence to bear upon them could have been conceived than to subsidize their clergy; but no doubt these measures could have been considered in a calmer atmosphere in an Imperial Parliament, where Catholics were represented by Catholics.

Cornwallis was not long in reaching the conclusion that the Union was so obviously necessary that a thinking man could hardly be an honest opponent. Before the end of the year he was writing: "That every man in this most corrupt country should consider the important question before us in no other point of view than as it may be likely to promote his own private objects of ambition or avarice, will not surprise you." He had a soldier's impatience of mixed motives. He had probably met no one in whom natural pride was wholly unalloyed with personal ambition, or in whom a distaste for British interference was not mingled with apprehension of some financial loss to himself. He was, moreover, a pessimist, and saw little except what disgusted him. At first, prospects for the Union were favourable. But he soon found that not only officials but great noblemen were averse from a measure calculated to diminish their importance. He characteristically found in this only an additional ground for perseverance. "There cannot", he wrote in the following July, "be a stronger argument for the measure than the overgrown Parliamentary power of five or six of our pampered borough-mongers, who are become most formidable to Government by their long possession of the entire patronage of the Crown in their respective districts." He was strongly of opinion that it was for the Viceroy to rule the country, and not for the Beresford or the Ponsonby or any other interest. He longed, he said, to kick those whom his public duty obliged him to court. In the face of all this opposition he failed to get the Union accepted by the Irish

THE FALL OF PITT'S ADMINISTRATION 235

House of Commons in the session of 1799. He now set himself with astonishing vigour to obtain a majority which should reverse that decision.

At first there was fear of another outbreak. Dublin in particular was greatly disturbed. Cornwallis was determined to give Parliament no excuse in the shape of a clamour out of doors. He toured the country. Cork and Belfast were won over. The Irish Government was not permitted to give any assurance to the Catholics, but the support of their spiritual and temporal leaders was obtained through confidence in the Viceroy's good intentions and the conviction that they had a better hope of obtaining their desires from a parliament sitting in London than in Dublin. Meanwhile, the reluctance of the borough patrons to part with their interests in a representation which it had been decided to reduce from three hundred to one hundred members gave scope to the abilities of the Chief Secretary. An Irishman of Presbyterian and Scottish extraction, Castlereagh had been an early Reformer. He elaborated the plan of buying up the rights of the patrons in all but the thirty-three most important boroughs. For this purpose £1,500,000 was set apart and handed over to Commissioners. These were described at the time by Barrington in a strain of Milesian exuberance as commissioners for the purpose of bribery, and the notion that the Union was carried through by a wholesale system of corruption passed into sober history. As a matter of fact the right to represent a borough was treated regularly as a species of private property on the west as on the east side of the Irish Channel. The patriotic party was no whit behind the Government in this. It is a significant fact that Grattan's dramatic return to Parliament in the heat of the discussions on the Union was due to a seat having been hastily purchased for him by some members of the Opposition. It was in the highest degree improbable that any patron would refuse to accept the compensation offered, and in the event none did, although it was indiscriminately and unconditionally tendered to supporters and opponents alike. The rate was £15,000 for each borough. Prominent among those compensated were John Foster, the former Chancellor, now Speaker, and the Honourable George Ponsonby, the men who in Grattan's absence had led the Opposition in the Lower House. Out of the £1,260,000 awarded, the largest sum received by any single individual was £52,500. This was the Marquis of Downshire, whose opposition to the Union had taken the violent form of the circulation of a paper for signature by the officers and men under him. For this he was dismissed from the command of his militia regiment and from the governorship of his county, and his name struck out of the Privy Council. But nothing of all this prevented his receiving the compensation to which he was entitled. Out of eighty-four disfranchised boroughs, only one, that of Swords, a small place near Dublin, was found to be without a patron. Even here the compensation was not withheld. The money was handed over to trustees for the benefit of the place.

The effect of these contemplated arrangements was to relieve borough patrons of any sense of grievance, while two members could be retained for each of the thirty-two counties. Dublin and Cork also each kept its two members. These sixty-eight, together with the single members for each of thirty-one remaining boroughs and for Trinity College, made up the prescribed number of one hundred members in all. The boroughs which were to send members to Westminster had been automatically selected on the basis of their hearth and window tax returns. To such a principle no objection could be made. In the event the patrons were left with only twenty-three Irish boroughs in the Imperial Parliament. The constituencies of the remaining seventy-seven members were entirely open, or became so shortly afterwards. The measure thus recommended to the House of Commons in Dublin by Castlereagh was approved in principle by 158 votes to 115, 37 out of the 64 county

THE FALL OF PITT'S ADMINISTRATION 237

members being of the minority. In the House of Lords there was no difficulty.

The majority had not been obtained without the employment of much more questionable methods than the compensation of the borough patrons. A number of places came under reduction with the Union of the two Parliaments, and for them compensation was legitimately given. The Government was pestered with claims—the most celebrated, and very probably not the least justified, being that made by the Lord-Lieutenant's rat-catcher. All this was public, but there were other objects to which English secret service money was devoted. The demands of the actual occupants of seats in parliament, as well as their patrons, had to be satisfied. A few thousands were spent in what amounted to direct bribery of members. Richard Lovell Edgeworth, that strange English figure which looms up so oddly on the Irish stage, and whose romantic attachment to principle and disdain of worldly advantage, even when it can be innocently obtained, was depicted in his daughter's novel, Patronage, stated in his place in the House that he had been offered 3,000 guineas for his seat during the few remaining weeks of that session. He spoke as a unionist, he argued for the Union; but he refused to vote for it on the ground that the measure was disapproved by five-sixths of the people of the country. The Opposition was taunted by Clare in the House of Lords with having adopted similar methods, a charge which it was impossible to refute. But the Government possessed advantages with which their adversaries were unable to compete. They could offer titles and posts and pensions. What the lofty Governor-General of India, who was at that moment consolidating his conquests in Asia, complained of to Pitt as a miserable reward for his services—a pinchbeck Irish Marquisate—this—or at least a peerage—was the common object of ambition to almost every Irish commoner who had a borough or a county interest at his disposal. The liberal bestowal of these honours, most of which had been made the subject of bargain in advance, was strenuously resisted by the King, and it was not until Cornwallis had tendered his resignation that he was able to carry his point. In the end twenty-one new Irish peers and peeresses were created. Besides, nineteen of the promotions which were made in that peerage during 1800 were more or less connected with the question of the Union. It was fair, however, that such compensation should be given to some of those whose consequence was reduced owing to the transfer of their Parliament. For the same reason five Irish peers obtained British peerages.

The remainder of the Irish House of Lords was to be represented at Westminster by twenty-eight temporal and four spiritual peers. The latter were to sit by rotation. In the case of the former, Scottish precedents were not followed. The Irish peers were to choose their own representatives for life, and not—as in Scotland—at the beginning of every parliament. The object of Government was to reduce political excitement to a minimum; and it was for this reason that it also avoided a general election. In order to interfere as little as possible with existing privileges, Irish peers were allowed (if not already representing their order in the House of Lords) to sit in the House of Commons, which Scottish peers were not permitted to do. Finally, titles in Ireland differed from those in Scotland in being entailed only upon heirs male. There was danger of the Irish peerage becoming considerably reduced if a power was not reserved to the Crown of maintaining the numbers existing at the Union by new creations. Another reason why in this case again the Scottish precedent was not followed, was that it had become customary to grant Irish peerages freely to Englishmen as well as to Irishmen, and it was very convenient that the King should retain this power.

Two important points remained. As regards finance, Ireland's contribution was for the next twenty years to stand at two-seventeenths of the joint expenditure of the

THE FALL OF PITT'S ADMINISTRATION 239

United Kingdom, after which it was to be revised upon a basis similar to that on which it had been worked out by Castlereagh. This was a comparison of a three years' average of the imports and exports of the two countries, taken along with a similar average of their consumption of certain articles. Ireland was to keep her own separate Chancellor of the Exchequer, and to arrange for the redemption of her debt as it existed at the Union. It was provided that in certain circumstances the Irish separate exchequer might be extinguished, and the finances of the two countries united. But no provision was made for the possibility of putting to an end, or reducing to smaller proportions, the separate system of administration known as Castle government, the continuance of which was bound to keep alive the idea of foreign domination.

The other matter which required regulation was trade. At the time of the Union, Great Britain was under considerable disadvantages. Ireland burdened trade between the two countries alike with an export duty and an import duty. The leather which she sent to Great Britain paid one duty on shipment as raw material, and another on its return in the shape of finished goods. She sent butter and meat to the value of over a million, linen, £2,400,000, oats, £200,000; and the only important commodities which she received in exchange were £800,000 worth of woollens, and less than £300,000 worth of iron, and the same of coal. Bounties were actually given from the British exchequer on Irish linen exported from Great Britain. On the other hand, the numerous restraints to which trade was subject were not beneficial. Property was unsafe in Ireland, capital was shy, and an Irish debenture stood at £70 in London when an English debenture, paying the same interest, was at £75. To break down these barriers and unite the resources of the two countries an arrangement was made of which the principal features were the abolition of duties wherever possible, the reduction to ten per cent. of the duties on some articles which it still seemed necessary to protect in the interests of Ireland, while those on calicoes and muslins were, as a special concession to Irish manufactures, not to be reduced until 1816. The fears afterwards expressed on behalf of Yorkshire by Fitzwilliam and Wilberforce in the two Houses of Parliament at Westminster, of the resuscitation of the dreaded Irish woollen manufacture, were brushed aside by Government.

Opposition to the Union in Ireland weakened as the measure advanced. It was easy for Castlereagh to show that, far from robbing Ireland of her independence, it raised her from a position of dependence to be a constituent part of the greatest empire in the world. On some points, however, the opponents of the Union had the best of it. They pointed, for example, to the evils of absenteeism as likely to be increased. Its supporters weakly offered some counterpoise for this in the inflow of British capital which they expected to follow. It was a pardonable error. The poverty of the resources of the country had not been sounded; nor was it yet understood how deeply ingrained in the national character were the qualities inimical to industrial improvement. But these were secondary considerations, and did not delay the passage of the bill, which became law on the first of August. It was then seen that the outside public had become almost completely reconciled. When Cornwallis communicated the royal assent not a murmur was heard in the streets. A few days later he wrote that the concourse of people as he passed on a state occasion was immense. "They all had cheerful countenances, and when I passed they cried out: 'There he is; that's he', and often added 'God bless him!'" "These are not unpleasant circumstances", he added, "to a man who has governed a country above two years by martial law." And Dublin had been the centre of opposition to the Union.

At Westminster there had been a vigorous opposition. But it was deprived of the services of Fox, who was in

THE FALL OF PITT'S ADMINISTRATION 241

temporary retirement from Parliament. In his absence the party was led by Grey, who pointed shrewdly to the evils likely to arise from combining a united parliament with a separate government and a distinct treasury. But what seemed to weigh with the Opposition most was the notion that the Irish members would follow the example of the Scottish in becoming servile adherents of the ministerial phalanx. Others, more penetrative, argued that their intrusion would change the character of the House and render it too popular and tumultuous an assembly. But there were very few to support these and similar criticisms by their votes, and the Bill of Union actually became law in England on July the 2nd, nearly a month before it did so in Ireland.

The first Parliament of the United Kingdom of Great Britain and Ireland met in January 1801 in unusually grave circumstances. The seasons of 1799 and 1800 had been bad. In the former year there had been a deficiency in the corn crop, amounting to one-third according to the estimates accepted by Government. That of the following year was computed by a special Committee of the House of Commons at a quarter in the case of wheat. The crops of barley and oats were not much below average. In February 1800 an emergency act had been passed compelling bread to be baked twenty-four hours before sale. The distilleries were prohibited from using wheat, and—later on—barley as well. Another temporary law was passed to establish a wholemeal loaf by prohibiting millers from supplying fine flour. They might only reject the broad bran weighing five or six pounds to the bushel. This became known as the Brown Bread Act. Members of the House of Lords had also, on the proposal of Doctor John Moore, the Archbishop of Canterbury, limited the consumption of wheaten bread in their families to one quarter loaf a head weekly, and discontinued pastry. This gave ten ounces a day for each individual, or 228 pounds a year, of bread, whereas in normal conditions the yearly consumption was supposed to be very nearly a whole quarter, of 480 pounds, of wheat. Riots having ensued on the failure of the harvest of 1800, the suggestions for economy were embodied in a royal proclamation. An autumn session was specially summoned to deal with the emergency. By the new year the quarter of wheat was selling at nearly £7 in London, and, though considerably less in some of the eastern counties, it was much higher in the midlands. The quartern loaf in the capital cost eighteen-pence. A calculation, interesting in itself and as an illustration of the poverty of the statistical resources then available, was made of the requirements of the country by the Commons Committee on the high price of provisions. No attempt was made to take the acreage under wheat and thus estimate the stocks of corn. There had been no census; but the population of Great Britain was computed at about ten millions. One-third was supposed not to consume wheaten bread. Allowing a quarter a head for the rest, the Committee believed themselves to be within the mark in taking the usual annual consumption at 7,000,000 quarters. From this they deducted the average importation of 125,000 quarters to obtain an average crop. But the deficiency in the 1800 harvest had been one-fourth. The produce was, therefore, roughly 5,000,000 quarters. The crop had not been good in northern Europe, and for the first time it had become necessary to depend upon other continents. 170,000 quarters of wheat had already been imported in the last three months of the year. Canada was expected to supply 30,000 and the United States the equivalent in flour of 580,000 quarters. Rice equal to 630,000 quarters of wheat was expected from South America and India. The rest it was expected to make up by the stoppage of distilleries, the use of coarse meal, and retrenchment, each of these three means of economy accounting for between 300,000 and 400,000. All this offered the prospect of a considerable margin over the 2,000,000 quarters required. Bounties were given to promote

THE FALL OF PITT'S ADMINISTRATION 243

an adequate import of corn. That on wheat ensured the importer a price of 100s. a quarter. Several methods were at the same time adopted to encourage a supply of fish. In the event it was after all northern Europe, including Holland, with which country England was at war during the whole period, which sent her most of the wheat received by her during the year ending the 30th of September, 1801. Ireland as a whole was not greatly affected by the scarcity. In Dublin, however, the distress was serious, and one of the first acts of the new United Parliament was to permit the Lord-Lieutenant to spend upon relief amounts not exceeding one-third of what was raised in voluntary subscriptions.

The other difficulties which the new Parliament would have to meet were occasioned by the serious state of foreign affairs. The war had now dragged on for eight years. It was impossible for France to do England much injury without command of the seas. It was impossible for England to do real harm to France without a good army with a sensible objective. Pitt's military administration was lamentable, and presents an excellent example of the fatal results of neglecting the most important of all strategic principles—that it is impossible to be too strong at the decisive point. The defect was observed by the King, whose strong common sense often gave him a glimpse of what much cleverer eyes had overlooked. He told Pitt as early as the eighth month of the war: "The misfortune of our situation is that we have too many objects to attend to, and our force consequently must be too small at each place." This was, in fact, the fault of almost every one of the numerous expeditionary forces sent out from Great Britain. There was no lack of good material and no lack of good generals—Stuart, Abercromby, Moore, Moira, and others, but they were almost wasted. England had no confidence in herself as a military power. In this state of distrust Pitt attempted to keep the war on the Continent going by subsidies to powers large and small, on which £8,195,940 was spent up to 1800.

It was one of the many Whig legends cleverly invented to vilify him that the system of continental alliances and subsidies was his special scheme. It would have been more correct to say that this was the Whig method of making war, and one to which Pitt, had he been a Tory, might have bitterly objected, as Tories in the past had done. But it remained true that the policy was a failure, because the expenditure was uncontrolled. With the power of the purse behind him, Pitt was in a position to maintain upon the Continent some British military adviser, or some diplomatist not wholly ignorant of the art of war, who might have offered authoritative advice upon all strategic questions with a single eye to the successful prosecution of the war—such a part as was afterwards happily played by Castlereagh in 1814. Had this been done the gallant Russian veteran Suvarov need not have died broken-hearted in 1800.

It was the misfortune of Great Britain to be opposed to an enemy now commanded by a man already proving himself the greatest genius in strategy whom the world has ever seen, while over against him was a continent mainly ruled by women and lunatics. Napoleon Bonaparte was now thirty-one years of age. It was one year since he had obtained for himself the position of First Consul, in name the head of a triumvirate, in fact the autocrat of France. He was fortunate in the heads of the states against which he was opposed. Towards the close of the eighteenth century the government of most of the principal countries in Europe had fallen at one time or another into the hands of women, either ruling in their own right or directing the wills of their weaker consorts. Among the former had been the great Catherine of Russia and Maria I, Queen of Portugal. Of the latter were the daughters of Maria Theresa, the great Austrian Empress—the ill-fated Marie Antoinette of France and Maria Carolina of the kingdom of the Two Sicilies, who still lived to bring misfortune upon herself, her family, and her country. Her husband Ferdinand IV, a Bourbon

THE FALL OF PITT'S ADMINISTRATION 245

and brother of King Charles of Spain, counted for very little in the corrupt court at Naples. The King of Spain was likewise in the hands of his Queen, Maria Luisa, herself a puppet of her paramour, the execrated Godoy. Another woman who put her husband in the shade was the noble and beautiful Luise, honoured and beloved by friends and foes alike, who shines in those tempestuous times like a star in dirty weather. She was consort of King Frederick William III of Prussia. The kings were, in several instances, worse than feeble-witted. Paul I, the son of Catherine and now Czar of Russia, Gustavus Adolphus of Sweden, and Christian VII of Denmark, were all, in some degree, insane. The last was completely so, and the country was ruled by Prince Frederic as Regent. The Sovereign of Portugal was both a woman and insane. Here, too, the government was in the hands of a Prince Regent—Don John. George III of Great Britain was the one sovereign who possessed vigour and clearness of head, although this, the sole constitutional monarchy in Europe, was the one in which those qualities were least needed in a hereditary ruler. But the dark shadow of insanity had twice fallen even upon him, and was to do so again in the year 1801, thenceforth obscuring the direction of the helm of the State by its abiding menace.

One country remained of which none of these things could be said—Austria. Its ruler, Francis II, was neither half-witted nor given up to female influence. But he was unfortunate in his advisers, and the Aulic Council which directed the operations of war from Vienna became proverbial for incompetence. Francis was the last of the Holy Roman Emperors, and as such possessed a shadowy authority over the mass of kingdoms, electorates, grand duchies, prince-bishoprics, and other petty states and free cities which made up Germany. But they were not even bound to follow him in peace and in war; and the Emperor was soon to yield up at the demand of France the few vestiges which remained of his ancient power and dignity.

In the last month of the century the Austrian defeat at Hohenlinden brought to an end the Second Coalition of European Powers against France. England now faced the victor of Europe alone. But worse remained behind. It was due to the confused plans of his allies rather than to the weakness of his own arms that the Czar of Russia had not succeeded in humbling France. Exasperated at finding himself on the losing side, Paul's distempered brain conceived a violent admiration for Bonaparte, who flattered him in return and concerted plans with him for the conquest of India, the inevitable goal of Russian ambition. He quarrelled with England, and made one of those right-about-turns so frequently made by Russian sovereigns in the wars of the time, and which were always accompanied by expressions of the loftiest idealism. Sweden and Denmark had claimed as a right that their merchantmen should be immune from search by British men-of-war, when accompanied by men-of-war under their own flag whose captains guaranteed that they had nothing liable to confiscation on board. But as Great Britain disagreed with them as to what goods were liable to capture, and had never recognized such a right, the claim had recently led to unfortunate collisions. Paul took advantage of this to renew the Armed Neutrality formed by his mother in 1780. Russia, Sweden, Denmark, and Prussia laid down as principles of natural equity five articles of international law which England had never recognized. Among them were the exemption of vessels under convoy, and the celebrated claim that enemy goods might pass in neutral vessels with the exception of contraband of war. All these the four nations bound themselves to maintain by force.

The right time in which to introduce a new code of maritime law was one of peace, and not an hour when one of two belligerents had just been completely victorious on land, and the other felt that its only hope lay in foregoing none of the advantages given to it by the command of the sea.

THE FALL OF PITT'S ADMINISTRATION 247

The Armed Neutrality was aimed directly at Great Britain, and inspired by Bonaparte, who looked forward to seeing these advocates of neutral rights converted into belligerents, ranging eighty sail of the line against her war fleet, and closing the whole coast of Europe down to the central Mediterranean against her mercantile marine. The character of peaceful protest soon dropped from the engagements into which the Northern Powers had entered. Already Paul had, with great injustice, not merely laid an embargo on British ships in Russian ports, but marched the crews off as prisoners into the interior, where they were almost starved. In January 1801 Great Britain replied with an embargo both on Russian ships and on Swedish and Danish ships as well, and moreover took the harsh step of ordering the temporary seizure of Swedish and Danish possessions in the West Indies. War had not been declared, and the embargo was justified as an act of just and necessary precaution. A similar precautionary measure was taken two months later by the King of Prussia, who, as charged with the duty of securing the neutrality of the various states in Northern Germany, was in the congenial position of being able to make war without being at war. He did more than join with the Danes in closing the mouths of the Ems, the Weser, and the Elbe, through which Great Britain's exports reached Central Europe—a trade which had trebled in the eight years of the war. He occupied Hanover with his army till long after the general peace, and made that country pay for the troops' support. When Parliament actually met, on the 22nd of January, the clouds were only gathering; yet the defiant manner in which the menaces of the Northern Powers were being faced made the event certain. The best, the strongest, and one of the most truly peace-loving ministries which England had ever known was to close its career without an active ally in Europe, and exposed to the hostility of every naval power worth the name.

The King, as usual, opened the session of Parliament

in person with a speech composed by his ministers, outlining the policy of Government. Reference was made to that happy Union which had just been consummated, as well as to the prevailing distress caused by high prices. As regards the war, it was, as usual, composed in the language of unshaken confidence. There was no hint that King George III was unwilling to face about to those enemies who had risen in the north, with the same resolution with which he had for years fronted France and Spain. In the House of Lords the debate on the Address of Thanks to the Crown turned largely on the military failures of Government. In the House of Commons the Address was moved and seconded by supporters of the Ministers in the usual way. Then rose Charles Grey, one whose position and the counsel which he offered might have recalled that Spirit whom Milton described as rising second in the synod of gods meeting after disaster. He appeared more graceful and humane than his allies, the gross Fox, the red-nosed Sheridan, the keen-faced, puny Erskine. A fairer person lost not the heaven of office. His whole bearing, with that thoroughbred air which Byron admired, suggested courage and dignity. Born in 1764, he was the son of a distinguished general, of a hard northern family. A general and two admirals were afterwards to be numbered among his sons. As often happened in those days, he had entered Parliament at an age at which half a century later a youth would still have been at college, but he had already not only been to Eton and Cambridge, but had spent nearly three years on the grand tour of Europe. Like his rivals he had instantly been hailed as a leader. He had the long nose and eagle eye, united with the lofty action, which marked other notable patricians of his day. His lips denoted passion—that passion which is expressed in his every limb and lineament in the great picture by George Hayter of Queen Caroline's Trial in the House of Lords twenty years later. But it was a passion now never violent and usually under control. Such was the man. He

THE FALL OF PITT'S ADMINISTRATION 249

stood up now to utter language of surrender. Russia, he allowed, was in the wrong. She had acted with unjustifiable violence. But had Malta, which had been taken from the French, not been retained in British possession, she would never have gone to such lengths. Then, as to Denmark and Sweden, why should we enforce our rights? We had not done so in 1780. But the national honour is involved. Be it so; we had failed to vindicate it in the case of Holland. Even now we feared to do so against Prussia. "Why, but because Prussia is strong and Denmark and Sweden are weak? . . . Behold how sacred the honour of the nation is in the hands of ministers! See them haughty to the little, and submissive to the mighty." Once there was a confederacy of all Europe against France. That failed. Now there is a confederacy of all Europe against us. We refused to treat for peace a year ago when we had Austria as our ally. Now that we were ready to treat we had none. Where was the military force raised four years ago for the public defence? Dissipated and destroyed in disgraceful expeditions. "Part have been wasted in the fatal descent upon Holland; part have mouldered away in the holds of transports; and the rest, after being driven about from Portsmouth to Belleisle, from Belleisle to Ferrol, from Ferrol to Cadiz, are, last of all, to perish in the burning sands of Egypt." There was, however, still hope if members of the House would but vote in public against ministers whom they cannot but censure in private; and he ended by moving one of the lengthy amendments usual at that day, the purport of which was that His Majesty's advisers ought to be changed.

The Minister against whom all this attack was mainly directed rose at once. He made what an Opposition speaker who followed called a splendid speech, but it was no occasion for one of Pitt's really great speeches. In a few words on the great and honourable efforts of the last nine years he brought the House back to its accustomed level. He then devoted himself to showing with overwhelming force how clearly his country was in the right on the question of the Northern Powers, as to which Grey had weakly doubted. He pointed out that she could now enforce her rights, and need not shrink from doing so, as in 1780 when French and Spanish ships rode supreme in the Channel. One characteristic episode occurred when Sheridan entered the House with the tedious Doctor Lawrence, usually an independent member. It was one of those interruptions which Pitt well knew how to turn to advantage. "I suppose I shall be answered by and by", he observed in one of his lofty asides, "as I see there is an accession of new members to the confederacy who will, I have no doubt, add to the severity and the length of the contest"; a hint that he placed additions to the ranks of his country's enemies in Europe and accessions to the thin ranks upon the Opposition benches in Parliament on the same level. Other speakers followed: but the best speech of the day was that of the Solicitor-General, Sir William Grant, who eloquently contrasted the mock lamentations of gentlemen whose fears for their country had never robbed them of their sleep or of their enjoyments, with the sober fortitude of the lower orders of the community. While Fox and Grey were enjoying the happiest times of their lives at Saint Anne's Hill or Howick, while parties of patrician malignants regaled themselves at Woburn or Holkham, only relieved by an occasional trip to Westminster to utter a parliamentary jeremiad, humbler persons had been stinting themselves to give their mites towards the patriotic contribution of voluntary gifts to the exchequer, or equipping themselves at their own charges for national defence. And with wheat bounding up to 160s. a quarter the comparative quietness of the people was in itself a high merit. The Opposition counted 63 votes against 245. But the day after the division in which the Government had presented so firm a front to its critics Pitt resigned, the longest administration of English history came to an end, and Ireland was the cause of its fall.

THE FALL OF PITT'S ADMINISTRATION 251

The Irish Catholics had supported Cornwallis in the previous year only in the confident hope that they would themselves obtain seats in the united Parliament which they were helping to bring into existence. They understood that he was himself in their favour, and that he anticipated no insuperable difficulty in satisfying them. This was all. There was no pledge, no bargain. But Cornwallis and Castlereagh recognized none the less the strong claim which the Catholics had; and on the first of January, 1801, when the new flags were hoisted and the guns fired in Dublin Castle, the latter wrote a long letter pressing the subject upon Pitt.

But that cause was already as good as lost. Six years before, when the same proposal was made by Fitzwilliam, the King had been given the opportunity of putting his views before the Cabinet. He did so in a paper drawn up with considerable ability, which he sent through Pitt before the subject was discussed. On this occasion he described the grant of the concessions proposed as "beyond the decision of any Cabinet of Ministers". He gained his point. There was very little hope indeed of changing views so strong, and so successfully maintained on the previous occasion. But the attempt was to be made. The principal struggle was expected to be over the Test Act, which excluded Catholics from Parliament as well as from many offices in Great Britain which they had been able to hold in Ireland since 1793.

The scheme which Pitt presented to his colleagues was comprehensive. The new test was to be political, not religious. It would enforce a pledge to be faithful to the constitution upon most classes of persons in a position to influence the opinions of others, whatever might be their religion. All members of Parliament, persons holding state or corporation offices, ministers of religion and teachers, were to take an oath of fidelity and allegiance to Church and State. This was to be accompanied by measures for regulating tithes, improving church discipline, and increasing the income of ministers whose poverty made them unable to reside in their parishes. There was to be some provision for the Catholic and dissenting clergy. It was a plan worthy of great statesmen like Pitt and Lord Grenville, who had probably an equal share in it from the first. But when put formally before the Cabinet on the 30th of September, 1800, Loughborough, the Chancellor, opposed it. If the King's objections were to be surmounted, there was no time to be lost. But Pitt delayed. Already, in 1795, the King had been furnished with a written legal opinion to the effect that the royal assent to the repeal of the Test Act would be a violation of the coronation oath. Loughborough exhausted himself in efforts to defeat the plan, in which he was seconded by Lord Clare who seems to have supplied the King with another memorandum. The Primates of England and Ireland were alarmed. Four more cabinet ministers were brought round to the Chancellor's side.

Pitt had postponed finally closing with the King upon the subject until he could bring him a definite scheme, supported by a united Cabinet. It was George himself who brought matters to a head. He spoke to Dundas at the levee on the 28th of January, and sent a message to Pitt through Henry Addington, the Speaker. This brought, three days later, a letter from the Minister outlining the whole scheme. He admitted that it had only reached the stage of being in accordance with what appeared to be the prevailing sentiments of the majority of the Cabinet, yet tendered his resignation if he should not be allowed to go on with it. He does not seem now to have hoped to shake the King. The chance of opening upon him with the whole weight of a united Cabinet behind him was gone. George sent his reply the very next day. He had no great respect for lawyers and did not borrow any of the materials with which his Chancellors had supplied him. His argument was a very simple one. He was bound by the coronation oath to maintain the constitution. A part of that constitution was the

THE FALL OF PITT'S ADMINISTRATION 253

Established Church. Those who hold employments in the State must therefore be members of it, and evince the fact by receiving the Holy Communion according to its rites. This view had not, however, prevented George from acceding eight years before to the proposal that Catholics should be eligible for employment in the Irish Army.

The case was not, in point of fact, one of conscience merely. The King laid stress on his oath because he felt this to be the strongest line to take. He soon worked himself into a dangerous state of excitement. His equerry, General Garth, afterwards described to Addington how he had had it read out to him about this time, and had burst out passionately: "Where is that power on earth to absolve me from the due observance of every sentence of that oath, particularly the one requiring me to maintain the protestant reformed religion? Was not my family seated on the throne for that express purpose? And shall I be the first to suffer it to be undermined, perhaps overturned? No; I had rather beg my bread from door to door throughout Europe than consent to any such measure." Two years earlier Dundas had, in this same connection, attempted to argue with him that the coronation oath bound him only in his executive capacity. "None of your Scotch metaphysics, Mr. Dundas!" was the reply which he received. It was George's cunning means of avoiding a discussion with a person with whom he disagreed. Even in the letter to Pitt just mentioned, although, from the same motive, he laid principal stress upon what he called a sense of religious duty, he did not omit to refer to political considerations; and when he wrote of the unchangeable opinions of forty years, he was thinking of policy and not of the meaning of his oath. When he could open his mind to a more sympathetic listener he showed this more clearly. On the 18th of February he saw the Duke of Portland. He told him he was himself an old Whig; and he considered those statesmen who made barrier-treaties and conducted the ten last years of the Succession War the ablest the country ever had. He considered, in fact, that he had a special duty, not so much by the terms of an oath as by the fact of the Hanoverian succession, to resist anything which might possibly lead to Catholic ascendancy. He had his place in the constitution, and the Parliament had theirs; but he would not have admitted that he ought to have deferred to the opinion of the House of Commons because it represented the people. Generations which have listened to opposition speakers rising at the opening sessions of successive reformed parliaments to explain, with a wealth of statistical detail, that the House of Commons then sitting was not representative of its constituencies, can hardly blame George III for thinking the same in the days of rotten boroughs and close corporations. He remembered that a former ministry had given him a fall on this very subject. In 1778 a measure of toleration to Catholics had been passed, which led to the terrible Gordon riots; and in that welter of incendiarism the King's Ministers were helpless, and it was the King himself whose resolution and courage put an end to the trouble. He was, no doubt, thinking of this occasion when he composed the paper of 1795. He feared, he then wrote, that religion was but little attended to by persons of rank, and went on to suggest that it was easy enough for those who were indifferent to talk about toleration, but that the bulk of the people felt otherwise. A religious man himself, there was no doubt that he understood the deeply felt Protestantism of the country. There was no doubt that in resisting his Ministers this time he had the nation with him.

There was another thing which hardened the King in his resistance. It would not be quite true to say that he was tired of Pitt. He did not wish to lose him as First Minister. He did not wish, even after his resignation, to lose him from his councils. But he was certainly tired of Pitt's ascendancy. He was inclined to set up against it a sort of court cabinet of his own intimates, among whom Loughborough was from time to time a moving spirit. They recalled to him the familiar counsel, "George, be King," which he had heard from his mother when first brought to the throne forty years before. It was the secret influence of an invisible power which at that time had driven Pitt's great father from the royal councils. But it was better than to remain with hands tied. The son understood the danger. It was Pitt who more than any other man established the principle that the First Minister was to be the First Minister in reality—that there should be no separate repository of His Majesty's political confidences. From this constitutional point of view the last sentence of his letter of the 31st of January is the most important of the whole:

"He has only to entreat your Majesty's pardon for troubling you on one other point, and taking the liberty of most respectfully, but explicitly, submitting to your Majesty the indispensable necessity of effectually discountenancing, in the whole of the interval, all attempts to make use of your Majesty's name, or to influence the opinion of any individual, or descriptions of men, on any part of this subject." He did not consider the King's answer satisfactory on this point either, as his final letter of resignation of the 3rd of February showed; and he afterwards told Canning that he had gone out, not merely upon the Catholic question, but upon the manner in which he had been opposed. He was consistent. It was upon this principle that, all the time that he was out of office, he refused every opportunity of seeing the King except upon the most formal occasions. He pressed this particular matter to the point of resignation because he refused to have the duty and privilege of being the King's principal adviser filched from him by a subterraneous cabal. And there can be no doubt that he was unconsciously influenced, like most ministers after many years of office, by a desire for rest.

Thus the country lost what was perhaps the most statesmanlike series of measures ever proposed for it. There was a close connection between them all, but the removal of the

Catholic disabilities was, in particular, an almost inseparable condition of the Union itself. A genuine grievance was allowed to remain, and the disturbances arising from it might have been met with less odium by measures approved in a local parliament. Moreover, the best time for religious reconciliation was passing by. Presbyterians had not been backward in hostility to Government, and were still almost as desirous as the Catholics themselves of seeing the claims of their fellow-countrymen met. But with the removal of the Irish Parliament most of the direct influence of Government, of high rank, of education—all making for tolerance—was to be reduced or withdrawn, and a Protestantism, sometimes savage in its puritanical fervour, left exposed to a Catholicism excluded from representation in the councils by which the nation was governed. Even the arrangements for improving the condition of the lower Catholic clergy, which might, as Grenville had hoped, have been taken up separately, were dropped; and all that remained to connect this influential body with the State was the grant of a few thousands to Maynooth College.

The King lost no time in forming an administration. He sent for Addington. The choice was a very natural one. As Speaker, Addington had been in close relations with the King, and they thought alike on the Catholic question. He agreed with Pitt as well as his Sovereign on every other. He was supposed to be an able man, and had been upon the whole a successful Speaker. Nor does this imply that he was a dumb member of the House except as regards his official duties. He had made, for example, a most important suggestion on one occasion when the House was in committee, and he was able, in consequence, to address it from the gallery; it led to the celebrated voluntary Patriotic Contribution to the cost of the war. His father had been the old Lord Chatham's physician, and the sons had known one another from boyhood. Addington was, in fact, almost Pitt's greatest friend. The retiring Minister was no great judge of

THE FALL OF PITT'S ADMINISTRATION

men, and had an opinion of his friend's abilities which few shared, and in which he was very soon to find himself woefully mistaken. Four seasons earlier he had patriotically planned the retirement of his ministry as an obstacle to peace with France in favour of a new one of which Addington was to have been the head. The projected arrangement must have been known to many, and have given colour to the infamous suggestion that a similar reason, although with a discreditable distinction, held now—that the Minister had found that he could make war no longer, and could make no peace with credit, and had invented a mean pretext for abandoning the helm of the State. Addington at once referred the King's offer to Pitt, who strongly advised him to accept the responsibility, and promised him his support. He could hardly have done otherwise. But from this time onwards, not through his own fault, he was led from one false position to another. His giving the new Government his support meant one of two things. Either he was regarded as responsible for measures which he knew nothing about until they were adopted; or he was shown some papers and asked to advise, although it was impossible to do so with justice to himself without being in the regular current of affairs. But this difficulty was to appear later. For the present he encouraged those of his colleagues who did not agree with him about the Catholics to remain. The result was expected to be the old Cabinet deprived of its best men, who would go with Pitt. This gave Sheridan a fine opportunity. "When the crew of a vessel was preparing for action", he said in parliament on the 16th of February, "it was usual to clear the decks by throwing overboard the lumber; but he never heard of such a manœuvre as that of throwing their great guns overboard." And he concluded with a withering reference to "this empty skull, this skeleton administration". In answering him Pitt was obliged, out of regard alike to his Sovereign and to his friend and successor, to observe a certain reticence, and could never do justice to the motives which had led to his resignation. Then the King went out of his mind, as he had twice before—partly in 1765 and completely in 1788. The malady commenced with a feverish cold, and was intensified by the political crisis, particularly in its religious aspect. On the 18th of February he was talking to Portland in a strangely loud tone of voice, on the 21st he had been put under restraint, and Addington, who was admitted, found that his mind was wandering, though for a day or two longer he was able to sign papers which required no detailed explanation. He then grew violent and became incapable of any business. The disease was not mental only. On the 2nd of March his life was thought to be in danger; but on that night he fell into a deep sleep and from the next day steadily mended. The familiar mode of talking—the "what? what? what?" which was regarded in his case as a sign of sanity—had returned. Four days later he sent messages to some of those most closely connected with him. That to Pitt ran: "Tell him I am now quite well —quite recovered from my illness; but what has not he to answer for who is the cause of my being ill at all?" Pitt, whose feelings were warm, and who had now realized the hopelessness of endeavouring to overcome the royal resistance on this subject, assured His Majesty in reply that he would not bring forward the Catholic question again during his reign. He has been rightly blamed for so completely binding himself. But the loss to the nation from the King's inability to perform his duties was generally regarded as extremely serious—even by Fox himself. "To keep his health safe is the cause of the country", wrote Abbot; and the feeling extended to foreign courts. Nicholas Vansittart, who was shortly afterwards sent on a mission to Copenhagen, found there that the news of his illness had greatly increased the influence of the French.

During the interval the prospect of a Regency, as well as discussions in Parliament and elsewhere, had thrown into high relief the incapacity of Addington for framing a

THE FALL OF PITT'S ADMINISTRATION 259

respectable administration. Some of Pitt's friends now pressed him to remain in office. He was willing to do so. He was still Minister. But Addington had been replaced as Speaker by Sir John Mitford, the Attorney-General. In these circumstances it was unfair to ask him to give up what he had been very eager for, and had resigned the Speakership in order to obtain. Pitt refused to do this, but some of his friends did on his behalf. He thus became exposed to the unfair charge of countenancing a discreditable intrigue. In any case, his willingness to remain, had Addington been able to see his way voluntarily to relinquish his claim of the Premiership, totally does away with the absurd charge afterwards made that he abandoned office in order not to have to end a discreditable war by a discreditable peace. One of the qualities most admired in Pitt by Wilberforce, who was not blind and who knew him as well as anyone, was his strict regard for truth. If others had recognized this, they might have spared themselves many weary wanderings in the mazes of error. But those responsible for contemporary political speculations are invariably credulous—credulous of every underground intrigue and disingenuous artifice attributed to those in high places.

On the 14th of March Pitt ceased to be Minister. But he had already introduced the budget for the year. Exclusive of the charges defrayed from the Consolidated Fund he had to find £42,197,000, of which £31,702,000 was shared almost equally between the Navy and the Army, and £1,938,000 was for ordnance. The rest was mainly made up of last year's deficit. He estimated as the Ways and Means of raising £16,744,000 within the year, £4,000,000 from customs and excise, £4,260,000 from income tax, £3,300,000 as surplus of the Consolidated Fund, and £4,324,000 to be provided from Ireland, besides minor items. He had, further, to raise a loan of £25,500,000. New taxes were imposed for the interest and sinking fund of the loan, amounting, as estimated, to £1,794,000. They included increased taxation of paper and horses. This last measure of the great finance minister was a triumph; it passed completely without opposition. The first budget for Ireland was introduced into the United Parliament a fortnight later by Corrie, the Irish Chancellor of the Exchequer. It provided for £7,000,000, out of which over £4,700,000 was the imperial contribution, and the remainder for purely Irish services. That country's principal source of revenue was customs, two and a half millions; she had a balance of almost that amount in hand, and he proposed to borrow a third two and a half millions. This also passed without difficulty. Another urgent measure was the repeal of the Brown Bread Act. This law had led to so much adulteration that it was thought necessary to obtain the King's signature on the 24th of February, when only his physicians could see him.

For his new Cabinet Addington was unable to count upon Dundas; nor on the Grenvilles or the old Whigs of the Portland group—Spencer and Windham—who soon went into violent opposition, not, however, over Addington's illiberalism regarding Ireland, but over his feebleness in foreign affairs. The old Duke himself became after a short interval President of the Council. As the member of the Cabinet responsible for Irish policy he should naturally have been among those who retired. But he never had strong opinions, and he was at this time too much embarrassed financially to be ready to resign office. The seals of the Foreign Office were entrusted to Hawkesbury. A solemn though a good speaker, he had always been something of a butt in the circle of Canning's friends. He was disrespectfully known by such refinements on his family name as Hawkinson and Jenky. "But only think of Jenky as Secretary of State!" wrote Lady Malmesbury to a friend. "I cannot endure that, nor will you, I think, easily." She was right. In charge of foreign affairs he proved unbusinesslike, unable to acquire the confidence and respect of foreign diplomats, and destitute of the art of pressing the demands of his government in the proper way

THE FALL OF PITT'S ADMINISTRATION

and at the proper time. Lady Hester Stanhope in her old age told how he used to come with bulging breeches pockets which he used to ram his hands into in search of some paper or another, just as if he were groping for an eel at the bottom of a pond.

Canning himself, Pitt's favourite disciple, followed him into retirement against his own wish, as did others of the junior men. Earl Hardwicke and Charles Abbot replaced Cornwallis and Castlereagh as Lord-Lieutenant and Chief Secretary for Ireland. Although possibly no one had had more connection than the last with the question upon which the late Ministry had resigned, it did not prevent him from becoming in the following year President of the Board of Control for the affairs of India with a seat in the Cabinet and Addington's best debater in the House of Commons.

The Navy presented a special difficulty. The post of First Lord of the Admiralty has often been supposed to be one easy to fill; not because the Navy is unimportant, but because it is so efficient and so loyal that the gentleman responsible for its affairs in the Cabinet and Parliament has an easy task. This was not the opinion of that day. After much consideration it was decided to offer the post to the distinguished Commander-in-Chief of the Channel Fleet, the Earl of St. Vincent. He accepted it with hesitation. Naval officers had usually failed as First Lords. He himself was to prove no exception to the rule.

George III settled the Lord Chancellorship himself. He knew Lord Loughborough. He had made use of him, but he had no intention of allowing him to profit by his opposition to Pitt. He chose the new Chancellor, as he had done his new Chancellor of the Exchequer (an office combined with the premiership when the latter was held by a member of the House of Commons); they were his men, and he was fond afterwards of writing of both of them in such terms as "His excellent Chancellor". His selection fell upon the Lord Chief Justice, Lord Eldon, Pitt's Attorney-General at the time of the political prosecutions, and one of the highest Tories who have ever existed. Born in 1651 the son of a Newcastle coal-factor, he had made the best possible use of a university education—early concluded, for he was a fellow of his college at sixteen—to rise by exemplary industry to the head of his profession. He was an able judge; but dilatory through excessive conscientiousness. In the Pindaric Poems, a typical specimen of Whig pleasantry of some years later, he was thus contrasted with Sir Edward Law, the new Attorney-General, who had come to be Chief Justice as Lord Ellenborough when the poem was written:—

> "First there's that *precious quiz* OLD B——GS,
> Who doubts and dreads and frets and fags;
> Then there's the judge, so fond of swearing,
> Who flouts and fumes beyond all bearing."

But slow as Eldon might have been on the bench, he was very different in the palace. A few years later, when George III had reached a stage at which, without requiring to be put under control, his strange behaviour was a cause of constant anxiety, he was thought to be the only person, certainly the only public man, who had any power over him. He could always decide there. His kindly and humorous nature endeared him to many besides his sovereign.

His predecessor gradually faded out of public life. He dangled round the Cabinet, going to one or two meetings uninvited. Then he dangled round the Court, partly consoled by promotion in the peerage to the title of Earl of Rosslyn. In 1805 he passed out of life altogether. The King asked whether he was really dead. On being reassured, he observed: "Then he has not left a greater knave behind him in my dominions."

The new administration certainly had modesty to its credit. The general impression which Ministers had of themselves was perhaps best expressed at the time by Vansittart, himself a new Secretary to the Treasury. Abbot records him as having been so little elevated with his new

THE FALL OF PITT'S ADMINISTRATION 263

honours as to have said—so early as the 9th of February —that he would go to Botany Bay willingly to bring the last ministers back.

The Cabinet as finally completed in July consisted of six peers and three commoners, and of these last all except Addington were the eldest sons of earls, so great was the reliance placed on the solid qualities of the aristocracy. Henry Addington was First Lord of the Treasury and Chancellor of the Exchequer; Lord Eldon Lord Chancellor; the Duke of Portland Lord President of the Council; the Earl of Westmorland Lord Privy Seal; Belham, Hawkesbury, and Hobart, of whom the first two were lords by courtesy only, Secretaries of State for the Home Department, the Foreign Department, and that of War and the Colonies respectively; Earl St. Vincent, First Lord of the Admiralty; and the Earl of Chatham, Master-General of the Ordnance.

No Irish official had a seat in the Cabinet, though both Pelham and Hobart had been Chief Secretaries to the Lord-Lieutenant. The most outstanding minister outside the Cabinet in the House of Commons was the Secretary at War, the Honourable Charles Yorke, Lord Hardwicke's brother. He was afterwards raised to the Cabinet as a Secretary of State. Even with the addition of Spencer Perceval, another earl's son, and a future Prime Minister, as Solicitor-General, the debating power of the Government in the Lower House could not be strong. But Addington trusted in Pitt and in patronage, and seems to have been sure of the House of Commons. It was the House of Lords in which he felt weakest, and his two commoner Secretaries of State found their way prematurely to the benches which would in course of time have become theirs by inheritance. Such were the lights set to guide England to victory now that France had at last arrayed all the sea powers of Europe against her.

CHAPTER IV

NORTH AMERICA—THE WEST INDIES—THE NAVY—THE ARMY—ADDINGTON'S ADMINISTRATION TILL THE CLOSE OF THE WAR

(MARCH—OCTOBER 1801)

AFTER the new Government had been established, an opportunity was given for debates in both Houses of Parliament upon opposition motions for a Committee on the State of the Nation. It might have been supposed that at a time when the price of corn had risen to the highest point ever known, and when, as Fox said in the course of debate, one-sixth of all the souls in England were supported by charity, including poor-law relief, the internal condition of the country would have formed the principal topic. But this was far from being the case. The Opposition did not possess an economist, and social distress was much too nearly allied to political economy, which was Fox's aversion, to be used by him except for the purpose of a passing rhetorical flourish. The debate in the Lower House on the 26th of March centred upon the change of ministry, the Catholic question, the conduct of the war, and the points at issue with the Northern Powers. It gave an opportunity for one of the last great argumentative duels between the two chiefs. In this Fox clearly had the better, disclosing a rich vein of scorn more characteristic of his adversary than of himself. Pitt had been conciliatory—almost genial. The opinion which had been expressed by Grey, the mover, of the poor qualities of His Majesty's present advisers gave him an opportunity of combining a high appreciation of Fox with a good-natured gibe at his abstentions. Pitt urged that the new Foreign Secretary, Hawkesbury, was as good as anyone that the Opposition could produce, "except one hon. gentleman"—so the official report runs—"whose attendance was of late so rare that he might almost be considered as a new member—whose

ADDINGTON'S ADMINISTRATION IN WAR 265

transcendent talents, indeed, made him an exception to almost any rule in everything that required uncommon powers." This was no random compliment, but a singularly well-judged appraisement of the most peculiar of the many peculiar gifts of Fox, that of making it seem perfectly reasonable that he should be a law to himself. He then went on to give a simple answer to the question why the Ministry had resigned. They were unable to bring in a measure for the relief of the Catholics, which they regarded as essential. Finally, he dealt in detail with the claim of the Northern Powers. He concluded in memorable words: "Whatever shape it assumes, it is a violation of public faith, it is a violation of the rights of England, and imperiously calls upon Englishmen to resist it even to the last shilling and the last drop of blood, rather than tamely submit to degrading concession, or meanly yield the rights of the country to shameful usurpation."

Pitt had spoken of a league to force upon Europe a new code of maritime law as acting upon a Jacobin principle. Fox quickly fastened upon this: "The right honourable gentleman's indiscriminate cry of Jacobin! Jacobin! to every thing and person that he dislikes, has brought utter contempt upon his continual cant." One asserter of this neutral claim, he scornfully added, had been "that implacable zealot in Jacobinical faith", Catherine the Great of Russia. Fox has usually been regarded as the greatest master of debate who ever spoke in that House, and his powers seldom showed better than on this occasion. Too well versed in foreign affairs to be able to argue that the British standpoint was wrong, he succeeded, by grasping tenaciously at every unwary illustration or allusion of his opponents, in making it appear that the Ministry had been ridiculous in insisting on it. After this it was an easy task to attack the genuine weak points of the late Secretary for War. Dundas had attempted to show that the expedition sent into the Mediterranean in the preceding year had been well thought out, and had failed only owing to accidents which could not have been foreseen. This was a fine opportunity for contempt. " 'But had the right honourable gentleman's expedition been able to sail sooner'—'If the battle of Marengo had not been lost'—'But!'—'If!' . . . I defy imbecility itself to string together a more motley pack of excuses than the right hon. gentleman has laid before the House this night." And he introduced a satirical summary of Dundas's speech. Returning to Pitt, he discussed the resignation and the Catholic claims, and argued with great force that it was a breach of duty on his part to commit himself to satisfying them, before he had made himself acquainted with his sovereign's opinion on the matter. Here Fox undoubtedly put his finger on a point which, tied as his adversary was by the impossibility of discussing the views of his colleagues and his and their communications with the King, was unanswerable. Touching on the constitutional point, he unreservedly admitted the Sovereign's right to place a veto in advance on legislation contemplated by his Ministers. In fact, he charged Pitt with "gross irreverence to the King". To the end of his speech he maintained a fine attitude of contempt, and left upon the House an impression that it owed him something for leaving his wiser retirement to tell the late Government, or its fatuous successors, what he thought of them. No wonder after such a speech that such a man as Addington offered an apology for even uttering the few words with which he attempted to obtain a confidence which he never could win—except numerically. When the division was called, as many as 105 voted against the Government's 291 ; some strong followers of Pitt having already refused to support the new Ministry. A similar tendency was seen in the Upper House.

Meanwhile the Government had to meet the difficulties of the internal situation of the kingdom without any assistance from parliamentary discussions. Remarkably little attention was paid in the debates of March to an evil which all the expedients of the previous year had only been able to palliate. The quartern loaf had risen in London to one shilling and ninepence in January, and though it had been kept from exceeding that price by the operation of the Brown Bread Act and such measures, it did not begin to fall till May. A large number of monopolists had been prosecuted in the previous year. This action was extremely popular out of doors. But no one dared to outrage the principles of Adam Smith by suggesting approval in parliament, and the Government had put a stop to the prosecutions. The people were driven to take the law into their own hands; and it was characteristic of the time that, although the authorities scrupled to interfere with free trade themselves, they did not stand in the way of the same thing being done by a free people. The traditions of disorder were strongest in the south-west of England. Thomas Poole, an acute local observer, told Coleridge in April that the whole people had risen from Land's End to Bridgwater; and the miners in the neighbourhood of Bristol were all up in arms. They had succeeded, he added, in doing what the Government ought to have done itself. They had brought down the loaf from 1s. 9d. to 10d., and enforced similar restrictions in the prices of dairy produce, bacon, and shambles meat. The mob even took it upon themselves in Totnes to fix the price of corn, for wheat at 10s. 6d. and 12s. a bushel, for barley at 5s. 3d. and 6s. The efforts of the Mayor and the local magistracy were paralysed. But in a few weeks the trouble passed by. Wheat came in from Prussia and Germany and flour from the United States. Imports were adequate, and the prospects of the year's harvest good. Indeed, it was found that some farmers, in their anxiety to make the best use of the emergency, had overreached themselves. Wheat, which had almost touched 19s. a bushel in April, fell by 2s. 6d. in the following month, and fell rapidly a few weeks later. The most important measure taken by Ministers, in addition to those already initiated by their predecessors, was the offer of premiums to the amount of £30,000 for the growth of potatoes. Ten pounds was to be given for each acre newly broken up for the purpose which should produce 200 bushels, and special rewards for the encouragement of potato-growing on small plots by cottages.

The prevailing scarcity was, as usual, turned to purpose by political agitators. Horsley, Bishop of Rochester, called the attention of his diocese to the opening of seditious Sunday schools. Sir Robert Peel had a letter from his partner in Lancashire to the effect that the country was ripe for rebellion. A Committee of the House of Commons found acute distress to exist in the manufacturing centres; and in Birmingham and in Yorkshire in particular the numbers upon poor relief rose to an alarming extent. Combinations among factory workers upon a large scale first began to be noticed in the autumn of 1800. Discontent showed itself in the most extravagant forms. There appeared in Yorkshire, one of the homes of religious eccentricity, a society known by the name of the New Jerusalemites, which upon the faith of pretended prophecies looked instantly for the coming of the millennium. Another millennium of a different character was promised by the Spensonians, who advocated a re-division of the land. Spence, the founder of this association of reformers, was thought by many to be insane. But this did not prevent his being fined fifty pounds and sentenced to twelve months' rigorous imprisonment for his book, Restorer of Society, as a seditious libel. All these elements of unrest together afforded sufficient reason for the re-enacting of the Habeas Corpus Suspension Act and the Seditious Meetings Act, both of which had been permitted to expire. But the general good sense of the people, and the usually firm handling of the situation by the magistracy throughout the country, prevented more serious developments.

In Ireland both these elements of stability were wanting. Trade depression and poor crops, though neither so grave

ADDINGTON'S ADMINISTRATION IN WAR 269

as in England, had had the effect of reviving in some degree the fires which had been smothered two years before. The popular method of dealing with monopolists was characterized by the greater directness and severity of such movements usual where the sister island is concerned. From one county it was reported that it was still the practice for bands of a couple of hundred armed and mounted men to descend upon the villages and flog the venders of provisions into a humane consideration for the purses of the public. The same parliamentary committee reproduced one of the earliest examples of that sinister growth of an anarchical authority established in defiance of the State with which later Irish history has been so familiar. A man named Price had taken a farm against the will of a popular self-constituted rent court. He received the following intimation:

LIBERTY HALL.

"Take notice that you have been tried and convicted of having taken —— farm—you have been sentenced to death—you are to give up the farm, otherwise the warrant for your execution is in the hands of the executioner. Given at the council chamber."

Price was impenitent. The council was as good as its word. He was shot in the open fields at noon. The murderer was allowed to depart at leisure, and none of those who were at work in the neighbourhood made any attempt to arrest him. In the face of occurrences like this it was thought necessary to continue the Irish Martial Law Act. At the same time very little use was made on either side of the Irish Channel of the severe powers which had been placed in the hands of the authorities. Those people who were not philosophers had grown tired of abstract rights. In Ireland Hardwicke conciliated all classes. The hospitalities of the Viceregal Court were renewed at the Castle, and after a time a new Dublin was in existence—no unworthy successor of the old splendid dissipated capital of the days of the separate Parliament. The Chief Secretary, Abbot, set to work on his part to clear the air of some of the fumes of corruption which had settled so thickly over the Castle in the last few years. As prices fell, discontent in Ireland subsided, while in England it disappeared altogether. It was well, for the war taxed to the full such powers as the Ministry possessed.

As carried on under Pitt, the struggle had been largely one for possessions in the New World. In this he had followed the precedent of the last three wars with France. But by this time the situation in North America had become established. Canada was irredeemably British. As a measure of security, possession was at once taken for the period of the war of the small islands of Saint-Pierre and Miquelon, off Newfoundland, which were all that remained to France of her North American colonies, (with the exception of her fishing rights on the coast of the main island;) and these were regularly lost to her in war and renewed in time of peace. The British colony itself had at this time a population of about 20,000. It lay outside the regular Canadian system, and had not as yet been granted the usual colonial constitution of a nominated Executive and Legislative Council with an elected Assembly. The home country supplied Newfoundland with a Governor, usually some resolute sailor, and with the thousand pounds or so necessary for the administration.

Westward, but on the south side of the Gulf of Saint Lawrence, lay the four maritime provinces of Canada—Nova Scotia, New Brunswick, Prince Edward Island, and Cape Breton Island. They first became important in 1783 when thousands of United Empire Loyalists, many of them men of high position in the seceded colonies, were cast out from the States, and threw themselves upon those inhospitable shores. Nova Scotia was the first of these. In Halifax it possessed one of the finest harbours in the world, and here the North American squadron had its headquarters. The "Blue Noses", as the people of Nova Scotia—which, as the name suggested, was predominantly Scottish—were called,

ADDINGTON'S ADMINISTRATION IN WAR 271

already amounted to 60,000 in 1800. That Province and Prince Edward Island, which had 9,000, were already established, but the other two provinces only received their first constitutions according to the usual colonial model in 1784. New Brunswick grew very rapidly and had over 30,000 inhabitants by the end of the century, but Cape Breton Island had hardly 2,000, and could not long retain a separate government from Nova Scotia. In all these provinces with one exception the rule was that the occupier of the land was its owner. But the two thousand acres of Prince Edward Island had a generation earlier been distributed by lottery in a single day to a handful of proprietors. This ill-considered act gave rise to a century of agitation.

Canada proper consisted of two main divisions. Lower Canada had been separated from Upper Canada by a line drawn westward up the river Ottawa from a point not far from its confluence with the river Saint Lawrence to a point almost due south of the head of what was then called Hudson's Bay. From here the border ran due north as far as the territories granted to the Hudson's Bay Company, and was prolonged to the Bay itself. Southward and westward of this line was Upper Canada. Towards its other extremity the line crossed the Saint Lawrence, and then ran eastward again along the north-eastern border of the United States until it separated the Lower Province from New Brunswick. This tract was settled by immigrants from the south towards the end of the eighteenth century. On the north bank of the Saint Lawrence lay Quebec, the capital of the Lower Province, and the port of Canada, and, nearly 200 miles higher up, the growing commercial centre of Montreal. Here also dwelt the French settlers, the most conservative and perhaps the most valuable and the most loyal element in the British colonial empire. In 1800 the Lieutenant-Governor of Lower Canada, Robert Milnes, estimated the whole population at 160,000, nine-tenths of whom lived in the 123 parishes outside the towns, occupying each its frontage of about three leagues along the river bank. Nearly everyone of these was French. The British were almost confined to the towns and can scarcely have numbered more than 20,000.

Generations before Wolfe's victory had given Canada to England, an offshoot of old feudal France had been planted here, and the change of rule had made little difference. A Canadian gentry of Seigniors still existed. Yet the trifling rent and the feudal dues which they were permitted to claim were not enough to enable them to maintain that position; they were without enterprise or influence; and they were being rapidly merged in the rest of the population. This consisted of the farmers or habitants. They were not as a people averse from adventure. It was these who furnished the intrepid boatmen who navigated the rapids of the Saint Lawrence, and the boats on the Great Lakes and rivers were known by their French name. In some parts the Frenchman in Canada showed his national gift of making himself at home with men of another colour and degree of civilization by intermarrying freely with the Red Indian, to whom he bore no slight resemblance with his sallow face and slim figure, encased in the long-skirted coat tied at the waist with a worsted sash adorned with beads, moccasins below, the red nightcap above, and in his mouth the everlasting pipe. But, generally speaking, New France exhibited in even greater measure another characteristic of the mother country—love of home. There was no need to travel. The habitants made everything which they required in those wooden huts stretched in long lines with strips of cultivated land spreading down from them to the river which formed the parishes of Lower Canada. There were no banks; money was hoarded; manuring the soil was only beginning to be known. They married early, had large families, and subdivided their land. Education scarcely existed; even members of the Assembly were sometimes unable to read and write. But there was much gaiety and real happiness, and few people can have enjoyed such freedom from war's alarms and the distresses of industrial vicissitude. In every parish one figure was supreme—that of the priest. He deserved to be so. There was not a more exemplary parochial clergy in the world. They usually exercised their influence in favour of Government. They might well do so. In no country in modern times has the Roman Church obtained such undisputed power and wealth as in French Canada and Ireland under the tolerant sway of the British Government.

A sharp contrast was furnished by Upper Canada with its population of 60,000 spread for some hundreds of miles along the Saint Lawrence and the Great Lakes. The colony was not twenty years old. Its nucleus was made up of soldiers who had fought in the American war, of whom rather more than a hundred of the officers in the settlement were still alive, and of other United Empire loyalists from the United States. In the last decade of the century they were joined by other refugees from the south, some of them men flying from their debts or their crimes, some of a very different stamp—Quakers from Pennsylvania, and the descendants of German Anabaptists—all who wished to escape the cramping political atmosphere of the Eastern States. Whatever their preference may have been for the Stars and Stripes, the fear of Red Indians if they moved westward, and the attractive offer of lands close to the lakes and waterways of Upper Canada, turned the scale. Some immigrants came from the Scottish Highlands, gradually increasing in number with the increase in the sheep-runs which dispossessed them. There was one notable example of an Irish colonel who had been attached to a Lieutenant-Governor and afterwards founded the settlement called by his name on the shore of Lake Erie—"the once gay Tom Talbot", as he called himself. "Could I but be seen", he wrote, "by some of my St. James' friends when I come back to my frugal supper, as black as any chimney-sweep, they would exclaim, What a damned blockhead you have been, Tom, but no, as I actually eat my homely fare with more zest than I ever did the best dinners in London." But the genuine backwoodsman spirit was rare in the colonist from England. If he came, it was to trade. There was a storekeeper aristocracy in the towns—Toronto, at this time called York, the capital, and Kingston. Little less ignorant than the French Canadians, the people of Upper Canada were more restless and more unscrupulous.

The two provinces had been divided in 1791 as the best means of satisfying without danger the claim made by the English colonists to some form of constitutional government. Difficulties over communications, and, still more, difficulties over uniting into one assembly the representatives of rival nations, opposed the establishment of a single legislature. Lower Canada was given, besides its Governor or Lieutenant-Governor with his Executive Council, a Legislative Council of 15, nominated for life, and an Assembly, elected upon a popular franchise every four years, consisting of 50. There was no French press. Few of the habitants understood or cared for democratic institutions. So little confidence had they in themselves that they elected 16 Englishmen to the first Assembly, whereas they might if they had chosen have returned a Frenchman for nearly every seat. A few only of the high Offices of State and of the seats in the Executive and Legislative Council were French. There were in this condition of things the elements of acute discord between the Assembly and the other Estates. Milnes looked to a characteristic Englishman's cure for a difficulty which Englishmen had themselves created. Influence was to be brought to bear upon the voters through their parish priests and the captains of militia. Some success was obtained in winning the support of the former, as the British Government was regarded as a bulwark against atheism; and the Catholic Bishop of Quebec was especially well disposed. The latter were already the regular though informal instruments of government policy in the parishes. Meanwhile the Governor found one curious source of satisfaction. "It is considered by the well-wishers of Government", he wrote, "as a fortunate circumstance that the Revenue is not equal to the Expenditure." It was taken for granted that the military expenses of the two Canadas, amounting to about £260,000 a year, should be defrayed by the mother country. But she had also to supply an annual deficiency of about £12,000 in the ordinary civil expenditure of Lower Canada, which amounted to £25,200. In these circumstances the apprehensions that the Government might have to depend on the will of a popular assembly were remote.

The difficulties which beset the ruler sent out from England were not over supplies but of a totally different character. He had ten million acres of land to dispose of, and the members of his Executive Council interested themselves in the matter. Undeveloped land had come to be worth fifteenpence an acre, which it was the policy to grant in plots of 1,200 acres to genuine settlers of the Protestant religion. But most of the members were interested in monopolies. The dispute between General Prescott, Governor-General of all the six provinces as well as Governor of Lower Canada, and his Council on the subject of the land grants became so serious that he was recalled in 1799, and was replaced by Milnes as Lieutenant-Governor. But he remained Governor —one of the numerous band of colonial officials residing in London—until 1807, and continued to draw his allowance of £2,000 a year. The quarrel was an obscure one, and it was impossible to decide whether Prescott's opponents were actually corrupt. But the general character of public men in Lower Canada was beyond dispute. When Prescott's recall was known, addresses of regret poured in. The members of Council were in general men of much the same type as Alexander Davidson, who had been one in 1784 and was sentenced in 1808 to a long term of imprisonment for a big fraud on Government; or Thomas Dunn, Acting Governor in 1807, whose anxiety for the interests of his stepson and neglect of those of the State received very contemptuous treatment from Castlereagh as Colonial Secretary in 1807.

Upper Canada had, as was natural, a much smaller Legislative Council and Assembly. The numbers were 16 and 7. She had her Lieutenant-Governor and Executive Council, her Chief Justice and Judges who held assizes, her Sheriffs and Grand and Petty Juries on the English model. Indeed, the lawyers, as is often the case in a new country where education is not widely diffused, rather overweighted the political machine. High judicial personages were apt to descend from the Bench to place themselves at the head of the Opposition, as was also the case in Lower Canada. Here, too, the Government enjoyed the advantage of a deficit treasury. Beyond Lake Superior lay wild territory, the hunting-ground of Indians and of the North-West Company of fur-traders, a recent rival to the Hudson's Bay Company in the north. Here Alexander Mackenzie had penetrated in 1789 down the great river which afterwards bore his name northward to the Frozen Sea. Four years later he was the first European to cross the Rockies and so reach the Pacific. But he had had no followers.

The principal preoccupation of both Governments was, however, with the southern border. No ruler in those days could feel perfectly safe. Yet it is significant of the loyalty of the French Canadians that when a seditious conspiracy was discovered in Montreal it was found to be the work of a parcel of Americans, and that the only man executed for treason at this time bore the name of David McLane. The danger came from the United States. In 1797 a vessel from Ostend, with 20,000 stand of arms besides artillery on board, had been captured by the British. It was given out by their owner that they were intended for the militia of Vermont State. But there was no doubt that he had intended to use them for a filibustering invasion of Canada from that part of the United States. It would have been no trifling matter. In 1798 the two Provinces had little more than 2,000 regular troops besides 400 French Canadian volunteers in Lower Canada, and 600 irregular troops in Upper Canada. The militia in the Lower Province alone counted nearly 38,000. But the number armed and trained was not more than a few hundred. Even Quebec and Montreal were not in a state of defence.

The official attitude of the United States was correct enough. Under George Washington's Presidency a treaty had been concluded in 1794 with Great Britain which settled the more serious questions then outstanding between the two countries. Unfriendly as the third President, Thomas Jefferson, who had been elected in 1800, was known to be, there was as yet no fear of the relations between the two countries becoming seriously disturbed. Meanwhile, Great Britain held firmly to Canada as a part of the Empire. There was little of that constant intercourse between the home country and her that there was with the West Indies. A country whose export trade with Great Britain was carried, even in 1802, a year of peace, in 211 vessels of 36,000 tons, had hardly yet begun to be regarded even as a possible source of wealth. But there was no idea of casting her adrift.

Another ancient British colony, the tempest-tossed Bermudas, enjoyed a compensation in being unvexed by the storms of war. Hardly another spot on the globe was so removed from any other land, the nearest point on the coast of the United States being nearly six hundred miles distant. The islands, reputed to be in number as the days of the year, covered, with their cedar-woods, their tiny houses, gardens, and piggeries, an area of about 12,000 acres, and supported a population of nearly one soul for every acre. About half were slaves. The chief articles of trade were at this time ducks and onions; but ship-building and—in war-time—privateering were their most remunerative means of support. Early in the war a naval dockyard was recommended; but it was not until 1810 that it was actually commenced.

There was a Governor, Council and Assembly, and the institutions brought out from the old country included a Court of Chancery, which mixed itself up in political squabbles.

Lying like a long, broken reef which stretched from Florida in North America to the mouths of the Orinoco in South America, the West Indian islands were first reached by ships sailing from Europe before the east trade winds near their southern extremity. Here was the first group into which the West Indies were divided—the Windward Islands. But before reaching them a call was made at Barbados, the metropolis or mother country of the other colonies. From its original settlement in 1626–7 it had always been English, and strong enough, too, to send out men to conquer and occupy other islands. In a climate mild for that part of the world, Englishmen were able to labour with their hands in the fields. There were about 16,000 white men and 60,000 coloured, the latter almost all slaves, on an area of 166 square miles. Sugar, mainly to Great Britain, and rum, mainly to the United States, were the principal exports. South of it, and divided only by narrow channels from the mainland of South America, lay the great sugar island of Trinidad, of 1,754 square miles, lately wrested from Spain, and now being harshly but ably governed by Brigadier-General Picton. Between it and Barbados was the smaller island of Tobago, with 115 square miles, which would have been more prosperous had it changed masters less frequently. Ceded to France at the last peace, it had been reconquered by England in 1793.

The Windward Islands, immediately west of Barbados, formed the next group of rather more than five hundred square miles. The three main islands, Saint Lucia, Saint Vincent, and Grenada, had experienced vicissitudes somewhat similar to those of Tobago. But by the end of the century Great Britain had re-established her authority in the last two islands, and taken Saint Lucia from the French. Here

John Moore had been Governor. The place was notoriously unhealthy. Even that man of iron, who was equal to walking thirty miles in a day under a tropical sun, succumbed to the climate at last, while in one of the regiments under his command, which had been 776 strong in May 1796, only fifteen were returned as fit for duty in November. Each island supported 1,500 to 2,000 white men with perhaps ten slaves for every man, besides a few hundred free coloured people and aboriginal Caribs.

North-west of these lay the Leeward Islands, the British portion of which amounted to over seven hundred square miles. Several of these islands were alternately French and English according to the fortunes of war, and had a partly French and partly English population. The largest of all, Dominica, lying as it did between the French islands of Guadeloupe and Martinique, was especially liable to attack. The population of the British Leeward Islands was between ten and twelve thousand whites, with the usual proportion of slaves.

Farther to the north-west again, reaching up to the coast of Florida, stretched the Bahamas, which, with Turks Island, formed a gigantic archipelago with an area of over 4,600 square miles. But they were very thinly inhabited—hardly more than a couple of thousand whites and as many blacks, and the former were strange fellows, the descendants of lawless buccaneers tempered by a recent admixture of loyalists, who had come over after the American War of Independence. Within the belt were the great islands of Cuba and San Domingo, both of them centres of unrest, and the smaller island of Porto Rico. They were mainly Spanish. Full of restrictions as the British colonial policy of that day was, it was liberality itself compared with that of Spain. So tempting were the chances of making money by a contraband traffic that the Spanish merchantman naturally turned to smuggling, and from this to privateering and piracy were but steps. It exceeded the power of Old Spain to prevent the enormous indented coast of such a possession as Cuba from becoming a network of the haunts of sea-robbers; and, indeed, the task would have been beyond the scope of any European government of that day. The island was almost equally troublesome as a neighbour whether Great Britain was at war with France, as now, or at peace. The greater part of San Domingo had been French, the rest Spanish. But the gospel of the Rights of Man had been preached somewhat too liberally, the emancipated slaves had risen upon and massacred their former masters, and the colony was lost to France.

Covered from the north by these mighty and turbulent neighbours lay the greatest British West Indian colony, Jamaica, with upwards of 4,000 square miles and a population of 30,000 whites, 300,000 slaves, and 12,000 free coloured people. It had been Spanish once, and right up almost to the close of the eighteenth century it had been distracted by wars with the Maroons, the descendants of Spanish slaves, who had fled into the mountains of the interior. Conveniently near the Spanish Main, it had, like the Bahamas, become the home of buccaneers. But it was that of peaceful, comfortable planters as well, who grew their cane and their cotton in its quiet valleys where English church bells pealed and counties called by the English names of Cornwall, Middlesex, and Surrey reminded them of the old country. Like the Bermudas, and the other British West Indian Islands or groups of islands, it enjoyed an English legal and administrative system. There was a Governor, a nominated Council of twelve, and an elected Assembly of 43. The Council had a threefold function—that of a privy council of advisers to the Governor in executive matters, a high court of appeal, and a second legislative chamber. The Governor was his own Lord Chancellor. Many of his hours were spent in the Court of Chancery.

The time of the Revolutionary and Napoleonic Wars was the heyday of West Indian prosperity, and Jamaica was the centre of it all. In 1800 it sent Great Britain, besides its ginger and the spice known as pimento, two-thirds of the sugar, rum, and coffee sent by the whole of the British West Indian Islands. Coffee made marvellous progress during the two wars. It was all that sugar could do to hold its own, but this it did for a considerable time after 1799, when it was reinforced by the introduction of the Bourbon cane. It was, indeed, a feverish, unreal, unstable prosperity. Some of the great sugar-planters could have taken their places without shame among the wealthiest Europeans. But there were clouds on the horizon. A hurricane like that of 1780 might blot their plantations and factories out of existence. Fires and earthquakes ranked as minor calamities. The islands of Trinidad, Tobago, Martinique, Saint Lucia, and Curaçao, and, on the mainland, Essequibo, Demerara, Berbice, and Surinam, had been captured from the Spanish, French, and Dutch. New fields were opened to British enterprise and there was a glut of sugar in the European markets. The Gazette price, which had been as high as 66s. 8d. a cwt. in 1798, had dropped by 1800 to 54s., exclusive of the 20s. duty, and was falling still more. The planter of the interior and even the merchant at Kingston existed under the constant apprehension of a slave rising. They were on the watch for omens. A saucy grin from a passing negro would send a chill into their marrows. On the other hand, the agitation for the abolition of the slave trade threatened their well-being. This was more particularly the complaint of the newer acquisitions such as Trinidad, where the conversion of the virgin forests into cane-fields took a heavy toll of the negroes occupied in the deadly work. Even in the old-established islands yellow fever claimed its victims. Hardly anybody endeavoured to escape. In 1801 nearly 2,500, or about a quarter, of the whole British force in the West Indies perished of disease, including 104 officers. Nobody was attacked at 3,000 feet above sea-level. But no one thought of avoiding this by cantoning any of the troops among the beautiful hills with which Jamaica and most of the greater islands were covered. Death might come in a moment in other forms besides that of yellow fever—the bite of a snake or even a venomous spider. At first these things were regarded with terror, but they soon grew common. The fever itself got its familiar name of yellow jack. Soldiers and other visitors soon looked upon the world with the same eyes as the Creoles or West Indian born. By them death was accounted nothing of. When men died no bell tolled; there was very little ceremony. To make a joke about the passing of a man who had been an hourly companion not many days before was a common thing. The roystering West Indian of that day determined, if he could not hope to reach middle age, that his short life should be a merry one. The wife of the Lieutenant-Governor of Jamaica, Major-General George Nugent, recorded in her diary the most astonishing descriptions of the enormous repasts of which she was expected to partake, and how sick the very sight of them made her feel. She complained that the men of the country ate like cormorants and drank like porpoises. Such a reckless way of living certainly brought the end of life nearer, but at any rate those who adopted it did not die before death came. The West Indian spirit was the same in business. Plunging speculation, boundless profusion, reckless waste of life were the order of the day. The West Indian frequently made large fortunes, but he borrowed vastly to enable himself to do so; and in unlucky years his losses were so immense that a careful contemporary observer, Sir William Young, calculated that the landowner did not receive upon the whole more than four per cent. on the money which he had laid out. His financial prospects were like his country, where there was much storm and much sunshine, and yet, as Mrs. Nugent noted after being two years there, only very rarely a whole day overclouded. Through all this two imperturbable figures serenely held the even tenor of their way. One was the careful Scot who came out as apprentice to an estate or counting-house, outlived with his strong stomach and stronger head a generation of less prudent revellers, and retired eventually as the shadow lengthened on life's dial to a snug villa on the banks of the Clyde. Of such was Michael Scott, author of Tom Cringle's Log, most romantic of novels as well as most faithful of pictures of those wild days. The other figure was that of the Jew—unerring sign that money was to be made and that there were imprudent people about. There were enough of the race in Spanish Town, Jamaica, to make a company which outdid the rest of the militia in absurdity, and furnished matter for unextinguishable laughter to the negro onlookers.

The total exports to all places of the British West Indian Islands amounted in 1800 to two and a half million hundred-weight of sugar, six and a quarter million gallons of rum, and ten and a half million pounds of cotton. Rum was exchanged with the United States for flour, rice, and lumber. These imports were absolutely necessary; and although the Government in England pursued on the whole a liberal policy, yet some uncertainty was introduced into the prospects of trade, and even of the very subsistence of the negro population, by the existence of the Navigation Act. It was only by Orders in Council, proclamations, and licences that the trade between the States and the West Indies was from time to time enabled to be carried in vessels belonging to the former country; and without them it could not go on. There was also a system of Free Ports comprising all the principal ports in the colonies. These were allowed to receive raw materials from any part of America in one-decked American vessels.

The prosperity of the West Indies was based upon coloured labour. It was not that it was impossible for white men to work with their hands. Leaving on one side the cases of Barbados and the Bahamas where some did so, and where there was much less than the usual proportion of one white to ten black men, even in Jamaica the European overseer, who followed the slaves about with his whip in all weathers, had almost as hard a life as the slaves themselves. He would have sworn that he could not have done their work, but it was more matter of custom than anything else. The listless lady who rang for a maid to pick up her handkerchief could dance all night and night after night. Men-of-war manned entirely by British were not lost owing to the enfeeblement of their crews in a tropical climate. Negroes were necessary because they provided an abundant supply of cheap labour, quickly acclimatized and subject to less wastage from disease than that of Europeans would have been. The British West Indies alone absorbed between fifteen and sixteen thousand slaves from West Africa yearly. Apart from the kidnapping and other outrages which attended the original seizure of the negroes, the ghastly nature of the trade is evinced by the fact that, even after the capacity of the slave-ships had been strictly regulated, the loss of life in the passage across was reckoned at above five per cent. When they arrived in the West Indies they suffered further loss in the process of acclimatization. They were then generally well treated. They had their own villages on the plantations, their gardens, and their own accumulations of pigs and poultry, furniture and money. Their Sundays were their own, devoted to marketing and merry-making. But they had no security against ill-treatment. The overseer might legally punish them with thirty-nine stripes for each offence, and if he exceeded the law he was protected by the infamous provision that a slave's evidence could not be received against a white man. The courts themselves could inflict death, dismemberment, and repeated floggings for such offences as striking a white person or being in possession of stolen goods; and mutilations actually were inflicted as late as 1783. The argument that men who owned human beings would take as much care of them as of their cattle did not hold so long as the slave trade lasted. Each estate, it is true, had its hospital. But the natural replacement of the black population by births was hindered by the insufficient importation of females, by the polygamous propensities of the white men, and by want of care for the mothers and infants. No one took long views in the West Indies. The price of a slave rose steadily, until at the end of the century it was over £70. The total slave population of the British West Indian Islands, exclusive of conquests made during the war, was about 500,000, against a white population of perhaps 55,000. The free coloured people, a class constantly increasing owing to manumission of slaves and concubinage with Europeans, numbered about 18,000.

Saving the temporary acquisitions from the Dutch of Surinam, and those settlements to the west of it which afterwards formed as British Guiana a permanent member of the Empire, Great Britain had no regular possessions on the mainland. But an informal colony had grown up in that part of Central America which looks eastward on to the Caribbean Sea. This was British Honduras, where settlers were permitted to cut logwood and mahogany under a treaty with Spain. They elected their own magistrates; and a Superintendent of the settlement was appointed from Jamaica. Force of circumstances was gradually depriving the Spanish power of the shadowy rights which yet remained to it under the Treaty of 1783.

There was a great deal in the state of the fighting services which demanded the closest attention of the new Government. It is not easy to realize that the spirit of the British Navy can have been so bad as it undoubtedly was, in several important respects, towards the end of the first phase of the war with France. Eight glorious years had passed, and the victories which the fleet had won under Howe, Jervis, Duncan, and Nelson, in a period which had been one almost unbroken success in every action great or small, should, it might have been supposed, have welded the whole service into what Nelson claimed that he and his captains at the Nile were—a Band of Brothers. True, there had been the mutinies at Spithead and the Nore; but the grievances of the men had been met, and the eruption should have purged the whole body of its distemper. The officers, at all events, should have learnt the need of standing together. Yet this was not the case. The chronicles of those years are full of courts-martial arising from the most dishonourable causes, such as violent quarrels between officers, disgraceful charges brought by juniors against their seniors—sometimes even men of the highest rank—and, in one case at least, of an officer who deliberately incited the men to insubordination. The new First Lord of the Admiralty, John Jervis, who had won the title of St. Vincent by his victory over the Spanish fleet in 1797, was even more remarkable for the vigorous steps which he subsequently took to maintain discipline in the Mediterranean Fleet, which he then commanded. A significant indication of laxity among officers in the Channel Fleet occurred in 1799. He had just been appointed to that command. At a dinner at which his predecessor, Lord Bridport, was present, the toast, "May the discipline of the Mediterranean never be introduced into the Channel Fleet," was actually suffered to be drunk. It was in reality not unnatural for such effects to be produced by a system which also produced acts of courage and endurance hardly paralleled in any other age or country. Whether the fool of the family or not, the boy who entered the Navy was almost sure to be distinguished for wildness and indiscipline. When on board ship he found himself among the roughest men living under the roughest conditions. He was formally addressed as a young gentleman, and treated as such—in the rugged naval way. But this was all. Even when he rose to be midshipman he had no commission. He might be given corporal punishment, or, if the captain wished, turned before the mast as a common seaman. Except in the few ships which carried schoolmasters, he received little encouragement to any form of study, even professional. He was cooped up for years together with men and boys like himself in the narrowest surroundings. The variety and distraction which officers could not get otherwise they were obliged to seek from one another. They had to find something to laugh at. They developed the oddities which fill the pages of Captain Marryat's and Michael Scott's novels. The light-heartedness for which the sailor has ever been famous was balanced by a dangerous tendency to grumble. The long war and the exhausting duties of blockading squadrons had severely tried both officers and men. Nelson regarded the average life of a seaman as finished from old age at forty-five. Much the same can be said of the officers who were young men at the beginning of the war, and served through it. Three years after the outbreak at the Nore it was the self-indulgence and the licentious insubordination of the officers which was to blame for the occasional recrudescence of mutiny, which ended on more than one occasion in men rising on their officers and carrying their ships into the enemy's ports. Such was the opinion of St. Vincent, who discovered, when he took command of the Channel Fleet, that it was the officers who were out of hand and that it was not advisable to brace the men up too tight. Many a good officer ruled his ship with a severity which, after a full consideration of all his difficulties, must be regarded as excessive. One or two captains adopted the horrible practice of flogging the last man who was down on deck after a piece of work up aloft; and there was one notorious case in 1805 of a man being flogged to death.

Besides, there were incompetent officers. The Whig party was very successful in obtaining currency for such legends, as that it was itself a democratic party, and that the Navy was a democratic service; the inference being that the service and the party were closely connected. Yet a strong contrast cannot be drawn with the Army in this respect. Of those who reached the quarter-deck through the hawse-holes, as the saying was, it would be hard to name any officer who attained distinction. Such men, starting life as ship's boys or seamen, usually got their promotion too late to rise above the rank of a lieutenant. There was a considerable class, on the other hand, of officers who by means of political and other interest obtained rank to which their merits did not entitle them, a state of affairs which rendered them dangerous and sometimes fatal to the ships and ships' companies confided to their care. St. Vincent complained bitterly in 1806 of the vast overflow of the young nobility into the service. The third class of officer was the most common one—the son of the poor gentleman—to whom Nelson belonged. But even he had naval interest; and had he entered the Army he would have found officers of dragoons among his relatives.

The important step in a naval career was not the mere entry into the Navy. It was comparatively easy for a boy to obtain from the captain of a ship the favour of being allowed to sling his hammock in the cockpit as a Boy of the First Class, although it was not until after he had been five years at sea that he could be rated as a midshipman. To rise to be one of the 2,300 lieutenants was the great difficulty. Above them there were over 400 masters and commanders, above them again 530 captains, and, highest of all, the 140 flag officers bearing the ranks of Admiral of the Fleet, Admirals of the White and the Blue, and Vice and Rear Admirals of the Red, the White, and the Blue respectively. But there were grey-headed lieutenants as well as dried-up midshipmen, and it was only when he saw himself as commander that a sailor could feel that a career was opened before him. Then might his sister write as Jane Austen did in 1798, after the usual correspondence had passed between the young man's father and a high-placed officer, and between him again and the First Lord of the Admiralty: "Frank is made. He was yesterday raised to the rank of Commander, and appointed to the *Peterel* sloop, now at Gibraltar." But it was often the officers under whom a young man had served and who knew his worth, and not necessarily his relations, who made interest for him.

How the system by which the British Navy was manned resulted in one of the most efficient instruments of war which the world has ever seen, is a problem which almost defies solution. There were several devices for raising men. Voluntary recruitment was not enough. The inhabitants of the inland feared the sea, those of the coasts found better reward for braving its terrors if they went as fishermen or into the merchant service. On rare occasions only were they swept by a wave of enthusiasm. When the war with France was about to be renewed, a Portsmouth paper recorded that there were twelve volunteers forthcoming to one pressed man, which was unprecedented. As a rule recourse was had to the press-gang. It has always been a subject of surprise to foreign critics that such a liberty-loving people as that of England, and particularly her seafaring population, can have borne such a system. The explanation is in itself a kind of paradox. Englishmen hated the notion of a paid body of armed men who might be a danger to their liberties in time of peace. When war came it was another matter. It was necessary, and therefore right, to catch men in haste, and force them to defend their country. Volunteers who knew nothing of the sea were not wanted in any number. Seafarers were required, and it was more in the strange spirit of British fair play to get what was wanted for the great game at haphazard. It was realized, on the other hand, that the State had its right, had indeed an obligation, to take from the trade which it protected its toll in men as well as money. The press-gang was to the sea service what the militia ballot was to the land service. In some ways at least it was not so harsh. It did not carry a man away to duties which were absolutely new and strange to him. It did not compel a man of peace to become a fighting man.

T

The merchant seaman had always to battle with the elements, and in war-time—the time of impressment—he might be called upon to resist the attack of a privateer or even a man-of-war. There was no such hard-and-fast line between the fighter and the trader afloat as there was between a soldier and a pedlar ashore. At sea trade was dignified as the merchant service, and Nelson himself was proud to have served in it, and of the lessons which it had taught him. Nor did the press-gang often drag a man from his wife and weeping children. A likely young foretopman of twenty-five was—in all probability—no family man, and if he was, three years before the mast afloat were just as much a separation under the merchant flag as under any other. Doubtless, wherever there was a hot press there was a good deal of resistance and even bloodshed, but a seafaring population enjoyed fighting. Once secure on board, most of them took to their new duties, even if they had not been in the service before, with a good enough grace. No doubt, also, individual cases occurred of very great hardship and even injustice. Officers were not always very particular whom they pressed. In 1804 a son of a Canadian judge had been serving two years in the Mediterranean before the mast; the case was brought to the attention of Nelson himself before he could be released. But perhaps the gravest abuse of the press was when half a dozen of the best seamen were carried off from a troopship which had already started on her voyage, or from a vessel homeward bound from some colonial port, which had no chance whatever of making up the loss. Naval officers were so used to navigating captured vessels with only a prize crew of a handful of men on board that they thought little of this. But captains of merchantmen were not. The lives of several hundreds of people were often endangered by such misuses of the press.

Other methods of raising men proved less satisfactory. In 1795 a requisition was made from shipowners for nearly 20,000 men. In the same year a levy was made from the

ADDINGTON'S ADMINISTRATION IN WAR

land, of 9,859 men from England and Wales, and 1,814 from Scotland. Corporations added their own to the government bounties to enable themselves to raise their quotas. In Liverpool the amount came to £31 5s. for an able seaman, £23 10s. for an ordinary seaman, and £17 10s. for what was known as a landsman. It was a grand opportunity for local authorities to shoot their rubbish. Although repeated in 1796, the experiment did not justify itself. The men so obtained fell usually into the class known as the King's Hard Bargains. But, without the encouragement of this bounty, the system of practically forcing men of supposed bad character on board His Majesty's ships went on. In Ireland this was done by magistrates first in undisguised contravention of law and subsequently made legal. In the case of convicted men there was no scruple. As many as a hundred men might be discharged from a jail on board a single ship at one time. Abroad all kinds were often taken. In 1803 Nelson was expected to complete the Mediterranean Fleet to war strength with Maltese, and that although Malta was as yet no regular part of the empire. Colour did not matter, as is shown by the case of the black man whose good work at his gun was noticed by Collingwood at Trafalgar. There was not much discrimination. In the foul, rat-ridden receiving ship volunteers were herded with the Lord Mayor's men, as those sent by the magistrates were called, and gratings put over them. They were soon introduced to skillagolee or burgoo, a nauseous imitation of porridge which they had to learn to eat. Once they were well out at sea salt-beef with its attendant danger of scurvy could not well be avoided, which made this callous disregard of them by their country at the very outset all the more reprehensible. When the mutiny of 1797 took place the pay of blue-jackets had not been raised since the days of Charles II. An able seaman henceforward received a shilling a day. The nation now felt that it had done its duty, and those who composed the Navy should do theirs. There was plenty of sentimental appreciation. Just about this time it was observed that Dibdin's ballad was obtaining a fresh popularity in the seaport towns:—

> "There's a sweet little cherub that sits up aloft,
> Will look out for the life of Poor Jack."

It was fortunate; for there were few willing to do so down below.

The nation hardly even troubled to clothe its defenders. They were at all times rather a motley crew. Yet they soon developed those little personal vanities which seem almost inseparable from valour. They wore their pigtails down to Trafalgar, and after; and in Poor Jack, Marryat has finely fancied the Greenwich pensioner whose brawling wife's unforgivable sin it was to cut his off while he was asleep. It was something of his own which made the sailor's pride; it was to his own enterprise that he looked for his reward. It was the idea of prize-money rather than the remembrance of a grateful country which helped both officers and men to swallow cheerfully their salt-junk and captain's biscuit. The amounts won in this way were enormous, and the complicated rules sometimes led to disputes and litigation between high officers which were discreditable. "George is gone down the Mediterranean, as I wish to put £10,000 in his pocket," wrote Nelson of one of his captains in 1803. The rough memorandum which he drew up in the summer of 1805 is a revelation of the enormous amounts in prize-money which were being made by a squadron whose main duties were of a totally different and a very urgent character. When Captain the Honourable Charles Paget found himself in command of a crack frigate at the outbreak of the war with Spain in 1804, he wrote: "My *whack* of Prize Money at a moderate calculation will be about fifty thousand Pounds"—a few weeks' work. British sailors would not have fought so well without this incentive. It was all they had; there were no medals for ordinary ratings or even for junior officers. But the pelf was after all not very much more than counters to be played for. Light come, light go, was notoriously the sailor's way with money. It was honour and the spirit of adventure which animated them most of all.

It was with such officers and such crews and such inducements that the men who commanded in the old Navy performed their difficult task. The oak of which it was fashioned was solid enough, but there was many a rugged knot which made it difficult to work. The results were marvellous. Feats of courage and endurance were performed that were unsurpassed in any service and in any age. Gratitude is due to crabbed old William James and the compiler of the Naval Chronology for the quiet matter-of-fact way in which they relate time after time how a boatful or two of men volunteered to cut out from under the guns of the enemy's batteries a vessel with a complement three or four times their number, armed and ready to receive them, and succeeded. The smallest embellishment of these narratives would have thrown doubt on the credibility of the whole.

The establishment of the Navy during the last year of the war with revolutionary France was 100,500 seamen and 30,000 marines. This last force corresponded in some measure to the large number of soldiers carried on board French men-of-war to enhance their fighting qualities. It had behaved so well, and, in particular, been so conspicuous for its loyalty during 1797, that it shortly afterwards obtained the honour of being called Royal. A new force, the Royal Marine Artillery, came into existence in 1804. There were 800 ships, exclusive of hospital and prison ships. Of these, leaving the hybrid 50-gun ships out of account, the first, second, and third rates carrying 64 guns and over numbered 125; 41 were on the Channel and Irish station, 14 in the Downs and the North Sea, 18 off the Spanish Peninsula, 24 in the Mediterranean, 4 in the West Indies, and 9 at the

Cape of Good Hope and in the East Indies. The principal duties of the capital ships were to guard the frontier—the enemy's coast—and to watch his ports. Of these the blockade of Brest, which fell to the lot of the Channel Fleet, was the most arduous. Generally speaking, the British enjoyed a superiority both in numbers and the size and quality of their ships over their opponents, although until Trafalgar the biggest ship in the world was the Spanish four-decker, Santissima Trinidad, and thereafter, until Duckworth's victory a few months later, the French Impérial.

On the English side the Victory was typical of the strongest class. Nominally a 100-gun ship, she carried, at Trafalgar, 28 twenty-four-pounders on her middle deck, and 30 each of twelve-pounders and thirty-two-pounders respectively on her main and lower decks, besides 10 twelve-pounders on the quarter-deck and forecastle, or 98 long guns in all. But besides these she had two sixty-eight-pounder guns of the type known after the celebrated Carron factory on the Firth of Forth as carronades, though this type of gun was by no means confined to Great Britain. They were used for close action. An eighteen-pounder carronade was one-third of the length and one quarter of the weight of the ordinary long gun throwing a projectile of the same weight. The commonest type of battleship in the whole Navy was, however, the two-decker 74—so-called—though she usually carried a few more than that number of guns. The war against the enemy's commerce, and that against the small craft and privateers which made war upon British commerce, was committed to a number of lesser vessels—frigates, sloops, and smaller craft still. The former had been so complete a success that the French Directory admitted in 1799 that there was not a single merchant-ship on the sea carrying the French flag. But this turned the attention of the seafaring population which remained to preying on commerce, and left the British no easy task. The Channel became infested with privateers. A coasting voyage between

Portsmouth and Plymouth might still usually be taken with tolerable safety. But even this was not always so. The inhabitants of the coast towns were often alarmed by the news that there was an enemy's privateer in the offing, and occasionally even by a shell being thrown into the town itself. The number of British vessels captured was over five hundred annually. Larger vessels usually sailed under convoy, itself one of the most onerous duties of the Navy, and in any case were generally strong enough and swift enough to escape capture by privateers. Making every allowance for the fact that the smaller merchantmen were most likely to fall victims, it is probable that, even in 1800, the toll taken by France and her allies from British trade was as much as two per cent. Satisfactory as it was that this was no more, it was enough to keep busy those upon whose shoulders the duty of protecting commerce rested. Even in 1800, 87 French privateers were captured, vessels commonly of 14 guns with a complement of about 80 men. The greatest number were taken in the Channel.

The supreme control of the Navy was vested in the Board of Admiralty, which at this time consisted of a civilian First Lord and four other Lords, as they were called, of whom two were naval men and two civilians, with two Secretaries, one of whom was in parliament. Spencer, the First Lord, who was excellent in everything relating to appointments and promotions, was no reformer. The Navy was served by a fortuitous concourse of offices, several of which were partly, and some completely, independent of the Admiralty. Building and repairs were dealt with by the Navy Board, presided over by the Comptroller, a naval officer, who was of course as such subordinate to the First Lord. But the Navy Office, where he worked, was in another part of London, and the claim made by Admiral Sir Andrew Hammond, who presided there, to be master in his own house, led afterwards to considerable friction under the strenuous administration of St. Vincent. This was natural, considering what that officer's views were, even before taking over the duties of First Lord. Having chiefly in his mind the gross corruption which existed in the dockyards, he had written to Spencer that the civil department of the Navy was rotten to the very core. Besides the Navy Board there was a Victualling and a Transport Board. The Pay Office was under the Treasurer of the Navy, and Dundas was free to take advantage of his long tenure of this post to introduce a number of excellent improvements in the system by which the pay of seamen and marines could be drawn at home by themselves or by their families. Provision for the spiritual and physical welfare of the men had not gone beyond a rudimentary stage. If religion existed among seamen, it was probably not due to what few chaplains there were. They brought it with them. The Evangelical Magazine published in 1807 an unsympathetic officer's account of his impressions of "a set of fellows called '*Methodists*' on board the Victory". They were left alone, and had their own mess. "Those men never wanted swearing at. The dogs were the best seamen on board." In the men's health such admirals as St. Vincent and Nelson took the greatest possible personal interest, both paying particular attention to such details as the provision of lemons to lessen the danger of scurvy. They did not throw the responsibility on the medical authority. St. Vincent at any rate preferred a man without qualifications. He had a contempt for the letters M.D.

The Army was under two separate Ministers in the Cabinet —the Secretary of State for War and the Master General of the Ordnance. This latter department had little to do with the Navy beyond providing it with guns and ammunition. On the military side it presided over both the Artillery and the Engineers; and the vote of supply for these arms was included in the Ordnance vote. When the Secretary for War furnished statements of the strength of the Army their numbers were always excluded. The Ordnance was an inefficient department; and this is the more strange because a good soldier, Cornwallis, was the Minister in charge during several years, and the professional head was for a long time Sir John Macleod, an excellent gunner officer. Yet as late as 1808 Lieutenant-Colonel William Robe, who commanded the artillery in the Peninsula, was sent with shells without any guns to fit them. The Navy came to the rescue. He was fortunately able to borrow from the fleet guns which fitted his ammunition. For trace-horses he was given blind cavalry casters which had to be replaced by oxen. Such details as the provision of spare shoes for the horses were completely overlooked. Up to the end of the eighteenth century and after it guns were provided in pairs to each battalion. There was no concentration. The expedition to the Helder in 1799 was the first in which a general officer was sent in command of the artillery. The old practice was again reverted to in 1807, when General Whitelock at Buenos Ayres had to depend for advice on artillery matters upon whoever happened to be the senior captain present. But in a country in which the affairs of the Ordnance had only a few years before been permitted to be under the control of a Minister whose principal business it was to govern Ireland and suppress a rebellion there, such an anomaly might escape notice. The Royal Horse Artillery again, started in 1793, was actually provided with three different sorts of gun for each troop. Both branches of the arm were rather under a cloud until 1800, after which improvement set in and the Gunners soon established a claim to be equal to anything in the whole Army. They were now recognized everywhere as worthy antagonists. Their strength at the end of the revolutionary war was 9 battalions of 1,190 men each. There was never any difficulty in obtaining an excellent stamp of man. The pay was the highest in the Army. A gunner received 1s. $3\frac{1}{4}$d. a day.

Of the other force under the Ordnance Department there is not much to be said. It was well remarked by the French general Foy, in his History of the War in the Peninsula, that it could no more be expected that the art of engineering as applied to military fortifications could be understood in a country which had none, than that of seamanship in one which had no ships. During his term of office as Master-General, Cornwallis paid some attention to the subject. Engineers, he complained, could only rise to colonel's pay in forty years; they had no prospect except by peculation. He recognized that, deprived as these officers were of the attractions of an exhilarating mess, they ought to have some compensating advantages which might make service in this corps an object of ambition to a clever young man who had been three or four years in the artillery. But little was done. It was only after a long time and at immense sacrifices that the engineering arm learnt its duties with a besieging force. The needless loss of life in the storming of Montevideo in 1807, no less than the failures before Bharatpur in 1805, and Badajos in 1811, are the proofs. At home unnecessary fortifications were constructed, for all of which it must be admitted that the Royal Engineers were not responsible. Large sums were spent on Martello towers along the south-east coast of England. The total expenditure on fortifications in the United Kingdom for the six years following the recommencement of war was nearly two and a quarter millions. The establishment of the Royal Military Artificers and Labourers, as the rank and file of the arm was called, was only 975, and it was nearly a quarter under strength. In time of war the necessary duties had to be hastily taught to troops of the line.

The Regular Army—cavalry and infantry—was—so far as the Cabinet was concerned—under Dundas, the Secretary of State for War, as well as Windham, the Secretary at War. It was only on account of the latter's peculiar abilities that he was permitted to sit in the Cabinet, holding the office which he held. He was also allowed his share in the organization of campaigns. But as a rule the Secretaryship at War

ADDINGTON'S ADMINISTRATION IN WAR

was a minor post, concerned mainly with military finance, and in 1806, when Windham himself was Secretary for War, the other Secretary was almost unnoticed. The supreme disciplinary control of the Army was under the Duke of York as Commander-in-Chief, a post in which he was almost independent of the Cabinet and directly responsible to the King. He had failed in the field, rather owing to orders from home and to the need for conforming his movements with the ill-conceived operations of his allies than to his own incompetence. At the Horse Guards he showed himself an excellent administrator. One of his acts was the opening, under Lieutenant-Colonel Le Marchant of the 7th Light Dragoons, of the High Wycombe College in Buckinghamshire, in 1799. The principal instructor was a French emigrant professor of the art of war, General Jarry. The standard for those who took the higher or staff course was, according to the young officer who afterwards became General Sir Charles Napier, a high one in draftsmanship and in French, the language in which the lectures were given. A junior department was added a few miles away at Great Marlow; it was intended for three hundred students of fourteen to sixteen years of age; one hundred to be sons of noblemen and gentlemen, one hundred sons of officers still serving, fifty sons of officers who had died in the service or been invalided out, and fifty cadets of the East India Company. It was far from being necessary to take this course in order to obtain a commission. Still, a beginning had been made of the idea of the professional officer for the Army as a whole, just as a separate training for the more scientific arms was already provided at Woolwich. The Duke introduced other measures which helped to mark the stage at which the profession of arms had definitely passed from the position of leadership or membership of a company of adventurers, such as the organizing of the system of purchase on a definite basis, and the introduction of a uniform drill manual for both cavalry and infantry. The former arm remained poorly trained. It was not taught the duties of a covering force—duties well understood both in the French and Austrian armies. But in the campaigns on the Continent in the earlier part of the war it had displayed plenty of dash, and its performances should have been enough by themselves to redeem the British Army from the low opinion in which it was held by the world. The infantry had not enjoyed such opportunities, and there is more excuse for despising it. It has been common in the British Army to apply somewhat too closely to European warfare the lessons learnt in colonial campaigns. During the wars which lasted until the Peace of Amiens the high command in England certainly avoided this fault. Prussian instruction and Prussian tactics were the word, and it almost seemed as if it was the object to make British soldiers pale copies of the veterans of Frederick the Great. Much importance was attached to mechanical precision. The contemporary prints of Rowlandson showed six positions for priming and loading a musket. Steadiness was almost everything; and the British relied so much upon this that it was felt by the enemy that, a breach once made in the wall of bayonets, the whole ball was at their feet. An important sacrifice of depth to breadth of front had, indeed, been made as a result of experience gained in more open warfare. The British now fought in double instead of the triple rank still in vogue on the Continent. But the fine skirmishing tactics of the American War had fallen into disuse. General Humbert, the victor of Castlebar, in a report drawn up in 1800, actually remarked that the English did not know how to employ light infantry. Before the work of Simcoe in America could be repeated by that of Craufurd in the Peninsula, there was a gap, partly filled by regiments of a foreign or colonial origin and composition, armed with the rifle, the weapon of the sharpshooter. Such were the Sixtieth Rifles and the Rifle Brigade.

The mass of the British Army was expected to consist of men who, in Oliver Cromwell's phrase, made some conscience of what they did—who fought with that majesty which William Napier magnificently described in his story of the storming of the fatal hill of Albuera. It was beneath the soldier even to pick his man. It was by becoming something of a fop that he was led to take a pride in himself. The orders even for Light Horse Volunteers began: "Hair powdered and greased, six inches long, close to the head." The pigtails of the regulars had grown so long in 1804 that a special order had to be passed reducing them to seven inches, and they were not abolished altogether until 1808. Coleridge, in a sermon against militarism, which William Hazlitt heard, gave a vivid picture of the change from civil to military life on its worst side—"A striking contrast between the simple shepherd-boy, driving his team afield, or sitting under the hawthorn, piping to his flock 'as though he should never be old', and the same poor country-lad, crimped, kidnapped, brought into town, made drunk at an alehouse, turned into a wretched drummer-boy, with his hair sticking on end with powder and pomatum, a long cue at his back, and tricked out in the loathsome finery of the profession of blood." But with all this he imbibed feelings of honour which struck refined persons in civil life with astonishment. Lady Bessborough described how her maid's brother, just returned from Buenos Ayres, told her of Whitelocke's shameful surrender. His honest rage was a novel experience to that fashionable lady. "I never saw such indignation in my life", she wrote. "He stamped and threw down his hat on merely naming him."

In one of his sublime passages Napier wrote that the British soldier conquered in the cold shade of aristocracy. How cold that shade was is evinced by Wellington's unfair generalization that they had, all of them, enlisted for drink. This was seldom true, except in the sense that a good drinking bout accompanied the recruit's enlistment. Mixed motives, in which a disgust with home usually predominated, made him take the king's shilling. There was, as Adam Smith observed, a contempt of risk and a presumptuous hope of success. "The son of a creditable labourer or artificer", he added, "may frequently go to sea with his father's consent; but if he enlists as a soldier it is always without it." It is curious that this should have been so. Criminals found their way into the Army by twos and threes. They were drafted into the Navy by scores. A military recruit had to be regularly attested before a magistrate, and that some hours after enlistment, when the effects of the drink had worn off and the cold fit had taken its place. Once on board ship the naval recruit was at the mercy of the captain. But Adam Smith's statement was no doubt true, and the reason was the one which he gives, that there was more money to be made at sea. But there was also the idea that the harvest of the country's wealth and greatness lay upon the sea, and it had to be defended, whereas the land fighter's profession of blood, as Coleridge called it, was not altogether a very necessary one, and might just as well be left to foreigners—who were, indeed, very much better performers, until it came to the hard fighting.

On the other hand, it would be a mistake to suppose that the officers were made up almost entirely of such aristocrats as the Napiers, whose mother, the beautiful Lady Sarah Lennox, might, had she wished it, have been Queen of England. The purchase system, indeed, suggests that it was so. By its aid the sons of the nobility could rise rapidly in the service. The greatest soldier in the Army may be quoted as an example. Arthur Wellesley was a Lieutenant-Colonel, commanding his regiment, at twenty-four. But he was not rich, and the amounts paid under the purchase system were not beyond the means of a respectable man of the middle class, such as Doctor Moore, the father of the great general. The commission of ensign cost 300 guineas, and a boy often became one at fifteen or sixteen, and could then earn a part of his livelihood, whereas if brought up for one of the learned professions he would earn nothing till many years later. The subaltern was far from living like a lord. Cobbett's Political Register for 1806 contains a budget of a typical ensign, whose yearly pay was £85 3s. 4d., and who spent, including taxes, more than double that amount. Yet his breakfast was only tenpence a day, his bread-and-cheese supper the same, and his dinner, with nothing stronger than small beer, two shillings. His washing bill was sevenpence a day. Splendid as his uniform was, it did not cost much. A regimental coat, with epaulets and waistcoat, came to £11 10s., and three lasted him two years. Pomatum and powder appear to have been important items, but pipe-clay and whiting cost him only 4s. 4d. in the year, and hair-ribbon, combs, and rosettes 10s. 6d. An officer was usually impecunious, like the Billy of Fielding's Amelia, in an earlier generation. Many officers would not afford to purchase their steps of promotion, and waited—often till they were many years older than the commanding officers of their regiments—for the coveted death vacancy which would give them their companies without being obliged to pay. "That Officer!" says a character in an old play, "The Farmer":—

"Ha, ha, ha! a captain lend money? That's a good joke."
"He's agent to fifteen regiments."
"Zounds, then he can lend me the King's money."

The agent was usually a financial assistant to the colonel, and it was not until an officer had reached that coveted rank, with the prospect, while he remained, of making a thousand a year in addition to his pay by clothing the regiment, and, when he retired, of making three or four thousand by selling out, that he was even decently well off. Another writer in the Political Register was, however, a colonel, who put his ordinary daily expenses at 10s. 7d. and could not live on his pay. All this shows that those who went into the Army must have had means to enable them to do so, but it also showed that they were not rich, and that the standard of living was a low one.

At the same time, Napier's suggestion that officers had little in common with their men was true. They were expected to lead an existence apart at quarters as in the field. At the siege of Hathras in India an officer who attempted to identify himself with his men by removing his epaulet, and the plate and feather from his cap, was ridiculed as a coward. The barrack system was only just being introduced, and the officers had no idea of responsibility for the welfare of their men while on home service, and very little when on foreign service. Moore noted in the West Indies that parades, firelock exercises, etc., took up only an hour or two in the day, and were all that claimed an officer's attention. His own readings in the classics suggested a wish that the discipline of the ancients, which consisted of bodily exercises, running, and marching, terminated by bathing, might be introduced, and greater attention paid to cleanliness and neatness. He was before his time. The lack of sympathy with the men was also shown by the brutal floggings. It was quite a different matter here from what it was in the Navy, where corporal punishment was only just ceasing to be a piece of routine. Marryat's famous boatswain, Mr. Chucks, was never without a rope's end in his hand, and that rope's end seldom for long out of use. Or a man might be triced up in a moment at the captain's word, and given his three dozen. A flogging in the Army was a much more serious thing. It was only awarded on the sentence of a court-martial, and, although lash for lash the punishment which the drummer administered was not nearly so severe as that inflicted by the boatswain's mate, it was a far more cruel punishment, for hundreds of lashes were commonly given. The soldier's saying was: "If we flog one devil out, we flog fifty in", and John Shipp wrote, as one twice promoted to officer from the ranks, that in thirty years' service he had only known of one case of a man who had been flogged, and had recovered his own respect and that of his fellows. This was peculiar to the British service,

ADDINGTON'S ADMINISTRATION IN WAR 305

as was another of the evils of a soldier's life. In order to fight he had to cross the seas, and the conditions on board the troopships in which he was often cooped up for many months were appalling. Grattan, of the Connaught Rangers, told how, on the voyage to the Spanish Peninsula, officers had parts of their bodies eaten by rats as they lay in their hammocks helpless from seasickness, but they were at least not confined to the ships for weeks before they sailed, as the men were. The military surgeons knew very little of tropical diseases. Even nearer home there were frequently mysterious epidemics. One of these carried off over four hundred men out of three regiments in Gibraltar in a few months in 1804. As regards the West Indies the case was infinitely worse. In 1800, a year of little or no fighting, 1,221 men died, or about a sixth of the European rank and file, besides 58 officers. In the following year 104 officers died. Of the total losses by death of troops in expeditions overseas between 1793 and the Peace of Amiens, estimated at 1,350 officers and 60,000 men, by far the greater number perished by disease in the West Indies. One feature of military administration redeemed the general inhumanity. A definite number of soldiers' wives were permitted to accompany each regiment upon active service abroad. A similar concession was made to the Navy in 1800.

One alteration was made for the better at home during these years. Until 1792 the Army and the civil population alike had been exposed to the annoyances inseparable from the system of billeting. In that year a Barrackmaster-General was appointed, and the construction of barracks commenced. The plan was absurdly attacked as savouring of military despotism—and it was certainly justified on the ground that men so housed were less exposed to the arts of the political agitator. Necessary as the scheme was, it is painful to relate that, at a time when the Army was harassed by so many petty economies in other respects, the country did not get good value for its money in this. There was

U

extravagance and dishonesty, and the buildings were bad. The men suffered from pneumonia. Abuses were constantly being brought to light, until, in 1807, the Barrackmaster-General was abolished, and the department placed under civil commissioners.

The first War Office return for 1801—which does not include Ireland—showed the Regular Army to consist, in cavalry and infantry, of 140,226 men out of an establishment of 162,805. Of these over 34,000 were in Southern Europe and the Mediterranean, of whom more than half formed the expeditionary force being collected under General Abercromby. Of the other troops abroad, North America, including the Bermudas, accounted for 4,000, the West Indies for 23,000, the East Indies for 16,000, and the Cape for 5,000. There were 53,000 in Great Britain and the Channel Islands. The total of 140,226 comprises a few thousand Fencibles—troops raised only for the period of the war—and Invalids. Some of these were to be found in the Mediterranean stations, but neither class could form part of any expeditionary force. The total also includes a regiment of Yorkshire Hussars—in reality Germans—stationed at Weymouth, coloured troops in the West Indies, several thousands of French royalists, or French prisoners of war who pretended to be so, Germans, Swiss, Corsicans, and others, as well as such units as the special New South Wales Corps, and the 5th battalion of the 60th Rifles, which, when formed, was of German composition under a German commanding officer. But so far as India is concerned it only includes the King's troops, and not the three European regiments and the native troops organized by the East India Company. The Irish Army, which was also excluded, consisted of about 17,000, according to the estimate presented to the House of Commons at the same time.

Very few regular troops were stationed north of the Trent, or in any of the industrial centres. So far as Great Britain was concerned, the Regular Army, apart from Fencibles, was regarded as a striking rather than a defensive force. Scotland could not have been supposed immune either from invasion or from internal disorder, and yet that country was left to depend almost entirely upon less than eight thousand militia, besides volunteers. The militia in England was 38,083 strong. There were also Yeomanry, Provisional Cavalry, Volunteer Infantry and Artillery, and Volunteer Associations for defence. All of these helped mildly to sustain the military spirit. Probably the experience of the Lancashire radical, Samuel Bamford, was fairly typical of early volunteering. When he committed what his aunt called the great sin of volunteering, he received 1s. bounty and a black-and-red cockade. His conscience was not severely tried. The corps was never called upon once even to parade. It is impossible to estimate either the nominal or effective strength of all these bodies. In comparison with the militia they were of little importance. The latter was permanently embodied during the war. Its drills and field exercises were occasionally made intentionally severe to tempt men to volunteer for the regulars. The militia being maintained by local ballot of able-bodied men, who were permitted, if drawn, to find substitutes, could always be kept up to strength. It was the best channel for filling the Regular Army. No other system produced such good results. The bounty for men enlisted from the civil population had been ten guineas at the beginning of the war; later on contracts were made to supply recruits at twenty guineas a head. Another method was to offer a step in rank as a reward for recruiting the men, which cost the officer not much less than if he had purchased the rank or commission in the ordinary way. The method of obtaining them by a levy from parishes failed in the Army as it did in the Navy. To obtain men for the line from the militia required, however, an Act of Parliament. In 1799 a bounty was offered of ten guineas to men so volunteering, and the standard of height fixed at 5 feet 4 inches only. The measure was a complete success;

and the men, engaged for Europe only, volunteered for service in Egypt, where they did themselves credit.

The Peace of Lunéville, signed on February the 8th, 1801, marked the break-up of the Second Coalition formed by Pitt against France. By it she obtained from Austria Belgium and the Rhine frontier from Holland up to Switzerland, while both countries recognized the independence of the Dutch, Swiss, Cisalpine, and Ligurian republics, and of the kingdom of Etruria. But these last three petty Italian states turned out to be at France's disposal. Switzerland was at her mercy. Holland's admirals were soon to take their orders direct from the First Consul or his subordinates. Supreme in this way upon land, France had nothing to contend with but Great Britain, who was equally supreme at sea. In these circumstances it became difficult for either party to carry on the war with vigour. British maritime supremacy, however, made it possible to enable her Army to carry out an expedition outside Europe in which the opposing military forces might contend on terms of equality. Within Europe itself new adversaries had risen to challenge that supremacy in the North. Hence the spring of 1801 was occupied with expeditions to Africa and to the Baltic.

Darkly as the new century had opened for England, it was illustrated in Egypt by the first signal success obtained by a British army during the war. It was not then the practice to attach naval and military officers to embassies; and in the absence of any other system of intelligence the greatest ignorance prevailed regarding suitable points of attack. Hence, difficult as it always has been in England to raise the most contemptible military force, the question where, when raised, it should be sent, served only to increase the embarrassments of the authorities. The troops of an island power need to be transported by sea to the place where they are to operate. There was little difficulty, however, in this, even for considerable bodies of troops, with so large a navy and mercantile marine. The real trouble was the failure to understand that a war is concluded by dealing heavy blows, not by what the Roman poet called making a huckster's business of it. Dundas's conception of warfare had been one better suited to a race of pirates than to a nation of soldiers and sailors. "It shall not be my fault", he wrote in May 1798, "if, with one expedition after another, the coast of France is allowed to sleep sound any one week during the summer." It was upon this principle that the forces collected in 1800 had been employed upon the coasts of both France and Spain in making pecks at Belleisle, Ferrol, and Cadiz. It was now that Dundas formed a plan for the conquest of Egypt. It was unwillingly accepted by his colleagues, and particularly so by the King himself, who afterwards paid him the high compliment of having proved right and the rest all wrong. Yet in truth his triumph over his friends at home was a gift from the incompetence of the enemy in Egypt.

When Bonaparte conquered that country from the Turks in 1798 he had carried there the flower of the French Army —the victors in the great campaign in Italy in 1796, which had first made him famous. During nearly three years' absence from their native land the army had deteriorated, and a book had been published in England whose title, Intercepted Letters, suggests its contents. These homesick and discontented effusions presented a vivid picture of the depression of the troops, and the indiscipline into which they had fallen. It had led the British Ministry to underrate their value. For, in spite of all, they were able on the day of battle to render perhaps as good an account of themselves as they ever had been. It was leadership which was wanting. The best generals had left, and the command had now fallen to General Menou, who was as presumptuous as he was incompetent. At his departure in 1799 Bonaparte had left a complete account of what the British would do, and how their plans should be met. They would land at Aboukir with 15,000 men, and a Turkish force would co-operate with them across the desert from the direction of Palestine. But the two operations would not be timed to coincide, and all that was necessary was to mass all the troops available to oppose the landing. Bonaparte had himself shown the way to hurl an invading army into the sea at that very spot. This remarkable forecast was lost on Menou, even when confirmed by the very early intelligence received by him through those in the French interest regarding the approach of the so-called "Secret Expedition", to which unfavourable critics denied the qualities of either expedition or secrecy.

On the side of the British every step was deliberate. The greatest caution seemed to be dictated, not merely by the Scottish characteristics of the generals who held high command before and during the expedition—Charles Stuart, Abercromby, who succeeded him in the chief command in the Mediterranean, Moore, and Baird—but by the imperative necessity of risking nothing with so small a force. For after a detachment had been made to Portugal—which eventually returned to England without striking a blow—just over 15,500 were left. To remedy this Dundas, who in his position as President of the Board of Control directed Indian affairs, as well as the Army, was able to concert with Marquis Wellesley, the Governor-General, for a force from India to co-operate by way of the Red Sea. In addition to this, the Ambassador in Constantinople, Lord Elgin, was to obtain the assistance of the Turks both by way of supplies and of arms. But nothing was done according to plan. The Turks knew and cared nothing for supplies, and—as to fighting—they preferred, after the heavy blows already received, to do as Napoleon had foretold—to wait and see what success the British might obtain.

For almost the whole of the first two months of 1801, General Sir Ralph Abercromby lay off the south-west coast of Asia Minor, but he had not been idle. The requirements of the expedition were partly met. Abercromby had learnt from the mistakes made in the disembarkation on the Dutch

ADDINGTON'S ADMINISTRATION IN WAR 311

coast in 1799 the need of constant practice in landing troops in the face of the enemy. He gave them a thorough training accordingly. Meanwhile he sent to Jaffa Major-General John Moore, his right-hand man and the best officer then in the whole Army, to endeavour to concert operations with the Grand Vizier who commanded the Turkish troops in Palestine. He found that army a wild, ungovernable mob. When the Vizier wished to muster them at Moore's request he was met by a few shots fired at his tent, the customary hint that an order was unpopular. The ration strength being above the fighting strength, an exact enumeration of the troops would have been awkward for the chiefs. Besides, plague raged in the camp. Moore returned and reported how little the Turks were to be depended upon. Abercromby replied that he had long been convinced that the British had only themselves to rely upon, and the plan for landing in Aboukir Bay was independently pursued.

Lower Egypt is embraced and watered by the channels into which the Nile divides itself, in its passage northward to the sea, a few miles below Cairo. The Mediterranean coast at the mouths of that river is characterized by long, narrow strips of sand-dunes, almost entirely separated from the rest of the mainland by large spaces of water. On the westernmost of these stands Alexandria, the Port of Egypt, regarded as its key by both Bonaparte and Abercromby. The waters of the Nile did not reach that city in their natural flow, but were carried to it by an aqueduct. West of the canal lay Lake Mareotis, then dry; east of it, Lake Maadi, which communicated with the sea near the Bay of Aboukir, at the east end of the strip of land which runs from Arab Tower in the west, past Alexandria, to Aboukir in the east. It was on this strip of land that Abercromby was to win the last three engagements of his life.

On the 1st of March the armament reached the coast; and almost at the same time two French men-of-war, in spite of the presence of the British fleet, sailed safely into

Alexandria. These repeated efforts to throw reinforcements and supplies into Egypt, which had met with some success during previous months, kept French hopes alive, and forced upon the British a policy of caution which subsequently protracted the campaign. The arrival of the fleet was known at Menou's headquarters in Cairo on the 4th of March, but he made no concentration. It was in vain that one officer, General Reynier, put before him Bonaparte's example, and described what that commander would have done. Menou was quite certain that the small force then in Alexandria would overwhelm the British, and he was encouraged in this bravado by Reynier himself, who expressed the greatest contempt for Abercromby. That general, on his side, had the gravest doubts of a successful landing, and possibly would not have made the attempt at all had he not wrongly believed Menou to have only 10,000 French and 5,000 auxiliaries in the country. The real number was upwards of 25,000. But of these only 1,600 infantry, two squadrons of dragoons, and fifteen guns were collected at Aboukir. For nearly a week bad weather made landing impossible, and the British had the mortification of watching, from their harassed ships, the preparations for defence. On the 8th the sea had fallen, and the expected moment had arrived. The careful orders issued by the Commander-in-Chief mark an epoch in the history of amphibious operations. Every precaution was taken so that every unit in the line should reach the exact position on the shore where it was intended to make its attack. To ensure their reaching land as soon as possible, the men were to sit down in the boats, to observe the strictest silence, and —it was positively ordered—not to load till formed on the beach. Covering fire was left to the gunboats on the flanks. Captain the Honourable Alexander Cochrane, R.N., was in command of the disembarkation, while the launches, carrying fourteen field-guns and a landing party of 350 seamen, as well as the gunners, were under Captain Sir

Sidney Smith, the hero of the defence of Acre, who was second to none in knowledge of the coast.

The boats rowed in perfect silence. Cochrane formed them in line on reaching the rendezvous; and now the gunboats opened fire to cover their advance—ineffectually, because there was no mark on which to aim. At last the signal on the French side was given. The artillery opened with a storm of round-shot, then with grape as the boats drew nearer; finally a hail of musketry broke on them three hundred yards from the beach. The British were fortunate. Three boats only were sunk, and not many men hit. Cochrane, who had Moore in his boat on the right of the line, gave the direction; and that general upon landing formed his division at the foot of a high sandhill which commanded the whole position. The men of the 40th, 23rd, and 28th regiments gallantly climbed the steep, and, as he recorded in his diary afterwards, never offered to fire until they had reached the top, whence they drove the French back with the loss of four guns. Meanwhile the Brigade of Guards and the 42nd Highlanders on the left were equally successful, though charged by cavalry soon after they had got on shore. The French had been beaten back with the loss of eight guns and three or four hundred men, the landing was secured, and the rest of the army quickly followed. The British losses in this gallant affair were nearly 700 men. Only thirteen miles now separated Abercromby from Alexandria; it only remained to press his advantage quickly home, and the campaign might have been finished.

It was, however, too rough for a day or two to land supplies, and the general advance did not take place until the 12th. On the 13th there was a general engagement about seven miles from the city with an enemy now amounting to about 4,500 men and 21 guns. On this occasion the French showed a resolute front, and used their artillery with destructive effect; and Abercromby, though he succeeded in driving back an enemy one-third of his strength, showed indecision, and failed to press his advantage home. He was hampered, too, by ignorance of the conditions of the East. The bed of Lake Mareotis, which was perfectly firm, looked from the nitrous salt on its surface like a marsh, and he did not dare to trust to a wide turning movement over it, which his superiority in numbers would have enabled him to attempt with success. He was deceived by another common hallucination of the desert, where forts and military positions appear much bolder from a distance than they are in reality. The result was that at a cost of 1,300 casualties against a French loss of 500 men and five cannon, he had secured a strong position three miles from Alexandria, with its right flank supported by a hill named Caesar's Camp, called after the ruins of a large walled enclosure dating from Roman times. Here he awaited his heavy artillery. Meanwhile Menou had at last arrived from Cairo, bringing the French force up to 10,000 men, including 1,400 cavalry, with 46 guns. The British were weaker in artillery, mounting only 36 guns upon the position, and also in cavalry, of which they had 200 against the French 1,400.

It was obviously to Menou's advantage to make the best use of the arms in which he was superior, there being an inferiority of about 1,000 in the total numbers. But he did not do so. He seems to have had no plan of his own. One of his generals of division, Lanusse, persuaded him to adopt the plan of attacking, not over the open plain on the British left, but on the side where his own division was, and against the Roman Camp. This position was not only the strongest part of the British line, but was supported by gunboats on the open sea. Even as it was, the attack was not pressed home by mass upon mass of infantry, as it should have been, but cavalry were used prematurely and met with disaster.

The intrepid Moore had always the fortune to see the best of the fighting. As Major-General of the day, he was visiting the left picquets at four in the morning of the 21st of March, when he heard shots fired there, soon followed by more shots from his own division on the right. He at once realized that the attack on the left was a feint, and said to his aide-de-camp: "This is the real attack, let us gallop to the redoubt." He soon found himself in all the confusion of battle. Under general orders the troops had stood to arms an hour before daylight, and were not taken unprepared. So violent, however, was the French attack that British troops were fighting to front, flank, and rear, one French battalion penetrating right through the line. Moore saw his opportunity. He wheeled the right wing of the 42nd, the regiment which was to have the honours of that day as they had had of the landing. The Frenchmen were driven into the ruins upon Caesar's Camp and forced to surrender. Lanusse had already been mortally wounded. The left and centre divisions were exhausted. And now, instead of bringing up men from the right, Menou ordered a cavalry charge, deaf to all remonstrances. These also penetrated through the line, the British opening to let them pass, but closing again when they had done so. They were repelled by the Minorca regiment of the foreign brigade under Brigadier-General John Stuart, who brought it up from the second line in support, and it was good to see the gallantry displayed by these Mediterranean troops disciplined by British officers. In that death ride the French General, Roise, gallantly fell, and two British generals were nearly taken— Moore, who had been wounded earlier in the day, and Abercromby himself, who was also wounded in the thigh but took no heed of it. It was now 10 o'clock, and Menou had failed. The troops on the British side which were actually engaged did not outnumber their assailants, and in the critical judgment of Moore excelled them in valour. "We were for an hour without a cartridge", he wrote, describing the last hour of the battle, a period when the infantry in the front lines were hurling stones at one another in default of ammunition; "the enemy during this time were pounding us with shot and shell, and distant musketry. Our artillery could not return a shot, and had their infantry again advanced we must have repelled them with the bayonet. Our fellows would have done it; I never saw men more determined to do their duty; but the French had suffered so severely that they could not get their men to make a second attempt." The British losses in this, the battle of Canopus, as the French called it, were 11 officers and 236 men killed, 1,243 wounded, and 32 missing, in both army and navy. The French lost over a thousand in killed alone, six or seven hundred wounded, over two hundred prisoners, two guns, and a standard.

A few minutes before the enemy sounded the retreat Abercromby sank on the ground fainting from his wound. He was put on a litter, and a blanket placed under his head. As he was being carried away—to die a week later—he gave one last instance of his punctual care for the good of his men. "What is that you are placing under my head?" he asked. "Only a soldier's blanket", was the reply. "Only a soldier's blanket!" cried the General. "A soldier's blanket is of great consequence, and you must send me the name of the soldier to whom it belongs, that it may be returned to him." It is by such conduct that armies are made the instruments of victory. Abercromby's work had in fact been almost done when the troops had landed on the beach at Aboukir. He had shown his confidence in them, and they had shown theirs in him, and with a weapon so perfected to his hand the success of the campaign was hardly in any doubt, if the Navy but kept the enemy's reinforcements out. All honour was given to his memory, and a peerage and pension granted to his widow. But the soldier-like phrases of his successor, Major-General Hely Hutchinson, in announcing his death, form his best epitaph: "Were it permitted for a soldier to regret anyone who has fallen in the service of his country, I might be excused for lamenting him, more than any other person; but it is some consolation to those who tenderly loved him that as his life was honourable so was his death glorious." Nor did he forget him five months later, when the campaign was happily ended. "To them", he wrote of his own and Abercromby's followers, "everything is due, and to me nothing. It was my fate to succeed such a man, who created such a spirit, and established such discipline among them, that little has been left for me to perform, except to follow his maxims, and to endeavour to imitate his conduct."

Want of enterprise prevented Hutchinson from making any further attempt upon Alexandria till reinforcements arrived. On the 25th of March he was joined by the Capitan Pasha, a Turkish general, with six men-of-war and a well-disciplined body of 4,000 troops, most unlike those of the Grand Vizier. The hordes of that chief himself were now crossing the desert. Hutchinson altered his plan. He seized the mouths of the Nile, moved southwards, ascending the river with the aid of a naval flotilla, and by the 10th of May had occupied Rahmanieh, cutting the communications between Cairo and Alexandria. A week later the Turkish army of about 20,000 men had reached the neighbourhood of the capital. Instead of attacking the Vizier at once with every available man before he could make his junction with Hutchinson, the French General, Belliard, made a feeble demonstration in front of him with 5,500 men—only two-thirds of his effective strength—and was thrown back into Cairo. The final surrender was now a mere matter of time. The Mamelukes, those swordsmen resplendent in gold and silver, who, under the name of slaves, had governed Egypt for a hundred years, making the Turkish Pasha no better than a prisoner in his own palace, came over to the British. Six thousand men, one-third being Indian troops, had arrived under Major-General David Baird from India at Cosseir, the nearest point to the Nile on the Red Sea, and were prepared to cross the desert and descend the river to Cairo. Reinforcements from England and Minorca had come or were on their way. Thus strengthened, Hutchinson set about the investment of Cairo in earnest. "France" had long been a talisman to the unhappy exiles, who could not but yield when surrender meant nothing but a safe conduct home on British ships. On June the 27th Belliard signed a convention for the surrender of nearly 13,000 men, of whom 8,000 who were fit for duty were marched down to the coast and shipped to France.

Lake Mareotis, south of Alexandria, had long been flooded, and the only communication between that city and the rest of Egypt was along the narrow strip on which it lay. This was occupied from the west as well as the east from August the 17th, the troops gradually advanced, the outworks were taken, and Menou surrendered on the 2nd of September with 10,500 men. The campaign was at an end. It received no higher eulogist than Napoleon Bonaparte, writing six years later. No operation, he said, was more hazardous; the French army was treble the English. He could ascribe its result to nothing else but a perverse destiny.

This first success obtained by the newly organized British Army over the undefeated troops of France was recognized by the thanks of Parliament, and the bestowal of a peerage and pension on the Commander-in-Chief, already a Knight of the Bath. The reconquest of Egypt, which was thus transferred from French aggression to Turkish misgovernment, did not carry its due weight in the subsequent peace negotiations. The Preliminaries were, in fact, signed in London on the day before Hutchinson's dispatch arrived. But Bonaparte's plans for the establishment of a French colony in what had been in ancient times the granary of Southern Europe, not to speak of his ulterior designs upon India or Constantinople, were for ever baffled. India had, indeed, for perhaps the first time in her history shown that, so far from waiting like a ripe plum for the conqueror to pluck, she was active, and could take the initiative in her own defence. Although it reached Cairo

ADDINGTON'S ADMINISTRATION IN WAR 319

and the coast successively too late to take a part in any engagement, the Indian contingent had its moral effect on the issue of the campaign, a British army had its first and a most useful experience of surmounting the hardships of desert marching between the Red Sea and the Nile, and the world had its first glimpse of the source of strength which lay in Indian battalions drilled by British officers. It was also the first campaign in which officers from the Staff College at High Wycombe bore a part. Apart from the splendid assistance rendered by it on the Nile and on the coast of Egypt itself to the military arm, the Navy in the Mediterranean could boast of very little. Stirred by Bonaparte, Vice-Admiral Ganteaume had most gallantly escaped from Brest in a gale of wind in January, and spent most of the half-year wandering about the Mediterranean in three efforts to land reinforcements in Egypt. He captured a 74-gun ship, the Swiftsure, and on one occasion he would have succeeded in landing troops west of Alexandria had it not been for the resistance displayed by the inhabitants. One more effort was still to be made, and the last laurel of this war to be added to the British Navy's crown.

The Spanish coasts being now left unwatched, Rear-Admiral Sir James Saumarez had been detached from the Channel Fleet in June with his flag flying in the 80-gun ship Caesar, Captain Jahleel Brenton, besides six 74-gun ships of the line. Meanwhile, three of Ganteaume's ships under Rear-Admiral Linois were on their way to join six Spanish ships at Cadiz. The combined squadron was then first to carry out a raid on Lisbon and afterwards to take reinforcements from Southern Italy to Egypt. The French ships had reached Algeciras, on the mainland of Spain facing Gibraltar across the Bay, when Saumarez heard of them. On the 6th of July he attacked with six of his ships, but the wind was light, and it was difficult to get them to stations from which they could bring an effective fire to bear. In attempting this, her captain ran the Hannibal aground. Linois ran two of his own ashore under protection of the Spanish batteries, which did good service in the action, and in the end Saumarez had to withdraw to Gibraltar, leaving a ship in the possession of the enemy. The honours of an action which had been broken off in this way rested with England; the enemy had suffered much heavier loss in killed and wounded, and Linois had his ships to refit and sent urgently to Cadiz for help. But the French success was made much of in Paris, where the wits said that the destruction of the Modern Carthage was now certain, since she had lost her Hannibal. They forgot that she possessed a Caesar, too. That ship was being refitted against time by the most heroic exertions of her crew; for it was now a race for the six Spanish ships to sail round from Cadiz to escort the French ships out before the British were ready for another adventure. It was on the 8th that they arrived, as did the Superb, one of Saumarez's ships which had been left behind off Cadiz. At noon of the 12th of July the combined squadron of nine ships with the dismasted Hannibal in tow were seen to be moving out. Saumarez could count upon three of the ships which had fought with him, and the Superb had just joined. One ship it had been impossible to attempt to refit. The flagship was to the last moment an uncertainty; and Saumarez had even changed his flag to the Audacious, when the crowd of onlookers, many of them soldiers hoping to behold the sister service perform another exploit in those waters which have been more often than any other part of the world the scene of British valour, saw the Caesar warping out of the mole. Brenton was not to be baulked. The Admiral was taken on board; the ship's band played "Come, cheer up, my lads, 'tis to glory we steer," the military band of the garrison answered with "Britons strike home", and such was the ardour of all to wipe off even the slight stain of the check off Algeciras from the national escutcheon that at the last moment a boat came off to the Caesar with several wounded

ADDINGTON'S ADMINISTRATION IN WAR 321

men who would not be denied their share in honours of which they did not feel a doubt. It seemed only natural that five British ships of the line—an 80-gun ship and four 74's—should be pursuing a squadron of six Spanish and three French ships of the line—of which two were 112-gun ships and all but three of a stronger armament than 74's; and that the latter should be making all haste to get away.

It took many hours, however, for those unwieldy ships to get clear, and even then it was found impossible for the Hannibal and the frigate towing her to keep company. They returned to Algeciras. The Superb, under Captain Keats, an officer who never failed, had the place of honour in the pursuit, and Saumarez sent her ahead to attack the enemy. It was night before he dashed, firing right and left, between the two sternmost ships. While the Superb shot ahead in the smoke, each of the two great 112-gun ships mistook the other for the enemy. One had already caught fire, and the other ran aboard her and caught fire also. Both exploded after a short interval with terrible loss of life. Meanwhile the Superb had brought to action and took with very little help a third Spanish ship now flying French colours, and commanded and partly manned by Frenchmen. All this was done without the loss of a man killed. During the rest of the night and well into the morning the pursuit towards Cadiz continued, but owing to the variable winds both squadrons were scattered, and the only other enemy ship engaged, the French Formidable of 80 guns, extricated herself after inflicting heavy loss upon her principal opponent. Whether regarded as an isolated exploit, or in relation to its strategic results, Saumarez's action had been a fine night's work. The old Earl at the Admiralty was in raptures. "This last enterprise of Sir James Saumarez has placed us all on velvet", he wrote, and he was particularly pleased with the efforts by which the ships were refitted at Gibraltar mole ready for the action on the twelfth—a service which he was of all men the most qualified to appreciate. Sir James, who was at the time a baronet in recognition of his previous services, was now made a Knight of the Bath, and obtained a pension of £1,200 a year. Keats's honours were to come.

A venture by Rear-Admiral Sir John Warren was less successful. Almost a year earlier the British community in the port of Leghorn in Northern Italy had been driven out by the French, and its members had successfully maintained themselves in Porto Ferrajo, the capital of the island of Elba between Italy and Corsica. They collected a few hundred Corsicans, Neapolitans, and local levies, and got supplies from Warren, who also brought them 300 soldiers, making their force up to about 1,500 men. The defence of the place was under Isaac Grant, the Vice-Consul, and was gallantly carried on against a French army of 5,000 men; but an attempt of Warren to throw in 3,000 men was foiled with heavy loss. Grant maintained his position, however, till the peace, and in a successful attack made by him upon a French post as late as November fired what were probably the last shots of the war in Europe.

One of the last acts of Pitt's Ministry had been to equip a fleet of 18 sail of the line, with 35 smaller vessels, under Admiral Sir Hyde Parker, to clear up the situation in the Baltic. Denmark was to be given forty-eight hours to abandon the Armed Neutrality of her own will, or to be coerced into doing so. The expedition sailed on the 12th of March. The officer selected as Second-in-Command was Vice-Admiral Horatio Nelson, who had been created Lord Nelson of the Nile for the victory in which he annihilated the French fleet on the 1st of August, 1798. Born the 29th of September, 1758, the son of a Norfolk rector, he had entered the Navy at the age of twelve under the care of an uncle, and served the usual rough apprenticeship to the sea. He had even done part of his time in a merchant ship, and had there acquired a sympathy with the seaman before the mast, which he ever afterwards retained. While still a boy he displayed a courage, a professional ability, and a devotion to the service which were very quickly recognized; and he became post-captain before he was twenty-one. In his early years he was remarkable for a taciturn disposition and a confidence in himself which mark the born man of action. Feeling the repugnance common to many men of this stamp from busying himself in matters in which he could not lead, he took little interest in affairs out of the way of his profession, and it is partly due to this that, although he possessed some friends in high quarters, notably the sailor Prince William Henry, Duke of Clarence, he never became a man of the world. But what distinguished him most of all was his power of leadership. This gift is impossible without professional capacity of a high order, which Nelson had. It was the fruit of careful and devoted study of all matters connected with the service, and of tactics in particular, although he was hampered by a lack of general education remarkable even in a sailor of the time. But the devotion with which he was able to inspire those who followed him was due especially to his activity, his readiness to be the foremost in danger, and above all to his love for those whom he led. It has been common to represent him as almost the typical dare-devil; and part at least of his success as due to the mystical law by which fortune favours the bold. Yet no fact in biography is better known than the amount of careful thought, often for weeks and months together, which he bestowed upon his battles before he fought them. And at the age which he had now reached, he displayed all the caution which his rank and responsibility required. In dealing with those under him he showed no little art. He was not in the habit of inculcating courage and devotion to duty in their minds. He rather assumed that those qualities were already there, and there are many stories of how he curbed the impatience or relieved the disappointment of those whose anxiety to close with the enemy against the heaviest odds was, he implied, at least equal with his own.

As has been said, he deliberately limited his own horizon. There are indications in his correspondence that, had he given his mind to world strategy, he might have given advice to the Government which would, if taken, have prevented some ghastly mistakes. His letters show how little confidence he reposed in the Great Powers of the Continent. Nor did he believe in expeditions to distant parts of the world. "A blow struck in Europe", he wrote to Lord Moira within a year of his death, "would do more towards making us respected, and of course facilitate a Peace, than the possession of Mexico or Peru." He was thinking of the support of a national resistance to French oppression of a Mediterranean people—such a resistance as Southern Italy had offered in 1799—by such a blow as was afterwards struck by British arms at Maida in 1806. A force so employed was able to communicate more easily by sea with England than a French army could overland with France. And the latter would be gradually exhausted in the efforts to reduce patriots struggling in their own mountain fastnesses. In the event, it was another Mediterranean people which made the successful effort. It is not difficult to imagine how warmly he would have welcomed the opportunity offered by Spain in 1808. But he never studied widely and developed his views. Had he done so, he might have saved Government from dissipating the strength of the nation in the way it did; but he could hardly have been a better sailor and might easily have been a worse. This want of breadth, however, hampered him in other and more serious ways. Confined as his vision was usually to the limits of his ship or his squadron, or at least to the area in which it was to operate, he was apt to regard the arrangements of his superiors at the Admiralty with a good deal of peevishness. He neither saw their point of view nor wanted to. This impatience of restraint is again common enough to leaders of war. He had another failing, less often found among men of that class, although by no means rare, namely vanity. He sometimes laughed at himself for it, even while he was giving it free play. He glorified himself and his achievements to an absurd extent. But if he spoke to people about them, he was only telling them what—in a full-blooded and uncritical age—they loved to hear. He always put those who had served under him before himself, and his country first of all. Much was forgiven him. Had he had more knowledge of the world, he could never have fallen so rapidly and so completely a victim to the celebrated adventuress Lady Hamilton, who had found a protector and then a husband in an elderly diplomatist who was Nelson's friend. She was a creature to be loved; she was made by the painter Romney the subject of the most beautiful of English portraits; and she had a rare gift of enthusiasm. But she was essentially vulgar, and it was ridiculous of Nelson to call her his sainted Emma.

One more curious weakness remains to be noticed, rare indeed in a fighting man. At this time he appeared the mere wreck of a man. He had lost an eye in Corsica, his right arm in Teneriffe, and had received a serious wound in the head at the Battle of the Nile, which seems to have seriously affected his judgment at the time when he first came under the thrall of Lady Hamilton. At a little over forty years of age he was somewhat wizened, and although really of the average height, his restlessness and vivacity combined with his general spareness of build and the smallness of his extremities to suggest a little man; and so he has been generally regarded. He was never constitutionally strong; he had been reduced by Mediterranean fever; and he suffered frequently from sea-sickness. Fretted by all this, he not only felt his body to be unequal to the demands of his aspiring mind, but constantly supposed it to be almost on the point of dissolution. But this was imagination. When there was a chance of getting to grips with the enemy, he invariably made a miraculous recovery. The hero was a good valetudinarian; and regular exercise, early hours, and careful dieting during the last years of his life, enabled his medical adviser, Doctor Beatty, to describe his health as excellent. What Nelson thought were mortal heart attacks were only spasms caused by indigestion; and his vital parts after death were found to be perfectly healthy and to resemble those of a much younger man.

Ships entering the Baltic Sea have to pass first north-eastward up the Skager Rack; then, after rounding the north coast of the Peninsula of Jutland, they turn due south through the Cattegat. Southward of this tract of sea, a line of islands almost joins the mainland of Denmark to Sweden. The largest and easternmost of these is Zealand, on the east side of which lies the city of Copenhagen. It is approached by a channel named the Sound, only three miles wide at its northern point. Here stands, well out to sea, Kronenburg Castle, and behind it and to the south the town of Elsinore. The "wild and stormy steep" of Campbell's contemporary poem is as much a dream as Shakspere's "cliff, that beetles o'er his base into the sea", to the dreadful summit of which Horatio feared the Ghost tempting Hamlet. Mariners, after passing the Strait, found themselves in what seemed to be a vast lake full of islands and shoals, surrounded by flat cultivated lands, the chief objects of the landscape being the gothic towers of the Danish capital. Nelson's plan, which he persuaded Parker to adopt, was for the whole fleet to sail boldly past the two frowning bastions, Danish and Swedish, which guarded either side of the entry to the Sound. Copenhagen was then to be passed by a channel which was out of reach of the batteries, and the main attack delivered from the southward. This plan had several advantages. The British fleet —or that part of it engaged in the main operation—being between the Danish fleet at Copenhagen and the Baltic Sea, where the Russian and Swedish fleets were, would be able to prevent a junction being made before the attack on the Danes was delivered. Again, sailing northward with a favourable wind, the British ships engaged would, if crippled, drift back among the friends whom they had left behind in Copenhagen Roads, instead of being carried by a northerly wind into the Baltic. Further, they would not have to depend only upon the wind, as the current setting northward would carry them to their assigned stations, and afterwards take them out of action when necessary. Finally—and this was the most important consideration from a tactical point of view—the town was strongly defended at its northern end by a battery formed upon two outlying artificial islands, called the Three Crowns Battery, commemorating the days when the crowns of Denmark, Norway, and Sweden were united. The southern approach had no such protection.

The Commander-in-Chief had informed the Governor of Kronenburg Castle that he intended to pass through the Strait on the west side of which that fortress stood, and had been refused permission. The authority which the Governor claimed was long established. All Europe had acquiesced in Denmark's right to command the Sound. For years traders had lowered their topsails and paid a toll for the privilege of entering or leaving the Baltic by the channels which the Danes had buoyed. The giant Russia—nay, Sweden herself, who held the opposite battery guarding the entrance—had recognized the claim. And now that the two guardians were united in their aims, the Governor thought himself safe. But, contrary to what the British had supposed, the Swedish battery turned out to have only eight guns, and even these did not so much as open fire on the fleet as it passed through. Finding that they could safely do so, the ships kept on that side out of range of the Danish batteries and to the general surprise found themselves anchored on the afternoon of the 30th of March at about fifteen miles from Copenhagen, without a single vessel having been touched. After moving ten miles nearer the admirals carefully examined the defences, and Parker finally decided to accept Nelson's offer to make the attempt. In the afternoon of the 1st of April a detachment of twelve ships of the line, with the usual following of smaller vessels, sailed southward, and anchored that evening two miles on the other side of Copenhagen.

Nelson had had an early training as a pilot, which had made him confident in himself among shoals and sandbanks, as he showed by the boldness of his attack at the Nile. He understood every difficulty and took every precaution. Up to now much of the rebuoying of the channel, the Danes having naturally removed or misplaced buoys, had been done through his personal and indefatigable exertions, spending hours and hours in a small boat amid the floating ice. He had with him an officer in whom he placed a peculiar trust—Captain Thomas Hardy, lent from the St. George, his flagship, which on account of her greater draught, being a 98-gun ship, had been left behind with the Commander-in-Chief. He sent him the same evening in a small boat to examine the King's Channel, as that nearest to the town was called, as far as the Danish line. This Hardy did, actually sounding with a pole, to avoid the noise of the lead, round the first of the enemy's ships and back. He reported to Nelson that the Channel was practicable.

That Admiral was no believer in fettering his subordinates with elaborate instructions as to what to do against a mobile enemy. But here he had to deal with a fixed line of ships and floating batteries, stretched in front of Copenhagen to prevent its bombardment. His orders for the attack were detailed and precise. The defending line consisted of seven two-deckers, mostly dismasted, the strongest of which, the Syaelland, carried 74 guns. Two of these were anchored together at each end. The remaining three, along with eleven floating batteries, filled the space between. The whole mounted 628 guns. Ten British ships of the line were to

ADDINGTON'S ADMINISTRATION IN WAR 329

attack this part of the enemy's force. These alone carried over 700 long guns, besides carronades. Victory was assured if they could be brought properly into action. Every ship was given her station. The stations were carefully arranged so that each ship should have an enemy worthy of her, two or three batteries counting for one ship. Nelson's own temporary flagship, the Elephant, was to be placed opposite the only enemy 74. The first five ships were to take up their respective positions opposite the nearest nine of the enemy, firing while on their way to their stations; in this way the nearest end of the line would soon be crushed. The rest were to pass outside them, each ship, as she became the leading ship of the column, anchoring by the stern on reaching her station in front of the leading ship already engaged. The two last ships to take their stations were to pass beyond the line, and to attack the two dismasted or block ships which, along with two ships of the line and other vessels, lay at the northern entrance of the harbour in front of the Three Crowns Battery. Minor parts were assigned to the gunboats, sloops, bomb-vessels, and fire-ships. Parker had, on his side, arranged that he with his eight ships of the line would weigh at the same moment as his Second-in-Command, and menace the Three Crowns Battery and the ships stationed there.

Nelson was prepared to wait for a fair wind. He had not to wait long. The day of the 2nd of April was heralded by a light wind from the south-east, and the various signals were given for the attack, concluding, after the ships had become actually engaged, with the favourite, Number 16, "Engage the enemy more closely". But, after giving him the wind which he wanted, Fortune had seemed to withdraw her favours. All the pilots refused to work. When a start was made the Agamemnon, not being able to weather the shoal and stand into the King's Channel, was obliged to anchor. Two 74's, the Bellona and Russell, ran aground, and were only able to engage at long range. But the nine which remained got into action very nearly in their assigned stations, no ships of the line being, however, available to attack the Three Crowns Battery, or the ships in front of it. A minor difficulty was that the wind, which was fair for Nelson, was foul for Parker, who was able to do no more than make a demonstration at three miles' distance from the Battery.

The Commander-in-Chief's inability to get into action nearly entailed a much greater calamity. Soon after one o'clock, when the battle had raged for about three hours, Parker became obsessed with his own difficulties, coupled with what he was able to see of those of his Second-in-Command, who had not yet achieved any notable success. He made signal Number 39—to discontinue the action. This gave occasion for the most famous episode in Nelson's career. Asked whether it should be repeated, he first said: "No! Acknowledge it!" There was a soldier on deck in command of the troops intended for a landing operation. This was Colonel the Honourable William Stewart, to whose forced inactivity history is indebted for several amusing traits of Nelson's character, recorded by him at the time. On this occasion he observed the Admiral pacing the deck in considerable agitation, a fact which, he wrote, "was always known by his moving the stump of his right arm". Then he stopped, and after a passing remark upon the signal to Stewart himself, he put his glass up. Like most great commanders he was no stranger to those touches of rugged humour which raise the spirit of the fighting man. "And then", adds Stewart, "with an archness peculiar to his character, putting the glass to his blind eye, he exclaimed: 'I really do not see the signal!'" On the contrary, the opposite signal, Number 16, was kept hoisted. Had the Commander-in-Chief's signal been obeyed, and an attempt made to discontinue the action, it would have been impossible to bring away the ships which were aground, other ships would probably have met with the same fate, and the general result would have been disaster.

But the event, as it turned out, was rather fortunate. Nelson's next in command, Rear-Admiral Thomas Graves, flew his flag in the Defiance, which was the leading ship of the line. Being so, she was also the nearest ship to the Commander-in-Chief. She, as well as the Monarch next to her, was heavily engaged by the Three Crowns Battery. He must have felt a special responsibility in this situation. He had just ahead of him a group of half a dozen frigates and sloops, which Nelson had detached to assist in the attack of the ships at the harbour's mouth; and they were being badly mauled in the attempt. Accordingly, without obeying the offending signal himself, he repeated it by hoisting it as an optional order below and to one side of the famous Number 16, which still held the place of honour. Not a ship of the line moved. But the "gallant and good Captain Riou", as Nelson called him, who was in command of the frigates and sloops, took the opportunity to draw off; and not a moment too soon. Hardly had he given the order when he was himself killed by a round-shot.

And now the enemy's fire began to slacken. At the south end of the line, where the Désiré frigate had done effective service in the absence of the Agamemnon, the Danish resistance was overborne. Near the centre, the Dannebrog, flagship of Commodore Fischer, who commanded the enemy's fleet, was set on fire by Nelson's own flagship. The Elephant had not been able to reach the Syaelland owing to the shortening of the British line. Nevertheless, the Danish 74 was properly taken in hand, her cables were shot away, and she was carried out of the line. Driven from one ship to another, the Commodore at length had to hoist his pennant ashore, in the Three Crowns Battery. Here the Danish resistance was unabated.

Fighting within gunshot of their own capital, under the eyes of their Prince, there was something of undisciplined fury in the behaviour of the defenders, many of whom were drawn straight from the plough or out of the streets; British boats on their way to take possession of ships which had struck their colours were fired upon, although the ships were useless for the purpose of effective resistance. For by this time the battle was being carried on mainly between the shore batteries and the British ships; shot from both sides struck the unfortunate Danish vessels, and in the interest of humanity it was necessary to remove them, which Nelson had every right to do. He decided that, unless permitted to do so, he would send fire-ships against them and burn them. He sent a letter ashore to the Crown Prince to this effect, addressed: "To the Brothers of Englishmen, the Danes." Meanwhile the battle continued with success against the northern part of the line, to which the near approach of two of Parker's ships contributed. At three o'clock a flag of truce came out, and the battle came to an end, only three out of the eighteen vessels forming the Danish line of defence escaping. The prizes were, however, too much battered to carry away; those that were not wrecked could only be burnt, except one ship of the line—the only trophy. On the British side the truce was very welcome. The Three Crowns Battery, even though it remained undefeated, for it was not thought advisable to land a force to attack it, as originally planned, could not have prevented a bombardment of the city. But, on the other hand, the British were in difficulties of their own, for the moment the cessation of fire allowed their ships to weigh and sail northward several touched the shoals, and as many as seven vessels were seen aground at the same time. The truce, which was extended after the Danish Adjutant-General had been sent four miles out to confer with Parker himself, gave time to get them off. But one frigate could not be floated until 7 a.m. on the 4th.

The conflict had been strenuous, and in five of the British ships the losses were severe. Of these the Monarch lost the most—56 killed, including her captain, Robert Mosse, and 164 wounded. The total casualties were 255 killed and

688 wounded, the slightly wounded not being included. The Danish killed and wounded amounted to between 1,600 and 1,800, according to Fischer's estimate, which he did not claim as complete. The prisoners amounted possibly to twice that number. The result was in every way satisfactory. The British obtained their object, and the Danes retained their honour and saved their capital. The intrepidity of the defence was admirable in every way. Ships were manned three times over, reinforcements arriving from the shore to replace casualties; and the Rear-Admiral, writing to his brother on the following day, told him how one of the captured ships had between two and three hundred dead on her decks besides those which had been thrown overboard. This preserved Copenhagen from bombardment, an event which would have produced a lasting bitterness between Dane and Briton, which Nelson was most anxious to avert. In this he was completely successful. So good a foundation for reconcilement had been laid by the communications which he had inaugurated, that he was directed by Parker to go ashore and open up negotiations for a regular armistice. This he did at noon on the 3rd. "A negotiator is out of my line" are the words with which he commenced one of the two letters to Addington in which he described his conversations with the Prince. Nothing can be less true. As usual with fighting men on such occasions, Nelson remarked upon his own unfitness for the job, but, as usual, he was at least as successful as a diplomatist would have been, because he enjoyed, in common with other soldiers and sailors, the benefit of a training which gave patience and courtesy with opponents, quickness of apprehension, clearness of mind, and the power of keeping to the main point. Besides, frankness is often necessary in diplomacy, and to exercise that quality in a manner which would not be permitted to the mere civilian is the prescriptive right of the fighting professions. In the postscript to the letter just quoted he wrote of the Danish Foreign Minister:

"I have the pleasure to tell you that Count Bernstorff was too ill to make me a visit yesterday. I had sent him a message to leave off his Ministerial duplicity, and to recollect that he had now British Admirals to deal with, who came with their hearts in their hands. I hate the fellow."

His landing in the enemy's capital, his reception by a populace in whose attitude anger was tempered by admiration, his dinner at the palace, at which he embraced and recommended for promotion to admiral an officer of seventeen who had attacked his flagship with the greatest courage, were ordinary incidents in his picturesque career. And nothing could have done more to bring about the right atmosphere of restored friendship, for which he had asked when he had penned his first note during the battle: "The brave Danes are the brothers, and should never be the enemies, of the English." In such circumstances there was no great difficulty in securing an armistice for fourteen weeks from the 9th of April, the date when it was signed, which gave Great Britain what she desired. The Treaty of Armed Neutrality was suspended, the fleet was allowed to get supplies in Denmark, and a free passage was assured for operations against Sweden or Russia. Danish trade was reopened and the prisoners returned.

The news of the victory was well received in England—so far as words went. In moving the thanks of the House of Lords to those engaged, St. Vincent gave it as his opinion that their conduct far surpassed anything that was to be found in the glorious annals of the British Navy. Writing to Nelson with this impression still in his mind on the 31st of May, he said:

"To find a fit successor, your Lordship well knows, is no easy task, for I never saw the man in our Profession, excepting yourself and Troubridge, who possessed the magic art of infusing the same spirit into others which inspired his actions, exclusive of other talents and habits of business not common to naval characters. . . . Your Lordship's whole conduct, from your first appointment to this hour, is the subject of our constant admiration; it does not become me to make comparisons. All agree there is but one Nelson; that he may long continue the pride of his Country is the fervent wish of your Lordship's truly affectionate

"St. Vincent."

The subject of this eulogy received a step in the peerage, becoming a Viscount. Rear-Admiral Graves was made a Knight of the Bath. This was all. No medals were conferred. Parker was first of all thanked, and then superseded in the command by Nelson on account of his indecision and moral cowardice—unworthy of one who had done brilliant service in his early career.

Meanwhile the head of the League was no more. The men about the Russian court could no longer tolerate Paul's savage exhibitions of mental derangement. Ten days before the Battle of Copenhagen he had been strangled in his palace. His son, Alexander the First, who succeeded him, released the British ships, and concluded a convention on the points in dispute, to which Sweden and Denmark also agreed. Danish devotion to the common cause had not been altogether in vain, and several advantages were secured. But on several main points, such as the right of search and the right to make prize of enemy goods in neutral bottoms, Great Britain had her way. The rivers of Germany were once more opened; the Armed Neutrality was at an end; and the British fleet was recalled.

Baulked of further hope of exercising pressure upon England through the aid of his northern allies, Bonaparte had turned his attention to the possibility of some demonstration in the narrow seas which separate England from the Continent. He proceeded to collect a flotilla in Boulogne, and made other preparations elsewhere. War could now bring him neither glory nor advantage. He desired peace, and he was aware that, by making such a feint (which could at any time be converted into a genuine attack), he was adopting the best way of affecting the morale of the civil population on the adverse side, and creating a similar disposition in Great Britain to his own. He placed his best admiral, Latouche-Tréville, in command of the invasion flotilla in March; that officer, still a Rear-Admiral in spite of his fifty years' service, set seriously to work. He turned his attention particularly to improving the defences of Boulogne, which he selected as the best port of embarkation. But he met with not much more than lukewarm support from Bonaparte, who was also considering an expedition from Brest to Trinidad and Tobago.

As the summer wore on it was necessary to be more serious with the preparations for invasion, in order to keep the minds of the British in increasing tension. In this Bonaparte was completely successful. St. Vincent now took the danger seriously, and on the 24th of July passed an order appointing Nelson to a command for which he was not well fitted—that of a miscellaneous squadron of about thirty vessels, and also of the south-eastern coastal defences, including the evasive Sea Fencibles. He was even kept there for some days after the eventual preliminaries of peace were signed. It was an appointment made almost entirely in order to reassure the public, and enable it to feel that their coasts were safe under England's greatest admiral. So far as the naval authorities were concerned, there was no alarm. But nothing was left to chance. "Our first defence", said Nelson, "is close to the enemy's ports." But assuming that line to be broken through, he looked forward to a possible invasion by row-boats crossing in calm weather in twelve hours from Boulogne to the Kentish coast simultaneously with another flotilla attacking Essex from Dunkerque and the Dutch ports. To meet these he designed three flotillas of flat boats and other small boats. The former was to be manned by the Sea Fencibles, who, had they been tested, would probably have proved inefficient.

Something better seemed to be wanted than to sit ashore organizing this unsatisfactory means of defence against an enemy whose exact point of attack could not be divined, and Nelson would not have been Nelson if he had spent his energy in the work of inspection only. He hoisted his flag on the 30th of July; and on the 3rd of August he made a reconnaissance in force of Latouche-Tréville's twenty-one gun-vessels moored in a line end to end in front of Boulogne. He followed next day with an attack by bomb-vessels which severely tested the defences of the port. The British admiral was able, referring no doubt to present conditions, to inform the Premier that in his belief the result had shown that an embarkation at Boulogne with a view to invasion was impossible; while on his side the French admiral was compelled to recognize the inadequacy of the vessels which he had placed for the protection of the harbour. His efforts to improve the defences were successful. On the 15th of August Nelson reappeared off Boulogne with a large force, and at night launched four divisions against the flotilla. Owing to the currents, for which due allowance had not been made, they did not reach the enemy's line at the same time, and one never arrived at all. Only one vessel was carried, and she was too strongly secured to be towed off. The check was a serious one, the losses in killed and wounded amounting to 172. At the same time Nelson was encouraged by the difficulty which—as his own failure had shown—the currents and tides would put in the way of a flotilla attempting to row across the Channel. Henceforward he confined his energies to inspection and to as close a blockade as possible. There could now be no danger of an invasion before the equinoctial gales would make it impossible. The situation had had its ironic features. While the British were alarmed, the French on their side had been led to believe stories of the preparation of shallow-draught vessels and of the assembly of troops for a descent on Boulogne or the island of Walcheren. But it was Bonaparte's menace which was the more effective. His demonstration corresponded to his calculations, and the peace for which all France and most of England hoped was being brought sensibly nearer.

CHAPTER V

ADDINGTON'S ADMINISTRATION DURING THE PEACE

(October 1801—May 1803)

The war had reached a stage at which its continuance seemed to be for the benefit of neither party, when a Gazette Extraordinary of the 2nd of October, 1801, announced that preliminary articles of peace had been signed the day before between the Foreign Secretary, Lord Hawkesbury, and Louis Otto on the part of France. This gentleman had been engaged in a former unsuccessful negotiation with Grenville, and had been ordered to remain in London as Commissioner for the exchange of prisoners of war by Bonaparte, who was anxious, now that he had disposed of his continental enemies, to pursue his further encroachments under the cover of universal peace. But if he was eager, the new British Ministry was none the less so; and as early as the 21st of March it had proposed to negotiate. The spring and summer were spent in a struggle for position, in which —had they only appreciated the fact—the British Government had an immense advantage. Once Abercromby's initial successes were known, the restoration of Egypt to the Turks might have been taken as certain; and the negotiations might well have been protracted until the French army surrendered.

Nor was the failure of British Ministers to do this their only mistake. Great Britain possessed a long list of conquests from France and her allies—mainly West Indian Islands. Of these, the most important in the West Indies were the great island of Trinidad and two smaller islands—Tobago, next to it, and Martinique, one of the more northerly of the chain of rocks and islands which forms the eastern boundary of the Caribbean Sea. In the East, she had, besides the French possessions in India, the Dutch possessions of Cochin on its south-west coast and Ceylon. Added to these were the Cape of Good Hope, captured from the Dutch, Minorca from the Spanish, and Malta from the French, who had themselves taken it from the Knights of the Order of St. John of Jerusalem, an outworn survival of the Crusaders. As early as the 14th of April, when the news of the success of Aboukir had not reached England, Hawkesbury was bold enough to demand the retention of Trinidad—or Tobago—Martinique, Malta, and Ceylon, besides some smaller conquests. These sanguine proposals were curtly refused, and new bases had to be found. Bonaparte employed the interval in hurling his unwilling vassal, Spain, against England's old ally, Portugal. The British brought themselves to suppose that, in return for further concessions, that country would be secured against loss, and obtained an article in the Preliminaries guaranteeing her integrity in general terms. But when it was elucidated afterwards in the Definitive Treaty, considerable cessions of territory by Portugal to both Spain and France were confirmed. British intervention had done very little good. The astuteness of the First Consul combined with the anxiety of Addington not to let slip the opportunity of appearing before the world as the author of a peace which Pitt had four times failed to secure, to effect an arrangement very greatly to Great Britain's disadvantage. Of all her conquests, she retained only Ceylon and Trinidad. She kept none of her gains in the Mediterranean. Not only did Hawkesbury fail to recover the independence of those parts of Italy which had passed under French control, but he obtained no provision against future encroachments; though separate stipulations were made for the evacuation of the Kingdom of Naples and the Roman Territory, which had been already provided for by separate treaties with the Powers affected. The situation in the Mediterranean was thus altered completely to Great Britain's disadvantage: in war because under the Preliminaries she would no longer retain the bases of Minorca and Malta; in peace because France had acquired, through her dominant influence on the mainland, the power to close the ports to British trade. As to Holland, the case was even worse. Great Britain had gone to war for the independence of the Low Countries, and in this she had completely failed. Nor was this all. Whereas by the Treaty of Lunéville Austria, who was considered to have gone to war for the security or recovery of her own possessions, had stipulated for the independence of the Batavian Republic, Great Britain had not merely not done so, but accepted the Dutch overseas possession of Ceylon by the good offices of the very enemy against whom she had been fighting by Holland's side. Similar was the case of another former ally, Spain, who gave up Trinidad. On the other hand, the French Republic maintained her proud boast as the "One and Indivisible", and gave up nothing. When the final Treaty, based upon these Preliminaries, was afterwards concluded and published, the sensation caused by the omission of all mention of Northern Italy or Switzerland, or of any commercial arrangements, was not confined to England. An observer in Berlin declared that he could not believe she would have been so inattentive to her interests. He supposed that there must be some equally elaborate secret treaty in existence.

The news of the peace was received with greater joy on the British side of the Channel than in France. But even in England discontent soon showed itself. Only a week after the peace was known Nelson wrote: "England called loudly for it, and now I see it is to be abused; but Englishmen are never satisfied, full or fasting." The French Envoy enjoyed a triumphal progress from Dover to London and the mob drew his carriage from Portland Place to Whitehall. But the cheers were for Bonaparte, and the Ministers got none. It was not a national rejoicing. That the joy was much greater among the English lower classes was admitted by Fox, who rightly held it to be an additional reason why peace should have been made. It did not matter if the

ADDINGTON'S ADMINISTRATION IN PEACE 341

people never stopped to inquire about the terms. This only showed how weary they were of war and high prices. As Sheridan asked a year later: "Did they rejoice that we had gained Trinidad and Ceylon? Would two farthing candles have been burnt less had we not obtained them?" It was not a Dutch spice island or a Spanish sugar island the more which contented them. They understood something of loyalty to their King, and to the national ideals enshrined in the British constitution, which was endangered by the revolutionary movement upon the Continent; but the niceties of a credit balance from colonial conquests were beyond them. Great Britain had given up much which she had won during the war; but throughout the eighteenth century it had been usual that she should do so. The colonies restored to her enemies became hostages held at the disposal of her predominant sea-power in any future war. The case of Malta was different. Not being a French or even a Spanish possession, it would not be possible for Great Britain to seize the island, once restored to the Order of St. John of Jerusalem, whenever she wanted it, in the manner in which Bonaparte had seized it on his way to Egypt in 1798. It was a mistake to give up Malta; and both Pitt and Fox, anxious as they were to support the Peace, did not disguise this fact in the debate which followed in the House of Commons a month after the publication of the terms.

Apart from this instance, the real vice of the Preliminaries lay broader and deeper than in any question of territorial cessions. Great Britain had gone to war over the affairs of the Continent, and everything now showed that the First Consul did not intend her to have a voice there. The encroaching arm of France was not thrust back, nor were bounds set to it. This became clearer still during the negotiations which followed. The British Plenipotentiary, Lord Cornwallis, though treated with the highest personal consideration, was kept waiting for months at Paris and Amiens, while the First Consul developed plans of further aggrandisement in Italy. One of these was the reorganization of the Cisalpine Republic, which submitted to a new constitution dictated at Lyons. Bonaparte himself became President of it by its new name of the Italian Republic. Master of this large territory, stretching from the northern border along a great part of the Adriatic coast, he held those other parts of Italy which were not yet annexed to France at his mercy, and the provision for the evacuation of Southern Italy in the Treaty lost most of its value. A part of Switzerland was also detached, and steps taken to compel the rest —the Helvetic Republic—to accept another constitution, although its independence, like that of the Cisalpine Republic, had been guaranteed by the Treaty of Lunéville. At the same time treaties were published, which were either hastily made immediately after the conclusion of the Preliminaries, or had been kept secret until that event took place, all of which contained something to the disadvantage of Great Britain. Even the separate treaty made by France with England's ally, Portugal, secured special commercial advantages for both parties. There was nothing of this in the Preliminaries signed in London; and the whole trend of treaties made with other countries was to exclude Great Britain from the trade of the Continent for the benefit of France. And it was for Peace and Plenty, as the mottoes displayed at the peace rejoicings showed, that she had sacrificed so much.

"A peace which every man ought to be glad of, but no man can be proud of." The phrase was used by Sheridan in his speech on the Address to the Throne, at the beginning of the new session of Parliament of October the 29th. The debates which followed were variations on the same theme. In the House of Lords it was severely attacked by the ex-Ministers Grenville and Spencer. It was supported, not merely by St. Vincent, who would naturally do so as a member of the Government, but by Nelson, who said, truly enough, that the great object was to keep Malta out of France's hands, and that the Cape of Good Hope was worse than useless as a place of call on the way to India. In the Commons almost every speaker who was not a Minister—even Pitt, Fox, and Wilberforce, who gave the Peace the strongest support they could—contributed his doubts and apprehensions. Here, too, there were a few who had no doubts at all. Thomas Grenville thought like his brother. Windham, who was reduced to the depths of despair, argued that so long as France's fixed purpose of accomplishing the final overthrow of the country was maintained, the peace was no more than an armed truce, during which it was fatal to throw away the advantages which had been gained.

Events which followed soon afterwards lent support to this view of the situation. In December Bonaparte sent a large expedition to the West Indies to subdue the revolted island of San Domingo. Nothing could have shown better how well he knew the Addington Ministry. Were the negotiations to fail, a superior British force might have easily fallen upon this detachment; and the knowledge of this ought to have enabled them to raise their tone. But it only proved a source of embarrassment. It was, of course, necessary to reinforce the fleet in the West Indies. When this was known, the seamen felt bitterly that the only result of the general peace for them was to be sent to that pestilential quarter which had already proved the grave of so many thousands of soldiers and sailors. A spirit of mutiny arose, which came to a head in the Temeraire. The ringleaders were sentenced to death, the disorder was put down, and the squadron sailed.

It was not as yet possible to make any reduction in armaments, and the only other point of a reassuring nature which had been touched upon in the King's Speech was the excellence of the harvest. It was a timely relief. It is probable that at this time almost the whole of the agricultural population labouring for weekly earnings were in receipt of poor-law relief. Some of the exceptional measures introduced to deal with the scarcity were now no longer necessary. The law prohibiting the consumption of bread until twenty-four hours after it had been baked was repealed. The distilleries were reopened. A proposal to continue the prohibition produced an interesting reply. Although, Addington said, a quantity amounting to less than one-tenth of the average barley crop was used in them, it was not all lost, as vast numbers of hogs were fed on the refuse. It was impossible, he added, to check the growth of illicit stills, which produced more moral evil than legal distilleries, and the defalcation of the revenue was estimated at £400,000.

Interesting disclosures regarding the imperfect state of the finances were also made on the occasion of an inquiry into the deficiencies in the Civil List. As he had often done before, George III had to ask Parliament to make a grant, this time of £990,000, to pay off deficiencies. He had not been extravagant; but the vice was in the system by which the person of the King, as an individual maintaining a family and household on the scale required for a sovereign, had never been fully separated from his position as head of the State. The consequence was that the Civil List comprised, not merely the King's privy purse, but a great deal besides; including the salaries of the Lord Chancellor, the Judges, the Ministers abroad, the Chancellor of the Exchequer, and the Lords of the Treasury. Some of these were not unnaturally eager to see the question brought up, seeing that their salaries, which were already three-quarters in arrear, would have been cancelled in another quarter according to rule. The grant was made, in spite of the unfair opposition of Fox, who was, however, quite right in complaining that this system freed Ministers from parliamentary control as regards some objects of expenditure. For the purpose of his satire he personified the Civil List: "Thus the civil list: 'I wish to have a new secretary of state.'—'But have you the means to pay for him?'—'No; but the House of Commons will pay cheerfully. I have good friends there.'—'But ask your friends first.'—'Oh, no! it is not necessary; I can use freedom; I know my friends very well; they will be quite delighted with the opportunity. They have brothers and cousins to provide for. Never fear; let the expense be incurred. Say nothing about the matter at present; the House of Commons will pay the money and ask no questions."

Meanwhile, at Amiens, where the negotiations for a Definitive Treaty of Peace were being carried on, Joseph Bonaparte, who represented his brother, the First Consul, was skilfully maintaining the position of the negotiator who is, of the two, less anxious to see the business through. On more than one occasion affairs reached a critical point. But there was no real danger of the negotiations failing altogether. The First Consul could not possibly have afforded to renew the war, for domestic reasons. It was only after the signature of peace with France's last remaining enemy that he was able to obtain from his supporters the proposal that, in recognition of his services to his country, he should be declared Consul for life—the coveted step on the road to the dignity of Emperor. The matter had really become urgent; and, once Bonaparte had settled the Italian question, it was found to be the Dutch and Spanish plenipotentiaries who caused delay by their reluctance to present themselves for the purpose of signing away rich overseas possessions as a penalty for having been compelled to fight on France's side against their original ally. At last, on the 27th of March, the Definitive Treaty between the United Kingdom on the one hand, and France, Spain, and the Batavian Republic on the other, was concluded. The articles left vague in the Preliminaries were all elaborated to the advantage of France. The most important one was the tenth, relating to Malta. The original arrangement was that it should be restored to the Order, and for the purpose of rendering it completely independent of either Great Britain or France it was to be placed under the protection and guarantee of a third Power, to be agreed upon in the Definitive Treaty. The obvious protector of the Order was the Czar. But Bonaparte refused to accept Russia as the single guarantee Power. The new article contained thirteen elaborate stipulations, almost impossible of fulfilment, the most important of which was the sixth, which ran: "The independence of the islands of Malta, Gozo, and Comino, as well as the present arrangement, shall be under the protection and guarantee of Great Britain, France, Austria, Russia, Spain, and Prussia." Thus the treaty depended for its fulfilment upon the consent of four outside Powers. Any or all of them might refuse the guarantee, or impose conditions, but no provision was made for this. It was afterwards argued on the part of France that the evacuation of the island was independent of this condition. But, if so, there was no guarantee for the arrangement which was to take place after the British had left. The French attitude upon the point in fact suggests that, while Great Britain was intent upon the most practicable means of rendering the island independent of both countries, France left matters purposely involved, in order to provide herself with an opportunity of selecting a favourable ground of dispute at a future date. The article was, in fact, instinct with occasions of quarrel, and if ever there were truth in the grim jest about the treaty, which, however deadly and disastrous it seemed, bore within it the seeds of a just and durable war, there was truth here.

Had France intended to take seriously any part of the tenth article, except that providing for the evacuation of Malta, she would have joined Great Britain without delay in approaching the four Powers with regard to the guarantee. But months passed without any instructions being sent. Her ambassador in Vienna had to act without them. Her representative in Berlin treated the business as one of little importance, and so did that court when pressed by the

British representative, justifying its indifference by the example of Spain. Yet Spain was represented at the signing of the Treaty of Amiens, and might in a moment have been induced by France to agree to the guarantee. Russia, when at last approached, made her adhesion depend upon conditions amounting to an alteration of the treaty. Other difficulties presented themselves, which France did not labour to remove, as she might have done, and in January 1803, the evacuation, which should have taken place within three months after ratification of the treaty, had not been begun.

Meanwhile, the people on both sides of the Channel rejoiced as if it had been a real peace. It was noted that, as usual, many Englishmen crossed to Paris for pleasure, while some few Frenchmen visited England on business. Fox hastened to admire the ruler of a country which, as he repeatedly said both publicly and in private, had ended a glorious war by a glorious peace. His intimates behaved even worse. Afterwards, when relations became strained, the Ambassador complained bitterly of men like the Earl of Lauderdale encouraging Prince Talleyrand, the Minister for Foreign Affairs, in the notion that the British would submit to any compromise. Sheridan was not one of these. He disapproved of such journeys altogether, and declared that for his part he wanted to be free to speak of Bonaparte as he wished.

On the 5th of April, Addington was able to place before the House of Commons a peace budget. He gave up the income tax, which was extremely unpopular, and which never produced three-fifths of the £10,000,000 originally estimated by Pitt. The machinery of returns was defective, and there existed no method of taxation at the source. The tax was now put aside as a war tax, but it was necessary to substitute miscellaneous taxation amounting to £4,000,000. The Army and Navy were not yet reduced to a peace standard. A loan of £23,000,000 for Great Britain and £2,000,000 for Ireland was also raised. The budget passed without much criticism, and the House went on to the consideration of the Treaty of Amiens, which was very warmly debated on the same lines as the Preliminaries had been.

The House also found leisure to discuss a bill to prevent bull-baiting, which had already been abolished in Ireland. On this occasion humour was on the side of the humanitarians. Sir Richard Hill, a highly respected county member, after describing the terrible cruelties often practised on the bull to make it give sport, added in a lighter vein that there were some gentlemen who hated a system of peace so much that they could not even bear to hear of a definitive treaty between a dog and a bull. This was aimed at Windham, and brought that strange embodiment of—often misdirected—chivalry upon his feet. So well known was his love of old English sports, and his determination that the poor should no more be deprived of their enjoyments than the rich, that on one occasion, when magistrates had dispersed a crowd assembled for one of those fights without gloves then called boxing matches, the men shouted "Windham and Liberty!" In a rather rambling speech, he complained that this particular amusement should have been selected. Why not stop horse-racing upon the same principle? A horse-race collected infamous characters of every kind, and was nothing more than a large gambling hell. The supporters of the bill, he continued, wished to drive the poor into the tabernacle or to jacobinism. Others wished to deprive them of their amusements to make them work harder. This was enough to jacobinize a whole country. John Courtenay, the member for Appleby, followed. In a strain of elaborate irony, of which he was a master, he congratulated his right honourable friend on having proved incontrovertibly that bull-baiting was the great support of Church and State. Besides, how could those ex-Ministers, who had just seen to their sorrow the death-warrant of the constitution signed by the peace, employ themselves if this bill passed? They must have a warlike sport, such as bull-baiting, to keep up their spirits. And he concluded with an ironical panegyric on the British bull-dog since Roman days. Among other speakers in favour of the bill was Sheridan. He rallied its opponents with characteristic humour, and then passed to a serious mood, detailing the almost incredible cruelties to the dogs themselves, to which the virtues of the British bull-dog breed were due. Indeed, the most agreeable feature of this debate, affording, as it did, a lamentable picture of the brutalized condition of the lower orders, is the circumstance that the practice only prevailed here and there, and, as Windham said, was decreasing all over the country. The bill was thrown out in a small House by a small majority.

A humanitarian measure of much greater importance actually passed into law this session. It originated with that unique body, the Manchester Board of Health, which had drawn up a report in 1796 suggesting factory legislation. In March 1802 Wilbraham Bootle brought before the House of Commons the objectionable character of the bargains between masters and parish authorities for children to be employed in the mills. The Manchester local body's interest in health was now reinforced by that national recognition of an obligation for the well-being of pauper children which had existed since Tudor times. As a great employer of apprentices Sir Robert Peel now brought in the first factory bill. At this stage he was unwilling to extend it to what was known as free labour, pointing out that there were technical difficulties in the way. But he was partially overruled by Perceval and Wilberforce, and the bill passed on to the Statute Book as an Act for the Preservation of the Health and Morals of Apprentices and others, employed in Cotton and other Mills, and Cotton and other Factories. It was still concerned mainly with apprentices. But it provided generally that the mills and factories should be registered, regularly whitewashed, and ventilated, and their inspection arranged by Justices of the Peace. Apprentices were not to work for more than twelve hours a day or to work at night, and provision was made for their accommodation, their clothing, and their education. But the whole measure depended upon the Justices. No great dependence could ever be reposed upon the executive activity of this type of authority in urban areas, and the Act could not be adequately enforced. Besides, as regards the apprentices, the problem was changing. Steam was making it possible to concentrate the factories in towns where the growth of an industrial population provided an increasing local supply of children whom it was not necessary to take as apprentices.

The session was also remarkable for a stupid attempt of Pitt's political opponents to take advantage of the situation for the purpose of moving a vote of thanks to His Majesty for removing him from his councils. They were signally discomfited. A resolution that he had rendered great and important services to his country was passed by a majority of four to one; and not this only, but in the City a subscription for a statue was raised for him, and 900 leading men joined in a dinner in his honour on his birthday, the 29th of May. Canning, who had been silent during the recent debates as he did not wish to offend Pitt by attacking Addington, found his opportunity on that day. He wrote a poem, which was sung on the occasion; the last verse was prophetic, and soon became famous:

> "And O! if again the rude whirlwind should rise,
> The dawning of peace should fresh darkness deform;
> The regrets of the good, and the fears of the wise,
> Shall turn to the pilot that weathered the storm!"

It was Canning's dearest wish to see Pitt at the helm again. But the retired Minister had so bound himself to Addington, that it was long before he could countenance even the most reasoned and temperate criticism of the weakness of his friend's administration.

A minor event of this year was the trial at the Old Bailey

of Joseph Wall—a remarkable illustration of the fact that neither rank, high connections, services, nor lapse of time and distance of place of commission of the offence could screen an offender from British justice—an illustration, too, of the callousness and brutality of the age. Forty years earlier he had risen into notice as a young soldier, distinguishing himself by his bravery; twenty years earlier, as Lieutenant-Governor of Goree in West Africa, he had, to suppress an incipient mutiny, ordered a sergeant to receive 800 lashes in his presence, which resulted in his death, five days later. The Garrison Surgeon was present, and also gave evidence at the trial. The sergeant had been able to walk back after the punishment, which had been inflicted with a small rope, as all the cats-o'-nine-tails were reported to have been destroyed. The Surgeon had not realized that a rope which did not cut the skin was more dangerous on that account, and did not interfere. The punishment followed the sentence of a hastily formed irregular court martial, none of the officers composing which were present at the trial. Wall was found guilty and sentenced to death. Although he no doubt deserved the extreme penalty, there were some circumstances in his favour, and there have been many murders more atrocious. But he received no mercy. He was sentenced to be hanged the next day but one; the royal clemency gave him only six days longer, and when he appeared at the scaffold three distinct shouts of exultation burst from the immense crowd. His miseries did not terminate even then. It might have been supposed that it had been learnt by this time how to hang a man. But the science was still so imperfect that Wall lived and was seen to move for a quarter of an hour. After three-quarters of an hour more, the body was cut down and taken away to be dissected. This was regularly treated as a punishment for murder additional to the death penalty. Only six years before, an increase in burglaries and highway robberies had induced a Member of Parliament to propose its infliction as an additional deterrent in their case also, hanging alone being—he thought—too good for such delinquents.

In February, Parliament had obtained a new Speaker in succession to Mitford, who on Clare's death was appointed Lord Chancellor of Ireland, taking the title of Lord Redesdale. This was Charles Abbot, who was succeeded as Principal Secretary to the Lord-Lieutenant by a member of the diplomatic service, William Wickham. It was now, however, six years since that Parliament had been called, and in the summer a general election was necessary under the Septennial Act, the first general election for the United Kingdom of Great Britain and Ireland. In this last country all passed off quietly. The Union was scarcely made an issue anywhere, and men who had taken a considerable share in bringing it about were elected by independent county constituencies. It was observed that, for the first time, Roman Catholics exercised their privilege of voting in large numbers. In Scotland the few thousand electors returned their Tory representatives without any more being heard about it. But in England considerable freedom was asserted. This was not due to any provocation on the part of those in authority. Two generations earlier, Ministers might have gone up and down buying the country; two or three generations later, they might have gone up and down stumping the country. Now they let it alone. "Never", said Sheridan, "did the Treasury interfere so little in the general election." In several places the rabble was encouraged by the Whigs to indulge in revolutionary orgies. In Liverpool two men were shot and one trampled to death. In Middlesex one of those returned was the patrician incendiary, Sir Francis Burdett. Just as if it had consisted of the fashionable ladies of the day, the mob faithfully followed the obsolete French fashion of ten years before, displayed revolutionary emblems, and paraded him before the royal palace to the accompaniment of a band playing a French revolutionary air, which would not have been

ADDINGTON'S ADMINISTRATION IN PEACE 353

tolerated in Paris in 1802. Nottingham, by a privilege of 400 years, enjoyed the benefit of an elected magistracy, consisting of the Mayor, Sheriff, and Aldermen. All were Whigs, and, though they appeared on the hustings, refused to keep order, so that the military had to be called in. A petition was afterwards presented to Parliament, signed by 537 persons, alleging that they had been intimidated from voting. Upon this it was decided to grant the county magistrates, who were appointed by the Crown, concurrent jurisdiction with the town magistrates, not without bitter protests from Fox as an invasion of constitutional freedom.

In all other respects, however, the general election merely fulfilled a constitutional requirement, and altered nothing. There was no discussion in parliament on its results; the parties which were in the minority took no opportunity of showing that the public had been misled, and that in any case the members returned did not represent those who had elected them. Only one passage in a speech made by a member to his constituents was discussed. Wilberforce, in his anxiety for peace to be maintained, had told the freeholders of Yorkshire that the people of his country were too honest to have much to do with continental connections. But this was not the view of the Government. In opening Parliament on the 23rd of November, 1802, the King, in a speech in other respects wholly colourless, ominously declared that he regarded the interests of other states as connected with those of the United Kingdom, and would not be indifferent to any change in their relative condition or strength. The allusions were not to be mistaken. In August, Bonaparte had annexed the island of Elba—so gallantly defended by the British, and given up by the Treaty of Amiens in the fond belief that it would remain with the King of Etruria, who was no more, it is true, than one of his vassals on the mainland of Italy. In September, Piedmont, the King of Sardinia's possession on the north-west of the peninsula, had been incorporated with France. In October, Switzerland was invaded, and its inhabitants were finally obliged to accept a new constitution, dictated not this time at Lyons, but in Paris.

The New Opposition, as those who were dissatisfied with the want of vigour shown by the Government were called, took a higher tone than ever. They were now joined in this by Canning, who had so long been restrained from discussing foreign policy by his regard for Pitt. The large peace establishments of 129,000 regular soldiers and 50,000 seamen were unanimously voted. In the debate on the Army vote, Sheridan gave a fine exhibition of his independence and patriotism. He was in the forefront of his time. While the New Opposition spoke of the humiliation of truckling to France, and the Old Opposition palliated her aggressions, he, with a rarer vision, divined precisely where the danger lay. "I see", said he, "in the very situation and composition of the power of Bonaparte a physical necessity for him to go on in this barter with his subjects, and to promise to make them the masters of the world, if they will consent to be his slaves." It was Great Britain which stopped the way. In a speech of great eloquence and power Canning followed, but did not surpass him. He made an attempt, which proved to be premature, to bring forward Pitt by acclamation, in Lord Sheffield's words. The finest passage in his speech was a tribute to his leader, Pitt, then absent at Bath, in which, after praising his disinterested efforts to efface himself in favour of Addington, he concluded that they were unavailing efforts: "He cannot withdraw himself from the following of a nation; he must endure the attachment of a people whom he has saved." Wilberforce and Fox spoke after him. Labouring for peace, they could not gainsay the growing danger.

Fox never concealed the strong sense which he entertained of the violence done to Switzerland, and it was this which chiefly struck the imagination of the people, who in their indignation paid no attention to the merits of the settlement which Bonaparte actually effected. In the sonnet which begins "Two voices are there", the poet Wordsworth described his regret that Liberty had been driven from one of her two homes—her mountain home—and his fears that she would be hard put to it to maintain herself in her last resting-place among the ocean waves. Hawkesbury had lost no time in making his formal protest upon a question on which his countrymen felt so deeply; but it was ineffective. Bonaparte successfully maintained the standpoint that Great Britain had no right to interfere in the affairs of the Continent, Portugal and Naples excepted. It none the less remained a motive of mistrust of France. There were other grounds of dispute which had originated soon after the Treaty had been signed. Bonaparte strongly objected to the entertainment in England of French emigrants who continued to hatch plots for his overthrow; and to the licence of abuse indulged by the press; and in this connection he named only one Englishman, the journalist Cobbett. He was throughout careful to base himself, with the precision of a lawyer, on the exact wording of the Treaty, and in this instance he could quote the last words of the first article: "They shall not afford any assistance or protection, directly or indirectly, to those who should cause prejudice to any of them." The note which Otto was instructed to present on this subject was brusque and offensive. At the same time Bonaparte had a genuine grievance, and although some steps were taken to meet it, such as the prosecution and conviction of the refugee Peltier for an abominable article inciting to assassination, more might have been done.

On the other side, Bonaparte, keeping strictly within his rights under the Treaty, and moreover within the law of the French Republic, had made Englishmen the subject of almost incredible outrages. It is not easy to realize that even under the savage guidance of Robespierre, and in time of war, France could actually have passed a measure confiscating all small vessels, under whatever flag, having any English goods on board, which should approach near the French coast. It is almost incredible that the First Consul, who prided himself upon the transformation which he had wrought in France since the days of the Terror, should have enforced so barbarous a law in time of peace. Yet it was done, and with the utmost rigour. A vessel bound for Jersey was forced by stress of weather into Cherbourg. She was confiscated, and her captain sentenced to six months' imprisonment. This occurred in December 1801, and yet the Treaty was signed while the innocent man was still in prison. Hawkesbury's remonstrances did, however, eventually reach the First Consul, who decided—to use his own phrase—that justice should take its course. There were other cases which formed the subject of fresh diplomatic correspondence. One of them was even more extraordinary. The freedom of the seas, which it was the boasted aim of Bonaparte to wrest from its English tyrants, did not include freedom of commerce. British goods were under Robespierre's law prohibited entry. But at least it was supposed that France would be glad enough to sell her brandy, and in October 1802 a vessel entered a French port in ballast, to take a cargo on board for London. She was condemned on account of four pounds' worth of table utensils, found in the captain's cabin. The British representative then in Paris asked Talleyrand whether the French Government expected the captain to eat off the table with his fingers. But no redress was obtained for any of these grievances. It is strange that public opinion was not more excited by all this, when diplomatic intervention had proved so ineffectual. But the failure to obtain, not merely a commercial treaty, but the most meagre permission to trade under any circumstances, at least robbed the Treaty of Amiens of all its popularity with the business classes, and prepared the way for the final rupture.

While relations were thus strained, a gleam of hope

appeared. At last, eight months after signing peace, the two Powers felt able to resume regular diplomatic relations. The British Ambassador, Lord Whitworth, an experienced diplomatist who had been ennobled for his services, reached Paris in November. He was received with the highest honours and even with popular enthusiasm. He was perfectly fitted for his delicate duties, his only fault being that, in spite of his thorough knowledge of French, he underestimated Bonaparte's character and the strength of his position. The channels through which Englishmen derived their views of France were then highly misleading. Bonaparte was misrepresented as extremely unpopular, and the whole country as seething with discontent; much as England was described to him as ripe for revolution, the resources of her government and the stability of her institutions being underrated.

Within a fortnight of his arrival, on the 27th of November, Whitworth was writing to Hawkesbury that the acquisition of Egypt was the object which the First Consul had most at heart, and emphasizing the importance of Malta remaining in British hands as increasing the risk to the French of attempting to occupy that country. The evacuation of Egypt, as well as Malta, had been delayed, but owing to a different reason—John Stuart, who now commanded the troops there, having misunderstood his instructions. The mistake was eventually corrected, but before this could be done, Bonaparte sent Colonel Sebastiani to make a military report upon the country. On his return at the end of January the report was officially published. The manner in which Stuart and the British generally were spoken of gave great offence, but the importance of the incident really attached, not to any of the report's contents, but to the fact of the mission having been sent, and to the publicity given by the report to Bonaparte's designs on Egypt, which in a subsequent conversation with Whitworth he made no attempt to disguise. "Sooner or later", he told the Ambassador, "Egypt would belong to France, either by the falling to pieces of the Turkish Empire, or by some arrangement with the Porte."

But Hawkesbury had already taken a strong line before learning of this admission. The French Government had been pressing for five months for the evacuation of Malta. There was a complete reply to any insinuation of bad faith in not having already done so. Great Britain had already taken all the steps in her power to obtain the fulfilment of the conditions necessary to enable the island to be restored to the Order. But they were not yet fulfilled. Russia, the only guarantee Power really independent of France, had imposed conditions which required the reopening of the Treaty, and a Grand Master had not yet been elected. The British Government was, therefore, still in possession of Malta, and not through its own fault or neglect of duty. It took full advantage of the position in which it found itself. In one of his original letters of instructions Hawkesbury had recommended Whitworth to say nothing which might engage His Majesty to restore the island, even if the requisite conditions should now be fulfilled. If Great Britain now chose to retain Malta as a counterpoise for aggressions made since the Treaty was signed and as a guarantee for the future, it had good reason to do so, resting its action on a general recital of the past proceedings of France and her present position in Europe, as well as the question of Egypt. The Treaty of Lunéville had guaranteed the independence of the Batavian, Helvetic, and Cisalpine Republics, and yet French troops were still in Holland, Switzerland had been invaded, and the Cisalpine Republic practically annexed. If the Treaty of Amiens had not mentioned them, their independence was none the less a British interest, as was perfectly well understood at the time; if it was not so understood—it was open to Great Britain to say—it might be so understood now.

In the note actually presented to the French Ambassador on the 15th of March, in reply to one demanding the evacuation of Malta, Hawkesbury began very properly by showing that the Treaty had been negotiated with reference to the actual state of possession of the different parties to it. The French Government had formally agreed, as a basis of negotiation, that Great Britain should keep a compensation out of her conquests for the important acquisitions of territory made by France upon the Continent. Fresh gains of territory and influence by France consequently gave a right to additional compensation. But after detailing these (although by no means fully) Hawkesbury threw over nine-tenths of his case. He preferred to waive all such claims, and rested his refusal to evacuate Malta upon Sebastiani's report. "Think of resting the whole grounds of a war on Sebastiani's report!" wrote Lord Grenville scornfully. And by going on, after he had once stated this refusal, to discuss the difficulties which had presented themselves in the way of the fulfilment of various clauses of the article relating to Malta, he merely weakened his case instead of strengthening it. But this was not the only mistake made by the British Government.

On the 8th of March a Royal Message had been delivered, acquainting the House of Commons that very considerable military preparations were going on in the ports of France and Holland. After it was read, Addington proposed a vague address of thanks for the vague statement which he had himself put into the King's mouth, together with the usual promise to support His Majesty in the adoption of such measures as the circumstances would appear to require. The address was, of course, adopted, but; as Fox observed, no vote was ever required from the House under circumstances of more utter darkness. But the surprising thing was that, vague as Ministers had been, they had not succeeded in avoiding inaccuracy. This public assumption of an attitude of self-defence by Great Britain afforded Bonaparte an opportunity of posing before the world as an ill-used devotee of peace who could not restrain his honest indignation. On the 13th of March he accosted Whitworth at a large reception given by Madame Bonaparte, and, before the ambassadors of Europe, violently upbraided Great Britain upon her warlike policy. All these measures of precaution, he said, were quite uncalled for. There were no armaments in the ports of France. There were no differences between the two Cabinets. True, Malta had not been evacuated, but His Majesty's word had been engaged to this. Then, with one of his quick changes, he expressed the hope that Whitworth's wife, the Duchess of Dorset, might yet spend the summer in Paris. "But ill speed those who do not respect treaties."

What he had said was true. French ports were almost empty of armaments and naval stores. In Holland barely 3,000 men had been collected for an expedition to America. The mistake was all the more extraordinary because in his last dispatch, dated the 3rd of March, Whitworth had enlarged upon France's weakness from a maritime point of view. But it was another part of the dispatch which had prompted Addington's Ministry. Talleyrand had told Whitworth that a note was on its way to the London Foreign Office demanding an immediate and categorical answer on the subject of Malta. Without waiting for this note, which was not presented till the 10th, the Ministry had assumed that preparations must have been made.

The reception of the Royal Message now showed them what degree of support they might count upon from Parliament and from the Russian Government. The former was unnecessary. In the latter expectation they failed. The Czar was ready to keep the French from Egypt, but he was actually opposed to the British retention of Malta for that purpose. Addington would have been much better advised had he based the Message on more unassailable grounds. For example, in an official summary presented by Bonaparte to the French Legislature on the 22nd of February, it was stated that there existed in England a war party which had sworn eternal hatred to France, and that, as long as this continued, the Republic must keep on foot 500,000 men, to undertake its defence and avenge its injuries.

Although the Message of the 8th of March had embittered relations, it did not render a breach inevitable. War might have been avoided altogether, had either side withdrawn on the question of Malta. The negotiations dragged on for the next two months on this subject, both parties in turn receding a little from their original positions, but never enough to meet one another's wishes. It is curious that, although it was France who originally made demands for the fulfilment of the Treaty as an aggrieved party, it was Great Britain who finally delivered the ultimatum. This was due to Bonaparte's fondness for manœuvring himself into the position of the party attacked; on the other hand, it provided George III's Government with an opportunity of proving its good faith. It demanded from France, at the price of war, the retention of Malta. It did not say, "Here we are, here we remain", and wait for the French ultimatum. It did not even adopt the more Napoleonic expedient of inveigling some members of the Order of St. John to Malta, wringing from them, through the pressure of British bayonets, a Grand Master entirely in the British interest, and then obtaining from him a request for the retention of the British garrison. Had it done either of these, it might have been charged with bad faith on good grounds.

Whitworth's ultimatum was rejected, and Addington's Government now saw that war was inevitable, and desired to make the interval as short as possible. In this it followed traditional British policy. The more sudden the declaration the greater the amount of money in the form of profits from confiscated enemy ships which would accrue to the Crown. And such sums, amounting to many hundreds of thousand pounds, under the name of Admiralty droits, were independent of the direct control of Parliament. France on her side made every effort to put off war. Whitworth could not get his passports, and was made to stop and listen to fresh proposals. Bonaparte, whose cry had been "All the Treaty of Amiens and nothing but the Treaty of Amiens", was ready to allow Malta to be handed over to a Russian, Austrian, or Prussian garrison. But this was refused. Even after Whitworth had left Paris an offer was sent after him to allow the British to keep Malta with compensation to France. It was of no use. By the 18th of May all was over, and war was declared—a war which need not have broken out as soon as it did, had Addington's Ministry had the power to make Bonaparte feel that he had men to deal with. So ended what George III—and not he alone—called an experimental peace, and the veteran diplomatist, Lord Malmesbury, thought little better than an armed truce. In bringing it to an end as she had done, England had, as the Emperor Alexander said, been technically in the wrong, but she was morally in the right.

So far as the French Government was concerned, the Peace had borne throughout the character ascribed to it by Malmesbury. The one exception was the extremely courteous treatment of British visitors, official and unofficial. But, even in war-time, this was enjoyed by those few who had permission to enter France, or found themselves there involuntarily. Claims of individuals who had suffered from the action of the French Government were almost completely disregarded. In the official Message to the Legislature of the 22nd of February, Great Britain had been spoken of in terms of undisguised hostility. And, as has been seen, the English merchantman was treated in time of peace as almost as great an enemy as an English man-of-war in time of war, and as a much greater enemy than an English merchantman in time of war. In war, if France required tropical produce, she usually had to receive it in British or neutral bottoms. Such ships, laden with coffee and sugar, entered French ports with very little disguise. When the Northern Powers closed their ports in the beginning of 1801,

ADDINGTON'S ADMINISTRATION IN PEACE 363

French speculators came over to London, and created such a demand for English goods, such as cottons and calicoes, as to raise the price ten per cent. If other ports were shut, they said, Boulogne would remain open. But this was now changed. There was a prospect, in time of peace, of bringing the produce of the West Indies in French ships; and Bonaparte was ambitious to be a restorer of the industries of Northern France. British trade of every kind with France was sternly suppressed, and a manifest intention entertained to exclude it from as much of the Continent as possible. What his power was appears from his having been able—immediately upon the outbreak of war—to confiscate British ships in the ports of Northern Italy, without going through the formality of consulting the governments of States supposed to be independent. Holland he treated entirely as a part of France, sending his orders direct to his Dutch servants.

The only remaining event of public notoriety which occurred in the United Kingdom during the Peace was the discovery, in November 1802, of a plot to destroy the King and Government, for which Colonel Despard, a distinguished Irish soldier, was hanged, with six of his associates. Another plot against the Government deserves greater attention. During the autumn of 1802, the failure of Addington became more and more apparent, and the problem how to get rid of him more and more pressing. Canning was the soul of the movement. His object was patriotic and highly honourable. But he loved mystery; when he was young it took the form of a practical joke—an elaborate quiz, in the language of the day—later on, that of a plot. He probably could not have asked three old schoolfellows to dinner without in some way suggesting a dark conspiracy. Pitt would not make a move to displace Addington. He had engaged himself to support him. He owned to Canning that he was ambitious, but, as he finely added, it was for character, not for office. This placed the young statesman in his element. He drew up a paper offering Addington the proposition of being replaced by Pitt, for which he canvassed signatures, writing mysterious letters. The "Paper Plot", as it was called, bored some people, and somewhat disgusted Pitt. It was dropped in favour of the plan of leading the Minister to reality along another road. So long as Pitt assisted him—as he had been doing—or was even supposed to do so, Addington stood. That prop taken away, he was bound to fall. It was essential, therefore, to keep Pitt out of the House of Commons, and to prevent even a meeting between the two, if possible. For even this would get into the papers, and strengthen Addington's position.

All that winter Canning watched Pitt like a cat. But he was only half successful. Only till the end of 1802 did Pitt remain at Bath for reasons of health—a considerable factor in almost all the resignations and retirements of public men, as it was in this case. His absence from Parliament had the desired effect. After the debates of the autumn of 1802, in which he had, as has been seen, a new adversary in Canning, and missed the support of Pitt, Addington felt his weakness. The friends met in January. They still signed themselves "yours affectionately" to one another. After feeling his way, as he thought, Addington made him a startling offer in the following March through Dundas, now Lord Melville. Chatham was to be at the head of the Government, with Addington and Pitt as twin Secretaries of State. It is hard to realize Melville carrying such a proposal to Walmer Castle, where Pitt resided as Warden of the Cinque Ports. Many years afterwards Wilberforce told how he had asked him which Secretaryship he had been offered. " 'Really', said Pitt with a sly severity—and it was almost the only sharp thing I ever heard him say of any friend—'I had not the curiosity to ask what I was to be!' " In the following month Addington made further sacrifices. He was ready to resign in favour of Pitt on the one condition that the Grenvilles and Windham, his bitter opponents, were excluded from the new administration. Pitt refused, and the breach was complete.

He now returned to his place in Parliament. On the 23rd of May, in a debate on the war, he enjoyed the greatest oratorical triumph of his life. There were so many to hear him after his long silence, that the arrangements for the reporters broke down for the day. The parliamentary history gives twelve columns to his speech, whereas Fox's three-hour speech of the following day has just a hundred. "Never was any speech so cheered", wrote Malmesbury, of Pitt's, "or such incessant and loud applause; it was strong in support of the war, but he was silent as to Ministers." Some of its powerful reasoning remains; in particular, a reply to the argument that had the French Government really entertained designs upon Egypt it would not have disclosed them. But the effect of the ominous omission of which Malmesbury wrote, and which so impressed his hearers, is lost. In the same debate Wilberforce and some others argued that war was not necessary, and urged a recourse to the mediation of Russia. Among these was Fox, whose speech was as powerful a defence of the position of France as could have been addressed to an English audience. This drew a feeble protest from Addington, and a violent one from Windham. He accused Fox of using poisoned arrows, and of supporting selfishness against patriotism. The scene ended with an apology from Windham for the warmth of his language, and a characteristic reply from the other to the effect that for himself he had a foible of not easily and slightly quarrelling with an old acquaintance.

Pitt was now no longer a supporter of the Ministry. Till its fall, he held himself free to defend or attack its measures on their merits; though he went no farther. It had failed in peace, and was now to be tried in war. The first great measure for which its head was responsible was well considered. In presenting his first war budget for £30,398,220 for Great Britain (Ireland's £3,500,000 being separate),

Addington proposed to increase both customs and excise, and to reintroduce the income tax as a war tax. He attempted to disguise it as a land and property tax, but this would not serve. The veil was rudely drawn aside, and it had to run the gauntlet of the usual criticisms. The irregular and precarious profits of industry were taxed equally with regular and permanent income; land, which bore other burdens, with investments in the funds, which bore none; the trading community would pass on the tax to the consumer; the inquisition into an Englishman's private affairs which it entailed was an outrage upon popular opinion, a violation of every principle of freedom. Moreover, two points upon which Addington deserves real credit as a financier met with Pitt's successful opposition. He had introduced for the first time the principle of taxation at the source. This, while ensuring a larger revenue to the Government, protected the individual from a great part of that vexatious interference of which so much was said. Pitt thought it quite right to assess the general income of a fund-holder, and to take five per cent. of it—the amount of the tax; but he entertained the curious idea that it was a breach of faith with the public creditor to deduct the five per cent. at the time of paying the interest, even when it was pointed out to him that it amounted to the same thing. He also disagreed over another thing. Addington was before his time in making a distinction between earned and unearned income. For this purpose he proposed to tax every landed proprietor and fund-holder, however small his income was. At that period the number of persons who had invested money in businesses with which they were personally unconnected appears to have been too small for that class of receivers of unearned income to be considered; if capital went into industry, the owner of that capital was assumed to go into it too. If earned income was not more than £150, the recipient was to receive an abatement; if under £60, to pay no tax at all. Pitt thought that all classes of capital should be treated alike. He regarded

ADDINGTON'S ADMINISTRATION IN PEACE 367

it as an interference with economic freedom that the State should, by its scheme of taxation, encourage capital to flow in one direction rather than in another. His authority prevailed on this point also; and Addington, who did not, like Pitt, enjoy the confidence of the City of London, gave all taxpayers equally the benefit of the exemptions. At the same time a loan was raised of £10,000,000 in the complicated manner of the time, the yield to the investor being a little over five per cent.

Three months of war were not allowed to pass before the usual advantage was taken of the opportunity offered by England's difficulties. The south of Ireland had been disturbed in 1802; and in January of the following year special judges had been commissioned to try offenders. Unrest was still in the air; leaders of revolt were wanting. There were still in existence a few incendiaries, not of the first class, some of whom had been residing in Paris, but returned to Ireland before the outbreak of war. The principal of these was Robert Emmet, son of a leading physician in Dublin. He had no personal grievance, and was not an Irishman half-turned Frenchman. In fact, he was without French support. He was a patriot, and his wish was to see Ireland independent. Hampered as the Government was by a most inefficient police, and by the 17,000 or so available regular troops being necessarily widely scattered, it was still unsafe for their enemies to presume upon its incompetence, and there was very little time. It was impossible to raise the country. Ulster, in particular, had grown cordial, the most dangerous element having been won over by the establishment of relations between the Crown and the Presbyterian Church somewhat resembling those between it and the sister Church of Scotland. Dwyer, a sturdy outlaw who had, since the Rebellion, maintained himself in the Wicklow hills not many miles south of Dublin, refused his help. Emmet finally decided to collect peasants from the adjoining county of Kildare, where a fellow-conspirator had been working, to arm them mainly with pikes from armouries which he had prepared, and to seize first the Castle, and then the other principal places in the city. The Government was warned in time. On the 16th of June there was an explosion in a house where gunpowder was stored; the owner disappeared, but the alarm had been given, and news soon began to come in. But, as often happens in such cases, the officials were afraid of being considered alarmists, and took no action. On the 23rd there no longer remained any doubt. The Commander-in-Chief in Ireland, General Henry Fox, the brother of Charles Fox, had 3,000 men in Dublin. He was sent for to the Castle, where he heard the situation elaborately explained to him and to the Lord-Lieutenant. Yet even now the official who did so, in spite of being certain in his own mind that there would be a rising, inconsistently admitted that there was a chance that it would not take place. Upon this Hardwicke elected to leave the responsibility to the military arm; and Fox, who was supine, to do nothing at all. The neighbouring villages had been emptying themselves into Dublin since the previous evening. But Emmet was not really ready, and when he met the local leaders in the afternoon he failed to satisfy them. A number withdrew, with many of their supporters. This was the moment to disperse the crowd, but it was not done; and preparations continued until eight or nine o'clock at night, when three thousand pikes were deliberately distributed to those who required them. There were only four muskets. The leaders had blunderbusses. Emmet, with his lieutenant-generals, all in green uniforms, appeared and tried to take the lead, but finding that he was not followed he left the city in despair. Those who remained committed a few murders, including that of Lord Kilwarden, Chief Justice of Ireland, before the casual arrival of one or two detachments of infantry put an end to the outbreak. Emmet and the other leaders were captured soon afterwards and hanged, to the number of eighteen, as well as three fellow-conspirators in the north. Moreover, the detention of suspected persons and other precautionary measures were continued for some time. Ireland was now quiet. Even Dwyer and his outlaws submitted. The whole episode would have been more quickly forgotten, had it not been for the pathetic interest which attaches to the early death of the ill-fated visionary who had tried to lead. Robert Emmet is remembered by the poet Moore's beautiful song: "She is far from the land" —in which he bewails the hard fate of the boy's betrothed, pining to death for her lover beyond the seas.

Unable to strengthen his Government with Pitt, Addington looked in precisely the opposite direction. Long before this he had made Grey's father a peer, and had offered a post to the son, but met with a refusal. He now made one more effort to recruit his strength from among Pitt's opponents. So ardent had been Tierney's opposition under the late Ministry, that after Fox had seceded from Parliament he still carried on with a party so minute that it was supposed to return home in a single coach when the House rose. He had fought a duel with Pitt, arising out of a dispute during a debate, which Addington as Speaker had failed to settle. His independence had drawn him away from Fox; he was interested in finance; and he accepted the post of Treasurer of the Navy. Addington also strengthened his Cabinet by promoting Yorke to the office of Home Secretary. Pelham took the Duchy of Lancaster. With such help, and the friendship and partial support of such other prominent members of the opposition as Erskine and Sheridan, Addington prepared to face criticism at home as well as the foe abroad.

CHAPTER VI

ADDINGTON'S ADMINISTRATION AFTER THE OUTBREAK OF WAR

(MAY 1803—MAY 1804)

IN 1809 Napoleon Bonaparte told Prince Metternich that he would never have been fool enough to have made a descent upon England unless a revolution had already broken out in that country, and that the army collected in Boulogne had always been intended against Austria. This was an easy thing to say after events had rendered invasion impossible. But there was no folly in the idea in 1803, and there are very good reasons for supposing that it was genuinely entertained and perfectly feasible.

Even before the temporary peace both the Admiralty and Nelson himself had believed in it. It was supposed that about 40,000 men might succeed in landing. In his memorandum of the 25th of July, 1801, when he was in charge of the defence of the south-eastern coast, Nelson had written: "Whatever plans may be adopted, the moment the Enemy touch our Coast, be it where it may, they are to be attacked by every man afloat and on shore: this must be perfectly understood." Bonaparte's ostentatious preparations were a feint, but the apprehensions entertained by the wisest heads in Britain were genuine, and the effect upon the people generally contributed to a wish for peace, of which he reaped the benefit. He told Whitworth, three months before war again broke out, that, if it did, he was determined to attempt the invasion, expatiating at length on its enormous dangers. It is dangerous to suppose that he spoke unguardedly; or, on the other hand, that he was pursuing the plan of bluff of 1801, known by now in England not to have been seriously meant. He would have presumed that when they had learnt what he had said British Ministers would have been thrown off their guard—convinced that he was at his old tricks

CLOSE OF ADDINGTON'S ADMINISTRATION 371

again. Even if they believed that he meant it, they would then also believe what he said about the difficulties of the expedition—which was no more than the truth—and would relax their preparations.

Bonaparte was surrounded by men who held that an invasion of some part of the British Islands was certainly possible, for the best of all reasons—because it had already taken place, and some of them had already taken part in it. General Humbert, in particular, who had been leader of the Irish expedition of 1798, said that he could conquer that country with eight or ten thousand men. Forty-five successful descents upon Great Britain were enumerated by students of military history, and the pigeon-holes of the Ministry of War were stuffed full of projects. Nothing would probably have suited Bonaparte but a landing as near the Straits of Dover as possible. But it was here that the most powerful defence could be concentrated. Even were he successful, it was certain that the invader's communications would be interrupted. Yet this would have mattered little to Bonaparte—marching on London, and soon to hold the richest city in the world at his mercy. The French General Staff had no opinion of the Sea Fencibles, volunteers, and other extemporized defensive forces. Regarding the volunteers, an agent in London reported that these gentlemen could do nothing without their morning tea, their coffee, and their carriages. The mounted units hired their horses, and they were often put in prison for not being able to pay the hire. There was one exception to this. The St. James's Dragoons consisted of the richest young lords in England. So far from being in danger of imprisonment for debt, each had five or six followers on horseback; one to carry his master's port-wine, another his liqueur, a third his plain-clothes so that he might change out of uniform as soon as he wished. Of the regulars the reports were not much better. Indeed, had Bonaparte been able to read English Ministers' private correspondence, he would have known that in 1800, while still in office, Thomas Grenville said of the Austrian defeats: "Our own Army could not have done worse", while even after Abercromby's victories two years later he still thought the Army in as bad a state as possible. With some exceptions the troops had not really done well in the Flanders campaigns of the last ten years, and apart from the indiscriminate admiration of a patriotic public for their gallant defenders, only, among those who thought, could a few officers like Moore discern the sterling stuff of which the British soldier was made—partly tested on the far-off sands of Egypt.

There was an example only a year or two back of a force which did not have to lay down its arms, even after its communications had been interrupted. Such was the case of Bonaparte's own army in Egypt after the Battle of the Nile. Although the General was cut off almost at once, not only was he able to escape back to France himself, but in January 1800, nearly eighteen months after the battle, the isolated force was strong enough to wrest from the Turks, under the auspices of a British officer, Sir Sidney Smith, the Convention of El Arish. By this the French army was promised a safe return, without any stipulation that it was not to bear arms again in the war. Though the Convention was not carried out, its conclusion was a good example of what good terms a powerful, though isolated, force can obtain for itself; and in fact the troops fared as well in 1801, when they finally surrendered, as they would have done under it. Another example of an army cut off, yet saved from destruction or captivity, may be seen in the excellent terms which General Junot was to obtain under the Convention of Cintra, in part because it was thought desirable to save Lisbon—a city not to be compared with London—from injury.

At first Bonaparte felt his way gradually, and treated the whole more as an enormous theme for combined naval and military staff-work, with real and not skeleton crews and troops, than as a project intended to be definitely carried out. This master of war had a great deal to learn, and was conscious of the fact. On one occasion he ordered a curious inquiry as to how many fishing-boats existed "stronger than 500 tons". About the same time, aware of the unseamanlike qualities of the crews, he directed manœuvres to be carried out in Brest Roads—of course quite impossible. At one time a belief was encouraged by one naval officer at least, that the flotilla gunboats were strong enough to take the offensive against British ships. But so far was this from being the case that they were constantly themselves attacked while moving to the points of concentration, and by September 1803 a very efficient system had been introduced of defence by means of mobile batteries, under which the detachments of the flotilla were able to take shelter. The four ports of concentration, Boulogne, Etaples, Wimereux, and Ambleteuse, were not completed until June 1804.

But the greatest revolution in Bonaparte's ideas was the gradual conviction of a fact long realized by naval experts on both sides of the Channel, namely, that the invasion was not one that could be made by stealth in the dark night of winter, but that it needed the calm weather which could only be relied upon in summer, and the temporary command of the seas. By the autumn of 1803 Bonaparte had ceased to display impatience. He had given the movement its initial thrust; and, though still keeping a very close eye on what was being done, he allowed the work to go on slowly as well as systematically. During that first year he toyed with the idea of an invasion of Ireland from Brest. The openness with which he allowed the preparations for the Irish expedition to go on, and his known mistrust of that people, show that he was not serious. He had other pretended plans, of which he took care that England should be informed through Méhée de la Touche, a pretended spy in communication with the British. These were for an invasion of Ireland from the Texel round the north coast of Scotland, an expedition to Morea from Taranto, and another to support it from Toulon. But in reality the fleet at this last port was intended to support the real invasion from Boulogne, where—as Méhée had orders to explain—the preparations were merely a blind. In his correspondence with Admiral Ganteaume, who commanded at Toulon, he showed that he recognized the strategic aspect of the project. "Eight hours of night", he wrote on the 23rd of November, "which should be favourable to us, would decide the fate of the universe." But he wrote as a searcher, inquiring from the Admiral how this favourable night was to be secured. In reply, Ganteaume pointed out that two things were to be postulated—a storm which should drive off the British, succeeded by a calm which should enable the flotilla to start; it was then next to impossible for a great number of vessels to leave in the first tide after the seas had fallen. It would be better for a surprise attack to be made by a French squadron on the British and to make sure of freeing the Channel passage for forty-eight hours instead of eight. Bonaparte rejoined that Ganteaume had divined his plans, which were for concentrating a superior force. The Admiral replied that none of the various plans would obtain a superiority over the forty or fifty vessels which the British could collect in the Channel; all that was necessary was to rush in a light division just strong enough to brush aside the British ships watching the Straits of Dover, and so to facilitate the invasion.

Upon the outbreak of war economies had seriously affected the efficiency of personnel, ships, and dockyards on both sides of the Channel, but of the two countries England was by far the readier. The Admiralty, moreover, under Lord St. Vincent, a believer in a close blockade, was prepared to exercise a stricter watch over the enemy's naval ports than had been maintained in the last war. The first important task before it was to intercept seven French ships of the line on their way to Europe from the West Indies. In this they failed. One reached Rochefort, one ran into Cadiz, and the other five into Coruña, gaining shelter in Ferrol, where the blockade was accordingly extended; and this treatment of their ports had some influence in hastening the entry of Spain into the war. The French fleets were then blocked in their own and the Spanish harbours, and continued to be so during the first year and a half of the war.

On the Texel the Dutch Navy was watched by Admiral Lord Keith with five or six ships. The French had no squadrons of line-of-battle ships in the Channel Ports, and the various sections of the invasion flotilla being collected there were left to be harassed by small craft, which could get as near as possible to the coasts and up the estuaries. Five sail of the line were, however, retained at Spithead as a reserve. On the Atlantic coast the French had at first three effective ships in Brest; in a year they had sixteen, and before another year had passed, twenty-one. Southwards of Brest lay Lorient and Rochefort, at the latter of which ports there were soon to be five ships ready for sea. The blockade of all these was in the charge of Admiral the Honourable William Cornwallis with a squadron made up by about the end of the year to twenty ships, twelve of which were to be constantly at sea—six with the Admiral, who was to cruise near enough to be able to attack the French as soon as they came out. The remainder formed—with frigates —the inshore squadron, penetrating the outer harbour and keeping the ships within actually in view, or else were detached for the watch of the other ports. Coruña was watched by Rear-Admiral Sir Edward Pellew, with a squadron, eventually raised to five ships, based upon Bantry Bay in Ireland. That port was under Admiral Lord Gardner, who was also ordered to keep a squadron of six ships in reserve off the south-west coast. Cadiz, which was in the Mediterranean command, under Vice-Admiral Lord Nelson, who had nine ships off Toulon, was watched by frigates only at the beginning of the war.

The above is the account of line-of-battle ships only, and does not include frigates and smaller vessels. There was always a shortage of these. It was partly their absence which allowed the West India squadron to slip through. Nelson bitterly complained of the lack of frigates—the eyes of the fleet as he called them; and when it is recollected that they had to be used not merely for scouting purposes, but to convey important dispatches and military and diplomatic officials, as well as to fetch supplies, it becomes a wonder that the few which there were were able to do so much.

For various reasons the blockades maintained on the Atlantic were of a far more stringent character than Nelson's in the Mediterranean. Once out, it would be impossible to get on the tracks of a ship in the ocean, whereas it would not take long to find out where a squadron escaped from Toulon had gone; and if through the Straits of Gibraltar, it was bound to be seen, and its direction of sailing noted, by the ships stationed there. Ships on the Atlantic stations had bases at no great distance in England and Ireland, where they could constantly return for repair or the refreshment of their crews. The Mediterranean fleet had only Gibraltar and Malta. For twenty-two months the fleet never went to anything better than an open roadstead or a neutral coast. The ships were greatly undermanned, and, having been allowed to run down, were in a very bad condition. When Nelson complained to St. Vincent, he was told to rely on the resources of his mind. What these were may be gathered from the fact that his crazy ships rode many a gale before the chase after Villeneuve to the West Indies in the spring of 1805; that they showed themselves to be far more seaworthy than that admiral's ships, fresh out of harbour; and that most of them would have been fit for action at the Battle of Trafalgar, though only five actually fought. Further, there were the climatic differences. Situated below a sort of funnel, formed by the converging Alps and

Pyrenees, the Gulf of Lions is proverbially a place of almost perpetual rough weather, with no swell or other indication as in the Atlantic to announce the approach of storms. The Atlantic gales were terrific, but it was generally possible for the inshore squadron to get some sort of shelter, and, if the wind was at all westerly, there was no danger of the blockaded fleet putting to sea. Further, there was a difference in the instructions of the two admirals, and in the manner in which they were interpreted. Cornwallis's duties were purely naval, including, of course, the protection of homeward convoys and the interruption of the enemy's trade. Nelson had political business as well. When he joined his command he did not even begin his watch before Toulon all at once. After a visit to Malta his earliest preoccupation was with Naples. As a reply to the English delay in evacuating the former island, Bonaparte had reoccupied Southern Italy, and had troops in the whole peninsula which amounted to 80,000 in all (according to Nelson's information). This portended a possible attack on the King of the Two Sicilies, or a crossing to Sicily, which Nelson thought possible if the French united their Toulon and Brest fleets. At the same time, these anxieties, together with fears for Egypt and the Levant trade as well, made him feel sure that the Toulon fleet was coming out and desirous of encouraging it to do so. Frequently, therefore, leaving a couple of frigates on the watch, he lay with his fleet in a central position off the northern end of Sardinia.

No individual, except Barham and Nelson, contributed more to the final success of the naval campaign than Admiral Cornwallis. That fine old officer, whose fighting experiences dated back nearly half a century, had been one of those who inspired Nelson with certain homely "sentiments", as the latter called them, such as, "that it was always to err on the right side to fight". And though as an admiral he did not have the good fortune to do so, and did not win renown, the unceasing vigilance maintained by him, and those under him, throughout those bitter Atlantic gales, deserves the highest praise. Still, the life of those mariners had its lighter side. They were constantly descending upon the islands, and even the mainland. One French report of the early days of the war describes an English officer who had done so making a bet with a local Frenchwoman of ten louis against one of her cows that he would succeed in capturing some coasting vessels known to be near the place at the time.

During the winter of 1803–4 the difficulties of the French flotilla took definite shape. As only a hundred vessels could be got out of the Boulogne harbour in a single tide, attempts were made to moor as many as possible in the Sound by way of experiment. This could only be done in fair weather; and on one occasion, in November 1803, a delay in bringing them in caused a disaster under the Consul's own eyes in which five were wrecked and many damaged. Even in the summer of the following year, in another visit which he made, now as Napoleon, Emperor of the French—a title which he had assumed in May—he was witness of another mishap. A sudden north-easterly breeze drove about fifty vessels to take refuge in the ports west of Boulogne, and twelve were lost, with twenty-nine men. Generally speaking, it was not found possible to keep vessels out for more than a week, or to a greater number than 150, without accident. Again, owing to storms and British attacks, it was very difficult to concentrate the flotilla. By June 1804 there were, out of 2,008 projected, only 1,103 vessels supposed fit to fight and to navigate collected in the Channel Ports and at Ostend. Of the 231 still in the ports of the Bay of Biscay, only 35 managed to get round, and the impossibility of bringing up the remainder in face of Cornwallis's vigilance, aided by the Atlantic storms, was formally, though most unwillingly, recognized. Even vessels at Havre suffered considerably from the exposed state of the roadstead and the energy of the English, who here, as well as in the narrow seas, where

CLOSE OF ADDINGTON'S ADMINISTRATION 379

the Dutch contingents were being brought from the east, cruised or moored as close to the coast as possible. Indeed, so great was the respect in which Britain was held, that to get a score of vessels from one port to the next without serious mishap, while protected by an elaborate organization of field batteries ready to appear on any threatened point at the call of a cavalry patrol, was almost regarded by Napoleon himself in the light of a victory.

During this period of waiting the seas were far from being devoid of incident. Many a gallant act on board of vessels large and small was recorded; many a deed of heroism and intrepidity outside it must have gone unchronicled even in the ephemeral records of the hour. But there was one that created a great sensation. On the 15th of February, 1804, Commodore Nathaniel Dance, of the East India Company's service, sailing with sixteen regular merchantmen and a few country vessels from China towards the Straits of Malacca, met Rear-Admiral Linois, who was on the look-out for him with a 74-gun ship, two frigates, a corvette, and a brig. The Frenchman was cautious; and it was not till the afternoon that he made an attempt to cut off Dance's rear, when the latter, seeing with what sort of an adversary he had to deal, actually made an attack with his Indiamen in line ahead. Armed as they were with nothing better than thirty or so 18-pounders each, the first three exchanged a number of broadsides with the enemy, and after an action of three-quarters of an hour put them to flight, with the loss of one seaman killed and one wounded, pursued them for two hours, and then turned back to their own course. The men of the leading Indiaman, the Royal George, afterwards exhibited as a trophy a 42-pound shell fired from the French flagship. Dance, whose dispatch to the Court of Directors speaks of his ships being in line of battle and his men at quarters, as if it were a squadron of ships of war that was in question, had evidently made Linois suppose that he was dealing with an enemy of this formidable kind. For the saving of their valuable property the East India Company voted £50,000, every seamen receiving six guineas. The Commodore was knighted, and rewards were showered upon him.

The acuteness with which Bonaparte had felt from the first the ignominy of being at war with a country which he could not seriously injure appears from two outrages committed the moment war was declared. Great Britain had, following the law of nations, attached French vessels then in British ports. This gave Bonaparte a pretext for imprisoning as possible soldiers—many of them for years—hundreds of British who then found themselves in France. Even the position of Lord Elgin, the late ambassador in Constantinople, who was returning home with the usual passports, was not respected. Bonaparte also refused to spare Hanover, as had been done in the last war. He knew that Prussia would no longer dare to assert her position as the protectress of the neutrality of the North German States, besides which she had been gorged to the full in his recent rearrangement of the German Empire. Early in the following month the occupation of the greater part of the country was complete. George was partly hampered in taking any steps for its defence by the old prejudice against the Electorate, which was still strong in Great Britain, but now that it was lost men found some cause to deplore the event. The two great rivers which carry the trade of northern Germany into the North Sea, the Elbe and the Weser, were closed to British vessels. Their Government, not choosing that their vessels should be made an exception, blockaded the mouths of both rivers. At a later date many of the electorate troops passed over to England, and won an honour in Spain as the King's German Legion which they had no opportunity of winning in their own country.

The French had more justification for reoccupying the southern ports of the Kingdom of Naples. It was an infringement of neutrality; but that country had been a close ally

CLOSE OF ADDINGTON'S ADMINISTRATION 381

of Great Britain in the last war, and the evacuation of Southern Italy by the French troops under the treaty of Amiens had been connected with the British evacuation of the Mediterranean Ports. It was, therefore, a reply, so far as Great Britain was concerned, to her retention of Malta. But in this as in so many other matters the interests of countries, whose only wish was to remain neutral, were sacrificed, according to Bonaparte's outspoken policy, to his designs against the one enemy with whom he was professedly at war.

Great Britain was even less able to touch France closely. In the West Indies, however, little time was lost in once more seizing St. Lucia and Tobago from the French. On the mainland of South America, Essequibo, Demerara, and Berbice were also taken in 1803 from the Dutch, whom it had been found necessary to include in the war. The force which had been sent to subdue the insurrection in San Domingo surrendered to the British, and the island became independent. Against this the French scored one colonial success. A force crossed the Atlantic from Cayenne, and, being reinforced at Senegal, recaptured the small island of Goree, captured from the French in the last war, and still in British hands, contrary to the Treaty of Amiens. But it was once more recaptured by the British in March 1804, only a few weeks later. In the following month the Government felt strong enough to seize Surinam. The operation was ably carried out by Major-General Sir Charles Green and Commodore Sir Samuel Hood from the West Indies. All those Dutch possessions upon the mainland, since known as Guiana, were now in British hands. Other adventures in that part of the world were avoided. The West Indies had been the grave of too many British soldiers in the last war, and the dread of yellow fever was a permanent hindrance to recruiting.

The principal preoccupation of Ministers was, indeed, for the land defence of the country, which, even under the best administrations, has usually in the United Kingdom been found to be in almost inextricable confusion. At the opening of the war they found themselves with a force of about 105,000 regulars—or 27,000 less than the establishment—and over 70,000 militia. On the 20th of June, 1803, Charles Yorke, then still Secretary at War, introduced a bill for the establishment of an Army of Reserve of 50,000 men, in order to set free some part of the Regular Army for offensive operations. But although it was to be raised by ballot of all males from 18 to 45 years of age, there was so much delay and interruption that in December it only stood at 27,500, besides 7,500 who had chosen to pass through it into the Regular Army. In the meantime, the Government forgot the importance which it had attached to the offensive, and turned their attention to the volunteers. Here they were confronted with precisely the opposite difficulty. A powerful burst of patriotism followed the outbreak of war—not so intense as occurred on some occasions during those years in France or in Spain—but still remarkable. Public places were placarded with speeches and other incitements to serve, the most telling being the speech which Queen Elizabeth made at Tilbury on the last occasion when a grand foreign invasion was impending. But it was observed that there wanted something of the devotion of those nobles and gentry who in that day rallied round the great Queen; while, on the other hand, those Catholic lords whose ancestors had done good service against a Catholic invader were now refused the rank which they requested in the forces of their country. None the less, Ministers very soon found themselves in the possession of a force entirely beyond their power to discipline or control. "They no sooner turned this cock", as Windham told them, "than it spurted in their faces." By December they had in Great Britain 340,000 volunteers; but they could only arm two-thirds with muskets, and two-thirds of the remainder with pikes. As the first year of the war drew to an end they became more and more involved in those difficulties which the tempered zeal of the volunteers presents—rights to exemption, rights to resign, rights to elect their own officers. On these questions they had no fixed opinions; on the more important questions of discipline and training they seem to have had none at all. But they had in parliament to meet the criticism of men who had very definite views—those of soldiers, such as Lieutenant-Colonel Robert Craufurd, afterwards the celebrated commander of the Light Division in the Peninsula; and those of civilian officers of volunteers who were actively engaged, when not in their places in parliament, in carrying the Government's scheme into effect. There were few leading men who had not served or were not serving. Addington himself had been till lately a volunteer colonel. But the most notable examples were Erskine and Pitt. The former had been distinguished as an opponent of the policy of the late war. But in the present war he consented to be, according to the legal joke of the day, "retained for the defence". He had been early thrust out to sea, and had served with credit in the Navy as a boy, and in the Army as a youth. He had left both professions, as they had offered him no prospects in time of peace; and impelled by the same inducement which had fired Eldon, whom he was so soon to succeed as Lord Chancellor—a very early marriage—had taken vigorously to the law. He had long been known as the first of advocates, and was famous for the gift of identifying himself with all the passions and interests of his clients. Although he had forgotten his military lore and was a poor officer, he commanded a corps which was reviewed by the King on a great occasion. His Majesty asked what was its composition. "They are all lawyers, Sir", said Erskine. "What! What!" was the royal reply. "All lawyers? All lawyers? Call them the Devil's Own! Call them the Devil's Own!" Pitt is credited with being inspired himself to a jest at the expense of his corps. As Warden of the Cinque Ports he had raised three battalions of nearly 3,000 men. In the draft rules submitted to him by one battalion the words, "except in case of actual invasion", constantly appeared. He showed his disgust at this by sarcastically making the same addition to another rule, which provided that at no time, and on no account whatever, were they to be sent out of the country. He did not hold with half-heartedness, even in volunteering. Under him the post of Lord Warden became what it had been hundreds of years before, and Walmer Castle the centre of an organization for the defence of all that part of the coast. Thus the accident of the King's method of disposing of what was then regarded as a sinecure led to this outpost of Empire being placed in the charge of the greatest British statesman of the day, just at the time when Britain's greatest living poet was addressing its people in glowing words:

> "Men of Kent,
> Ye children of a Soil that doth advance
> Her haughty brow against the coast of France."

In November, when the new session opened, Ministers had to stand a fire from several directions. Pitt, whose own efficiency as an officer made him a recognized authority, pressed strongly for adjutants to be lent from the Regular Army. After much delay the Government partly accepted this suggestion. On the other hand, Windham, although himself another colonel of volunteers, rated their value low, and complained that the Regular Army was starved. Fox supported him. Both of them believed that the volunteers were largely a sham, and thought an armed peasantry better. Craufurd developed the idea. Such a body would, he said, form a valuable force of genuine irregulars, three or four times as large as the volunteers. They would be taught the use of their arms by gamekeepers and poachers; they would learn to use ground, lining hedges where possible; they would be able to form themselves into a mass and dash into any opening which might present itself, and to retire with equal rapidity when pressed. Fifty officers of the stamp of Moore, who was at that time at Shorncliffe training the celebrated Light Brigade, and Craufurd himself, who afterwards commanded it, might, had they existed, have shaped this force; but even this is doubtful. And, as Pitt said, the enemy, once landed, would pass "with the rapidity of a torrent" over the sixty miles which separated them from London. There would be little time for all these tactics. The country was, therefore, thrown back upon the volunteers. Several generals had pronounced them efficient, but it is dangerous to take literally the encouraging cirtificates granted by a regular officer. It was not till the autumn of 1804 that the Officer Commanding the forces in Kent and Sussex, Sir David Dundas, a cautious Scottish general of great experience in training, who would have been far from trifling with Pitt, pronounced his corps fit to take the field with regulars. Accidentally tested by false alarms in Yorkshire and on the east of Scotland as vividly described by Walter Scott at the end of the Antiquary, the volunteers showed that they possessed a readiness in getting themselves in movement which deserved all praise. The proceedings which were published by the association formed for the defence of this extremely vulnerable part of Great Britain throw an interesting light on their difficulties, and the energetic steps taken to meet them. For example, in several volunteer companies every fifth or sixth shot took effect on a target of three feet in diameter at a hundred yards. "This with the common battalion firelock", it was claimed—no doubt truthfully—"is a high degree of precision." Yet it is unlikely that, had the invasion taken place during Addington's Ministry, the volunteers would have been of much use.

The general opinion—held by both Ministers and others —appears to have been that in the event of a successful invasion of England, London must fall. A landing on the east coast to the north of the Thames was not very probable. Southwards, it was not to be feared on any part of the coast near the entrenched camps of Chatham and Dover. There remained the south coast of Kent and Sussex. It was Dundas's intention, if beaten on the shore, to leave the way open to London, falling back towards his own left upon Dover. Should Bonaparte neglect to leave a force to mask that place, Dundas would be free to attack his right and threaten his communications. On the other hand, if he were to leave one, his advance would be very considerably delayed. By the time he had reached London troops from Essex and the city itself would be collected to dispute the enemy's passage in the suburbs south of the Thames. But it was not intended to risk a pitched battle in the open. On Christmas Day, 1803, Addington gave Abbot what he believed to be the French plan. The Irish expedition was to sail that day simultaneously from Brest and the Texel, in 220 transports protected by twenty sail of the line. When they had landed, the Boulogne army was to cross. So ingeniously had he been misled. Lord Cornwallis was sent for, and took command of the Central Army. If the landing was in Essex, the King, with Addington and Yorke, was to move to the inland fortified camp of Chelmsford; if in Kent, to Dartford, half-way on the road to the corresponding camp of Chatham. The Queen and the Princesses, as well as the exchequer and the treasure, and the duplicate books of the Bank of England, would be escorted to Worcester. The bank-books in regular use would be moved to the Tower, and the artillery and stores from Woolwich transported inland by the Grand Junction Canal. In the event of an invasion also, and not before, the press would be prohibited from publishing movements of troops, and there would be a general arrest of suspected persons.

As the New Year opened it came to be acutely felt that the Government was inadequate to the crisis. The Grenvilles made overtures to Fox, who had shown himself at times uncertain whether to join the Ministry or to co-operate in overthrowing it. Many of his own party—those in particular who were most closely connected with the Prince of

Wales, such as Sheridan and Erskine—objected strongly to any union with Grenville. These difficulties were, however, got over, and an understanding reached with Pitt, who would not agree to a closer alliance. On the 23rd of April, 1804, Fox moved that the various measures which the Government had introduced and tinkered and trifled with for the exasperation of the country for whose benefit they were proposed, should be referred to a committee of the whole House. Pitt supported him in a complete review of those measures, in which he showed—but without the smallest trace of undue self-assertion—that it had borrowed his ideas but spoilt them in the adoption. Only the Attorney-General, Perceval, attempted a vigorous defence, and he made two curious admissions. He praised Pitt in terms which showed that he felt that it was he, and not Addington, who was required at the head of the Government. He also objected to efforts which had been made to collect members from the country for this debate. He had put his finger on the real weakness of his case. As a rule, members who do not attend regularly are not the best judges of how they should vote. But this was a special case. All county members who owed their seats to local importance, and whose business usually kept them down on their estates, had a great deal to do with questions of national defence, and when they listened to Fox and Pitt, they heard a great deal which they could have supported from their own experience. It was these, and not the placemen and members for rotten boroughs, that carried weight—a weight visibly attested by the spurs which they alone were privileged as knights of the shire to wear in the House. Wilberforce was one of them, although of course a regular attendant. He knew that the people could be stirred, and he knew how to stir his own Yorkshiremen; his diary at this time was full of complaints of the Government's neglect of its opportunities, its throwing cold water upon enthusiasm, and its unbusinesslike methods. The business men, such as Sir Robert Peel, and the City interest had no confidence in Addington's Ministry. It saved itself, but by fifty-two votes only.

Two days later it was Pitt's turn to introduce a motion which Fox supported. The Government had now deserted its own favourite measure, the Army of Reserve Act, which had been, upon the whole, a failure. But to close down the Army of Reserve while increasing the militia, as the Government wished to do, would put an end to all recruiting for the Regular Army. Pitt therefore outlined a scheme, putting the recruitment of the Army of Reserve and the Regular Army also upon a territorial basis, and opposed the suspension of the Army of Reserve Act. The motion was lost, the votes being 203 to 240; but the fate of the Government was decided.

In the days of a House of Commons which was so unequal a representative of the nation, it was not the mere figures in the division which counted; it was the character of those who formed the opposition; and it was opinion out of doors which turned the scale. What complexion this bore was no longer in any doubt. For a year past Canning had made merry in verse with ideas suggested by Addington's popular nickname, "The Doctor", and his pious provision for what Cobbett in his Political Register called "The Family"—"Brother Bragge and Brother Hiley". He summed up the position in the lines:

> "Pitt is to Addington
> As London is to Paddington."

Having none of the epigrammatic wit of Canning, the friends of the Ministry had recourse to a war of pamphlets with "Cursory Remarks upon the State of Parties by a Near Observer". But here, too, they had the worst of it. A misfortune, moreover, which occurred to the British Ministers in Bavaria and Württemberg made the Government ridiculous in the eyes of Europe. The pretended French conspirator and spy, Méhée de la Touche, took money from the

CLOSE OF ADDINGTON'S ADMINISTRATION 389

first of these, along with instructions regarding blowing up of powder magazines in France, seducing the troops by the promise of higher pay, and so on. The Minister in Würtemberg was similarly involved. All these directions and correspondence were published with caustic comments about British gold going astray, and forwarded with a circular letter of Talleyrand calling the attention of all the courts of Europe to what he described as the profanation of the sacred character of an ambassador, metamorphosed into that of an agent for plots and corruption. Matters like these gave the Government a very unfavourable press.

There had also been a very serious outcry upon naval administration. Pitt had taken it up strongly. But he had not been so successful in pressing the matter home in parliament as he had been in the case of the Army, owing to St. Vincent's reputation and influence. But that distinguished admiral, in his zeal as an economist and a reformer of abuses, had failed as a First Lord, as was admitted by Addington a year before in attempting to replace him. Skilled artificers had been dismissed in large numbers from government dockyards, and, as he would not trust private yards, there was a shortage of sea-going ships of the line. Of 81 in commission, which Melville found after he had succeeded St. Vincent, against 65 owned by France and Holland—to say nothing of Spain, a very probable enemy—17 were fit for home service only. Besides this there were 32 ships unfit to be put into commission and 6 building. This was altogether insufficient for blockade. Again, seamen had been encouraged during the peace to take service abroad in large numbers, and when war broke out again Nelson was expected to complete establishments of seamen and marines with Maltese, Italians, or anything else he could find in the Mediterranean. And in April 1804 the press got wind of a plan (which came to nothing) for blocking the invading flotilla in Boulogne harbour by sinking ships filled with stones in the entrance. In the undisciplined fashion of the time this "stone expedition" was ridiculed in a letter to the Morning Chronicle openly dated from the British squadron off Boulogne, and presumably from some discontented officer. Of these there were many, owing to St. Vincent's personal severity when afloat, and to the strictness of the blockade which he enforced. No doubt, also, those who no longer profited, as they had during the last war, by the embezzlement of stores amounting to a sum put by the Attorney-General, when prosecuting one of them, at half a million pounds yearly, out of the royal dockyards, knew how to make their grievances felt. But, just as were all his endeavours, it was right that he should pay the penalty of those who in time of war, or of precarious peace, handle the delicate question of economy and correction of abuses with misdirected vigour.

The King's anxiety for his own position was another factor. He had had a two months' attack of gout, followed by partial paralysis and mental aberration, earlier in the year, and still was difficult to deal with. George held firmly by his right to choose his ministers. If the nation pressed him to change them he was ready to do so, but for that very reason would not wait to have the alteration forced upon him by government defeats, which were possible in the House of Commons, and almost certain in the House of Lords. In his own words, he feared his closet being forced. He was most averse to a change. He was ready for a general election. But, to his honour, Addington was willing to spare both his country and his King. He had, previously to the 23rd of April, made a last attempt to secure his retreat by opening up negotiations with Pitt. But the latter refused to communicate except with the King himself. He had already prepared the way for a return to office by a letter to His Majesty, explaining that he should consider it his duty to his Sovereign and to the country to attack the Government. He closed with an assurance that he would not commit himself to any party or policy which should be objectionable to him. The reference was to Fox, and to the Catholic claims. Eldon carried the letter. He did nothing of himself to undermine Addington's position, but his willingness to be the bearer of such a communication places his loyalty to his colleague in an unfavourable light. He could not deliver it till the 27th. Two days later, the Cabinet decided to resign; and Pitt, as desired by the King, entrusted the Lord Chancellor with his plan for a new administration on a broad basis. His Majesty's comments upon it were most caustic. He reproached Pitt with having agreed with such colleagues as Dundas, who upon the Catholic question "showed that he was become the follower of all the wild ideas of Mr. Burke", and Grenville, who acted from "obstinacy, his usual director". Fox he could not possibly have, and he was astonished at his name being even mentioned. In his letter to Eldon he did not spare Pitt himself, and described his letters as essays containing empty words and little information.

In fact, the King was very unwilling indeed to part with Addington or any of his present Ministers. It was not till the 7th of May that Pitt obtained an audience. By this time George, with that happy disposition to which he owed much of his peace of mind, had resigned himself to the inevitable. "I must congratulate Your Majesty", said Pitt, "on your looking better now than on your recovery from your last illness." "That is not to be wondered at", replied the King. "I was then on the point of parting with an old friend; I am now about to regain one." The interview which followed lasted for three hours. There was some trouble over both the Grenville and Fox parties, but finally the King was willing to waive his objections to all except Fox himself. No doubt much of the three hours was spent by Pitt in an endeavour to obtain his admission. But the King was obdurate. His principal objection to Fox was that he had encouraged the Heir-Apparent in a life of dissipation and in opposition to himself—an objection which he had a strong right to entertain both as a sovereign and as a parent. But in arguing with Pitt he was on even stronger ground. The inclusion of Fox was pressed upon him on the ground of the importance of enlisting all the abilities of the country in the present crisis. Yet this was the man who had done more than any other man, and almost as much as man could do, to weaken the hands of Pitt in meeting the former danger during his former administration, and who had even argued strongly against the policy of the present war. It was a subject which raised George's powers to unusual activity. Pitt told Eldon afterwards that he had never been so baffled by him in any conversation he had with him in his life. But the King had no objection to Fox being sent on a foreign mission of importance, should this be desired. He demurred only to personal relations with him.

Had Pitt persisted, the King would probably have accepted his refusal, and recalled Addington. Another return of his madness was also to be feared. There was, however, every likelihood of his aversion being eventually surmounted, and Pitt subsequently more than once endeavoured to do so, but without success. Fox was ready to wait. When he heard the King's decision, he generously disclaimed ambition for office for himself, and advised his friends to accept. In loyalty to him they refused, whereupon Grenville refused also, carrying his friends with him. His motive equally was loyalty. Fox had been an enemy, he was now a friend, and Grenville could not bear the notion of using him to return to power, and then allowing him to be cast aside. But the motive operated upon prepared ground. He and his cousin were both stiff, nor did their relationship help the matter. For Pitt could not think of himself as a Grenville except as one of a family which in the old Whig way treated the State as a means for its own enrichment and aggrandizement; and this was not his way. He held himself apart from most of the old aristocracy, and indeed it was partly for this reason that he had by large creations of peers made a sort

CLOSE OF ADDINGTON'S ADMINISTRATION 393

of aristocracy of his own. His friends were chiefly the old, like Malmesbury, or the young, like Canning. One great friendship which he had, that for Addington, whom he was so long in bringing himself to oppose, had drawn him away from his old political associates; and he held a lonely course. Grenville, on the other hand, was leagued with Windham, the most attractive public man of his day, whose quarrel with Fox was a political legacy from his master Burke, and far from due to natural antipathy. The two were bound to come together again; indeed, they had already done so. Thomas Grenville, who had none of his brother's stiffness, was another link; others, such as Spencer and Fitzwilliam, who had been zealous members of the New Opposition, were joined to Fox by still older bonds, which intervening years had not snapped. Through such social ties as these, and through the essential opposition of Whig ideas to that peculiar union of jobbery in Scotland with national feeling, commercial interests and personal devotion in England, which formed the strength of Pitt, what had begun as a mere co-operation between the New and the Old Opposition for the purpose of turning out Addington became a close union.

Grenville displayed in his refusal of office another instance of his characteristic obstinacy. He preferred to force Fox upon the King, rather than to join Pitt and unite with him in gradually removing His Majesty's objections. In the powerful letter which he wrote to his cousin on that occasion, concluding with the words, "Most affectionately yours, Grenville"—but which nevertheless closed their personal relations—he wrote of the refusal of his party to join the administration: "We rest our determination solely on our strong sense of the impropriety of our becoming parties to a system of government which is to be formed, at such a moment as the present, on a principle of exclusion." He was right in holding Pitt constitutionally responsible; but it was grossly unfair to send him a letter which he could not have answered without bringing in the Sovereign's name, and therefore did not answer at all. And, to make matters worse, the letter was published in the newspapers. Thus Pitt was left to make up by his own personal followers, and such of Addington's Ministers as would remain, for the splendid national administration which he had designed; in which he had intended to offer the post of Foreign Secretary to Fox, who would almost certainly have accepted on the understanding that he would obtain a free hand, such as Grenville had enjoyed in the former Cabinet. Once more he had been frustrated in what would have been a fine piece of statesmanship, by the astuteness and pertinacity of a Sovereign in whom those qualities had been sharpened by impending insanity.

In the event, five members of the old Cabinet, including Castlereagh, were simply transferred to the new with the same offices as before. A sixth, Hawkesbury, was moved to the Home Department, his place being taken at the Foreign by Lord Harrowby. An attempt had been made to induce Lord Moira, the chief adviser of the Prince of Wales, to accept this last post, but it was unsuccessful. Harrowby was, however, an acquisition of some value, the only one of which this can be said, except Pitt himself, the Chancellor of the Exchequer, and Melville, the First Lord of the Admiralty. No person of greater ability than the mediocre Camden could be found for the important post of Secretary of State for War and the Colonies. The last two members were Lord Mulgrave, Chancellor of the Duchy of Lancaster, and the Duke of Montrose, President of the Board of Trade. The last appointment is interesting as being the first occasion of that Minister having Cabinet rank.

Outside the Cabinet the judicious and popular Hardwicke was kept as Lord-Lieutenant of Ireland, and Perceval as Attorney-General. Irish affairs in the House of Commons were in the hands of an Irish member as usual, John Foster, eventually appointed Chancellor of the Irish Exchequer.

CLOSE OF ADDINGTON'S ADMINISTRATION

No better places were given to Pitt's devoted followers, the veteran George Rose and the brilliant George Canning, than those of Joint Paymaster of the Forces and Treasurer of the Navy respectively. Pitt had only one Cabinet Minister, Castlereagh, to support him in the Lower House. But, secondrate as most of them were, each of his ten colleagues carried a kind of weight in council which Rose and Canning did not. The younger man was most deficient in judgment, and he was himself very ready to recognize that his own promotion to a higher post would have involved his chief in a charge of favouritism.

Even this weak Cabinet had the misfortune to be reduced by a casualty in the following December. Harrowby fell on his head, and was obliged to give up all work for some months. It was Mulgrave who succeeded him. This gave occasion to a saying at his expense by Lady Hester Stanhope, Pitt's unbridled niece, who was now living with her uncle. Mulgrave was at his chief's breakfast-table, and displayed with indignation a broken egg-spoon, the only one he could find. The lady became nettled, and—according to the tradition, handed down by Pitt's Private Secretary to his biographer, the third Earl Stanhope—she employed these words: "Don't you know, have you not yet discovered, that Mr. Pitt sometimes uses very slight and weak instruments to effect his ends!" The great contemporary continental critic of foreign policy, Friedrich von Gentz, afterwards said that he did not suppose posterity would believe that it was possible to select such a Foreign Minister in such a crisis. Such was the Ministry which took office from May the 12th, after first leaving it to Addington to introduce the budget providing for £15,400,000 of war taxes, and a loan amounting to £10,000,000 for Great Britain alone. It had been agreed to, like that of Pitt three years before, without a word of criticism.

CHAPTER VII

PITT'S LAST ADMINISTRATION

(MAY 1804—JANUARY 1806)

UPON accepting office the new Ministers had before them the task of repairing the failures and deficiencies of their predecessors in the Navy, the Army, and foreign relations. Melville took up the first with his usual efficiency. By the middle of June of the following year there were 91 sail of the line in commission, besides twelve 50-gun ships.

For the Army, Pitt introduced the measure which he had already partly outlined. He found himself with sufficient troops for home defence; but the Regular Army was starved. This was due to Government competing against itself. In the nine months ending on the 30th of April, 1804, 31,758 men were raised for the Army of Reserve; but of these only 2,531 were balloted men, the rest were substitutes. Many of these were the right men for the Regular Army. But the usual price of a substitute paid by the unlucky person balloted was fifty pounds, and a man could take this and go into the Army of Reserve with a bounty of twelve guineas, and then, if he wished, take another of ten guineas to become a regular soldier. But if he went into the Regular Army direct, he only received sixteen. There was similar competition between the Militia and the Regular Army. It was, therefore, necessary to cut down the former, and this the bill proposed to do for Great Britain from 79,000 to 51,489. The field of possible recruitment being thus enlarged, there remained the method of recruitment. The dreaded ballot had produced a system of insurance, which, as might naturally have been expected, was carried to a high point of perfection in Scotland. The tendency was for those in a village on whom the ballot might fall to subscribe to a fund. It then did not matter who was drawn. He did not have to serve, and the fund provided the substitute. The inference was that the ballot might be abolished altogether, and a quota fixed upon each parish. The regular parish authorities, namely, the churchwardens and overseers, were to provide the men for the new force, in which service was to be for five years, or until six months after the end of the war; and, if they could not, the parish was to be fined £20 for every man deficient. The bounty was to be twelve guineas, or only three-fourths of that for the Regular Army. But a man who chose to enter the Regular Army through the Additional Force thus created would receive a bounty of ten guineas in addition to his former twelve. The force was to be formed into second battalions to the regular regiments. The bill would, therefore, furnish a permanent body of men for home defence, and a constant supply of regular soldiers for the striking force.

The plan was violently attacked from almost every quarter. The second reading passed by a majority of 40 only; in one division in the course of its stormy career the Ministry was in a minority of 6; and at a later stage Pitt was reduced to declaring that if the House threw out the bill they would not get rid of him, it being the right of His Majesty to choose his own Ministers. Finally it passed on the 29th of June. No other measure of the first importance was introduced in the session, but before it closed Pitt obtained the consent of the House to the grant of £591,842 3s. 10½d. for defraying the arrears of the King's Civil List, and also to its being permanently raised by £60,000 to £900,000, the increase being made necessary by the rise in the cost of living.

The Additional Force Act soon proved to be a dead failure. Before the next session opened, it became indispensably necessary to strengthen the Government. By January 1805 Pitt was safe. The exasperated Opposition learnt that he had been reconciled with Addington, an arrangement with which the good offices of the King had much to do. Addington, accepting a peerage as Lord Sidmouth, took Portland's place as President of the Council. His friend Hobart, now the Earl of Buckinghamshire, also entered the Cabinet as Chancellor of the Duchy instead of Mulgrave, now Foreign Secretary. An abler member of the party, Vansittart, went to Ireland as Chief Secretary. But it was numbers rather than talent to which Pitt looked. Addington's party brought him forty votes. Pitt had by this time lost much of his popularity; and the reconciliation of two men who had only disagreed upon one important question of principle—the Catholic claims—was severely criticized. "I think they are a little hard upon us", he said wistfully to Wilberforce, "in finding fault with our making it up again, when we have been friends from our childhood, and our fathers were so before us, while they say nothing to Grenville for uniting with Fox, though they have been fighting all their lives." Some of these opponents, after the manner of the feminine sex, concealed their mortification under the pretence of being very much amused, and, in the war of gibe and retort which followed in Parliament, Sheridan showed himself, as usual, a very fair match for Pitt himself.

The recruiting failure furnished excellent material for attacking the Government. The parish officers turned out to have been the wrong agency, natural though the selection was. They neither had the knowledge of recruiting officers and sergeants, nor carried with them the prestige of men of local influence rallying their tenants and friends around them for national service. Indeed, the absence of any attempt on the part of the aristocracy and squirearchy to animate the people by their example (except as regards the volunteers) is one of the strange things of the time. The explanation is not difficult. The Army was a profession, and recruiting for it the business of the Crown. The farmers, who formed the natural link between the great lords and squires and the labourers, were far too busy making money to do anything to help. They enrolled themselves as volunteers, and this was enough. If the enemy came to them, they would fight. In the whole compass of Jane Austen's novels—all dealing with country life during the years of the war—apart from the naval references due to her own brothers having been sailors there is nothing whatever to suggest that war existed, and that it was incumbent upon young men of leisure to enter the Army. One novel is so far an exception that it shows that the militia was embodied, and formed an attraction for idlers. An even more remarkable instance of the way in which these things were regarded is seen in one of Maria Edgeworth's novels, The Absentee. The hero, disappointed in a love-affair, has a mind to serve a campaign or two if he can get a commission in a regiment going to Spain. The whole matter is discussed with characteristic solemnity, and he is told: "A martial spirit is now essential to the liberty and the existence of our country." But it finds no harbour in the bosom of the hero, exemplary young nobleman though he is, and as soon as the love-affair is smoothed out again, his country's call, if he ever felt it, is forgotten. One instance deserves to be added from actual life. Few families were more zealous in the cause of volunteering than that of which Lord Buckingham was the head. Yet in 1808, when service in the Army meant also the opportunity of striking a blow in the fascinating cause of Spanish liberty, his two brothers write to the Marquis on the question of the future of his younger son, who had expressed some desire to be a soldier. Buckingham himself was against it, and his brothers gravely weighed the disadvantages of the military profession against those of total idleness, pointing out that in these days of reform and economy a provision for a noble younger son by office or sinecure was growing difficult, and that soldiers are often to be found in the highest situations. When such was the attitude of men with some chivalry in their blood, little could be expected from the captains of industry in the manufacturing centres.

The result of this neglect was that, as Sheridan showed, when moving for a repeal of the Additional Force Act in March 1805, it had merely produced 2,427 effective soldiers, out of whom 386 had enlisted for general service. However, recruiting had been quicker in the last few weeks, and, after all, the position was not desperate. In meeting a similar motion in the House of Lords, Hawkesbury pointed out that the military force of the United Kingdom (excluding volunteers) was 400,000, or a tenth of the number capable of bearing arms, which he put at 3,800,000, being one-fourth of the whole population. The corresponding figures in France were 362,000 and 8,000,000.

Across the Channel steady preparations were being made meanwhile for the decisive blow. The flotilla and the army which it was intended to convey were gradually being concentrated. By the end of 1804 the number of so-called war-vessels alone concentrated at Boulogne was 532, while there were 319 more at the neighbouring ports of Etaples, Wimereux, and Ambleteuse. In October an attempt was made to destroy a part of the Boulogne flotilla. The "catamaran project", as it was called from the design of the tiny torpedo-like vessels which carried the explosives, brought upon Pitt's naval administration even more ridicule than the "stone expedition" had upon Addington's, as— unlike that one—it was actually carried out; particularly when it was noised abroad that Melville had gone afloat to witness the destruction of Napoleon's hopes, and that the Lord Warden had prepared what Sheridan called a sort of Alexander's feast for him at Walmer Castle on his return. Though no British lives were lost, the plan was a failure. One more attack that year merely gave an opportunity to Marshal Soult, who commanded the camp, for edifying reflections on British barbarity. The period of waiting, on the other hand, had been trying for the French. The army had, encamped as it was upon the bleak cliffs of the Channel coast, suffered in morale and in health, particularly the Italian troops. The Navy, too, had deteriorated. Ships certainly had been completed, but the problem of proper supplies, repairs, and manning had never been

PITT'S LAST ADMINISTRATION

really taken up. It cannot be said that Vice-Admiral Decrès, the Minister of Marine, though a most gallant officer, showed any gifts for organization. He was, moreover, too junior and too retiring a man to carry weight, either with his imperial master, who needed someone near him to throw into practical form his visions on naval matters, or with the service generally. Vice-Admiral Ganteaume, who had replaced in June 1804, at Brest, an admiral who had not even given the officers and men that training which it was possible to give in a blockaded harbour, complained that his ships were undermanned. In August, France had lost her finest admiral, Latouche-Tréville, dead—it was believed —of walking so of tenup to the signal-post at Toulon to watch the British fleet; and he was succeeded, after some hesitation on the Emperor's part over the choice, by Vice-Admiral Villeneuve, on the recommendation of Decrès, who had served under him. Villeneuve, in his turn, complained of desertions, and of the state of his ships, which he seems to have done very little to remedy.

And now the position of Spain with respect to the war took a definite shape. For a long time Great Britain had permitted her to discharge her obligations as an ally of France under the Treaty of San Ildefonso of 1796, by paying what was for her the enormous subsidy of nearly a quarter of a million pounds a month. Neither of the three Governments believed a war between Great Britain and Spain to be in its own interests. But the difficulties of maintaining this extraordinary state of things grew. It was not inconsistent with the international law of the time for belligerent vessels to enter a neutral harbour and to remain there. Consequently, while the French ships which had escaped from the West Indies lay at Ferrol, the British blockading squadron often entered the harbour and obtained provisions. But the French objected. Their own ships, they said, had come as refugees, but there was no reason for the British to be there at all. On the other hand, they had sent soldiers and sailors through Spain to the blockaded squadron; and defended this enforced breach of her neutrality by the argument that that neutrality itself was compromised by the prolonged stay of their ships, which they were anxious to get to sea as soon as reinforcements could be put on board. In the West Indies, French privateers made use of Spanish possessions such as Havana in the most bare-faced way, and at one time the Bahamas were threatened by bodies of troops which had escaped from San Domingo, and were now collected in other ports on the north coast of Cuba. Such violations of Spanish neutrality, added to the way in which the Treaty of San Ildefonso was enforced, as well as Spain's naval preparations—natural as these were—made war inevitable. But the way in which it broke out was not to England's credit.

In September, Rear-Admiral Alexander Cochrane, then blockading Ferrol, reported the existence of warlike preparations there, and in the ports of Carthagena and Cadiz. As a measure of precaution Spain must be prevented from prolonging negotiations until her galleons were safe and then declaring war; so orders were sent from the Admiralty to meet and detain Spanish vessels laden with naval and military stores, and in particular certain treasure-ships known to be leaving Montevideo. Unfortunately Cornwallis had no information of more than two of these last being on their way on the 22nd of September, when he issued orders to Captain Graham Moore, of the Indefatigable, brother of the great soldier, to stop them. That officer sailed from Brest at once, and, being joined by three frigates off the south-west of Spain, met four large frigates under a Rear-Admiral on the 5th October. Not being in anything near overwhelming force, he was resisted; and an engagement ensued, in the course of which, though the damage was otherwise inconsiderable, one of the Spanish vessels unluckily blew up, and all whom she contained except forty perished, including a number of passengers. The other ships were captured, with a treasure of 3,200,000 out of 4,000,000 dollars. No blame can attach to Moore, but such stringent orders should not have been issued without steps to secure their humane fulfilment. The Spaniards on their side do not seem to have felt bitter. The captain of the French ship in Cadiz, the Aigle, complained of the calm way in which the people there took the occurrence. It did not even, by itself, make war inevitable. The Spanish Ambassador did not ask for his passports at once. The head of the British Embassy in Madrid obtained his on the 7th of November, because he had received no satisfactory explanation concerning the armaments and the nature of the subsidy; and the subject of the galleons was not raised. In its declaration of war dated the 12th of December the Spanish Government took its stand not merely upon this occurrence, but upon the vigour and violence with which the precautionary orders issued by the British Government had been carried out generally. Ministers had, however, to meet much criticism in parliament, Grenville's censure in the House of Lords being particularly severe.

By a convention concluded on the 4th day of January, 1805, the King of Spain agreed to commission seven ships of the line at Ferrol, twelve at Cadiz, and six in the Mediterranean at Cartagena. But Napoleon was never under any illusion as to the value of the assistance which Spain could offer. With small vessels her people showed no little skill, and Spanish privateers became a formidable menace to the traffic passing through the Straits of Gibraltar. But their abilities, as was afterwards found to be the case on land, were confined to that petty or partisan warfare for which their own language has given the English a name: "guerrilla" warfare. A ship's company requires discipline— the training which enables a body of men to act as one— and in this they were deficient. In these matters, Admiral Gravina, who commanded the Spanish squadron at Cadiz, had many of the characteristics of his race. To chivalry, loyalty, and courage he added energy and a knowledge of his profession. But as to making ships with their companies into efficient instruments of war, he hardly seems even to have known what was required.

In the struggle to win the public opinion of Europe, Napoleon gave Great Britain one advantage, a few days after the Spanish treasure fleet was attacked. On the 24th of October, 1804, under orders from Paris, a French officer seized Sir George Rumbold, the British Minister in Hamburg, a free town of the German Empire, and under the protectorate of the King of Prussia. That sovereign remonstrated. Napoleon ordered Rumbold's release, but his papers were kept.

For the last year Russia had been drawing closer to Great Britain and away from France, whose incessant aggressions and outrages had driven Alexander to break off direct relations with that country in June 1804. It was now his object to bring about, with the help of British gold, a combination of Powers on the Continent strong enough to set bounds to Napoleon's ambition. Austria was encouraged to make warlike preparations. In January 1805 Napoleon saw the formation of a new coalition to be imminent, and addressed an overture of peace to his "brother", King George. The reply was sent by Mulgrave to Talleyrand. It was to the effect that His Majesty must first communicate with the Powers on the Continent which saw eye to eye with him, particularly the Emperor of Russia. At the same time a dispatch was sent to St. Petersburg, proposing that that Government should offer peace to France upon the condition of North Germany, Holland, Switzerland, and Italy being freed from French control. The suggestion was accepted. In order to put on foot an army to enforce this demand, the British Government agreed to give Russia £1,250,000 for every 100,000 men. A treaty to this effect was signed on the 11th of April, 1805, and it was provided that other Powers might join in order to complete the force of 500,000 men

PITT'S LAST ADMINISTRATION 405

contemplated. To avoid the dissensions which had broken out during the last war over the terms of peace when the French should have been defeated, and over the plan of campaign, it was settled that Russia should come to a direct understanding with Austria upon both points. This was done.

In December 1803 the First Consul had entertained the plan of an expedition to the West Indies to save Martinique, under Latouche-Tréville, now Vice-Admiral. This was, however, dropped, when the colony was found not to be in danger of attack; it was not till the following summer that Napoleon again turned his thoughts seriously to the movement of his fleets, and the first definite plan was not drawn up till the 29th of September, 1804. The principle underlying it was by threatening, if not attacking, the British in as many parts of the world as possible, to distract and disperse their energies, and then, before they had located the danger, to concentrate as great a strength as possible in the Channel—the decisive point. The actual shape assumed by the plan of 1804 fulfilled the first of these conditions better than the later one, actually adopted. It comprised two expeditions from Toulon and one from Rochefort, directed respectively against the Dutch colony of Surinam, now in British hands, against St. Helena, and against the British West Indian Isles. Napoleon intended that the English should feel the East Indies to be threatened, as well as the West. Shortly after these had started the Brest squadron was to go out, and, after landing 18,000 men in Ireland, enter the Channel and protect the invading flotilla. But the British got wind of the scheme through their intelligence officers, and it was dropped.

During the winter of 1804–5 invasion plans fell into the background. In Boulogne harbour, in particular, the banks had been allowed to silt up. Napoleon valued economy, and at this time it did not seem improbable that he would find himself obliged to turn the army of England against an eastern enemy, as he afterwards did. Austria had already been assuming a threatening attitude. But this was premature, as she was far from ready. By the end of February his menaces had induced her to draw back, and he felt himself free to put the ports in order. The winter plan for the fleet bears the impression of this policy of dropping invasion temporarily. A combined military and naval force was to sail both from the Mediterranean and the Bay of Biscay, and, after recovering the Dutch colonies on the mainland of South America, capturing some British, and strengthening the French, West Indian Islands, to return united to Rochefort. The blockade of Cadiz was to be raised on the outward voyage, and that of Ferrol on the return. The addition of the six ships which had taken refuge in the Spanish harbours would have given France a total of 22 ships of the line at Rochefort—or double that number, including the Brest ships—in the following spring, a formidable concentration, apart from a possible Spanish reinforcement of another 22 ships. Rear-Admiral Sir Thomas Graves, who had the blockade of Rochefort under Cornwallis, kept no adequate watch at that difficult station, and Rear-Admiral Missiessy had no trouble in getting away on the 11th of January, 1805, with a fresh easterly wind. He had five ships of the line with frigates and smaller vessels, and nearly 3,500 soldiers. Villeneuve on his side took advantage of a strong north-westerly wind, blowing up to a gale, to leave Toulon on the 18th with a force which included eleven sail of the line. Nelson had two frigates on the watch, and had the news next day in harbour near the Straits of Bonifacio. He was instantly off in pursuit, but, convinced as he was that the fleet was bound for the east, he went as far as Alexandria in search of it. Villeneuve meanwhile had suffered some injuries in the gale, and showing a very poor spirit—totally unlike that of Ganteaume in the Bay of Biscay in 1801—had returned by the 21st to Toulon, whence he vexed Paris with bitter complaints. His crews were not trained to storms; he was lucky to have escaped back without serious loss; he wished that the Emperor would relieve him before he became "the byword of Europe"—a phrase of which he appears to have been particularly fond. He seems, in fact, to have been in constant terror of Nelson from the moment when he started; and the excellent plan of leaving in a north-westerly wind, which confirmed his enemy in the belief that his destination was easterly, came from his fears rather than from his strategical insight.

Missiessy was accordingly left to carry out his mission alone; and by the end of February, when the Austrian crisis was passed, a new plan was matured in Napoleon's mind. Twenty-one ships—not 23 as he had at one time hoped—were all that could be expected to sail from Brest. These were to break the Ferrol blockade, to join the combined Toulon and Rochefort squadrons in Martinique, and, brushing aside the British ships at the mouth of the Channel, to present themselves before Boulogne. Even if all these ships were unable to join Ganteaume, 25 ships of the line would make him superior to Cornwallis, and enable him to fulfil his mission.

But the Brest fleet was never to leave harbour. Ganteaume was urged to break out of port, but without risking a battle, as he had succeeded in doing in 1801. It was not till much later that permission was given to fight if the odds were good enough. On the 24th of March, Ganteaume, who had a deal of fighting spirit, telegraphed for leave to force his way out. He had 21 against 15; he promised success; yet he was refused. Such a chance never occurred again; and his service remained confined to occupying a blockading force usually exceeding his own, if ships under repair are included.

Villeneuve had better fortune. On the 30th of March he broke out again with nineteen sail, including eleven ships of the line, taking over three thousand troops. Once more the English frigates did not watch him long enough, and Nelson, who seldom blamed a subordinate even in thought, recorded in his private diary an unusual note of dissatisfaction with the senior captain. On the 7th of April, Villeneuve appeared off Cartagena, but, in his anxiety to get forward, gave no time for the Spanish ships to join him. He allowed very little more at Cadiz, which he reached on the 9th, driving the small British squadron under Vice-Admiral Sir John Orde before him, picked up the French ship and the six Spanish ships which were ready under Gravina, and set sail for the West Indies, which he reached on the 13th of May. Nelson had most certainly been again outwitted. Had not a variety of circumstances, including the known movements of French troops in Southern Europe, convinced him that some Mediterranean expedition was intended, he might possibly have dispatched a frigate to the Straits of Gibraltar. As it was, only on the 16th of April did he learn the westward direction of the French fleet. He was delayed by foul winds, and then had to water and revictual and make other arrangements. The delay gave him time to collect and sift the indications as to where Villeneuve had gone. He could not have gone north or he would have been met with; and there would have been little object in sending so fine a fleet southward to the Cape or to the East Indies. He decided for the West Indies. On the 11th of May he took the strong step of leaving his command and taking ten of his ships to Barbados in pursuit. The French derived no strategical advantage from having a larger force followed and kept under observation by a smaller force; and it was this decision of Nelson's, together with the manner in which it was carried out and the steps to which it directly led, which was the immediate cause of the frustration of Napoleon's plans.

The Toulon fleet did not find Missiessy in the West Indies. Upon its return to port in January orders had been at once issued to the Rochefort squadron to do the same, and the subsequent orders that it should remain did not arrive in time. Missiessy returned hastily, expecting that a superior force would be in search of him. As a matter of fact, Rear-Admiral Cochrane, who had been sent in pursuit of him, had left most of his ships in Jamaica, which the ingenious system of false intelligence set at work by the French had indicated as the objective; so he need not have been alarmed. He only captured a few merchant-ships—winning some prize-money—levied contributions from the three small islands of St. Christopher, Nièvres and Montserrat, and left reinforcements intended for the reconquest of San Domingo from the revolted negroes. He left that island on the 28th of March for Rochefort, which he did not reach till the 20th of May.

Villeneuve did rather more. Tied as he was by the necessity of making his junction with Ganteaume, he felt himself free to carry out one operation of some importance which Missiessy had refused to undertake. This was the capture of "H.M. Sloop Diamond"—so shown in the Navy list—a rocky islet seized and fortified by Commodore Hood in 1803, as a station for harassing the enemy's trade and communications. Lying just off Fort de France, the Port of Martinique, and their headquarters in the West Indies, it was a source of bitter humiliation to the French to see the British flag flying there. With the large force at his disposal Villeneuve had no great difficulty in reducing the rock, which could not be relieved. The curious lenience shown towards prisoners of war in those days permitted Captain Maurice, who had commanded the captured "sloop", to send Nelson a dispatch which gave him the first accurate intelligence of the whereabouts of the French fleet.

The British admiral had been unfortunate. He had, indeed, gained ten days on Villeneuve, reaching Barbados on the 4th of June, two days after the fall of the Diamond Rock. He had then been sent south by false intelligence to save Tobago and Trinidad, and he was almost off the mainland of South America when he heard from Maurice. "But for wrong information", he complained, "I should have fought the battle on June the 6th where Rodney fought his"—between the British island of Dominica and the French island of Guadeloupe to the north of it. He now had twelve ships of the line against twenty. Each admiral had been reinforced with two ships, the British by a part of Cochrane's squadron, the French by a detachment under Rear-Admiral Magon from Rochefort. From this time onward Nelson trusted to his own judgment. With a vision of an equal or superior force against him, Villeneuve had lost little time, after he had heard of the arrival of the Mediterranean fleet from those on board of a convoy of merchant-ships which he had captured, in making for Europe with all speed. This was what Napoleon, writing from Italy, had realized that he would be sure to do (though contrary to his orders) once he knew that Nelson was after him. The British admiral was no less certain. He had turned back north with all speed, reaching Antigua on the 8th of June, still four days behind Villeneuve. After weighing what further information he could collect, he set sail for Europe. Taking himself a shorter passage to the Straits of Gibraltar, the quarter where it was his duty to anticipate the enemy, Nelson detached the Curieux brig, Captain Bettesworth, in advance upon the northerly course which he foresaw that the French would actually take. That officer caught the French fleet up on the 19th of June, and, hastening on to Portsmouth and London, placed his information in the hands of the First Lord of the Admiralty on the 9th of July.

Meanwhile there had been considerable alarm in England, where the enemy's movements had been better known than to Nelson himself. The Government was severely criticized, both in the press and in parliament, for imperilling the West Indian Islands. Pitt had been, in fact, beset by difficulties. He had solved the military question for the time being by the simple expedient of an Act, passed in April, to permit 17,000 militiamen to take bounties to enlist in the line. That was the number in excess in the militia, it

PITT'S LAST ADMINISTRATION

having been already decided to reduce it to the old strength—in privates—of 40,000 for England and 8,000 for Scotland. This and other measures taken by Government, such as the recruiting of several thousand Hanoverians, gave the country an effective disposable force so considerable that three expeditions left it during the year. The first, of 6,000 men, under Lieutenant-General Sir James Craig, left for the Mediterranean in March, in pursuance of an agreement with Russia. The second was very naturally intended for the West Indies upon their being threatened by Missiessy, and after him by Villeneuve. But, that danger removed, it was decided on the 25th of July to send Major-General Sir David Baird to reconquer the Cape of Good Hope. His force also consisted of 6,000 men. By the autumn, besides these 12,000 men and 63,000 other troops in foreign stations, the regular forces stood at 106,000 men; and there were also nearly 75,000 militia in the United Kingdom. This enabled a large expedition to be sent to Germany at the close of the year. It was unfortunate that Pitt, who stood for loyalty against revolution in his own country, did not trust to the former principle rather than to the latter abroad. All through those years, British Governments had a strange faith in their ability to stir up discontent against established governments which were hostile to them. They always failed. When the popular elements were on their side, as in Southern Italy in 1799 and in Spain in 1808, they were also on the side of their own legitimate rulers. Had Pitt trusted to Hanoverian loyalty, and thrown a force of 60,000 men into that country, he might have had not much less than 100,000 men operating in the electorate by the close of the year—an army which Prussia would have respected and Napoleon himself could not have despised.

But it was a naval matter which involved the Government in its most serious difficulties. Under St. Vincent's administration five Commissioners of Naval Inquiry had been appointed, with an admiral at their head. They drew up twelve reports dealing in a most searching manner with various classes of frauds and irregularities. When the tenth reached Pitt, Wilberforce happened to be with him. "I shall never forget", he told his sons afterwards, "the way in which he seized it, and how eagerly he looked into the leaves without waiting even to cut them open." It was the report which dealt with the office of the Treasurer to the Navy, held by Lord Melville, while still Henry Dundas, during Pitt's first ministry. It was proved against him that he had applied naval money to other services, the nature of which he refused to disclose; and also that he connived at the Paymaster of the Navy (who was also his private agent, and kept an account at Coutts's Bank, in which his chief's, his own, and the public money were all mixed up) speculating with thousands of pounds of the public balances. All this was contrary to law. Private use of public money had been a recognized source of income until 1782, when it was expressly forbidden and the Treasurer's salary raised in compensation. The feeling both in Parliament and out of doors was very strong. When the vote of censure was moved upon Melville on the 8th of April, Pitt had some difficulty at one time in obtaining a hearing. The Opposition, which included those of Dundas's former colleagues who now followed Grenville, frankly treated the occasion as one for party triumph. Pitt tried to save his friend by getting the matter referred to a Select Committee. A higher note was struck by Wilberforce. When he rose, Pitt turned on him an appealing look, but he refused to be moved. After a reference to the universal sentiment of persons of every rank, and to the fact that English history had shown that the mischief of a corrupt judgment was worse than that of the abuse itself which was brought to judgment, he added: "It is not only Lord Melville but we ourselves that are upon our trial, and a fearful trial it is." That fine though small body of independent voters of which Sir Robert Peel was the type followed his lead. When the result of the vote was brought

PITT'S LAST ADMINISTRATION 413

to the Speaker, it was found that they were exactly equal—216 both for and against the motion. Abbot had to give the casting vote, and after much hesitation he gave it in a short speech in favour of the way which justice imperatively demanded. The tension removed, the Opposition broke out into wild triumph; and one fox-hunting baronet gave a view halloo and called out, "We have killed the fox!". Pitt almost broke down; and his friends had to crowd round him to hide his tears.

Melville was forced to resign the Admiralty; his name was removed from the list of privy councillors; and it was decided to impeach him. A harsh fate had befallen one who even as Treasurer of the Navy had carried out many excellent reforms, by which prompt payment was assured to sailors and pensioners, and who was thought to be the ablest colleague whom Pitt possessed. But the result was strangely fortunate for the country. To succeed him, Pitt made the unexpected choice of Sir Charles Middleton, a retired admiral of nearly eighty years of age, and the greatest head which the Admiralty has ever had. He was raised to the peerage as Lord Barham. Another misfortune for Pitt turned out almost equally well. Sidmouth disliked the appointment, and difficulties arose over his friends joining in the attacks upon Melville. Finally he resigned, followed by Buckinghamshire, whose place as Chancellor of the Duchy was taken by Harrowby, now partially restored to health. Camden became President of the Council; and the Secretaryship for War and the Colonies passed into the far more able hands of Castlereagh, who, without leaving the office of President of the Board of Control, had a fair field for the display of abilities now becoming generally recognized.

There were difficulties, too, over the budget. By bringing the income tax up to 1s. 3d. in the £, Pitt was able to increase the war taxes to £15,750,000. But he needed also to borrow £20,000,000, and although he was able to get more favourable terms than Addington had for the loan which he had negotiated the year before, the interest being only £5 3s. 2d. per cent., yet he had to budget for £1,560,000 to meet the charge. It is strange to see the petty expedients to which so great a financier was reduced. The sum was made up of no less than eight items. An increase was proposed in the salt tax. This was strongly attacked, but Pitt got it accepted. The House, however, by 76 votes to 73, refused to agree to the tax on agricultural horses, which amounted to a tax on food, being raised from 12s. 6d. to a pound. It was, in fact, an excellent example of a thoroughly bad tax. Only estimated to bring in £200,000, the increase would have borne most hardly on those farmers who were trying to grow something on heavy soils and hilly land, and so to meet the wants of an increasing population.

The rest of the session was mainly taken up in an attempt to draw Pitt into difficulties over the Roman Catholic question. Grenville in the Upper and Fox in the Lower House moved for going into committee upon a petition from the Roman Catholics of Ireland for the removal of their disabilities. Honourable as their zeal was, it was a waste of time, for, as both knew, neither public, Parliament, nor King was converted to the change, in spite of its being just as necessary a change as it had been four years before. Nor was the question treated sufficiently in its practical bearings. Lengthy historical and theological essays were gravely read on both sides of the question. Pitt extricated himself with his usual skill from the dilemma of either being untrue to his former convictions or being bound to support the motion. The debates are chiefly interesting, on the part of the opponents of the claims, for some remarkable predictions. They were quick to realize that once Catholics might sit in Parliament, the Catholic tenants would vote not as their landlords but as their priests bade them. The Earl of Limerick said: "I will suppose that, at some distant day, a struggle of parties may take place, that the parties may be pretty nearly balanced; what if then the Catholic representation, acting in a mass, should offer their assistance to the party which should favour their views? Ministers may wish to cling to their situation"—and so on. "I am apprehensive, as long as human nature remains unchanged, that the resistance to their wishes would not be very strong." In the other House, Foster said that the object of this united and formidable mass of Catholic members of Parliament would be the restoration of Irish legislative independence. The other side of the question was distinguished by the wit and eloquence of Grattan, then heard at Westminster for the first time.

But now the time had come for the decision of greater matters which could brook no delay. Foreseeing Ganteaume's inability to escape from Brest unaided, Napoleon had sent further orders through Magon to Villeneuve. After picking up the Ferrol squadron, he was to attack and defeat the British fleet blockading Brest; Ganteaume would join him; united they would sweep the Channel until they should reach Boulogne, where the Emperor awaited them. Here the French National Flotilla had reached its highest point of organization. At no moment, indeed, were the ships accurately allocated to the troops which they were to carry, and there might have been some confusion on the day of embarkation. Still, there were collected at Boulogne, and in the subsidiary ports of Etaples on the west and Wimereux, Ambleteuse, Calais, Dunkerque, and Ostend on the east, not far short of 2,500 vessels, of which nearly half formed the war flotilla supposed to be able, though—it had been afterwards realized—only with the help of a protecting fleet of battleships, to fight their way across. Leaving on one side the three last-mentioned ports, as an embarkation from them could not have formed part of the same plan as one from the four westerly ports, there were enough vessels in these to transport the 90,000 men collected there under Marshals Lannes, Davout, and Soult. To be ready in that decisive hour, Napoleon had hastened home with extraordinary speed from Italy, where he had just been crowned King. He hoped that the invasion plan, threatened for so many months, might have passed from the minds of his enemies as an empty boast. He expected, by putting them on a false track, to send the British fleets away on distant cruises in empty seas. "Nothing", he said, "looks ahead less than the English Government—a government occupied with internal intrigues and turning its attention wherever there is a noise." Whatever truth there was in this as a general proposition—and it was certainly true of the captious opposition of the time—it did not apply in the least in the present case. The British Navy had refused to be led astray. The news that the West Indies and the West Indian trade were safe and that Villeneuve would be forestalled at the Straits of Gibraltar had brought a general thrill of relief. But at the Admiralty it was known that the larger task remained— to hinder a union between the Toulon and Ferrol squadrons, and in any case to prevent the combined fleet appearing in force off Brest, and making a victorious progress up the Channel.

Barham was not a believer in the system of close blockade, and felt that it could not be kept up for a third winter. He was ready to relax it even in summer for a definite object. When Missiessy had returned to Rochefort, five ships were again occupied in the blockade. To move them meant the escape of that squadron. But the certainty of this evil was balanced by the probability of the attainment of a much greater object, greater—he wrote—than any that he knew. In his manner of meeting the situation he took advantage of the suggestions made by a secret correspondent who afterwards disclosed his identity as Nicholas Brown, the Secretary of Admiral Lord Keith. Without loss of time he wrote a private letter to Admiral Cornwallis, embodying the substance of the official orders of the Admiralty, which were also dated the day when the news reached him.

PITT'S LAST ADMINISTRATION 417

"DEAR SIR,—If we are not too late, I think there is a chance of our intercepting the Toulon fleet—Nelson follows them to Cadiz and if you can immediately unite the Ferrol and Rochefort squadrons and order them to cruise from 30 to 40 leagues to the westward, and stretch out with your own fleet as far and continue 6 or 8 days on that service, and then return to your several ports, I think we have some chance of intercepting them. Official orders will follow as fast as possible.

"Yours,
"BARHAM.

"Time is everything."

It would be difficult to find a naval strategical disposition fraught with greater consequences to the history of the world. Villeneuve's fleet, the hope of the Grand Army, was to be met and defeated before it could reach any French port, or any port in northern Spain. The orders reached Cornwallis and were passed on to Rear-Admiral Sir Robert Calder, commanding the squadron of ten sail of the line off Ferrol, on the 11th, and by the 15th, the date when he received them, he was joined by the five ships off Rochefort and was on his way to his cruising-ground. On the 17th July, Captain Allemand, with a squadron of five sail of the line and the usual accompaniment of smaller vessels, had escaped out of Rochefort. Napoleon instantly realized that the blockade must have been raised; that the British squadron had gone to meet Villeneuve; and that he must therefore be nearing home waters. He believed that Cornwallis had equally raised the blockade of Brest, and that Ganteaume had at last got his opportunity. But that admiral realized that the blockading squadron was still near, and did not make the venture.

Calder, who had interpreted his instructions liberally, met Villeneuve nearly 300 miles westward of Ferrol, sailing straight towards that port, on July the 22nd. There were four three-deckers of 98 guns among his fifteen ships, while the combined fleet of twenty, though stronger than had been expected, had no ships of more than 80 guns. As the fleets drew towards each other for action, the fog thickened, and during the battle which followed it closed down on the

DD

combatants and lifted again. There was, of course, very little wind. Calder lost some time in manœuvring to cut the centre of the enemy's line from leeward, and it was half-past five in the afternoon before battle was joined. The wind was from the north-west, and both fleets, being close hauled on the port tack, were steering in column in nearly an east-north-easterly direction, but the British rather nearer the wind, to bring them up to the enemy. Villeneuve ordered his ships to wear in succession, the effect of which was to bring the leading ships round parallel but in an opposite direction both to his enemy's ships and to those of his own which had not yet changed their course. He would thus double his line at the point of attack, and so protect his rear. Upon this, Captain the Honourable Alan Gardner, of the Hero, which led the British line, tacked. The Admiral confirmed this well-timed movement, and, the rest of the fleet following, a general action was brought on. The fleets were again so far as possible in two columns close together, but now steering in nearly the opposite direction from that which they had held before. Gravina, who with his six ships led the combined fleet, carried out his manœuvre smartly and well, and had the gunnery of his squadron been good the British ships should have been heavily mauled as they tacked successively under the Spanish broadsides. As it was, two Spanish ships were badly damaged, fell to leeward, and were taken, Calder thus reaping the advantage of the leeward position which he had sought. Partly for this reason also those British ships which were damaged, particularly the Windsor Castle, which had to be taken in tow, escaped. Only the first three of the French ships were heavily engaged; and Villeneuve did very little to save the Spanish ships, of one of which he had caught a good view, in her dismantled state, during a lift in the fog. The battle lasted till nine o'clock, when it was broken off in the mist and smoke and night.

When day broke, both sides supposed that they had

gained a victory. Calder reported that it had been a "very decisive action", although he added that he hoped to renew the battle as soon as he had put things to rights. Villeneuve found the two Spanish ships missing. But he was not sure that they were captured. On the other hand, there were no signs of the Windsor Castle, and he believed that she had foundered; besides which, other British ships had been damaged. And it was Calder who had drawn off in the night, to cover his prizes and injured ships, and was found a long way to leeward in the morning. Again on the 23rd it was Villeneuve who wished to renew the engagement; but he delayed, night came on, and on the 24th the wind was contrary. Calder was afterwards court-martialled, and severely reprimanded—with reason—not for anything which he failed to do on the day of battle, but "for not having done his utmost to renew the said engagement, and to take and destroy every ship of the enemy". Prevented by contrary winds only from making Ferrol, Villeneuve reached Vigo Bay to the southwards on the 27th. Calder made some show of resuming the blockade of the former place, but kept at a considerable distance, and the combined fleet reached it unhindered on the 2nd of August, the day before Napoleon's arrival at Boulogne, and set sail again, after being joined by the French and Spanish squadrons there, on the 13th of the same month.

Yet, incomplete as it was, Calder's action had been in a true sense decisive. As soon as the full effects of it had come to be realized, Villeneuve, and Gravina also, became profoundly discouraged. Calder's readiness to engage them with fifteen ships against twenty was in itself a moral blow. There were numbers of sick. Two Spanish and one French ship sailed badly, and had to be left behind at Vigo. Villeneuve's dispatches were full of his misfortunes. He had had nothing but contrary winds. Even Heaven—he complained—was against him: his flagship had been struck by lightning. From the point of view of strategy both Villeneuve and Gravina represented to Decrès that, as suddenness was of the essence of the plan of campaign, the circumstance that the English had received information of it in time to take counter-measures had made it useless, excellent as it was.—It was, as a matter of fact, ignorance of the prevailing winds which had caused a wrong course to be taken, and made the passage from Martinique last so long.—The French admiral added in his letter that the navy of his country possessed only a superannuated tactic. The battle which he was expected to offer off Brest would be one between two large fleets, and the larger the fleets the worse would it be for the side which had this disadvantage.

Had Villeneuve been able to effect a union with Allemand, he might have obtained, besides an increase of five ships of the line, a reinforcement of that vigour, resource, and judgment which the enterprising commander of the "invisible squadron" was afterwards to show so abundantly on his successful five months' cruise. Unfortunately for France, the Didon, sent to the rendezvous to fetch the Rochefort squadron, was on the 10th of August captured by the Phoenix, Captain Baker, after a fine frigate action. On the 16th Allemand was off Vigo, where he was met by orders, which proved illusory, to follow the combined fleet to the northward. Still undecided when he led the combined fleet, now of twenty-nine ships, out of Ferrol on August the 13th, Villeneuve found himself met by northeasterly winds, directly contrary to vessels sailing from Brest. On the 15th he came to a decision. "The Emperor"—so ran his instructions—"has foreseen the eventuality in which, in consequence of incalculable contingencies, the position of the fleet would not permit you to undertake the execution of these plans which would have so great an influence upon the fortunes of the world. . . . In that case the Emperor wishes to collect at Cadiz a mass of imposing forces." The case had arisen. It was in vain that Napoleon, who still trusted that Austria would not—in his own phrase—be so mad as to make war upon him, had addressed on the 13th to Ferrol a last exhortation to Villeneuve to carry out his mission; to appear off Boulogne for three days—nay, only for twenth-four hours—and enable him to descend upon the shores of that Power which had oppressed France for six centuries. The letter did not reach him. The die was cast. Villeneuve turned southward, the Grand Army never obtained its covering fleet, and the day of invasion was postponed for ever.

The great sea battle which followed, two months later, fought while the "Army of England" was enjoying a triumph in Bavaria, was a sort of epilogue to the naval campaign, albeit transcending in grandeur not only every event since the peace, but all the past sea fights of history. Here the leading parts were reserved for Nelson and Collingwood. The latter, an old friend of Nelson from West Indian days, like him a vice-admiral, was his junior in the service, his senior in age, and his brother in comradeship. Unsurpassed in patriotism and devotion to duty, of a retired and stern temperament, he had flashes of rare vision; but he was a man who could no more win the implicit confidence of his subordinates than their hearts. He had been sent down when it was known that Villeneuve had left the Mediterranean, and when Nelson returned from the West Indies he was off Cadiz with four ships. He realized that the object of Napoleon was not the West Indies, but a powerful concentration with a view to operations in home waters. "They will now", he wrote to Nelson in a remarkable letter on July the 21st, the day before the action above related took place, "liberate the Ferrol squadron from Calder, make the round of the bay, and, taking the Rochefort people with them, appear off Ushant, perhaps with thirty-four sail, there to be joined by twenty more." As he very rightly added: "The French Government never aim at little things while great objects are in view." Meanwhile Nelson had anchored in Gibraltar Bay, and recorded in his diary: "On the 20th I went on shore for the first time since June 16, 1803, and from having my foot out of the Victory, two years wanting 10 days." He had done a short passage, his ships were sound, and his men—always a very special point with him—"in the most perfect health", a great contrast to Villeneuve's condition. There was no intelligence of that admiral's movements, but on the 25th he learnt from a Lisbon newspaper the news brought by the Curieux as to the course taken by the French squadron, and this determined him to go north at once. Delayed by foul winds, and obliged to fetch to the westward, he could not join Cornwallis till August the 15th, the day on which Villeneuve had finally abandoned the great campaign. Here he received orders to proceed on leave—a leave long since applied for and sanctioned, but of which he had not availed himself so long as he hoped to catch the French fleet. He arrived in the Victory, leaving the rest of his ships with Cornwallis, who now had at most 38 sail of the line, including 20 ships which he had detached under Calder. Ganteaume had 22; Villeneuve 29, including 5 French and 9 Spanish ships which he had picked up in Ferrol. In other quarters the British were equally outnumbered. Alike at Cadiz and Cartagena six Spanish ships were being watched with four, while Allemand with his five was free in the Atlantic.

The plan of invasion had, however, been already dropped. Austria had become a party to the Russo-British treaty on the 9th of August, and the Third Coalition was now in being. Its object was negotiation if possible; in the alternative, war. But Napoleon was not the man to listen to overtures made from behind the points of his enemies' bayonets. He had not even waited for news of Villeneuve's destination. From the admiral's despairing letters, combined with what could be known even in Paris as to the contrary winds, it was possible to divine that he would turn south; and Napoleon accepted Decrès's representation that, if this happened the great combination was hopeless. On the 23rd he wrote a letter to Talleyrand, announcing his resolution to break up his camp and to march on Austria; and on the back of a letter of Decrès' of the same date he outlined a plan of giving up the concentration of his fleet in favour of a division of thirty-one ships of the line and fourteen frigates among seven cruising stations. The Grand Army was already in movement, and by the 1st of September the Boulogne camp had broken up for ever as a serious menace. But it was necessary to mask his intentions, and as late as August the 27th there took place one of the periodical movements in Boulogne harbour, in which as a British officer noted, the French put more vessels outside in the roads than ever before. In any case, a considerable fleet was known to be still at large on the high seas.

So serious was the threat to British trade and security that Nelson, when approached for his opinion by Pitt and Castlereagh, submitted that even the defeat of Calder, supposing Villeneuve again to have met with him and to have taken him at a disadvantage, was not a thing to be deprecated; the damaged enemy ships, even though victorious, would no longer be a menace. This uncertainty lasted till the 2nd of September, when Captain the Honourable Henry Blackwood, of the Euryalus, arrived at the Admiralty with the reassuring news that the combined fleet was safe in Cadiz. London breathed again. "If they had captured our homeward-bound convoys", wrote Lord Minto in his diary of the following day, "it is said the India Company and half the City must have been bankrupt." And they would have captured the future Duke of Wellington as well. "What a squeeze we had like to have got yesterday!" wrote Collingwood to his wife on August the 21st from off Cadiz. "While we were cruising off the town, down came the combined fleet of thirty-six sail of men-of-war; we were only three poor things, with a frigate and a bomb, and drew off towards the Straits, not very ambitious, as you may suppose, to try our strength against the odds." The pursuit was half-hearted, and the next day he was looking into Cadiz again, gazing at a forest of masts. It was gallant work, although it could not be said that he with his full number of four sail of the line was actually blockading Villeneuve with as many as twenty-nine, besides any more Spanish ships in Cadiz which might be ready to sail. The need of repairs, stores, munitions, and the recruitment of the men's health, had rendered some stay in port a necessity for the allies—prolonged owing to shortness of money. Financial resources did not exist for the Spanish Government. That of France, in its attempts to get as much as possible out of the Spanish without payment, bungled, and it is a wonder that Villeneuve ever got his supplies at all.

It is a strange proof of the daring—almost recklessness—of Pitt's Ministry that Baird's expedition was allowed to leave Cork on the 31st of August, two days before Blackwood's good news had reached London. On the very next day, in fact, Napoleon informed Villeneuve that that convoy was about to sail—it was supposed for the Mediterranean, its ostensible destination—and ordered him to intercept it. Yet the troops had been for many weeks in the transports, and it was doubtless felt that no more time should be lost in seizing the colony before it could be strengthened so as to serve as a base for predatory descents upon the East Indian trade. No doubt this dissemination of the country's resources was wrong. But the enemy's aims were thwarted; the settlement, which was only defended by a mixed force of a couple of thousand men, was conquered in the following January with very little loss, and a French squadron which escaped from Brest in December, bound for the Cape, had to turn aside on receiving the news that the place had fallen.

On hearing the great news that Villeneuve had been found, Nelson was prompt in offering his services. He was ordered back to Cadiz, as he had desired, to reassume command of the Mediterranean Station. Barham offered him his choice of officers. "Choose yourself, my Lord," he replied, "the same spirit actuates the whole profession; you cannot choose wrong." This confident speech must have blown into the musty board-room like the free breath of the Atlantic Ocean, scattering the foul mists of suspicion and dissension and corruption which then hung about it, littered as it had been with Naval Inquiry papers, and with proceedings connected with a number of highly dishonourable charges which had been brought by one highly placed officer against another in the last few months. The Navy was after all united at the call of honour. Nelson went determined that the victory which he intended to win should be complete and adequate to the expectations of his country—that it should be the greatest of all naval victories—full also of the presentiment that he would not survive. How their champion was honoured by the people of London at this time was recorded by Lord Minto, who found himself alone with him in the middle of a tumultuous crowd. "It is beyond anything represented in a play or a poem of fame." How he left Portsmouth is told by Southey, the most picturesque of his biographers: the people kneeling before him and blessing him as he passed, and pressing upon the parapet, undeterred by the soldiers' bayonets, to gaze upon him after his barge had pushed off. Two Ministers, Rose and Canning, dined with him on board the Victory before he sailed. He arrived on the 28th of September in time to celebrate his birthday on the following day among the "band of brothers" whom he loved. All felt the change to Nelson's gay and hospitable sway from that of the strict and reserved Collingwood; and his personality soon impressed those who had not known him before. "He is so good and pleasant a man", wrote Captain Duff, of the Mars, "that we all wish to do what he likes, without any kind of orders." After his death there was handed about an extract of what was believed to be the last private letter which he ever wrote. It was dated the 3rd of October. It ran: "The reception I met with on joining the Fleet caused the sweetest sensation of my life. The Officers who came on board to welcome my return forgot my rank as Commander-in-Chief in the enthusiasm with which they greeted me. As soon as these emotions were passed, I laid before them the Plan I had previously arranged for attacking the Enemy; and it was not only my pleasure to find it generally approved, but clearly perceived and understood." This plan had special reference to the importance of obtaining complete victory, and suffering as few as possible of the enemy to escape. "It is, as Mr. Pitt knows," he wrote to Rose, "annihilation that the Country wants." Moral ascendancy it already enjoyed.

The document in which this was laid down is perhaps the most famous tactical paper in history, and has been the most discussed. It is unique in having been made the subject of appeals to the emotions and even of poetry under its author's quaint title of the "Nelson touch". The memorandum provided for an attack by two divisions, in two methods, according to whether it was made from leeward or windward. It was the latter which was carried out. First of all the divisions were to be brought nearly within gunshot of the enemy, obviously in the most suitable formation for doing so as quickly as possible. The business of the admiral commanding the line farthest from the wind—or lee line—which would be opposite the enemy's rear, would then be to set every sail and cut through it, beginning at the twelfth ship from the end. That of the Commander-in-Chief was to manage the remainder, and to see that the operations of his Second-in-Command were as little interrupted as possible. Nelson's own line was to lead through the centre of the enemy, and every effort would be made to capture the opposite Commander-in-Chief. "I look", he added, "with confidence to a Victory before the Van of the Enemy could succour their Rear." In all these points the memorandum was exactly followed. The part dealing with the windward attack, however, included a diagram showing the actual advance being made in lines parallel to that of the enemy, Nelson's being, of course, to windward of Collingwood's and farther from the enemy, though somewhat overlapping it; and this arrangement could not be followed in the weather conditions which prevailed.

Meanwhile it was essential that Villeneuve should come out of port. Pressure of different kinds was brought or proposed. When Nelson arrived, he found a blockade in full swing, which he vigorously continued. In days of very poor land communications, outlying ports, like Brest, Marseilles, and Cadiz, were very dependent upon the sea for supplies; and an increase to the population of thirty thousand ablebodied men was a heavy tax on the resources of the lastmentioned place. To force the enemy out by hunger was one hope. Other expedients were possible attacks upon the port by Major-General William Congreve's rockets, or the catamarans of Francis, better known as Fulton. But it was his imperial master who finally determined Villeneuve. He was bitterly censured by Napoleon, who naturally felt it a disgrace for his fleet to be blockaded by an inferior force. In computing what was an inferior force he allowed Spanish ships to be counted as two for one, on account of their crews' want of experience, and the large proportion of soldiers carried. Account was also made of the British superiority in three-deckers. Nelson told with him for nothing. The rapidity of his movements, and the impetuosity of his onset, had impressed the French; he had been called the "fiery admiral"—the flame and smoke of battle which were his element concealed all else from Napoleon and Decrès themselves. Villeneuve was accordingly ordered to attack any force inferior to his own that might cross his path, and after defeating it, and joining the Cartagena squadron, to land troops near Naples, destroy the convoy carrying Craig's force there, and generally to operate upon the coasts of Italy. Finally, he heard that he was superseded. His spirit rose, and he determined, as he said, to do something to show that he was worthy of a better fortune. He took advantage of the absence of six of Nelson's ships, refitting or escorting Craig's convoy, with Rear-Admiral Thomas Louis, to set sail from Cadiz.

Nelson had spent the time keeping a careful watch on that port. Frigates communicated by means of an inshore squadron of sail of the line under Duff, with the main fleet, lying fifty miles or so west of it, in order to screen its strength and to draw the enemy out. In those few days he won the hearts of all under him. His sympathy took practical form. One of his last orders provided for the names and families of all killed and wounded men to be reported to him, in order that he might pass on the information to the Chairman of the Patriotic Fund, from which such cases were relieved; and another that when a man was sent to hospital an account of his case should accompany him. His insight made him a pioneer in introducing humane provisions, which should have been the matters of routine which they afterwards became. But his generosity led him into an act of disobedience to orders, which, however much approved in the fleet, was utterly unjustifiable. Calder having to return home for his court-martial, Nelson let him take his flagship—a three-decker. But four more ships arriving from England brought the number up to twenty-seven, after deducting the six whose absence Villeneuve had ascertained. These included the Royal Sovereign, Captain Rotheram, just refitted to be Collingwood's flagship, and, last of all, an old ship of Nelson's, the Agamemnon, under Sir Edward Berry. That officer had a great reputation for luck in not missing a general action. "Here comes Berry! Now we shall have a battle", Nelson is reported to have exclaimed.

"How would your heart beat for me, dearest Jane", wrote young Captain Codrington, of the Orion, to his wife, on October the 19th, "did you but know that we are now under every stitch of sail we can set, steering for the enemy, whom we suppose to be come out of Cadiz!" For early that

PITT'S LAST ADMINISTRATION

morning the long-looked-for signal that the enemy was coming out of port had been hoisted by the frigate on the watch off the harbour, and passed on by Blackwood, who commanded the frigate squadron, to Duff, and so reached the Commander-in-Chief. Nelson's hospitable "dinner flag" of invitation to several of his captains was at that moment up, but was immediately altered to one for a general chase to the south-east, to prevent the enemy escaping through the Straits of Gibraltar. But this was premature. The whole of the combined fleet was not under sail until noon of the 20th Nelson turned back to the north-west, keeping far enough away to allow the enemy to get well out of port. During the darkness the fleets drew nearer together, still with the frigate screens between, and the predestined ships' companies of the enemy had leisure to admire the horizon to the westward, picturesquely lit up by the blue signal lights which Nelson had introduced. Villeneuve somewhat prematurely ordered line of battle to be formed, which could not be done properly in the dark, and all night long his men were kept in expectation of an action. It was different on the other side, where most of the sailors had had a good rest. Dawn of the 21st found the two fleets in sight of one another at about eight miles' distance, the British in no regular formation, sailing in a direction a little east of north, the French and Spanish sailing in an opposite direction, in almost equal disorder in spite of all their efforts, with Cape Trafalgar another ten miles beyond them. There were very light breezes from the north-west, shifting to west in the course of the day.

As soon as the signal flags were visible Nelson ordered his battle fleet to be formed in two columns, and to sail down the wind in the direction of the enemy. He himself, with eleven ships, led towards Villeneuve's rear, the Second-in-Command, with fifteen, towards his van. There was a mile between the two columns. To meet Nelson's manœuvre the French admiral reversed direction by wearing his ships all together, in order to save his rear from being overwhelmed, and to secure his retreat towards Cadiz. The effect of this, however, was that, the combined fleet now sailing to the northward, the southern—Collingwood's—column was directed so as to cut off and overwhelm what was formerly the enemy's van, but had now become his rear. Both British columns were sailing nearly E.N.E., but converging slightly towards the enemy. The main conditions contemplated in the memorandum were, in fact, fulfilled. The Second-in-Command would be able to carry out his assigned task, while the Commander-in-Chief would be in the best position to secure that the hostile van and centre ships should not interrupt him. A further effect upon the combined fleet of the manœuvre which they had just carried out was to bring their line into the shape of a bow, the imaginary string of which was about five miles long, and was on the side at which the British attack was to be delivered. This gave the French and Spanish ships the benefit of being in a position to render one another mutual support against ships advancing into the hollow thus formed. The advantage, such as it was, was accidental, but in other respects Villeneuve, who was no mean tactician, had foreseen Nelson's method of attack, and taken steps to meet it. In an order issued to his captains, he had pointed out that the onset, if the enemy attacked from windward, should be awaited in a well-closed-up line. Foreseeing that the British would attempt to break through the allied line and overwhelm the rear, making manœuvre impossible, he added that they should take counsel of their own courage and love of glory rather than look to the signals of the admiral, which probably would not be seen in the smoke of battle. A captain who was not under fire would be away from his post, and a signal to call him there would be a stain of dishonour. There is a close parallel to this in the "Nelson touch".—"But in case signals can neither be seen or perfectly understood, no Captain can do very wrong if he places his Ship alongside that of an enemy." The event was to show how far these stirring words of the two Commanders-in-Chief would find an answer in the deeds of those to whom they were addressed.

When ships are travelling at a rate of no more than two knots, communication by boat between them is easy, and Nelson had called on board the Victory to receive his orders Blackwood and the other captains of frigates, whose work it was to transmit signals and to perform such duties as the towing of disabled vessels, but to take no regular part in a general action between ships of the line. He made a round of inspection of his flagship, cautioning the gunners particularly against premature fire. In this there was nothing new. The old tradition of the British was: "Hold hard! Let us see the white of their eyes first—they will never stand the singeing of their whiskers." But it was different on the other side. Admiral Villeneuve had made a similar round of the Bucentaure, which carried his flag, and the whole ship's company swore between his hands and upon the imperial eagle to fight to the last extremity—as indeed they did. But far from ordering his people to reserve their broadsides he made a signal to commence firing as soon as the British should be within cannon-shot.

At about the same time, namely a little before noon, Nelson was making a signal of a very different kind. The Victory was now nearing the enemy, leading her own line. Collingwood had the management of his. To the restless mind of the Commander-in-Chief a last word of encouragement seemed called for. There was very little time, he desired a signal which could be quickly made, and it has been said that he originally suggested the hoisting of something to the effect: "Nelson confides that every man will do his duty," words which would have expressed a characteristic reliance upon the reciprocal confidence existing between him and every man in the fleet. Lieutenant Pasco, however, who being signal officer should have known, though his memory may have failed him thirty-five years afterwards, when he gave his account, wrote that the first two words of the signal as it came to him direct from the Admiral were, "England confides". Whether the change which Pasco suggested was of one word or two, Nelson made no objection. "Nelson" and "confides" would have needed six and eight flags respectively; "England expects" only two. "England expects that every man will do his duty" could be quickly made and read; it was hoisted; a round of cheers answered from the fleet; and the reverberations of that loyal shout have not yet died away.

It was not until the Victory was actually under fire that Blackwood took leave of the Admiral. Writing afterwards to his wife, he said: "He told me, at parting, we should meet no more; he made me witness his Will, and away I came, with a heart very sad." In a more solemn private moment, while making his last entry in his diary that morning, Nelson was evidently filled with the same presentiment which he had expressed to Blackwood, though he thought for his enemies as well as himself. "May the Great God whom I worship grant to my Country, and for the benefit of Europe in general, a great and glorious victory; and may no misconduct in anyone tarnish it; and may humanity after Victory be the predominant feature in the British fleet. For myself, individually, I commit my life to Him who made me, and may His blessings light upon my endeavours for serving my Country faithfully. To Him I resign myself and the just cause which is entrusted me to defend. Amen. Amen. Amen."

A little before nine in the morning Collingwood had signalled to his division to form line of bearing. This manœuvre, which, however, was only partly carried out, would have brought up his ships from their present position astern of him so as to form a line on his right hand to the southward as well as westward. They would thus have been more nearly parallel to the enemy, particularly to that part of his fleet which formed the rear end of the curve. In this way they would have got into action more nearly together. In order to permit of such a change it was obviously necessary for the Royal Sovereign to go slower or for the other ships to go faster, but they could not catch up the flagship, a splendid sailer, which kept every stitch of canvas set. The Victory kept all her sail set, and her sister flagship was bound to follow her example. It was also Nelson's known wish that, particularly on a short autumn day, as little time as possible should be lost in manœuvring. So the two admirals raced for the enemy's line like leaders in the days of chivalry, throwing themselves into the heart of the hostile array, as this was the quickest means of bringing their followers into battle. Moreover, had there been any shortening of sail, the ships that lost speed would also have lost some of the immense advantage which they enjoyed. They were moving through the water four times as fast as those of the enemy ships which were moving—indeed, some of these last were hove to to close the line as much as possible. They could select their point of attack where they pleased, and, even after passing between the enemy ships and changing direction to the northward, they still had way on and thus more freedom of manœuvre. Moreover, for a single ship to have the broadsides of three or four antagonists directed on her for a few minutes was not so serious as it appears. Not only was French and Spanish gunnery known to be poor. A swell from the west, the sure forerunner of a storm, brought the British ships bounding down upon them—a difficult mark to hit from the batteries of the allied ships as they rolled heavily from side to side. And, as if this were not enough, the allies had a mistaken custom of firing at the masts and rigging of ships instead of their hulls—the resource of the privateer against the man-of-war—of one who seeks to escape and not of one who expects victory. Also the lines were led by three deckers: Nelson's by three—the Victory, Temeraire, and Neptune; Collingwood's by one—the Royal Sovereign; and it was not likely that such formidable vessels would come to much harm in a short space of time. There were no ships of this class in the French fleet; the Spanish had four, but would have done almost as well in smaller ships; while the British had seven altogether. Such and similar considerations were not lost on the mind of either admiral, and the issue of a battle so joined could not be doubtful.

Collingwood was expected to cut the line twelve ships from the rear, thus obtaining with his fifteen ships a one-fourth superiority over those cut off. It was about noon when he reached the enemy. There was a gap of three-quarters of a mile in front of a Spanish three-decker, the Santa Ana, carrying Vice-Admiral de Alava's flag. Three out of the fourteen ships astern of her had fallen away out of the line to leeward. He selected her as his antagonist. Finding room to pass behind her in spite of the efforts of the next ship to close up, he swung round, pouring a tremendous broadside into her stern ports, which swept the ship from stern to bow, and then ranged up on the opposite side. For a quarter of an hour Captain Rotheram's ship found herself not only engaged in close combat with one more powerful, but surrounded by enemies and alone. The Belleisle, Captain Hargood, now came up to her support, only to be surrounded and almost isolated in her turn until relieved by the Mars. That ship was engaged from the stern by the fourth ship from the Santa Ana, the Pluton, commanded by the most enterprising of Villeneuve's captains, Cosmao-Kerjulien, who poured in a devastating fire, by which her Captain, "the worthy Duff", was killed. The Royal Sovereign was upwards of two hours engaged with the Santa Ana before she took her, and then was left herself not much more than a sheer hulk, and perfectly unmanageable. The Belleisle was in not much better case. These were the only ships of Collingwood which had to be towed in after the battle, but all the first six, including the Tonnant, Captain Tyler, the Bellerophon, Captain Cooke—the only other British captain killed—and the Colossus, Captain Morris, suffered heavily. The casualties in these six ships amounted to 202 killed and 589 wounded, against only 127 killed and 242 wounded in the remaining nine ships of the division, none of which could get into close action for as much as an hour, or in some cases two hours or more, after the Royal Sovereign.

In the meantime the Commander-in-Chief was engaged upon his self-imposed task of managing the remainder of the enemy's fleet. Finding it advisable not merely to prevent those ships coming southward and disturbing Collingwood, but also to hinder as many as possible from escaping northward into Cadiz, he decided to push through the enemy's line, and made known his intention accordingly at about eleven. But the first object being still the essential one, he kept his formation of line ahead, allowing his ships to trail behind him, until he was himself nearing the enemy. Then a change in the Victory's course permitted of a slight deployment being made. It was now just after noon. He turned slightly northward, making a feint upon the van, and then ran almost down the line, past the Santissima Trinidad and the Bucentaure, the flagships of Rear-Admiral Cisneros and Vice-Admiral Villeneuve respectively. It was the last which he had marked out for his prey. So close was the line here that it was impossible to pass between the ships, and Hardy, the Flag Captain, was obliged to sail right on to the Redoutable, and to run on board her, as the phrase went. As he did so, he poured a terrible fire into the Bucentaure, the ship immediately ahead, clearing her from stem to bow with much the same destructive effect which the Royal Sovereign had produced on the Santa Ana, and he found himself in much the same condition of dangerous isolation as Captain Rotheram. The Redoutable was commanded by a fine officer, Captain Lucas, who had specially trained men to fire from aloft, to throw grenades, and to board. At about a quarter past one, as Nelson and

Hardy were walking the quarter-deck, a shot from her mizen topmast struck the Admiral. "They have done for me at last, Hardy", he said; and to an "I hope not", he added: "Yes, my backbone is shot through." The Admiral was immediately carried below, a number of other officers and men were killed or wounded at the same time, and the upper-deck was almost cleared of men. Lucas deemed that the time had come to board. The ships did not quite touch each other, and he had ordered his main yard to be cut down to serve as a bridge, when Captain Harvey brought up the Temeraire on the opposite side, and delivered a broadside on her deck, crowded as it was with troops and men awaiting the signal to board, with terrific effect. This ended all hope for the French ship, which shortly afterwards surrendered with the honourable loss of 300 killed and 222 wounded out of 643. The Victory was now free to devote her attention to the ships on her left. These, the Bucentaure and the great four-decker Santissima Trinidad, had been now surrounded in their turn. In crashing into the Redoutable, the Victory had forced her down to leeward, and the Neptune, Captain Fremantle, was able to make way past her bows, and to pour her broadsides successively into the sterns of the French and Spanish flagships, which were soon dismasted, and the doomed vessels were left helplessly exposed to the repeated blows of several British coming up freshly one after the other. The Victory and Temeraire had been dismasted also, and enjoyed, like the two leading ships of the rear line, the distinction of being towed off after the action, but were not in so evil a case as they were. Harvey, indeed, was able to complete the capture of one of the ships which had been engaged with Collingwood.

That admiral's division had, in the meanwhile, been completely successful. As his ships came up successively on his rear and right, all those of the enemy astern of the Santa Ana found themselves under fire. The Tonnant, which was his fourth ship, being denied a passage through the line, fell on board the Algésiras, Rear-Admiral Magon's flagship. The two vessels were locked in a death grapple, and the French, who had some advantage in small arms, attempted to board, but a murderous fire hurled them back. Wounded twice and severely, the intrepid Magon refused to leave the deck till a cannon-shot in the breast laid him low. The Algésiras, which was also engaged by other ships, shortly afterwards struck to her antagonist. The three-decker Principe de Asturias, Gravina's flagship, was heavily beset, and the Admiral received a wound from which he afterwards died. Soon after four o'clock, rescued from destruction by two of her own ships, she was towed out of action by a frigate and followed by ten ships from every part of the fleet into Cadiz, leaving eleven out of the combined rear in the hands of the British, and one, the Achille, which was only saved from surrender by blowing up. Collingwood had done his work nobly.

The separation of the rear from the rest of the combined fleet had been complete. Nelson's feint had been successful, aided by the gallant behaviour of a 64-gun ship, the Africa, Captain Digby. She had become detached to the northward during the night, and in rejoining the van division ran right down the enemy's line, engaging each ship in turn as far as the Santissima, which she helped to capture. The effect was that the van of the combined fleet believed itself to be already engaged, and made no movement, and it was not until after Villeneuve had made the signal to come to his help—that signal which he had said would be a dishonouring stain upon the ships to which it was made—that Rear-Admiral Dumanoir, who commanded those ten ships, began to bring them round. But a calm had succeeded the heavy firing; the ships with Dumanoir had to be towed tediously round by boats, and only five succeeded in coming to windward of the line. It was near three o'clock; the Bucentaure and the Santissima lay, dismasted and helpless, on the point of surrender, and Dumanoir had not the boldness to bear down into the angle formed by the ships which were still engaged with them and those remaining ships of Nelson's division which had not yet got into action. He sailed onward and away from the scene of battle to the south-west, and met his fate on a later day. His fifth ship was cut off by the two last ships of the British column. Of the other five which failed to follow him, two found their way into the mellay and were captured, the others joined Gravina. The Santissima and Bucentaure had already surrendered—the French Commander-in-Chief and his staff being still on board the latter. Six ships, including perhaps the most formidable in the combined fleet, had fallen to the van division. It had not been so heavily engaged, but had carried out completely the two tasks designed for it in the "Nelson touch", the containing of the enemy's van, and the encircling and capture of the French Admiral. The losses of the Victory in killed, however (57), were more than in any other British ship—those of the Temeraire and Royal Sovereign being next with 47 each—and her losses in killed and wounded together were 159, only exceeded by those of the Colossus (200). The total losses of the twelve ships of the division, including the Africa, were 571 out of 1,690 for the whole fleet, of whom 449 were killed, the rest wounded. The losses of the French in killed and drowned were afterwards computed in Cadiz at 3,373, those of the Spanish at 1,022, but these figures include many drowned subsequent to the action. The prisoners ran into many thousands. One French was burnt, and eight French and nine Spanish ships taken.

Had Nelson been on deck, he would never have tamely watched the great Spanish flagship being towed off out of action to the northward, or Dumanoir escaping with four ships to the southward, while he had several ships in both divisions which had never been heavily engaged, twelve which had not lost a single spar, and one which had not even had a single man hit. But he was in the cockpit of the

Victory, surrounded by other wounded and dying men. Cheer after cheer from the decks told of the surrender of one enemy ship after another, and as his last moments approached, and his officers gathered round him, his Flag Captain was able to grasp him warmly by the hand, and to congratulate him on a victory which was complete. He was certain of fourteen or fifteen ships having surrendered. "That is well", answered Nelson, "but I bargained for twenty." Then he pressed on Hardy the need for anchoring the fleet. He knew well that the storm was coming, and had made the preparative signal for anchoring before the battle. After some talk on personal matters, he said, "Kiss me, Hardy". His old friend kissed his cheek and forehead in farewell, and then returned to his duties. There were only a few minutes more. It was his private secretary, Doctor Scott, who, bending over him, was able to catch what he said. "Doctor, I have *not* been a *great* sinner", he murmured; and later on, in a tone of thanksgiving, more than once, "Thank God, I have done my duty"; and in the end, "God and my country".

History loves to linger over a scene so touching and so glorious: the dying hero in the terrible cockpit below; above, the deck of the shattered Victory clustered around with her followers and prizes; the Royal Sovereign a short way off—like her, broken but undaunted, with her own group of prizes, and the ships which had helped to win them; in the water, the broken masts and sails and the boats, now on an errand of mercy among the drowning men—all labouring heavily in the swell; Dumanoir's four ships speeding away to the south-west, Gravina's eleven to the northward; the Cape from which the battle takes its name visible eight miles to the south-east; the gathering storm and the setting sun. All these things stand out clearly as the smoke of battle dies away, but the completeness of the victory itself remains one of those things which can never fully be explained. In his letters Collingwood laid repeated stress on the premeditated character of the attack. To Admiral Sir Thomas Pasley he wrote of his chief: "I cannot separate from the glory of *such* a day the irreparable loss of *such* a hero. He possessed the zeal of an enthusiast, directed by talents which Nature had very bountifully bestowed upon him, and everything seemed as if by enchantment to prosper under his direction. But it was the effect of system and nice combination, not of chance." But he has left very little light on what that system was. There are many imponderable things in war; and although Nelson was a great student of tactics from an early age, although Napoleon advised soldiers to read and re-read the battles of great captains, although Wellington kept Caesar's commentaries at his bedside, it is not possible to define in what way study brings to birth the crowning act which snatches victory from the skirts of opportunity. It is not even possible in the case of all battles, and certainly not in the case of Trafalgar, to say precisely what was in the Commander's mind when he issued an order the results of which proved decisive. This is all the more so with Nelson, since, though we have countless letters, notes, and memoranda of his, though they contain phrases which ring down the decades as clearly as a bell, yet the defects of his education make it hard for us to plumb his mental qualities to our satisfaction. He has left many things which posterity can never unravel, but it would be the greatest mistake to cut the Gordian knot and to say that his men's seamanship and gunnery, their courage and confidence, were the secret of his victory, even although these were among the best cards in his hand. There was little difference in all these respects in the fleets which his predecessors had commanded. Yet they had been raised to earldoms, and highly honoured, for inflicting no more than severe defeat upon their country's enemies; in fact, until his time it had been thought almost impossible to do more; whereas in each of the three great battles in which he commanded he had dealt overwhelming disaster.

Confidence in his abilities confirmed that lasting devotion inspired by his courage, his patriotism, and his love of those serving under him which prompted Captain Hoste to go into action in 1811, with the signal "Remember Nelson", and to which the aged St. Vincent alluded in writing of the bombardment of Algiers five years later still: "From what I can gather of his conduct in the battle, the Captain of the Granicus surely must have thought Lord Nelson was looking at him."

When the news reached England, the people, from the Ministers to the humblest, showed that they understood what they had lost—a "mind which inspired ideas superior to the common race of men"—to quote Collingwood's dispatch; and felt—in words from the same source—"a grief to which even the glorious occasion in which he fell does not bring the consolation which, perhaps, it ought". Their gratitude was no less. Nelson's brother William was made an earl, a grant of £5,000 was voted to the title for ever, and £100,000 for an estate. Collingwood was made a peer, with a grant of £2,000 a year, and Hardy a baronet. The only Companionship of the Order of the Bath granted—so few were the military honours then bestowed—was to Rear-Admiral the Earl of Northesk.

In the following March, Napoleon in one of his speeches made a curious passing allusion to the battle. "Storms", he said, "have caused the loss of some ships after a battle imprudently fought." He did not add that these same storms had deprived the British of most of their prizes, and of the glory of escorting them to England. It is often the hard fate of those whose warfare is on the sea, while their brethren on land, after a fight well fought, can enjoy a sleep on their bivouacs, or the luxuries of welcome or pillage in a captured town, to have to brace themselves, short-handed, with broken masts and spars, torn rigging, and sails in shreds, to meet a deadlier foe with whom no terms of surrender can be made. Had Collingwood followed the dying injunctions of Nelson to anchor, most of the misfortunes which followed would almost certainly have been avoided. Four hours after the battle, indeed, he made a signal which was carried out by the Defence and three prize ships only, all of whom by anchoring rode out the storm; and these three, with one other which had not received much damage, were the only prizes which were ultimately saved. Instead of anchoring his remaining ships, or even proceeding to Gibraltar, he remained off Cadiz "to show the enemy", as he wrote, "that it was not a battle nor a storm which could remove a British squadron from the station which they were directed to hold". It was nobly intended, but what remained of the hostile fleet were not at all impressed. The gale arose, and wrecked and sank several of the prizes; and the difficulty in which the British were seen to be, encouraged the gallant French captain, Cosmao-Kerjulien, to bring out five ships of the line in order to recover what prizes he could. He recaptured two, which were cast off by the ships towing them, but at the cost of one of his own ships first captured and then wrecked. The prize crews of three other ships, including the two French flagships Bucentaure and Algésiras, being too few to work them themselves, had to call up from under hatches the original crews, and were thus made prisoners in their turn and taken into Cadiz. The Bucentaure was, however, wrecked. Four prize ships, including the giant Santissima Trinidad, had to be destroyed. The brave battered Redoutable sank. The remaining three were wrecked.

A number of British as well as of the enemy were drowned during those days, and many men of the prize crews fell into hostile hands. This gave the Spaniards the opportunity to show the best side of their national character. They turned their own soldiers out of their beds to make room for British shipwrecked seamen. An officer described to Codrington a sort of triumphal procession in which he was driven from the harbour to the lodgings prepared for him. Nothing had been wanting on the British Admiral's side to fulfil one of Nelson's last wishes, and as early as six days after the action he had proposed, in the interest of humanity, a direct exchange of wounded prisoners on board his ships, in return for the British in Cadiz, which was duly carried out. The latter being comparatively few, he sent many more against receipts, with a promise that they would not serve in the war until exchanged. This was very highly appreciated, and Spanish courtesy went to the point of the dispatch by the Captain General of Andalusia of a cask of wine to Collingwood, who sent a cheese and a cask of porter in exchange.

Meanwhile, Dumanoir's four ships, all French, were attempting to make their way to a port of safety in the north. While off the north-west coast of Spain, however, they fell in with Captain Sir Richard Strachan, who was looking for Allemand. Although they had not been heavily engaged at Trafalgar, they were in no condition to meet four fresh sail of the line accompanied by four frigates. These also, contrary to the usual custom, took part in the battle, on the 4th of November. After a severe engagement in which Dumanoir, who was twice wounded, did much to redeem his character, all four ships struck their colours. Strachan was extremely surprised when he found who his captives were, as he had expected to meet with Allemand's "invisible squadron", as it came to be called by the French. Those ships, after many narrow escapes from falling in with a British force, completed their cruise in safety. So elaborate were their commander's precautions, that he actually sank as many as twenty-two neutral vessels, after providing for the safety of the crews, to prevent their giving information of his movements, during his first month. He had made every effort to join Villeneuve, but that admiral had sent him word to meet him to the northward of Ferrol, and then went south himself. Finding that he had been sent in the wrong direction, and that the main fleet was in Cadiz, which was blockaded, he had turned off into the Atlantic and preyed on the trade-routes according to his instructions. He showed great enterprise, made a number of prizes, and finally reached port on the 25th of December with the Calcutta, a 50-gun ship which he had taken.

Allemand's Odyssey was the one bright page in the naval history of France during the year. Nelson had done his work. Including the Achille, which must have struck her colours if she had not blown up, as well as the ship captured three days after Trafalgar, his ships took only one less than the twenty for which he had bargained. In the end five French and six Spanish only remained; the former were commanded by Villeneuve's successor, Vice-Admiral Rosily, in the port of Cadiz till June 1808, when Cadiz became hostile, and compelled him to surrender. Trafalgar completed Napoleon's conversion to the view that all hope of an even temporary command of the seas must be abandoned. The only use for a French fleet was to occupy the British in blockading it, while select squadrons of ships or frigates occasionally dashed out on filibustering expeditions.

While Trafalgar was being fought, Napoleon had just reached a definite stage in the most brilliant of all his campaigns. On that very 21st of October he was holding triumph at Ulm in Bavaria. Thirty thousand beaten Austrians laid down their arms before him, and while they did so he spoke to their officers about his aims. There was no real quarrel, he said, between him and the Emperor. Let him hasten to make terms. "I want nothing on the Continent. It is ships, colonies, and commerce that I want, and that is good for you as well as for us." But they were the one thing which he could not obtain. All hope of destroying England by force of arms was lost. Nor did Francis sue for peace; and Napoleon was definitely launched upon the succession of wars of aggression and aggrandizement which led to his downfall. He was trebly impelled—by personal ambition, by a sense that it was safer to make the kings of Europe his vassals than to live surrounded by baffled but unreconciled enemies, and by hatred of England, which he borrowed in part from French tradition. It is at the last point that he touches British history. His services even to the peoples whom he conquered and oppressed were great; the British Empire owes him only the indirect benefit of awakening her manhood.

Apart from furnishing the gold, without which it could not have come into being at all, Great Britain's share alike in the diplomacy and in the operations of the Third Coalition was secondary only. The Russian Government had displayed the greatest anxiety for British co-operation, both in the Mediterranean and in Northern Europe. It would have been disgraceful to have been nothing more than a paymaster; and accordingly Pitt had dispatched Craig's 6,000 men to Gibraltar in April. Delayed by naval alarms, they did not reach Malta till July. The presence of the combined Russian and British force was then used to tempt the Neapolitan Court, in which the Queen was the ruling spirit, into an act of bad faith towards France, for which Craig was not responsible. The allied troops were invited to Naples—not much more than 20,000 in all—and were to have marched forward and co-operated with the Austrians in driving the French from Italy. They landed on the 20th of November to learn of the surrender of Ulm, and that Marshal Masséna was free to turn upon them with his full strength. There was no hope of resistance, and in January 1806 southern Italy was evacuated and left to her fate. The force sent to northern Germany was still more unfortunate. A very considerable armament had been prepared. A force of 25,000 British and Hanoverian troops was actually landed in Hanover, Lieutenant-General Lord Cathcart being put in command; and it was intended to raise it to 65,000 in all, dispatched in 257 transports. These troops were to have co-operated with Russian and Swedish in the recovery of Holland. But the latter contingent was driven back by a storm, eight transports being wrecked with heavy loss of men, and no move forward could be made till it was seen what Prussia would do.

Pointed overtures from that country for a subsidy had encouraged Pitt to send Harrowby, who was now in a better state of health, to make a vigorous effort to get Frederick William actively upon the British side. But he did not reach Berlin before the middle of November. All that could be done had been done a fortnight earlier by the Czar's visit to Potsdam. Frederick William at this time, in the interests of his policy of balance, kept two advisers upon foreign affairs, according as he wished to pursue a policy favourable or unfavourable to France. It was, however, the friend of France, Count Haugwitz, who was sent to Napoleon with a proposal of mediation upon the basis of the treaty just concluded between Russia and Prussia. He carried also an ultimatum to be presented, if those terms were still refused, on the 15th of December, by which date the Prussian Army was to be ready. But Napoleon was not waiting for this. On the 13th of November he had entered Vienna; on the 2nd of December he crushed the armies of the two Emperors at Austerlitz. Alexander withdrew his beaten troops. Francis, helpless, now asked for peace; and the miserable Haugwitz ended his mission by signing on the 15th of December a treaty of offensive and defensive alliance with the Power to which he was to have presented an ultimatum. Austrian incapacity, Russian temerity, and Prussian timidity had ruined the Third Coalition.

And now the great British statesman was dying. On the 9th of November he had delivered his most celebrated, and —it may be presumed—his shortest, speech. It was at the London Guildhall dinner, where his popularity, which had been waning, had returned with the knowledge that the convoys were safe, and the combined fleet securely bottled up; its destruction was only known three days before. The crowd had drawn his carriage through the street. The Lord Mayor proposed his health as "the Saviour of Europe".

Pitt replied: "I return you many thanks for the honour you have done me; but Europe is not to be saved by any single man. England has saved herself by her exertions, and will, as I trust, save Europe by her example." These grand words were the last which he ever spoke in public.

Sir Arthur Wellesley, who had safely returned in that Indian convoy which had been in danger, was present at the dinner, and afterwards described the life lived by Pitt when staying with Camden in Kent in the same month. He was by way of being an invalid at the time. But he would ride eighteen or twenty miles a day, and on their return the party would put on dry clothes and hold a Cabinet, for almost all those staying in the house were members. Then followed dinner, at which Pitt took a great deal of port-wine and water. He was certainly overtaxing his strength, and he was advised to go to Bath for the winter. Here he remained till the 9th of January, 1806. The waters first threw the gout from which he suffered into his feet— a good sign; but the news of Austerlitz proved fatal to him. It was long before the correct news came. A battle was known to have been fought on that 2nd of December, at which the allies had been defeated. But then it had been continued—so the accounts ran—on the 3rd and 4th, and the tide had been completely turned in their favour. Incorrect reports of this kind, gratifying as they were to a public which would not believe in defeat, were extremely common in those years, and it is to Pitt's discredit that he attempted to thwart the praiseworthy efforts of John Walter, of The Times, to provide correct information of what occurred on the Continent. It was not until the new year that he heard that an armistice had been signed, and that the Russian troops were in full retreat. The gout left his extremities and he fell into a general weakness.

His physician, Sir Walter Farquhar, was now with him. Always hopeful, Pitt wrote on the 6th of January to Castlereagh, who was now not merely Secretary of State for War, but by force of character the virtual leader of the Cabinet, deprecating the recall of the troops from northern Germany. He went on to say: "My attack of gout is now subsiding, and I hope to recover from it quicker than from the former"; but he added that he had much ground still to gain. He was, in fact, worn to a shadow. The Bath waters had done all the good which could be expected from them, and Farquhar did not oppose his return for the meeting of Parliament. He reached his villa at Putney on the 11th. In some more despondent moment—although even the biographer Lord Stanhope possessed no family tradition to enable him to fix the time and place—he observed a map of Europe. "Roll up that map!" he said. "It will not be wanted these ten years." Yet the old sanguine temperament usually prevailed. On the 12th the doctors who were called in to assist Farquhar gave a hopeful report, and Pitt wrote to his old friend Lord Wellesley, just returned from India after his brother, that he believed that he was now in the way of real amendment. Even a visit on the 13th from Hawkesbury and Castlereagh to obtain his consent to the bitter necessity of the recall of Cathcart's troops did not quench his soul. On the following day Wellesley found his spirits high and his mind as vigorous as ever. But it was too much. After that visit he fainted.

He never again left the house or attempted business. Two days later he took to his bed. Almost unable to receive nourishment, he grew weaker and weaker. On the 22nd he received the last spiritual comfort from his old tutor, Doctor Tomline, whom he had made Bishop of Lincoln. Although he had complied with the outward forms of religion, had always lived a pure and honourable life, and lived and died in charity with all, he knew that this was not enough. He expressed remorse that he had not been a religious man, and this sense of his own unworthiness showed that he understood what it was to be one. He took comfort, as he said, from the innocency of his life. Then his mind fell again into its old track. James Stanhope, the brother of Hester, who watched by him all that night, wrote notes of his last hours. He cried "Hear! Hear!" as if in the House of Commons. His thoughts then turned to Harrowby in Germany. He asked the direction of the wind. "East! ah, that will do; that will bring him quick." In the coldest hours of the night he ceased moaning, and the chill of death began to come over him. "I feared he was dying", wrote Stanhope; "but shortly afterwards, with a much clearer voice than he spoke in before, and in a tone I shall never forget, he exclaimed, 'Oh, my country! how I love my country!'" The words bear a strange resemblance to those caught from the dying lips of the hero in the cockpit of the Victory three months before. On the 23rd of January, 1806, at half-past four in the morning, he was dead. He had reached his forty-seventh year.

"Pitt never was a boy", Windham told that valuable diarist, Francis Horner. True, no doubt, in one sense; and yet there were more ways than one in which he was always a boy. He retained the simplicity and transparent sincerity of a boy. He had a boy's hopefulness; indeed, his sanguine temper was at once his great merit and his great defect—good in that it made him refuse to accept defeat—evil in that it made him lax to provide against its possibility. He sometimes strangely abandoned his own judgment for the ill-advised counsels of others, usually older men, not with the weakness of one who is unable to make up his mind and wishes others to do so for him, but with a boy's frank surrender. He had a boy's frank impulsiveness in friendship, and thus, in the case of Melville, he was led wrong by what Wilberforce called "that false principle of honour which was his great fault". His spirit was stirred to its greatest depth by the distresses and sufferings of mankind. The greatest of all his speeches was almost certainly that of the 2nd of April, 1792, on the Slave Trade, for the last twenty minutes of which Windham and Wilberforce agreed that he really

FF

seemed inspired. Even when he spoke on less rousing subjects, that oratory which has been admired for the frozen harmonies of a perfect state paper, with no word misplaced and no word redundant, derived a warmth from the animation of his manner. It appeared to Horner not that it was too cold, but that there was too much passion; in his eagerness to convince he threw away the advice of Hamlet to the players altogether, and sawed the air not with the hand only, but with the whole body. He flashed sympathy with any tale of generosity, and this virtue was alive in the last days of Bath, when he added some lines in praise of Collingwood's humanity to an ode which Mulgrave had sent him upon the death of Nelson. He could abandon himself to the most childish fun—surpassing Fox in this respect. "He was very attractive", wrote William Napier, telling the story of a frolic in which he and the Stanhopes got Pitt down and blackened his face with burnt cork, while two Ministers waited in the next room for him to wash his face—and then of his sudden transformation and the awful majesty with which he received them. And this was not merely the unbending of the statesman. He was a natural idler, albeit, as the second Lord Malmesbury wrote, an "accomplished" one. He never acquired method. He was terribly careless about his meals, and almost criminal in his mismanagement of his private concerns. In days when men were at their offices by nine, and official visits were often paid at that or even an earlier hour, he would sleep almost round the clock, and begin work at noon or later. The state of his desk was well enough known; an ambassador, Count Woronzow, said he was sure that if a paper were left with him he would not be able to find it himself next day. George III himself had to put up with the fact that the royal missives were occasionally not merely not answered, but left unopened; and later in life he "contracted the bad habit of never writing to anyone", according to a letter from Grenville to Wellesley in India, which, falling into the hands of Napoleon, was published for the edification of Europe. He was, it is true, a good farmer and a good colonel of volunteers, but these were businesses to which he set his mind as he did to matters of state, and for such purpose made an exception to his natural habits. He was shy—particularly with the opposite sex. Not merely had he never been out of his own country but once for a few weeks, and never travelled farther south than Paris or farther north than Northamptonshire; he was never in any sense really out in the world—never really knew men except in official relations. Windham, who mentioned this also, said he thought more of how his measures would succeed in the House of Commons than where they were to operate. It was true. This was the place which he knew like an old nursery, habituated to it from childhood almost as a carpenter's son knows his father's workshop.

It might be wondered why such a man should not have lost touch with realities. But he was saved by several things. He was first of all a financier, and the hard yet delicate materials with which a financier has to deal demand a firm and accurate touch; no magic passes in the air have any effect. He was only through his misfortune the First Minister of a War Cabinet. His own War Minister he never was, except during the first year of his last Ministry. Where he had weak colleagues he did the work himself; but the correspondence of Grenville, Dundas, Spencer, and Windham shows that such men were well able to settle the points which affected their departments with little or no reference to their chief.

Again, though he was a man of words—perhaps because he was a man of words—he saw them in their true relations. If they did not represent things they were nothing to him. Some forms of rhetoric—those, for instance, in which there is a great deal of dialectical fence, of personal reference, or of attractive imagery—provide excuses for inertness—and cloaks for incapacity. But Pitt's eloquence was of that clear-cut type which is closely associated with action.

Then there was his dominating will—indicated to the world by the lineaments of that haughty face, every muscle of which was under complete control, passion being only betrayed by the fire darting from the eyes. Napoleon's saying that he could control the House of Commons with a sign from his eyebrows can hardly be an exaggeration, if Byron's story be true that it was the approval of Grattan's oratory conveyed by his significant nods, anxiously watched for by a subservient House, which determined whether he should be applauded or damned. His was a will always in search of material to act upon. With perhaps only one exception—the deplorable tendency which he shared with the British statesmen of his time, to suppose that war could be carried on by a series of diversions—a pounce here and a nibble there—he did things in a great way, and he carried them through. In 1808 Sir John Moore, writing to Lady Hester about his ignominious flight from a city to which he had come as an ally, added that he would not have fled had her uncle still been Minister—Pitt would have seen him through. Even his mistakes, such as the Additional Force Act, were of use. They showed clearly how much could be done or not done in a certain direction, and were of far more value than the gropings of purblind politicians in the limbo between truth and error. One of his greatest—and it was in the field where he was at his best—was his failure for many years to recognize that the war should be defrayed as much as possible out of increased taxation. This error, and his subsequent frank recognition of it, were used by William Ewart Gladstone with very great effect in 1854 to justify the doubling of the income tax, and meeting as much as possible of the expenses of the Crimean War from the country's present resources.

And all this might of mind and will, this proud rectitude of character, were moved by an ardent patriotism. The quality was not common among statesmen of the eighteenth century. The word itself had got into bad odour. To Wilberforce, whom friendship could never have seduced to speak one syllable beyond what he felt to be due, this seems to have appeared almost as astonishing as what he called Pitt's "strictness in regard to truth". "The love of country", he wrote, "burned in him with as ardent a flame as ever warmed the human bosom."

Pitt would never have called himself anything but a Whig. But by a strange fate he became after his death a Tory tradition; and a tradition handing down ideas which he would never have embraced in his lifetime. It did not greatly matter.

His legacy was his inflexible determination to bring his country safe through the death-struggle upon which she was embarked. For the moment, it seemed as if no one was able to take up the task which he had laid down. Well might Walter Scott write:

> "Hadst thou but lived, though stripp'd of power,
> A watchman on the lonely tower,
> Thy thrilling trump had roused the land,
> When fraud or danger were at hand;
> By thee, as from the beacon-light,
> Our pilots had kept course aright;
> As some proud column, though alone,
> Thy strength had propp'd the tottering throne:
> Now is the stately column broke,
> The beacon-light is quenched in smoke,
> The trumpet's silver sound is still,
> The warder silent on the hill!"

REFERENCES

(*Full titles of books and dates of editions are not given where they are in the bibliography—either in the general list or one of the two lists for the chapter concerned.*)

CHAPTER I

Pp. 17–20.—*The Country.*—The complaint of labourers refusing an offer of work is made in John Arbuthnot's Inquiry, p. 81; Young's account of the prosperity of Axholme is from his Agriculture of Lincoln, p. 17; the reference to Adam Smith's Wealth of Nations is to Book V, Chapter II, Part II, Article IV: and the remark on the discontinuance of churchgoing is taken from Davies's Case of Labourers in Husbandry, p. 28. The prevalence of leases for the duration of three lives is noticed by Marshall in his Rural Economy of the West of England, pp. 43 ff. The notices of feudal customs in Cheshire and Cumberland are made in the Reports to the Board of Agriculture of those counties, H. Holland's Cheshire, 1808, p. 103, and Bailey and Culley's Cumberland, 1799, p. 11. Lord Ernle in English Farming summarizes the counties in which the yeomanry were numerous, pp. 292, 293. The Isle of Man is included on the authority of B. Quayle's General View of . . . the Isle of Man, 1794, p. 10.

Pp. 20–22.—Young's list of employments in a Norfolk market town is from pp. 111, 112, of his Agriculture of Norfolk. Wendeborn's observations are in his Reise durch einige . . . Provinzen Englands, II, pp. 23 ff. The Yorkshire girl's superior vigour is observed by Marshall in his Rural Economy of the Midlands, II, 151. Brown's Yorkshire poems are quoted by S. Baring Gould in Yorkshire Oddities, etc., 1871, II, 126. Eden's list of a labourer's requirements is on p. 556, Vol. I, of his book; his remark on the greater variety of cooking in the north of England on pp. 496, 497; he also gives the bill of fare of many poorhouses. The description of the diet of the West of England is taken from the Second Report of the Lords Committee on the Dearth of Provisions, Parliamentary History, XXXV, 847.

Pp. 22–28.—*The agrarian revolution.*—Gilbert Slater, in English Peasantry, etc., gives the areas of parliamentary enclosure in the various counties. Young made the remark on the Vale of Aylesbury in his Tour through the East of England, 1771, I, 19, 23, and that on Norfolk's miserable condition as a pastoral county, II, 150. The evidence as to the periods when different parts of Wales were enclosed is resumed in J. H. Clapham's Economic History of Modern Britain, pp. 25–27, which has also the facts as to the relative numbers of agricultural occupiers who did and who did not hire labourers, pp. 113 ff., and the extent to which the hired labourer no longer boarded, etc., with the farmer, pp. 121 ff. and 453. A typical example of forced emigration into the towns is given in the Hardwicke Papers, British Museum Add. MSS. 35646 ff. 247–250. The reference to the holdings of three acres and a cow in Lincolnshire is p. 35 of Young's Agriculture of Lincoln, that to its general benefit is the Annals of Agriculture for 1801, XXXVI, 509 ff., also XXXVII, 597 ff.; and those to Winchelsea's experiments in Rutlandshire and to Carrington's in Lincolnshire to Vol. I, 1798, pp. 116 ff., and Vol. II, 1800, pp. 187 ff., respectively of the Reports of the Society for Bettering the Condition, etc., of the Poor. Eden's State of the Poor is the authority for the diet of the northern and southern labourers, I, 496 and 499. There is a notice of the chance of an agricultural labourer bettering himself in years of high prices in Observations on the Enormous High Price of Provisions, 1801, p. 12. The price of the cheapest tea is inferred from Pitt's budget speech of 1796 in Parliamentary History, XXXII, 1259.

Pp. 28–31.—*Agricultural wages.*—Criticism of the system of encouraging imports of corn by bounties was expressed in Sir John Sinclair's Report on the Cultivation of Waste Lands, etc., Parliamentary Reports, IX, 224; the failure of the Enclosure Act of 1801 to effect economy is described in J. S. Trelawny's speech in 1845 in Hansard, Third Series. Vol. LXXXII, p. 25. The Speenhamland meeting is described in J. L. and B. Hammond's Village Labourer, pp. 137 ff. Lord Grenville's criticism of subsidizing wages is in Buckingham's Memoirs of . . . George III, Vol. III, 97, 98; his brother's in Historical MSS. Commission, Fortescue MSS., VI, 344. Young's Norfolk budget is in his Agriculture of that county, pp. 493, 494. The connection of early marriages with the allowance system is brought out in G. Talbot Griffith's Population Problems of the Age of Malthus, p. 169. The decay in the habit of saving against marriage is mentioned by Sir Thomas Bernard in Reports of the Society for Bettering the Condition, etc., of the Poor, III, 1801, p. 20.

Pp. 31–33.—Corn prices are taken from Lord Ernle's English Farming, p. 441. The authorities for actual wages are, generally, Eden's State of the Poor, I, 566 ff.; the Agricultural Surveys of Yorkshire, Brown's W. Riding, App. 28, and Leatham's E. Riding, p. 32—in the case of a boarded servant; and Marshall's Rural Economy of the West of England for the wage there, I, 107 ff. A rise of 65 per cent. in earnings (£20–£33) is computed for 1780–1800 by A. L. Bowley in Royal Statistical Society's Journal, Vol. LXII, for 1899, p. 562. Davies describes cheese as having become a luxury in his Case of Labourers in Husbandry, pp. 18, 19. Bishop Watson's remark is in his Life, II, 253. The rate of rental enhancement is taken from Pitt's Agriculture of Stafford, p. 33, and a paper of Thomas Poole's in Coleridge's Essays on his own Times, II, 441. The figures of Coke's improvement of his estate are from A. M. W. Stirling's Coke of Norfolk, I, 301. Young's View of . . . Oxfordshire, 1809, has his comparison of the classes of farmers, p. 35, and Eden's book gives figures for the two Buckinghamshire parishes, II, 27 ff.

Pp. 34–35.—*The rise in prices.*—The amount of wheat used in starch

REFERENCES

is from the Committee's Sixth Report in Parliamentary History, XXXV, 827. The quotation from the Telegraph about flour is in the Life of Thelwall, 1837, I, 323.

Pp. 35–36.—*The stoppage of cash payments.*—Tooke's History of Prices, I, 204, gives the note circulation of February 1797. The earlier is given by Thornton in his Enquiry into the Nature and Effects of the Paper Currency of Great Britain, p. 73.

Pp. 36–38.—*Country Banks.*—Thornton also gives the number and the typical account of the origin of country banks, p. 154.

Pp. 38–40.—*Changes in agricultural methods.*—Marshall in his books on the Midland Counties, I, 99, on Yorkshire, I, 32, and on the West of England, I, 116, mentions the retention of oxen. Young's Norfolk has the steam-thresher, p. 73. Marshall's Midland Counties has his account of yeomen and farmers having ceased to despise their own calling, I, 84. Rennie mentions the farming recreations of manufacturers in his Agriculture of the West Riding of Yorkshire, pp. 39 and 114.

Pp. 40–41.—*Yorkshire.*—Wilberforce's speech on Yorkshire clothiers is in Parliamentary History, XXXV, 138.

Pp. 41–43.—*Manchester.*—Aikin in his Description, etc., describes the roughness of the manufacturers there, p. 188 note.

Pp. 43–44.—*Liverpool.*—The History of Liverpool, by J. Corry, has figures for vessels entering its docks, p. 280; the cockpit which became a church, p. 385; the account of the town's rowdiness, pp. 192, 202; and the number of its inhabited cellars, p. 268. The author of a Tour through the South of England, etc., describes the pests of flies, p. 354.

Pp. 44–45.—*Newcastle.*—J. Aikin in England Delineated, p. 29, mentions the depopulation consequent upon the engrossment of farms in the Cheviots. Reports of the Society for Bettering the Condition, etc., of the Poor, gives the wages of hewers and their families, Vol. I, 1798, pp. 380, 381, as well as the Derbyshire and Cornwall systems of contracting, p. 368. The Nelson Despatches mention the forest free miners, V, 25.

Pp. 45–47.—*Birmingham.*—The description of Birmingham is taken from p. 742, Vol. I, of the Encyclopædia Britannica, 1802; also W. Hutton's History, which in particular has its Hotel, p. 131, and its clubs, pp. 136 ff. The Spirit of the Public Journals, Vol. III, 1805, p. 389, quotes the satire on Messrs. Humbug & Company. Thomas Osler gave evidence before the Select Committee on Artizans and Machinery on the ingenuity and independence of the workmen, p. 320 of the Reports. The author of the Tour through the South of England, etc., described the dirtiness of the people and their streets, and the business of the place, pp. 373, 378, 379.

P. 47–48.—*Wales and Bristol.*—The same Tour has mention of the Welsh harpers, pp. 349 ff.

Pp. 48–50.—*Effects of machinery on the condition of the cotton weavers.*—The tourist in Derbyshire who came across Arkwright's mill was a friend of Sir John Sinclair—Correspondence, I, 361. J. James's History of the

Woollen Manufacturer, 1857, has the refusal of Bradford to admit a steam-engine, p. 592. Radcliffe, Origin of the New System of Manufacture, has an account of cotton weavers' lives, pp. 59–67, which is supplemented by the Report of the Select Committee on Emigration, 1827, p. 5, and Bamford's Early Days, p. 94. The cost of their food is taken from the Select Committee on Hand-loom Weavers' Petitions, p. 432, and the wages from that on Artizans and Machinery, p. 392.

Pp. 50–51.—*Conditions of the cotton spinners. Rise of Owen and others.*—Spinners' wages for 1810 ff. are in Baines's History of the Cotton Manufacture, p. 438. Bamford in Early Days describes the Weavers' Christmas, p. 120.

Pp. 51–53.—*Condition of labouring children.*—Gregory's Robert Raikes has Porteus's criticism, p. 78. The observation on children in Manchester is from Southey's Espriella, II, 141; the contracting for wagon loads from Cottle, Early Recollections, II, 320.

Pp. 53–55.—*Obstacles to the introduction of machinery.*—Lancashire fighting is mentioned in E. Baines's Lancashire, 1836, III, 75, 76; the intimidation of employers by W. Hirst, History of the Woollen Trade, p. 19. E. Baines's Account of the Woollen Trade in Yorkshire has the weaver's bet, p. 690, and the woollen spinners' wage, p. 651. The knitter's wage is in Felkin's History of the Machine Wrought Hosiery, etc., pp. 228 and 434.

Pp. 55–58.—*Wealth of the Country.*—The food prices are taken from Eden's State of the Poor; in the case of meat from Vol. I, pp. 568 ff., and from Vol. II, p. 204, for ale; the cost of a labourer's outfit is on p. 557. The frugal meals of Coleridge and his friends are mentioned in Cottle's Recollections, I, 321; the landlord's interest in pulling down cottages in Young's Farmers' Letters, I, 301. Pitt's income-tax estimate is in Parliamentary History, XXXIV, pp. 10 ff.

Pp. 58–61.—*Trade.*—The trade figures are in the Commons Journals, Vol. LIX, pp. 584–586. Radcliffe's account of his markets is in his Origin of the New System of Manufacture, p. 68. Baert's admiration for English leather work, etc., is in Tableau de la Grande Bretagne, III, 301. Raw cotton and wool imports are given in Baines's History of the Cotton Manufacture, 347, and his Account of the Woollen Trade in Yorkshire, pp. 637, 638 respectively. Alexander Baring describes the round trade in An Inquiry into causes, etc., of the Orders in Council, 1808, pp. 138 ff. B. G. Niebuhr mentions the superiority of the products of foreign to British colonies in his Mémoire sur la Guerre in Nachgelassene Schriften, p. 419. The account of English and foreign vessels sailing to France is in Commons Journal, Vol. LVI, p. 861; the tonnage of ports in Naval Chronicle, XIV, 45 ff. Edwards's account of himself is in Historical MSS. Commission, Fortescue MSS., Vol. VI, 289 ff.

Pp. 61–62.—*Canals.*—The comparison of coastal trade is taken from the abstract opposite p. 215 of Colquhoun's Treatise on the Police of the Metropolis. The opening of the Paddington Canal is described in the Annual Register for 1801, Chronicle, p. 24. The opposition to its use for

REFERENCES 459

coal appears from Hansard V, 8, 183, 184. J. H. Clapham's Economic History of Modern Britain, p. 79, shows how little coal actually came.

Pp.62-63.—*Roads.*—Southey describes the western roads in his Espriella, I, 8-16. Hansard VII, 101, which contains a misleading reference to 13 G. III, cap. 84 (the General Turnpike Act), shows that interest was then being taken in the weights carried by wagons and their teams. The badness of the Gloucestershire roads is described in Marshall's Gloucestershire, I, 14, and in Communications to the Board of Agriculture, VI, 1808, p. 182. The pace at which the various coaches went and the cost of travelling are given by Middleton, View of the Agriculture of Middlesex, p. 394. Niebuhr's impressions are in his Life by the Chevalier Bunsen, I, 121; that of another traveller is J. E. Campe's Reise durch England, I, 49, 55. Travelling in Wales is mentioned in Life of W. Hutton, p. 145. Baert observed the peculiarity of the English as regards walking, Tableau de la Grande Bretagne, IV, 168, 170. Faujas Saint-Fond describes the roads near London, Voyage en Angleterre, I, 71-73.

Pp. 64-68.—*London.*—Baert remarks on the nobility appearing to be only encamped in the metropolis, Tableau de la Grande Bretagne, I, 56. Malcolm, in Anecdotes of London, describes the disadvantages of the long building-lease system, II, 388, 389, and how the streets were cleaned, II, 400 f. Babeau, Les Anglais en France, pp. 28, 29, mentions pavements as an English idea. The account of Vauxhall is taken from the Ambulator, 1793, p. 251. Colquhoun's Treatise on the Police of the Metropolis, 1800, has the desertion of the tea-gardens, p. 346, the figures as to theft, p. 10, the iniquities of the hackney coachmen, p. 105, the figures as to gin, p. 327 note, and as to the effect of closing the distilleries, p. 328 note, the change in the apprentices' morals, p. 316, the figures as to prostitutes, p. 346. Middleton's View of the Agriculture of Middlesex gives the value of fermented liquor sold, p. 475, and Observations and Facts relating to Public Houses, 1796, pp. 6, 7, the number of these. Haydon's visit to the porter is in his Autobiography, 1853, I, 102. The move of the alderman is mentioned in Spirit of the Public Journals, IV, 1801, 363 ff. French remarks on English depravity are made by Fiévée, Lettres sur l'Angleterre, pp. 87, 88, and Ferri de St. Constant, Londres et les Anglais, I, 182, 216.

Pp. 68-71.—*Manners.*—The poverty of the three London parishes is discussed in a Committee's Report in Parliamentary History, XXXV, pp. 817 ff. Malcolm's Anecdotes of London has remarks on the journeyman, II, 409 ff.; the tradesman, pp. 415 ff. The Spirit of the Public Journals has the unfashionableness of coming to town till May, Vol. XII, 1809, p. 67, the jokes about the thermometer, III, 1800, p. 63, and about the absence of old women in public places, II, 1799, pp. 370, 371. Baring Gould gives details of a sale of a wife in Old Country Life, p. 267. Fiévée, Lettres sur l'Angleterre, p. 58, comments on the youthful dressing of old women. The anecdote in the Lady's Monthly Museum is in Vol. III, p. 179; an example of female toleration of coarseness also in III,

p. 211. Baron Baert, Tableau de la Grande Bretagne, 1800, censures English dancing, IV, 181. Niebuhr's complaint of British formality is in his Life by the Chevalier Bunsen, I, 113, 122. W. Hickey on the smoker is in his Memoirs, Vol. IV, 1925, p. 158. Faujas Saint-Fond describes his entertainment with the Quaker in his Voyage en Angleterre, I, 42-45, and that at Inverary, pp. 290 ff. Windham Papers, II, 107, has the mention of cold baths; Young's is in his Autobiography, 1898, p. 354; Beaumont's is in the Farington Diary, Vol. V, p. 112.

Pp. 71-74.—Malcolm's Anecdotes of London has the change in heads due to the powder tax, I, 356, and the labourer's dress, p. 406. Young's Autobiography has also the sensation created by Fox, p. 425. Beau Brummell's story is in Clubs of London, I, 255 ff. Baert, Tableau de la Grande Bretagne, praises the example of Lord Lansdowne's brother, IV, 141 note. Mary Wollstonecraft's complaint is in her Vindication of the Rights of Women, p. 42. The Spirit of the Public Journals, VI, 1803, p. 84, describes the Bond Street Lounger; Southey, in his Espriella, adds the detail as to his neckcloth, II, 333, and the Sporting Magazine, Vol. XIX (Oct. 1801), p. 23, that as to his manner of speech. The Annual Register for 1803 has the duel of that year, pp. 380-382. The Morning Chronicle's correspondent is quoted in Spirit of the Public Journals, IV, 1801, p. 46.

Pp. 74-75.—*The race for wealth.*—Fiévée's remark on the English is in his Lettres sur l'Angleterre, p. 193; the reference to Southey's Espriella, is to Vol. I, p. 77; that to the lottery office is to Malcolm's Anecdotes of London, II, 403.

Pp. 75-83.—*Treatment of women.*—Those who remarked on the intelligent female public were Fiévée, Lettres sur l'Angleterre, p. 205, and Ferri de St. Constant, Londres et les Anglais, II, 100; the last notes also the neglect of women, I, 385. The Diary of Frances Lady Shelley mentions parties mainly of men dining without their wives, pp. 39, 40. Madame de Staël mentions the freedom enjoyed by girls in Corinne, Livre XVI, 5. The Annual Register for 1804 has the Address to the King, pp. 898 ff.; Whyte's History of the British Turf, II, 57 ff., gives Mrs. Thornton's racing career. "Speculation" at the Malmesburys is in the first Earl's Diaries and Correspondence, IV, 154. The letter to Mackintosh is in his Memoirs, I, 150. The objection to any but a very quiet wedding is illustrated by Lady Holland's Journal, I, 218. The facts as to decrease in crim. con. cases appear from Sir W. Scott's speech on Auckland's Bill, Parliamentary Register, XII, 1800, p. 46. The Spirit of the Public Journals, Vol. VII, has the proposal made in the Morning Chronicle, pp. 15 ff., Vol. IV, the complaint of a man on 'change, p. 101, and the lines beginning "If Eve", pp. 95, 96, Vol. VII, has the contrast of male and female attire, p. 3. Brown's lines are quoted in S. Baring Gould's Yorkshire Oddities, 1874, II, 134. G. Rose has George III's remarks in his Diaries, 1860, Vol. I, pp. 94, 95. The Clubs of London describes Norfolk's character, Vol. II, p. 119. Cobbett's observations are in the Political Register, Vol. X, 1806, pp. 385 ff.

REFERENCES 461

Pp. 84–90.—*The Church.*—Examples of Horsley's insistence on the divine origin of the church are in the First Charge of the Bishop of St. David's, 1791, pp. 34 ff., and Hansard, II, 127 ff. Sir W. Scott's speech, Parliamentary History, XXXIV, 481, has figures of livings. Cobbett's Political Register, Vol. I, 1804, pp. 938, 939, has an account of the class of clergy taken from the plough. Porchester's estimate of non-residents is in Hansard, VI, 924. A Young complains of the clergy of Norfolk in his Agriculture of Norfolk, p. 104, of the Suffolk clergy in his Autobiography, p. 336, and of the Lincolnshire clergy in Agriculture of Lincoln, 437. Tomline's letter is in Buckingham's Memoirs . . . of George III, Vol. III, 61, 62; Horsley's generosity to his curates is detailed in J. H. Overton's English Church in the 19th century, p. 20; his speech is in Parliamentary History, XXXVI, 1582. Mary Wollstonecraft in her Vindication of the Rights of Women, p. 240, mentions the irreverent performance of the Cathedral services, H. Gunning in his Reminiscences, Vol. II, 145, the locked pews, and Southey in Espriella, the poor being expected to stand, I, 201. Porteus's complaint is in his Lectures on St. Matthew, 1804, I, 205 note. Overton, *op. cit.*, p. 157, has mention of the free church in Bath. W. F. de Levis's remarks on religion in England are in his L'Angleterre au Commencement du 19me Siècle, pp. 269, 270. Thomas De Quincey mentions Bishop Watson's Deism in his Works, 1863, II, 111. Leigh Hunt on his father is in his Autobiography, I, 21, 22.

Pp. 90–91.—*The Evangelicals.*—The references to W. Wilberforce's Practical View, etc., are to Chapter IV, Section 2, and—as to religion being in a declining state—Chapter VI.

Pp. 91–94.—*The Nonconformists.*—A New History of Methodism, by W. J. Townsend and others, gives the figures and distribution of methodism, I, 369. S. Bamford's reminiscence is in his Early Days, I, 60. The passages referred to in Sydney Smith's articles are in Edinburgh Review, Vol. XIV, p. 151, Vol. XI, p. 344, and Vol. XIV, p. 44. R. W. Dale, in his History of English Congregationalism, pp. 580 ff., describes the relations of the Independents to the other sects. The Rev. J. Berrington's State and Behaviour of the English Catholics, 1780, gives their number, p. 111.

Pp. 94–95.—*Philanthropy.*—Lansdowne's letter is in Lord E. Fitzmaurice's Life of Lord Shelburne, III, 478. Clarkson's observations on giving up sugar are in his History of the Abolition of the Slave Trade, II, 349.

Pp. 95–97.—*Intellectual condition of the people.*—The quotation from Silas Marner is from Chapter VI. The charity schools are described in Mrs. Trimmer's Education of Children, p. 11, and the schools of the north in the Life of Dr. Porteus, pp. 10 ff.; Cumberland education in W. Wordsworth's Prose Works, 1876, I, 336, and the education of working children touched on by a Bradford (Wilts) witness before the Committee on the Woollen Manufacture, 1806, p. 309 of the Report. The difficulties over educating sergeants appear from the Trial of an action for False Imprisonment brought by Sergeant Richard Warden, 1811, pp. 111–113 and 142.

Pp. 97–98.—*The Press.*—The sale of the Morning Post is taken from Stuart's article in the Gentleman's Magazine, N.S., Vol. IX, 1838, pp. 490 ff. Windham mentioned the poor being reached by the London newspapers, and the popularity of the parliamentary debates, Parliamentary History, XXXIV, pp. 162, 164.

Pp. 98–102.—*Higher education.*—P. J. Grosley's remark on the knowledge of French possessed by Londoners is in Londres, 1788, I, 165, and P. Colquhoun's in his Treatise on the Police of the Metropolis, p. 530. Fiévée ascribes superiority to the English in middle-class education in Lettres sur l'Angleterre, p. 231. The diners-out are described by Frances Lady Shelley in her Diary, p. 39. Parr's retort is in Recollections of the Table Talk of Samuel Rogers, p. 48. Tomline's tribute to Eton is in a letter to his wife of May 9, 1804, in the Pitt Correspondence at Orwell House, Suffolk. Baert's remark on Cambridge is in his Tableau de la Grand Bretagne, I, 82, 83; the lives of the senior members of the community are described in H. Gunning's Reminiscences, II, pp. 62, 63, 113, 114, 117. Temple's letter to Hare is in Sir H. Bulwer Lytton's Life of Lord Palmerston, 1870, I, 8. Education at Christ's Hospital, and Coleridge reciting Homer in his Greek, are described in Charles Lamb's Essay on Christ's Hospital five and thirty years ago. Southey in Espriella, III, 194 ff., mentions the existence of persons who professed a belief in classical mythology. Macaulay's discussion is in his Life by Sir G. Trevelyan, 1877, I, 211. Sir R. Wilson's classical comparison is in his Life, I, 192. The remark on High Wycombe College is in Gen. Sir William Napier's Life of General Sir Charles Napier, 1857, I, 26.

Pp. 102–105.—*Recreations.*—The reference to the 1801 census is to page 497, and that to the 1851 census to pp. ccxxiii and ccxxix of Population Tables II, Part I. Wendeborn's observation is in his Reise durch einige . . . Provinzen Englands, II, 25. In Sir Walter Scott's St. Ronan's Well, Chapter IV, there is mention of the setter as the poacher's dog. The Roxby hounds are described in The Cleveland Hounds, by A. T. Pease, 1887, p. 12. Edge's walk is from Annual Register for 1806, p. 437.

Pp. 105–107.—*National vigour.*—St. Vincent's being slapped on the back is mentioned in J. S. Tucker's Life of him, 1844, I, 256. Bentham's acknowledgment of his debt to Shelburne is in his Works, 1843, X, 115; Windham's dinner to Pitt and Cobbett in the Windham Papers, II, 159. Baron Baert writes of adventuresomeness in trade and thoroughness as English characteristics in his Tableau de la Grande Bretagne, IV, 139. The quotation from A. Smith's Wealth of Nations is from Book I, Chapter X. Those from Cobbett are from his Life by himself, p. 12.

REFERENCES 463
CHAPTER II

Pp. 109–115.—*The House of Commons.*—The Petition from the Society of the Friends of the People, which is the authority for there being 35 places where the right of voting was mere matter of form, etc., is in Parliamentary History, XXX, 788 ff. Grey's mention of the steward's holding the election round a table is on p. 805. Oldfield's Representative History is the authority for the price of a vote being fifty or sixty pounds, III, 516; for that of a borough being £5,000, V, 415; for the price of Gatton, IV, 607; for Lonsdale's arrangements at Haslemere, IV, 599; and generally for the facts as to the government boroughs. There is an example of a constituency with about half of the voters men on weekly wages in the List of Exeter voters in Political and other Broadsides, in the British Museum. "Down with your ten pounds", etc., is from Spirit of the Public Journals, II, p. 271; the Liverpool incident from Picton's Memorials of Liverpool, I, 228; the decay of Taunton from J. Billingsley's General View of . . . Somerset, 1794, p. 167. The number of electors in Scottish counties is in Political State of Scotland, edited by Sir C. E. Adam, 1887, p. xxxi. Chesterfield's letter on his offer for a seat was read in parliament by Sir P. Francis with his own observations; they are in Parliamentary History, XXX, 848, 849. The Memoir of Sir S. Romilly has his intention to purchase a seat, I, 442; II, 55, 56. Holcroft's Narrative of Facts relating to a Prosecution, etc., 1795, has the passage quoted, App. pp. 30–43. The circumstance about Royston is in British Museum Add. MSS. 35646, ff. 36 ff. The restriction of the privilege of wearing spurs is mentioned in Colchester's Diary, I, 45, 46. The Life of Wilberforce by his Sons, 1838, has the expenses of the Yorkshire election, III, 335, and the account of his first victory in the county, I, 53 ff. Fox's letter is in his Memorials, etc., IV, p. 429.

Pp. 116–117.—*The House of Lords.*—The totals of the classes of peers are taken from Beatson's Register of the British Parliament, III, 112.

Pp. 117–123.—*The Sovereign.*—The joke against Kenyon is in Twiss's Life of Eldon, I, 403; the talk on proofs with Miss Burney in Diary, etc., of Madame d'Arblay, 1905, V, 275. Camden's saying is in the Life of Wilberforce, II, 415.

Pp. 123–125.—*The Cabinet.*—The objections of Fox's party to the notion of Cabinet responsibility appear from passages in Hansard, VI, 309 and 278. Instances of the King's independence of his Ministers are in J. H. Rose's William Pitt and the Great War, p. 477, and Diaries, etc., of the First Earl of Malmesbury, IV, 326. The power of the King to delay or refuse to take action is discussed in Jeffrey's article in the Edinburgh Review, XX (for 1812), pp. 337, 338. Stanhope's Life of Pitt has Pitt's avoiding the royal presence for three years, IV, 169. Leveson-Gower's letter is in his Private Correspondence, I, 128. The honour of a Privy Councillorship is compared to that of the Bath by William Wickham in the Historical MSS. Commission, Fortescue MSS., VII, p. 53. Abbot's account of the Privy Council ceremony is in Pellew's Life of

Sidmouth, I, 402. Fox's audience of 1797 is mentioned in the Annual Register for 1806, p. 904. The account of George III's routine is in Letters from an Irish Student, II, 12.

Pp. 131–134.—*Pitt's home policy.*—The estimate of 150,000 men is from the British Museum Add. MSS., 27, 808, ff. 38, 39 (Place MSS.). The connection of the London Corresponding Society with Irish rebellion is brought out in the Report from the Committee of Secrecy, 1799, Parliamentary History, XXXIV, 599; its suppression appears from p. 601 of that volume; the number imprisoned without trial, p. 1485; the interest taken in Despard's confinement, pp. 515, 566.

Pp. 135–138.—*Pitt's colleagues.*—Historical MSS. Commission, Fortescue MSS., VI, has evidence of the inner Cabinet, pp. 247, 249, and has the letter mentioning Castle Rackrent, p. 400. The Duke of Buckingham's Memoirs . . . of George III has Grenville's letter on his own shortcomings, IV, 1855, p. 133. The incident of the horse is in Lord Minto's Life, III, 357. Lady Holland's story is in Vol. II, 29, of her Journal. The epigrams are in Spirit of the Public Journals, I, 1802, pp. 7, 12. Windham's illegitimacy is mentioned in a letter of Lady Malmesbury in Lady Minto's Lord Minto in India, 1880, p. 236. Romilly's Memoirs has Mackintosh's remark, II, 143.

Pp. 138–140.—*Minor Ministers.*—H. W. V. Temperley's Life of George Canning has his drafting dispatches after resigning office, p. 60.

Pp. 140–146.—*Fox.*—Russell's Life of Fox has his saying: "I do not see sufficient prospect", etc., III, 318. Recollections of the Table Talk of Samuel Rogers mentions his pronunciation of "London", p. 248. His saying on British sea power is in Parliamentary History, XXII, 702. Georgiana, Duchess of Devonshire, describes his temperamental indiscretion in W. Sichel's Sheridan, II, 401, which has also, on p. 2 note, his observation on movements out of doors. Lieut.-Gen. C. Grey's Lord Grey has the latter's complaint of Fox, in Some Account of the Life . . . of . . . Earl Grey, 1861, p. 11. The convivial commencement of the Friends of the People movement is recounted in Lady Holland's Journal, I, 101.

Pp. 147–148.—*The Prince of Wales.*—The same book is the authority for the Prince calling himself the head of the party, II, 196; and the dinner party to him, I, 190. Sir N. Wraxall describes his memory in his Memoirs, V, 354, 355, and his conversation about the Prussian Army, p. 360.

Pp. 148–151.—*The Opposition, Nobility and Press.*—Bedford's false return is mentioned in the Anti-Jacobin, I, 1799, 254 ff., which has also the exposures of Whig press indecency, I, 348, and 536, 537. The desire of the Whigs for church property is in the Life of Wilberforce, I, 261. Parr's comment on the young man is in Stirling's Coke of Norfolk, I, 361. Sydney Smith's joke at Perceval's expense is in his Works, 1840, III, 448. The Albion is mentioned in E. V. Lucas's Life of Charles Lamb, 1910, 199, 214. Grenville's letter in Historical MSS. Commission, Fortescue MSS., VI, 409, shows the ministerial attitude towards The Times.

REFERENCES 465

Pp. 151–154.—*The Opposition in the country.*—Coke's claim to appear before the King in boots is from Stirling's Coke of Norfolk, I, 208, 209, as is Parr's levy of subscriptions for Fox, pp. 400 ff. An example of Stanhope's activities in Kent is given in G. P. Gooch's Life of him, 1914, pp. 155 ff. Oldfield's Parliamentary History has the tendency to split county representation between the two parties, III, 440, the Birmingham representation, V, 64, and that of Preston, IV, 97, 98. The Jerningham Letters has the mobbing of one of the family, I, 217, 218, and the commission held by another, p. 179; other examples are discussed in F. Plowden's History of Ireland, 1811, I, 269 note. The position of the Nonconformists as regards office is given by Professor F. W. Maitland in Lectures on the Constitutional History of England, 1908, p. 517. The removal of a Baptist minister is from J. Ivimey's History of the English Baptists, 1830, pp. 77 ff.

Pp. 154–159.—*The Judicature.*—J. L. de Lolme's observations are in his Constitution of England, p. 452 note. Colquhoun's Treatise on the Police of the Metropolis, p. 585, has the estimate of the cost of a suit for £20, and the number of persons arrested annually for debt, p. 587. Hutton's Courts of Requests has his account of the Birmingham court, pp. 29 ff., and mentions the non-attendance of commissioners, p. 74. A civil-court prisoner begging through the gratings is described in Tour through the South of England, 1791, pp. 235–237. Sinclair's arrest is mentioned in Arthur Young's Autobiography, p. 437, and Mrs. Fitzherbert's danger in W. H. Wilkins's Mrs. Fitzherbert and George IV, 1905, II, 275.

Pp. 159–161.—*The criminal administration.*—P. Colquhoun's observations on acquittals are in his Treatise on the Police of the Metropolis, p. 424; his figures of those discharged, p. 446; his remarks on failure of prosecutors to appear, pp. 423–425; and his enumeration of capital offences, pp. 437 ff. Romilly's remarks on acquittals are in his Memoirs, II, 85. Porter, Progress of the Nation, has the comparison of commitments to convictions, pp. 635–636.

Pp. 161–164.—*Prisons and punishments.*—John Howard, in his State of the Prisons, etc., mentions his being obliged to go on horseback, p. 9. The Parliamentary History, XXXV, 463 ff., has the debate on Cold Bath Fields Prison, and on p. 1240 the bills about the vagrants. Letters from an Irish Student, I, 190, mentions the stories about that prison. James Neild, in his State of the Prisons, etc., describes the condition of those at Bristol, pp. 78 and 80. The treatment of an Anabaptist prisoner in Carmarthen gaol, described in H.O. 42, 66, in Public Records Office, under date 23/11/02, is an example of good treatment in 1802 of a prisoner confined for sedition. Instances of private prisons are given in S. and B. Webb's English Prisons under Local Government, pp. 3, 4 note. H.O. 42. 65 has Neild's report and the letter on the moral effect of hulk confinement on a prisoner, under dates 16/3/02 and 19/3/02. Colquhoun's condemnation of hulk confinement and transportation is on pp. 471 and 480 of his Treatise on the Police of the Metropolis; p. 480

has also his estimate of the cost of transportation. J. H. Campe mentions the pillory in his Reise durch England . . . 1803, II, 110. The other instance of it is in Annual Register, 1806, 363. The Spirit of the Public Journals, V, 354, has the ducking of the scold; that of the pickpockets is in Porter, Progress of the Nation, p. 634.

Pp. 164–166.—*Independence of the Courts.*—J. Bentham, Works, V, 1843, pp. 79, 121, describes the Guinea Corps. Lady Holland's entry about Fitzgerald is in her Journal, I, 186. The difficulty of Halifax, etc., getting justice is mentioned in S. and B. Webb's English Local Government, The Parish and the County, p. 583 note. The case of a theft at Bath being tried at Taunton is from W. and R. A. Austen-Leigh's Life of Jane Austen, 1913, pp. 131 ff. The Report from Commissioners on Municipal Corporations, 1835, gives details as to their criminal jurisdictions, p. 39.

Pp. 166–168.—*Activity of the Criminal Courts.*—The papers relating to the prosecution of the offender in 1802 are in the Public Records Office, H.O. 42. 65, under date 7/5/02. The Lincolnshire case is in the Place MSS., British Museum Add. MSS. 27808, f. 110. W. Marshall mentions manor courts dealing with public nuisances in his Rural Economy of Yorkshire, 1796, I, 28. The proceedings of the Portsmouth Commissioners 1800 to 1816 are in a book bound under that name preserved among the municipal records. There are complaints about false weights, etc., in Morning Chronicle for 1/4/1803. The special authority given to the High Constables is mentioned in S. and B. Webb's English Local Government, the Parish and the County, pp. 496 ff. J. Malcolm's Anecdotes of . . . London, 1810, gives the cases taken up by the Society for the Suppression of Vice, I, 215 ff.

Pp. 168–170.—*Police.*—P. Colquhoun mentions the foreign view of the inadequacy of the police in his Treatise on the Police of the Metropolis, p. 522. The saying of the King of Sweden is in The Life . . . of Henry Lord Brougham, I, 169. The horse patrol is described in Capt. Melville Lee's History of the Police in England, p. 194, S. and B. Webb's English Local Government, The Parish and the County, is the authority for the constable being usually appointed by the justices, pp. 27, 28. H.O. 42. 95 in the Public Records Office has the Committees of 1808 and 1810; as also the collection of weavers' shuttles by force by a mob, and Buckingham's letter, under date 4/6/08 and 8/5/08 respectively. The miners' riot is from Three Centuries of Derbyshire. Annals by Rev. J. Cox, 1890, I, 8, 9.

Pp. 170–171.—*Local Government.*—The case of the Richmond Justices is from H. Heaton's The Yorkshire Woollen and Worsted Industries, 1920, p. 429. The amount and distribution of the county rate is taken from Accounts and Papers (15), 1839, XIV, p. 19. Examples of complaints to quarter sessions about the roads are to be found in Hertford Sessions Rolls, 1905, II, passim.

Pp. 171–175.—*The Poor Law.*—Sir F. Eden's account of the Manchester Poor House is in his State of the Poor, 1797, II, 343 ff., which has also

REFERENCES 467

instances of labourers on rounds, II, 30, 384. The reference to S. Bamford is to his Early Days, 1893, p. 62; that to the Memoirs of Robert Blincoe, by John Brown, 1832, is to pp. 17 ff. Elizabeth Fry's story is in her Life, I, 117, 118. The churchwardens' electorate is taken from S. and B. Webb's English Local Government, The Parish and the County, pp. 21, 22. How those overseers who were not churchwardens were appointed is in J. Adolphus's Political State of the British Empire, III, 564, 565. The lawsuit about the paupers' marriage is from Hertford Sessions Rolls, II, 180. The poor-rate figures are from Commons Journals, LXI, pp. 802 ff. Sir C. Poole's speech in Hansard, XIV, 809, 810 mentions relief to militiamen's families.

Pp. 175–178.—*The Municipal Corporations.*—S. and B. Webb's English Local Government, The Manor and the Borough, Part II, has details for London as to status of freemen of a guild, 1908, p. 579 note, representation of wards by aldermen, 576, selection of Lord Mayor, 578, constitution of Court of Common Council, 577, that of Commission of Sewers, etc., 641, 642; and an example elsewhere of freemen choosing the Mayor, p. 532. The number of municipal corporations in England and Wales is given by the Journal of the Statistical Society, V, 1842, p. 104; the constitutions on p. 132. Gneist in Self-Government gives an estimate of the numbers in which the corporation was self-elected, and in which the freemen chose the corporation, p. 594 and note. There are examples of presentations of shopkeepers by the Grand Jury in the Cheshire Quarter Sessions Records for 1800–1802 preserved at Chester. W. Hutton's History of Birmingham, 1783, has that place's petitioning for a corporation in 1716, pp. 324 ff. The work of the Board of Health in Manchester appears in the Report of the Society for Bettering the Conditions of the Poor, I, 1798, pp. 98 ff. The account of Fox's welcome is from the Annual Register, 1806, p. 899. The Times article is of 5/11/1803. S. and B. Webb's English Local Government, The Parish and the County, has a description of financial irregularities in Manchester, pp. 72 ff. The Steward's Charge of 1799, in Manchester Court Records, IX, 1899, p. 256, mentions the failure to work the Act of 1792.

Pp. 178–179.—*Trade Control.*—Auckland's letter to Grenville is in Historical MSS. Commission, Fortescue MSS., VII, p. 350.

Pp. 179–180.—*The Post Office.*—W. Levins's His Majesty's Mails, 1864, has the prognostications of Palmer's failure, pp. 78 ff. Joyce's History of the Post Office, 1893, has the rapidity of communication in London, pp. 304, 305, and the rates, p. 330. Commons Journal, LVI, 717, gives the post-office income.

Pp. 180–182.—*Finance—Taxation.*—The Letter to Cobbett's Political Register is in Vol. IX, 925 ff. Sinclair's History of the Public Revenue, 1803, has details as to various branches of expenditure, II, 148 ff.

Pp. 182–185.—*The National Debt.*—The state of the debt in 1801 is taken partly from the Account in Commons Journal, LVI, 812 f., and partly from Accounts and Papers, 1864, (1) XXXII, pp. 150, 151, and 1857–1858, (1) XXXIII, p. 203. A. Young describes his successful venture in his Autobiography, pp. 379, 380. Newland's fortune is given in J. Francis's History of the Bank of England, I, 280, and he also mentions Jewish stockbrokers applying for loans in his Chronicles and Characters of the Stock Exchange, 1850, p. 180. Grelliers gives the terms of all the loans in question in his book so called, pp. 34 ff. The terms for 1800 are from Parliamentary History, XXXIV, 1518.

Pp. 185, 186.—*Excise.*—Dowell's History of Taxation has the facts as to the taxation of salt, IV, 1, paper, p. 326, advertisements, p. 347, newspapers, p. 343, and bricks, p. 379.

P. 186.—*Customs.*—Pitt in his budget speech of 1796, in Parliamentary History, XXXII, 1259, 1260, expressed his repugnance towards these taxes. Dowell's History of Taxation has the French-wine tax, IV, 130.

Pp. 186–187.—*Miscellaneous taxation.*—The same book has the tax on coaches, III, 52, 53, and the attempt to tax canals and parcels, p. 57, compared with Parliamentary History, XXXII, 1261. Commons Journals, LVI, 876, has the amount of stamp revenue.

Pp. 187–188.—*Income Tax.*—Newbury's Thoughts on Taxation, 1799, pp. 9–11, contains observations on the advantage of taxation being voluntary. The amount of the voluntary gifts of 1798 is taken from J. H. Rose's William Pitt and the Great War, p. 331. Bedford's criticism of direct taxation is in Parliamentary History, XXXIV, 205; his evasion of a tax is commented on in Anti-Jacobin, 1799, I, 254 ff., his voluntary contribution is mentioned in Earl Russell's Life of Fox, III, 240. Lady Bessborough's misfortune is described by her in Lord Granville Leveson-Gower's Private Correspondence, I, 205.

Pp. 188–191.—*Expenditure.*—The cost of the Board of Agriculture is in the account given on p. 772 of Vol. LVI of Commons Journals; the payment to the four parishes on p. 774. George Canning's sinecure is given in Black Book, p. 25, and the others on pp. 6 and 47. Pitt's emoluments are given in his Life by Lord Rosebery, App. C. The praise given him in the Annual Register for 1806 is on p. 880. The customs reductions are described in The King's Customs, by H. Atton and H. H. Holland, 1908, pp. 405–407, and the total number of persons employed in public departments in 1797 taken from the Extraordinary Black Book, p. 393. Loughborough's pension is mentioned in Campbell's Lives of the Chancellors, VI, 320.

Pp. 191–192.—*The Mint.*—Lord Liverpool's unfavourable criticisms are on pp. 204–206 of his book; he mentions the copper coinage at Boulton's on pp. 195–197; the issue of Spanish dollars, pp. 193–194; the silver coins being now mere counters, p. 168; the loss of weight at the assay of 1798, p. 187; his estimate of gold coin is on p. 177. Haden's letter is in H.O. 48. 413 under date 13/11/04.

Pp. 192–194.—*Idea of the Three Estates.*—The date of the Chairman of Committee being made permanent is from Porritt's Unreformed House of Commons, p. 532.

Pp. 194–195.—*Composition of the House of Commons.*—The proposed

REFERENCES 469

General Enclosure Bill of 1796 is discussed in Annals of Agriculture, XXVI, 1796, pp. 67 ff.

Pp. 195–198.—*Parliamentary conception of industrial legislation.*—Holland's declaration in support of Portland is in Parliamentary History, XXXV, 506; that against the Combination Act in Parliamentary Register, IX, 1799, 562 ff. The millwright's petition is in the Journal of the House of Commons, Vol. LIV, pp. 405, 406. There is an example of an exhortation to J.P.s, etc., to send up the names of men taking excessive wages in the Cheshire Quarter Sessions Records, preserved at Chester, for 1800–1802. Perceval's refusal to prosecute Trade Unions is in Yonge's Life of Liverpool, I, 166–169.

Pp. 198–201.—*Parliamentary conception of commercial legislation.*—The belief in the superiority of English wool appears in A. Callwell's Enquiry concerning the Restrictions laid on the Trade of Ireland, p. 758. The estimate of 7,000,000 acres of waste is from Communications to the Board of Agriculture, I, 1797, p. 126. Smith's saying about defence is from Book II, Chapter II, of the Wealth of Nations. The legislation modifying the Navigation Act is summarized in Strictures on the necessity of inviolably maintaining the Navigation and Colonial System, by Lord Sheffield, pp. 5–7.

CHAPTER III

Pp. 202–209.—*Ireland—National character and economic condition.*—Wakefield's Account of Ireland has the superiority of the Irish in education, II, 804, the passage quoted about the self-subsistent home, I, 760, the outrage at Carlow races, II, 773, 774, the population of Belfast, II, 694, and the observation about the rich Presbyterian's change of religion, II, 594. Arthur Young's tribute to the Irish peasant's prosperity is in his Tour in Ireland, II, Pt. II, 23, his remark on the brutality with which they were treated on pp. 40 ff. Tighe, in Statistical Survey of Kilkenny, p. 412, observes on the farmer's loose methods of husbandry. The peasant's drawing home the tithe-farmer's corn, etc., free is from a speech of Grattan in his Memoirs by his son Henry Grattan, III, 322. The £2,000,000 of rent spent outside Ireland is from Foster's speech, Hansard, I, 650. The History of Dublin by Warburton, etc., has mention of the tradesman's villa in the Wicklow hills, II, 1271. The reference to Maria Edgeworth's Memoirs of R. L. Edgeworth is to Vol. II, p. 219. The passage in the Memoirs of Miles Byrne is in Vol. I, p. 3. Luke Fox is the authority for the relative numbers of Church of England and Presbyterians, in the Memoirs, etc., of Viscount Castlereagh, II, 409. Dr. A. Ure describes the growth of the Belfast cotton industry in his Cotton Manufacture of Great Britain, 1861, pp. 294 ff.

Pp. 209–211.—*The Capital.*—The population of Dublin is taken from Rev. J. Whitelaw's Essay on the population of Dublin, p. 23. Baron

Baert's remark is in his Tableau de la Grande Bretagne, I, 370 note. Wakefield's Account of Ireland has the thanking of the Sheriff, II, 343, the examples of Irish vanity, p. 787, the lives of the poor in Dublin, p. 789, the Foundling Hospital, pp. 424, 425, and 436. The traveller of 1791 who is quoted is the author of the Tour through the South of England, 1793, pp. 312, 325 ff. Examples of Dublin's failure to advance are given by G. O'Brien, The Economic History of Ireland in the Eighteenth Century, pp. 270, 277, 278.

Pp. 211–215.—*The system of government.*—Wakefield's Account of Ireland gives information on the qualifications of J.P.s, II, 339, the Catholic magistrates, p. 340, recovery of debts at quarter sessions, p. 345, the charter schools, pp. 410 ff., the clergyman's oath, p. 441, the figures as to stills seized, I, 730, the term hearth-tax collectors, II, 326; the rate at which that tax fell is from G. O'Brien's Economic History of Ireland in the Eighteenth Century, p. 332. The difficulty over the uneducated squireens is described in the Memoirs of R. L. Edgeworth, by Maria Edgeworth, II, 184 ff. Lord Cloncurry mentions the baronial constable's qualifications in his Personal Recollections, p. 198, and his father's loan to Government on p. 19. Young describes the road-rate system, Tour of Ireland, Pt. II, 56. Walsh describes the hedge schools in his Sketches of Ireland Sixty Years Ago, 1847, pp. 102, 103. Opinions as to the effect of the duties on leather and salt upon the poor are in Lecky's History of Ireland, IV, 7, 8. The financial figures are taken from Sir E. Hamilton's Memorandum in the Report of the Royal Commission on Financial Relations, pp. 322, 323. Wakefield's book has Irish customs and excise receipts, II, 276; the custom of paying by tally, p. 182; the issue of tokens through the Bank, p. 178; the number of bankers issuing notes in 1800, p. 171; the rascally system of the estate agents' traffic, pp. 177, 178. The Killarney story is from Clubs of London, 1828, II, 289.

Pp. 215–217.—*Wealth of Ireland.*—The reference to Tighe's Statistical Survey of the County of Kilkenny is to p. 492; he also describes the effect of the introduction of the apple potato, p. 234. Other wage details are taken from the article by A. L. Bowley in the Royal Statistical Society's Journal, Vol. LXII, pp. 397 and 400. Wakefield's Account of Ireland has the increase in exports, II, 34, and the official values of exports and imports, pp. 33, 34, and 38 ff. G. O'Brien, in The Economic History of Ireland in the Eighteenth Century, has the number of yards of linen, p. 275.

Pp. 217–221.—*The Viceroys and Parliament.*—Earl Russell's Life of Fox has his opposition to the Convention, II, 15 ff. E. Porritt, in his Unreformed House of Commons, Vol. II, notes the dissensions in the Privy Council, p. 362, and describes the uninhabited boroughs, pp. 187 and 299. The failure of the Cabinet system is from the Cornwallis Correspondence, II, 385, and note. The numbers in the House of Lords are from J. W. Stewart's Gentleman's Almanac for 1801, pp. 52 ff. The nature of the control of the proprietary boroughs is given in App. 53 to Vol. IV of F. Plowden's History of Ireland, 1811; their origin as colonies is described in Porritt's book, II, 192 ff. The House's enjoyment of Roche's bulls is mentioned by Barrington in his Recollections, p. 135. The figures regarding placemen, etc., are from the Chancellor of the Exchequer's speech in Parliamentary Debates, Ireland, XIII, 448.

Pp. 221–224.—*The Catholic Question.*—Lecky's History of Ireland, III, 270, quotes Fitzwilliam's letter on Ireland being already in a state of rebellion in Feb. 1795. The King's action is from Lord Stanhope's Life of Pitt, II, 304, and App. XXIII–XXV.

Pp. 224–231.—*The Rebellion.*—Lecky's History of Ireland has the seditious notices mentioned by Camden, III, 387, Knox's complaint, IV, 59, Fitzwilliam's constabulary plan, III, 267, 268, Camden's yeomanry plan, III, 472–475, and the estimate of losses in the rebellion, V, 105, 106. Bristol's letter is in Documents relating to Ireland, 1795–1804, edited by Gilbert, pp. 121 ff.; Abercromby's in Lord Dunfermline's Memoirs of him, 1861, p. 84. W. J. MacNeven's Pieces of Irish History, New York, 1807, has the relations between volunteers and Catholic bodies, pp. 14, 15, and his statement before the Secret Committee of the House of Commons about the cause of the insurrection, pp. 206 ff. Wakefield in his Account of Ireland, II, 582, describes the advanced condition of S.E. Ireland. Grattan's letter is in his Miscellaneous Works, 1822, p. 42. Gosford's meeting is from Seward's Collectanea Politica, III, 157 ff. Sir Jonah Barrington's bargain is from his Recollections, pp. 166–169, and the duel from p. 190.

Pp. 231–235.—*The Union.*—Castlereagh's expression is in his Memoirs, III, 333. Lansdowne's observation is in Parliamentary History. XXXIV, 679. Camden's refusal to support the Orange Society is in Lecky's History of Ireland, V, 349. The Cornwallis Correspondence, Vol. III, has his refusal to be in the hands of the officials, which is in his letter to Portland of 16/9/98, pp. 404, 405; "that every man", etc., p. 8; "there cannot be", etc., p. 110; his longing to kick people, p. 101.

Pp. 235–241.—*The Terms of the Union.*—The same authority has the disturbed state of Dublin, p. 111; the arrangement for compensation for seats, pp. 321 ff.; the dismissal of Downshire, pp. 178, 179; the number of boroughs left with patrons, p. 324; the division figures on the Union, pp. 181 and 206; Clare's taunts, pp. 184–186; the tender of Cornwallis's resignation, pp. 262 ff.; and the peerage arrangements, pp. 257 ff., and 318, 319. Jonah Barrington's description of the object of the Commissioners is in his Rise and Fall, etc., pp. 450 ff.; he mentions the rat-catcher's claims, p. 452 note. Lecky has the purchase of a seat for Grattan in his History of Ireland, V, 349. The system of selection of boroughs is given in the Memoirs of Viscount Castlereagh, III, pp. 423–433. R. L. Edgeworth's speech is from Maria Edgeworth's Memoir of him, II, 230, 231. The exports are from Wakefield's Account of Ireland, II, 46 ff., and the imports from pp. 38 ff. Parliamentary History, Vol. XXXIV, has the belief in Irish subserviency, pp. 468, 469; the argument that the Irish members would introduce disorder is on pp. 929, 930. The Cornwallis Correspondence has the manner in which the royal assent was received in Dublin, III, 285, and his own personal popularity, p. 288. Coote's History of the Union has Grey's point about a separate government and a distinct treasury, p. 464.

Pp. 241–243.—*The scarcity of corn.*—The estimate of deficiency in corn for 1799 is taken from a Committee Report in Parliamentary History, XXXIV, 1490; that for 1800 from one in Vol. XXXV, pp. 778 ff.; Moore's proposal, XXXIV, 1497, 1498; the price of the quartern loaf in London being 1s. 6d. from XXXV, 716; the calculation of requirements from the Report in XXXV, 825 ff.; the manner of computing the bounty from p. 777. The prices of wheat in the New Year are in Annals of Agriculture, 1801, XXXVI, 446; the wheat imports from the Annual Register, 1801, Chronicle, etc., p. 137.

Pp. 243–247.—*Foreign affairs.*—The King's strategical observation is on p. 225 of Pitt and Napoleon by J. H. Rose. The amount of the subsidies is taken from Lord Rosebery's Pitt, App. A. That the method of subsidies was Whiggish appears from a letter in Young's Autobiography, p. 108. Schlosser mentions Paul's treatment of the British crews in his Geschichte des achtzehnten Jahrhunderts, VI, p. 331. The justification of the seizure of the West Indian Islands is in Hawkesbury's Note in the Annual Register, 1801, Chronicle, etc., p. 246, and the action of the King of Prussia on p. 287. The figures showing increase in the tonnage with North Germany are given in Mahan's Influence of Sea Power, etc., 1892, II, 28.

Pp. 247–250.—*Meeting of Parliament.*—The debate is in Parliamentary History, XXXV, 887 ff.

Pp. 251–256.—*Fall of Pitt's Administration.*—The extent of the assurances given to the Catholics appears from Castlereagh's letter to Pitt, which is in the former's Memoirs, IV, 11; George III's saying "beyond the decision of any Cabinet of Ministers" is in Lord Stanhope's Life of Pitt, II, App. p. xxv. Buckingham's Memoirs . . . of George III has the outline of Pitt's proposals, III, p. 129. Vol. III of Stanhope's book has Loughborough's opposition, p. 270; his furnishing legal opinions in 1795 and 1800, pp. 264, 271; the defection of four ministers, p. 273; Pitt's letter of Jan. 31st and subsequent correspondence, App. pp. xxiii ff.; Pitt's subsequent refusal of opportunities to see the King, III, 309, and IV, 169. Pellew's Life of Sidmouth has the legal memorandum, I, 500–512, and on p. 286, note, the King's outburst, "Where is that power", etc. His speaking to Dundas at the levy is mentioned in the Life of Wilberforce, III, 7; his earlier saying to him, "None of your Scotch metaphysics," in Life of Sir J. Mackintosh, I, 171; his saying to Portland in Diaries of the First Earl of Malmesbury, IV, 44, which also has Pitt's account to Canning of why he had gone out, p. 75. Mention is made of the King's inner body of advisers by Cooke, in Correspondence of Viscount Castlereagh, IV, 64, which has also the removal of tolerant influences in Ireland (T. M'Kenna's letter), p. 65; and Grenville's hope to retain the measure for the clergy, p. 89.

Pp. 256–259.—*Addington's succession as Premier.*—Colchester's Diary

REFERENCES 473

has Addington's speech from the gallery, I, 121; the account of the crisis in the King's health on March 2nd, pp. 249, 250; the "What? what? what?" as a sign of improvement, pp. 247, 248; Abbot himself on the importance of his health, p. 498. Bishop Tomline's Life of Pitt, Chapters XXIII, etc., published 1903, mentions Pitt's earlier intention to retire, p. 101. Sheridan's speech is in Parliamentary History, XXXV, 968, 969. Fox's regard for the King's health appears in the Diaries of the First Earl of Malmesbury, IV, 41. Lord Stanhope's Life of Pitt has his being pressed to remain, III, pp. 299, 305, 306. The Life of Wilberforce has his admiration of Pitt's truthfulness, II, 249, 250.

Pp. 259-260.—*The Budget.*—The two budgets are in Parliamentary History, XXXV, pp. 972 ff. and 1269 ff.

Pp. 260-263.—*The new Administration.*—The Farington Diary mentions Portland's embarrassments, I, pp. 127, 128. Hawkesbury's nicknames are mentioned in Bagot's George Canning and his Friends, pp. 180 and 127. Lady Malmesbury's letter is on pp. 126 ff. Lady Hester Stanhope's saying is from her Memoirs, I, 218. The lines on Eldon are from The R—L Spectre, by "Monk Lewis", 1813, p. 12. Eldon's gift for restraining George III appears from Twiss's Life of him, I, 418 ff. Vansittart's remark is in Colchester's Diary, 1861, I, 230.

CHAPTER IV

Pp. 264-270.—*The Scarcity.*—The prices of bread and wheat are taken from the Annual Register for 1801, Chronicle, pp. 168, 182; it has also the account of Spence, p. 20. Mrs. Sandford's Thomas Poole and his friends has Poole's account of the West of England rising, II, 42, 43. The occurrences in Totnes are in Public Records Office, H.O. 48. 10 ff., 175 ff. Parliamentary History, XXXV, has the measures taken to encourage food production, pp. 1004, 1005, and the Committee's Report on Secrecy, pp. 1302 ff., containing its findings on distress in the manufacturing districts, p. 1304, and mention of the Spensonians, pp. 1307-1309; the state of poor relief in Yorkshire is mentioned by Grey, pp. 1064, 1065; the reports as to Ireland, pp. 1313 ff. The Charges of Samuel Horsley, 1813, has mention of the seditious schools, pp. 145-147. Peel's letter from his partner is quoted from J. L. and B. Hammond's Skilled Labourer, 1919, p. 66. Warburton's, etc., History of Dublin, Vol. II, 1168-1171, has its improvement under Hardwicke.

Pp. 270-276.—*The North American Colonies.*—The figures of population, except where otherwise stated, are taken from Porter's Progress of the Nation, pp. 783 ff. Milne's estimate for Lower Canada is in the published Canadian Archives, 1892, p. 12; it has also details as to the old soldiers in Upper Canada, pp. 375-377; Talbot's letter, pp. xix, xx; Thorpe's phrase, "storekeeper aristocracy", p. 90; the system of land grants, pp. 13 and xi; and Castlereagh's censure of Dunn, p. iv. Garneau is the authority for the small British population of Lower Canada, Histoire du Canada, III, 76, and for the election by Frenchmen of 16 English deputies to the First Assembly, p. 85. The resemblance of the French Canadian to the Red Indian appears from the illustration facing p. 158, in Lambert's Travels through Lower Canada, etc., Vol. I; it also describes the gaiety of the people, pp. 173 ff. The local ignorance of agriculture appears from Heriot's Travels through the Canadas, p. 259. Canniff's History of the Settlement of Upper Canada has the character of the immigrants from the U.S., pp. 279 ff.

Pp. 276–277.—*Relations with the United States.*—The volume for 1891 of the published Canadian Archives has McLane's career, p. xlii, and the account of the capture of arms in 1797, p. 63. The volume for 1892 has the discovery that the conspiracy was the work of a parcel of Americans, p. 172; the evidence that the arms captured in 1797 had been intended for a filibustering expedition, p. 170; the number of the militia, p. 12; the fact of only a few hundred being trained, p. 269; the defenceless state of Quebec, the only place attempted to be put in a state of defence, pp. 269, 271. The strength of the Canadian forces is taken from Kingford's History of Canada, VII, pp. 454, 455. The export trade of 1802 is given in Heriot's Travels through the Canadas, pp. 230, 231.

Pp. 277–278.—*The Bermudas.*—The troubles of the Court of Chancery in the Bermudas are mentioned in Williams's Account, p. 116; the population is taken from Edwards's History of the British Colonies in the West Indies, Vol. II, 2.

Pp. 278–285.—*The West Indies.*—The same page has the populations of Barbados, the Windward Islands (cp. p. 3 note), the Leeward Islands, the Bahamas, and Jamaica; pp. 329, 330 have details as to the Council in Jamaica. The account of Moore's vigour and his eventually succumbing is in his Diary, I, 249, 251. Young's West-India Common-Place Book has figures of exports and imports of the West Indies, pp. 29, 30, 33; the mortality in St. Lucia in 1796, pp. 222, 223; the smuggling habits of the Spaniards in Cuba, pp. 168, 169; the Jamaica trade in 1800, pp. 16, 17; the fall in sugar prices, p. 48; the sickness of the troops in 1800, p. 218; the calculation that the landlord made only 4 per cent., p. 26. Lady Nugent in her Journal mentions the apprehensions of Europeans from negro risings, p. 289; their callousness, p. 62; the repasts, pp. 95, 127; the peculiarity of the climate, p. 224; and the Jew review, p. 76. Michael Scott's Tom Cringle's Log, Chapter XI, has the immunity at 3,000 feet; the Farington Diary, Vol. V, p. 166, the fact that no bells tolled for a funeral. Young's book is also the authority for the effect of the Navigation Act, pp. 130, 139, 140; he also notices the system of free ports, pp. 174 ff.; gives the yearly import of slaves, pp. 5, 12, and the loss of life among them, p. 10, and the total British W.I. population of all three classes, p. 3. Gardner, in his History of Jamaica, mentions the overseer's right to inflict stripes, p. 221, and the punishments ordered by the courts, pp. 177, 178.

REFERENCES 475

Pp. 285–290.—*The Navy*.—Examples of the courts-martial referred to are in Naval Chronicle, VII, pp. 166, 167, XIII, pp. 329, 330, XIV, pp. 84, 85; and Schomberg's Naval Chronology, III, 356. Tucker's Memoirs of St. Vincent, Vol. II, has the offensive naval toast, p. 10, and his complaints of the inflow of the young nobility, pp. 270, 285. The Nelson Despatches has the view that a seaman's life is finished at forty-five, Vol. V, p. 45. St. Vincent's views on discipline when in command of the Channel Fleet are in his Letters, printed for the Navy Records Society, Vol. I, p. 345, and the Historical MSS. Commission, Various MSS., Vol. VI, 1909, p. 396. Steele's Marine Officer mentions the case of a man flogged to death, II, 14. "T. Foley's" Nelson Centenary, 1905, has Nelson's relationships, pp. 24, 25. The rule as to period of qualification for midshipmen is mentioned by St. Vincent in Brenton's Life of him, II, 125. Schomberg's book gives the totals of officers, III, 538. Jane Austen's letter is in her Life by W. and R. A. Austen-Leigh, 1913, p. 121. The Morning Chronicle for 19th of April, 1803, repeats the Portsmouth paper's report as to enthusiasm for joining the Navy in that year. The case of the Canadian judge's son is from the volume for 1892 of the published Canadian Archives, p. 227.

Pp. 290–293.—The bounty payments in Liverpool are from J. E. Picton's Memorials of Liverpool, 1875, I, 241. The working of the system is discussed in an article by F. W. Brooks in the English Historical Review, XLIII, for 1928, pp. 236 ff. There is an instance of a hundred and eighty bad characters being sent on board a single ship in Bowers's Naval Adventures, I, 158, 159. The Nelson Despatches, Vol. V, has Nelson's recruitment of his fleet with Maltese, p. 231, and Elliot's prize-money, p. 198. Collingwood's notice of the black-man at Trafalgar is from the Selection from his Correspondence, 1829, p. 129. Nautical Economy, by a Sailor, describes the treatment of volunteers along with the Lord Mayor's men, p. 2, and Sinclair's Royal Navy, p. 37, the skillagolee. Fletcher's Naval Guardian, Vol. I, 1805, pp. 60 ff., has the popularity of Dibdin's ballad about 1797. Paget's letter on prize-money is in Sir A. Paget's Paget Papers, 1896, II, 162.

Pp. 293–296.—The number and distribution of line of battle ships at the end of the war of 1793–1801 is from Steel's Naval Chronologist, p. 103, which has the capture of privateers in 1800 also, pp. 83 ff. Victoires, Conquêtes, etc., Vol. XVII, 1820, p. 268, has the claim made for the Imperial. The strength of the Victory is taken from the MS. lists preserved in the Admiralty Library. The Directory's admission that there was not a merchant ship on the sea carrying the French flag is on p. 482 of the Moniteur for 1799 (An 7). There is an example of a privateer firing into a coast town in Lady Nugent's Journal, p. 347. The calculation that the toll of merchant shipping taken by privateers was as much as 2 per cent. is in Mahan's Influence of Sea Power, etc., Vol. II, 223 ff. Tucker's Memoirs of St. Vincent, Vol. II, has his complaint of the civil department, p. 146, his interest in lemons as preventive of scurvy, pp. 26 ff., and his contempt of medical qualifications, p. 111.

Dundas's improvements are detailed in Parliamentary History, XXIX, 548 ff. The account of naval Methodists is in the Evangelical Magazine for 1807, p. 120.

Pp. 296–298.—*The Army*.—Duncan's History of the Royal Artillery, Vol. II, has Robe's difficulties in the Peninsula, pp. 198, 199, and 211; the fact of the Helder expedition being the first in which a general officer was sent in command of the artillery, p. 89; the three different guns for the R.H.A., pp. 44, 45; the strength at the end of the war of 1793–1801, p. 136. Recognition of British gunnery is displayed in a book reviewed in the Edinburgh Review, Vol. IV, for 1803–1804, p. 451, and in Foy's Histoire des Guerres de la Péninsule, Vol. I, 294–296, which has also the observations on the R.E., pp. 301 ff. Cornwallis's observations about an R.E. officer's pay are in his Correspondence, III, 219, 229. The expenditure on foritfications is taken from the Ordnance Return, 1810, Commons Journals, LXIII, 335. Conolly's History of the Royal Sappers and Miners has their strength, I, 127.

Pp. 298–303.—The opening of the High Wycombe College is from Denis le Marchant's Memoirs of Major-General le Marchant, 1841, p. 68. Sir W. Napier's Life of Gen. Sir Charles Napier mentions the standard required for the staff course, I, 26. The details as to the educational scheme are from Commons Journals, Vol. LVI, p. 878. The ignorance of their duties by cavalry is set out in The British Army, by Hon. J. Fortescue, 1905, pp. 34; 85, 86; 109, 110. J. Grego's Rowlandson the Caricaturist has a list of prints for priming and loading, I, 377. The belief that once a breach made in the British line victory was easy is from Gen. Humbert's report, which is in Desbrière's Projets et Tentatives, etc., Tome II, pp. 282, 283. The order for Light Horse Volunteers is in the Diary of Lord Colchester, I, 114 note; an account of the gradual abolition of pig-tails in Lt.-Col. J. Luard's History of the Dress of the British Army, 1852, 98, and that of Coleridge's sermon in the Collected Works of W. Hazlitt, XII, 1904, p. 261. Lady Bessborough's account of the soldier's indignation is in Lord Granville Leveson-Gower's Private Correspondence, II, 310. Adam Smith's observation on the soldier is in Wealth of Nations, Book I, Chapter X. Cobbett's Political Register, Vol. X, has the cost of the ensign's commission, p. 155, his budget, p. 27, the colonel's, p. 154. The reference to The Farmer, 1792, is p. 30—volume in British Museum of farces performed at the Theatre, Smoke Alley, Dublin. G. Dyer's Complaint of the Poor People of England, 1793, mentions the position of a retiring colonel, p. 44.

Pp. 304–308.—The Memoirs of John Shipp has the Hathras incident, II, 186, and the sayings on flogging, II, 204, and 163. Moore's W. Indian observation is in his Diary, I, 236, 239. W. Grattan's account of a troopship is in his Adventures of the Connaught Rangers, 1847, I, 2. The Gibraltar epidemic is described in Sir J. Fellowes's Reports of the Pestilential Disorder of Andalusia, 1815, pp. 122–141. Young's West-India Common-Place Book, p. 218, is the authority for the deaths in the West Indies in 1800, and Lord Rosebery's Pitt, p. 148, that for the estimate for the whole war. The concession to sailors' wives is mentioned in Fletcher's Naval Guardian, Vol. I, p. 162, note. Clode's Military Forces of the Crown describes the annoyances of the billeting system, I, 232 ff., and the abolition of the Barrackmaster-General's as a separate department, p. 255. Sir W. Napier's Life of Gen. Sir Charles Napier contains reference to the bad barracks, I, 83, 86. The War Office return utilized is W.O. 17, 1161, in the Public Records Office; the contemporary Irish Army estimate is in Commons Journals, Vol. LVI, p. 685. The miscellaneous bodies formed for national defence are taken from History of the British Army, by Hon. J. Fortescue, Vol. IV, pp. 891 ff. Bamford describes his own volunteering in his Early Days, p. 153.

Pp. 308–311.—*The Expedition to Egypt.*—Dundas's boast is in Historical MSS. Commission, Fortescue MSS., Vol. IV, 1905, p. 224. The King's compliment to him is in the Farington Diary, VI, p. 48; Bonaparte's prediction in L'Expédition d'Égypte, by C. de la Jonquière (État-Major de l'Armée, Paris, Section Historique), V, 1907, pp. 603, 604. Menou's information is in Cartons de l'Armée d'Orient, preserved in Ministère de la Guerre, Paris, for Jan. and Feb. 1801—especially letters from Tunis of 7th Feb., Reynier of 12th, Friant of 23rd and 25th. Moore's difficulties in Jaffa and Abercromby's comment are in the former's Diary, I, 395, 397; on p. 386 is the description of Alexandria as the key of Egypt. Wilson's History of the British Expedition to Egypt has the incident of the shots being fired into the Vizier's tent, p. 6 note.

Pp. 311–314.—*Landing of the British.*—General Reynier's De l'Égypte mentions the date on which the fleet's arrival was known at Cairo, p. 188. Wilson's Expedition to Egypt has Abercromby's mistaken view of Menou's strength, p. 8. Jomini gives the real number in his Histoire des Guerres de la Révolution, XIV, p. 316. The authority for the disembarkation orders and the number of men furnished by the Navy is Anderson's Journal of the Secret Expedition, pp. 201 and 220.

Pp. 314–317.—*Battle of Canopus.*—The naval losses are added to those in Hutchinson's despatch from James's Naval History, III, 102. Hutchinson's casualty returns and his tributes to Abercromby are in Walsh's Journal of the Late Campaign in Egypt, 22*, 19*, 110*.

Pp. 317–319.—*Conquest of Egypt.*—Napoleon's remark on the campaign is in Correspondance, 1861, XV, No. 12361; the part borne by the High Wycombe officers is mentioned in D. Le Marchant's Memoirs of Major-General Le Marchant, 1841, p. 102.

Pp. 319–322.—*Saumarez's naval actions.*—The naval strategic situation in June is from Memoirs of Lord de Saumarez by Capt. Sir J. Ross, II, 21. Brenton's Naval History, 1837, describes Saumarez's departure from Gibraltar on July 12th, I, 549, 550. The incident of the boat coming off with the wounded men is in Naval Chronicle, VI, 1801, 113. The account of the action is from Dundonald's Autobiography of a Seaman, I, 133, 134. St. Vincent's appreciation is from his Letters printed for the

Navy Records Society, Vol. ,I p. 206. Grant's defence of Porto Ferrajo is in the Annual Register, 1801, pp. 70–72.

Pp. 322–326.—*Character of Nelson.*—The Nelson Despatches has his letter to Moira, VI, p. 310, and Dr. Beatty's account of the appearance of his body after death, VII, 1846, pp. 259 ff.

Pp. 326–328.—*The Expedition to Copenhagen.*—The same work has his own labours in rebuoying the channel off Copenhagen, IV, 312, and Hardy's, p. 304.

Pp. 329–334.—*Battle of Copenhagen.*—Stewart's account of the blind-eye incident is in Clarke and McArthur's Life of Nelson, II, 403; that of Nelson's reception in Copenhagen on pp. 409, 410. The movements of Commodore Fischer are from his report in Naval Chronicle, VI, 342, 343. Capt. Fremantle's letter in Buckingham's Memoirs of . . . George III, Vol. III, 152, is the authority for seven ships being aground at once. The Nelson Despatches has his two letters to Addington, IV, 1845, 332 ff. and 339 ff.

Pp. 334–335.—*Dissolution of the Armed Neutrality.*—St. Vincent's letters are in his Letters printed for the Navy Records Society, Vol. I, pp. 100, 101. The advantages obtained by the Armed Neutrality appear in the Convention with Russia, published in Parliamentary History, XXXVI, 18 ff.

Pp. 335–337.—*Operations in the English Channel.*—There is a letter of Latouche-Tréville mentioning his long service in E. Desbrière's Projets et Tentatives, etc., II, 329; Bonaparte's plan of an expedition to Trinidad, etc., is from pp. 277, 278; the 21-gun vessels are as shown on the plan opposite p. 336; the stories of English projected descents in France and Holland current in France are from pp. 386 and 372. Nelson's views on the defence of England are from his memorandum printed in Mahan's Life of him, pp. 509 ff.; p. 522 has his ideas as to the difficulties of rowing a flotilla across the Channel.

CHAPTER V

Pp. 338–342.—*The Signature of Peace Preliminaries.*—E. Driault, La Politique Extérieure, etc., has Otto's earlier negotiations with Grenville, pp. 39 ff., the first steps in those of 1801, pp. 165 ff., 176 ff., and 185 ff., and the Berlin view of the Treaty, pp. 257, 258. Nelson's comment is in his Despatches, IV, p. 507; Fox's in Parliamentary History, XXXVI, 75; p. 1068 has Sheridan's inquiry. W. Cobbett showed that it was not the Ministry which was popular with the mob in Letters to Lord Hawkesbury, 1802, pp. 4–13. The Franco-Portuguese treaty is in Annual Register, 1801, Chronicle, pp. 293–295.

Pp. 342–344.—*The Armistice.*—Windham's argument is in Parliamentary History, XXXVI, pp. 116 ff. The statement that almost the whole of the agricultural labourers were on relief is on the authority of Communications to the Board of Agriculture, III, 1802, 41. The account of the debate on reopening the distilleries is in Annual Register for 1802, p. 69.

Pp. 344–345.—*Parliamentary discussion on the Civil List.*—The facts about the Civil List are in Pellew's Life of Sidmouth, II, 62; Fox's impersonation of the Civil List is in Parliamentary History, XXXVI, 393.

Pp. 345–347.—*Treaty of Amiens.*—Critical stages in the negotiations are noted in Pellew's Life of Sidmouth, II, 24, 27, 31. Driault's La Politique Extérieure, etc., gives Bonaparte's opposition to Russia as guarantee power, pp. 250 ff. Annual Register for 1803 has Andréossy's note of 10/3/03 on the evacuation of Malta, pp. 694 ff. Papers presented to Parliament, 1803, pp. 69 and 73, show how the Maltese question was disregarded in Vienna and Berlin. Whitworth's complaints of Lauderdale are in Browning's England and Napoleon in 1803, pp. 135 and 139. Sheridan's disapproval of visits to Paris is in Windham's Diary, 1866, p. 440.

Pp. 348–349.—*Parliamentary Debate on Bull-baiting.*—The debate is in Parliamentary History, XXXVI, 829 ff. Windham's reception by the boxing enthusiasts is referred to in the Life of Wilberforce, by his Sons, II, 366.

Pp. 349–350.—*The first Factory Act.*—The movement for factory legislation is traced to the Manchester Board of Health by P. Mantoux in La Révolution Industrielle, 1906, p. 493; the Parliamentary Register, XVII, 1802, has Bootle's speech, p. 199, and the discussion on applying the bill to free labour, pp. 446 ff.

P. 350.—*Popularity of Pitt.*—The honours to Pitt in the City are described in Annual Register, 1802, p. 184.

Pp. 351–352.—*Trial and Execution of Wall.*—The same volume has Wall's Trial and Execution, pp. 363, 364, and 560 ff. The proposal that dissection should be made an additional deterrent in case of burglaries, etc., is in Parliamentary History, XXXII, 918 ff.

Pp. 352–353.—*General Election.*—The Annual Register for 1802 mentions how the elections went in Ireland, p. 194, the riots in Liverpool, p. 424, and the demonstration in Middlesex, p. 186. Parliamentary History, XXXVI, has Sheridan's remark, p. 1065, and the debate, etc., on Nottingham affairs, pp. 1230 ff.

Pp. 353–356.—*Growing alarm at French aggression.*—The same volume has the debate on the army vote, p. 1044, and Fox's views on Switzerland, p. 1087. Lord Sheffield's words are in his letter in Lord Auckland's Correspondence, IV, 174. Papers presented to Parliament, 1803, has Bonaparte's complaint of Cobbett, pp. 19 ff., Otto's note, pp. 23 ff., and the complaint of the confiscation of the ships in 1802, pp. 240, 241. The confiscations of merchandise generally are dealt with in M. Philippson's article in the Revue Historique, Vol. LXXV, pp. 304, 305. The Annual Register for 1803 has the confiscation of 1801, p. 223.

Pp. 357–363.—*Rupture of the Peace.*—Browning's England and Napoleon in 1803 has Whitworth's first letter to Hawkesbury about Malta, pp. 16, 17; the Egyptian difficulty, p. 80; the Russian attitude about Malta, p. 54; Hawkesbury's note of 15th March, pp. 121 ff.; Bonaparte's scene with Whitworth on the 13th March, p. 116; Whitworth's despatch of 3rd March, pp. 95, 96; Bonaparte's concessions as to Malta being handed over to a Russian garrison, etc., p. 224; his disregard of the claims of individuals, pp. 48, 97, 232, 233. The passage regarding Malta in Whitworth's instructions is given in A. J. Grant and Harold Temperley's Europe, etc., p. 121 note. Grenville's scornful remark is in Buckingham's Memoirs of . . . George III, Vol. III, p. 268. The authority for the condition of French ports at the time is Desbrière's Projets et Tentatives, etc., 1902, III, 8. The idea of arming to test the views of Russia appears from the Diaries of the First Earl of Malmesbury, IV, 225; this also has his opinion of the peace as an experimental truce, p. 63; and the visit of the French speculators to London, p. 30. Alexander's observation is mentioned by Sorel, L'Europe et la Révolution Française, VI, 285. Bonaparte's summary of public affairs is in the Annual Register for 1803, p. 760. Driault has the French final offer in his Politique Extérieure de Premier Consul, pp. 411, 412. The undisguised entry of British ships into French ports appears from a letter in Historical MSS. Commission, Fortescue MSS., VI, p. 292.

Pp. 363–365.—*Pitt's relations with Addington.*—The Diaries of the First Earl of Malmesbury has Pitt's avowal of ambition to Canning, IV, 78, and the progress of the "Paper Plot", pp. 98 ff. The meeting between Pitt and Addington in January 1803 is in Pellew's Life of Sidmouth, II, 112; the offer to Pitt in March on p. 114. Pitt's reply to Wilberforce is in the latter's Life, III, 219; and the further offer in Stanhope's Life of Pitt, IV, 32 ff.

Pp. 365–366.—*Budget of 1803.*—Parliamentary History, XXXVI, has the budget, pp. 1594 ff., and the income tax debate, pp. 1662 ff. Addington's unpopularity in the City is mentioned in the Diaries of the First Earl of Malmesbury, IV, 259.

Pp. 367–369.—*Disturbances in Ireland.*—The Memoirs . . . of Viscount Castlereagh, IV, has the disturbances of 1802, p. 262; the arrangement of troops, pp. 282, 294, 295; the conciliation of Ulster, pp. 282, 286; the episode of the green uniforms, p. 334. The Annual Register for 1803 has the nature of Emmet's plot, pp. 296 ff., and the course of the rebellion, pp. 303 ff. Plowden's History of Ireland, 1811, gives how it was punished, I, 211–222.

P. 369.—*Addington's endeavours to strengthen his position.*—The story of the party going in one coach is Vansittart's in Pellew's Life of Sidmouth, II, 135 note.

CHAPTER VI

Pp. 370–372.—*Feasibility of an invasion of England.*—Napoleon's saying to Metternich is in the latter's Mémoires, 1880, I, 38 note. Nelson's

REFERENCES

memorandum is in Mahan's Life of him, pp. 509 ff. Desbrière's Projets et Tentatives has Bonaparte's idea of making the enemy believe the preparations for invasion to be a blind, III, 591; Humbert's boast, II (pubd. 1901), 286; and the agent's report, III, 329. The 45 successful descents on Great Britain are mentioned in Observations sur le manifeste du roi d'Angleterre, Paris, 1803, p. 45. Buckingham's Memoirs . . . of George III has T. Grenville's remarks, III, 64.

Pp. 373–374.—*Bonaparte's Plans.*—Desbrière's Projets et Tentatives, etc., III, has Bonaparte's inquiry about the fishing-boats, p. 25; order about manœuvres in Brest Roads, pp. 42, 43; the mobile batteries, pp. 121 ff.; the completion of the four ports, p. 467; the pretences of an invasion of Ireland from Brest, p. 575, or from the Texel, p. 577; his plans to make the British believe these as well as the expeditions to the Morea to be genuine, pp. 591, 592; the correspondence with Ganteaume, p. 632.

Pp. 374–378.—*The naval situation.*—The same volume has the numbers of French ships of the line escaped from the West Indies, pp. 43 and 246, 247; and the three in Brest, p. 41. P. 149 of Vol. IV gives the figure in Brest a year later, p. 363 the final number. The Blockade of Brest, Vol. I, has Keith's strength, pp. 169–174; the arrangement of Cornwallis's ships, Introduction, p. xxx; his and Pellew's numbers in 1803, pp. 175–179; the bet about the coasting vessels, p. 81. St. Vincent's reply to Nelson's complaint is in the latter's Despatches, V, pp. 283, 284.

Pp. 378–379.—*The French flotilla.*—Desbrière's Projets et Tentatives, etc., has the French disaster of November 1803, III, 544; that of 1804, IV, 107–110; the number of vessels of the flotilla projected, III, 94; of those ready in the Channel and Ostend and the Bay of Biscay, III, 566–568; the number which got round from there, IV, 74; Napoleon's unwillingness to recognize the impossibility of bringing round more, IV, 67 note.

Pp. 379–380.—*Dance's action with Linois.*—Dance's letter is in Naval Chronicle, XII, 137 ff.

Pp. 381–386.—*The land defence of the United Kingdom.*—The numbers of the forces at the opening of war are taken from Hon. J. Fortescue's County Lieutenancies, etc., pp. 9, 10. Yorke's introduction of the Army of Reserve Bill is in Parliamentary History, XXXVI, 1603 ff. Hansard has the strength in December 1803, I, 1723. Windham's remark on the flow of volunteers, p. 1686; the total in December, pp. 1725, 1726; the acceptance of the adjutant suggestion, II, 218, 219; Fox's scepticism as to volunteers, I, 1736; Craufurd's ideas, p. 587; Pitt's criticism of them, p. 628; the false alarm in Yorkshire, VI, 1003. Horner observed on the lack of the enthusiasm of Tudor times and failure to bring the Catholics in, in his Memoirs, I, 231. Stanhope has the King's joke and Pitt's, Life of Pitt, IV, 96 and 82. William Pitt and the Great War, by J. H. Rose, has Dundas's pronouncement in favour of Pitt's corps, p. 492. The Annual Register for 1804 has the proceedings of the Scottish Association, pp. 522 ff. Sir H. Bunbury's Great War with France, 1854, gives the military plans of Dundas, etc., I, 176 ff. The Diary of Colchester has the invasion scare of Christmas, 1803, and plans, I, 469 ff.

Pp. 386–390.—*Criticism of the measures of Government.*—Horner describes Pitt's speech in Fox's support in a letter in his Memoirs, I, 248, 249. The Annual Register for 1804 gives the Méhée de la Touche affair, pp. 162 ff., 600 ff., 616 ff. The Letters and Papers of Lord Barham, Navy Records Society, 1911, Vol. III, gives the naval strength under St. Vincent, p. 43. Melville's account of the state of the ships is in Hansard, V, 81, 82. Nelson's Despatches show how he was expected to man the fleet, V, 231, 403. The letter to the Morning Chronicle is in the number for April 17, 1804. The Attorney-General's statement is in Naval Chronicle, VI, p. 242.

Pp. 390–391.—*Resignation of Addington.*—Colchester's Diary gives an account of the King's illness, I, 476–482. Stanhope's Life of Pitt has Addington's negotiations with Pitt, IV, 151 ff., the latter's letter to the King, App. i ff., and Eldon's part in all this, App. viii ff., and p. 166.

Pp. 391–395.—*Pitt's second Administration.*—The same volume contains the account of Pitt's interview with George III, pp. 169 ff., and the story about the egg-spoon, p. 87. The Diaries, etc., of George Rose has Pitt's efforts to bring George to accept Fox, II, 126 ff., and 198 ff. Holland discusses Pitt's aloofness from the aristocracy in his Memoirs of the Whig Party, I, 130. Windham appears as go-between with Fox in the Windham Papers, II, 230. The attempt to obtain Moira is from Yonge's Life of Liverpool, I, 150. The observation of Gentz is in Briefe von und an Friedrich von Gentz, 1913, III, i, p. 49.

CHAPTER VII

Pp. 396–400.—*The new Ministry's task in the Navy and Army.*—Camden's statement showing the number of ships in commission is in Hansard, V, 471; Pitt's declaration that he would remain in office if it was thrown out in Vol. II, p. 748; the Civil List grant on p. 906; Sheridan's criticism, III, 732; and Hawkesbury's defence, p. 803; Commons Journals, Vol. LX, p. 626, has the strength of the Additional Force. Hon. J. Fortescue's County Lieutenancies, etc., describes the insurance system, pp. 40 ff. The Life of Wilberforce has Pitt's complaint to him, III, 211. The correspondence on Buckingham's views for his son is in Buckingham's Memoirs . . . of George III, Vol. IV, 244 ff.

Pp. 400–401.—*The menace of invasion.*—The totals of war-vessels are given in Desbrière's Projets et Tentatives, etc., IV, 225; Soult's remarks, pp. 226, 227; Villeneuve's complaints, pp. 266, 267 and 272. The jokes about the catamaran project are in Hansard, III, 784.

Pp. 401–404.—*Outbreak of War with Spain.*—Desbrière has the details of the subsidy, Projets et Tentatives, etc., III, 76; the disputes as to

REFERENCES

breaches of neutrality in Spain, IV, 240–243; and the convention of 1805, pp. 258 ff. The two breaches of Spanish neutrality in the West Indies appear from Hansard, III, 204, 206, 237; Grenville's censure, pp. 354 ff. The account of Moore's capture of the treasure ships is from his despatch, published in the Annual Register, 1804, pp. 555 ff., which has also the Spanish declaration of war, pp. 699 ff.

Pp. 404–405.—*Formation of the Third Coalition.*—The same book has the Treaty with Russia, pp. 656 ff.

Pp. 405–407.—*Napoleon's naval plans.*—Desbrière's Projets et Tentatives, etc., Vol. III, has the plan of an expedition to save Martinique, p. 604. Vol. IV has the plan of the 29th of September, 1804, p. 188; that for Ireland, p. 192; the dropping of the scheme, pp. 199 ff. and 210 ff.; the neglect of Boulogne harbour, p. 378; Napoleon's winter plan of campaign, pp. 273 ff.; Missiessy's escape, p. 306; Villeneuve's, p. 298; his complaints, p. 329; his fear of Nelson, p. 296; Napoleon's revised plan, pp. 363, 364; his refusal of leave to Ganteaume to fight, p. 469.

Pp. 407–410.—*Nelson's pursuit of Villeneuve to the West Indies.*—The same volume has Villeneuve's departure, pp. 479, 480; his passage to the West Indies, p. 529; the fears for Jamaica, pp. 497–499; Missiessy's successes, pp. 319, 320; and Napoleon's divination of Villeneuve's return, p. 636. The reference to Nelson's Diary is to the MS. in the British Museum under date April 16, 1805. Maurice's information is from Corbett's Campaign of Trafalgar, p. 164.

Pp. 410–411.—*Military measures of the Government.*—The reduction of the militia, etc., is from Hansard, IV, 73. The destination of the second expedition is from Castlereagh's Memoirs, VI, 151, and the total strengths from p. 28.

Pp. 411–413.—*The Tenth Report and the Fall of Melville.*—Wilberforce's Life has his account of Pitt's reading the Report, III, 218, and that of his appealing look just before Wilberforce made his fatal speech, p. 221. Pitt's difficulty in getting a hearing appears from Hansard, IV, 279, 280; Wilberforce's speech and the rest of the debate is on pp. 317–320; the general description of the debate, including the episode of the view halloo, from Stanhope's Life of Pitt, IV, 281–284; Pitt's tears from Malmesbury's Diaries, IV, 347 note.

Pp. 413–414.—*Budget of 1806.*—The budget debate is in Hansard, III, 543 ff., and the debate on the horse tax on pp. 861 ff.

Pp. 414–415.—*Debates on the Catholic petition.*—The passage from Limerick's speech is in Hansard, IV, 727.

Pp. 415–417.—*Measures to counteract Napoleon's naval schemes.*—Desbrière, Projets et Tentatives, etc., IV, has Napoleon's orders to Villeneuve, pp. 513 ff.; the arrangement of transport, pp. 464 ff.; and Napoleon's divination of Villeneuve's arrival, pp. 659, 660. Barham's Letters, III, 258, has that to Cornwallis.

Pp. 417–420.—*Battle of the 22nd of July.*—Desbrière, Projets et Tentatives, IV, has Villeneuve's impressions afterwards, pp. 716, 717; the state of his men and ships, p. 723; his depression, p. 726; Gravina's and his own representations as to the situation, pp. 775–777.

Pp. 420–424.—*Villeneuve's retirement to Cadiz.*—The same volume has Villeneuve's decision of the 15th of August, p. 786; Napoleon's saying on Austria, p. 751 note; his exhortation to Villeneuve of the 13th, p. 752; the note of Decrès upon which he abandoned the plan of ordering Villeneuve to the Channel, p. 814; his letter to Talleyrand, pp. 816, 817; and his breaking up of the Boulogne camp, p. 819; Collingwood's letter of July 21st is in the Selection from his Correspondence, p. 107, his letter of August 21st on p. 109. Desbrière's Campagne Maritime de 1805 has the strength of the naval forces under Ganteaume, Villeneuve in Spain, and under Allemand, pp. 98, 99, 79, 76; the conjecture that Villeneuve would turn south, pp. 110 ff. and on p. 9 of the Documents Annexes in that volume. The plan of the seven cruising stations is on p. 15. The movement of August 27th is noticed in Naval Chronicle, XIII, 53–55.

P. 424.—*Expedition to the Cape of Good Hope.*—Desbrière's Projets et Tentatives, IV, gives Napoleon's order about the convoy, p. 823.

Pp. 424–428.—*Nelson's departure for the fleet off Cadiz.*—The saying, "Choose yourself", etc., is from Rev. J. S. Clarke and J. McArthur's Life of Nelson (1840), III, 118. Disputes between naval officers were dealt with in Parliament, vide Hansard, III, 261 ff. and 635 ff.; other charges are noticed in Naval Chronicles, XIII, p. 329, XIV, pp. 84, 85. Minto's observation is in his Life, III, 363. Nelson's Despatches, VII, has Duff's remark, p. 71; Nelson's letter to Rose, p. 80; his order about the Patriotic Fund, p. 106; that about men going to hospital, p. 102; and the saying about Berry, p. 117. The circumstances of his last private letters are in Naval Chronicle, XV, 37. Napoleon's censure of and instructions to Villeneuve are in Desbrière's Projets et Tentatives, etc., IV, 752 ff., 813, the expression "fiery admiral", p. 746, the orders to join the Cartagena squadron, etc., pp. 823, 824. The same author has the motives which decided Villeneuve to go out, Campagne Maritime de 1805, Documents Annexes, p. 102.

Pp. 428–438.—*Battle of Trafalgar.*—Codrington's letter is in Lady Bourchier's Memoir of him, I, 57. Desbrière, Campagne Maritime de 1805, has the French night before the battle, Documents Annexes, pp. 197 and 247; Villeneuve's order as to meeting the attack, ib. 122; his order as to commencing firing, ib. 129; the difficulty of hitting the British ships, ib. 180; the losses of the Redoutable, p. 201; and Magon's death, pp. 234, 235. The Admiralty Committee's Report on Trafalgar is the authority for the position of the British fleet on the morning of the 21st, the various tactical signals, and the manner in which the battle was engaged. The accounts of the "England expects" signal are in Nelson's Despatches, VII, 150, which has also Blackwood's letter to his wife, p. 224. The naval tradition of close battle is in Naval Chronicle, XV, 305. Nelson's prayer is copied from his brother Earl Nelson's copy ("several times repeatedly compared with the original"), in British Museum, Add. MSS. 34992 f. 15. The various British losses are taken from

James's Naval History, IV, 79; the French and Spanish losses from Desbrière's work cited above, Documents Annexes, pp. 224 and 226.

Pp. 438–441.—*Death of Nelson.*—The general scene after the action is from logs, etc., in Great Sea Fights, particularly pp. 153 and 251. The details as to Nelson's death are from Beatty's and Scott's accounts in Nelson's Despatches, VII, 252, etc., which has also Collingwood's letter to Pasley, p. 241. J. S. Tucker's Memoirs of St. Vincent, 1843, has his remark on the bombardment of Algiers, II, 412. Collingwood's despatch is in the Selection from his Correspondence, p. 119.

Pp. 441–443.—*Sequel to the Battle of Trafalgar.*—Napoleon's speech is in the Moniteur of 3rd March, 1806. Collingwood's reason for remaining at sea is in the Selection from his Correspondence, p. 156; the letters which passed between him and the Spanish on pp. 142 ff. Desbrière, Campagne Maritime de 1805, in his Documents Annexes, has Cosmao-Kerjulien's effort, pp. 219 ff., and the recapture of the three ships by their own crews, pp. 185, 225, 237. The rest of the fate of the prizes is taken from James's Naval History, IV, 92. The Spanish treatment of shipwrecked sailors is mentioned in Naval Chronicle, XIV, 458, and that of the friend of Codrington in Lady Bourchier's Memoir of him, I, 73.

Pp. 443–444.—*Strachan's action with Dumanoir.*—Desbrière, Projets et Tentatives, IV, has Allemand sinking 22 neutrals, p. 785; his movements and instructions, pp. 791 ff.

Pp. 444–446.—*Napoleon's defeat of the Third Coalition.*—The intention to raise Cathcart's force to 65,000 men in 257 transports is on the authority of J. H. Rose's William Pitt and the Great War, p. 551.

Pp. 446–447.—*Pitt's last days.*—Wellesley's account of Pitt is in Stanhope's life of him, IV, 346, 347; Pitt's letter to Castlereagh on pp. 366 ff. His relations with The Times are in H. R. Fox Bourne's English Newspapers, 1887, Vol. I, 281.

Pp. 447–450.—*Death of Pitt.*—Horner's Memoirs, Vol. I, has Windham's disparaging remarks on Pitt, p. 316, and Horner's own criticism on his speaking, p. 12. Wilberforce's saying about the false principle of honour is in his Life, III, 220; the opinion of his speech on the Slave Trade, II, 345, 346; his excellence as a farmer, III, 71, 72. William Napier's story is in his Life, I, 31, 32. The second Lord Malmesbury's opinion is in the Diaries of the First, IV, 347 note. Pitt's sleeping hours are mentioned by Farington, Diary, V, 162. Woronzow's remark is in Historical MSS. Commission, Fortescue MSS., VI, p. 259. Pitt and Napoleon, by J. H. Rose, is the authority for what George III had to put up with, p. 94. The Memoirs of Lady Hester Stanhope has the fire darting from Pitt's eyes, II, 69. Napoleon's tribute is in A. Thiers's Histoire du Consulat et de l'Empire, 1861, XIX, 620, and Byron's in Thomas Moore's Life of him, 1832, Vol. II, 211.

BIBLIOGRAPHY

OF BOOKS, ETC., CHIEFLY CONSULTED, WITH DATES OF EDITIONS USED

The first of the two lists under each chapter gives the more important authorities.

As the lists are long, asterisks have been used to mark books and articles of importance for the subjects of which they treat, or—in the case of biographies—of importance for general history.

A dagger denotes the presence of valuable original authorities.

GENERAL

 Alison, Sir Archibald. Lives of Lord Castlereagh and Sir Charles Stewart. Vol. I. 1861.
†Annual Registers.
*Auckland, The Journal and Correspondence of William, First Lord. Vol. IV. 1862.
 Bamford, Samuel. Early Days. 1893.
 Brougham, Lord, Life and Times of. By himself. Vol. I. 1871.
  Historical Sketches of Statesmen who flourished in the time of George III. 1839.
 Brougham and his Early Friends. London. Privately printed. 1908.
*†Buckingham, Duke of. Memoirs of the Court and Cabinets of George III. Vol. III. 1855.
*The Cambridge History of British Foreign Policy. Vol. I. 1922.
 Cambridge Historical Journal.
*The Cambridge Modern History. Vol. IX. 1906.
 Campbell, John Lord. Lives of the Lord Chancellors. Vols. VI, VII. 1847.
*†Castlereagh, Memoirs and Correspondence of Viscount. Vols. I–VI. 1848–1851.
*Clowes, W. Laird. The Royal Navy. A History. Vols. IV, V. 1899–1900.
†Commons Journals.
*†Cornwallis Correspondence. Vols. II, III. 1859.
 Creevey Papers, The. Vol. I. 1904.
 Dictionary of National Biography.
 Edinburgh Review.
 English Historical Review.
 Farington Diary, The. Vols. I–VI. 1922–1926.
 Fox, Memorials and Correspondence of. 1853–1857.
 Gillray, James. Works. 1873.
 Gower, Lord Granville Leveson-. Private Correspondence. 1916.

Grego, J. Rowlandson the Càricaturist. 1880.
*†Hansard's Parliamentary Debates.
*†Historical MSS. Commission. Fortescue MSS. (Dropmore). Vols. VI, VII. 1908–1910.
*†Holland, Lord. Memoirs of the Whig Party during my Time. 1852.
Holland, Journal of Elizabeth Lady. 1909.
Holland, Lady. Memoir of Sydney Smith. Vol. I. 1855.
Horner, Francis. Memoirs and Correspondence. 1843.
*James, W. Naval History. Vols. III, IV. 1837.
Mackintosh, R. J. Memoirs of the Life of Sir James Mackintosh. Vol. I. 1835.
*Mahan, Capt. A. T. The Influence of Sea Power upon the French Revolution and Empire. Vol. II. 1892.
* Life of Nelson. 1899.
*†Malmesbury, Diaries of the First Earl of. Vol. IV. 1844.
Minto, Life and Letters of Sir Gilbert Elliot, First Earl of Minto. Vol. III. 1874.
†Naval Chronicle. 1799 ff.
*†Nelson, Despatches and Letters of Lord. Vols. IV–VII. 1844–1846.
†Newspapers, as Morning Chronicle, Morning Post, Times; also Moniteur or Gazette Nationale.
*†Parliamentary History.
*†Pellew, Hon. George. Life of Viscount Sidmouth. Vols. I, II. 1847.
Phipps, Hon. Edmund. Memoirs of the Political and Literary Life of R. Plumer Ward. Vol. I. 1850.
*Porter, G. R. The Progress of the Nation. 1851.
Public Characters. 1803–1809.
*Romilly, Memoirs of the Life of Sir S. By himself. 1841.
*Rose, The Diaries and Correspondence of the Right Honourable George. 1860.
*†Rose, J. Holland. W. Pitt and National Revival. 1911.
*† W. Pitt and the Great War. 1911.
†Pitt and Napoleon. 1912.
*Rosebery, Earl of. Pitt. 1891.
*†Russell, Earl. Life and Times of Fox. 1866.
Sandford, Mrs. Henry. Thomas Poole and his Friends. Vol. II. 1888.
*†Sichel, Walter. Sheridan. 1909.
*Smart, William. Economic Annals of the Nineteenth Century. Vol. I. 1910.
*Sorel, A. L'Europe et la Révolution Française. Vols. VI, VII. Paris. 1903–1904.
Spirit of the Public Journals, The. 1801 ff.
*†Stanhope, Earl. Life of Pitt. 1861–1862.
Stanhope, Memoirs of Lady Hester. 1845.
Stirling, A. M. W. Coke of Norfolk and his Friends. 1908.

BIBLIOGRAPHY

*Temperley, H. W. V. Life of Canning. 1905.
*Treitschke, Heinrich von. Deutsche Geschichte im 19ten Jahrhundert. Vol. I. 1879.
*Trevelyan, G. M. Lord Grey of the Reform Bill. 1920.
*†Twiss, Horace. The Public and Private Life of Lord Chancellor Eldon. Vol. I. 1844.
*†Walpole, Spencer. The Life of Rt. Hon. Spencer Perceval. Vol. I. 1874.
*†Wilberforce, Life of. By his Sons. Vols. I–III. 1838.
Wilson, Sir Robert, Life of. 1862.
Windham Papers, The. 1913.
Yonge, C. D. Life and Administration of Lord Liverpool. Vol. I. 1868.
Young, Arthur. Autobiography. 1898.

CHAPTER I

*†Baert, Baron. Tableau de la Grande Bretagne. Paris. 1800.
*†Census Abstract for 1801. 1802.
*Clapham, J. H. An Economic History of Great Britain. 1926.
*Cunningham, W. Growth of English Industry and Commerce. Vol. I. 1903.
*†Davies, Rev. D. Case of Labourers in Husbandry stated and considered. 1795.
*†Davies, E. The Small Landholder, 1780–1832, in the Light of the Land Tax Assessments. Economic History Review. Vol. I, No. 1. 1927.
*†Eden, Sir F. State of the Poor. 1797.
*Ernle, Lord. English Farming Past and Present. 1919.
†Ferri de St. Constant, J. L. Londres et les Anglais. 1804.
Fiévée, J. Lettres sur l'Angleterre. 1802.
**Halévy, E. Histoire du Peuple Anglais. Vol. I. 1923.
*†Hammond, J. L. and B. The Skilled Labourer. 1919.
†The Village Labourer. 1920.
*Hasbach, Dr. W. History of the English Agricultural Labourer. Translation. 1920.
*Slater, Gilbert. English Peasantry and the Enclosure of Common Fields. 1907.
*Smith, Adam. An Inquiry into the Nature and Causes of the Wealth of Nations. (Editions from 3rd onwards.)
*Tooke, T. History of Prices. Vol. I. 1838.

Abu Taleb Khan, Travels of Mirza. 1814.
†Agricultural State of the Kingdom. 1816.

Aikin, J. A Description of the Country from thirty to forty miles round Manchester. 1795.
England Delineated. 1795.
†Annals of Agriculture. 1796–1805.
(Arbuthnot, John.) An Inquiry into the Connection between the Present Price of Provisions and the size of Farms, etc. 1773.
Attempt to estimate the increase of the Number of Poor during the interval of 1785 and 1803, etc. 1811.
†Austen, Jane. Novels.
Babeau, Albert. Les Anglais en France. Paris. 1898.
*Baines, (Sir) Edward. An Account of the Woollen Trade in Yorkshire. Included in Yorkshire Past and Present, by T. Baines, Vol. I. (1871.)
* History of the Cotton Manufacture in Great Britain. 1835.
Baring Gould, S. Old Country Life. 1890.
Beyträge zur Kentniss vorzüglich des Innern von England und seinen Einwohnern. Lemgo. 1796.
Bowley, A. L. Wages in the United Kingdom. 1900.
* Articles on Wages in the Journals of the Royal Statistical Society. Vols. LXI, LXII, LXV. 1899–1902.
†Brown, John. Memoirs of Robert Blincoe. 1832.
Brown, Robert. General View of the Agriculture of Yorkshire. West Riding. 1799.
Bunsen, Baron. Memoirs of B. G. Niebuhr. Vol. I. 1852.
Campe, J. H. Reise durch England u.s.w. Braunschweig. 1803.
*Chapman, S. J. The Lancashire Cotton Industry. 1904.
*Clarkson, T. History of the Abolition of Slave Trade. 1808.
Clubs of London, The. 1832.
Cobbett, William. Life of himself. 1809.
Rural Rides. 1885.
Coleridge, S. T. Essays on his own Times. Vol. II. 1850.
Colquhoun, P. A new and appropriate System of Education for the Labouring People. 1806.
*† A Treatise on the Police of the Metropolis. 1800.
†Communications to the Board of Agriculture. 1797–1806.
†Comparative Account of the Population. 1801–1831. (Government Account.) 1831.
†(Corry, J.) History of Liverpool. 1810.
Cottle, Joseph. Early Recollections. 1837.
Curtler, W. H. R. The Enclosure and Redistribution of our Land. 1920.
*Dale, R. W. History of English Congregationalism. 1907.
*Daniels, G. W. The Early English Cotton Industry. 1920.
De Lévis (Duke). L'Angleterre au Commencement du 19me Siècle. Paris. 1814.
English Encyclopædia. 1802.

BIBLIOGRAPHY 491

An Enquiry into the advantages and disadvantages resulting from Bills of Inclosure. 1780.
*Felkin, William. A History of the Machine-Wrought Hosiery and Lace Manufactures. 1867.
Fitzmaurice, Lord Edmond. Life of William Earl of Shelburne, afterwards first Marquis of Lansdowne. Vol. III. 1876.
(Forster, Nathaniel.) An Enquiry into the Causes of the Present High Price of Provisions. 1767.
*Fox Bourne, H. R. English Newspapers. 1887.
*Galloway, Robert L. Annals of Coal-mining. 1898.
"George Eliot." Novels—Adam Bede, Scenes from Clerical Life and Silas Marner.
General Report on Enclosures. Drawn up by order of the Board of Agriculture. 1808.
*Gonner, (Sir) E. C. R. Common Land and Enclosure. 1912.
Paper in Journal of the Royal Statistical Society. Vol. LXXVI, p. 261. 1913.
Gregory, A. Robert Raikes. 1890.
*Griffith, G. T. Population Problems of the Age of Malthus. 1926.
Gunning, H., Reminiscences. 1854.
Hammond, J. L. and B. The Town Labourer. 1917.
†Hardwicke MSS.—British Museum Add. MSS. 35646, ff. 247–250— Letter on decay in a rural parish in the North of England.
Held, A. Zwei Bücher zur socialen Geschichte Englands. Leipzig. 1881.
Hirst, W. History of the Woollen Trade for the last sixty years. Leeds. 1844.
Hunter, A. Georgical Essays. York. 1803–1804.
Hutton, William. History of Birmingham. 1783.
† Life of himself. 1816.
Inquiry into the connection between the present Price of Provisions and the Size of Farms. 1773.
Ivimey, J. A History of the English Baptists, etc. Vol. IV. 1830.
Jesse, Capt. W. Life of Beau Brummell. 1927.
Lady's Monthly Museum.
Langford, J. A. A Century of Birmingham Life. 1868.
Leatham, I. General view of the Agriculture of the East Riding of Yorkshire. 1794.
Leigh Hunt. Autobiography. 1850.
A Letter to Sir T. C. Bunbury on the Poor Rates, etc. By a Suffolk Gentleman. 1795.
Levy, Hermann. Large and Small Holdings. 1911.
Lewis, John. Uniting and Monopolizing Farms plainly proved disadvantageous to the Landowners, etc. Ipswich. (1802.)
*Lipson, E. History of the English Woollen and Worsted Industries. 1921.
Lucas, E. V. The Life of Charles Lamb. 1910.

*Malcolm, J. P. Anecdotes of the Manners and Customs of London. 1810.
*Mantoux, P. La Révolution au XVIIIme siècle. 1906.
*Marshall, W. A Review . . . of the Reports to the Board of Agriculture, Midland Department. York. 1815.
* A Review . . . of the Reports to the Board of Agriculture, Southern and Peninsular Department. York. 1817.
* Rural Economy of Gloucestershire. 1796.
* Rural Economy of the West of England. 1796.
* Rural Economy of Yorkshire. 1796.
Middleton, John. View of the Agriculture of Middlesex. 1798.
*Muir, Ramsay. History of Liverpool. 1907.
Nicholls, J. F., and John Taylor. Bristol Past and Present. Vol. III. 1882.
Niebuhr, B. G. Mémoire sur la guerre entre l'Angleterre et la France. 1806. In Nachgelassene Schriften. Hamburg. 1842.
Observations on "An Enquiry into the advantages and disadvantages resulting from Bills of Inclosure." 1781.
*Overton, J. H. The English Church in the 19th Century—1800–1833. 1894.
*Owen, Robert. Life of himself. Vol. I. 1857.
Parish Registers. 1801. (Report.) 1802.
Picton, (Sir) J. A. Memorials of Liverpool. 1875.
Pitt, William (of Wolverhampton). General View of the Agriculture of the County of Stafford. 1808.
Political Inquiry into the consequences of enclosing waste land. 1785.
Porteus, Life of Dr. By a Layman. 1812.
Pratt, S. J. Cottage Pictures. 1803.
†Radcliffe, W. Origin of the New System of Manufacture, commonly called "Power-loom Weaving", etc. Stockport. 1828.
Recollections of the Table Talk of Samuel Rogers. 1856.
Rennie, G. General View of the Agriculture of the West Riding of Yorkshire. 1794.
†Report from the Select Committee on Hand-loom Weavers' Petitions. 1834.
†Report from the Select Committee on the Woollen Manufacture of England. 1806.
†Reports from the Select Committee on Artizans and Machinery. 1824.
†Reports of the Society for Bettering the Condition of the Poor. 1798–1808.
*Richardson, Charles. The Complete Fox-Hunter. (1908.)
(Rogers, Samuel. See "Recollections", etc.)
Rogers, Thorold. Six Centuries of Work and Wages. 1903.
Saint-Fond, B. F. Voyage en Angleterre. 1797.
Sandford, Mrs. (Margaret E.). Thomas Poole and his friends. 1888.
Shelley, Diary of Frances Lady. 1912.
†Simond, Louis. Voyage en Angleterre pendant 1810 et 1811. 1817.

BIBLIOGRAPHY 493

Sinclair, Correspondence of the Right Honourable Sir John. 1831.
†(Southey, Robert.) Letters from England by Don Manuel Alvarez Espriella. 1807.
Steffen, Gustaf F. Studien zur Geschichte der englischen Lohnarbeiter. Translation into German. 1904.
Stone, Thomas. Suggestions for rendering the Inclosure, etc., a source of population and riches. 1787.
*Taylor, W. Cooke. Notes of a Tour in the Manufacturing Districts of Lancashire. 1842.
*Thornton, H. An Enquiry into the Nature and Effects of the Paper Currency of Great Britain. 1802.
Tour through the South of England, etc. 1793.
*Townsend, W. J., and others. A New History of Methodism. 1909.
Transactions of the Royal Society of Arts. 1801–1805.
Trimmer, Mrs. Sarah. Reflections upon the Education of Children in Charity Schools, etc. 1792.
Tuke "Junior". Agriculture of the North Riding of Yorkshire. 1794.
Unwin, G. Samuel Oldknow and the Arkwrights. 1924.
Ure, Dr. A. Cotton Manufacture of Great Britain. 1861.
*Wallas, Graham. Life of Francis Place. 1898.
Watson. Anecdotes of the Life of Richard Watson, Bishop of Landaff. 1818.
Wendeborn, G. F. A. Reise durch einige. . . . Provinzen Englands. 1793.
Whyte, J. C. History of the British Turf. 1840.
Wilberforce, W. A. Practical View of the Prevailing Religious System of Professed Christians.
Wollstonecraft, Mary. Vindication of the Rights of Woman. 1891.
Wood, G. H. History of Wages in the Cotton Trade. 1910.
†Young, Arthur. Farmer's Letters. 1771.
* General View of the Agriculture of Norfolk. 1804.
Political Arithmetic. 1774.
* Six Months' Tour in the North of England. 1771.
* View of the Agriculture of Lincoln. By the Secretary to the Board of Agriculture. 1799.

CHAPTER II

*Dowell, Stephen. History of Taxation and Taxes in England. 1888.
*Liverpool, Earl of. A Treatise on the Coins of the Realm. 1805.
*May, T. E. Constitutional History of England. 1861–1863.
*Oldfield, T. H. B. Representative History of Great Britain and Ireland. 1816.
*Porritt, E. Unreformed House of Commons. 1903.

*†Webb, Sidney and Beatrice. English Local Government: The Manor and the Borough. 1908.
*† English Local Government: The Parish and the County. 1906.
*† English Local Government: Statutory Authorities. 1922.
*† English Prisons under Local Government. 1922.

Adolphus, John. The Political State of the British Empire. 1818.
*Anson, Sir William. Law and Custom of the Constitution. 1897–1908.
Anti-Jacobin. 1799.
Attempt to estimate the increase of the Number of the Poor during the interval of 1785 and 1803, etc. 1811.
Atton, H., and H. H. Holland. The King's Customs. 1908–1910.
Bagot, Josceline. George Canning and his friends. Vol. I. 1909.
Bastable, C. F. Public Finance. 1892.
Beatson, R. Chronological Register of both Houses of Parliament. 1807.
Bentham, Jeremy. Works, Vol. IV. (Prisons, etc.) 1843.
Black Book, The. 1820.
†Bucks Quarter Sessions Records, preserved at Aylesbury. Vol. XXVI, for 1800–1801.
Callwell, Sir J. An Enquiry concerning the Restrictions laid on the Trade of Ireland. Appended to "Documents relative to the Affairs of Ireland." 1766.
†Cheshire Quarter Sessions Records preserved at Chester. For 1800–1802.
*Clapham, J. H. The Economic History of Great Britain. 1926.
Clubs of London, The. Vol. II. 1832.
*Colquhoun, P. A General View of the National Police System. 1799.
* A Treatise on the Functions and Duties of a Constable. 1803.
A Treatise on Indigence. 1806.
*† A Treatise on the Police of the Metropolis. 1800.
De Lolme, J. L. The Constitution of England. 1807.
*Dicey, A. V. Law and Public Opinion in England. 1905.
Law of the Constitution. 1889.
Dudley, Rev. (Sir) H. B. (Rev. Henry Bate). A few Observations respecting the present state of the poor, etc. 1802.
Extraordinary Black Book, The. 1831.
Fletcher, Joseph. Article on Statistics of the Municipal Institutions of the English towns, in Journal of the Royal Statistical Society. Vol. V, p. 97. 1842.
Francis, J. History of the Bank of England. (1847.)
Fry, K. F. (Katherine Fry) and R. E. C. Memoir of the Life of Elizabeth Fry. Vol. I. 1847.
*Gneist, Dr. Rudolf. Self-government—Communalverfassung und Verwaltungsgerichte in England. 1871.

BIBLIOGRAPHY

Grellier, J. J. The Terms of all the Loans, etc. 1802.
Hardwicke MSS.—British Museum Add. MSS. 35646, f. 26—Letter of October 1806 from Lord Charleville, naming £3,000 as regular price for a parliamentary borough for the duration of Parliament.
†Hertford Sessions Rolls. Vol. II. 1905.
Holcroft, T. A Narrative of facts relating to a prosecution for High Treason. 1795.
*†Howard, John. The State of the Prisons in England and Wales, etc. 1780.
†Howell, T. B. State Trials. Vols. 22–27.
*Hutchins, B. L., and A. Harrison. A History of Factory Legislation. 1911.
†Hutton, W. Courts of Requests. 1787.
Jerningham Letters, The. 1896.
*Joyce, H. The History of the Post Office. 1893.
*Kennedy, William. English Taxation. 1913.
*Lee, Captain W. L. Melville. A History of the Police in England. 1901.
Letters from an Irish Student. 1809.
Lewins, William. Her Majesty's Mails. 1864.
McCulloch, J. R. Essay on the Circumstances which determine the Rate of Wages and the Condition of the Labouring Classes. 1826.
Manchester Court Leet Records. Vol. IX. 1889.
(Newbury, Francis.) Thoughts on Taxation. By a Commissioner of Taxes. 1799.
Neild, J. Account of Persons confined for Debt in the various Prisons. 1800.
  State of the Prisons in England, etc. 1812.
Papendick. Mrs. Papendick's journals. 1887.
Paris Archives—A.F. IV, Cart. 1597, Plaq. 2, pp. 41 ff.—for strength of revolutionary feeling about 1795.
†Place MSS.—British Museum Add. MSS. 27808—containing historical sketch of Corresponding Society's activities.
†   British Museum Add. MSS. 27810, ff. 91 ff.—Letter on reform agitation under Pitt.
Portsmouth Guildhall Records (Muniment Room). Volume entitled "Court Records 1800–1816."
  Volume entitled "Portsmouth Commissioners 1800."
Recollections of the Table Talk of Samuel Rogers. 1856.
Reflections on the Increase of the English Peerage. 1798.
†Reports from Commissioners on Municipal Corporations. 1835.
Report from the Select Committee on Sinecures. First Report. 1810. Second Report. 1811.
Ricardo, David. Works. 1846.
(Rogers, Samuel. See "Recollections", etc.)

496 ENGLAND IN THE NINETEENTH CENTURY

Rose, George. A Brief Examination of the increase of Revenue, etc., of Great Britain from 1792 to 1799. 1799.
Sheffield, Lord. Strictures on the Necessity . . . of the Navigation and Colonial System. 1804.
Sinclair, Sir J. History of the Public Revenue. 1803.
Tawney, R. H. The Assessment of Wages by the Justices of the Peace. From page 307 of Vierteljahrschrift für Sozial- und Wirtschaftsgeschichte, Vol. XI. Leipzig. 1913.
*Trevelyan (Sir), G. O. Early History of Charles James Fox. 1881.
*†Webb, Sidney and Beatrice. English Local Government. The Story of the King's Highway. 1913.
* The History of Trade Unionism. 1902.
†Wraxall, Memoirs of Sir Nathaniel. Vol. V. 1884.

CHAPTER III

*Lecky, W. E. H. A History of Ireland. Vols. III–V. 1903.
*O'Brien, George. The Economic History of Ireland in the Eighteenth Century. 1918.
*O'Connor, Sir James. History of Ireland. Vol. I. 1925.
*Porritt, E. Unreformed House of Commons. Vol. II. 1903.
*†Wakefield, Edward. An Account of Ireland. 1812.
*†Young, Arthur. A Tour in Ireland. 8vo. edition. 1780.

---

*†Baert, Baron. Tableau de la Grande Bretagne. Vol. I. Paris. 1800.
Barrington, Recollections of Jonah. Pubd. by T. Fisher Unwin. (1918).
Barrington, Jonah. Rise and Fall of the Irish Nation. (Paris?) (1833?)
Bushe, C. K. Cease Your Funning. Dublin. 1798.
*Byrne, Memoirs of Miles. Vol. I. Dublin. 1907.
Cloncurry, Lord. Personal Recollections. 1850.
Coote, C. History of the Union. 1802.
Edgeworth, Maria. Memoirs of R. L. Edgeworth. Vol. II. 1821.
† Novels—The Absentee, Castle Rackrent, Ormond.
†Gilbert, J. T. Documents relating to Ireland, 1795–1804. 1893.
Grattan, Henry. Miscellaneous Works. 1822.
*Grattan, Henry (junior). Life and Times of the Rt. Hon. Henry Grattan. Vols. III–V. 1841–1846.
Holt, Memoirs of Joseph. Vol. I. 1838.
Lever, Charles. Novels—Charles O'Malley and Knight of Gwynne.
Luckombe, P. A Tour through Ireland. 1783.
Macneill, J. G. Swift. The Constitutional and Parliamentary History of Ireland till the Union. 1917.
Macneill, J. G. Swift. The Irish Parliament. 1886.

BIBLIOGRAPHY

Newenham, T. A. A Statistical and Historical Enquiry into the progress and magnitude of the population of Ireland. 1805.
View of the . . . circumstances of Ireland. 1809.
Parliamentary Debates, Ireland. Vol. XIII.
†Pitt Correspondence—MSS. preserved in Orwell House, Sussex—a letter from Redesdale to Pitt, dated 31/10/03, on interference of Commander-in-Chief, and suggesting the existence of a court party.
*Report of the Royal Commission on Financial Relations between Great Britain and Ireland—Sir E. Hamilton's Memorandum. 1895.
Report from the Select Committee of the House of Commons. Dublin. 1798.
    Ditto, House of Lords. Dublin. 1798.
Schlosser, F. C. Geschichte des achtzehnten Jahrhunderts. Vol. VI. 1846.
Seward, W. W. Collectanea Hibernica. Vol. III. Dublin. 1812.
Stokes, Whitley. Project for re-establishing internal peace and tranquillity in Ireland.
*†Tighe, W. Statistical Survey of the County of Kilkenny. Dublin. 1802.
Tomline, George. Life of William Pitt. Ch. XXIII. 1903.
Tour through the South of England, etc. 1793.
*Townsend, Rev. H. Statistical Survey of the County of Cork. 1810.
Walsh, J. E. Sketches of Ireland Sixty Years Ago. 1847.
*Warburton, J., J. Whitelaw, and R. Walsh. A History of the City of Dublin. Vol. II. 1818.
Whitelaw, J. Essay on the Population of Dublin in 1798. Dublin. 1805.

CHAPTER IV

*Edwards, Bryan. The History of the British Colonies in the West Indies. 1794.
*Fortescue, Hon. (Sir) J. History of the British Army. Vol. IV. 1906.
*   The British Army. 1905.
*Kingsford, William. History of Canada. Vol. VII. 1894.
*Lucas, (Sir) C. P. Historical Geography of the British Colonies. The West Indies. 1890.
*   History of Canada. 1909.
*†Moore, Diary of Sir John. Edited by Sir F. Maurice. 1904.
*†Tucker, J. S. Memoirs of the Earl of St. Vincent. 1843.

Anderson, Aeneas. Journal of the Secret Expedition. 1802.
†Barham, Letters and Papers of Lord. Vol. III. Navy Records Society. 1910.

Bolingbroke, H. A Voyage to the Demerary. 1807.
†Bowers, W. Naval Adventures. Vol. I. 1833.
*Bradley, A. G. The Making of Canada. 1908.
Brenton, Capt. E. P. Life . . . of John, Earl of St. Vincent. 1838.
    The Naval History of Great Britain. Vol. I. 1837.
Bryce, George. A History of the Canadian People. 1887.
*Bunbury, Sir Henry. Narrative of some Passages in the Great War with France. Vol. I. 1854.
†Canadian Archives, Reports on. D. Brymner. 1890, 1891, 1892.
Canniff, W. History of the Settlement of Upper Canada. 1869.
Christie, Robert. History of Lower Canada. 1848.
Clarke, Rev. J. S., and J. McArthur. Life of Nelson. Vol. II. (1840.)
Clode, C. M. The Military Forces of the Crown. 1869.
*Conolly, T. W. J. The History of the Corps of Royal Sappers and Miners. Vol. I. 1855.
*†Desbrière, Édouard. Projets et Tentatives de Débarquement aux Iles Britanniques. Tome II. Paris. 1901.
*Duncan, Major F. History of the Royal Artillery. Vol. II. 1874.
Dundonald, Earl of. Autobiography of a Seaman. Vol. I. 1860.
Dunfermline, Ld. Lieutenant-General Sir Ralph Abercromby. 1861.
Egerton, H. G. A Historical Geography of the British Dominions. Canada. Part II. 1893.
Fletcher, C. Naval Guardian. 1805.
Foy, Général M. Histoire de la Guerre de la Péninsule. 1808.
Gardner, W. J. History of Jamaica. 1873.
Garneau, F.-X. Histoire de Canada. Tome III. Montréal. 1882.
Gourlay, R. A Statistical Account of Upper Canada. 1822.
†Heriot, George. Travels through the Canadas. 1807.
Hook, Theodore. Life of General Sir David Baird. Vol. I. 1833.
*Jomini, Baron A. H. de. Histoire des Guerres de la Révolution. Tome XIV. Paris. 1824.
†Lambert, John. Travels through Lower Canada, etc. 1816.
†Marryat, Captain Frederick. Novels.
Napier, Lt.-Gen. Sir W. Life and Opinions of General Sir Charles Napier. Vol. I. 1857.
†Nautical Economy, etc. By a Sailor Politely called by the Officers of the Navy, Jack Nastyface. (1831.)
†Naval Miscellany, The. Navy Records Society. 1901–1927.
†Nugent, Lady (Maria). Journal. Edited by F. Cundall. 1807.
†Paris unpublished records in Section Historique, Ministère de la Guerre, 3a/9 34–40, and Cartons de l'Armée d'Orient, Jan. 1801.
†Public Records Office. H.O., 48.20—riots in West of England. 1801.

BIBLIOGRAPHY

†Public Records Office. Returns of military strength for 1800—
W.O. 17. 1161 General.
1587 Cape of Good Hope.
1507 North America.
1747 East India.
Reynier, Le Général. De l'Égypte après la Bataille d'Héliopolis. 1802.
Robinson, Commander Charles N. The British Fleet. 1894.
Ross, Sir J. Memoirs and Correspondence of Lord de Saumarez. Vol. I. 1838.
Royal Society of Canada, Proceedings. II, Series IV, sect. i. p. 73. Article on Bédard by M. N. E. Dionne.
†St. Vincent, Letters of Lord. Navy Records Society. 1922–1927.
Schomberg, Isaac. Naval Chronology. 1802.
†Scott, Michael. Novels—The Cruise of the Midge and Tom Cringle's Log.
†Shipp, Memoirs of John. 1829.
†Sinclair, Capt. A. Reminiscences of . . . the Royal Navy. (1859.)
†Spencer Papers, The. Vol. IV. Navy Records Society. 1924.
Steel, D. Steel's Naval Chronologist. (?1801.)
†Steel, Sir Robert. The Marine Officer. 1840.
Walsh, Capt. Thomas. Journal of the late Campaign in Egypt. 1803.
Williams, W. F. An Historical and Statistical Account of the Bermudas. 1848.
Wilson, (Sir) Robert. History of the British Expedition to Egypt. 1803.
†Windham MSS.—British Museum Add. MSS. 37845, ff. 180ff., on Council in Lower Canada.
Young, Arthur. The Question of Scarcity plainly stated and remedies considered. 1800.
Young, Sir W. West-India Common-Place Book. 1807.

CHAPTER V

*†Browning, Oscar. England and Napoleon in 1803. Being the Despatches of Lord Whitworth and others. Edited by O. Browning. 1907.
*†Driault, Édouard. La Politique Extérieure du Premier Consul. Paris. 1910.
*Grant, A. J., and Harold Temperley. Europe in the Nineteenth Century. 1927.
†Papers relative to the Discussion with France presented to Parliament in 1803.

Le Bon Sens d'un Manufacturer. Paris. 1801.
Cobbett, William. Letters to Lord Hawkesbury. 1802.
Coquelle, P. Napoléon et l'Angleterre. Paris. 1904.
Garden, Comte de. Histoire des Traités de Paix. Tome VII. Paris. 1848–1887.
†Hardwicke MSS.—British Museum Add. MSS. 35703, regarding outbreak in Dublin in 1803, and—f. 234—Pitt's position.
†Hawkesbury—Lord Hawkesbury's Diplomatic Letter Book, 11/11/01–6/12/02—British Museum Add. MSS. 38319, showing unwillingness of Spain to take part in Treaty of Amiens and cede Trinidad (ff. 1 and 8).
Jackson, Diary and Letters of Sir George. Vol. I. 1872.
Lefebvre, Armand. Histoire des Cabinets de l'Europe. Paris. 1845.
Observations sur le manifeste du roi d'Angleterre. Paris. 1803.
Paget, Sir Arthur. The Paget Papers. Vol. II. 1896.
†Papers relative to France presented to Parliament in 1800.
Philippson, M. Articles in Revue Historique, Paris. Vols. 75, pp. 286 ff., and 76, pp. 48 ff. 1901.
Plowden, Francis. The History of Ireland from 1801 to 1810. 1811.
†Public Records Office. F.O. 27.59 and 60, relating to Treaty of Amiens.
†Public Records Office. H.O. 42.66, relating to clothiers, etc., and their combinations in 1802, especially Mayor of Leeds's letter enclosed with Fitzwilliam's of 21/8/02.
H.O. 42.65—similar correspondence to above.

CHAPTER VI

†Blockade of Brest. Navy Records Society. Vol. I. 1898.
*†Desbrière, Édouard. Projets et Tentatives de Débarquement aux Iles Britanniques. Tomes III, IV. 1902.

---

*Fortescue, Hon. John. The County Lieutenancies and the Army. 1909.
Hardy, Thomas. The Trumpet-Major.
†Nelson MSS.—British Museum Add. MSS. 34935, f. 18, instructions to Nelson of 18/5/03.
Paris. Archives Nationales. A.F. IV, Cart. 1597, Plaq. 1 and 2, Papers regarding possibility of invading England.
Pitt Correspondence —MSS. preserved in Orwell House, Suffolk— Correspondence of Tomline in 1804, showing genuineness of Pitt's desire to obtain George III's consent to Fox, with his own view that Pitt had not done all that he might.
Regnier, C. A. Second Rapport du Grand Juge au Premier Consul. Paris. (1804.)
Secret Correspondence connected with Mr. Pitt's return to office. 1852.

BIBLIOGRAPHY

CHAPTER VII

†Barham, Letters and Papers of Lord. Navy Records Society. 1911.
†Blockade of Brest. Navy Records Society. 1899–1902.
†Collingwood. A Selection from the Public and Private Correspondence of Vice-Admiral Lord Collingwood. 1829.
*Corbett, Julian. The Campaign of Trafalgar. 1805.
*†Desbrière, Édouard. Projets et Tentatives de Débarquement aux Iles Britanniques. Tome IV. 1902.
*† Campagne Maritime de 1805. 1907.

---

*Fortescue, Hon. John. The County Lieutenancies and the Army. 1909.
Fraser, E. The Enemy at Trafalgar. (1906.)
Gentz, F. von. Briefe von und an Friederich von Gentz. III, i. München. 1913.
†Great Sea Fights. Navy Records Society. Vol. II. 1900.
Jurien de la Gravière, L'Amiral. Guerres maritimes. s8vo. n.d.
Mikhaïlovski-Danilevski. Campagne de 1805. 1846.
†Nelson's Private Diary, 1805. British Museum Add. MSS. 34968.
†Public Records Office. Russia. 55–59.
*†Report of a Committee appointed by the Admiralty . . . relating to the Tactics employed by Nelson at the Battle of Trafalgar. 1913.
†Rose, J. Holland. Despatches relating to the Third Coalition. Publications of the Royal Historical Society, Series III, Vol. VII. 1904.
Southey, Robert. Life of Nelson.
*Tatistcheff, Serge. Alexandre 1er et Napoléon. 1891.
Thursfield. Nelson and other Naval Studies. 1909.

INDEX

ABBOT, Right Hon. CHARLES, his account of Privy Council, 123; on the King's health, 258; Chief Secretary, 1801, 261; quoted, 262; Speaker, 1802, 352; informed of French plan of invasion, 386; gives his casting vote against Melville, 413.

ABERCORN, Marquis of, nicknamed Don Magnifico, 71.

ABERCROMBY, Gen. Sir RALPH, opinion of Irish unrest when Commander-in-Chief in Ireland, 224, 225; in chief command in Mediterranean, 310; preparations for Egyptian expedition, 310, 311; lands at Aboukir, March 8, 1801, 311 ff.; defeats French, March 13th, 313, 314; wins Battle of Canopus, March 21st, 314, 315; death, 316; honours to, 316, 317; mentioned, 136, 243.

ABOUKIR, Egypt, landing and defeat of the French, March 8, 1801, 311 ff.

ABSENTEE LANDLORDS, in Ireland, 205, 206.

ADDINGTON, HENRY, early career, 256; Speaker to 1801, 193; an incident during his Speakership, 369; becomes Prime Minister, 256; incapacity for Premiership, 258, 259; formation of his administration, 260 ff.; weakness in debate, 266; lack of support, 266; correspondence of Nelson with, 333; anxiety for peace, 338 ff.; weakness in foreign policy, 342, 343; speech on distilleries, 344; introduces peace budget in 1802, 347; Pitt's relations with, 350; policy during general election, 352; foreign policy, 1803, 359 ff.; weakness of his ministry, 362; attempts to bring him to resign, 363, 364; negotiations with Pitt, 364, 365; in war debate of May 1803, 365; introduces 1803 budget, 365, 366; City's want of confidence, 367, 387, 388; his attempts to strengthen his ministry, 369; belief in an immediate invasion, Christmas, 1803, 386; general proofs of unfitness, 386 ff.; Canning's epigram, 388; his difficulties, 388 ff.; resignation, 391; possibility of the King's recalling him, 392; introduces 1804 budget, 395.

a volunteer colonel, 383; Pitt's friendship, 256, 257, 393, 397, 398; mentioned, 122.

ADMIRALTY: admiralty boroughs, 113; composition and authority of the Board, 295. *Also see* FIRST LORD OF THE ADMIRALTY.

ADMIRALTY DROITS, 361.

ADULTERY, growing frequency, 82; law of divorce, 157, 158.

AFRICA, cheap guns exported to, 46.

AGRICULTURAL LABOURER, condition in 1800, 17 ff.; women, 21, 22; effect of Poor Law, 27 ff.; wages, 31; enlistment in army, 31; and emigration, 31; hours of labour, 51; longevity, 102.

Ireland, 202 ff., 215 ff.

AGRICULTURE, methods of, 38, 39; respect shown to, 40; cultivated area in 1798, 57; estimated national income from, 57; tithes, 84, 85; number engaged in 1801, 102; popular encouragement of, 104, 105; its interests sacrificed to woollen interests, 198; protection and state encouragement, 198 ff.; effect of tax on agricultural horses, 414. *Also see* BOARD OF AGRICULTURE.

AIKIN, JOHN, his description of Manchester, 42.

ALAVA, de, Vice-Admiral, Spanish Navy, flies flag in Santa Ana at Trafalgar, 434.

ALBION, newspaper, 150, 151.

ALDERMEN, as magistrates, 166; status in London, 175, 176; elsewhere, 176.
ALEXANDER I, succeeds Paul as Emperor of Russia, 1801, 335; obvious protector of the Knights of St. John, 346; opposed to English views as to Malta, 360; on the merits of the rupture of the Peace of Amiens, 362; joins in Third Coalition, 1805, 404, 405; Visit to Potsdam, 446; defeat at Austerlitz, 446.
ALEXANDRIA, the key of Egypt, 311; Abercromby's march towards, 1801, 313 ff.; its surrender, September 2nd, 318.
ALGIERS, bombardment of, 1816, mentioned, 441.
ALIEN OFFICE, RECEIVER-GENERALSHIP OF, sinecure held by Canning, 189.
ALLEMAND, Captain, French Navy, escapes from Rochefort with a squadron in July, 1805, 417; successful five months' cruise after failure to effect junction with Villeneuve, 420, 443, 444.
AMBLETEUSE, French port of concentration, 373, 415.
AMERICA, trade in 1800, 48, 58, 59, 60, 61.
AMERICA, NORTH, British troops in, 277, 306.
AMERICA, SOUTH, import of wheat from, 242.
AMIENS, TREATY OF, signed March 27, 1802, 345; Preliminaries of October, 1801, on which it was based, 338 ff.; their reception, 342, 343; character of the actual Treaty, 345 ff., 358, 362, 363; sayings as to it, 362; provisions as regards Mediterranean, 381; not carried out as regards Goree, 381; mentioned, 355, 356.
AMSTERDAM, trade, 59.
ANABAPTISTS, in Canada, 273.
ANGLESEA, copper mine, 47.
ANIMALS, punishment of cruelty to, in 1803, 168; cruelty mentioned, 140.
ANTI-JACOBIN, Canning's, 139, 150.
APPRENTICES, London, 66, 67; debates in parliament leading to the Act for the Preservation of the Health and Morals of Apprentices and Others, 1802, 349, 350.
ARCHBISHOP, *see* MOORE, DR. JOHN.
ARCHITECTURE, domestic, in London, 65.
ARKWRIGHT, RICHARD, inventor of water-frame: his Derbyshire cotton mill, 48, 49; a mill of his burnt, 53, 54.
ARMED NEUTRALITY, 246, 247; ultimatum to Denmark regarding, 322; its dissolution, 334, 335.
ARMORIAL BEARINGS, tax on, 181.
ARMY, general account, 299 ff.; recruiting, 31, 301, 302, 307; powdering the hair, 34; education of officers, 101; low standing army, 115; royal control of, 120; York as Commander-in-Chief, 120, 148; its reduction in 1792, 129; objections to its use in suppressing riots, 132; Scotsmen, 136; Catholics, 153, 253; incitement of soldiers to sedition, 166, 167; General Defence Act of 1803 mentioned, 178; cost, 181; small estimation in which held, 243, 371, 372; Grey on dissipation of its resources, 1801, 249; Cabinet control, 296 ff.; artillery and engineers, 296 ff.; strength in 1801, 306; French reports on, 371; recruitment in 1803, 382, 388; Army of Reserve Act, 382; the Act a failure, 388; Additional Force Act, 1804, 396, 397; the Act a failure, 397, 398, 399; general indifference to the Army, 398, 399; strength in 1805, 400; law permitting militiamen to enlist, 1805, 410, 411; recruitment of Hanoverians, 411; prolonged detention of troops in transports, 424.

INDEX 505

ARMY, Canadian army, 277.
  West Indian, 279, 281, 282, 306.
ARTILLERY, Royal, placed under the Ordnance Department, 296, 297; its strength and efficiency, 297; R.H.A. started, 1793, 297.
  volunteer, 307.
ARTISTS, in debtors' prisons, 159.
ASSESSED TAXES, 186, 187.
ASSIZES, 159; in Taunton, 166; in Ireland, 209.
ASTON, Sir W., bet at Brooks's, 178.
ATHLONE, Countess of, mentioned, 83.
ATHLONE, Earl of, mentioned, 83.
ATTORNEY, in the pillory, 163.
ATTORNEY-GENERAL, his advice in sedition cases, 167; Eldon, a former Attorney-General, 261; Mitford in 1800, 140; Law in 1801, 262; Perceval in 1804, 387.
  in Ireland, member of Irish Cabinet, 218.
AUCKLAND, Lord, his bill regarding adultery, 80; Joint Postmaster-General in 1800, 139, 179, 180.
AULIC COUNCIL, 245.
AUSTEN, Rev. GEORGE, father of Jane Austen, 87, 88.
AUSTEN, JANE, her Emma quoted, 27, 78; her Love and Friendship, 77; silence as to the war, 398, 399; idea of the militia, 398, 399.
AUSTERLITZ, Battle of, December 2, 1805, 446; its news fatal to Pitt, 447.
AUSTRIA, relations with France, 1792, 129; government of, 245; concludes Peace of Lunéville with France, 1801, 308; made a guarantee power under Treaty of Amiens, 346; a proposal of Bonaparte's affecting Austria, 362; his intention to use Boulogne army against her, 370, 423; question of joining Third Coalition, 1805, 404; Napoleon's disbelief in her going to war, 420, 421; joins Coalition, 422; Napoleon marches against her, 423; her defeat, 444; peace concluded, 446; Austrian incapacity one of the causes of the failure of the Coalition, 446; mentioned, 246, 249.
AUTHORS, in debtors' prisons, 159.

BACON, export from Ireland, 215, 216, 239.
BADAJOS, siege mentioned, 298.
BAERT, Baron, French traveller, observations on the English, 72, 99, 106; on the Irish, 209.
BAHAMAS, West Indies, character, 279; a home of buccaneers, 279; threatened invasion of, 402; mentioned, 283, 306.
BAINES, EDWARD, story of the weaver's bet, 54.
BAIRD, Lt.-Gen. Sir DAVID, commands Indian detachment in Egypt, 1801, 317; designated for command of expedition to Cape of Good Hope, 411; despatched, August, 1805, 424; conquers the colony, January, 1806, 424; mentioned, 310.
BAKER, Capt., R.N., in command of Phœnix, captures Didon, 1805, 420.
BALDWIN, Councillor, his election to Parliament, 112.
BALTIC POWERS, effect of their hostility on the corn-supply, 199.
BALTIC TRADE, its extent and character, 59, 60, 61.
BAMFORD, SAMUEL, his accounts of a Methodist family, 92; of the Manchester poor-house, 172; his volunteering experiences, 307.

BANKING HOUSES, tender for government loans, 184.
BANK OF ENGLAND, its general position in the country, 35–37; favour shown as regards government loan, 184; issue of Spanish dollars, 191; arrangement for its books in case of invasion, 386.
BANKS, country banks in England, 36, 37; banks in Ireland, 214, 215; Coutts's bank mentioned, 412.
BANTRY BAY, Ireland, French landing in 1796, 214, 226; base for squadron blockading Coruña, 375; in Gardner's command, 375.
BAPTISTS, their strength, 93; and loyalty, 154.
BARBADOS, West Indies, 278, 283, 408, 409.
BARHAM, Admiral Lord: Admiral Sir Charles Middleton takes this title and becomes First Lord of the Admiralty, 1805, 413; not a believer in the system of close blockade, 416; orders to Cornwallis of July 9, 1805, 416, 417; reception of Nelson in September, 1805, 424, 425.
BARLEY, as food of the West of England, 22; crop in Great Britain in 1799 and 1800, 241; its use prohibited for distilleries in 1800, 241; price fixed by rioters in Totnes in 1801, 267.
BARONS OF EXCHEQUER, 156.
BARRACKS, introduced for the army in 1792, 305, 306; mentioned, 304.
BARRINGTON, Sir JONAH, on the Irish rebellion, 230; on the Union, 235.
BASTARDY, 78, 79.
BATAVIAN REPUBLIC, *see* HOLLAND.
BATE, Rev. HENRY, fighting parson and editor of the Morning Post, 87, 150.
BATH, a free church in, 89; Irishmen at, 206; mentioned, 364, 448.
BATH, ORDER OF THE, Companionship bestowed on Lord Northesk for Battle of Trafalgar, 441; mentioned, 123.
BATHS, HOT AND COLD, 70, 71.
BATTLE OF JULY 22, 1805, 417, 418.
(For other battles see names of places after which they are known.)
BAVARIA, British Minister deceived by pretended French spy, 388, 389.
BEADLE, 169.
BEATTY, Dr., as Nelson's medical adviser, 326.
BEAUMONT, Sir GEORGE, on baths, 71.
BEDFORD, Fifth Duke of: his annual sheep-shearing, 40; his London house replaced by squares, 64; his pride, 149; his false return of his manservants, 149; his voluntary contribution to the exchequer, 187; mentioned, 82.
BEEF, the traditional British meat, 40; export from Ireland, 215, 216, 239.
BEER, home-brewed, 18, 28, 67; drinking, become a vice, 31; cost, 55, 66, 67; brewing a domestic trade, 57; sale in London, 67; public-houses in London, 67; beer at table, 70; taxation of, 185; mentioned, 18.
BELFAST, rise, 208, 209; its political views, 225, 229; accepts the Union, 235.
BELGIUM, annexation to France, 308.
BELLEISLE, expedition to, 249, 309.
BELLIARD, General, French army, in command at Cairo, 1801, 317; surrenders, June 27, 1801, 318.
BENTHAM, JEREMY, his debt to Lansdowne, 105; attack on Blackstone, 192, 201.
BENTINCKS, a Whig family, 148. *Also see* PORTLAND.
BERBICE, South America, captured from Dutch, 281; captured again, 381.
BERESFORDS, a ruling family in Ireland, 234.

BERKSHIRE, yeomen in, 20; meeting of magistrates at Speenhamland regarding agricultural wages, 29, 30, 173.
BERLIN, a criticism of the Treaty of Amiens from, 340.
BERMUDAS, account of, 277, 278.
BERNARD, Sir THOMAS, his Society for Bettering the Condition of the Poor, 95.
BERNSTORFF, Count, Foreign Minister in Denmark, Nelson's remark on him, 334.
BERRY, Capt. Sir EDWARD, R.N., in command of Agamemnon, joins fleet off Cadiz, October, 1805, his good luck, 428.
BESSBOROUGH, Lady, friend of Canning, 139; fined for non-payment of tax, 188; her experiences in Ireland, 205; quoted, 301.
BETTESWORTH, Capt., R.N., in command of Curieux, brings home information of Villeneuve's return from West Indies, July, 1805, 410.
BHARATPUR, siege mentioned, 298.
BIRMINGHAM, described, 45–47; its political views, 110, 152; its Court of Requests, 156; its administration, 177; Boulton's works, 191; riots of 1792, 197; distress in 1801, 268.
BISHOPS, *see* CHURCH OF ENGLAND.
BLACKSTONE, views on the constitution attacked by Bentham, 192, 201.
BLACKWOOD, Capt. Hon. HENRY, in command of Euryalus; on September 2, 1803, brings news of the combined fleet being located at Cadiz, 423; in command of frigate squadron at Trafalgar, 429; sent for on board Victory on morning of the battle, 431, 432.
BLINCOE, ROBERT, Life of, mentioned, 172.
BLIND, Institution for, at Liverpool, 95.
BLOMFIELD, ROBERT, poet, his popularity, 105.
BOARD OF AGRICULTURE, its establishment in 1793, 188; survey of Somersetshire mentioned, 110, 111; mentioned, 194, 199.
BOARD OF CONTROL, Dundas President in 1801, 136, 310; Castlereagh in 1802, 261; retained on change of administration in 1804, 394.
BOARD OF HEALTH, MANCHESTER, institution in 1796, 42, 177; report in same year in favour of factory legislation, 349.
BOARD OF TRADE, abolition in 1782, restored by Pitt under its old name, 178; Montrose first President to be in Cabinet, 1804, 178, 394; succeeded by Auckland, 179.
BOLTON, home of Samuel Crompton, 56.
BONAPARTE, JOSEPH, negotiator of Treaty of Amiens, 345.
BONAPARTE, NAPOLEON, his rise, 244; conquest of Egypt in 1798 mentioned, 309, 310; forecast of the British attack, 309, 310; his influence after the Peace of Lunéville, 244; instigates Northern Powers against England, 246, 247; anxiety for peace in 1801, 338, 345; astuteness in negotiating, 339; plans of aggrandizement in Italy, 341, 342; made President of Italian Republic, 342; sends expedition to San Domingo, 343; low opinion of the Addington Ministry, 343; made Consul for life, 1802, 345; annexations of Elba, etc., 353, 354; annoyance at British press, 355; outrages on British merchants, 355, 356, 362, 363; misunderstands and is misunderstood by England, 357; views as to the Near East, 357, 358; despatch of Sebastian to Egypt, 357; scene with Whitworth, March 13, 1803, 360; saying as to the Treaty of Amiens, 362; proposals as to Malta, 362; ambition to restore French industries and exclude British goods, 363; control over European trade, 363; care

for French trade, 363; assertions regarding the invasion of England, 370; his preparations of 1801 a feint, 370; reports received by him, 371; plans for invasion, 372, 373, 374; witnesses disasters in Boulogne harbour, 378; becomes Emperor, 378; arrest of British in France in 1803, 380; invasion of Hanover, 380; need of a good naval adviser, 401; appraisement of Spanish assistance, 403; seizure of Rumbold, 404; sends peace overture, January, 1805, 404; plan of expedition to West Indies, 405; plan of 1804, 405; returns from Italy, 416; his view of the English Government, 416; realizes Villeneuve's return, 417; reaches Boulogne, August 3rd, 419; his alternative plan of concentrating at Cadiz, 420; final exhortation to Villeneuve, 421; his plan as divined by Collingwood, 421; drops plan of invasion, 422; fresh naval plan, 423; information regarding British oversea movements in September, 424; orders Villeneuve to leave Cadiz, 427; his low opinion of Nelson, 427; reference to Battle of Trafalgar, 441; success in Bavaria, October, 444; his statement of his aims, 444; definitely launched on a policy of aggression, 444; services to Europe and England, 445; enters Vienna, 446; defeats Coalition at Austerlitz, December 2nd, 446; obliges Austria and Prussia to withdraw from the Coalition, 446.

His despatch of Fiévée to England, 74; opinion of the British expedition to Egypt, 318; of the value of military history, 440; remark on Pitt, 452.
BONAPARTE, Madame, her reception at the Tuileries, March 13, 1803, 360.
BOOTLE, WILBRAHAM, Member of Parliament, his interest in children in mills, 349.
BOROUGH REEVE, in Manchester, 177.
BOROUGHS, PARLIAMENTARY, representation in England and Wales, 108–111; in Scotland, 111; price of a borough, 112; subservience of, 112, 113; their possession by government departments, 113; importance of independent boroughs, 114, 115; Irish boroughs, 219; how dealt with at the Union, 235, 236; account of them after the Union, unimportance in parliament of members for rotten boroughs as compared with county members, 387.
BOULOGNE, armament at, in 1801, 335, 336, 337; in 1803 ff., 370 ff., 400, 415; French disasters in the harbour, 378; abortive British attempt to block entrance to harbour, 389, 390; break-up of the Boulogne camp, 423.
BOULTON, MATTHEW, his works, 46; used for government coin, 191.
BOUNTIES, on linen, 239; on imported corn, 242, 243; for potato growing in 1801, 268; for naval recruits, 291.
BOW STREET RUNNERS, 168.
BOXING, as recreation, 103; professional, 103; matches, 348; mentioned, 170.
BOYNE, traditions of the, 227.
BRADFORD, attitude of the town towards steam engines, 49.
BRAGGE, one of Addington's family, 388.
BREAD, the quartern loaf as basis of poor law relief, 29; doubled in cost between 1780 and 1800, 31; emergency measures in 1800, 241, 242; price in 1801, 242, 267. *Also see* BROWN BREAD ACT.
BRENTON, Capt. JAHLEEL, in command of Caesar, 1801, 319, 320.
BREST, expeditions projected from, 336, 373; strength of fleet in, 375; blockaded, 294, 401, 415, 416, 417, 420.
BRIBERY, in parliamentary elections, 110; of members of the Irish Parliament, 237.

INDEX

BRICKS, duty on, 186, also 180.
BRIDGES, how maintained, 171.
BRIDGEWATER, unrest in 1801, 267.
BRIDPORT, Admiral Lord, in command of Channel Fleet, 1799, 286.
BRIGHTON, without a resident magistrate, 165; mentioned, 68.
BRISTOL, Earl of, Bishop of Londonderry, his opinion on Irish unrest, 224.
BRISTOL, population and description, 48; distanced by Liverpool, 43, 48; sledges at, 62; the port for Wales, 48, 63; Burke as member for, 115; foulness of its gaol and bridewell, 161, 162; unrest near, in 1801, 267.
BROOKS'S CLUB, gambling at, 141; a bet at, 178; mentioned, 82.
BROWN, NICHOLAS, Secretary to Admiral Lord Keith, 416.
BROWN, Rev. THOMAS, Yorkshire dialect poet, quoted, 22, 81.
BROWN BREAD ACT, introduction, 241; failure and repeal, 260; mentioned, 267.
BRUMMELL, Beau, mentioned, 72.
BRUTALITY, in punishments for crime, 163; towards poor in Ireland, 207; examples in England—in bull-baiting, 348, 349; in Wall's case, 351.
BUCKEENS, in Ireland, 206.
BUCKINGHAM, Marquis of; as Earl Temple, Viceroy of Ireland, 1783, 217; mentioned, 135.
BUCKINGHAMSHIRE, Earl of, enters Cabinet as Chancellor of the Duchy of Lancaster, 397, 398; resigns, 413. *Also see* HOBART, Lord.
BUCKINGHAMSHIRE, pasture land in, 23; Winchelsea's system of cottage holdings, 26; two villages compared, 33.
BUDGETS, general attitude of the House of Commons towards, 193.
    Budget of 1801, 259, 260.
    Budget of 1802, 347, 348.
    Budget of 1803, 365, 366, 367.
    Budget of 1804, 395.
    Budget of 1805, 413, 414.
    Budget, Irish, of 1801, 260.
BUENOS AYRES, Whitelocke's surrender at, mentioned, 301.
BULL-BAITING, 103; parliamentary debate on, 348, 349.
BURDETT, Sir FRANCIS, elected M.P. for Middlesex, 1802, 352.
BUREAUCRACY, non-existent in 1800, 194.
BURGAGE TENURES, 109.
BURKE, EDMUND, his parliamentary doctrine, 115; his Act of 1782, 178; praise of Pitt as a young man, 127; fervour against the French Revolution, 131; as Windham's master, 138, 393; and Fox's, 143; a friend of the Prince of Wales, 147; his economic reforms, 189; George III on his "wild ideas," 391; quoted, 132.
BURNEY, FANNY, novelist, interview with George III, 118.
BUTTER, export from Ireland, 239.
BYRNE, MILES, a Wexford rebel, 208.
BYRON, Lord, on Grey, 248; and Pitt, 452.

CABINET, position in the constitution and general formation, 119 ff.; inner cabinet, 135; cabinet responsibility imperfect, 201.
CABINET, IRISH, 218.
CABINETS, Pitt's in 1801: Pitt, Loughborough, Grenville, Portland, Dundas, Spencer, Cornwallis, Chatham, Westmorland, Windham, Camden, 137 ff.

510 ENGLAND IN THE NINETEENTH CENTURY

CABINETS, Addington's, 1801-1804: Addington, Eldon, Hawkesbury, Pelham, Hobart, St. Vincent, Chatham, Portland, Westmorland, 263; Castlereagh added in 1802, 261; Pelham replaced by Yorke, 1803, 369. Pitt's, 1804-1806: Pitt, Eldon, Harrowby, Hawkesbury, Camden, Melville, Chatham, Portland, Westmorland, Montrose, Mulgrave, Castlereagh, 394, 395; Harrowby replaced by Mulgrave, 395; Portland by Sidmouth and Mulgrave by Buckinghamshire, 397, 398; Melville by Barham, 413; Camden by Castlereagh, Sidmouth by Camden, and Buckinghamshire by Harrowby, 413.

CADIZ, expedition against, mentioned, 249, 309; escape of French ship to, 375; watched by frigates, 1803, 375; Villeneuve watched by Collingwood in, 1805, 420 ff.; connection with Battle of Trafalgar, 424 ff.; and with its sequel, 442, 443; final surrender of French ships there in 1808, 444.

CAIRO, captured by British, 1801, 317, 318.

CALDER, Rear-Admiral Sir ROBERT, in command of squadron off Ferrol, order to meet Villeneuve, 417; his action of July 22, 1805, 417 ff.; court-martialled and severely reprimanded, 419; return from Cadiz, 428; mentioned, 421, 422, 423.

CALICOES, duty on, 186; protection in Ireland, 240.

CAMBRIDGE UNIVERSITY, clerical profligacy at, 99; connection with Simeon, 90; Pitt, 126; and Grey, 248; representation in parliament, 108; mentioned, 86, 101.

CAMDEN, first Earl, remark on George III, 119.

CAMDEN, second Earl, in Cabinet without office in 1800, 138; his Viceroyalty of Ireland, 1795-1798, 223 ff.; features of his Viceroyalty mentioned, 218, 232, 233; becomes Secretary for War, 394; resigns, and becomes President of the Council, 413.

CAMPBELL, poet, mentioned, 326.

CANADA, its four maritime provinces, 270, 271; Upper and Lower Canada, 271; people of Lower Canada, 271, 272, 273; of Upper Canada, 273, 274; administration of Lower Canada, 274, 275, 276; of Upper Canada, 276; relations with the United States, 276, 277; value to Great Britain, 277; export of wheat from, 242.

CANALS, total income from in 1798, 57; canal speculation, 62; attempt to tax, 186; mentioned, 43, 48.

CANNING, GEORGE, character and early career, 138, 139; Foreign Under-Secretary before 1800, 139; his Anti-Jacobin, 139, 150; his phrase "candid friend," 151; relations with Pitt, 189, 393; takes Receiver-Generalship of the Alien Office, 189; his friends, 260; follows Pitt into retirement in 1801, 261; silence in parliament, 1801-1802, 350; verses in praise of Pitt, 350; speech in parliament, 1802, 354; "paper plot" to bring back Pitt, 363, 364; ridicules Addington, 388; becomes Treasurer of the Navy, 395; dines with Nelson, 425.

love of mystery, 363; lack of judgment, 395.

CANOPUS, Battle of, March 21, 1801, 314 ff.

CAPE BRETON ISLAND, population and constitution, 270, 271.

CAPE OF GOOD HOPE, Dutch possession captured by British, 339; strength of British garrison, 306; restored by Treaty of Amiens, 339; Nelson's low opinion of, 343; expedition to, decided upon, 411; again captured by British, January, 1806, 424.

CAPITAN PASHA, Turkish general, joins Hely Hutchinson, 1801, 317.

INDEX 511

CARD-PLAYING, 76, 141.
CARICATURES, 151.
CARIBS, West Indian aboriginals, 279.
CARLOW, incident at the races, 207.
CAROLINE OF BRUNSWICK, Princess of Wales, marriage, 1795, 147; gives birth to a daughter, 147; picture of her trial, mentioned, 248.
CAROLS, sung by weavers, 51.
CARRIAGES, tax upon, 181, 186.
CARRINGTON, Lord, his qualifications as a public man, 117; satirical charade on his name, 117; his speculations in the funds, 184.
CARRON gun factory, 294.
CARTWRIGHT, EDMUND, his power-loom factory destroyed, 54.
CASH PAYMENT, prohibition of payment for notes by Bank of England, 1797, 35.
CASTLE RACKRENT, Grenville's allusion, 135.
CASTLEBAR, Battle of, 300.
CASTLEREAGH, Viscount, 139; Chief Secretary for Ireland under Cornwallis, 1798–1801, 218; opinion as to need for the Union, 232; his work for it, 235, 236; presses Catholic claims on Pitt, 251; enters Cabinet as President of Board of Control, 1802, 261; and is Addington's best debater in House of Commons, 261; keeps his office in 1804, 394; becomes Secretary for War, 1805, 413; makes an inquiry from Nelson, 423; becomes virtual leader of Cabinet during Pitt's illness, 447, 448; visit to Pitt, 448.
    a pronouncement of his as Secretary to the Colonies, 276; allusion to his mission in 1814, 244; mention of his suicide, 144.
    his abilities, 413.
CATHERINE THE GREAT of Russia, 244, 245; mentioned by Fox, 265.
CATHOLIC FRANCHISE, granted in Ireland in 1793, 204, 222, 223.
CATHOLICS, ENGLISH, 93, 94; concessions to, 221; difficulties in the way of their military service, 153, 382. *Also see* ROME.
CATHOLICS, CANADIAN, 272, 273.
CATHOLICS, IRISH, position, 206, 207; penal laws, 207, 217; exclusion from magistracy, 211; wealth, 216; concessions to, 221, 222, 233, 253; no emigration among, 225; question of admission to parliament in 1795, 222, 223, 233; and in 1801, 251 ff.; foundation of Maynooth College, 223; relations with Presbyterians, 222, 226 ff.; support of the Union, 233, 235, 251; question of subsidizing the clergy, 233; their vote in general election of 1802, 352; debate in parliament on their disabilities, 414, 415; mentioned, 273, 136.
CATTLE breeding, 40; maiming as an Irish crime, 231.
CAVALRY, regular, 299, 300; provisional, 307.
CAVENDISHES, a Whig family, 148.
CENSUS, of 1801, reliability, 21; employment details, 21, 34.
    of 1811, mentioned, 34.
CEYLON, Dutch island captured by British, 339; retained by Treaty of Amiens, 339, 340.
CHAIRMAN OF COMMITTEES, in House of Commons, first made permanent in 1801, 193.
CHANCELLOR, Lord, the office and its peculiar place in the constitution, 121, 157, 164, 165; his Court, 157, 158; Loughborough Chancellor in 1801, 138, 164; succeeded by Eldon, 261.

512 ENGLAND IN THE NINETEENTH CENTURY

CHANCELLOR, Lord, in Ireland, Clare, 218; Redesdale, 1802, 352; mentioned, 223.
CHANCELLOR OF THE DUCHY OF LANCASTER, the office, 125; Pelham, 1803, 369; Mulgrave, 1804, 394; Buckinghamshire, 1805, 397, 398; Harrowby, 1805, 413.
CHANCELLOR OF THE EXCHEQUER, the office, 125; Pitt to 1801, 125; Addington, 1801, 263; Pitt, 1804, 394.
   Irish, before the Union, 216, 220; Corrie, 1801, 260; Foster, 1804, 394.
CHANCERY, see CHANCELLOR, LORD.
CHARITIES, subscription to, by members of parliament, 110.
CHARLES II, ancestor of Fox, 141.
CHARLES IV, King of Spain, 245.
CHARLOTTE, QUEEN, a caricature of, 118; arrangements for, in case of invasion, 386.
CHATHAM, fortified camp, 385, 386.
CHATHAM, WILLIAM PITT, first Earl of, his education of the Younger Pitt, 126; driven from power by secret influence, 255.
CHATHAM, second Earl of, President of the Council in 1800, 137; Master-General of the Ordnance, 1801, 263; proposed for Premier by Addington, 364; retained in 1804, 394.
CHELMSFORD, fortified camp, 386.
CHELTENHAM, mentioned, 62.
CHESHIRE, feudal survivals in, 20.
CHEVIOTS, depopulation of, 44, 45.
CHIEF BARON, 156.
CHIEF JUSTICE OF THE KING'S BENCH, how far independent of party, 164.
CHIEF JUSTICES, 156.
CHIEF SECRETARY TO THE LORD-LIEUTENANT OF IRELAND, 1798–1801, Castlereagh, 218; previous Chief Secretaries, Pelham and Hobart, mentioned, 263; some subsequent Chief Secretaries: Abbot, 1801, 261; Wickham, 1802, 352; Vansittart, 398.
CHILD LABOUR, in cotton-mills, 43, 52, 53, 349, 350; in collieries, 45, 53; views of Wilberforce, 41; of Southey, 52; chimney-sweeps, 53; mentioned, 74.
CHIMNEY-SWEEPS, 53, 95.
CHINA, the trade, 59; vessels protected by Dance, 379.
CHRISTIAN VII, King of Denmark, 245.
CHRIST'S HOSPITAL, education at, 100.
CHURCH: discontinuance of church-going, 19, 89; churches in Liverpool, 43, 44; neglect and misuse of churches, 87 ff.
CHURCH, IRISH, unpopularity, 205; wealth and indifference, 206.
CHURCH OF ENGLAND, historical position and connection with the State, 84, 85; views of high churchmen, 84; debt of England to the clergy, 85; position of the clergy, 85 ff.; absenteeism, 86 ff.; Evangelicalism, 90 ff.; High Church Tories, 93; Whig Latitudinarians, 93; profligacy of Cambridge clergy, 99; representation in House of Lords, 116; relations with the King, 120; Whig attitude towards, 149, 150; connection with the land, 157; parish priest's share in appointment of churchwardens, 40, 173.
CHURCH RATES, 181.
CHURCHWARDENS, 172, 173; use for recruitment, 397.

INDEX

CIDER, mentioned, 18, 21.
CINQUE PORTS, LORD WARDEN OF THE, Pitt's salary as, 189; his conversion into an active office, 383, 384.
CINTRA, CONVENTION OF, allusion to, 372.
CISALPINE REPUBLIC, French influence over, 308. *Also see* ITALY.
CISNEROS, Rear-Admiral, Spanish Navy, at Trafalgar, 435.
CITIES, parliamentary representation, 109.
CITY OF LONDON: habits of city men, 64; its constitution, 175, 176; confidence in Pitt, and the reverse in Addington, 367, 387, 388.
CIVIL LAW, administration of, 156, 157.
CIVIL LIST, amount of, 182; debate in Addington's administration, 344; its anomalous character, 344; debate, 1804, 397.
CIVIL SERVICE, 194.
CLAPHAM, 64; place of education of the poet Shelley's sisters, 72.
CLARE, Earl of, his Catholic origin, 206; first Irishman to be Irish Lord Chancellor, 218; view as to a Protestant garrison, 233; speech in Irish House of Lords, 237; death, 1802, 352.
CLARENCE, WILLIAM, Duke of, connection with Mrs. Jordan, 83; a Whig leader, 148; a friend of Nelson, 323.
CLARKSON, THOMAS, quoted, 94.
CLASSICS, study of, 99 ff.
CLERGY, *see* CHURCH OF ENGLAND.
CLERKSHIP OF THE PELLS, refused by Pitt, 189; given by Addington to his son, 189.
CLOCKS, tax upon, 186.
CLONCURRY, Lord, 206, 214.
CLOTH INDUSTRY, in Yorkshire, 41; in relation to legislation, 198.
CLUBS, benefit, 46, 47; decline of London club life, 80.
COACHES, 62, 63; mail-coaches, 179; duty on stage-coaches, 186.
COAL, carried by Paddington Canal to London, 62; export from England to Ireland, 216, 239; coalfields in Ireland, 216. *Also see* MINES.
COALITION, Second, 246, 308.
Third, formation, 404, 422; defeat, 444 ff.
COBBETT, WILLIAM, early life, 51; career to 1802, 97, 98; befriended by Windham, 105; patriotism, 106, 107; treatment in prison, 162; his Political Register, 180; Bonaparte's objection to him, 355; ridicules Addington, 388.
COCHIN, Dutch possession on S.W. coast of India, captured by British, 338; and restored by Treaty of Amiens, 339.
COCHRANE, Capt. Hon. ALEXANDER, R.N., in command of disembarkation at Aboukir, 1801, 312; in command as Rear-Admiral of squadron blockading Ferrol, 402; reports warlike preparations, 402; pursues Missiessy, 409; two of his ships reinforce Nelson, 410.
COCK-FIGHTING, 103.
CODRINGTON, Capt., R.N., letter before Trafalgar, 428; mentioned, 442.
COFFEE, general import trade, 59; West Indian trade, 59, 60; in Jamaica, 281.
COINAGE, state in 1800, 191.
COKE, THOMAS, of Holkam, his system of leases, 19; his successful estate management, 32, 33; asserts rights of a country member of parliament, 151, 152.
COLD BATH FIELDS PRISON, maladministration, 161.

514 ENGLAND IN THE NINETEENTH CENTURY

COLERIDGE, poet, his allowance from Wedgwood, 55; his frugality, 56; his religion, 91; a contributor to the Morning Post, 97, 151; his education at Christ's Hospital, 100; letter from Poole to, 267; on recruiting for the army, 301, 302; mentioned, 42, 85, 105.

COLLINGWOOD, Vice-Admiral, character, 421; watches Cadiz, 421; observations on the enemy's strategy, 421; driven from Cadiz, 423, 424; contrast with Nelson, 425; flies flag in the Royal Sovereign, 428; in Battle of Trafalgar, 430 ff.; his view of the Battle and of Nelson, 439, 440; awarded a peerage, 441; injudicious movements after the battle, 441, 442; exchanges courtesies with Spaniards, 443; mentioned, 291, 450.

COLONIAL ADMINISTRATION, brutality of Governor Wall in Goree, 351.

COLONIES, superintendence of, transferred from Home to War Secretary by Addington, 1801, 125; sinecures relating to, 190; as a source of wealth, 199; usual constitution, 270, 280.

COLQUHOUN, PATRICK, stipendiary magistrate—his book on London quoted, 67, 98; his statistics as to debtors, 159; and criminal convictions, 160; observations on a prisoner's chances, 160; on transportation, 163; on duties of police, 169.

COMBINATION ACTS, enactment and effect, 196 ff.

COMBINATIONS, legislation regarding, 196, 197; first noticed on a large scale among factory workers in 1800, 268.

COMMANDER-IN-CHIEF OF THE ARMY, post held by Duke of York, 120; duties, 299.

COMMERCIAL INTERESTS, unfriendly to Addington, 387, 388; support Pitt, 393.

COMMERCIAL TREATY, failure to make one with France in 1802, 340.

COMMERCIALISM, 72, 74.

COMMITTEE OF PUBLIC EXPENDITURE, finding as to sinecures, 189, 190.

COMMON COUNCILMEN, as magistrates, 166; of London, 176; elsewhere, 176.

COMMON LAND and COMMONS, *see* ENCLOSURE.

COMMON LAW, 155; its treatment of marital relations, 158; of forestalling, 195; of trade relations, 196.

COMMON PLEAS, COURT OF, 156.

COMMONS, the third Estate of the Realm, 108, 201. *Also see* HOUSE OF COMMONS, under PARLIAMENT.

CONGREGATIONALISTS, 93.

CONGREVE, Major-General WILLIAM, his rockets mentioned, 427.

CONNAUGHT, houghing of cattle in, 231.

CONNAUGHT RANGERS, mentioned, 305.

CONSOLIDATED FUND, nature, 183, 186; surplus in 1801, 259.

CONSOLS, price in 1800, 185.

CONSPIRACY, LAW OF, applied to pauper marriages, 174; to trade unions, 196.

CONSTITUTION, BRITISH, its merits, 108; popular checks, 114, 115; place of Crown in, 119, 120. *Also see* CABINET, PARLIAMENT, etc.

CONVICTIONS, infrequency of, 159, 160.

CONVOY DUTY, 186.

INDEX

COOKE, Capt., R.N., killed when in Command of Bellerophon at Trafalgar, 434, 435.
COPENHAGEN, situation, 326, 327; Battle of, 328 ff.
COPENHAGEN FIELDS, meeting at, in 1795, 96, 133.
COPYHOLDERS, 20.
CORK, a centre of the provision trade, 216; accepts Union, 235; its parliamentary representation, 236.
CORN, bounties, 28, 35; prices, 29, 31, 34, 35; imports, 59; trade with France, 61; export from Ireland, 216, 239; scarcity in 1801, 267, 268; riots, 267 ff. *Also see* WHEAT, etc.
CORN LAWS, of 1689, 1774, 1791, 198, 199; of 1804, 200, also 152, 194; Foster's corn law in Ireland, 216.
CORNWALL, mines, 45, 46; methodism, 92; recreations, 103; representation in parliament, 109.
CORNWALLIS, Admiral Hon. WILLIAM, in charge of Atlantic blockade, 375 ff.; an inspirer of Nelson, 377; receives orders for seizure of Spanish treasure ships, September, 1804, 402; and for intercepting Villeneuve, July, 1805, 416, 417.
CORNWALLIS, General, Marquis, Master-General of the Ordnance and Viceroy of Ireland, 138, 298; his work as Viceroy, 231 ff., 251; abolition of Cabinet system in Ireland, 218; resignation, 261; negotiates Treaty of Amiens, 1802, 341; sent for in 1803 to command central army in England, 386.
CORPORATIONS, parliamentary representation, 109 ff.; power to grant freedom of a borough, 109; constitution in London, 175, 176; elsewhere, 176 ff.
CORRIE, ISAAC, Chancellor of the Irish Exchequer before the Union, his quarrel with Grattan, 220; introduces first Irish budget in United Parliament, 260.
CORRUPTION, of public men in Canada, 274, 275, 276. *Also see* BRIBERY.
CORUÑA, escape of French ships to, 375; blockade of, 375. *Also see* FERROL.
COSMAO-KERJULIEN, Capt., French Navy, at Trafalgar, 434; exploit afterwards, 442.
COTTAGE INDUSTRIES, 18; decay, 27; agricultural labourers' dependence on, 30; cottage woollen industries in Yorkshire, 41.
COTTAGERS, ENGLISH, 17 ff.; their distress, 25; cost of building a cottage, 56.
COTTAGES, IRISH, 202, 203.
COTTIERS, IRISH, 202 ff., 215, 217, 224.
COTTON, the industry in Manchester, 41 ff.; importance of cotton-spinning by machinery to the industrial revolution, 48 ff.; opposition to machinery, 53; cotton fabrics worn only by the few, 55, 61; export trade, 58, 59; import trade, 59; re-export trade, 59; Indian piecegoods, 59; duty on, 186; legislation for children in cotton-mills, 195, 349; the industry in Ireland generally, 203; in Belfast district, 209; export from England to Ireland, 216; in Jamaica, 280; in West Indies, 283.
COUNTIES, parliamentary representation, 108, 109, 111.
COUNTRY BANKS, account of, 36 ff.; a run on, 35; financing of farmers, 38.
COUNTRY GENTLEMEN, additions to the peerage from, 116; taxation of, 181. *Also see* JUSTICES OF THE PEACE.
COUNTY MEMBERS OF PARLIAMENT, their importance, 114, 387.
COUNTY RATE, 171.

COURTENAY, JOHN, M.P. for Appleby, wit and humanitarian, 348.
COURTIERS, 154.
COURT-LEET, at Manchester, 177.
COURT OF RECORD, at Portsmouth, 157.
COURTS OF JUSTICE, *see under* CHANCERY, COURT OF, etc., *also* JUSTICE.
COURTS OF REQUESTS, 156.
COUTTS'S BANK, mentioned, 412.
CRABBE, Rev. GEORGE, mentioned, 85.
CRAIG, Lieut.-Gen. Sir JAMES, in command of expedition sent to Mediterranean, 1805, 411, 445; its arrival, 445; withdrawal, 445; mentioned, 427.
CRAUFURD, Col. ROBERT, leader of Light Infantry, 300; speech in parliament on volunteers, 383, 384, 385.
CREOLES or West Indian born Europeans their characteristics, 282.
CREWE, his bet at Brooks's, 178.
CRICKET, stage reached in the development of the game, 103.
CRIME, 67. *Also see* THEFT, etc.
CRIMINAL ADMINISTRATION, in England, 159 ff.; severity in the case of Wall, 351; an additional deterrent to hanging, 351, 352.
CRIMINAL CONVERSATION, cases, 82, 157, 158.
CRIMINAL COURTS, procedure in, 159, 160; convictions, 161; in towns, 166; seditious cases, 166, 167.
CRIMINAL LAW, its sanguinary character, 161.
CROMPTON, SAMUEL, inventor of the spinning-mule, mentioned, 56.
CROMWELL, Irish traditions of, 208, 227, 229; quoted, 300, 301.
CROWN PRINCE OF DENMARK, *see* FREDERIC, CROWN PRINCE OF DENMARK.
CRUELTY TO ANIMALS, punishment of, 168; mentioned, 140.
CUBA, West Indies, Spanish possession, 279, 280; *also see* HAVANA.
CUMBERLAND, feudal survivals in, 20; household economy, 22; education, 96; recreations, 103.
CURAÇOA, West Indies, Dutch possession, 281; captured by British, 281; and restored by Treaty of Amiens, 339.
CURRENCY, bank-notes and inflation, 35 ff.; the coinage, 191; Irish currency, 214, 215.
CURSORY REMARKS UPON THE STATE OF PARTIES, ministerial pamphlet, 388.
CUSTOMS, English, 186; unpopularity, 170; various duties on wheat, 198, 199; in budgets for 1801, 259; and 1803, 366.
Irish, 214, 239, 240.

DAIRY FARMING, increase in, 40.
DALE, DAVID, proprietor of the New Lanark Mills, 51.
DALTON, JOHN, discoverer of the atom, 42.
DANCE, NATHANIEL, Commodore, East India Company's service, 379; action with Linois, 1804, 379, 380.
DANCING, 68, 70.
DANISH WEST INDIES, temporary seizure by Great Britain, 1801, 247.
DARTFORD, use of, in case of invasion, 386.
DARWIN, ERASMUS, 102.

INDEX

DAVIDSON, ALEXANDER, Member of Council, Lower Canada, 1784, sentenced for fraud, 1808, 275.
DAVOUT, Marshal, French Army, commands part of army of invasion in 1805, 415.
DAVY, HUMPHRY, lectures on chemistry, 102.
DEBT, law of, 158, 159.
DECRÈS, Vice-Admiral, French Navy, Minister of Marine, 401; recommends Villeneuve for Toulon command, 1804, 401; is moved to represent impossibility of plan of invasion, August, 1805, 420, 422, 423; poor opinion of Nelson, 427.
DEISM, 89, 90.
DE LÉVIS, DUC, emigrant, writer on England, quoted, 89.
DE LOLME, JEAN LOUIS, on the English constitution, 155.
DEMERARA, South America, captured from Dutch, 281; captured again, 381.
DENMARK, Royal family of, 245; joins Armed Neutrality, 246, 247; under French influence, 258; claim to toll on ships passing Sound, 327; expedition against, 322, 326 ff.; truce with, 332; Convention, 333 ff.
DEPARTMENTS OF GOVERNMENT, restriction of, 194.
DEPOPULATION of country areas, 56.
DERBY, Earl of, founder of Epsom races, 104.
DERBYSHIRE, mines, 45; Arkwright's mill, 48; disturbances in 1797, 170.
DESPARD, Col., is imprisoned, 133; plots against Government, November, 1802, and is hanged, 363.
DEVONSHIRE, early enclosed, 33; outbreak in 1801, 33, 267; woollen manufactures, 48.
DEVONSHIRE, GEORGIANA, Duchess of, as political hostess, 75, 80; interest in Fox, 115; mentioned, 139.
DIBDIN, his ballad mentioned, 292.
DIET, of agricultural labourers, 18; poorhouses, 18; in various parts of England, 22, 34; calculation of a quarter of wheat a head as yearly requirement, 34; beef and mutton, 40; general simplicity of, 56; effect on female beauty, 74.
DIGBY, Capt., R.N., in command of Africa at Trafalgar, 437.
DINNER PARTIES, 75.
DIPLOMATIC SERVICE, how maintained, 120; authority of King over, 120.
DISRAELI, quoted, 127.
DISTILLING, a domestic trade, 57; distilled liquor in London, 67; effect of closure of distilleries, 67; prohibition of wheat and barley in distillation, 241; one-tenth of average barley crop so used, 344.
DIVORCES, how procured, 157.
DOCKYARDS, ROYAL, St. Vincent's preference to private yards, 389; embezzlement from, 390.
DOGS, sporting, 103; tax on dogs, 181, 186; bulldogs, 348, 349.
DOMESTIC SERVICE, mentioned, 48.
DORSET, Duke of, mentioned, 103.
DORSET, Duchess of, wife of Lord Whitworth, 360.
DOWNSHIRE, Marquis of, Irish borough patron and opponent of Union, 236.
DRESS of male Londoners, 72; of fashionable women, 74, 80; and men, 72, 81.
DRUNKENNESS, the general habit mentioned, 77, 78, 80; at elections, 110.

DUBLIN, landlords resident at, 206; tradesmen, 206; description, 209, 210; unrest in, before Union, 217, 218; parliamentary representation, 236; under Hardwicke's Viceroyalty, 269; outbreak of June, 1803, 367, 368, 369.
DUBLIN CASTLE GOVERNMENT, 218, 219.
DUCHY OF LANCASTER, *see* CHANCELLOR OF THE DUCHY OF LANCASTER.
DUCKING, punishment for scolds, 164.
DUELS, in general, 73; Pitt and Tierney, 73; Grattan and Corrie, 220; a Wexford duel, 230, 231.
DUFF, Capt., R.N., in command of Mars, 1805, 425; appreciation of Nelson, 425; commands inshore squadron off Cadiz, 428; killed at Trafalgar, 434.
DUIGENAN, Dr., 206.
DUMANOIR, Rear-Admiral, French Navy, commands van at Trafalgar, 437; fails to come to the help of the centre, 437, 438; escapes with four ships to the north, 438, 439, 443; taken by Strachan, 443.
DUNCAN, Admiral, mentioned, 285.
DUNDAS, Gen. Sir DAVID, in command of troops in Kent and Sussex, 385; reports on Pitt's corps, 385; plans in event of invasion, 386; mentioned, 136.
DUNDAS, HENRY, Secretary for War, Treasurer of the Navy, and President of the Board of Control, 135, 296, 298; character, 136; possible squib upon, 190; fails in arguing with the King, 253; resignation in 1801, 260; his idea of war, 309; plans Egyptian campaign, 309; satirized by Fox in House of Commons, 265, 266; raised to peerage as Lord Melville, 364.
  a follower of Burke over Irish questions according to George III, 391; his earlier Home Secretaryship mentioned, 218; other mentions, 166, 252, 451. *Also see* MELVILLE.
DUNN, THOMAS, Acting-Governor in Lower Canada, 275, 276.
DUNSTABLE, mentioned, 170.
DURHAM, methodism, 92.
DWYER, Irish outlaw, 367; submission in 1803, 369.

EAST INDIA COMPANY, cadets trained at Great Marlow, 299; rewards Dance for defence of its fleet, 379, 380.
EAST INDIANS, spoil the market for rotten boroughs, 112.
EAST INDIES, strength of British army, 306; apprehensions for security of trade, 423; connection of Cape of Good Hope with protection of the East Indies trade, 424.
ECCLESIASTICAL COURTS, matrimonial separations in, 157.
EDEN, Sir FREDERIC, his State of the Poor quoted, 22, 33, 172.
EDGE, fast walker, 104.
EDGEWORTH, MARIA, novelist, account of tenants in The Absentee, 205; quotation from Life of her father, 207; Grenville's admiration for Castle Rackrent, 135; verses from Ormond, 219, 220; picture of her father in Patronage, 237.
EDGEWORTH, RICHARD, experiences as a landlord, 205; his Life quoted, 207; views on the Union, 237.
EDINBURGH, parliamentary representation, 111; the old town mentioned, 140; cost of letters to, 180.

INDEX

EDINBURGH REVIEW, an article by Sydney Smith, 93; by Jeffrey, 124.
EDINBURGH UNIVERSITY, scientific superiority, 101.
EDUCATION, condition in England, 95, 96, 99 ff.; not a public charge, 171, 188; provision for parish apprentices under the first Factory Act, 350.
EDWARDS, a visitor to Paris, 61.
EGYPT, conquered by Bonaparte, 1798, 309; British conquest projected, 249, 309; carried out, 310 ff.; French designs upon, in 1802–1803, 357, 358, 365; delay in British evacuation, 357; Nelson's fears for, 377; mention of the expedition and events leading to it, 372.
EL ARISH, Convention of, 1800, 372.
ELBA, partly occupied by British in 1800–1801, 322; annexed to France, 1802, 353.
ELDON, Lord, Lord Chancellor, 1801, 261, 263; career and character, 261, 262; his independence in 1804, 122; channel of correspondence between King and Pitt in 1804, 391; effect of his early marriage, 383.
ELDON, Lady, mentioned, 87.
ELECTIONS, parliamentary, 109 ff.; Middlesex, 153, 155; general election of 1802, 352, 353.
ELGIN, Lord, Ambassador in Constantinople, his share in the Egyptian campaign of 1801, 310; arrested when returning through France, 380.
ELIOT, GEORGE, novelist, her Silas Marner quoted, 95.
ELIZABETH, QUEEN, a statute of her reign, 17; her speech at Tilbury, 382.
ELLENBOROUGH, Lord, Sir EDWARD LAW, Attorney-General 1801, 262; afterwards made Lord Chief Justice and created Lord Ellenborough, 262; lines on him, 262.
EMIGRATION, prohibition of, of skilled workmen, 201.
EMMET, ROBERT, leader of a rebellion in Dublin, June, 1803, 367, 368; hanged, 368, 369.
ENCLOSURE: the village before enclosure, 17 ff.; the process of enclosure, 22 ff.; advantages, 23, 24; disadvantages, 25 ff.; General Enclosure Act, 1801, 29; General Enclosure Bill, 1796, 194.
ENGINEERS, ROYAL, 298.
ENGLAND: appearance of the country, 17; unwillingness of Englishwomen to work in the fields, 21, 48; beauty of the women, 74; change in the physiognomy of the men, 73; Fiévée's strictures on, 74, 83; pride, contradictions in the English character, 83; spiritual state, 84 ff.; intellectual, 96 ff.; physical, 102; recreations, 103 ff.; adventurous spirit, 106; love of freedom, 105; patriotism, 106, 340, 341, 382; Nelson on the English, 340.
ENGLAND, EAST OF: arable land, 23.
ENGLAND, NORTH OF: yeomen, 20; diet, 22; early enclosure, 24; household economy, 28; wages of and system of boarding the farm-labourer, 31; depopulation of the Cheviots, 44, 45; coal industry, 45; education, 86, 96; parliamentary representation, 109.
ENGLAND, SOUTH OF: economic development, 21; diet, 22; household economy, 28.
ENGLAND, WEST OF: leases for three lives, 19; yeomen, 20; diet, 22; early enclosures, 24; wages, 31; oxen, 39; woollen trade, 48, 54; education, 96; parliamentary representation, 109; unrest in 1801, 267.
ENTAIL, mentioned, 158.
ERIE, LAKE, Upper Canada, 273.

ERSKINE, Hon. THOMAS, early life, 140, 145; friend of the Prince of Wales, 147; independence as Lord Chancellor in 1807, 122; partial support of Addington, 369; mentioned, 83, 248.
ESSEQUIBO, South America, captured from Dutch, 281; captured again, 381.
ESSEX, yeomen in, 20; early enclosure, 22; plan for, in case of an invasion, 385, 386.
ÉTAPLES, French port of concentration, 373.
ETON, Tomline on, 99; Fox on, 99; education at, of Canning, 138; of Fox, 141; of Grey, 248; mentioned, 72.
ETRURIA, Kingdom of, under French influence, 308.
ETRURIA, Wedgwood's workshop, 55.
EUROPE—"Europe's balance", 137; general state in 1801, 244 ff., 338 ff.; how affected by Peace of Lunéville, 308.
EUROPE, NORTHERN, export of wheat from, 243. *Also see* ARMED NEUTRALITY.
EVANGELICAL MAGAZINE, letter in, on crew of Victory, quoted, 296.
EVANGELICALISM, 90, 91.
EXCHEQUER, CHANCELLOR OF THE, 125. *Also see* PRIME MINISTER.
EXCHEQUER, COURT OF, 156.
EXCISE, failure of Walpole's Bill, in 1733, 115; unpopularity, 170; amount and details, 185; loss from illicit distillation, 344; in budgets for 1801, 259; and 1803, 366.
  Irish, 213.
EXECUTIONS, their infrequency, 160, 161; public behaviour at Wall's execution, 351; his unscientific suspension, 351.
EXPENDITURE, NATIONAL, amount, 181, 182; limitations, 188.

FACTORIES, in Manchester, 42, 51, 52; Wilberforce on, 41; attacks on factories, 53; hours worked, 53; Owen's small factory, 51; relations between employer and employed at a Lancashire factory, 58; unrest in factories, 1800, 268; first Factory Act, 1802, 349, 350; mentioned, 195.
FARMS: engrossment of farms, 24 ff., 56; wealth of farmers, 27, 32; boarding in, in the north, 31; rents, 32; large and small farms, 37, 38; assistance from country banks, 38; changes in farming, 38 ff.; respect of farmers for their own calling, 40; Welsh labour on English farms, 48; aggregate income of farmers in 1798, 57; injury from tithe system, 84, 85; grievances against the game laws, 168; taxes on farmers, 181; attitude towards army and volunteers, 398; how affected by tax on horses, 414.
  in Ireland, *see* IRELAND.
FARQUHAR, Sir WALTER, Pitt's physician, 447, 448.
FASHIONS, 67 ff., 76 ff.
FAUJAS ST. FOND, French traveller, quoted, 70.
FENCIBLES, 306.
FERROL, expedition against, mentioned, 249, 309; French squadron takes refuge in, 1803, and is blockaded by a British squadron, 375, 417; orders issued regarding former, 407, 415; and regarding latter, 1805, 417; Villeneuve enters Ferrol and leaves with the blockaded squadron, August, 1805, 419.
FIELDING, novelist, mention of his novels generally, 75; his Tom Jones, 152; his Amelia, 303.

INDEX 521

FIÉVÉE, JEAN, French traveller and writer, 74; his strictures on the English, 74, 83.
FIFE, Earl of, his forests in Scotland, 40.
FINANCE, English, general account, 180 ff. *Also see* BUDGETS, CIVIL LIST, TAXATION, etc.
  Irish, before Union, 213, 214; after Union, 238, 239.
FIRST LORD OF THE ADMIRALTY: the office, 261; Spencer to 1801, 137; St. Vincent, 1801, 261; Melville, 1804, 394; Barham, 1805, 413.
FIRST LORD OF THE TREASURY: the office, 125. *Also see* PRIME MINISTER.
FISCHER, Commodore, Danish Navy, commands fleet at Battle of Copenhagen, 331, 333.
FITZGERALD, Lord EDWARD, Irish rebel, 165.
FITZHERBERT, Mrs., real wife of Prince of Wales, 147; in danger of arrest for debt, 159.
FITZWILLIAM, Earl, a borough proprietor, 112; Whig leader, 148; his Irish Viceroyalty, 222, 223; view of Irish unrest, 223, 224; plan for an Irish constabulary, 228; on danger from Irish competition to Yorkshire woollen trade, 240; his political position in 1804, 393; mentioned, 251.
FLANDERS, campaigns in, during war of 1793–1801, 372.
FLAX, in Ireland, 203.
FLOUR: wholemeal flour made compulsory in 1800, 241; American, 242; import from United States into Jamaica, 283. *Also see* BROWN BREAD ACT.
FOREIGN SECRETARY, Grenville to 1801, 134; Hawkesbury, 1801, 260; Harrowby, 1804, 394; succeeded by Mulgrave.
FORESTRY, encouragement of, 40.
FORT DE FRANCE, 409.
FORTIFICATIONS, cost of, 298.
FOSTER, JOHN, his Corn Law as Chancellor of the Exchequer in Ireland before the Union, 216; as Speaker of the Irish House of Commons opposes Union, 236; becomes Chancellor of the Irish Exchequer under Pitt, 394; his prediction in debate on Catholic petition, 415.
FOUNDLING HOSPITAL, in Dublin, 210, 211.
FOX, CHARLES JAMES, birth and early career, 140, 141; elected to parliament before he was of age, 113; Irish policy when minister, 218; Coalition with North, 127, 128, 137, 217; hostility to France under old order and friendliness under new, 130, 139, 145; supports Grey in 1792, 145, 146; attempt to get Test Act repealed, 153, 154; obtains audience of King in 1797, 124; witness for O'Connor in 1798, 146; retirements from parliament, 146, 240, 241, 250; relations with Prince of Wales, 147; his friends, 148 ff.; subscription for him, 152; recognizes importance of the King's health, 258; Pitt's compliment to, 264, 265; speech in parliament, March, 1801, and censure of Pitt's treatment of the King, 265, 266, 124; on popularity of the peace, 340; speech on the Civil List, 344, 345; views on the peace terms, 341, 343, 347, 354; visit to Paris, 347; defends the Whig magistrates of Nottingham, 353; censure of Addington, 359; speech in favour of France and scene with Windham, May, 1803, 365; decision to oppose Addington, 1804, 386, 387; Pitt declines a close alliance with, 387, 392; King's rejection of, as a minister, 391; and approval of a foreign mission for, 392; attitude

of Fox and his friends, 392, 393; intended by Pitt to be Foreign Secretary, 394.

gives up powdering, 71; his contest for Westminster mentioned, 115; George III's influence over, 119; remark on Pitt's early promise, 127; low opinion of him, 143.

general character, 141 ff.; a wit, 98; an idler, 99; his view of Eton, 99; a cricketer, 103; a racing-man, 104; his vitality and versatility, 141; indolence, 141; nature of his patriotism, 142; love of liberty, 143; limitations, 143; powers, 144; charm, 144, 148; statesman rather than party leader, 145; in caricature, 151; master of debate, 264, 265; dislike of economics, 264; "foible of not easily quarrelling with an old acquaintance", 365.

mentioned, 126, 248, 368.

FOX, Gen. HENRY, brother of Charles, failure as Commander-in-Chief in Ireland to stop outbreak in Dublin in June, 1803, 368.

FOY, Gen., French Army, on the Royal Engineers, 298.

FRAMEWORK KNITTERS, condition in 1801, 55.

FRANCE, effects of war with, of before Pitt's first administration, 128; the French Revolution, 129, 134, 145; foreign relations during Revolution, 129; declares war with Great Britain, 131; rebels in the kingdom in sympathy with France, 133; influence of French ideas in Ireland, 225, 226; French invasions of Ireland, 214, 226, 231; strength of France and successful conclusion of war on the Continent in 1800, 243 ff.; Peace of Lunéville concluded with Austria, 1801, 308; relations with Great Britain in 1801-1802, 338 ff.; English tourists in France during the peace, 347, 362; disputes with Great Britain, 1802-1803, 353 ff.; treatment of British trade, 355, 356, 362, 363; rupture, 358 ff.; discussion of French policy in parliament, 365; relations with Spain, 401 ff., 424; and Russia, 404; at war with Third Coalition, 422, 423, 444 ff.; treaties concluded with Austria and Prussia, 446.

trade, 61, 362, 363; change in national physiognomy, 73; French war enthusiasm mentioned, 382.

Also see WAR WITH FRANCE, and headings under FRENCH.

FRANCHISE, English, *see* PARLIAMENT, BOROUGH.

Irish; the forty shilling franchise, 204.

FRANCIS, *see* FULTON.

FRANCIS II, Emperor of Germany and King of Austria, 245. *Also see* AUSTRIA.

FRANCIS, Sir PHILIP, speech on price of boroughs, 112.

FRANKFURT, trade with, 59.

FREDERIC, CROWN PRINCE OF DENMARK, Regent during King of Denmark's insanity, 245; Nelson's letter to, 332, 334; reception of Nelson, 334.

FREDERICK THE GREAT, mentioned, 300.

FREDERICK WILLIAM III, King of Prussia, 245. *Also see* PRUSSIA.

FREEHOLDERS, 113, 114; no gatherings of, in Scotland, at elections, 111.

FREE TRADE, in corn, 195; in labour, 195, 196; exemption from Navigation Laws of Free Ports in West Indies, 283.

FREELING, FRANCIS, Secretary to the Post Office, 179.

FREEMEN OF A BOROUGH, in parliamentary elections, 109, 110; their municipal rights, 175, 176.

FREMANTLE, Capt., R.N., commands Neptune at Trafalgar, 436.

FRENCH, in British Army, 306.

INDEX 523

FRENCH CANADIANS, 271 ff.
FRENCH LANGUAGE, acquaintance with, by London tradesmen, 98; by officers in British Army, 101.
FRENCH POSSESSIONS IN NORTH AMERICA, 270.
FRENCH REVOLUTION, 129, 130; in what sense inevitable, 134; attitude of the Whigs, 131, 148; of Fox, 145; of dissenters, 154; of the Irish, 221 ff.
FRENCH WEST INDIES, 278 ff.
FRIENDLY SOCIETIES ACT, 1799, 196.
FRIENDS OF THE PEOPLE, Club formed by Grey and others in 1792, 145.
FRY, ELIZABETH, 172.
FULTON, his catamaran scheme for attacking combined fleet in Cadiz, October, 1805, 427.
FUNDHOLDERS, total income in 1798, 57.
FURNITURE, of Lancashire weavers, 49; furniture a domestic manufacture, 56.
FUR-TRADERS, of Canada, 276.

GAMBLING, 76, 80.
GANTEAUME, Vice-Admiral, French Navy, escapes from Brest, and tries to throw reinforcements into Egypt, 1801, 319; in command at Toulon, 1803, 374; correspondence with Bonaparte, 374; in command at Brest, 1804, 401; failure to break out, 407, 415, 417; mentioned, 406.
GARDENS, NURSERY, of Chelsea and Kensington, 64.
GARDNER, Admiral Lord, in command in Bantry Bay, 375.
GARDNER, Capt. Hon. ALAN, R.N., in command of Hero in action of July 22, 1805, 418.
GARTER, ORDER OF THE, worn by Lord Abercorn, 71.
GARTH, Gen., George III's equerry, mentioned, 253.
GATTON, parliamentary borough, auctioned, 112.
GENTZ, FRIEDERICH VON, observation on Mulgrave, 395.
GEORGE III, position in the constitution as King, and methods of government, 117 ff., 123; insistence on retaining Thurlow as Chancellor in 1782, 122; offers Pitt premiership, February, 1783, 128; insanity in 1788, mentioned, 82; opposition to Catholic claims in 1795, 223, 251; opposition to large creation of peers in 1800, 237, 238; opening of parliament, 1801, 247, 248; opposition to Catholic claims, 252 ff.; view of the position of parliament, 254; selects Addington as premier, 256; temporary insanity, 258; obtains pledge from Pitt, 258; selects Eldon as Chancellor, 261; asks for extra grant for Civil List, 344; describes the Peace as experimental, 362; difficulties as Elector of Hanover, 380; arrangements for, in case of invasion, 386; insistence on his right to choose his own ministers, 390, 391; correspondence and conversation with Pitt, leading to formation of new administration, 391, 392; graceful saying of his to Pitt, 391; resentment at bad influence of Fox over Prince of Wales, 391; grant for Civil List, 397.

   character, 117, 118; interest in agriculture, 40; address to him at Weymouth, 75; remark on Eldon, 87; wit, 98, 383; in satire and caricature, 118, 151; observation on strategy, 243; comparison of him with foreign sovereigns, 245; description of himself as an Old Whig, 253; Eldon's influence over, 262; early attachment to Lady Sarah Lennox, men-

524 ENGLAND IN THE NINETEENTH CENTURY

tioned, 302; causticity, 262, 391; sharpness and pertinacity, 391, 392; his communications with Pitt not attended to, 450; mentioned, 24, 62.

GEORGE, PRINCE OF WALES, birth, talents, and character, 147, 148; wives, 147, 159; friends, 147; in caricature, 151; the King's resentment at Fox's bad influence over, 391; Moira his chief adviser, 394.

GERMANS, in British Army, 306.

GERMAN SCHOOL, of romances, 76.

GERMANY: the German Empire, closing of German rivers to British trade, 247; their reopening, 335; importance of corn from, 267; Prussia as protector of North Germany, 380; North German trade, 380; liberation of North Germany from French control an object of Third Coalition, 404; British expedition to, 411, 445; its recall, 448.

GIBRALTAR, naval actions near, in 1801, 319 ff.; epidemic in 1804, 305; importance as a Mediterranean base, 376.

GILBERT'S ACT, amending Poor Law, 173.

GILLRAY, caricaturist, 118, 151.

GINGER, an export from Jamaica, 281.

GLADSTONE, Sir JOHN, of Liverpool, father of the following, 43.

GLADSTONE, WILLIAM EWART, his allusion to Pitt's delaying war taxation, 452.

GLASGOW, the New Lanark Mills near, mentioned, 51.

GLEANING, 21, 22.

GLOUCESTER, mentioned, 52, 62.

GLOUCESTERSHIRE, woollen trade of, 48; roads, 62.

GOLDSMITH, his lines on a peasantry mentioned, 32.

GORDON, Duchess of, political hostess, 75, 80.

GORDON, Lord GEORGE, riots connected with him, mentioned, 67.

GOREE, French island off West Africa, its vicissitudes, 381.

GOSFORD, Lord GEORGE, Governor of Armagh, on supineness of the magistrates, 227.

GOTHIC SCHOOL, of romances, 76.

GOVERNMENT OFFICES, at Somerset House, 72.

GOVERNMENT SERVANTS, their number, 190, 191.

GOVERNOR, title of the head of a county in Ireland, 210.

GOWER, Lord, Postmaster-General in 1800, 180.

GOWER, Lord GRANVILLE LEVESON, mentioned, 123.

GRAND VIZIER, Turkish General, *see* TURKEY.

GRANT, ISAAC, Vice-Consul of Leghorn; his defence of Porto Ferrajo, 322.

GRANT, Sir WILLIAM, Solicitor-General, his speech on the Address, 1801, 250.

GRATTAN, of the Connaught Rangers, on troopships, 305.

GRATTAN, HENRY, Irish patriot, obtains legislative independence for Ireland, 217; his support of Government, 220; "Grattan's Parliament", 219 ff.; his insistence on reforms, 223; belief in subsidence of religious animosities, 226, 227; return to parliament during Union debates, 235; provocation of Corrie to a duel, 220; speech in British House of Commons in 1805, mentioned, 415; Pitt's approval of his oratory, 452.

GRAVES, THOMAS, Rear-Admiral, flies flag in Defiance as Nelson's Second-in-Command in Battle of Copenhagen, 331; his part in the battle, 331; his letter on it, 333; made a K.B., 335; while in command of squadron blockading Rochefort in 1805 allows Missiessy to escape, 406.

INDEX 525

GRAZIERS, IRISH, 205, 216.
GREATHEAD, HENRY, rewarded for invention of life-boat, 188.
GREAT MARLOW, training-college for military cadets at, 299.
GREEN, Major-Gen. Sir CHARLES, captures Surinam jointly with Hood, 381.
GRENADA, West Indies, 278.
GRENVILLE, Lord, Foreign Secretary, 134; free hand enjoyed as such, 394; Auditor of the Exchequer, 189; his unsuccessful negotiations with Otto, 338; share in proposed measure for Catholics, 1801, 252; resigns and passes into opposition, 260; attacks the peace terms, 342; scornful observation on Hawkesbury's negotiations, 359; Addington's objections to his holding office, 364; overtures to Fox, 386, 387; Erskine's and Sheridan's objections to him, 387; his position in May, 1804, 392, 393; breach with Pitt, 393, 394; censures treatment of Spain, 403; action of his party in motion on Catholic petition, 414.
  his condemnation of the Speenhamland system, 30; remark on Pitt in an intercepted letter of his, 450.
  character, 135; George III on his obstinacy, 391; a fresh instance of it, 393.
  mentioned, 412, 451.
GRENVILLE, THOMAS, member of Pitt's first administration, 135; resigns and passes into opposition, 260; objects to the peace terms, 343; Addington's objection to his holding office, 364; overtures to Fox, 386, 387; a link between him and Lord Grenville, 393.
  his condemnation of the Speenhamland system, 30; poor opinion of the army, 372.
GRENVILLES, a Whig family, 148.
GRETNA GREEN MARRIAGES, 79.
GREY, CHARLES, early career, 248, 145; opposes Irish Union in parliament, as leader of Opposition in Fox's absence, 241; speech on Address, 1801, 249; motion in parliament in March, 264; his father made a peer by Addington, 369; refuses office under Addington, 369.
  remark on Fox in after life, 145; mentioned, 140.
  character, 248; zeal for Reform, 145, 146, 152; happiness at Howick, 250.
GROSLEY, French visitor to England, quoted, 98.
GUADELOUPE, French West Indies, 279.
GUARDS, BRIGADE OF, at Aboukir, March 8, 1801, 313.
GUIANA, 381.
GUILDHALL, Pitt's speech at the banquet, November 9, 1805, 446, 447.
GUILDS of London, 175.
GUNS, naval, 294.
GUSTAVUS III, King of Sweden, his remark on the English police, 168.
GUSTAVUS ADOLPHUS, King of Sweden in 1800, 245.

HABEAS CORPUS ACT, so-called Suspension of, 133, 164, 166; re-enaction of "Suspension", 1801, 268.
HAIR-POWDER, a waste of flour, 34; disuse, 71; effect of the tax on, 71; incidence of the tax, 181; one of the assessed taxes, 186, 188; the tax mentioned, 34.
HALIFAX, without a resident magistrate, 165.
HALIFAX, NOVA SCOTIA, value of its harbour, 270.

HAMBURG, a Free Town, mentioned, 404.
HAMILTON, Lady, connection with Nelson, 325.
HAMMOND, Admiral Sir ANDREW, head of Navy Board, 295.
HANOVER, French invasion of, 380; British prejudice regarding, 380; recruitment for Great Britain in, 411; troops landed in, 445.
HARDWICKE, Earl, Viceroy of Ireland, 261; his success, 269; failure to prevent outbreak in Dublin, June, 1805, 368.
HARDY, Capt. THOMAS, R.N., commands St. George, Nelson's flagship, in 1801, 328; intimate relations with him, 328, 435, 436, 439; his work before Battle of Copenhagen, 328; commands Victory, Nelson's flagship at Trafalgar, 436; with him when dying, 439; made a baronet, 441.
HARE, FRANCIS, friend of Harry Temple, 100.
HARGOOD, Capt., R.N., in command of Belleisle at Trafalgar, 434.
HARGREAVES, JAMES, inventor of spinning-jenny, mentioned, 53.
HARROWBY, Foreign Secretary, 1804, 394; accident to, December, 1804, and resignation, 395; rejoins Ministry as Chancellor of the Duchy of Lancaster, 413; mission to Berlin, November, 1805, 446; Pitt's dying mention of him, 449.
HARROW SCHOOL, tastes of Temple (Lord Palmerston) at, 100.
HARVESTS, bad harvests towards end of 18th century, 33, 34; in 1799 and 1800, 241, 242, 248; good harvest in 1801, 343.
HARVEY, Capt., R.N., in command of Temeraire at Trafalgar, 436.
HARWICH, a Treasury borough, 113.
HASLEMERE, parliamentary borough owned by Lord Lonsdale, 113.
HASTINGS, WARREN, his trial mentioned, 102.
HATHRAS, siege mentioned, 304.
HAUGWITZ, Prussian Count, French policy of, 446; concludes Treaty of Alliance between Prussia and France, December, 1805, 446.
HAVANA, superiority of its coffee, 60.
HAVRE, mentioned, 378.
HAWKESBURY, Lord, a member of Pitt's first administration, 139; Foreign Secretary, 1801, 260; his abilities defended by Pitt, 264; proposes peace terms to Otto, 338; agrees to the Preliminaries, 338; remonstrates against subjugation of Switzerland, 355; and treatment of British vessels, 356; instructions to Whitworth, 357; note on Malta, 358, 359; Home Secretary, 1804, 394; speech on Army, 1805, 400; visits Pitt, January, 1806, 448; Home Secretaryship of 1808 mentioned, 170.
 character, 260, 261.
HAYDON, BENJAMIN, painter, mentioned, 67.
HAYTER, GEORGE, picture by, mentioned, 248.
HAZLITT, WILLIAM, account of a sermon by Coleridge, 301.
HEALTH, of the people of England, 102; of Bristol, 177; of Dublin, 210. *Also see* BOARD OF HEALTH, MANCHESTER.
HEARTH TAX in Ireland, 213; reduction, 224.
HELDER, expedition to, in 1799, mentioned, 297.
HELVETIC REPUBLIC, *see* SWITZERLAND.
HENRI IV, King of France, ancestor of Fox, 141.
HEREFORDSHIRE, a cider and agricultural county, 21.
HERTFORD COLLEGE, OXFORD, education of Fox at, 141.
HESIOD, mentioned, 18.
HICKEY, WILLIAM, of Calcutta, on smoking, 70.

INDEX 527

HIGH WYCOMBE, Staff College opened at, in 1799, **299**; officers trained there take part in Egyptian campaign, 319; mentioned, 101.
HILEY, "BROTHER", one of Addington's family, 388.
HILL, Sir RICHARD, M.P., introduces bill to prevent bull-baiting, 348.
HOBART, a former Chief Secretary, 263; Secretary for War, 1801, **263**; becomes BUCKINGHAMSHIRE, Earl of, 397, 398, q.v.
HOHENLINDEN, Battle of, 1800, 246.
HOLCROFT, THOMAS, speech in his own defence on a charge of high treason, 112.
HOLKAM, mentioned, 250. *See also* COKE.
HOLLAND, Pitt's policy with reference to, before and after 1792, **128, 130**; French attack upon, 130, 131; export of wheat from, 243; under French influence in 1800, 308; how affected by Treaty of Amiens, 338 ff.; warlike preparations incorrectly alleged to exist in, March, 1803, 359, 360; treated as a part of France, 363; share in French plans against England, 373, 375, 378, 379; loses West Indian and South American possessions, 381; liberation from French control an object of Third Coalition, 404; proposal for its reconquest by the Third Coalition, 445; mentioned, 249.
HOLLAND, first Lord, father of Fox, 140.
HOLLAND, Lord, Fox's nephew; his zeal for negro emancipation, **149**; supports freedom of trade, 195.
HOLLAND, Lady, her education, 101; a friend of Canning, 139; dinner to Prince of Wales, 148; quoted, 136, 165.
HOLY ROMAN EMPIRE, 245.
HOME SECRETARY, Portland to 1801, **137**; Pelham, 1801, **263**; Yorke, 1803, **369**; Hawkesbury, 1804, **394**.
Colonies also under Home Secretary until 1801, 125.
Powers of the office under so-called Habeas Corpus Suspension Act, 164.
HONDURAS, BRITISH, 285.
HOOD, Commodore Sir SAMUEL, captures Surinam jointly with Green, 381; seizes a fortified islet off Fort de France, 409.
HORNER, FRANCIS, quoted, 449, 450.
HORROCKS, JOHN, cotton spinner and M.P., 152.
HORSE-RACING, Mrs. Thornton's matches, 76; condition of horse-racing in 1800, 104; Windham on, 348.
HORSES, owned by small-holders, 19; supersede oxen in husbandry, 39; horse-breaking and breeding, 39; taxes on, 181; taxation, 181, 259, 260; increase in 1805 rejected by Parliament, 414.
HORSLEY, SAMUEL, Bishop, leader of the High Church school, 84; an absentee, 88; a writer, 88; as Bishop of Rochester, on seditious Sunday schools, 268.
HOSTE, Capt., R.N., his signal "Remember Nelson", 441.
HOUSES, Elizabethan law relating to, 17; in Manchester, 42, 44, 53; Liverpool, 44; Birmingham, 45, 46; general adequacy and cheapness, 56; suburban, 64; in London, 64; English contrasted with Scottish and continental, 65; coolness of, 74; taxes on, 181; Dublin overcrowding, 210.
HOWARD, JOHN, his visits to jails, 161.
HOWARDS, a Whig family of influence in Yorkshire, 114, 148.
HOWE, Admiral, mentioned, 285.
HOWICK, Grey's home, 250.

528   ENGLAND IN THE NINETEENTH CENTURY

HUDSON'S BAY COMPANY, 271, 276.
HULKS, for convicts, 162.
HULL, trade of, 61; Wilberforce member for, 113; mentioned, 90.
HUMBERT, Gen., French Army, commander of force which invaded Ireland in 1798, on light infantry tactics, 300; on possibility of conquering the island, 371.
HUNT, LEIGH, journalist, his account of his father, 90; his treatment in prison, 162.
HUNTING, by farmers, 38; by women, 75; condition of the sport in 1800, 103, 104.
HUNTINGDON, Countess of, mentioned, 75.
HUTCHINSON, Major-Gen. HELY, succeeds Abercromby in command of forces in Egypt, March, 1801, 316; admiration for him, 316, 317; diffidence, 317; captures Cairo and Alexandria, 317, 318; made a K.B. and a peer, 318.
HUTTON, WILLIAM, his account of the Court of Requests, 156.

INCOME, NATIONAL, difficulties in the way of computing it, 56; Pitt's attempt, 57.
INCOME TAX, first imposition in 1798, 57, 187; estimate for 1801, 259; abolished, 1802, 347; estimate of receipts exaggerated by Pitt, 347; reintroduction, 1803, 366; criticisms, 366; taxation at the source, 347, 366; distinction between earned and unearned income, 366.
INDEPENDENTS, religious sect, 93.
INDIA, trade, 59; its unimportance compared with that with Northern Europe, 60; duties on calicoes and muslins from India, 186; export of rice, 242; Russian and French designs on, 246; siege of Hathras mentioned, 304. *See also* BOARD OF CONTROL and EAST INDIES.
INDUSTRY, representation in parliament, 195. *See also* separate industries under their own heads, as COTTON.
INDUSTRY, CENTRES OF, an instance of shortage of magistrates in, 165; political views in, 152; patriotism in, 177, 178; revolutionary propaganda in, 196; disturbances in, 197, 268.
INFANTRY, ignorance of Light Infantry tactics in 1801, 300.
INFORMERS, REVENUE, their ingenuity, 188.
INTELLIGENCE OFFICERS, mentioned, 405.
INTERCEPTED LETTERS, name of a publication containing letters from the French army in Egypt intercepted by the British, 309.
INVALIDS, in the Army, 306.
INVASIONS of Ireland, 214, 226, 231; feasibility of invasion of the United Kingdom generally, 370 ff.; French plans, 1803, 1804, 370 ff., 386, 400, 401, 405 ff.; British defensive measures, 381 ff.; alarms of invasion, 385; French plans temporarily dropped in winter of 1804, 405; renewal in 1805, 407, 415; finally dropped, 420, 421, 422.
IRELAND, agricultural labourers from, 18; connection with Liverpool and Bristol, 43, 48; income from, 58; Irish setter dogs, 103; charge against Government of Ireland of provoking 1798 rebellion, mentioned, 132; primitive economy of the country, 202, 203, 204; its peasantry, 202, 203, 204; Church, 205; gentry, 205, 206; religious oppression and proselytization of Catholics, 206, 212; ill-treatment of the poor, 207, 224; population, 208; magistracy, 211, 227, 228, 231; agrarian dis-

INDEX 529

turbances, 211, 224, 269; roads, 212; finance before Union, 212 ff.; education, 212, 213; banking, 214, 215; trade, 215, 216, 239, 240; agriculture, 216; industries, 216, 239, 240; obtains legislative independence in 1782, 217; subsequent events, 217, 218; nature of the Viceregal government, 218, 219; corruption, 219, 220; the Catholic question, 221, 222; causes of the 1798 rebellion, 222 ff.; the rebellion, 229, 230, 231; the Union, 231 ff.; French invasions, 214, 226, 231; finance at the Union, 238, 239; economic weakness, 239, 240; how far affected by scarcity of 1799, 243; Pitt's proposals for satisfying the Catholics, 251 ff.; result of his failure to carry them, 254 ff.; Irish budget, 1801, 260; distress in 1801, 268; unrest, 269; continuation of Irish Martial Law Act in 1801, 269; success of Hardwicke's Viceroyalty, 269; strength of troops in the country, 306; abolition of bull-baiting in Ireland, mentioned, 348; general election of 1802, 352; budget for 1803, 365; disturbances in 1802–3, 367; reconciliation of Ulster, 367; outbreak in Dublin, June, 1803, 368; pacification, 368, 369; facility of conquering Ireland according to Humbert, 371; projects of invasion after renewal of French war, 373, 386; debates in parliament on Catholic petition, 414, 415; predictions in this connection, 414, 415.

national characteristics—lawlessness, 205, 207, 217, 227, 228; religious feelings and animosities, 222, 225 ff., 233, 234; vindictiveness, 202, 207, 208, 227; dirt and ostentation, 209, 210; callousness, 210, 211; want of enterprise, 212, 216. *Also see* PARLIAMENT, IRISH; VICEROY; etc.

IRON, the industry, 45, 46; export of, from England to Ireland, 216.
ISLE OF MAN, 20.
ITALY, trade with, 60; how affected by Peace of Lunéville, 308; omission of arrangements for, at the Peace between Great Britain and France, 339; a criticism on this, 340; Bonaparte's plans for, 341, 342; Cisalpine Republic reconstituted as Italian Republic, 342; recruitment of British Navy from Italy, 389; liberation from French control an object of Third Coalition, 404. *Also see* NAPLES, etc.

JACKSON, GEORGE, diplomatist, his precocity, 100.
JACOBINISM, methods of, 166; connection with trade-union activity, 197; effect on Ireland, 222; mentioned in parliament, 265; connection discovered between it and the abolition of bull-baiting, 348.
JAMAICA, West Indies, 280 ff.; mentioned, 409.
JAMES, WILLIAM, naval historian, 293.
JARRY, General, French emigrant, Professor at High Wycombe Military College, 299.
JEFFERSON, THOMAS, elected President of the United States in 1800, 277.
JEFFREY, FRANCIS, views on the power of the Crown, 124.
JENNER, EDWARD, rewarded for discovery of vaccination, 188.
JERNINGHAMS, a Catholic family, 153.
JERVIS, JOHN, *see* ST. VINCENT, EARL OF.
JEWS, as stockjobbers, 184; in West Indies, 283.
JOHN, Prince Regent of Portugal, 245.

LL

JOHNSON, EDWARD, inventor of penny post in London, 179.
JOHNSON, Dr. Windham's master, 138; on excise, 170; mentioned, 99.
JORDAN, Mrs., 83.
JUDGES, English, *see* CHANCELLOR; etc.
   Irish, 209.
JUNOT, General, French Army, mentioned, 372.
JURIES, independence of, 164; defects, 164, 165.
   grand, 159; duties in certain cases, 176; in Ireland, 212.
   petty, 159.
   special, 164.
JUSTICE, the independence of the law-courts a British advantage, 108.
JUSTICES OF THE PEACE, their independence of Government and reliance on local interests, 115, 165; as the agency by which the laws were carried out, 115; number and distribution, 165, 166; character and duties, 165, 166, 169 ff.; duties under the first Factory Act, 349, 350.

KEATS, Capt., R.N., commands Superb in action near Gibraltar, October, 1801, 321, 322.
KEITH, Admiral Lord, blockade of Dutch ships by, 375; a suggestion of his Secretary, 416.
KENT, yeomen in, 20; a county of early enclosure, 22; Stanhope's influence with the freeholders, 152; sonnet of Wordsworth addressed to the men of Kent, 384; plans for, in case of invasion, 384, 385, 386.
KENYON, Lord, Chief Justice, mentioned, 118.
KEUGH, Capt., Wexford landlord and rebel, 230.
KILKENNY, wages, 215; coalfields, 216.
KILLARNEY, an English traveller in, 215.
KILWARDEN, Lord, Chief Justice of Ireland, murdered, June, 1803, 368.
KING, power of, 108, 119 ff.; use of prerogative of mercy, 161; cursed by seditious agitators, 166, 167.
KING'S BENCH, COURT OF THE, 156; its criminal jurisdiction, 159.
KING'S GERMAN LEGION, mentioned, 380.
KINGSTON, a scold ducked at, 164.
KINGSTON, a town in Jamaica, 281.
KINGSTON, a town in Upper Canada, 274.
KIRWAN, Dean, his Catholic connection, 206.
KNITTERS, *see* FRAMEWORK KNITTERS.
KNOX, Brigadier-Gen. JOHN, views on Irish unrest, 225.

LABOUR AGITATION, in 1801, 267 ff. *Also see*
LABOURERS, combinations and the Combination Acts, 195 ff.; emigration of skilled labourers prohibited, 201. *Also see* AGRICULTURAL LABOURERS, FACTORIES, MINES, etc.
   Irish, 202, 203, 210; wages of, 215, 224.
LAKE, GENERAL, a friend of the Prince of Wales, 147; mention of, in Ireland, 230.
LAMB, CHARLES, as contributor to the Morning Post, 97; mentioned, 100.
LANCASHIRE, population and importance, 41 ff.; cotton industry in, 49, 50; roughness of the men, 53; a Lancashire mill, 58; trade of, 61;

INDEX

531

Methodism, 92; recreations, 103; a Tory county, 152; Lancashire interest in protection, 186; restriction of certain exports, 201; unrest in 1801, 268.
LAND, its redivision advocated by Spence, 268; Irish land troubles, 269; taxation on, 181, 366. *Also see* following entries:
LANDOWNERS, 19; decay of smaller landed gentry, 32; total income of landholders in 1798, 57; landed property not liable to be sold for debt, 158; taxation on landowners, 181.
   in Ireland, land system, 203, 204, 206, 216, 217; landed gentry, 203, 205 ff., 216, 217.
LAND-TAX, 186; mentioned, 181.
LANNES, Marshal, French Army, commands part of army of invasion in 1805, 415.
LANSDOWNE, Marquis of (formerly Earl of Shelburne), quoted on Slave Trade, 94; a patron of Bentham, 105; his administration, 127; views on Union with Ireland, 232; mentioned, 217.
LANUSSE, General, French Army, at Battle of Canopus, 314; mortally wounded, 315.
LATITUDINARIAN WHIGS, 93.
LATOUCHE-TRÉVILLE, Rear-Admiral, French Navy, in command at Boulogne, 1801, 336, 337; as Vice-Admiral designated for command of a naval expedition in 1803, 405; death, 1804, 401.
LAUDERDALE, Earl of, unpatriotic conduct in 1803, 347.
LAURENCE, Dr., M.P., 250.
LAW, Sir EDWARD, *see* ELLENBOROUGH.
LAW, knowledge of, widely diffused in England, 156, 157; impossibility of enforcing an unpopular law, 108, 115; English respect for law, 155; legal fictions, 156.
LAW-COURTS, *see* CHANCELLOR, etc.
LAW, INTERNATIONAL, views of the Northern Powers in 1801, 246.
LAWYERS, income, 57; influence in a new country such as Canada, 276; as volunteers, 383.
LEEDS, population, etc., 41; mentioned, 54.
LEEWARD ISLANDS, West Indies, 279.
LEGHORN, mentioned, 60.
LEINSTER, Duke of, sole Irish duke, 219.
LE MARCHANT, Lt.-Col., at head of High Wycombe College for Officers, 299.
LENNOX, Lady CAROLINE, her marriage to the first Lord Holland, 141.
LENNOX, Lady SARAH, becomes by marriage mother of the Napiers, 302.
LENNOXES, a Whig family, 148.
LEVANT, trade, 60; apprehensions regarding, 377. *Also see* TURKEY.
LIBERTY HALL, headquarters of gang of intimidators in Ireland, 269.
LIFEBOAT, reward for its invention, 188.
LIGHT BRIGADE, trained by Moore at Shorncliffe, 384, 385.
LIGURAN REPUBLIC, French influence over, 308.
LIMERICK, a centre of the provision trade, 216.
LIMERICK, Earl of, speech on the Catholic petition, 1805, 414, 415.
LINCOLNSHIRE, small-holders in, 19, 26; wages, 31; non-resident clergy, 88; sentence on a blacksmith in, 167.
LINEN, worn by labourers, 19; export from Ireland, 216, 239; bounties, 239.

LINOIS, Read-Admiral, French Navy, actions with Saumarez, July, 1801, 319 ff.; action with Dance, 1804, 379.
LISBON newspaper mentioned, 422.
LITERATURE, not assisted by Government, 188.
LIVERPOOL, population and description, 43, 44; trade, 61; institution for the blind, 95; a parliamentary election at, 110; recruits for the Navy, 291; election riot in 1802, 352.
LIVERPOOL, Earl of, Tory statesman, 139; his work on coinage, 191, 192; his view of the Crown, 192.
LOANS, GOVERNMENT, how raised, 184, 185; £16,744,000, £23,000,000, £10,000,000, £10,000,000, £20,000,000, borrowed in 1801–1805 respectively, 259, 347, 367, 395, 413.
  Irish, £2,500,000 and £2,000,000, borrowed in 1801 and 1802 respectively, 260, 347, 348.
LOCAL SELF-GOVERNMENT, in the country, 169 ff.; in towns, 175 ff.
LOGWOOD, trade from British Honduras, 285.
LONDON, its meat supply, 23; cost of a labourer's clothes, 55, 56; Docks, 61; canal communication with, 62; the neighbourhood, 64; population and description, 64 ff.; shortage of churches, 89; press, intelligence of Londoners, 98; its courts, 166; police, 168, 169; administration, 175, 176; its penny post, 179; millwrights' dispute, 196; Spitalfields weaver riots, 197; riots of 1780, 197; heaths near, 199; intended abandonment in case of invasion, 385, 386; apprehensions for, 423.
LONDON CORRESPONDING SOCIETY, activities, 133.
LONDONDERRY, Presbyterian traditions of, 227.
LONDONDERRY, Bishop of, *see* BRISTOL, EARL OF.
LONSDALE, Earl of, his parliamentary boroughs, 113, 149.
LORD CHANCELLOR, *see* CHANCELLOR.
LORD-LIEUTENANT, *see* VICEROY.
LORD MAYOR OF LONDON, 175, 176.
LORD OF THE MANOR, 20, 177.
LORD PRESIDENT OF THE COUNCIL, the office, 125; held by Chatham to 1801, 137; Portland, 1801, 263; Sidmouth, 1805, 399; succeeded by Camden, 413.
LORD PRIVY SEAL, the office, 125; held by Westmorland in Pitt's first and the two following administrations, 137, 263.
LORDS, the title, by whom borne, 116. *Also see* PARLIAMENT.
LORIENT, French port on Atlantic coast, blockaded, 375.
LOTTERIES, STATE, demoralizing effect, 74, 75; in Ireland, 214.
LOUGHBOROUGH, Lord, Lord Chancellor in 1800, 138; opposes Pitt on Irish question, 252; secret adviser of the King, 254; attempt to remain in office after change of Ministry, 164; retirement, 261, 262; pension, 191; created Earl of Rosslyn, 262; death, 262; George III's judgment on, 262.
LOUIS XVI, King of France, his dethronement, 129.
LOUIS, Rear-Admiral THOMAS, in command of a squadron detached by Nelson, October, 1805, 428.
LUCAS, Capt., French Navy, at Trafalgar, 435, 436.
LUISE, Queen of Prussia, 245.
LUMBER, import of, from United States into Jamaica, 283; in British Honduras, 285.
LUNÉVILLE, Peace of, 308; mentioned, 358.
LUTTRELL, Col., society wit, 98.

INDEX

MACAULAY, mentioned, 101.
MACHINERY, pumping engines for mines, 46; machinery for spinning and weaving, 48, 49; resistance to, 53, 54; superiority of machine-spun cotton, 59; export of machinery prohibited, 201.
MACKENZIE, ALEXANDER, Canadian explorer, 276.
MACKENZIE, HENRY, his "Man of Feeling", 77.
MACKINTOSH, Sir JAMES, law reformer, his defence of Peltier, 97; Parr's rebuke of him, 99; remark on Windham, 138; mentioned, 77.
MACKINTOSH, an anticipation of the, 74.
MCLANE, conspirator executed for treason in Canada, 276.
MACLEOD, Sir JOHN, R.A., professional head of the Ordnance Department, 297.
MACNEVEN, Dr., Irish rebel, on causes of the rebellion, 228.
MAGISTRACY, *see* JUSTICES OF THE PEACE, *also* NOTTINGHAM.
    Irish, constitution and duties, 211; opened to Catholics in 1792, 222; failure of, 227 ff., 225.
MAGON, Rear-Admiral, French Navy, reinforces Villeneuve in West Indies, 410, 415; killed at Trafalgar, 437.
MAHOGANY, trade from British Honduras, 285.
MAIDA, Battle of, mentioned, 324.
MAILS, how carried, 63; establishment of mail-coaches, 179.
MALACCA, Straits of, Dance's naval action, 379.
MALCOLM, JAMES, author of a book on London, 65.
MALMESBURY, Earl of, retired diplomatist, a friend of Pitt, 76, 393; his opinion of the Peace of Amiens, 362; on Pitt's speech of May 23, 1803, 365.
MALMESBURY, second Earl of, on Pitt, 450.
MALMESBURY, Lady, letter of, on Hawkesbury, 260.
MALTA, taken by French from Order of St. John, 1798, 339, 341; taken by British, 339; position at the Peace of 1801-1802, 339 ff.; Pitt and Fox on, 341; obstacles to British evacuation, 346, 357 ff.; final French proposals and their refusal, 362.
    recruitment of Navy from, 291, 389; mentioned, 249, 376, 377, 445.
MAN, ISLE OF, yeomen in, 20.
MANCHESTER, population and description, 42, 43; weavers, 49, 58; self-made men, 50; Owen in Manchester, 51; Southey on child-labour in, 52, 53; political views of, 110, 152; administration of, 177, 178; mentioned, 62. *Also see* BOARD OF HEALTH, MANCHESTER.
MANORIAL COURTS, 167, 177.
MANUFACTURES, *see* INDUSTRY.
MARCUS AURELIUS, mentioned, 90.
MARENGO, Battle of, mentioned in parliament, 266.
MAREOTIS, LAKE, in Egypt, 311, 314, 318.
MARGATE, visits to, 68.
MARIA I, Queen of Portugal, 244, 245.
MARIA CAROLINA, Queen of the Two Sicilies, 244.
MARIA LUISA, Queen of Spain, 245.
MARIA THERESA, former Austrian Empress, mentioned, 244.
MARIE ANTOINETTE, former Queen of France, mentioned, 244.
MARINE ARTILLERY, started in 1804, 293.
MARINES, strength in 1801, 293; their good service, 293.
MARLOW, GREAT, *see* GREAT MARLOW.

MAROONS, in Jamaica, 280.
MARRIAGE SETTLEMENTS, 158.
MARRYAT, Capt., R.N., his novels mentioned, 287, 292, 304.
MARTELLO TOWERS, 298.
MARTINIQUE, French West Indies, 279; its superiority in sugar, 60; captured by British, 281; French fears for its capture again after renewal of war, 405; mentioned, 338, 339, 420. *Also see* FORT DE FRANCE.
MASSENA, Marshal, French Army, in command in Italy, 1805, 445.
MASTER-GENERAL OF THE ORDNANCE, the office, 296 ff.; held by Cornwallis to 1801, 138, 297, 298; Chatham, 1801, 263.
MASTER OF THE ROLLS, 164.
MAURICE, Capt., R.N., commands islet off Fort de France in 1805, and is forced to surrender, 409.
MAYNOOTH, Catholic College founded in 1795, 223; mentioned, 256.
MAYORS, as magistrates, 166; in a civil court, 157; election of, 176.
MEATH, a typical Irish county, wages in, 215.
MEDICAL PROFESSION, estimated total income in 1798, 57; no expenditure on medical service for the public, 188; naval medical service, 296; military, 305.
MÉHÉE DE LA TOUCHE, used by French Government as pretended spy for British, 373, 388, 389.
MELVILLE, Lord, attempted mediation between Addington and Pitt, 1803, 364; becomes First Lord of the Admiralty, 1804, 394; his administration and services to the Navy, 396, 400, 413; resigns on censure of House of Commons, 412, 413; mentioned, 389, 449. *Also see* DUNDAS, HENRY.
MENOU, General, French Army, in command in Egypt, 1801, 309 ff.; failure to resist British landing effectually, 312, 313; fights Battle of Canopus, 314 ff.; surrenders Alexandria, 318.
MEN-SERVANTS, tax on, 181, 186.
MERCHANT SERVICE, 289, 290; loss to, from privateers, 294, 295.
MEREDITH, GEORGE, novelist, quoted, 78.
METHODISTS, 91, 92; attitude towards established Church and Government, 154.
MIDDLESEX, parliamentary election, 1802, 153, 155, 352.
MIDDLETON, Sir CHARLES, becomes First Lord of the Admiralty and takes title of Lord Barham, q.v., 413.
MILDMAY, Sir HENRY, reports on convict hulks, 162.
MILITIA, the ballot, 90; difficulty over education of N.C.O.s, 96; unpopularity of service in, 170; families of militiamen provided from poor fund, 175; strength in 1801, 307; strength in 1803, 382; comparison with regular army, 396; strength reduced in 1804, 396; Jane Austen's view of militia officers, 398, 399; militiamen pass into the Line, 1805, 410, 411.
    Irish, 231.
MILLWRIGHTS, trade dispute, 196.
MILNES, ROBERT, Lieut.-Governor of Lower Canada in 1790, 271, 275.
MILTON, poet, mentioned, 248.
MINES, conditions in England, 45; Birmingham pumping engines for, 46; Welsh coal used for smelting Cornish ore, 47; Anglesea copper mine, 47; Somerset coal mines, 48; total estimated income in 1798, 57; Methodism among miners, 92; Cheddar miners, 95; turbulence of miners, 170, 267.

INDEX

MINORCA, Spanish possession, taken by British and restored at the Peace, 339; a regiment from, 315; mentioned, 317.
MINT, ROYAL, its inefficiency, 191.
MINTO, Earl of, mentions Grenville, 135; the danger to trade in 1805, 423; Nelson's popularity, 425.
MIQUELON, French island off Newfoundland, taken by British in war and restored in peace, 270.
MISSIESSY, Rear-Admiral, French Navy, escapes from Rochefort, 1805, 406; sails to West Indies and returns, 407, 408; mentioned, 411.
MITFORD, Sir JOHN, Attorney-General till 1801, 140; Speaker, 1801, 259; Lord Chancellor of Ireland, 1802, with title of Redesdale, 352.
MOIRA, a friend of the Prince of Wales, 147, 148; letter of Nelson to, 324; refuses post of Foreign Secretary, 394; mentioned, 243.
MONMOUTHSHIRE, mines in Forest of Dean, 45.
MONOPOLISTS, prosecution of, 267; riots against, 267.
MONTE VIDEO, siege of, mentioned, 298.
MONTREAL, Lower Canada, commercial town, 271; conspiracy in, 276; its military weakness, 277.
MONTROSE, Duke of, President of the Board of Trade, 1804, 394.
MOORE, Dr., 302; father of the two following:
MOORE, Capt. GRAHAM, R.N., seizes Spanish treasure-ships, 1804, 402, 403.
MOORE, Major-Gen. Sir JOHN, Governor of St. Lucia, 278, 279; under Abercromby in Mediterranean and sent to Jaffa, 311; in actions of March 8, 1801, 313; and March 21st, 314, 315; commands Light Brigade at Shorncliffe, 384, 385.
 on the soldier's training, 304; his confidence in Pitt, 452; mentioned, 136, 310, 402.
MOORE, Dr. JOHN, Archbishop of Canterbury, proposes voluntary rationing of bread, 241.
MOORE, THOMAS, poet, a wit, 98; his song on Emmet's betrothed, 369.
MORALS, 68, 73 ff.; at Cambridge University, 99.
MORE, HANNAH, her work, 95; mentioned, 75, 80, 90.
MOREA, plan of French expedition to, 374.
MORNING CHRONICLE, letters in, 73, 390; satire on female dress, 80; position of, in 1801, 97; its indecent political attacks, 150; a satirical advertisement, 190; quoted, 167.
MORNING POST, its descriptions of Society, 71; Rev. Henry Bate, editor, 87; position of, in 1801, 97; its indecent political attacks, 151.
MORRIS, Capt., R.N., in command of Colossus at Trafalgar, 435.
MOSSE, Capt. ROBERT, R.N., killed at Battle of Copenhagen, 332.
MULGRAVE, Chancellor of the Duchy of Lancaster, 1804, 394; made Foreign Secretary, 395, 398; his unfitness, 395; reply to peace overture, 404; poem by, 450; mentioned, 106.
MUNICIPALITIES, dissenters in, 153; administration of, 175 ff.
MURPHY, Father JOHN, Irish Catholic priest and rebel leader, 229.
MUSEUM, BRITISH, mentioned, 188.
MUSKETRY, volunteer proficiency, 385.
MUSLINS, duty on, 186; protection of, in Ireland, 240.
MUTINIES, NAVAL, at Spithead and the Nore, 286; during the Peace 343.

NAPIER, Gen. Sir CHARLES, observation when a young officer, on the high standard required for High Wycombe College, 101, 299.

NAPIER, WILLIAM, on the Battle of Albuera, 301; on the British soldier, 301, 304; anecdote of Pitt, 450.

NAPLES, or THE TWO SICILIES, Kingdom of, ruled by Ferdinand IV and Maria Carolina, 244, 245; French evacuation under Treaty of Amiens, 339, 342, 355; Nelson's interest in, 377; French reoccupation of the southern ports, 377; allied troops at Naples, November, 1805, 445; bad faith of Neapolitan court towards France, 445; popular rising of 1799 mentioned, 324, 411.

NATIONAL DEBT, arrangements for, made through Bank of England, 35; amount during Pitt's first administration, 182, 184; operations of Sinking Fund, 182, 183; method of borrowing, 184. *Also see* LOANS, GOVERNMENT.

NAVAL CHRONOLOGY, book mentioned, 293.

NAVIGATION ACT, 200.

NAVY, general account of, 285 ff.; waste of flour upon, 34; mutinies and mutineers, 107, 133, 286, 287, 343; impossibility of a Scottish Navy, 136; Fox on naval greatness, 142; cost of the navy, 181; Irish bad characters sent into the navy, 229; punishments, 286, 287, 304; seamen's wives, 290, 305; distribution at outbreak of war, 1803, 374 ff.; strength, 389; the five Commissioners of Naval Inquiry, 411; and their twelve Reports, 412; scandals, 425; hospital arrangements, 428; night signals, 429; part played by frigates in a general action, 431; traditions of close gunnery action, 431; advantage of three-deckers, 427, 433, 434; hardships of naval warfare after a victory, 441. *Also see* ADMIRALTY, FIRST LORD OF THE ADMIRALTY, and TREASURER OF THE NAVY.

NEGROES, in West Indies, etc., 277 ff.; treatment, 284, 285; in Navy, 291. *Also see* SLAVE TRADE.

NEILD, JAMES, his visits to prisons, 161; and hulks, 162.

NELSON, HORATIO, LORD, early career, 322, 323; services as Second-in-Command of Baltic expedition, 322, 326 ff.; fights Battle of Copenhagen, April 2, 1801, 329 ff.; negotiates with Danish Government, 333, 334; receives letter from St. Vincent, 334, 335; supersedes Parker, 335; made a Viscount, 335; commands on south-east coast, 336, 337; remarks on English dissatisfaction with peace, 340; defends it in House of Lords, 342; believes in practicability of an invasion, 337, 370; in command in Mediterranean as Vice-Admiral, 291, 375; complains of want of frigates, 376; nature of his work, 376, 377; pursues Villeneuve, January, 1805, 406, 407; pursues him to West Indies, April–May, 407 ff.; returns to Europe, July, 410, 421, 422; his view of the situation, 423; offers services and returns to the fleet, 424, 425; his "Nelson touch", 426, 427; fights Battle of Trafalgar, October 21st, 427 ff., 444; death, 426, 439; honours given to him, 440, 441; his last injunction neglected by Collingwood, 442.

friendship with Clarence, 323; Collingwood, 421, 423; Canning and Rose, 425; liaison with Lady Hamilton, 325; wounds, 325; views on early deaths in the Navy, 287; on merchant service, 290; on prize-money, 292; French opinion of, 427.

his courage, 323; devotion to duty and patriotism, 323, 324; taciturnity, 323; ignorance of the world, 323; tactical studies, 323, 440; strategical

INDEX

insight, 323, 324; leadership of men, 323; caution, 323; an instance of this, 328; narrow outlook, 324; vanity, 325; physique, 325, 326; knowledge of pilotage, 328; indefatigability, 328; diplomatic qualifications, 333; confidence in those under his command, 425, 431, 432; popularity ashore, 425; and afloat, 425, 426, 428; generosity, 428; piety and humanity, 432; want of education, 440; genius, 440, 441.
   mentioned, 85, 100, 288.
NEW BRUNSWICK, population and constitution in 1800, 270, 271.
NEWCASTLE, population, 45; coal industry, 45; trade, 45; Eldon's original home, 262; mentioned, 47.
NEWFOUNDLAND, population and government in 1800, 270.
NEWGATE PRISON, mentioned, 162, 163.
NEW JERUSALEMITES, a sect, 268.
NEWLAND, ABRAHAM, Chief Cashier of the Bank of England, 184.
NEW SOUTH WALES, strength of troops in, 306; transportation of convicts to, mentioned, 163.
NIEBUHR, statesman and historian, his impressions of England, 63, 70.
NILE, Battle of, mentioned, 322, 325, 372.
NONCONFORMISTS, 91 ff.; political position, 153, 154.
NORFOLK, leasing system in, 19; variety of employment, 20, 21; improvement under enclosure, 24; a labourer's budget, 30; agricultural steam mill erected, 39; non-resident clergy, 88; returns Coke to Parliament, 151, 152.
NORFOLK, eleventh Duke of, mentioned, as a club man, 82; gives evidence for O'Connor, 146; a Protestant, 149, 153; mentioned, 149.
NORTH, Lord, effect of his American War, mentioned, 32, 128; fall of his Ministry, 121; coalition with Fox, 127, 128, 137, 217; Fox's attacks on, mentioned, 143.
NORTHAMPTON, mentioned, 40.
NORTHAMPTONSHIRE, a county of late enclosure, 23.
NORTHESK, Rear-Admiral the Earl of, awarded C.B. after Battle of Trafalgar, 441.
NORTHUMBERLAND, Methodism in, 92; Grey returned for the county, 152.
NORTH-WEST COMPANY of fur-traders in Canada, 276.
NORWICH, its woollen industry, 54.
NOTTINGHAM, elected magistracy's failure to act, 353; county magistrates given concurrent jurisdiction, 353.
NOVA SCOTIA, population and constitution in 1800, 270, 271.
NOVELS, influence of, 75, 76, 77.
NUGENT, Major-General George, mentioned as Governor of Jamaica, 282.
NUGENT, Mrs., wife of above; her diary, 282.
NUISANCES, how judicially dealt with, 167, 168.

OATS, increase in area under, 38; export from Ireland, 216, 239; harvests in 1799 and 1800, 241.
O'BEIRNE, Bishop of Meath, his Catholic connection, 206.
O'COIGLEY, Irish conspirator, tried for treason, 99.
O'CONNOR, ARTHUR, Irish rebel, tried for treason, 1798, 146.

538 ENGLAND IN THE NINETEENTH CENTURY

OPPOSITION, its character in parliament, 140; its strength, 145 ff.; the New and the Old Opposition, 354, 393, 412.
ORANGE SOCIETY, foundation, 226; Orangemen, 229; Camden's refusal to encourage, 232, 233.
ORDE, Vice-Admiral Sir JOHN, driven off Cadiz by Villeneuve, 1805, 408.
ORDER OF ST. JOHN OF JERUSALEM, rulers of Malta before 1798, question of restoration of Malta to, 339, 341, 358; mentioned, 361.
ORDNANCE DEPARTMENT, possession of boroughs by, 113; cost of, 181. *Also see* MASTER-GENERAL OF THE ORDINANCE.
ORINOCO, river in South America, 278.
OSTEND, Dutch port of concentration for invasion flotilla, 378, 415.
OTTAWA, river in Lower Canada, 271.
OTTO, LOUIS, French diplomatist, negotiates Preliminaries of Peace, 1801, 338; mentioned, 355.
OVERSEERS, PARISH, 173, 174; used for recruitment in 1804, 397; the experiment a failure, 398.
OWEN, ROBERT, industrialist, early career, 50, 51; mentioned, 42.
OX, use in husbandry, 38, 39. *Also see* CATTLE.
OXFORDSHIRE, farmers in, 33.
OXFORD UNIVERSITY, parliamentary representation, 108; place of Fox's education, 141.

PAGET, Capt. Hon. CHARLES, R.N., his prize-money, 292.
PAINE, THOMAS, his Rights of Man, 96, 97; popularity of his works, 105; their influence in Ireland, 227.
PALMER, JOHN, inventor of mail-coaches, 179.
PAPER, taxation of, 185; increased, 1801, 259, 260.
PAPER PLOT, 363, 364.
PARCELS, attempt to tax, 186.
PARIS, trade with, 59; British visitors to, during the Peace, 347.
PARISH, *see* CHURCH, CHURCHWARDENS, and OVERSEERS, PARISH.
PARKER, Admiral Sir HYDE, appointed to command expedition to the Baltic, 1801, 322; adopts Nelson's plan, 326; forces the Sound, 327, 328; his part in Battle of Copenhagen, 328 ff.; sends Nelson to negotiate, 333; thanked and afterwards superseded, 335; his brilliant early service mentioned, 335.
PARLIAMENT, duration, 110; responsibility of Ministers to, 119, 120, 201; King's right to dissolve, 121; disagreement of the British with the Irish Parliament, 221.
    Seditious Meetings Act, 132; so-called Suspension of Habeas Corpus Act, 133; an Act of Parliament necessary for divorce, 158; Turnpike Acts, 171; Burke's Act of 1782, 178; Act establishing pensions for Judges, 191; Combination Acts, 196, 197; Friendly Societies Act, 196; Corn Laws, 198 ff.; Navigation Act, 200; Act of Union, 240, 241; miscellaneous measures dealing with scarcity before 1801, 241 ff.
    First Parliament of the United Kingdom meets, January, 1801, 241, 248; repeal of enactments dealing with scarcity, 260, 344; re-enactment of coercive Acts, 268; King's speech at opening of new Parliament, 1802, 353. *Also see*—for Acts relating to them—ARMY, ENCLOSURE, and POOR LAW.

INDEX 539

PARLIAMENT, HOUSE OF COMMONS, composition, 108 ff.; petitions to, 115, 192, 196; corruption of, 120; position in the State, 192 ff.; Speaker and Chairman of Committees, 193; work of Committees, 193; private bill legislation, 194; representation of industry, 195; attitude towards trade, 195 ff.; intimidation of, 197; traditional fiscal policy, 198 ff.; unrepresentative character of parliament, 251; influence of county members, 387; independent votes, 412.

before 1801: Wilberforce on woollen trade, 41; Porchester on non-resident clergy, 88; Cold Bath Fields Prison inquiry, 161; master millwrights' petition, 196; debate on the Union, 240, 241; dissection as an additional punishment to execution, 351, 352; Pitt's speech on the Slave Trade, 449, 450.

Session of 1801: debate on the Address, 248 ff.; on the change of Ministry, 257, 258; on the State of the Nation, 264 ff.

Session of 1801-2: on the Peace Preliminaries, 342, 343; on distilleries, 344; on the Civil List, 344, 345; debate on Treaty of Amiens, 348; on bull-baiting, 348, 349; passing of the First Factory Act, 349, 350; motion against Pitt, 350.

Session of 1802-3, New Parliament: debate on army vote, 354; King's Message, 359; debate on the war, 365.

Session of 1803-4: attacks on the Ministry, 384; Addington's fear of defeat and resignation, 390; Pitt's difficulties on succeeding him, 396; Civil List raised, 397; Western's Corn Bill, 152, 194, 200.

Session of 1805: Pitt strengthened, 398; criticism of his treatment of Spain, 403; also imperilling of West Indies, 410; vote of censure on Melville, 412, 413; debate on Irish Catholics, 414, 415.

Also see BUDGETS, ELECTIONS, and OPPOSITION.

PARLIAMENT, HOUSE OF LORDS, composition and place in the State, 116, 117; Lord Chancellor as President, 121.

before 1801: Warwick on farmers, 27; Auckland's Adultery Bill, 80; Holland on freedom of internal trade, 195, 196; Archbishop's proposal regarding bread, 241.

Session of 1801: debate on the Address, 248; Suffolk's proposal regarding country bank notes, 37; debate on the State of the Nation, 264, 266; vote of thanks moved for victory of Copenhagen, 334.

Session of 1801-2: debate on the Peace Preliminaries, 342, 343.

Session of 1802-3: Horsley on a non-resident rector, 88.

Session of 1803-4: weakness of Addington's Ministry, 390.

Session of 1805: Hawkesbury on strength of the Army, 400; Grenville on the treatment of Spain, 401 ff.; debate on Irish Catholics, 414, 415.

Picture of Queen Catherine's trial mentioned, 248. *Also see* OPPOSITION.

PARLIAMENT, IRISH, Grattan's Parliament, 1782–1800, 217; an experiment in working the parliamentary system without complete possession by the Administration of the confidence of Parliament, 201; its subsequent history, 217 ff.; refuses free trade with Great Britain, 221; attitude on the Regency question, 221; Catholic franchise granted, 1793, 204, 221 ff.; question of the Union of the British and Irish Parliaments, 231 ff.; Bill of Union finally passed, 1800, 236, 240, 241.

resolution on tithes, 205; procession at opening of Parliament, 210; management of Parliament, 219 ff., 232; composition of House of Lords, 219; composition and character of House of Commons, 219 ff.; the "borough-mongers", 234 ff.

540 ENGLAND IN THE NINETEENTH CENTURY

PARLIAMENTARY REFORM, petitioned for in 1793, Fox's attitude, 145, 146; demand for, in Ireland, 222, 223; reform of Irish Parliament at the Union, 235, 236; mentioned, 178.
PARR, Dr., a leading Whig divine, 149; his rebuke of Mackintosh, 99; view of the Church, 150; collection of subscriptions for Fox, 152.
PASCO, Lieutenant, his reminiscences of Nelson's Trafalgar signal, 431, 432.
PASLEY, Admiral Sir THOMAS, Collingwood's letter to, 440.
PATRIOTIC FUND, Nelson's arrangements for supplying information, 428.
PATRIOTISM in England, 106, 107, 341; eighteenth-century contempt of patriotism, 143; burst of patriotism in 1803, 382; its limitations, 382, 398, 399.
PATTERSON, ROBERT, attorney, condemned to the pillory, 163.
PAUL I, Emperor of Russia, 245; breaks with Great Britain, 246, 247; his savagery and insanity, 335; strangled, March, 1801, 335.
PEASANTRY, decried in England, 32.
 in Ireland, 202 ff.; oppression of, 207; vindictiveness, 207, 208; not heavy drinkers, 213.
PEEL, Sir ROBERT, First Baronet; origin, 41; share in labour legislation, 194, 195; introduces first Factory Bill, 349, 350; has no confidence in Addington, 387, 388; votes for censure of Melville, 412; mentioned, 268.
PEERAGE, in Great Britain, 116; distinctions in, 72; Pitt's additions, 72, 116, 117.
 in Ireland, 219, 237, 238.
PELHAM, Lord, a former Chief Secretary, Home Secretary, 1801, 263; becomes Chancellor of the Duchy of Lancaster, 1803, 369.
PELLEW, Rear-Admiral Sir EDWARD, blockades Coruña, 375.
PELTIER, French emigrant and author, Mackintosh's defence of, 97; convicted of incitement to assassination, 355.
PEMBROKE HALL, CAMBRIDGE, Pitt's education at, 126.
PENSIONS, substitution for sinecures in Great Britain, 191.
 in Ireland, 221.
PERCEVAL, Hon. SPENCER, Solicitor-General, 1801, 263; satirized, 150; on silver notes, 191; his working of the Combination Acts, 197; helps to widen the scope of the first Factory Bill, 349; his defence of Addington's Administration as Attorney-General, 387; retained by Pitt in that capacity in 1804, 394.
PERRY, JAMES, editor of the Morning Chronicle, his coarseness, 97, 150.
PERSIA, mentioned, 59.
PETITIONS to House of Commons, 115, 192; master millwrights' petition, 196; Irish Catholic petition, 414.
PICKPOCKETS, popular punishment of, 164.
PICTON, Brigadier-General, Governor of Trinidad, 278.
PIEDMONT, incorporated with France, 1802, 353, 354.
PIGTAILS, in Navy, 292; in Army, 301.
PILLORY, 134, 163.
PILNITZ, Declaration of, 1791, 129, 131.
PIMENTO, export from Jamaica, 281.
PINDAR, PETER, name taken by the obscene Dr. Wolcote, Whig clerical writer, 150; his joke at George III's expense, 118.
PIRATES, Spanish, 279, 280.
PITT, WILLIAM, birth and early life, 125 ff.; elected to parliament as a nominee, 113; becomes Prime Minister, 1784, 128; economic policy,

INDEX 541

128; policy of toleration, 221; foreign policy to 1792, 128, 129; contest with Thurlow in 1792, 122; reduces army, 129; policy towards France, 129 ff.; joined by Portland Whigs, 131; extends policy of toleration to Ireland, 221 ff.; success in maintaining order, 131, 132; war administration, 243 ff.; willingness to retire in 1797, 257; stoppage of cash payments, 35; estimate of the national income, 57, 58; decides for Union with Ireland, 231; introduces pensions for judges, 191; meeting with Cobbett, 105, 106; speech on the Address, 1801, 249, 250; his Irish policy, 251; difference with the King and resignation, 252 ff.; promises to drop the Catholic question, 258; introduces budget of 1801, 259, 260; avoids seeing King when out of office, 122, 123, 255; speech in March, 1801, 264, 265; Fox on his resignation, 266; break-up of his Second Coalition against France, 308; supports the Peace, 343; regrets stipulation to restore Malta, 341; motion of his parliamentary opponents, 350; honours shown to him, 350; continued support of Addington, 350; Canning's attempt to bring him forward, 354, 363, 364; negotiations with Addington break down, 1803, 364; his great speech of May, 1803, 365; criticizes Addington's income tax proposals, 366; energy as Warden of Cinque Ports and Colonel of volunteers, 383, 384; presses for adjutants for volunteers, 384; in pronounced opposition to Addington, 1804, 387; his military proposals, 388; attacks the Government's naval policy, 389; correspondence and conversation leading to formation of his second administration, 390, 391; George III's description of his letters, 391; breach with Grenville, 392, 393; forms administration, 394, 395; his Additional Force Act, 396 ff., 452; provides for Civil List, 397; strengthened by Addington's support, 1805, 397; interested in catamaran project, 400; passes Act to enable militiamen to enlist in Line, 410; his overseas expeditions, and inability to understand national feeling on the Continent, 411; failure to protect Melville from censure, and emotion on the occasion, 412, 413; replaces him by Barham, 413; breach with Sidmouth, 413; his last budget, 413, 414; displays his skill in debate on Catholic question, 414; rashness in allowing the Cape expedition to sail, 424; sends Harrowby to Berlin, 446; regains his popularity, 446; speech at Guildhall, November 9th, 446, 447; journey to Bath, return, and death, January 23, 1806, 447, 448.

effect of his French War, 32; his new peerages, 72, 116; his duel, 73, 369; reduces personal power of the King, 121; reliance on Dundas, 136, 449; Fox's low opinion of him, 143; his so-called Habeas Corpus Suspension Act, 164; revives Board of Trade, 178, 179; introduces mail-coaches, 179; invention of Consolidated Fund, 182; his Sinking Fund, 182 ff.; methods of raising loans, 184; and of taxation, 185 ff.; economic reforms, 188 ff.; his income from public money, 189; favours to Pretyman, 189; treatment of his budgets by House of Commons, 193; friendship with Addington, 256, 257, 364, 393, 398; failure to make peace with France on four occasions, 339; City's confidence in him, 350, 367; character of his friendships, 393; incident of his home life with Hester Stanhope, 395; relations with Nelson, 423, 426; manner of his life in 1805, 447; discreditable opposition to The Times, 447; his greatest speech that on the Slave Trade, 449, 450; anecdote of his playfulness, 450; financial mistake of delaying war taxation 452; Scott's lines on him, 453.

general character, 126, 127; conviviality, 126, 137; amusements, 76, 447,

450; a wit, 98; adherence to the better part of Whiggism, 136; integrity, 189; veracity, 259; ambition for character, not office, 363; reserved disposition, 392, 393; sanguine temper, 448, 449; precocity and boyishness, 449 ff.; "false principle of honour", 449; eloquence, 449 ff.; humanity, 450; unbusinesslike habits, 450; other intellectual qualities, 452; dominating will, rectitude and patriotism, 452, 453; mentioned, 123, 124, 153, 166.

PLACE, FRANCIS, democratic leader, 167.

PLACEMEN, 154, 189, 190; unimportance of, in parliament, compared with county members, 387.

    in Ireland, 221, 237.

PLATE, tax on, 186.

PLYMOUTH, mentioned, 45.

POACHING, 168.

POLICE, general account, 168, 169; inadequacy, 115, 132.

    Irish, inadequacy of, 228; plan for a constabulary, 228.

POLITICAL REGISTER, newspaper started by Cobbett, 1802, 98; quoted, 180, 303, 388.

PONSONBY, a leading Irish family, 234.

PONSONBY, Hon. GEORGE, opposes Union in Irish Parliament, 236.

POOLE, THOMAS, on riots of 1801, 267.

POORHOUSES, 171 ff.; diet in, 18; children sent from, to factories, 53.

POOR LAW, 171 ff.; its operation, 29, 30, 31; relief in aid of wages, 31, 173; one-seventh of population on relief in 1803, 31; law of settlement, 31, 173, 174; poor rate in Bucks, 33; inadequacy of the rate in East London, 68; apprentices, 95, 349, 350; estimated number under some form of relief in 1801, 264, 268, 343, 344; unsatisfactory treatment of pauper children leads to first Factory Act, 349.

    Ireland free from its demoralizing effects, 203.

PORCHESTER, Lord, on non-resident clergy, 88.

PORCUPINE, newspaper edited by Cobbett, 98.

PORK, export of, from Ireland, 215, 239.

PORTEUS, BEILBY, Bishop of London, preacher and theologian, 89; his lectures, 102; mentioned, 52.

PORTLAND, Duke of, Premier of Coalition Ministry in 1783, 131; joins Pitt, 1792, 131; Home Secretary to 1801, 137, 170; a suggestion of his rejected by Camden, 232, 233; King's observation to him, 253; President of the Council, 1801, 260; his place taken by Sidmouth 1805, 397.

    protects freedom of internal trade in 1800, 195.

    character, 137.

    mentioned, 112.

PORTO RICO, West Indies, Spanish possession, 279.

PORTSMOUTH, Court of Record at, 157; its Paving and Cleansing Commissioners, 168; a Portsmouth newspaper quoted, 289.

PORTUGAL, trade of, 60; royal family of, 244; attacked by Spain, 339; position of, as affected by Peace between Great Britain and France, 339, 342, 355.

POST, see MAILS.

POSTMASTERS-GENERAL, Auckland and Gower in 1800, 139, 180.

POTATOES, as a common diet in West of England, 22; in Ireland, 217, 224; encouragement of potato growing by the State in 1801, 268.

POTTERIES, Staffordshire, 55; their productions mentioned, 49

INDEX 543

POTWALLOPER, a class of parliamentary elector, **109**; Taunton a potwalloper borough, **111**.
POUNDS, used for vagrants, **163**.
PRELIMINARIES OF PEACE concluded between Great Britain and France, October 1, 1801, **338** ff.; mentioned, **318**.
PRESBYTERIANS, religious sect in England, **93**.
  Scottish Presbyterian church in Liverpool, **44**.
  in Ireland, **208**, **209**; sedition among, **222**, **225**, **256**; faction fights with Catholics, **222**; friendliness towards Catholics in 1795, **225**, **226**; Presbyterian traditions, **227**; Pitt's intentions for them, **252**; growing hostility towards Catholics, **256**; relations with the Crown, **367**.
PRESCOTT, Gen., Governor-General of Canada to 1799, **275**.
PRESS, rudimentary provincial press, **94**; the London press, **97**, **98**; freedom of the press, **132**, **155**; the party press, **150**, **151**; taxation of the press, **185**; Bonaparte's complaints, **355**; unfavourable to Addington, **389**; criticizes Government, 1805, **410**; Nelson's use of a Lisbon newspaper, **422**; Pitt's treatment of the press, **447**.
PRESS GANGS, **289**, **290**.
PRESTON, its political views, **152**.
PRETYMAN, GEORGE, afterwards TOMLINE, q.v.
PRICE, name of a farmer murdered in Ireland, **269**.
PRIESTLEY, Dr., riots against, **47**.
PRIMATE of Ireland, member of Irish Cabinet, **218**.
PRIME MINISTER, his position in the Privy Council and Cabinet, **123** ff.; Fox's view of, **119**, **120**; Pitt's, **122**.
  Pitt to March, 1801, **259**; Addington, March, 1801, to May, 1804, **259**, **390**, **391**; Pitt, May, 1804, to his death, January, 1806, **391**, **392**.
  earlier Prime Ministers: Rockingham, **122**; Shelburne, **127**; Portland, **137**.
PRINCE EDWARD ISLAND, **270**; population and constitution in 1801, **271**.
PRINCE OF WALES, *see* GEORGE, PRINCE OF WALES.
PRISONS, administration of, **161**, **162**; interest in, **133**.
PRIVATEERS, from Bermudas, **277**; Spanish, **279**, **280**; losses from, **294**, **295**.
PRIVY COUNCIL, constitution and functions, **123**, **124**. *Also see* LORD PRESIDENT OF THE COUNCIL.
  Irish, **218**.
PRIZE MONEY in the Navy, **292**, **293**.
PROSECUTION, weakness in criminal cases, **160**; a case of Treasury prosecution, **167**.
PROTECTION, of corn, **198** ff.; of shipping by Navigation Act, **200**; of industries by prohibition of export of yarn and machinery, and of skilled workmen, **201**.
PROVISION TRADE, in Ireland, **216**.
PRUSSIA, relations with France in 1792, **129**; royal family of, **245**; joins Armed Neutrality, **246**; seizes Hanover, **247**; military ideas imported from, **300**; import of corn from, **267**; made a guarantee power under Treaty of Amiens, **346**; her attitude in this connection, **346**, **347**; a proposal of Bonaparte affecting Prussia, **362**; impotence in 1803, **380**; uncertain policy in 1805, **446**; Harrowby's mission to, **446**; French policy successful, **446**; mentioned, **147**.
PUBLIC OPINION, on the Slave Trade, **94**; how brought to bear on Parliament, **115**; public opinion on the "English Bastille", **161**; on the police, **168**, **169**; public objection to uniformity, **194**; on the war, **250**;

in favour of Pitt, 393; on Melville's case, 412, 413; on the death of Nelson, 441; on Pitt in 1805, 446; optimism on the war, 447.
PUMP, as a means of punishment, 164.
PUNISHMENTS, CRIMINAL, their severity, 160 ff.; some miscellaneous punishments, 163, 164; efficacy of public punishment, 134.

QUAKERS, 93; their good living, 70; in Canada, 273.
QUARTER SESSIONS, 171; orders to sheriffs regarding, 197; in Ireland, 212.
QUEBEC, capital of Lower Canada, 271; its military weakness, 277.
QUEENSBERRY, Duke of, sportsman, 104.

RADCLIFFE, WILLIAM, Lancashire employer, 58, 59.
RAIKES, ROBERT, journalist, establishes Sunday schools, 52.
RAILWAYS, at the Newcastle collieries, 45.
RATES, rate-paying as a qualification for a parliamentary elector, 109, 110; county rates, 171; estimated at 8s. in the pound, 181.
RED INDIANS, 272.
REGENCY, question of, in 1788–1789, 145, 221.
REGIMENTS—
    23rd, at Aboukir, March 8, 1801, 313.
    28th, at Aboukir, March 8, 1801, 313.
    40th, at Aboukir, March 8, 1801, 313.
    42nd, Highlanders, at Aboukir, March 8, 1801, 313; at Canopus, 315.
REIGATE, parliamentary borough, 113.
RELIGION, contemptuous attitude adopted towards, by persons of rank, 79, 254; neglect of religious teaching, 102; religious eccentricity in Yorkshire, 268.
REVOLUTION, FRENCH, 129, 130; its influence on English morals, 77.
REYNIER, General, French Army, his advice to Menou, 312.
REYNOLDS, the painter, 73.
RICHMOND (Yorkshire), a decision of the justices, 170.
RICHMOND, Duke of, grandfather of Charles Fox, 141.
RIFLE BRIGADE, character and composition, 300.
RIFLES, 60th, character and composition, 300, 306.
RIOTS, in Liverpool, 44; in Birmingham, 47; against machines, 53, 54; in London, 67; at elections, 110; difficulty of suppressing, 132, 133; at general election of 1802 in Liverpool, 352; and Nottingham, 353.
RIOU, Capt., R.N., killed in Battle of Copenhagen, 331.
ROADS, the traffic, 62, 63; their badness, 62, 63; travelling by road, 63, 64; their insecurity, 168, 169; upkeep, 171; not a government charge, 188; upkeep in Ireland, 212.
ROBE, Lt.-Col. WILLIAM, R.A., in Peninsular War, 297.
ROBESPIERRE, his confiscatory measures against British trade, 355, 356.
ROCHE, Sir BOYLE, M.P., Irish Parliament, his bulls, 220.
ROCHEFORT, escape of French ships to, and blockade of, 375; mentioned, 405 ff.; Rochefort squadron, 416, 417. *Also see* ALLEMAND.
ROCKIES, North America, crossed by Mackenzie, 276.
ROCKINGHAM, Premier in 1782, 122; his Irish policy, 217; mentioned, 189.
ROGERS, SAMUEL, as a society wit, 98; on a mannerism of Fox, 142.
ROISE, General, French Army, killed in Battle of Canopus, 315.

INDEX 545

ROMAN TERRITORY, French evacuation stipulated for by Treaty of Amiens, 339.
ROME, religion of, institutions and beliefs retained in the Church of England, 84.
ROMILLY, SAMUEL, his purchase of a borough, 112; on the criminal law, 160.
ROMNEY, painter, his paintings of Lady Hamilton, 325.
ROSCOE, WILLIAM, of Liverpool, 44.
ROSE, GEORGE, a minister in Pitt's first administration, 139; joint paymaster of the Forces, 1804, 395.
ROSILY, Vice-Admiral, French Navy, Villeneuve's successor, his surrender to Spanish in 1808, 444.
ROSSLYN, Earl of, *see* LOUGHBOROUGH.
ROTHERHAM, Capt., R.N., commanding Royal Sovereign, October, 1805, 428.
ROWLANDSON, caricaturist, 151; his prints of drill, 390.
ROXBURGH FENCIBLES, 170.
ROYAL ACADEMY, mentioned, 67, 118.
ROYAL FAMILY, interest in Sunday schools, 95.
ROYAL SOCIETY OF ARTS, rewards for agriculture from, 39, 40.
ROYSTON, Lord, election for parliament as a minor, 113.
RUM, in Barbados, 278; Jamaica, 281; West Indies generally, 283.
RUMBOLD, Sir GEORGE, British Minister in Hamburg, French outrage on, 404.
RUSSELLS, a Whig family, 148.
RUSSIA, Pitt's policy with regard to, 128; royal family of, 244, 245; forms Armed Neutrality, 246; designs upon India, 246; Grey on Russia, 249; concludes Convention with Great Britain, 1801, 335; as guarantee of Malta under Treaty of Amiens, 346, 358; Czar's views on Malta and Egypt, 360; proposal to hand Malta over to a Russian garrison, 362; forms Third Coalition against France, 1805, 404, 405; joint Russian and British force in Mediterranean, 411, 445; relations with Prussia, 446; defeat at Austerlitz and withdrawal, 446, 447.
RUTLANDSHIRE, Winchelsea's system of cottage holdings, 26.

ST. ANNE'S HILL, Fox's home, 146, 250.
ST. HELENA, French plan of expedition to, 405.
ST. LAWRENCE, river in Canada, 271, 272, 273.
ST. LUCIA, West Indies, French possession taken by British, 278, 281; again taken in 1803, 381.
ST. PETERSBURG, mentioned, 60.
ST. PIERRE, French island off Newfoundland, taken by British in war and restored in peace, 270.
ST. VINCENT, West Indies, French possession taken by British, 278.
ST. VINCENT, Admiral Earl of, victor over Spanish fleet in 1797, 286; appointed to command Channel Fleet, 286; First Lord of the Admiralty, 1801, 261, 286; encomium on Saumarez, 321; on the work of the fleet at Copenhagen, 334; on Nelson, 334, 335; defends the Peace in the House of Lords, 342; a believer in a close blockade, 374, 390; his naval economies, 376, 389; his hostility to the Naval Board, 295; his Commissioners of Naval Inquiry, 411, 412; succeeded by Melville, 1804, 389, 394.

a liberty taken with him, 105; remark on Dundas, 136; as disciplinarian, 286; on noblemen in the Navy, 288; regard for the men's health, 296; contempt for M.D.'s, 296; testimony to the Nelson spirit, 441.
SALLUST, mentioned, 101.
SALT, tax on, 185; raised, 414.
SAN DOMINGO, West Indies, 279; French and Spanish possession, 280; French expeditions to, 343, 409; becomes independent, 381.
SAN ILDEFONZO, Treaty of, 1796, 401, 402.
SANITATION, sanitary administration in London, 176; elsewhere, 177; in Manchester, 177; sanitation not a government charge, 188.
SARDINIA, Piedmont taken from the Kingdom of, and incorporated with France, 353, 354; mentioned, 377.
SAUMAREZ, Rear-Admiral Sir JAMES, actions with Linois, July 6 and 12, 1801, 319 ff.; honoured and rewarded, 322.
SCARCITY, of 1799–1800, 241; of 1800–1801, 242, 243, 248, 267 ff.; mentioned, 134.
SCHELDT, question of the, in 1792, 130.
SCHOOLS: charity and other elementary schools, 95; grammar schools, 95; northern grammar schools also mentioned, 86; public schools, 99; boarding-schools for girls, 68, 72.
SCHOOLS, SUNDAY, 52, 95, 96; seditious, 268.
SCIENCE, not assisted by Government, 188.
SCOT AND LOT, a local tax, payment of which qualified for parliamentary vote, 109.
SCOTLAND, cattle, 23; afforestation, 40; connection with Liverpool, 43, 44; houses, 65; representation in parliament, 111, 116; Dundas's patronage of Scotsmen, 136; her separate legal system, 155; Scottish and Irish Union compared, 232, 238; how defended, 307; Tory in general election, 1802, 352; alarm of invasion, 385; Pitt supported by jobbery in Scotland, 393; insurance against militia ballot, 396; strength of militia, 411.

Scottish contrasted with Irish, 209; Scottish in Ulster, 208, 209; in Nova Scotia, 270; in Canada, 273; in the West Indies, 282, 283.
SCOTT, Dr., Nelson's Secretary, at his death-bed, 439.
SCOTT, MICHAEL, novelist, author of Tom Cringle's Log, 283; mentioned, 287.
SCOTT, WALTER, his Antiquary quoted, 385; his lines on Pitt, 453.
SEA FENCIBLES, mentioned, 371.
SEBASTIANI, Colonel, French Army, his mission to Egypt, 357; and report, 357, 359.
SECRETARIES OF STATE, see HOME, FOREIGN, and WAR SECRETARY.
SECRETARY AT WAR, the office, 298, 299; Windham in Pitt's first administration, 138, 298; Yorke in Addington's, 263, 382.
SECRET SERVICE MONEY, use of, for bribery of Irish members, 237.
SEDITION, Pitt's measures dealing with, 132, 133; Addington's, 268.
SEDITIOUS MEETINGS ACT, 132, 133; re-enacted, 1801, 268.
SENECA, mentioned, 90.
SENEGAL, French expedition from, captures Goree, 381.
SERVANTS, DOMESTIC, tax on (male), 181, 186.
SHAKESPEARE, quoted, 76, 83; on Elsinore, 326.
SHEFFIELD, its steel industry, 55.

INDEX 547

SHEFFIELD, Lord, quoted, 354.
SHELBURNE, Lord, see LANSDOWNE, Marquis of.
SHELLEY, poet, mentioned, 72.
SHERIDAN, RICHARD, a leader of Opposition to Pitt in House of Commons, 138, 140; gives evidence for O'Connor, 146; speech on change of administration in 1801, 257; on the Peace, 341, 342; refuses to visit France, 347; speech against bull-baiting, 1802, 349; remark on general election, 352; on Bonaparte, 354; partial support of Addington, 369; attacks Pitt, 1805, 398; moves repeal of Additional Force Act, 399; a joke against Pitt, 400.
    his character, 140; a society wit, 99; a friend of the Prince of Wales, 147; in caricature, 151; mentioned, 72, 126, 145, 248, 250.
SHERIFFS, 153, 197; Irish, 209.
SHIPP, JOHN, 106; on punishments in the army, 304.
SHIPPING, 60, 61.
SHORNCLIFFE, Light Brigade at, 384, 385.
SHREWSBURY, mentioned, 63.
SICILY, French project of invasion, 377. *Also see* NAPLES.
SIDMOUTH, becomes President of the Council, 397; resigns, 413. *Also see* ADDINGTON.
SIMCOE, light infantry leader, mentioned, 300.
SIMEON, Rev. CHARLES, mentioned, 90.
SINCLAIR, Sir JOHN, first President of the Board of Agriculture, 188; arrested for debt, 159.
SINECURES, partial abolition in 1782, 178; their amount, 189; how far justified, 191; mentioned, 399.
SINKING FUND, Pitt's, general account, 182, 183.
SLAVES, in Bermudas, 277; in West Indies, 278 ff.
SLAVE TRADE, on what ground defended, 60; enthusiasm for abolition, 93, 94, 115; figures of, 284; mentioned, 43, 149.
SLEDGES, in Bristol, 62.
SMALL-HOLDERS, 17, 18. *Also see* FARMS.
SMITH, ADAM, author of Wealth of Nations, on the use of soap, 19; on going to sea, 106; his conclusions used by Pitt, 57; his free trade principle, how far accepted by Government, 195, 196, 267; on the Navigation Act, 200; on the Army and Navy, 301, 302; mentioned, 101, 203.
SMITH, Capt. Sir SIDNEY, R.N., hero of Acre; at Aboukir, March 8, 1801, 312, 313; his Convention of El Arish mentioned, 372.
SMITH, Rev. SYDNEY, attack on Methodism, 93; a society wit, 98; a tutor, 99; lectures on moral philosophy, 102; satire on Perceval, 150.
SMITHFIELD MARKET, 23.
SMOLLETT, novelist, mentioned, 75.
SOAP, use of, by poor, 19.
SOCIETY FOR BETTERING THE CONDITION OF THE POOR, 95.
SOCIETY FOR THE SUPPRESSION OF VICE, 168.
SOCIETY OF THE FRIENDS OF THE PEOPLE, petition for parliamentary reform, 111; its foundation, 145.
SOCINIANISM, 91.
SOMERSET HOUSE, Government offices at, 72.
SOMERSETSHIRE, coal, 48; wool, 48; Cheddar miners, 95; Board of Agriculture's Survey quoted, 110, 111.

548 ENGLAND IN THE NINETEENTH CENTURY

SOULT, Marshal, French Army, commands part of army of invasion in 1805, 400, 415.
SOUTHEY, ROBERT, on child labour, 52, 53; on London shops, 74; on Nelson, 425.
SPAIN, general trade with, 60; woollen trade, 48, 59; Pitt resists her claim to the North American coast, 128; the war of before 1783 mentioned, 128; Spanish dollars in England, 191; attacks Portugal, 339; how affected by the Peace between Great Britain and France, 339, 341, 345, 346, 347; French ships in Spanish harbours, 1803, 375; Spanish war enthusiasm mentioned, 382; Treaty of San Ildefonzo, 401, 402; outbreak of war with Great Britain, 1804, 402, 403; the Spanish Navy, 403, 427; Convention with France of January 4, 1805, 403; popular rising in 1808 mentioned, 411; financial weakness, 424; Spanish hospitality, 442, 443; capture of French ships in Cadiz, 1808, 444. *Also see* WAR.
SPEAKER OF THE HOUSE OF COMMONS, the office, 193; right to address House while in committee from gallery, 256.
Addington to 1801, 193, 252, 256; Mitford, 1801, 259; Abbot, 1802, 352; gives his casting vote on Melville's question, 413.
Irish, the office held by Foster, 236.
SPEECH, FREEDOM OF, 132, 166.
SPEENHAMLAND, scale of poor-rate allowances fixed at, 29, 173.
SPENCE, his views, 268; imprisoned for seditious libel, 268.
SPENCER, Earl, First Lord of the Admiralty, 137, 295; resigns, 1801, and passes into opposition, 260; attacks the Peace, 342; his position in 1804, 393; mentioned, 296, 451.
SPENCER, Lady, playful letter of, 71.
SPIES, absence of politica, 188.
SPINNING: hand-spinning, 21, 22, 54; decay of hand-spinning, 27; spinning in Manchester, 42; by machinery, 49, 50, 51, 53, 59; wages of spinners, 50, 54; fortunes made by, 50, 51; in Irish homes, 203; in Belfast, 209.
SPITALFIELDS, weavers, 67; poverty, 68; riot of weavers, 197.
SPORT, in England, 103, 104; discussed in parliament, 348; in Ireland, 206.
SQUATTERS, 17, 18, 25.
SQUIREENS in Ireland, 206; as magistrates, 211.
STAFF COLLEGE, *see* HIGH WYCOMBE.
STAFFORD, a sentence at, 167.
STAFFORDSHIRE, pottery, 49; the Potteries, 55; Methodism, 92.
STAMPS, duty on, 186.
STANHOPE, Earl, his extreme views, 154.
STANHOPE, Earl, Pitt's biographer, 395, 448.
STANHOPE, Lady HESTER, niece of Pitt and housekeeper for him, joke against Hawkesbury, 261; and Mulgrave, 395; frolic with Pitt, 450; Moore's letter to her, 452; mentioned, 449.
STANHOPE, Hon. JAMES, Pitt's nephew, account of Pitt's death, 449; frolic with Pitt, 450.
STARCH, effect on wheat consumption, 34.
STATE TRIALS, their paucity during the years 1791-1800, 166.
STEAM ENGINES, in agriculture, 39; in Leeds, 41; in Manchester, 43; in mines, 45; made at Boulton's works, 46; at Bradford, 49.
STERNE, LAURENCE, his Sentimental Journey, 77.

INDEX 549

STEWART, Col. Hon. WILLIAM, in command of troops in Danish expedition, his account of Nelson's "blind eye" episode, 330.
STOCK-JOBBERS, first connection with government loans, 184.
STOCKS, punishment of the, 134, 163.
STONE EXPEDITION, 389, 390.
STRACHAN, Rear-Admiral Sir RICHARD, successful action with Dumanoir, November 4, 1805, 443.
STRATEGY, British ignorance of, 243; George III's observation, 243.
STUART, CHARLES, general officer, succeeded by Abercromby in chief command in Mediterranean, 310; mentioned, 243.
STUART, DANIEL, editor of Morning Post, 97.
STUART, JOHN, Brigadier-General, at Battle of Canopus, 315; left in command in Egypt, 357.
STUARTS, in British Army, 136.
SUFFOLK, clergy, 88.
SUFFOLK, Earl of, on banking, 37.
SUGAR, general account of the crop in West Indies, 278, 280 ff.; warehouses in Liverpool, 44; trade, 59, 60; a luxury, 61; caricature of royal economy in, 118, 119; taxation of, 186; import into Ireland, 216; import into France, 362.
SUNDAY, neglect of observance of, 90.
SUPERIOR, LAKE, Upper Canada, 276.
SUPERSTITIONS, Welsh, 47, 48.
SURINAM, South America, captured from Dutch, 281; captured again, 381; project of a French expedition to, 405.
SURVEYS: Agricultural Surveys of counties of England conducted by Board of Agriculture, 188; that of Somersetshire quoted, 110, 111; Statistical Survey of County of Kilkenny quoted, 215.
SUSSEX, plans for, in case of invasion, 386.
SUVAROV, Russian general, 244.
SWANSEA, population, 47.
SWEDEN, royal family of, 245; joins Armed Neutrality, 246; hostilities towards, 247; convention with, 335; co-operates with British and Russian in 1805-1806, 445; mentioned, 249, 326, 327.
SWEDISH WEST INDIES, temporary seizure by British, 1801, 247.
SWITZERLAND, falls under French influence, 308; guaranteed by Treaty of Lunéville, 342; becomes Helvetic Republic, 342; subsequent treatment by France, 342, 354; Fox's and Wordsworth's interest in, 354, 355; liberation from French control an object of Third Coalition, 404. Swiss in British Army, 306.
SWORDS, Irish borough, 236.

TALBOT, Colonel, settler in Upper Canada, 273.
TALLEYRAND, Prince, Lauderdale's dealings with, 347; mentioned, 356, 360, 404, 423.
TARANTO, French project of expedition to Morea from, 374.
TARLETON, General, M.P. for Liverpool, his successful candidature, 110.
TAUNTON, 111; assizes, 166.
TAXATION, general account, 185 ff.; popular restraint, 108, 115; incidence on a small landowner, 181.

TAXATION in Ireland, 213, 214.
  Also see BUDGETS, etc.
TAXATION, LOCAL, 170, 171, 181; payment of, as an electoral qualification, 109.
TAYLOR, Lieut.-Colonel, Secretary to the King, 125.
TEA, consumption in poor families, 28; trade, 59; duty on, 186; import into Ireland, 216.
TEMPLE, Earl, *see* BUCKINGHAM.
TEMPLE, HENRY, afterwards Lord Palmerston, his precocity, 100.
TEST ACT, 154; Fox's proposal for its repeal, 154; Pitt's, 251 ff.
TEXEL, French project of invading Ireland from, 373, 386; blockade of Dutch ships in, 375.
THEFT: crop pilfering, 52; in London, 67; training of a thief in the hulks, 163; treatment of a thief by the mob, 164.
THELWALL, demagogue, character of his speeches, 96, 97.
THORNTON, HENRY, banker and M.P., on country banks, 37; distributes government aid to East End parishes, 188.
THORNTON, Mrs., sportswoman, 76.
THRESHING, 18, 27; by steam, 39.
THURLOW, Lord, his retention as Lord Chancellor in 1782, 122, 164; dismissal in 1792, 122.
TIERNEY, GEORGE, Whig leader, 140; his duel with Pitt, 73, 369; sometime leader of Opposition in parliament, 369; becomes Treasurer of the Navy under Addington, 1803, 369.
TIMBER, income from, in 1798, 57. *Also see* LOGWOOD.
TIMES, THE, newspaper, a letter to, 38; position in 1801, 97; quoted, 112; a candid friend of Government, 151; its praise of Manchester patriotism, 177, 178; an advertisement for government situations, 190; enterprise of its editor, Walter, 97, 447.
TITHES, origin and character, 84, 85; total income from, 57; Whig attitude towards, 149; incidence of, on a small landowner, 181.
  in Ireland, 204, 205; tithe jobbers, 217; grievances, 224, 225; Cornwallis on, 233.
TOBACCO, smoking, 70; import into Ireland, 216.
TOBAGO, West Indies, French possession taken by British, 278, 281, 338; mentioned, 339.
TOLERATION, RELIGIOUS, Whig attachment to, 149, 150, 153, 154; Pitt's, 153, 221; characteristics of 18th-century toleration, 227.
TOMLINE, GEORGE, formerly Pretyman, Pitt's tutor, made Bishop of Lincoln and a Dean, 189; his pluralism, 88; opinion of Eton, 99; at Pitt's death-bed, 448.
TOOKE, Rev. HORNE, mentioned, 150.
TORIES, High Church, 93; in Lancashire, 152; supporters of Pitt, 154; the Tory view of the State, 192.
  in Scotland, 352.
TORONTO, also known as York, capital of Upper Canada, 274.
TOTNES, rioting in, 267.
TOULON, project of French expedition to Morea from, 374; Ganteaume in French naval command at, 374; blockaded by Nelson, 375, 376, 377; project of French expeditions to Surinam and St. Helena from, 405; Latouche-Tréville succeeded in command by Villeneuve, 401; departure of the Toulon fleet, return and final departure, 406 ff.

INDEX 551

TOWNS, parliamentary representation, 109, 114, 115; administration, 176 ff.
TRADE, general, 57 ff.; wheat, 34, 35; Liverpool, 43; Birmingham, 45, 46; Bristol and West of England, 47, 48; Pitt's estimate of profits from, 57, 58; West Indian trade, 280 ff., 363; Baltic trade, 60; effect of war, 61; internal and coasting trade, 61, 62; scope of government interference, 178, 185, 186, 195 ff.; French designs against British trade, 247; Russian embargo, 247; trade with France in time of war and peace compared, 362, 363; protection of maritime trade, 289, 294, 295; apprehensions for, in 1805, 423; Allemand's injury to trade, 443, 444.
  Irish, 215, 216; failure of Pitt's attempt to introduce free trade with Ireland, 221; advantages expected from Union, 232, 239, 240.
TRADE UNIONS, effect of Combination Acts, 196, 197; power, 197.
TRAFALGAR, Battle of, October 21, 1805, 432 ff.; dispositions before the battle, 429 ff.; reception of the news in England, 441; sequel, 441 ff.; reference to, by Napoleon, 441; final result, 444; mentioned, 291, 294, 376.
TRANSPORTATION, 163.
TRANSPORT BOARD, 296.
TREASURER OF THE NAVY, 296, 412; the office held by Dundas in 1801, 136, 296; Tierney in 1803, 369; Canning in 1804, 395; Dundas's misconduct as, 412.
TREASURY: Treasury boroughs, 113; the Treasury and the general election, 1802, 352. *Also see* FIRST LORD OF THE TREASURY.
TRINIDAD, West Indies, Spanish possession taken by British, 278, 281, 338; ceded to Great Britain by Treaty of Amiens, 339, 340, 341.
TRINITY COLLEGE, DUBLIN, Catholics at, 206, 212; parliamentary representation, 219, 236.
TROOPSHIPS, 305.
TRUE BRITON, newspaper, 81.
TURKEY, Pitt's policy towards, 128; French conquest of Egypt from Turks, 309; Turkish unreliability, 310, 311; their co-operation with British in reconquest of Egypt, 317; Bonaparte on the approaching dissolution of the Turkish Empire, 358.
TWO SICILIES, *see* NAPLES.
TYLER, Capt., R.N., in command of Tonnant at Trafalgar, 434.
TYRONE, coal-fields in, 216.

ULM, Austrian surrender at, October, 1805, 444, 445.
ULSTER, Presbyterians in, 208, 209; republicanism, 208, 209; prosperity of, 208, 209; pacification of, 229, 367.
UNION—of the British and Irish Parliaments—steps leading to, 231 ff.; character of the measure, 237 ff.; becomes law, 1800, 241; Union flag hoisted in Dublin, January 1, 1801, 251; first United Parliament meets, 241; accepted in Ireland at general election, 1802, 352.
UNITARIANISM, 91.
UNITED EMPIRE LOYALISTS, 270, 273.
UNITED IRISHMEN, Belfast revolutionary society, 225, 226.
UNITED STATES, relations with Great Britain and Canada under Presidents Washington and Jefferson, 276, 277; connection of Liverpool with, 43; trade with, 58, 59, 60, 201; War of Independence mentioned, 128;

influence of, in Ireland, 225; import of flour from, 242; exile of loyalists from, 270, 273; emigration into Canada, 271, 273; trade with West Indies, 283.
UNIVERSITIES, English and Scottish university education compared, 101, 102; parliamentary representation of English universities, 108.

VACCINATION, reward for its discovery, 188.
VAGRANTS, 174; punishment of, 163.
VANSITTART, NICHOLAS, mission to Denmark, 1801, 258; a Secretary to the Treasury, 262; remark on the Cabinet, 262, 263; becomes Chief Secretary, 1805, 398.
VICEROY, system of government of Ireland by, 218; Fitzwilliam, 1795, 222; Camden, 1795, 223; Cornwallis, 1798, 231; Hardwicke, 1801, 261; Temple, Viceroy in 1783, mentioned, 217.
VICTUALLING BOARD, 296.
VILLAGE, English, in 1800, 17 ff.
VILLENEUVE, Vice-Admiral, French Navy, succeeds to command of Toulon fleet, 1804, 401; breaks out of Toulon and returns, January, 1801, 406; sails for West Indies in March, 407, 408; captures the Diamond rock, 409; returns, 410; plan to intercept him, 417; fights Battle of July 22nd, 417, 418; subsequent movements, 419 ff.; decides to leave Cadiz, 427, 428; fights Battle of Trafalgar and is made a prisoner, 429 ff.; his misleading instructions to Allemand, 443.
VIRGIL, mentioned, 18, 142.
VOLUNTARY CONTRIBUTION TO THE STATE, 1798, 187.
VOLUNTEERS, 301, 307; French contempt for, 371; general character in 1803, 382 ff.; number in December, 382.

WAKEFIELD, EDWARD, author of An Account of Ireland: on Irish economy, 203; on Catholic magistrates, 211.
WALES, population and description, 47, 48, 63; Methodism, 91, 92; parliamentary representation, 108.
WALKER, Rev. ROBERT, his life, 86, 87.
WALL, JOSEPH, trial and execution for murder, 351.
WALPOLE, Sir ROBERT, his Excise Bill, 115.
WALTER, JOHN, of The Times, 97; his enterprise, 97, 447.
WAR, general, on the Continent, 129 ff.; terminated by Peace of Lunéville, 1801, 308.
Great Britain and France, declared February 1, 1793, 131; danger of French invasion, 133, 335 ff.; Pitt's methods, 243, 244; debated in parliament, 248 ff.; public attitude, 250; Egyptian expedition, 1801, 308 ff.; Saumarez's naval actions, 319 ff.; British defence of Elba, 322; war terminated, October 1, 1801, 338.
war again declared May 18, 1803, 362; projects of invasion of Great Britain, 370 ff., 378, 379, 386, 400, 401, 405 ff.; naval situation at the outbreak of war, 374 ff.; incidents of the naval war, 379; French occupation of Hanover, 380; British colonial expeditions, 381, 424; French colonial expeditions, 381, 407 ff.; interception of Villeneuve on return, 417; Battle of July 22, 1805, 417, 418; abandonment of French scheme of invasion in favour of new principles of naval warfare, 419 ff.; events

INDEX

leading to Battle of Trafalgar, 423 ff.; Battle of Trafalgar, 429 ff.; sequel to it, 441 ff.; Strachan's action of November 4th, 443; infructuous British expeditions to Italy and North Germany, 445; failure of Third Coalition, 446.
    War with the Baltic Powers, 1801; its causes, 246 ff.; attack on Copenhagen, 322, 326 ff.; conclusion of hostilities, 335.
    internal effects of war: price cutting, 50; impossibility of undertaking an unpopular war, 108, 115; effect of war on fiscal policy, 199, 200.
WARDEN OF THE CINQUE PORTS, 189; Pitt's work as, 383, 384.
WARREN, Rear-Admiral Sir JOHN, services in Mediterranean, 1801, 322.
WAR SECRETARY, 298, 299; Dundas to 1801, 136, 298; Hobart, 1801, 263; Camden, 1804, 394; Castlereagh, 1805, 413.
    colonies included under War Secretary from Hobart's time, 263.
WARWICK assize, 156.
WARWICK, Earl of, on farmers, 27.
WASHINGTON, GEORGE, President of the United States; his Treaty with Great Britain, 1794, 277.
WATCHES, tax on, 186.
WATCHMEN, 169.
WATERFORD, a centre of the provision trade, 216.
WATER POWER, its importance, 43, 48.
WATERWORKS, in Liverpool, 44.
WATSON, RICHARD, Bishop of Llandaff, on decay of the smaller landed gentry, 32; a pluralist, 88; a political writer, 88; inclined to deism, 89.
WEAVING, condition of the industry, 49, 50; its decay about 1800, 50; opposition to power-looms, 54; relations between an employer and his men, 58, 59; strikes of weavers, 169; Spitalfields weavers, 197, 67.
WEDGWOOD, JOSIAH, the elder, 55.
WEDGWOOD, JOSIAH, the younger, 55.
WEDGWOOD, THOMAS, 55.
WEIGHTS AND MEASURES, control of, 168.
WELLESLEY, Marquis, his disgust at his title, 237; co-operates in the conquest of Egypt, 310; arrival from India and interview with Pitt, 448.
WELLESLEY, Sir ARTHUR, his rapid rise, 100, 302; account of Pitt, 447. *Also see*
WELLINGTON, Duke of, on recruiting, 301; his opinion of the value of military history, 440; mentioned, 423. *Also see* WELLESLEY, Sir ARTHUR.
WENDEBORN, German chaplain, his observations, 21, 103.
WENTWORTHS, a Whig family, 114, 148.
WESLEY, JOHN, religious leader, 90, 91, 92, 93.
WESTERN, CHARLES, Whig county member; his Corn Act, 1804, 152, 194, 200.
WEST INDIES, general description, 278 ff.; connection with Liverpool, 43; importance to Britain, 43, 59; rents from, 58, 59; trade, 59, 60, 61; wealth of West Indians, 112, 281; Danish and Swedish West Indies seized by British, 247; health of the troops, 305; their strength, 305; British conquests, how dealt with at the Peace, 338 ff.; French expedition to San Domingo, 343; unpopularity with the Navy, 343; escape of French ships from, in 1803, 374, 375, 376; capture of French possessions, 381; objection to further expeditions, 381; French violation of Spanish neutrality, 402; Missiessy, Villeneuve and Nelson in the West Indies, 408 ff.; mentioned, 405, 406.

554 ENGLAND IN THE NINETEENTH CENTURY

WESTMINSTER, Fox's election for, 115.
WESTMINSTER SCHOOL, George Jackson at, 100.
WESTMORLAND, tenth Earl of, Lord Privy Seal during Pitt's first and the two following administrations, 137, 263, 394.
WEXFORD, a rebel of, 208; the rebellion in, 229 ff.; a Wexford duel, 230, 231.
WEYMOUTH, King and Queen at, 75.
WHEAT: wheaten bread, 22; prices of, up to 1795, 29, 34; subsequent prices, 34, 250; trade in, 34, 35; duties from 1689 to 1804, 198 ff.; encouragement of wheat growing, 199; the wheat supply, 199; scarcity of 1799–1800, 241, 242; estimate of national consumption, 242; measure taken to ensure supply, 242.
WHIGS, Latitudinarian, 93; Pitt's Whiggism, 136; Whigs in parliament, 140; noblemen, 148, 149; clergy, 149, 150; press, 150, 151; Whig criticism of the subsidy system, 244; George III, as an "Old Whig", 253; misconduct of Whig magistrates in Nottingham, 353; points upon which Pitt was opposed to Whiggism, 392, 393.
WHIPPING, punishment of, 163.
WHITBREAD, SAMUEL, a leader of Opposition to Pitt in House of Commons, 140; a zealous social reformer, 195.
WHITELAW, Rev. JOHN, on population of Dublin, 210.
WHITELOCKE, General, his surrender at Buenos Ayres mentioned, 301.
WHITWORTH, Lord, Ambassador in Paris, 1802–1803, 357 ff.; his complaint of Lauderdale, 347; remark of Bonaparte to, 370.
WICKLOW, villas, 206; outlaws, 231.
WIGS, disuse of, 71.
WILBERFORCE, WILLIAM, M.P. for Yorkshire, birth and character, 90; on the Yorkshire woollen industry, 41; his Practical View, 90; leader of the evangelical party, 90, 91; a wit, 98, 99; expense of his electoral contests, 113, 114; his first success for York in 1784, 114; an observation on George III, 119; his share in first labour legislation, 194; fears for Yorkshire from Irish competition, 240; on Pitt's truthfulness, 259; supports the Peace, 343, 353, 365; favours isolation in foreign policy, 353; anecdote about Pitt and Addington, 364; criticizes policy of home defence, 387; a saying of Pitt to him, 398; speech against Melville, 412; on Pitt's "false principle of honour", 449; on his eloquence, 449, 450; other remarks on Pitt, 453.
WILSON, ROBERT, mentioned, 101.
WILTSHIRE, woollen trade of, 48.
WIMEREUX, French port of concentration, 373.
WINCHELSEA, its local court, 166.
WINCHELSEA, Lord, his cottage holdings experiment, 26, 28, 203.
WINDHAM, WILLIAM, enthusiasm against French Revolution, 131; befriends Cobbett, 105; Secretary at War to 1801, 138, 298; resigns and passes into Opposition, 260; despondency at the Peace, 343; speaks for bull-baiting and against horse-racing, 348, 349; Addington's objection to his holding office, 364; scene with Fox, 365; becomes a link between Grenville and Fox in 1804, 393.
    letter to, 71; a wit, 98; popularity as a lover of the poor man's sports, 348; his attractiveness, 393; Burke's influence, 131, 393; remarks on Pitt, 449, 451; mentioned, 451.
WINDOW TAX, 181, 187.

INDEX

WINDWARD ISLANDS, West Indies, 278, 279.
WINE, price, 66; drinking at table, 70; duty on, 186.
WOBURN, mentioned, 250.
WOLCOTE, Dr., *see* PETER PINDAR.
WOLFE, his victory in Canada mentioned, 272.
WOLLSTONECRAFT, MARY, authoress of Vindication of the Rights of Women, 79; her miserable life, 79, 80; her severe rationalism, 80.
WOLVERHAMPTON, silver notes at, 191.
WOOL, basis of English prosperity, 40, 198; woollen trade in Yorkshire, 41, 48, 49, 54, 61; in the West of England, 48; wages, 54; export of woollen goods, 58, 239; import of wool, 59; legislation, 198.
  in Ireland, a home manufacture, 203; fall in exports, 216; fears for Yorkshire from Irish competition, 240.
WOOLWICH, training for artillery and engineers at, mentioned, 299; arrangements for artillery stores in case of invasion, 386.
WORCESTER, Queen to repair to in case of invasion, 386.
WORDSWORTH, DOROTHY, sister of the following, mentioned, 56.
WORDSWORTH, WILLIAM, poet, his account of Walker, 86; a contributor to Morning Post, 97; his letter to Fox, 144; on subjugation of Switzerland, 355; on the defence of England, 384; mentioned, 56, 105.
WORK-HOUSES, 172.
WORONZOW, Count, Russian Ambassador, remark on Pitt, 450.
WRAXALL, Sir NATHANIEL, anecdote of the Prince of Wales, 147.
WRESTLING, 103.
WURTEMBURG, British Minister in, deceived, 388, 389.
WYCOMBE, *see* HIGH WYCOMBE.

YARN, export of, prohibited, 201.
YEOMANRY, 307; use of, in suppressing disturbances, 170.
  in Ireland, 228, 229, 231.
YEOMEN, where prevalent, 20; effect on, of economic changes, 32; respect for their own class, 40; cotton lords partly recruited from them, 41.
YORK, parliamentary election at, 114.
YORK, name temporarily given to Toronto, 274.
YORK, FREDERICK, Duke of, second son of George III, made Commander-in-Chief of the Army, 1798, 120, 148; his work, 299.
YORKE, Hon. CHARLES, brother of Hardwicke: Secretary at War, 1801, 263; his Army of Reserve Act, 382; Home Secretary, 1803, 369.
YORKSHIRE, population and importance, 40, 41; industry of women, 21, 22; woollen trade, 41, 48, 49, 54, 61; Methodism, 92; parliamentary elections, 114; religious eccentricity, 268; distress in, 268; a false alarm of invasion, 385; Yorkshiremen mentioned, 387.
YORKSHIRE HUSSARS, 306.
YOUNG, ARTHUR, agricultural author, on Lincolnshire, 19, 26; Norfolk, 20, 21, 30, 39; Buckinghamshire, 23; Oxfordshire, 33; his conclusions used by Pitt, 57; his bathing, 71; on clergy, 88; an investment in the Funds, 184; the first Secretary to the Board of Agriculture, 188; on Ireland, 203, 207, 215.
YOUNG, Sir WILLIAM, an authority on the West Indies, 282.

GEORGE ALLEN & UNWIN LTD
LONDON: 40 MUSEUM STREET, W.C.1
CAPE TOWN: 73 ST. GEORGE'S STREET
SYDNEY, N.S.W.: WYNYARD SQUARE
AUCKLAND, N.Z.: 41 ALBERT STREET
WELLINGTON, N.Z.: 4 WILLIS STREET
TORONTO: 77 WELLINGTON STREET, WEST

The Struggle for the Freedom of the Press (1819-1832)
Demy 8vo.   By WILLIAM H. WICKWAR   16s.

"It is clear from this admirable volume that Mr. Wickwar is a recruit of great promise to English historiography."—HAROLD J. LASKI in *Time and Tide*.

The Decline of the West
By OSWALD SPEOGLER
TRANS. BY MAJOR C. F. ATKINSON

Royal 8vo.   2 vols. 21s. each

"Colossal in its learning, vast in its range, and almost superhuman in its intellectual control."—*Evening Standard*.

"It shows him to be a man of immense historical erudition and brilliant historical imagination. . . . His generalizations are worked out with extraordinary wealth of historical illustration."—*Nation*.

Economic History of Europe
in Modern Times
By MELVIN M. KNIGHT, PH.D., HARRY E. BARNES, PH.D., AND FELIX FLUGEL, PH.D.

Demy 8vo.   EDITED BY A. A. YOUNG   15s.

The economic history of Europe in modern times is both the history of the industry, agriculture, and commerce of a continent over a period of five centuries, and the history of a series of changes in economic organization which have been dominant factors in making the modern world what it is. The authors have given due weight to both these aspects of their subject; but their sole aim in writing this volume has been to make the course of European economic development as intelligible as possible. The "Economic History of Europe to the End of the Middle Ages," by M. M. Knight, was a compact introduction to the present work.

Vol. I (to the End of the Middle Ages) 12s.

Nationality: Its Nature and Problems
By DR. BERNARD JOSEPH

Demy 8vo.   INTRODUCTION BY G. P. GOOCH   10s. 6d.

This is a critical study of the entire question of nationality. The various attributes of nationality, such as race, language, tradition, religion, culture, national consciousness, etc., are analysed in detail in an effort to establish the importance of each in the formation, development, and preservation of nationality. The principal nationalities of the world and the factors which have contributed to their formation are considered in detail in order to establish the fundamental basis of nationality. The book deals further with the various problems affecting nationality, such as the relationship between nationality and cosmopolitanism, nationality and the State, nationality, patriotism, and war, etc. It indicates the real nature of nationality and its importance in the social order.

A Diary of St. Helena
By Lady MALCOLM

La. Cr. 8vo.   Edited by Sir ARTHUR WILSON   6s.

Lady Malcolm's diary for 1816-1817 contains full and accurate reports of Admiral Sir Pulteney Malcolm's numerous conversations with Napoleon at Longwood. From this contemporary record we get a very vivid impression of the ex-Emperor. Originally published in 1899, it is now re-issued with a new Introduction by Muriel Kent.

Napoleon and His Family
By WALTER GEER

Sm. Royal 8vo.   *Illustrated*   3 vols. 18s. each

This is the second of the three volumes in which Mr. Geer traces the influence of Napoleon's family upon his plans, acts, and destiny, and shows that his brothers and sisters played a larger part than has hitherto been imagined in the downfall of the man best endowed by Nature, best served by Destiny, that History has ever known. Volume III will take us down to St. Helena, and will bring to a close this amazing story of an amazing family.

    Vol. I. Corsica–Madrid, 1769–1809.
    Vol. II. Madrid–Moscow, 1809–1813
    Vol. III. In preparation.

Fouché : The Man Napoleon Feared
By Dr. NILS FORSSELL

Translated from the Swedish by ANNA BARWELL

Demy 8vo.   *Illustrated*   12s. 6d.

" His book is a sound and competent piece of research, a nice example of historical reconstruction, and at the same time a very readable biography."—*Birmingham Post.*

" Dr. Forssell forces us to acknowledge the enormous historical importance of the underground work which Fouché did at the Ministry of Police under Napoleon."—*Saturday Review.*

Napoleon
By EMIL LUDWIG

Translated from the German by EDEN and CEDAR PAUL

Royal 8vo.   *Illustrated. Eighth Printing*   21s.

" The most readable and the most illuminating book about Napoleon Bonaparte that has ever been written. . . . It would be difficult to overpraise the translation."—J. C. Squire in the *Observer.*

The Amorous Adventures of Augustus of Saxony

Containing several transactions of his Life, not mentioned in any other History, together with Diverting Remarks on the Ladies of the Several Countries thro' which he travell'd

By CARL LUDWIG von PÖLLNITZ

Translated from the French by *A Gentleman of Oxford*

Narrow Pott 4to.   *Illustrated*   18s.

Here is the world of *Jew Süss* as seen by a contemporary. Von Pöllnitz was a soldier and adventurer, a favourite of Frederick the Great, and an inveterate gossip; his polite chronicle of Frederick-Augustus' scandalous life is one of the curiosities of eighteenth-century literature. Possibly his account is not always reliable, but it is quaint and amusing, and brings before us vividly the cheerful vulgarity of what was considered at the time "the most brilliant Court in all Europe."

William the First
By PAUL WIEGLER
Translated by CONSTANCE VESEY

Royal 8vo.   *Illustrated*   21s.

In these pages we see the makings of the German Empire, the passing of the eighteenth century, the coming of the modern spirit. The central figure is, of course, the King who was so loath to be Emperor. But all the great figures of the century are here. Herr Wiegler's unfailing eye for anecdote, drama, and character has made a piece of historical research as vivid and animated as a novel.

The Hohenzollerns
By HERBERT EULENBERG
Translated by M. M. BOZMAN

Royal 8vo.   *Illustrated*   18s.

"His picture of the exile of Doorn is the most cruel one that has ever been drawn by any author."—*Evening Standard.*

"Admirable."—*Morning Post.*

Bismarck
By EMIL LUDWIG
Translated from the German by EDEN and CEDAR PAUL

Royal 8vo.   *Illustrated. Second Impression*   21s.

"The personality of the great Chancellor is brought before us with all the resources of a vivid, vigorous, and imaginative style, and he lives as he has never yet lived in literature."—*Daily Telegraph.*

Some Fascinating Women of the Renaissance
By GIUSEPPE PORTIGLIOTTI
Translated by BERNARD MIALL

Demy 8vo.   *Illustrated*   12s. 6d.

In his new book of historical studies, Signor Portigliotti has chosen ten women of the Italian Renaissance whose brilliant, tragic, or remarkable lives are the very stuff of romance—Isotta da Rimini; La Bella Simonetta; Tullia d'Aragona, the great courtezan; the "blessed" Cecilia Gonzaga, and that Giulia Gonzaga who was loved by Cardinal Ippolito de Medici; Tommasina Spinola, whose platonic friendship with Louis XII was famed throughout Europe; and four others. Their stories contain a great variety of incident and character, and are told with all Signor Portigliotti's gift for making the past alive and vivid.

The Woman of the Eighteenth Century
By EDMOND AND JULES DE GONCOURT
Translated by RALPH ROEDER and JACQUES LECLERCQ

Demy 8vo.   *Illustrated*   18s.

"A very interesting and amusing book. . . . The eighteenth-century woman . . . from birth to the grave, is discussed in these light and witty pages."—*Times Literary Supplement.*

Christian IV
A Picture of the Seventeenth Century
By JOHN A. GADE

Med. 8vo.   *Illustrated*   18s.

Christian IV, one of the most famous and best-loved kings of Denmark and Norway, had, both in public and private affairs, an astonishing career. Succeeding to the throne while still very young, he held a splendid and pleasure-loving court, but found time to strengthen the Danish Army and Navy, to defeat Gustavus Adolphus, and increase his own power and territory.

"This most human and entertaining biography."—*Spectator.*

"A brilliant and accurate picture of life in seventeenth-century Denmark."—*Birmingham Post.*

Richelieu
By KARL FEDERN
Translated by BERNARD MIALL

Demy 8vo.   *Illustrated*   12s. 6d

". . . In Herr Federn's pages the great, cold, inscrutable figure moves and lives again. A memorable book, and a noteworthy addition to our knowledge of one of the most tumultuous and most interesting periods of European history."—*Sunday Times.*

All prices are net.

LONDON: GEORGE ALLEN & UNWIN LTD

For Product Safety Concerns and Information please contact our EU representative GPSR@taylorandfrancis.com
Taylor & Francis Verlag GmbH, Kaufingerstraße 24, 80331 München, Germany

www.ingramcontent.com/pod-product-compliance
Lightning Source LLC
Chambersburg PA
CBHW071133300426
44113CB00009B/956